GIANNI (GIANGUERRINO) BARBIERO, Ph. D. (1998) Phil.-Theol. Hochschule St. Georgen - Frankfurt, is Professor at the Pontifical Biblical Institute of Rome. He has published on the legal texts of Pentateuch (*L'asino del nemico*) and on the Psalms (*Das erste Psalmenbuch als Einheit*).

Song of Songs

Supplements
to
Vetus Testamentum

VOLUME 144

Song of Songs

A Close Reading

By

Gianni Barbiero

Translated by

Michael Tait

BRILL

LEIDEN • BOSTON
2011

First published as *Il Cantico dei Cantici* by Gianni Barbiero, 2004 Paoline Editoriale Libri, Milano. © Figlie di San Paolo via Francesco Albani, 21 – 20149 Milano, Italy.

This book is printed on acid-free paper.

Library of Congress Cataloging-in-Publication Data

Barbiero, Gianni, 1944–
[Cantico dei cantici. English]
Song of songs : a close reading / by Gianni Barbiero ; translated by Michael Tait.
p. cm.
Includes bibliographical references and index.
ISBN 978-90-04-20325-9 (hardback : acid-free paper)
1. Bible. O.T. Song of Solomon—Commentaries. I. Tait, Michael. II. Title.

BS1485.53.B3713 2011
223'.9077—dc22

2011007833

ISSN 0083-5889
ISBN 978 90 04 20325 9

FSC www.fsc.org MIX Paper from responsible sources FSC® C004472

PRINTED BY DRUKKERIJ WILCO B.V. - AMERSFOORT, THE NETHERLANDS

To the women who have been near to me:
mothers, sisters, friends and daughters.
Marvelling at their love.

CONTENTS

PREFACE

The present work is intended to introduce to the English-speaking public my recent work on the Song of Songs which appeared in Italian.[1] By contrast with the original, this volume is new in several respects. Following the editorial requirements of the *Supplements to Vetus Testamentum*, the work has now a less confessional character and is more narrowly exegetical in view of its being addressed to the community of scholars of the Old Testament. Accordingly, the introduction and the conclusion, together with the closing sections of each chapter, have been reworked. The exegetical sections themselves remain virtually unchanged. Another modification is the removal of the illustrations taken from the commentary of O. Keel as this is well known in the English-speaking world.

Until fairly recently and now adopted anew,[2] the allegorical reading of the Song has been dominant. By contrast, it is my conviction that the poem should be interpreted literally, as a poem about human love. This is the prevailing reading today, but one which frequently goes to the opposite extreme in eliminating everything of a theological nature. I believe that love, as it is presented in the Song, is open to a dimension that is supernatural, even theological. However, this dimension is not something external to love, as is the case in the allegorical interpretation, but of its very essence. Moreover, this corresponds to a close reading of the text.

A fundamental thesis which underlies my study is that the Song is a unitary work with a very precise structure and ideological programme. In my opinion, however, the unity of the Song is not of the dramatic order (and here I take my distance from the recent work of Stoop-van Paridon,[3] which relaunches ancient theses), or of the narrative one (as the encyclopaedic book of Davidson has recently suggested),[4] but of the lyrical.

---

[1] Barbiero (2004).
[2] Cf., for example, the recent study of Kingsmill (2010).
[3] Stoop-van Paridon (2005).
[4] Davidson (2007).

I would like to thank the publishers, Brill, in the persons of Ms Liesbeth Hugenholtz and Ms Gera van Bedaf, for their editorial assistance, and Professor H. M. Barstad, editor of the *Supplements to Vetus Testamentum*, for having believed in the value of the present research and welcomed it into this prestigious series. Dr. Michael Tait has translated the work and improved it with pertinent observations. Dr. Silvia Ahn has patiently corrected the drafts and compiled the indices. The Pontifical Biblical Institute of Rome and the Library of the Graduate Theological Union of Berkeley, CA, have granted me a sabbatical semester in which to complete the work.

LIST OF ABBREVIATIONS[1]

AAWLM.G	Abhandlungen der Akademie der Wissenschaft und der Literatur in Mainz. Geistes- und sozialwissenschaftliche Klasse
AB	Anchor Bible
ACFEB	Association catholique française pour l'étude de la Bible
AJSL	*American Journal of Semitic Languages and Literature*
AKM	Abhandlungen für die Kunden des Morgenlandes
ANEP	J. B. Pritchard (ed.), *The Ancient Near East in Pictures Relating to the Old Testament* (Princeton, 1969²)
ANET	J. B. Pritchard (ed.), *Ancient Near Eastern Texts Relating to the Old Testament* (Princeton, 1969³)
AnBib	Analecta biblica
AOAT	Alter Orient und Altes Testament
Aq.	Aquila
Ar.	Arabic version
Aspr.	*Asprenas*
ATD	Das Alte Testament Deutsch
AthR	*Anglican Theological Review*
AUSS	*Andrews University Seminary Studies*
BBB	Bonner biblische Beiträge
BC	Biblischer Commentar über das Alte Testament
BDB	F. Brown, S. R. Driver and C. A. Briggs, *A Hebrew and English Lexicon of the Old Testament* (Oxford 1976³)
BEAT	Beiträge zur Erforschung des Alten Testaments und des Antiken Judentums
BET	Beiträge zur biblischen Exegese und Theologie
BEThL	Bibliotheca ephemeridum theologicarum lovaniensium
BHK	R. Kittel (ed.), *Biblia Hebraica*
BHQ	*Biblia Hebraica quinta editione*
BHS	*Biblia Hebraica Stuttgartensia*
Bib	*Biblica*
BibInt	*Biblical Interpretation*
Bijdr.	*Bijdragen*
BiRe	*Bible Review*
BiTr	*Bible Translator*
BJ	*La Bible de Jérusalem*
BJSt	Brown Judaic Studies
BK	Biblischer Kommentar

[1] S. M. Schwertner, *Internationales Abkürzungsverzeichnis für Theologie und Grenzgebiete* (Berlin and New York, 1994²) is the guide generally followed here.

BLS	Bible and Literature Series
BN	*Biblische Notizen*
BTB	*Biblical Theology Bulletin*
BUR	Biblioteca universale Rizzoli
BZ	*Biblische Zeitschrift*
BZAW	Beihefte zur Zeitschrift für die alttestamentliche Wissenschaft
CBC	Cambridge Biblical Commentary
CBQ	*Catholic Biblical Quarterly*
CChr.SL	Corpus christianorum. Series latina
CÉg	*Chronique d'Égypte*
CEI	*La Sacra Bibbia della Conferenza Episcopale Italiana (1984)*
ChH	*Church History*
CRB	Cahiers de la Revue Biblique
CSCO	Corpus scriptorum christianorum orientalium
CTePa	Collana di testi patristici
DB(V)	F. Vigouroux (ed.), *Dictionnaire de la Bible* (Paris, 1895–1912)
Div.	*Divinitas*
DJD	*Discoveries in the Judean Desert*
EAEHL	M. Avi-Yonah and E. Stern (eds.), *Encyclopedia of the Archaeological Excavations in the Holy Land* (London, 1975–1978)
EeT	*Église et théologie*
EJ	*Encyclopaedia Judaica* (Jerusalem 1971–1982)
EHS	Europäische Hochschulschriften
EstBib	*Estudios bíblicos*
Et.	Ethiopic version
EtB	Études bibliques
EThL	*Ephemerides theologicae lovanienses*
FS	Festschrift
FV	*Foi et vie*
G	Septuagint (= LXX)
G^A	The LXX according to the Codex Alexandrinus
G^B	The LXX according to the Codex Vaticanus
G^S	The LXX according to the Codex Sinaiticus
GCS	Die griechischen christlichen Schriftsteller der ersten drei Jahrhunderte
GKC	W. Gesenius, E. Kautzsch and A. E. Cowley, *Hebrew Grammar* (Oxford, 1910)
Gr.	*Gregorianum*
GThT	*Gereformeerd theologisch tijdschrift*
GTJ	*Grace Theological Journal*
HAH	W. Gesenius, *Hebräisches und aramäisches Handwörterbuch* (Berlin – Göttingen – Heidelberg, 1962^{17})
HALAT	W. Baumgartner *et al.*, *Hebräisches und aramäisches Lexikon zum Alten Testament* (Leiden 1967–1995)
HAT	Handbuch zum Alten Testament
HBS	Herder biblische Studien
HebStud	*Hebrew Student*

HK.AT	Handkommentar zum Alten Testament
HOTTP	D. Barthélemy *et al.*, *Preliminary and Interim Report on the Hebrew Old Testament Text Project*, vol. III, *Poetical Books* (New York, 1979)
ICC	International Critical Commentary
IDB.S	G. A. Buttrick (ed.), *Interpreter's Dictionary of the Bible. Supplementary volume* (Nashville and New York, 1976)
Interp.	*Interpretation*
JAAR	*Journal of the American Academy of Religion*
JAC	*Jahrbuch für Antike und Christentum*
JANES	*Journal of the Ancient Near Eastern Society*
JAOS	*Journal of the American Oriental Society*
JB	*Jerusalem Bible*
JBL	*Journal of Biblical Literature*
JEA	*Journal of Egyptian Archaeology*
JETS	*Journal of the Evangelical Theological Society*
JJS	*Journal of the Jewish Studies*
JPOS	*Journal of the Palestine Oriental Society*
JQR	*Jewish Quarterly Review*
JSNT.S	Journal for the Study of the New Testament. Supplement Series
JSOT	*Journal for the Study of the Old Testament*
JSOT.S	Journal for the Study of the Old Testament. Supplement Series
K	Ketib
KAT	Kommentar zum Alten Testament
KBANT	Kommentare und Beiträge zum Alten und zum Neuen Testament
KHC	Kurzer Hand-Commentar zum Alten Testament
KJV	*King James Version*
KTU	M. Dietrich *et al.* (eds.), *Die keilalphabetischen Texte aus Ugarit, Teil I*, AOAT 24 (Kevelaer - Neukirchen-Vluyn, 1976)
LD	Lectio divina
LHVT	F. Zorell, *Lexicon hebraicum Veteris Testamenti* (Roma, 1989)
LND	*La Nuova Diodati*
LoB	Leggere oggi la Bibbia
LThK	*Lexikon für Theologie und Kirche*
Ms(s)	Manuscript(s)
MT	Masoretic Text
MThZ	*Münchener theologische Zeitschrift*
NAS	*New American Standard Bible*
NEB.AT	Neue Echter Bibel. Altes Testament
NET	*New English Translation*
NICOT	New International Commentary of the Old Testament
NIVAC	New International Version Application Commentary
NJB	*New Jerusalem Bible*
NKJ	*New King James Version*
NKZ	*Neue kirchliche Zeitschrift*
NT	New Testament

NRS	*New Revised Standard Version*
NRTh	*Nouvelle Revue Théologique*
NRV	*La Sacra Bibbia Nuova Riveduta*
NV	*Nova et vetera*
NVB	*Nuovissima versione della Bibbia*
OBO	Orbis biblicus et orientalis
OCD	Ordo Carmelitanorum Decalceatorum
OT	Old Testament
OTE	*Old Testament Essays*
OTM	Oxford Theological Monographs
OTP	J. H. Charlesworth (ed.), *The Old Testament Pseudepigrapha*, 2 vols. (New York, 1983–1985)
pap.	papyrus
PEQ	*Palestine Exploration Quarterly*
PW	A. Pauly, G. Wissowa and W. Kroll (eds.), *Realencyclopädie der classischen Altertumwissenschaft* (Stuttgart, 1894).
Q	Qere
QD	Quaestiones disputatae
Qui.	Origen's Quinta
RA	*Revue d'assiriologie et d'archéologie orientale*
RAC	Reallexikon für Antike und Christentum
RB	*Revue Biblique*
RHPhR	*Revue d'histoire et de philosophie religieuses*
RIA	Reallexikon der indo-germanischen Altertumskunde
RSO	*Rivista degli studi orientali*
RSV	*Revised Standard Version*
RV	*Revised Version*
RTL	*Revue théologique de Louvain*
RVS	*Rivista di vita spirituale*
RWB	*Revised Webster Update*
S	Syriac version
Sal.	*Salesianum*
S-B	H. L. Strack and P. Billerbeck, *Kommentar zum Neuen Testament aus Talmud und Midrash*, 6 vols. (München, 1922–1969)
SBFLA	*Studii biblici franciscani liber annuus*
SBL	Society of Biblical Literature
SBL.DS	Society of Biblical Literature. Dissertation Series
SBL.MS	Society of Biblical Literature. Monograph Series
SBS	Stuttgarter Bibelstudien
SB[T]	La sacra Bibbia (Torino)
SC	Sources chrétiennes
SJOT	*Scandinavian Journal of the Old Testament*
SS	*Semitic Studies Series*
SR	*Studies in Religion*
Sym.	Symmachus
Tab.	*Table*
TB	Theologische Bücherei

TDNT	G. Kittel and G. Friedrich (eds.), *Theological Dictionary of the New Testament* (Grand Rapids, 1981–1982)
TDOT	G. J. Botterweck and H. Ringgren (eds.), *Theological Dictionary of the Old Testament* (Grand Rapids, 1977–2003)
Tg	Targum
Th.	Theodotion
THAT	E. Jenni and C. Westermann (eds.), *Theologisches Handwörterbuch zum Alten Testament* (Gütersloh, 1994–1995^5)
ThPh	*Theologie und Philosophie*
ThQ	*Theologische Quartalschrift*
ThR	*Theologische Rundschau*
TILC	*Traduzione interconfessionale in lingua corrente*
TOB	*Traduction oecuménique de la Bible*
tr.	translate/translator
TRE	Theologische Realenzyklopädie
TUAT	O. Kaiser (ed.), *Texte aus der Umwelt des Alten Testaments*
UF	*Ugarit-Forschungen*
USQR	*Union Seminar Quarterly Review*
UT	C.H. Gordon, *Ugaritic Textbook*
VL	Vetus Latina
Vg	Vulgate
VT	*Vetus Testamentum*
VT.S	Vetus Testamentum Supplements
WThJ	*Westminster Theological Journal*
WUNT	Wissenschaftliche Untersuchungen zum Neuen Testament
ZAH	*Zeitschrift für Althebraistik*
ZAW	*Zeitschrift für die alttestamentliche Wissenschaft*
ZB	Zürcher Bibel
ZBK.AT	Zürcher Bibel Kommentar. Altes Testament
ZE	*Zeitschrift für Ethnologie*
ZDPV	*Zeitschrift des Deutschen Palästina-Vereins*
ZThG	*Zeitschrift für Theologie und Gemeinde*
ZThK	*Zeitschrift für Theologie und Kirche*

CHAPTER ONE

INTRODUCTION

1. Position in the Canon

The Song of Songs forms part of the canon of inspired books in both the Jewish and Christian traditions. How and when it entered into the canon is not clear. Explicit quotations of the Song are absent from the other books of the Old and New Testaments. The most ancient witness to the Song probably goes back to Josephus (c. A.D. 100): in his enumeration of the books of the Bible, after having spoken of the Pentateuch and the prophetic books, he affirms that "the remaining four books contain hymns to God and instruction for people on life":[1] he is referring to the Psalms and the three 'Solomonic' books, Proverbs, Qoheleth and the Song of Songs. Around 200 A.D., the Song of Songs is mentioned in the *Mishnah* in a text which reflects the problematic canonical status of the book. After having established the principle that "all sacred scripture 'defiles the hands'", that is that they are canonical,[2] the *Mishnah* adds:

> The Song of Songs and Qohelet impart uncleanness to hands. R. Judah says: "The Song of Songs imparts uncleanness to hands, but as to Qohelet there is dispute." Rabbi Simeon says, "Qohelet is among the lenient rulings[3] of the house of Shammai and strict rulings[4] of the house of Hillel."[5] Said R. Simeon b. Azzai, "I have a tradition from the testimony of the seventy-two elders, on the day on which they seated R. Eleazar b. Azariah in the session,[6] that the Song of Songs and Qohelet do impart uncleanness to hands." Said R. Aqiba, "Heaven forbid! No Israelite man ever disputed concerning Song of Songs that it imparts uncleanness to

[1] Josephus, *Ap* 1:8, 40.
[2] The sense of this expression is not at all clear. Cf. Luzarraga (2002), pp. 6–22; Goodman (1990), pp 99–107.
[3] That is, it does not belong to the canon. Cf. Barthélemy (1985), p. 14.
[4] In other words, normative, canonical.
[5] This means, therefore, that the canonicity of the Song "was established among the Pharisees before their division into two schools at the beginning of our era" (Barthélemy [1985], p. 14).
[6] This is the so-called Council of Jamnia in A.D. 90.

> hands. For the entire age is not so worthy as the day on which the Song of Songs was given to Israel. For all the scriptures *(k^e^tûbîm)* are holy, but the Song of Songs is holiest of all. And if they disputed, they disputed only about Qohelet." Said R. Yohanan b. Joshua the son of R. Aqiba's father-in-law, according to the words of Ben Azzai, "Indeed did they dispute, and indeed did they come to a decision."[7]

That the Song appears alongside Qoheleth is hardly surprising. Both books are somewhat 'heterodox' in comparison with the other biblical books. The praise of sexual love within the Song contrasts with the reserve generally encountered in the Old Testament. R. Aqiba argued strongly against the literal interpretation of the Song. He was a firm believer in the allegorical interpretation that was to become usual in Israel and in the primitive Church: "He who warbles the Song of Songs in a banquet-hall and makes it into a kind of love-song has no portion in the world to come".[8] He is echoed by the *Talmud*:

> Our Rabbis taught: "He who recites a verse of the Song of Songs and treats it as a [secular] air, and one who recites a verse at the banqueting table unseasonably, brings evil upon the world."[9]

Frequently, introductions to the Song conclude from these quotations that the book's inclusion within the canon was tied to its allegorical interpretation. In fact, the two passages quoted above testify to the fact that beside the allegorical interpretation, the 'literal' one was widespread: so widespread that the rabbis felt bound to contest it sharply.[10] The *Abot de Rabbi Natan* form part of this tradition:

> Originally, it is said, Proverbs, Song of Songs, and Ecclesiastes were suppressed; for since they were held to be mere parables *(m^e^šalôt)* and not part of the Holy Writings *(k^e^tûbîm)* (the religious authorities) arose and suppressed them; (and so they remained) until the men of Hezekiah[11] came and interpreted them.[12]

---

[7] m.Yadayim 3:5.

[8] t.*San* 12:10. Cf. Augustin (1988), p. 403; Urbach (1971), p. 249.

[9] b.*San* 101a.

[10] Cf. Keel (1994), pp. 5–7.

[11] The translator notes: "Text erroneously, 'Men of the Great Assembly'". Cf. *Abot de Rabbi Natan*, p. 176. In this case it would be a legendary assembly held in the time of Ezra. The Tannaitic sources hover between the two attributions. Cf. *Abot de Rabbi Natan, Version B*, p. 27.

[12] *Abot de Rabbi Natan*, 1d, p. 5. Cf. *Abot de Rabbi Natan, Version B*, 3, p. 27.

The allegorical reading of the Song is not original.[13] In fact there is nothing in the text of the Song, in so far as it has come down to us from the Hebrew tradition, which alludes to such a reading. On the contrary, there are passages that are absolutely incompatible with an allegorical reading. The attribution to Solomon (1:1)[14] is clearly apocryphal. It could be that this attribution had an influence in the canonical reception of the book; however, this did not prevent Solomon's being severely criticised in the Song (cf. 6:8–9; 8:11–12).

The Mishnah also gives direct testimony to a secular use of the Song:

> There was no days better for Israelites than the fifteenth of Ab and the Day of Atonement. For on those days Jerusalemites girls go out in borrowed white dresses [...]. And the Jerusalemites girls go out and dance in the vineyards. What did they say? "Fellow, look around and see—choose what you want! Don't look for beauty, look for family: *Charm is deceitful and beauty is vain, but a woman who fears the Lord will be praised* (Prov 31:30). [...] And so it says, *Go forth, you daughters of Zion, and behold King Solomon with the crown with which his mother crowned him in the day of his espousals and in the day of the gladness of his heart* (Song of Songs 3:11)".[15]

We must suppose, therefore, that the Song was originally read as a song of love,[16] even if the spiritual reading has to be very ancient. Traces of such a reading are to be found both in the presence of the Song of Songs at Qumran (where it was certainly not taken in a literal sense) and in the ancient versions where, here and there, an allegorical allusion surfaces. In the Hebrew text, I found only one trace of allegory, and that is the fact that the term *dôdî* ('my beloved') is uttered in the Song exactly 26 times, a sacred number in Hebrew gematria: it is, in fact, the numerical value of the tetragrammaton, YHWH. This is a rather minor indication in a text in which the literal sense is wholly coherent. The establishment of the allegorical interpretation is subsequent to the canonisation of the Song of Songs,[17] and, as

[13] Cf. Luzarraga (2002), pp. 26–56.
[14] Cf. Luzarraga (2002), pp. 22–25.
[15] m.*Taan* 4:8, pp. 315–316. Cf. also b.*Taan* 30b–31a, pp. 162–165.
[16] Cf. Bentzen (1953), pp. 41–47.
[17] So too Riedel (1898), p. 3; Gerleman (1965), p. 51. The dating of the entry of the Song into the canon is disputed. It is more a question of a slow process than of a precise date. The presence of the Song of Songs at Qumran favours a date prior to the Christian epoch. Cf. Sæbø (1996), p. 268 ("Current scholarship tends to view the

Augustin suggests,[18] is probably connected with the period in which Rabbi Aqiba lived, between the destruction of Jerusalem in A.D. 70 and the dispersal of the Jews following the revolt of Bar Kochba (135 A.D.). The time was hardly fit for making the "voice of the bride-groom and the bride" be heard (cf. Jer 16:9).

In the Hebrew canon, the Song of Songs is numbered among the *k^{e}tûbîm* (hagiographa or writings) after the Torah and the prophetic books.[19] Within this group, its position is disputed. The *Talmud* places it in sixth place after Ruth, Psalms, Job, Proverbs, Qoheleth, and before Lamentations, Daniel, Esther, Ezra and 1–2 Chronicles.[20] Such a position does not take account of the group of five 'scrolls' (*m^{e}gillôt*) meant for liturgical reading at the feasts (Song of Songs, Ruth, Lamentations, Qoheleth, Esther). It follows from this that the reading of the Song during the feast of Passover, still the practice today, is subsequent to the redaction of the *Talmud*: it goes back probably to the 8th century A.D.. Theodore of Mopsuestia (d. 428) was also unaware of a public reading of the Song either by Jews or by Christians. Some manuscripts order the five books 'chronologically'. The Song of Songs, therefore, as 'Solomonic', comes in second place, after Ruth, which was held to have been composed by Samuel, and before Qoheleth, also 'Solomonic' but a work of his old age (cf. *BHS*).[21] Others follow the order of the feasts and so place the Song of Songs in the first place since Passover is the first feast of the year. The Greek Bible, followed by the Christian tradition, places the 'writings', after the so-called 'historical books', before the prophets. Among the writings, the Song of Songs occupies the fourth place, after the Psalms and the other two 'Solomonic' books, Proverbs and Qoheleth. It should be noted that both the Hebrew and the Christian tradition place the Song among the sapiential books: this is not without importance for its interpretation.

---

canonization of the Hebrew Bible as less localized, rejecting the older connection with the so-called 'council' of Jamnia, at the end of the first century C.E.").

[18] Augustin (1988), p. 404.

[19] Cf. Riedel (1898), pp. 6–7; Rudolph (1962), pp. 77–78.

[20] Cf. b.*BB* 14d.

[21] *ShirR* 1:1, 10.

2. The Text

Our text of the Song of Songs follows the Hebrew (MT) as closely as possible. It was fashionable, above all in the twentieth century, to introduce conjectures in order to explain certain obscure passages,[22] and to shift verses from one position to another, as if the Hebrew text were irremediably corrupt.[23] Gradually, it was realised that this was to do violence to the text, subjecting it to preconceived ideas.[24] It is revealing that the critical apparatus of *BHS* (and still more that of *BHQ*) is much more prudent in suggesting conjectures than that of the previous *Biblica Hebraica* of Kittel. After examining all the emendations proposed by exegetes one by one, Hamp reaches the conclusion: "The Hebrew text of the Song, at least in its consonantal form, is very well preserved".[25] He retains as possible, though not certain, only six minimal conjectures.[26] To anticipate the results of the present work, I can say that, in my opinion, the MT shows itself superior to the conjectures in every case.

Claiming that the MT is the product of a moralising revision, Giovanni Garbini has reconstructed a hypothetical original Hebrew text which departs significantly from the Masoretic one. However, the textual evidence speaks against such an operation. The ancient versions show themselves to be wholly dependent on the Hebrew text, sometimes in a slavish way. Murphy observes: "The extant evidence preserves little if any trace to suggest that more than a single Hebrew recension or edition of the Song has existed".[27] Decisive here is the

---

[22] Cf., for example, Graetz (1871), or Budde (1898).

[23] Paradigmatic here are the champions of the mythological school, who, in order to discover the development of a fertility rite, change the order of the sections completely: cf., for example, Wittekindt (1925); Schmökel (1956). The same goes for Haupt (1907).

[24] Cf. the pertinent observation of Lacocque (1998), p. 2: "Every single verse of the Song has been one way or another hypothetically or tentatively altered by traditional reuse or by textual reshaping. If those 'corrections' were to be brought together in a modern edition, the Song as transmitted and canonized would all but completely disappear under a new, artificially reconstructed text".

[25] Hamp (1957), p. 212.

[26] The recent commentary of R. E. Murphy is even more minimalist. Cf. Murphy (1990), p. 7: "The only verse in the Song which seems to defy cogent decipherment is 6:12". On the MT of Song 6:12, cf. Barbiero (1997a), pp. 174–189. Another verse which has given rise to innumerable conjectures is Song 3:10b on which I refer to another work of mine, Barbiero (1995), pp. 96–104.

[27] Murphy (1990), p. 7.

witness of Qumran where passages from the Song have been found in three manuscripts from cave 4 and one from cave 6.[28] If this last fragment is rather small (Song 1:1–7),[29] the other three, published by E. Tov,[30] offer a fair sample. Manuscript 4QCant[c] is a small fragment containing Song 3:7–8; 4QCant[a] contains, in two columns, Song 3:7–4:7 + 6:11–7:7; 4QCant[b] has the following passages in four fragments: Song 2:9–3:5; 3:9–11; 4:1–3; 4:8–5:1. We have here, in the words of Tov, 'abbreviated texts', that is, a kind of anthology of passages (thus is to be explained their 'abbreviated' character). The passages depart from the MT at various points, but here too: "the assumption that they represented early literary crystallisations of the book differing from the one represented by other textual witnesses, though not impossibile, is discarded".[31]

The testimony of Qumran is decisive because it takes us back to the first century B.C.,[32] exactly the time in which Garbini places his supposed 'primitive Song'.

There is still no definitive critical edition of the Greek text of the LXX for the Song of Songs: we must content ourselves here with partial results. J.-M. Auwers, who is preparing the edition of the Song for the series "La Bible d'Alexandrie", sums up the result of his research thus:

> La version grecque du *Cantique des Cantiques* a été rédigée tard, probablement au Ier siècle de notrre ère, sans doute en Palestine, avec un grand souci de littéralisme, qui annonce la manière d'Aquila.[33]

In fact, the primary characteristic of the LXX is its "almost slavish fidelity"[34] with regard to the Hebrew original. Sometimes, the translation is a mechanical reproduction of the Hebrew, and one has to ask oneself whether the translator has understood the text.

---

[28] 4QCant[a], 4QCant[b], 4QCant[c], and 6QCant respectively.

[29] Edited by M. Baillet in *DJD*, vol. III, pp. 112–114, tab. XXIII.

[30] Tov (1995), pp. 88–111

[31] Tov (1995), p. 89.

[32] For 4QCant[a], Tov speaks of the "early Herodian period"; for 4QCant[b] of "the end of the first century B.C.E.". Cf. Tov (1995), pp. 92 and 99 respectively.

[33] Auwers (1999), p. 37, bases himself on the studies of Barthélemy, who has traced a revision of the ancient text of the LXX along the lines of greater fidelity to the MT, the so-called *kaige* revision, cf. Barthélemy (1963), p. 47, and *id.* (1985), p. 22, even if the indications that the LXX of the Song is part of this revision are not wholly convincing.

[34] Cf. Gerleman (1965), p. 77.

Be that as it may, the text of the LXX is clearly secondary in relation to that of the MT.[35] Its 'additions' often betray themselves to be explanations and harmonisations of the MT. Codex Sinaiticus and Codex Alexandrinus—but not Codex Vaticanus—have introduced some stage directions, explaining the names of the 'actors' (*hē nymphē* or *nymphios*, respectively) and their interlocutors.[36] Here the Christian allegorical interpretation is already clearly perceptible (cf. 7:1, *pros ton nymphion christon*). In the text itself, this interpretation is not evident, even if hints in this direction are not absent. Thus, for example, the geographical names are often read as common nouns. The MT's "from the summit of Amana" (4:8) becomes "from the beginning of faith" (*apo archēs pisteōs*); "as Tirzah" (6:4) becomes "as graciousness" (*hōs eudokia*); "at the gate of Bath-Rabbim" (7:5) becomes "at the gates of the daughter of the multitude" (*en pylais thygatros pollōn*). In 1:4, the Hebrew *mêšārîm ʾăhēbûka* ("rightly do they love you") is rendered by *euthytēs ēgapēsen se* ("righteousness has loved you"). The translation of the Hebrew *ʾahăbâ* with the Greek *agapē* is certainly also tending in an allegorical direction, but this is a choice made by the entire Greek translation of the OT which almost never uses the term *erōs* to indicate sexual love. All things considered, the signs of an allegorical interpretation are very discreet, and that is surprising given the dating (it is the period of R. Aqiba). It is to be explained by the respect of the translators towards the text received from the tradition. The rabbis were entitled to interpret it in an allegorical sense, but the text itself was not to be touched.

According to Rudolph and Gerleman, the Syriac version is even more faithful than the Greek to the Hebrew text.[37] The expansions are fewer than in the LXX; here too they are often harmonisations with parallel passages. Often the Syriac agrees with the LXX against the MT which could result from a dependence of the Syriac on the LXX,

---

[35] So too Garbini (1992), p. 135: "The Hebrew Masoretic text is by far the most correct from the formal point of view, that is to say that where the text has not been tampered with for ideological reasons, it presents itself as the better one". Naturally, we distance ourselves from the last remark: a correction for ideological motives is foreign to the canonical tradition which sees in the received text a word of God to be accepted as it is, not to be changed at will (cf. Deut 27:26; Matt 5:17–19).

[36] Cf. the "Corollarium" at the end of Rahlfs' edition.

[37] Cf. Rudolph (1962), pp. 80–81; Gerleman (1965), pp. 82–84. On the Peshitta (or Syriac version) of the Song, cf. Bloch (1921–1922), pp. 103–139; Euringer (1901), pp. 115–128.

though it could also be the product of a common *Vorlage*. At times, however, the Syriac is distinct from both the LXX and the MT. In other cases, the MT and LXX agree while the Syriac goes its own way. So, for example, in 2:9, the LXX *diktya* ('lattice partition') agrees with the Hebrew *ḥărakkîm* while the Syriac has *ṣjrṭ'* ('hinges of the door'); in 5:16, the Greek *holos* is a correct translation of the Hebrew *kullô* whereas the Syriac has *m'nwhy* ('vessel', probably reading *k^e^lî*). 8:1 is particularly singular: here the Syriac reads "my lambs have sucked my breasts",[38] a reading which finds no echo in either the MT or the LXX and is probably of an allegorical nature.

Clearly of an allegorical stamp is the variant in 8:5: the Syriac reads a feminine pronoun as the object of the verb 'to awaken' (*'yrtky*) while the MT has a masculine pronoun. According to the Hebrew text it is the woman awakening the man; according to the Syriac, the man awakening the woman, something more comprehensible in an allegorical interpretation.[39] Despite the fact that 8:5 is incompatible with an allegorical interpretation, it has remained in the MT, which means: first of all, that the Hebrew tradition has not changed the received (vocalic!) text even when this does not conform to its interpretative agenda; and second, the MT is better than the Syriac version.

Of the two Latin versions, the Vetus Latina is of scant textual value because it depends on the LXX. The Vulgate, on the other hand, is a witness to the quality of the MT, even if at times it differs slightly from it (one speaks of a 'proto-Masoretic text').[40] The most obvious case is the translation of 'Solomon' with *Pacificus* in 8:11–12 which allows a glimpse of an allegorical intention. Elsewhere, however, Jerome translates in a rather realistic form, as in 4:1, where the MT *mibba'ad l^e^ṣammātēk* ('behind your veil') is rendered: *absque eo quod intrinsecus latet*.[41]

3. Poetic Language

The undeniable difficulty in interpreting the Song of Songs is due not to the corruption of the Hebrew text but to the poetic character of

[38] Cf. Rudolph (1962), p. 81.
[39] Cf. p. 435, n. 3, and pp. 448–449.
[40] Cf. Murphy (1990), p. 10.
[41] Cf. p. 177, n. 36.

the book.[42] Against a tendency, in the past, to consider the Song as a collection of popular songs, recent commentaries have increasingly underlined its refined language,[43] which, in the words of H. P. Müller, sometimes borders on mannerism.[44]

Like no other book in the OT, the Song of Songs abounds in *hapax-legomena*. Greenspahn has counted a good 37:[45] at times, the meaning can be deduced from the context or from similar vocables in the Oriental languages, but at other times the translation remains uncertain.[46] Sometimes, it is a matter of archaisms, at other times of neologisms which reflect the cosmopolitan environment of the author, drawn, as they are, from Aramaic, Persian, Greek, Sanskrit and even Malayan.[47]

The Hebrew text is an exquisite sonorous piece of work: for example, there are frequent uses of paronomasia and alliteration, rhyme and assonance, together with forms of onomatopoeia.[48] These phenomena are discernible from the first to the last line of the poem, and speak in favour of the unity of the book.

From the rhythmical point of view, the basic element is the *stich* (called by others the *colon*), the 'line', which the present translation seeks to respect.[49] It is generally composed of two, three, but rarely four, accents.[50] As is typical of Hebrew poetry, the stich is almost never solitary (when it is, it has the value of an introduction or conclusion, as in 1:6e and 1:11). Generally, it is paired with a second stich (forming a *distich*) according to the *parallelismus membrorum*. The use of the *tristich* is also not infrequent (cf. 5:11–12). Parallelism is a particular example of the phenomenon of repetition which can be considered

[42] "The terseness of poetry [...] is a prime reason why poetry lacks semantic precision. [...] Poets relish this intentional ambiguity that results in an emotional richness" (Longman [2001], p. 10).

[43] Cf. Gerleman (1965), pp. 52–62; Krinetzki (1964), pp. 46–82; Murphy (1990), pp. 67–91; Reventlow (1986), p. 501.

[44] Müller (1992), p. 6.

[45] Greenspahn (1984), pp. 232 and 183–189. Cf., however, the corrections in Murphy (1990), pp. 75–76.

[46] This is the case, for example, with *talpîyôt* ('bulwarks' [?], Song 4:4); *taltallîm* ('date flowers' [?], Song 5:11); *bāter* ('division'[?], Song 2:17).

[47] Cf. Müller (1992), p. 51; Krinetzki (1964), pp. 44–45.

[48] The individual examples will be indicated in the course of the exegesis. For a comprehensive summary, we refer to Krinetzki (1964), pp. 55–60.

[49] Here we are following Watson (1984), pp. 87–103.

[50] The debate over Hebrew meter is still open. With Watson (1984), pp. 97–104, we prefer to follow the counting of accents rather than of syllables. Cf. also Alonso Schökel (1989), pp. 49–52.

the basis of the poetry of the Song. It is like the repetition of a melodic motif in the course of a symphony. The repetitions are never mechanical: they are, as it were, the breath of the poem and the sign of its profound unity.[51] Thus the forms of parallelism are extremely varied: synonymous (cf. 1:4cd; 2:1ab), antithetical (cf. 5:6ab), synthetic (cf. 7:11a).[52] A particular example of parallelism is the so-called climactic parallelism in which the second member repeats the first adding to it a new element (cf. 6:8–9).[53]

A form of repetition dear to Hebrew poetry is the *chiasm* in which the initial element is repeated by the final one while the two middle ones are linked together (a-b-b'-a). This compositional form can be encountered in small literary units (cf. 1:6de), but also at the macrostructural level to the extent that W. Shea has delineated a chiastic structure for the entire book.[54] Similar in function is the *inclusion* in which one element (a lexeme or a motif) from the beginning of a composition is repeated at the end (cf. 4:1, 7).

The smallest compositional unity is the *strophe*. The division into strophes is marked above all by repetition: the repeating of words significant at the beginning of the strophe (cf. in 4:8–5:1, the function of the appellative 'bride' in vv. 8, 9, 10, 11, 12) and phenomena of inclusion. The strophe is not an independent lyrical unity, however: it is the subdivision of a poetic composition which we call the *song*. In the *Prologue* (1:2–2:7) and in the *Epilogue* (8:5–14), the separate strophes have a marked autonomy so that they could be considered almost independent songs, but this is due to the character of these two sections which, as the beginning and conclusion of the book, enjoy a particular function. A characteristic method of composition used by

---

[51] As far as parallelism is concerned, it is clear, today, that the second member is never a simple repetition of the first. "The biblical poet is doing more than saying the same thing twice. The second part always nuances the first part in some way" (Longman [2001], p. 11). On parallelism, cf. Alonso Schökel (1963), pp. 195–230; *id.* (1989), pp. 65–83; Watson (1984), pp. 114–159; Alter (1985), pp. 3–26; Berlin (1992); Kugel (1981).

[52] Murphy (1990), p. 88, prefers to speak of two basic forms of parallelism: *balanced* (*symmetrical*) (cf. Song 1:4cd; 2:13ab; 8:3ab) and *echoing*, characterised by the ellipsis of an element in the second member (cf. 8:2cd; 8,6ab).

[53] Cf. Watson (1984), pp. 150–156; Murphy (1990), pp. 90–91; Grossberg (1989), pp. 77–81.

[54] Shea (1980), pp. 73–93, structures it in this form: a-b-c-c'-b'-a'. For his part, Dorsey ([1990], pp. 378–396) has discovered a central (palindromic) structure in the Song: a-b-c-d-c'-b'-a'.

the author is the so-called *surprise-effect*,[55] by which, as in a classical epigram, he condenses all the verve into the final verse which often assumes an enigmatic character (cf. 1:6e; 1:8cd; 2:17e; 3:10ef; 6:2a; 6:12b; 8:12; 8:14).

Another characteristic of the poetry of the Song is the *figurative language*. The poet expresses himself not through concepts but through similes and metaphors. This too confers an allusive and open character on his text. A concept is clear and distinct, but the expression "your eyes are doves" (1,15b) is highly pregnant. Moreover, this kind of language is more suited to speaking of love because it speaks directly to the senses yet allowing a glimpse of spiritual significance. Symbolic language is the language of incarnation, of the union between flesh and spirit, between body and soul.

Scholars distinguish between the metaphor and the simile.[56] The latter is introduced by the comparative particle *k*ᵉ ('like/as'; cf. 1,5b: "like the tents of Kedar, like the curtains of Solomon"), while the former sets up the superimposition of two objects. The expression of 1,12b, "My nard pours forth its fragrance" superimposes on to the person of the beloved woman the image of nard. What links the two objects is their attractiveness: the sex appeal that emanates from the woman, that is to say, her charm, is like the perfume emanating from nard. While the simile remains external to the object compared, the metaphor works a unification of the two objects. To say "Your eyes are doves" is to identify the eyes of the beloved woman with the animal that is characteristic of the goddess of love.

Hans-Peter Müller has underlined the mythological character of the metaphors of the Song.[57] In the background, there is still discernible a magic significance, an appropriation of the vital force present in the object compared, an overcoming of the barrier that separates man from the cosmos. In the mythological mentality, doves, gazelles, apples possess a soul, they have a vital force which man makes his own by means of the rite. The world of the Song is no longer that of myth; the latter's function is now being performed by the lyrical imagination. In this way, the cosmos is integrated once again with the human world. In this process, a divine value is attributed to the forces of love, and this

---

[55] This expression derives from Heinevetter (1988), p. 140.

[56] Cf. Alonso Schökel (1989), pp. 133–137; Watson (1984), pp. 254–271.

[57] Müller (1984); *id.* (1976), pp. 23–41. Discernible as the basis is the thought of P. Ricoeur. Cf., above all, Ricoeur (1975).

is naturally understood within the context of the Yahwistic religion. This value is expressed in the 'profession of faith' of 8:6: "[Love is] a flame of Yah".

Othmar Keel has studied the metaphors of the Song against the background of Oriental iconography.[58] He too has emphasised their mythological content. Moreover, he points out that their significance is often different from that of our modern Western world. While, in fact, in our poetry, the metaphor has a predominantly 'visual' dimension, in Oriental poetry it has a primarily functional dimension. Thus the expression "Your eyes are doves" (1:15b) is not to be referred to the form of the eyes (the eyes of the dove are not particularly beautiful), but to their communicative function which corresponds to the significance of the dove as the messenger of love. Similarly, in comparing the woman's neck to a tower (4:4; cf. 7:5a), the *tertium comparationis* is not the slender form of the tower but its defensive character which corresponds to the proud self-awareness of the woman. Even if, inevitably, his individual interpretations are debatable, Keel's work has made a fundamental contribution to the understanding of the metaphors of the Song. In the course of the analysis, we shall be making frequent reference to his illustrations.

In the light of Oriental iconography, the *šôšannâ*, the typical flower of the Song (2:1, 16; 4:5; 5:13; 6:2, 3; 7:3), is to be understood not as the 'lily' of Christian tradition but as the 'lotus flower' dear to Egyptian tradition.[59] To the documentation of Keel we must add that of Grober,[60] who points out how all the passages which use this metaphor are profoundly coherent. He proposes, therefore, to discover the unity of the Song not at the narrative but at the metaphorical level. It is, in fact, unthinkable that such a coherent use of metaphor is to be attributed to different hands. J.M. Munro has arrived at a similar result through a global study of the metaphors.[61]

As a refined work of poetry, the Song of Songs has not appeared out of thin air but is the heir to a long tradition of amorous lyrics of which traces have been conserved in both Egypt and Mesopotamia and in the Hellenistic literature, as also, later, in Arab literature and

[58] Keel (1984a); *id.* (1994).
[59] Cf. Keel (1984a), pp. 63–78. On the significance of the lotus flower in Egyptian love lyrics, cf. Derchain (1975), pp. 65–68.
[60] Grober (1984).
[61] Munro (1995).

Palestinian folklore. A comparison leads us to recognise in the Song literary forms that were widespread in the Ancient Orient, as well as motifs and situations typical of poetry everywhere. The parallels will be indicated as we proceed. Moreover, these literary forms and motifs are not reproduced in the Song as compositions isolated from their context.[62] They are always inserted into a unitary design and almost never recognisable in their pure state. The author, that is, uses a literary language widespread in his cultural environment, but he does so freely, adapting the traditional material to his own ends. The literary forms most clearly recognisable are the *waṣf* and the *paraklausithyron*.

The *waṣf* is an Arab term to indicate the description of the body of the beloved woman, a literary genre very widespread in amorous Arab lyrics[63] and one which, still in the modern period, has a place of honour in the nuptial ceremonies.[64] The most ancient witnesses take us to Egypt where the *waṣf* has characteristics very close to those of the Song.[65] In the poem itself, this literary genre can be identified in 4:1–7; 5:10–16; 6:4–7; 7:2–9. Three of these passages refer to the woman; the fourth, 5:10–16, is a description of the beloved man, something that is not found in the Arab world. It is found, however, in Egyptian culture where the description of the body of the pharaoh often takes as its model the statue of a god.[66] The description of 5:10–16 seems to have been inspired by a similar model. Typical of the *waṣf* is the use of metaphor drawn both from the world of nature and from that of the city and human art. To our Western taste, these metaphors can sound grotesque:[67] we must interpret them, as Keel suggests, not on the basis of a visual model but on that of a functional one.[68] In the body of the

---

[62] The study of Horst (1981), pp. 176–187, found a large echo, above all in the German world, in which the commentaries, even the most recent, are characterised by the fragmentation of the poem into minute compositional units corresponding to supposed primitive literary genres. An extreme example of this fragmentation is the last commentary of G. Krinetzki (1981) which recognised 52 independent poems in the Song. But the authoritative commentaries of Gerleman, Keel and Müller follow along the same lines. The unique exception is the work of Heinevetter.

[63] Cf. Horst (1981), pp. 180–182; Gerleman (1965), p. 65.

[64] Wetzstein (1973), p. 291.

[65] Cf. Mathieu (1996), p. 179; Gerleman (1965), pp. 67–72; White (1978), pp. 114–116, 148–149.

[66] Keel (1994), pp. 22–24.

[67] Cf. Black (2000), pp. 302–323; Brenner (1990), pp. 251–276.

[68] Cf. Keel (1984a), pp. 32–39; Soulen (1967), pp. 183–190.

beloved woman, the poet distils the vital force of the entire surrounding universe, above all of the land of Israel.

The term *paraklausithyron* is of Hellenistic derivation: it indicates the lament at the closed door of the beloved woman, a literary form widespread in the Graeco-Roman world,[69] but one which also has precedents in Egyptian love poetry.[70] In the Song, 2:8–17 and 5:2–8 are inspired by this form. Also in this case, the literary genre is adopted with a certain freedom, being merged with motifs that are foreign to it.

Another procedure typical of the poetry of the Song is the *role-playing*.[71] The beloved man is presented sometimes as a king ('Solomon'; 1:4, 12), sometimes as a shepherd (1:7). The beloved woman assumes the role of a 'keeper of the vineyards' (1:5–6), of a shepherdess (1:8), and of an Oriental princess (3:6–11; 7:2). This is not historical information but literary artifice, psychological projection. The 'burlesque' occurs in two directions: one towards the high, in which the lovers are transported to a higher social sphere. The courtly literature speaks of 'ladies and cavaliers'.[72] Love transfers its participants into a sphere of nobility, of feasting and wealth in which the social conventions and conditions of daily life no longer apply. However, to this burlesque to the high there corresponds a 'burlesque to the low' typical of peasant culture in which the two lovers are projected into a rustic or pastoral situation that is close to nature. This type of

[69] Cf. Müller (1992), p. 30, n. 76 (in this connection, Müller cites Theocritus [*Idyll* 3] and Callimachus [*Epigram* 63]).

[70] Cf. White (1978), pp. 117–118, 149–150; Fox (1985), p. 282; Mathieu (1996), p. 179; Gerleman (1965), p. 123. Cf., for example, Papyrus Chester Beatty IC: "(I) passed by her house in a daze. / I knocked, but it was not open to me. / A fine night for our doorkeeper! / Bolt, I will open (you)! / Door, you are my fate! / You are my very spirit. / Our ox will be slaughtered inside. / O Door, exert not your strength, / so that oxen may be sacrificed to (your) bolt, / fatlings to (your) threshold, / a stout goose to (your) jambs, / and an oriole to (your) lintel (?). / But every choice piece of our ox / will be (saved) for the carpenter lad, / that he may fashion us a bolt of reeds, / a door of grass (?)." (17:8–12; tr. Fox [1985], p. 75). Cf. Keel (1994), Fig. 158, p. 281.

[71] The term travesty/burlesque goes back to the German *Travestien* employed in Jolles (1932), pp. 281–294. For application to the Song, cf. Gerleman (1965), pp. 60–62; Müller (1976), pp. 26–27; *id.* (1992), pp. 13 and 40; Heinevetter (1988), p. 173. On the other hand, critical of this interpretation is Görg (1983), pp. 101–115.

[72] Even today, in Italy, the expression '*principe azzurro*' or 'blue prince' is used in a jocular way to indicate the fiancé.

'burlesque' reminds us of the bucolic poetry of Hellenism,[73] even if it has precedents in Egyptian love lyrics.[74]

This background of Oriental, above all Egyptian, love poetry, allows us to define the overall literary genre of the Song of Songs as 'lyrical', distinguishing it from both the 'narrative' and the 'dramatic'. Characteristic of the lyric is the strong subjectivity of the composition in which the author tends to communicate states of mind, emotions, rather than external facts. It will be appropriate to keep in mind this literary situation in order not to seek for a coherent narrative plot in the Song. If there is unity, it is unity of another kind. More subtle is the distinction between the lyrical and dramatic genres, so much so that G. Genette, clarifying the poetics of Aristotle, distinguishes only two literary 'modes', the narrative and the dramatic:

> In the narrative mode, the poet speaks in his own name, in the dramatic it is the characters themselves who speak, or, more accurately, it is the poet who speaks in the clothes of the various characters.[75]

Along the same lines, Mathieu considers the lyrical genre as "a sub-modal category of dramatic imitation",[76] and he situates Egyptian love poetry in the dramatic literary genre. In fact, in the Song, the author's voice is absent. He speaks through the characters who are three:[77] the *beloved woman* to whom are entrusted, apart from the *Prologue* (1:2–2:7) and *Epilogue* (8:5–14), another three series of poems (I. 2:8–3:5; II. 5:2–6:3; III. 7:10b–8:4); the *beloved man* who responds to the woman's words in two sequences of songs (I. 4:1–5:1; II. 6:4–7:10a), and a plural figure who takes on various guises (from the 'daughters of Jerusalem', 5:9; 6:1; 8:5; to the 'companions' of the man, 1:8, 11; 7:1; to the 'women of the *harem*', 6:10; and the 'brothers' of the woman, 8:8).

---

[73] The parallel is indicated in Müller (1997), pp. 555–574, and Heinevetter (1988), p. 173.

[74] Cf. Hermann (1959), pp. 111–112; Gerleman (1965), pp. 60–62; White (1978), pp. 109–114, 146–148.

[75] Genette (1986), pp. 98 and 150.

[76] Mathieu (1996), p. 133.

[77] Unfortunately, the text of the Song does not say explicitly who is speaking nor to whom the discourse is addressed (it is only Sinaiticus and Alexandrinus that have the stage directions). So it must be deduced from the context which is often disputed. Even though convinced that some attributions are speculative, we have chosen nevertheless to indicate the names of the individual actors, each time giving the reasons: the text is, in fact, clearly dramatised.

Sometimes this figure has the function of a voice 'off-stage' which could be identified with that of the 'narrator' (3:6–11; 8:11). The similarity to Greek tragedy is obvious.[78] For this reason, we call this figure by the general name of *chorus*. There is one sole occasion when the author speaks personally and not through his characters, and that is in 5:1ef where he comments benevolently on the union of the two lovers: "Eat, my friends, drink, get drunk, my dears!"[79]

By contrast with the Egyptian love songs which are characterised by monologues from the protagonists even when they are addressed to the partner,[80] the Song is a real and proper dialogue,[81] in this way too coming close to the world of the Greek theatre. However, the numerous attempts that have been made in the past to consider it as a classical drama are not convincing.[82] Today there are few who favour this theory,[83] and rightly so. Like narrative, drama too needs a plot, and the Song does not have one. Moreover, the different kinds of literary 'role-playing' make a dramatic interpretation impossible.[84] We prefer,

---

[78] Cf. Lacocque (1998), p. 42, n. 96.

[79] Even in the Egyptian love songs, the monologue of the two lovers is sometimes interrupted by the voice of the narrator. Mathieu (1996), pp. 145–149, speaks in this connection of refined 'transgression modale'.

[80] Mathieu (1996), p. 143.

[81] On the theological dimension of this literary genre, cf. Kristeva (1983), pp. 92–93; Rosenzweig (2005), pp. 188–189. Rosenzweig sees in the 'I-you' of the Song of Songs the prototype of every discourse on the human person and on God. So too Sonnet (1997), pp. 481–502.

[82] Already Origen defined the Song as an "epithalamium [...] which Solomon wrote in the form of a drama" (Origen, *Commentary*, p. 21). The dramatic theory, introduced by J. F. Jacobi at the end of the seventeenth century, enjoyed widespread popularity in the eighteenth. It assumed two basic forms: one with three characters (Solomon—the shepherd—the shepherdess), the other with two (Solomon—the Shulamite). The first form is more widespread. We record, for example: Ewald (1826); Löwysohn (1816); Renan (1884); Harper (1907); Cicognani (1911); and Pouget-Guitton (1934). Representatives of the second form are Delitzsch (1875) and Minocchi (1898). In the second group, the figure of Solomon is that of the beloved man while in the first he is the rival of the true beloved who is the shepherd; this observation alone leads us to doubt the suitability of this approach.

[83] We cite, for example: Mazor (1990); Provan (2001); Stoop-van Paridon (2005), who have taken up again the hypothesis of a drama with three characters; and Di Bianco (2000), who applies to the Song the tools of modern dramatological analysis.

[84] For a criticism of the dramatic interpretation, cf Murphy (1990), p. 58; Keel (1994), pp. 15–16; Elliott (1989), pp. 12–14. We have to dissent from the last author, however, when in confirmation of the fact that the Song cannot be a drama, she adduces the fact that this form of literature is foreign to the biblical world (*ibid.*, p. 13). Actually, this is a further element with which to date the Song in the Hellenistic period; besides, the love lyric is not typical of biblical literature either.

therefore, to define the Song, with D. Lys, as a "lyrical work with dramatic elements".[85]

4. Structure

The question of structure is closely connected to that of literary genre, Those who uphold the dramatic genre clearly presuppose the unity of the text even if, on this account, they have to introduce elements foreign to it.[86] Even the allegorical interpretation, traditional in rabbinic and patristic exegesis, assumes an organic development in the Song whether from the historical or the spiritual point of view. The commentary of Robert and Tournay is a typical example of this.[87] By contrast, the cultic interpretation, of which we shall speak below, upsets the order of the poem (and, often, the text too): the question of the structure is completely ignored.[88]

The placing of the Song in the sphere of the love lyric and the study of the smaller forms bound up with this genre have led to its being considered an anthology of disparate love lyrics.[89] This conclusion is

---

[85] Lys (1968), pp. 23–24. In the same sense already, Vaccari (1959), p. 113: "Is the Song a drama? Is it a lyric? It is a bit of both; but nothing which corresponds exactly to our literary categories. It is a lyrical dialogue accompanied by some dramatic movement". Cf. also Ravasi (1992), pp. 97–98, who compares this genre, a mixture between lyric and drama, to the 'idyll' and the 'mime' of Hellenistic literature.

[86] Cf. the structure proposed by Delitzsch (1875), pp. 143–161: "First act: the kindling of mutual love between the two lovers (1:2–2:7); Second act: mutual searching and finding by the lovers (2:8–3:5); Third act: procession of the bride and wedding (3:6–5:1); Fourth act: love rejected, but renewed (5:2–6:9); Fifth act: the Shulamite, attractive but humble princess (6:10–8:4); Sixth act: consolidating of the bond of love in the country of the Shulamite (8:5–14)".

[87] Robert – Tournay (1963) divide the Song into five poems: First poem: 1:5–2:7; Second poem: 2:8–3:5; Third poem: 3:6–5:1; Fourth poem: 5:2–6:3; Fifth poem: 6:4–8:5a, framed by a Prologue (1:2–4) and an Epilogue (8:5b-7). In 8:8–14, Robert-Tournay see a series of appendices added to the text successively.

[88] Wittekindt (1925) begins the poem with Song 6:8–10 to which there follow 1:7–8; 1:5–6; 1:9–10; 4:1–7; 4:12–5:1; 4:9–11; 7:1–6. Equally free is the sequence suggested in Schmökel (1956), pp. 45–46, in which he traces three scenes of sacred marriage in the Song. The first scene, for example, consists of the following sections in this order: Song 8:13; 6:10.5a; 1:5–6; 6:1; 6:2; 6:11–12; 3:1–2; 5:7; 3:4; 5:2–6; 3:3; 5:8; 5:9; 5:10–16; 1:7; 1:8; 8:1–2.

[89] One of the pioneers of this kind of consideration is Haupt (1907) who arrives at a disturbing of the order of the songs similar to that of Wittekindt and Schmökel, so much so that he needs a special table to trace the individual verses. According to him, the Song begins with 3:6–11*, continuing with 6:9, 12; 7:1; 7:7, 5, 4, 9, 6, 2 (and so on).

the most widespread today:[90] at most there is recognition of the hand of a redactor who has added some unifying motive here and there.[91] A similar result is reached by those who see in the Song a collection of nuptial songs: here too the link uniting the various poems is seen as something external,[92] in this case the ceremonies of the nuptial week.

Such a classification is not without consequence, however. If the Song is not a unitary composition, a consideration of the poem's content at the global level is rendered impossible. Moreover, the recourse to Oriental parallels often obscures the position of the Song within the Bible, putting the theological content of the book in second place.[93]

Our survey of the poetry of the Song leads us to recognise in it the work of an unmistakable personality: the refined literary artifice, the play of the metaphors, the repetition of terms and themes, coherent from beginning to end,[94] speak ineluctably in favour of the unity of the work. Clearly this is not a narrative unity but, precisely, a poetic, lyrical unity.[95] The Song is the work not of a redactor but of an author.[96]

---

[90] Cf., for example, Falk (1982); Gordis (1974); White (1978), p. 33; Rudolph (1962); Keel (1994); Krinetzki (1981); Müller (1992); Gerleman (1965); Morla (2004), p. 49: "Among current specialists, the opinion is prevalent that the Song is a collection of originally independent poems, without visible articulation, and arranged by association of ideas"; Luzarraga (2005), p. 121: "What appears in the Song is a generic argument, and as such does not allow us to speak of a fixed structure, a coherent development or a uniform dynamism, but only of a unity of theme and style". Cf. the judgement of Eissfeld (1965), p. 486: "Justice is best done to the text by the interpretation of the book as a collection of disconnected songs".

[91] Cf. Murphy (1990), pp. 62–64; Bonora (1997), pp. 139–140: "It appears to me preferable to read the Song of Songs as a collection of love poems, originally independent and then assembled together whether by unity of theme (love between man and woman) or through a certain homogeneity of ideas, style, vocabulary and images"; Longman (2001), interprets the title of the book thus: "It is a single Song composed of many different Songs".

[92] Following Wetzstein (1873), pp. 270–301, Budde (1898), p. XVI, sees in the Song a collection of twenty four nuptial songs.

[93] So, rightly, Elliott (1989), p. 32.

[94] We distance ourselves from those who would wish to conclude the Song with 8:7 (cf. Robert – Tournay [1963], p. 308), or with 8:6 (cf. Heinevetter [1988], pp. 166–169). On the basis for this position we refer to pp. 438–441.

[95] Elliott (1989), p. 33, speaks of the "organic unity" like that of a living organism, and she explains it thus: "In an organic unity each of the parts functions in virtue of the whole and, without each part, the whole lacks either integral or essential unity".

[96] We find ourselves in complete agreement with Ravasi (1992), p. 82, when he writes: "We are convinced that the text which has come down to us presents a unity that is difficult to contest, except at the price of textual disruption, except at the price of external 'logics', except for a scant structural analysis. We are convinced that this

By contrast with the Egyptian 'songs of love', the very title 'Song of Songs' (1:1) introduces the poem in unitary form.[97] However, the reader is disorientated by the fact that even those exegetes who recognise the unity of the poem still do not agree on the fundamental lines of its structure.[98] Undoubtedly the recovery of a literary structure is not something mechanical; it is an undertaking which leaves room for the poetic sensibility of the critic. It seems, however, that, even if opinions can diverge over the details, research has converged on various points. The proposal presented here is original, but it is based on observations made by more than one party: it is indebted above all to the work of M. T. Elliott[99] and H.-J. Heinevetter.[100]

In my opinion, the Song of Songs is composed of a *Prologue* (1:2–2:7), an *Epilogue* (8:5–14), and the Poem proper which is divided into

---

unity is not merely superficial, that is, the fruit of redactional interventions, because these would almost coincide with the proper activity of an author". Landy (1983), p. 37, reaches a similar conclusion: "The poem is a unity, such as it is, in part because of its thematic coherence, its erotic mode; and in part because of the reappearance of the same elements in diverse contexts, such as leitmotivs, refrains, episodes that repeat each other with variations, confluences of images". Cf. also Fox (1985), pp. 218–222; Lacocque (1998), p. 51; Garrett (1993), p. 376 (building on R. L. Alden); Hwang (2003); Wendland (1995); Davidson (2003); Davidson (2007), pp. 559–561; Exum (2005), pp. 33–41: 'The present commentary assumes that only by reading it as a whole can we do justice to its poetic accomplishment" (p. 37). By contrast, the attempts to detect redactional strata in the Song, seem to be without foundation, as in the case of Loretz (1971), pp. 59–63; Angénieux (1965), pp. 96–142; *id.* (1969), pp. 65–83, who recognises eight successive poems in the Song; or Heinevetter (1988), who distinguishes an original anti-Solomonic redaction from a final pro-Solomonic one.

[97] Elliott (1989), p. 34.

[98] Ravasi (1992), pp. 90–91, lists a series of thirty eight works in which the number of poetic units in the Song varies from a minimum of four to a maximum of fifty two.

[99] Elliott (1989), presents a structure in four parts framed by a prologue (1:2 –2:7) and an epilogue (8:5–14): first part: 2:8–3:5; second part: 3:6–5:1; third part: 5:2–6:3; fourth part: 6:4–8:4. This is a doctoral thesis defended at the Pontifical Biblical Institute in Rome under the moderation of Professor M. Gilbert: it is a work which, on the basis of the most detailed observations of form and content, demonstrates in a convincing way that the Song could not have been a redactional work.

[100] Heinevetter's work is a doctoral thesis presented at Münster under the direction of E. Zenger. Heinevetter recognises in the Song an introduction (1:2–2:7) and a body divided into two large symmetrical units (2:8–5:1 and 5:2–8:6. 8:7–14 he regards as an addition, cf., *supra*, n. 96). One has the impression that the analysis of the last part and, above all, of the addition is a little hurried and not of the same quality as that of the first two parts. Recently, there has appeared the posthumous thesis of D. Roberts (2007). The present work was not able to take it into account, but it is striking how, in what regards the small units of the poem, Roberts's conclusions coincide for the most part with those which I have arrived at by different ways.

Table 1

Prologue 1:2–2:7			Sick with love 2:5 Embrace 2:6 Awakening 2:7
Part I 2:8–5:1	*Songs of the beloved woman*	Matinée 2:8–17	Mutual belonging 2:16 Grazing among the lotus flowers 2:16 Passage of the day 2:17 The young stag on the mountains 2:17
		Nocturn 3:1–5	Awakening 3:5
	Choral Intermezzo	Nuptial procession 3:6–11	Ascent 3:6
	Songs of the beloved man	Contemplation 4:1–7	Grazing among the lotus flowers 4:5 Passage of the day 4:6 The young stag on the mountains 4:5–6
		Encounter 4:8–5:1	
Part II 5:2–8:4	*New songs of the beloved woman*	Separation 5:2–8 Remembrance 5:9–16 Love found again 6:1–3	Sick with love 5:8 Mutual belonging 6:3 Grazing among the lotus flowers 6:3
	New songs of the beloved man	Contemplation 6:4–12 Desire 7:1–11	Mutual belonging 7:11
	Final songs of the beloved woman	Union in nature 7:12–14 Union in the city 8:1–4	Embrace 8:3 Awakening 8:4
Epilogue 8:5–14			Ascent 8:5 The young stag on the mountains 8:14.

two parts that are almost symmetrical: 2:8–5:1 and 5:2–8:4 (cf. *Tab. 1*). The criteria on which my proposal is founded are various:

1) The first criterion is that of the *characters* who take part. Apart from the Prologue (1:2–2:7) and the Epilogue (8:5–14)—both entrusted to the woman but characterised by a lively dialogue between three voices—the two main parts are made up of three series of 'songs of the beloved woman' (I = 2:8–17 + 3:1–5; II = 5:2–8 + 5:9–16 + 6:1–3; III = 7:12–14 + 8:1–4), to which correspond two series of 'songs of the beloved man' (I = 4:1–7 + 4:8–5:1; II = 6:4–12 + 7:1–11). A single song

is entrusted to a voice off-stage which we identify with the 'chorus' (3:6–11). The dialogic principle, therefore, has a value which is not only ideal, as has been demonstrated by Rosenzweig[101] in an exemplary way, but also formal, structural.[102]

2) A second, important criterion is that of the *repetition* of words and themes. This type of approach has come into prominence above all from modern structural research. However, Rupert of Deutz already divided the Song into four parts on the basis of the 'refrain of awakening' (2:7; 3:5; 8:4).[103] The structural importance of the refrains has been underlined in the work of Angénieux[104] and Elliott.[105] From the latter we obtain the following list:[106]

a) Embrace, 2:6; 8:3.
b) Awakening, 2:7; 3:5; 8:4.
c) Mutual belonging, 2:16; 6:3; 7:11.
d) Passage of the day, 2:17; 4:6.
e) The young stag on the mountains, 2:17; 4:5–6; 8:14.
f) Grazing among the lotus flowers, 2:16; 4:5; 6:3.
g) Ascent, 3:6; 6:10; 8:5.
h) Sick with love, 2:5; 5:8.

The refrain of ascent (g) opens a poetic unit while all the others have a concluding function. It is interesting to note the accumulation of several refrains in some passages, as in 2:6–7 and 8:3–4 (a + b); in 2:16–17 and 4:5–6 (d + e + f). Of particular importance is the phenomenon in 2:6–7 and 8:3–4 because these are the signals for the conclusion of the Prologue (1:2–2:7) and of the body of the poem (2:8–8:4).[107]

---

[101] Cf., *supra*, n. 82.

[102] The structural function of the dialogue is pointed out in Webster (1982), p. 74; in Rendtorff (1985), pp. 262–263; and in Murphy (1990), p. 66 ("Elements of dialogue seem to provide the strongest evidence of sequential arrangement of poetic units within the Song and thus also suggest the work's overall coherence"); Fokkelman (2001), p. 202 ("The change of voice not only is of crucial significance for the understanding of each verse, but also proves to be a prominent criterion for the main outline"); Exum (2005), p. 38 ("Dialog is what determines the poetic development of the Song").

[103] Cf. *PL* 168:839.

[104] Angénieux (1965), pp. 96–142; *id.* (1969).

[105] Elliott (1989), pp. 36–41.

[106] Elliott (1989), p. 38. For other lists, cf. Murphy (1990), pp. 76–78 (five refrains); Angénieux (1965), pp. 104–105 (four principal refrains and two secondary ones). Watson (1984), p. 295, defines the refrain thus: "a block of verses which recurs more than once within a poem. Such a block can comprise a single word, a line of poetry or even a complete strophe".

[107] Cf. Elliott (1989), p. 39.

The works of J. C. Exum,[108] W. H. Shea,[109] E. C. Webster[110] and D. A. Dorsey[111] elaborate a structure for the Song founded on the tiniest literary observations, basically on the repetition of lexemes and themes. Although H.-J. Heinevetter[112] and E. Bosshard-Nepustil[113] have highlighted the defects of such an approach, it remains fundamental nevertheless. From these observations one obtains the conviction that the Song is a poem in two parts in which the second part repeats with variation the content of the first one: the caesura between the first and second parts is often placed after 5:1, considered by several authors to be the centre of the poem.[114]

3) Already Bossuet divided the Song on the basis of six transitions from night to dawn (2:7; 3:1; 5:2; 6:9; 7:11–12; 8:4):[115] he saw in this a description of the seven days of the nuptial ceremonies. Even if such a rigid framework seems foreign to the poetry of the Song, the principle of a certain coherence in the *determination of time* is present in the structure of the poem. For example: the passage from 2:7 (refrain of awakening) and 2:8–14 (morning theme) and that from 2:17 (evening theme) to 3:1 (night theme) is clear. Moreover, the temporal frame has a relevance which is far from secondary in Egyptian amorous lyrics as well.[116]

4) Beside the temporal dynamic, the spatial one also has importance in the structure of the Song. Heinevetter has rightly pointed out

---

[108] Exum (1973), p. 77, traces a structure in six parts in which the first (a. 1:2–2:6) corresponds to the last (a'. 8:4–14); the second (b. 2:7–3:5) corresponds to the fourth (b'. 5:2–6:3) and the third (c. 3:6–5:1) to the fifth (c'. 6:4–8:3).

[109] The structure proposed in Shea (1980), pp. 73–93, is chiastic and, like that of Exum, comprises six parts: a) 1:2–2:2; b) 2:3–17; c) 3:1–4:16; c') 5:1–7:10; b') 7:11–8:5; a') 8:6–14.

[110] Webster (1982), p. 74, delineates a palindromic structure around a central element. Beside 'repetition', he attaches value to the dialogic principle, arriving at the following proposal: a) 1:2–2:6 + 2:7–3:5 (woman); b) 4:1–7 + 4:8–15 (man); c) 4:16–6:3 (woman); b') 6:4–10 + 6:11–7:10 (man); a') 7:11–8:3 + 8:4–14 (woman).

[111] Dorsey (1990), pp. 93–94, also comes to a centric structure in 7 (!) units: a) 1:2–2:7; b) 2:8–17; c) 3:1–5; d) 3:6–5:1; c') 5:2–7:11; b') 7:12–8:4; a') 8:5–14.

[112] Heinevetter (1988), pp. 35–39: "Structural analysis with neglect of the global interpretation".

[113] Bosshard-Nepustil (1996), p. 48. But the structure proposed by Bosshard-Nepustil is discredited by ideological prejudices. He returns to a reading of the allegorical type, even if translated into modern terms, suggesting a (forced!) alternation of two themes: 'king + queen' and 'shepherd + shepherdess'.

[114] So Heinevetter (1988), p. 133.

[115] Bossuet (1732), pp. 195–199. The seven parts into which Bossuet divides the Song are: 1:1–2:6; 2:7–17; 3:1–5:1; 5:2–6:8; 6:9–7:10; 7:11–8:3; 8:4–14.

[116] For a parallel, cf. Mathieu (1996), pp. 159–162 ("Le temps amoureux").

a critical attitude in the poem concerning the relationship with the city and the search for a more simple life in contact with nature.[117] The juxtaposition of 2:8–17 with 3:1–5, like that of 7:12–14 with 8:1–4, is in the service of a contrast between nature, as the place of love, and the city, as the place potentially hostile to it. If love originates in nature, the desert or the steep mountains (3:6; 4:8; 8:5a), it is consummated in the city, or rather in the garden (5:1; 8:5c.14) which is the synthesis between nature and culture, which is nature humanised and the city vitalised by nature.[118] The journey from the desert to the garden is the structural principle in 3:6–5:1; 8:5–14.

5) Finally, it is typical of the amorous lyric that it progresses from separation to union by means of a gradual drawing together of the lovers. Medieval literature speaks of the *gradus amoris* ('amorous journey').[119] B. Mathieu has found this development in Egyptian love poems.[120] D. Buzy has observed it in the individual units of the Song, the structure of which would be characterised by the passage from contemplation to union.[121] Even if a rigid application of the principle is to be avoided, I believe that in many poetic units of the Song a similar progression can actually be noted.[122] It is the case, for example, in the Prologue in which in the first strophe the woman dreams of being brought into the king's chamber (1:4). The dream will come true at the end of the unit in 2:4 ("He has brought me into the banqueting chamber"), passing through the intermediate situation of 1:12 ("While the king is in his triclinium, my nard pours forth its fragrance"). Moreover, all the refrains listed above, with the exception of the refrain of

---

[117] Heinevetter (1988), pp. 179–190 ("Culture and nature: the 'green' vision of the Song").

[118] Cf. Landy (1983), p. 190.

[119] "Les nobles poètes disent que cinq lignes il y a en amours, c'est-à-dire cinq points ou cinq dégrés expeciaux, c'est assavoir le regard, le parler, l'attouchement, le baiser, et le dernier qui est le plus désiré, et auquel tous les autres tendent, c'est celui qu'on nomme par honnêté le don de merci" (Lemaire of Belgium, cited in Rousset [1984], p. 46, n. 10).

[120] Mathieu (1996), pp. 163–175: the passages listed are very close to those of the Song.

[121] Buzy (1940), pp. 172–190 and (1951), pp. 289–290, delineates seven units within which this movement is demonstrable: a) 1:5–2:7; b) 3:1; 2:8–14; 3:2–5; c) 4:1–5:1; d) 5:2–6:3; e) 6:4–12; f) 7:1–14; g) 8:1–7. It should be noted, however, how Buzy alters the order of the sections.

[122] "There is a dynamic movement of longing that becomes a structural principle in the poem as it moves forward incrementally from one stage of yearning to the next" (Fisch [1990], p. 86).

ascent refer to the union of the two lovers. Thus they have a concluding function.

Is it possible to detect this principle also within the macrostructure of the poem? Goulder claims this is undoubtedly the case, but he ends up in delineating a narrative plot similar to that of the dramatic hypothesis and forcing the text.[123] Against a continuous development of the text stands the fact that union is described right in the middle of the poem. Segal, therefore, proposes to see a development from separation to union in each of the two parts of the Song.[124] Here too we must avoid a mechanical symmetry: we are dealing with a principle which the poet employs freely. It is also possible that he is utilising existing material as a result of which his compositional freedom is limited. At any rate, a progress from an initial situation of separation to a final one of union is discernible both in 2:8–5:1 and in 5:2–8:4.[125] Leaving a thorough demonstration to the exegetical analysis, we sketch here the principal steps of this development.

Table 2

1. The two lovers are separated. He is searching for her.	2:8–17	5:2–5
2. She is searching for him	3:1–5	5:6–6:3
3. The two lovers are before each other: admiration and desire	4:1– 7	6:4–7:11
4. Union	4:8–5:1	7:12–8:4

[123] Goulder (1986), p. 2, delineates in the Song "a semi-continuous sequence of fourteen scenes, moving in a progression from the arrival of the Princess at Solomon's court to her acknowledgment by the King as his favourite queen". But the lady of the Song is never presented as a princess!

[124] Segal (1962), pp. 470–490, arrives thus at a structure for the Song which is very close to ours. He distinguishes: introductory stanza (1:2–8); body of the poem, divided into two symmetrical parts (1:9–5:1 and 5:2–8:6a); concluding stanza (8:6b–14).

[125] *Contra* Davidson (2007), pp. 592–601; Garrett and House (2004), p. 193, who think rather of a single plot. There would be only one description of the union of the spouses, precisely in 5:1. What happens before would be preliminary to the sexual union, what happens after would be moments in the life of the couple after their marriage. The thesis is certainly stimulating and is correct in certain of its elements, but, in my opinion, there are certain other elements which do not allow themselves to be incorporated into this vision: for instance, 5:2–6 is unthinkable if the two are married, not to mention the fact that sexual union is also described in 2:6.

5. Historical-Cultural Environment

Once the literary unity of the Song has been established, the question of its place in the history of literature is unavoidable.[126] To this day, however, the answer is far from clear: it ranges from the tenth century B.C., the era of Solomon,[127] up to the first century B.C.[128] Before formulating our proposal, it is appropriate to have a look to the literary parallels of the poem.

Here too the spectrum is rather wide, hardly to be wondered at since love is a universal theme of literature. Wherever love has been sung, it is natural to find assonances with the Song. At times, however, the similarities do not go beyond a vague similarity of themes and motifs: this is the case, for example, with the parallels drawn with Indian,[129] Tamil,[130] or Ethiopic literature.[131] More suitable, it seems to me, is the comparison with the modern Palestinian and Arab world. Here we find preserved certain literary forms such as the *waṣf*, which are also characteristic of the biblical poem and where the metaphorical language has clear analogies.[132] In 1873, the Prussian consul in Damascus, J. G. Wetzstein, published his observations on the nuptial customs of the peasants of Hauran, discovering there surprising analogies with the Song:[133] this has led many exegetes to see the nuptial week, something also characteristic of the Jewish tradition, as the original *Sitz im Leben* of the poem.[134] But the lady of the Song is called 'bride' in only one particular section (4:8–5:1), whereas the recurring appellatives

[126] If we were to assume the text to be an anthology, the question could be avoided as is the case for example with Gordis: "Being lyrical in character, with no historical allusions, most of the songs are undatable" (Gordis [1974], p. 23, cf. also Provan [2001], p. 335; Longman [2001], p. 19). It is my conviction that lyric poetry is not isolated from its historical circumstances.

[127] So, for example, Delitzsch (1875), p. 11; Segal (1962), pp. 481–483; Gordis (1974), p. 23; Gerleman (1965), pp. 76–77.

[128] So Garbini (1982), pp. 39–46; *id.* (1992), pp. 293–296 (exactly 68 B.C.).

[129] Cf. Ravasi (1992), pp. 46–47 (we refer to this work for further bibliography). Much space is reserved for Indian mythology in Pope (1977).

[130] Cf. Rabin (1973), pp. 205–219, and, above all, Mariaselvam (1988).

[131] Cf. the presentation in Robert – Tournay (1963), pp. 418–421.

[132] We shall make use of theses parallels many times in the detailed analysis. Cf. Dalman (1901); Stephan (1922), pp. 199–278. For a critical review, cf. Robert—Tournay (1963), pp. 382–417.

[133] During the nuptial week, the two spouses are called 'king' and 'queen'; the bride is eulogised with the *waṣf*; she executes the 'sword dance', etc. (cf. Wetzstein [1873]; *id.* [1875], pp. 162–177).

[134] Typical, in this sense, is Budde (1898). Cf. also Siegfried (1898), pp. 87–90.

between the two lovers are *raʿyātî* ('my friend') and *dôdî* ('my beloved'), terms which allude to a friendly rather than an institutional relationship: it is love that is being celebrated here, not marriage.

Archaeological discoveries have led scholars to compare the Song of Songs with the amorous literature of the cultures of the Ancient Near East. Throughout the ancient Orient, the cult of the sacred couple, whose union guaranteed fertility to the earth and to living beings, was widespread. This union was represented in cultic terms by means of the ceremony of the sacred marriage, above all on the occasion of the new year when the divine couple were personified by a priestess and the king or a priest.[135] In Mesopotamia, in the Sumerian epoch, the divine couple were called Inanna and Dumuzi; in the Akkadian epoch, Ishtar and Tammuz. At Ugarit, the two deities were Anat and Baal, in Egypt, Isis and Osiris. The most ancient love poems, popularised in the version of S. N. Kramer,[136] are precisely those Sumerian ones which refer to the sacred marriage. A whole current of exegesis has seen in the Song a Hebrew version of this ancient myth the existence of which is attested even in the Old Testament.[137] The commentary of D. Lys[138] is influenced by this vision when he sees in the Song the taking of a position, in a secularising direction, against the sacred marriage. Those elements which the myth attributed to the divine couple would have been demythologised in the Song and referred to a concrete couple of lovers.

The Mesopotamian texts on the sacred marriage are very direct: sex is described explicitly by contrast with the Song where genitality is not so open. The approach to sexuality is different in the two cases. The ceremonies of the sacred marriage are intended to secure the fertility

---

[135] Cf. Jacobsen (1975), pp. 65–97.

[136] Cf. Kramer (1969); Wolkstein – Kramer (1983); *ANET*, pp. 496, 637–645. Not all the Sumerian and Akkadian texts which speak of love refer to the sacred marriage: Jacobsen (1987), p. 2, attributes some compositions to the genre of 'courtship', connected only indirectly with the cult; Alster (1985), pp. 127–159, speaks, for other compositions, of 'royal love songs' which celebrate a secular, human love. Be that as it may, the majority of the Sumerian love lyrics are of a cultic, mythological character. For other parallels, cf. Cooper (1971), pp. 157–162; Lambert (1975), pp. 98–135; Nissinen (1998), pp. 585–634.

[137] Cf., above all, Wittekindt (1925); Schmökel (1952); *id.* (1956), but also, for example, Haller (1940); Ringgren (1962). In English, the leader of this tendency is T. J. Meek (cf. Meek [1922–1923]; *id.* [1924a]; *id.* [1924b]). More recently, the monumental work of M. H. Pope has devoted much space to the Mesopotamian and Ugaritic parallels (Pope [1977]).

[138] Lys (1968).

of the country whereas in the Song fertility plays a very secondary role: at the centre is the relationship and the feelings of the two lovers.[139] However, even if the attempts to interpret the Song in the same way as a cultic drama are not convincing, some themes take on new light against the background of the cuneiform literature,[140] and we shall not hesitate to point them out in the course of this study: for example, the motif of the identification of the woman with the earth (1:6e), the theme of the garden (4:12–5:1),[141] the identification of the woman with heavenly phenomena (6:10: Inanna was the morning star!), the strange use of the plural in the description of loving intimacy (cf. 1:4).[142] The equivalence of Love and Death (8:6) makes us think of the Ugaritic myth of Baal and Mot.

Among all the texts of the Ancient Orient, those which come closest in form and content to the Song are certainly the Egyptian love songs. We are talking here of four collections: Papyrus Chester Beatty I, Papyrus Harris 500, the Turin Papyrus and the Vase of Deir el-Medineh, beside some minor fragments.[143] The date of composition is between the nineteenth and twentieth dynasties, that is, between 1300 and 1150 B.C.: we are at the beginning of the 'New Kingdom', and the influences of the el-Amarna epoch are clearly being felt.[144] The environment in which these songs have arisen is not a cultic but a sapiential one, the court schools designed to prepare public officials.[145] As in the Song, one can often understand a reference to other sapiential compositions;[146] while in these, however, there is often a warning against the perils of love, any moralising concern is absent in the songs. Love is celebrated in itself with ecstatic admiration. Preoccupation with fertility and the safety of the family is not in the foreground (even if such aspects are not ignored); rather the emphasis is on the relationship between the two lovers.

---

139 Keel (1984a), pp. 18–19; *id.* (1994), p. 246.

140 Cf. Westenholz (1992); Watson (1995).

141 In this connection, cf. Paul (1997), pp. 253–271.

142 Paul (1995).

143 For the citations, we follow Mathieu (1996). For the translation we usually employ that of Fox (1985), sometimes also that of Bresciani (1990), pp. 452–477.

144 Fox (1985), pp. 183–186.

145 White (1978), pp. 71–81.

146 Cf. Mathieu (1996), pp. 218–219, 223–226; Krinetzki (1981), pp. 25–26.

Previously we noted the relationship to the dramatico-lyrical literary genre,[147] with the difference that the songs are characterised by the interior monologue of the two lovers whereas the Song is fundamentally a dialogue. Even in the songs, though, one hears, beside the protagonists, either the external voice of the narrator or that of a chorus, the group of his or her companions.

The basic rhythmical measure in the songs is the heptametrical distich consisting of two lines, the first with four accents, the second with three. Here too the similarity to the *qinâ* (the distich of 3 + 2 accents) with which the greater part of the Song of Songs is composed is notable. Like the Song, the Egyptian love songs do not belong to popular poetry but are works of exquisite literary construction: paronomasia, rhyme, alliteration, the phenomena of anaphora and epiphora, parallelism in its various forms are frequent. Each song is divided into 'stanzas' each with its own structure, often characterised by inclusion. The number 7 is favoured in the compositions.[148]

Egyptian amorous lyrics are characterised by the frequent use of metaphor and simile. Most of the time, the metaphors are drawn from the world of nature: plants, animals, the landscape of the Nile Delta with its canals and its swamps.[149] The place of love is the garden under the shadow of some tree. Naturally, in these songs, the 'lotus flower' (*sšn*) plays a big part; it too is the favoured flower of the Song (*šôšannâ*, cfr. 2:1–2, 16; 5:13; 6:2–3; 7:3).[150]

Hermann has noted the phenomenon of burlesque in the Egyptian songs—both that to the high, where the two lovers are clothed as characters of high class ('royal burlesque'), and that to the low, where, for example, one of the two characters is represented as the 'servant' of the other ('servile burlesque'), or as gardener or peasant ('pastoral burlesque').[151] Other *topoi* common to the two compositions are the

[147] Mathieu (1996), pp. 133–149.
[148] Cf., again, Mathieu (1996), pp. 189–215.
[149] Cf. Niccacci (1991), pp. 71–76.
[150] Cf., *infra*, pp. 83–84.
[151] Hermann (1959), pp. 111–124; White (1978), pp. 109–114, 146–148; Gerleman (1965), pp. 60–62. We have previously pointed out this same phenomenon in the Song. Cf., *supra*, pp. 14–15.

waṣf and the *paraklausithyron* of which we spoke above,[152] and again the 'love sickness'[153] and the 'love trap'.[154]

The surprising appellation 'sister' with which the beloved woman is designated in the Song (cf. 4:9, 10, 12; 5:1) is the common appellation of the woman in the Egyptian love songs (the beloved man is called 'brother', cf. Song 8:1). The term *yāpeh/yāpâ* ('fair'), which recurs eleven times in the Song (1;8, 15, 16; 2:10, 13; 4:1, 7; 5:9; 6:1, 4, 10), is rather rare in the rest of the OT but it finds correspondence in the Egyptian love songs.[155] Also common to the two compositions is the role of the mother in connection with love:[156] the paternal figure is completely absent. A surprising likeness is provided by the theme of the 'mother's house' (Song 3:4; 8:2). In the songs, the house of the mother (of the bride) is the place where the first encounters between the two take place before the marriage proper when the bride is taken into the house of her husband.[157]

The affinity with the world of Egypt reveals itself also in other particulars. The understanding of the kiss as an exchange of perfumes (Song 1:3; 4:10–11; 7:9) is typical of the Egyptian literature where the 'kiss' is understood as 'the perfume of the nose'.[158] Also characteristic of the Egyptian love songs is the representation of night, not in its negative aspect as the 'domain of evil' but in its positive guise as 'time of love' (cf. Song 2:17; 3:1).[159] Moreover the connected theme of the morning awakening after the night of love (Song 2:7; 3:5; 8:4) is well-known in the Egyptian world.[160]

We take our inspiration for understanding the dynamic of the Song from Mathieu's analysis of the 'amorous journey' in the Egyptian love songs.[161] Mathieu finds the following steps in the songs: look, desire,

---

[152] Cf., *supra*, p. 14.

[153] Cf. Niccacci (1991), pp. 62–65. For the Song, cf. 2:5; 5:8; for the Egyptian love songs, Papyrus Chester Beatty IA 1:8; 4:6–8; Papyrus Harris 500A 2:9–11 (cf., *infra*, p. 153, n. 204).

[154] Cf. Song 7:6 with Papyrus Harris 500A 1:12–2:1 (cf., in this connection, *infra*, p. 388).

[155] Cf. Ravasi (1992), p. 50; Murphy (1990), p. 70.

[156] Cf., *infra*, p. 136, n. 150.

[157] Cf., *infra*, p. 135, n. 147; also p. 144, n. 10.

[158] Cf. Niccacci (1991), p. 82; White (1978), p. 138; Gerleman (1965), p. 203.

[159] "Le thème des dangers de la nuit, si caractéristique de la littérature sapientiale et didactique, s'efface dans le cadre du genre amoureux, devant une entité complice" (Mathieu [1996], p. 160).

[160] Cf., *infra*, p. 93, n. 217.

[161] Cf., *supra*, p. 23.

agitation, Love (with a capital letter), union, expressed indirectly by means of the *topoi* of the embrace and the nuptial chamber. These details also find their match in the Song. For the 'agitation' caused by the 'look', cf. Song 4:9 and 6:5. For the representation of union, cf. 2:6; 8:3 (theme of the embrace) and 1:4; 2:4; 3:4; 8:5 (theme of the chamber).

The reciprocity which constitutes a fundamental characteristic of love in the Song is present also in the Egyptian love songs.[162] Often the words of one of the partners are echoed in the words of the other.[163] Like the love of the Song, so too the love of the Egyptian songs, though not being explicitly bound to the institution of the family, is not an occasional adventure: it sings of the 'uniqueness' of its own partner,[164] and of the 'eternity' which is typical of every authentic experience of love.[165]

By contrast with the Sumerian poems on the sacred marriage, the protagonists of the Egyptian love songs, like those of the Song, are not gods, simply mortals: in both cases, they do not have names, thus identifying themselves with every person who is in love. And it is typical of the Egyptian songs, as of the Song to emphasise the religious dimension of love. Love personified is felt to be a divine power which emanates from the person loved who therefore assumes, in the eyes of his partner, a supernatural character.[166] The Egyptian *waṣf*s take up the same structure as the hymns to a divinity[167] or imitate the descrip-

---

[162] Cf. Niccacci (1991), pp. 69–71.

[163] Cf., for example, Papyrus Chester Beatty IA. In the first stanza, he says of her: "One alone is my sister, having no peer: / more gracious than all other women" (1:1; tr. Fox [1985], p. 52). In the sixth stanza, she says of him: "Love of him captures the heart / of all who stride upon the way—/ a precious youth without peer! / A brother excellent of character!" (4:1; *ibid.*, p. 54). We shall often find a similar situation in the Song.

[164] Cf., for the Song, 6:9, and, for the Egyptian love songs, the two passages from Papyrus Chester Beatty I cited in the preceding note.

[165] For the Song, cf. 8:6. For the Egyptian love songs, cf., for example, Papyrus Harris 500: "I have obtained for ever and ever / what Amon has granted to me" (B 5:2–3; tr. Fox [1985], p. 21); "How lovely is my hour (with you)! / This hour flows forth for me forever—it began when I lay with you" (C 7:5–6; *ibid.*, p. 26). Often, also, the stability of the couple is affirmed. We cite again Papyrus Harris 500: "We say to each other: / 'I will never be far away. / (My) hand will be with (your) hand, / as I stroll about, / I with (you), / in every pleasant place'" (B 5:7; *ibid.*, p. 23; cf. Mathieu [1996], pp. 37–38).

[166] Cf. Mathieu (1996), pp. 168–172; Niccacci (1991), pp. 65–69.

[167] Cf. Mathieu (1996), pp. 235–240.

tion of the statue of a god.[168] It is a universal human experience: in the eyes of one in love, the person loved becomes a god. We too are apt to speak of 'adoring' the person loved (and at times this is not just a manner of speaking): he who loves has the clear impression of living an experience of transcendence, of the supernatural. We shall find this element again in the Song of Songs.

The correspondence between the Egyptian love songs and the Song is so exact as to make us conclude that there existed a dependence of the latter on the former. The author of the Song was undoubtedly aware of this kind of poetry. This observation has led authors like Gerleman and Keel to locate the biblical poem either in the Solomonic era[169] or in that of Hezekiah,[170] that is, periods when the contacts between Israel and Egypt were particularly intense. However, the linguistic data is opposed to such a dating. It is true that there are archaisms in the Song, but they can be explained as a literary device; more difficult to explain is the presence of neologisms which testify indubitably in favour of a more recent date for the poem. Frequent above all are the Aramaisms and the Neo-Hebraisms. There leaps to the eye, for example, the constant use of the prefix *še-* instead of the relative particle *ʾăšer* (unique occurrence, 1:1), a use which is matched in the OT only in Qoheleth while it is very widespread in Aramaic and Mishnaic Hebrew (above all in conjunction with the preposition *ʿad*: compare Song 1:12; 2:7; 2:17; 3:4...with Dan 7:4, 9, 11).[171] Among the lexemes of Persian origin, one that catches the eye is *pardēs* ('garden', Song 4:13; cf. Neh 2:8 and Qoh 2:5), which, through the Greek *paradeisos*, is the origin of our 'paradise'. If these parallels tend in favour of the Persian period, the Graecisms lead us to lower the date still further to the Hellenistic period. The most evident is *ʾappiryôn* (Song 3:9), a term

---

[168] Cf., *supra*, p. 13.

[169] Gerleman (1965), pp. 75–77.

[170] So Keel (1994), pp. 4–5. More recently, Keel (1991–), col. 189, has lowered the date to the Persian period.

[171] Cf. Graetz (1871), pp. 43–45. The judgement remains valid even if the presence of the prefix in Judg 5:7 and in other Semitic languages leads us to think also of a North Israelite dialectal influence. Cf. Murphy (1990), pp. 74–75, with further bibliography. According to Wagner (1966), pp. 17–121, the list of lexical Aramaisms in the Song comprises: *ʾêkâ* (1:7); *ʾommān* (7:2); *ʾĕgôz* (6:11); *bᵉrôtîm* (1:17); *ginnâ* (6:11); *ṭānap* (5:3); *kōtel* (2:9); *mezeg* (7:3); *nāṭar* (1:6; 8:11–12); *sûgâ* (7:3); *sᵉmādar* (2:13, 15; 7:13); *sansinnîm* (7:9); *sᵉtāw* (2:11); *qāpaṣ* (2:8); *rᵉhāṭîm* (7:6); *rᵉḥāṭîm* (1:17); *šallāmâ* (1:7); *šalhebet* (8:6). Cf. also Fox (1985), p. 189. Graetz (1871), pp. 45–52, and Garbini (1992), pp. 297–299, offer more comprehensive lists.

that passed into Mishnaic Hebrew, the derivation of which from the Greek *phoreion* ('stretcher') is difficult to contest.[172] Furthermore, the use of the preposition *ʿim* with the value of a conjunction ('and'; cf. Song 4:14–5:1) reflects the Greek use of *hama*.

More decisive is the presence in the Song of Songs of customs typical of the Hellenistic world. The 'triclinium' (*mēsab*, 1:12), that is reclining at table along the three sides of a room, forming a semicircle, is a practice of the Graeco-Roman world, and one unknown in ancient Israel.[173] The use of the litter (3:6–10) is also unthinkable in monarchical Israel while it became fashionable in the Hellenistic period.[174] The same goes for the coronation of the bridegroom (3:11): this is not mentioned in ancient Hebrew tradition whereas it was usual in Hellenism.[175] A typical Hellenistic institution is that of the *peripoloi*, that is, the patrols of soldiers with a policing function who made the rounds of the city to prevent disorder (cf. 3:3; 5:7).[176] The 'sentinels' spoken of in Isa 62:6 and Ps 127:1, are a quite different institution: their function was to guard against external dangers not to safeguard order within.[177]

The city-nature opposition typical of the Song fits in well with the Hellenistic period.[178] Fundamentally, the city is presented as an enemy of love. The beloved man is not found in the streets and squares of the city (3:1–5): they are the place of the 'watchmen' who treat the woman with brutality (cf. 5:7). Also representative of the urban world are the 'daughters of Jerusalem' who must be supposed to be frequent

[172] Cf. Graetz (1871), pp. 54–55. Other terms suggested by Graetz, however, cannot be sustained, as, for example, the term *talpîyôt* (4:4) which he derives from the Greek *tēlōpis* ('vision from afar'). The same goes too for various of Garbini's proposals which suppose an emendation of the Hebrew text (cf. Garbini [1992], p. 297). Thus, for example, *ʾgwn* ('contest, competition') in place of *ʾĕgôz* ('nut') in 6:11. The translation of *šwʿlym* (2:15) with 'lumbar muscles', and that of *lḥym* (1:10; 4:3, 13; 5:13) with 'buttocks', through a presumed influence of the Greek (*ibid.*), seems frankly tendentious; the terms have a totally different significance in Hebrew.

[173] Graetz (1871), pp. 61–62 ("Tafelrunde"); cf. Heinevetter (1988), p. 212. Keel (1991–), col. 189, objects, making reference to the banquet of Asshurbanipal with his wife, reproduced in *ANEP*, fig. 451, p. 155. But here there is a 'divan' not a circular 'triclinium' as suggested by the term *mēsab* (from the root *sbb*, 'around').

[174] Here we refer again to Graetz (1871), pp. 60–61; Heinevetter, p. 212. Even Keel (1994), p. 131, points out the Hellenistic character of the costume.

[175] Graetz (1871), p. 62; Keel (1991–), col. 189.

[176] Graetz (1871), p. 63.

[177] Heinevetter (1988), p. 108, n. 5; contra Delitzsch, Krinetzki (citations there), and Ravasi (1992), pp. 231–232.

[178] Cf., *supra*, p. 23.

disturbers of love if they are being prayed *not* to disturb it (2:7; 3:5; 8:4). In 1:5–6, the refined and decadent beauty of the sophisticated young women of the city is opposed to the simple 'bucolic' beauty of the beloved, burnt by the sun. To the hostile world of the city, 2:8–17 opposes with enchanted eyes the springtime awakening of nature, and 7:12–14 is a summons to savour love 'outside' the city ("Come, my beloved, / let us go out into the country…").

The Egyptian love songs also have nature as their background, but, as Heinevetter rightly notes, here nature is the place for the intimacy of love, far from social control (cf. also Deut 22:23–27): but it does not have the idealisation that is typical of the Song of Songs.[179] There nature is not something concrete lived by a peasant, but something dreamed of by a city dweller who is 'tired of civilisation' (*zivilisationsmüde*)[180] and desires a type of life that is simpler and closer to nature. Such an idealisation of nature is characteristic of bucolic poetry of which the most typical is that of the Syracusan Theocritus.

The links of the poetry of Theocritus with the Song have often been pointed out. We mention here some exact correspondences[181] which will be developed in the course of the textual analysis: the 'bed of fresh grass' (Song 1:16; cf. Theocritus, *Idylls* 7:133–136);[182] the foxes that damage the vineyards (Song 2:15; cf. Theocritus, *Idylls* 1:46–47; 5:111–112);[183] the sheep (or goats) who are 'mothers of twins' (Song 4:2; 6:2; cf. Theocritus, *Idylls* 1:25);[184] the dark colour of the woman (Song 1:6; cfr. *Idylls* 10:26);[185] 'Pharaoh's mare' (Song 1:9; cf. *Idylls* 18:30–31).[186]

The dramatic, dialogic form of the Song with the presence of the chorus has a certain correspondence in the Egyptian love songs; however, it comes much closer to the Greek theatre and to that form of theatre which we know as the mime.[187] Here too, the *Poems* of Theocritus, often stylised as a dialogue, can be looked on as a model. Graetz

179 Heinevetter (1998), p. 213; differently, Keel (1991–), col. 189.
180 The term is from Müller (1992), p. 14.
181 For this list, cf. Graetz (1871), p. 71; Garbini (1992), p. 299.
182 Cf., *infra*, p. 33, n. 157.
183 Cf., *infra*, p. 118, n. 73.
184 Cf., *infra*, p. 180, n. 52.
185 Cf., *infra*, p. 60, n. 63.
186 Cf., *infra*, p. 71, n. 108.
187 This is emphasised in Gebhardt (1931), pp. 20–21.

also notes a correspondence between the use of the refrain in *Idylls* 2 ('The Enchantress') and Song 5:2–6:3.[188]

However, a reading of Theocritus, like that of other lyric poets of the Hellenistic epoch also throws into prominence the distance of this world from that of the Song. Keel rightly observes that the closeness to the Egyptian love songs is much greater than that to Hellenistic poetry.[189] In the Hellenistic poets, love has nothing of the sacred: homosexual love, gallant adventures, typical of a decadent world are often encountered. Beyond the formal similarities, there is, in substance, an abyss of difference.[190]

Graetz thinks that the Song is a moralising writing with which the Hebrew culture wished to affirm its own identity in the face of the dominating Greek culture, precisely in the field of love.[191] Behind the figure of Solomon, who is the object of a hardly veiled criticism in the Song (cf. 6:8–9; 8:11–12), there is the Hellenistic court of Alexandria, behind the 'city', the world of the Hellenistic cities and of the Hellenising Jews.[192] The 'return to nature', then, would not only be a bucolic flight from the city but also acquire the sense of a recovery of one's own roots: the patriarchs were, after all, shepherd and peasants. In fact, not a few signals lead to the discovery in the Song of an affirmation of the Jewish national identity. The body of the bride assumes the contours of the Palestinian landscape. The places most typical of Israel are evoked: Mount Lebanon (3:9; 4:8, 11; 5:15; 7:5), Mount Carmel (7:6), Mount Hermon (4:8), the mountainous *massif* of Gilead (4:1; 6:5), the plain of Sharon (2:1), the oasis of Engeddi (1:14). The cities most rich in tradition are mentioned: Jerusalem (1:5; 2:7; 3:5, 10; 5:8, 16; 6:4; 8:4), Tirzah (6:4), Heshbon (7:5). Along with Solomon

---

188 Graetz (1871), pp. 72–73. A dating in the Hellenistic period is shared by Eissfeldt (1965), p. 490; Fox (1985), p. 190; Kaiser (1975), pp. 365–366.

189 Keel (1994), p. 5: "No one who knows the ancient Egyptian love songs can fail to see that these are much more close to the Song than the *Idylls* of Theocritus (third century B.C.) and similar Hellenistic poetry" (cf., also, Keel [1991–], col. 189).

190 That has to be said against a unilateral tendency (Garbini is an example) to interpret the Song solely against the background of erotic Alexandrian poetry. Fisch (1990), p. 81, rightly observes: "The Hebrew poet has really little or nothing of the artificiality, the posing, the playfullness of Theocritus. [...] Love for the Shulamite and the *dôd* is not a lighthearted game but a consuming fire".

191 Graetz (1871), pp. 85–91.

192 In fact, the Hellenistic world is fundamentally an 'urban' world while the traditional Jewish world does not know this phenomenon. Cf. Heinevetter (1988), pp. 215–216.

(1:1; 3:7, 9, 11) David is remembered (4:4). With pride, the guards who escort the litter are called "the mighty men of Israel" (3:7): the counterposing with the "watchmen who make their rounds through the city" (3:3; 5:7) is evident. Perhaps these last represent the forces of occupation of the Hellenistic period who were little loved by the Jewish population.

For his part, Heinevetter discovers in the Song of Songs an ambivalent position over and against Hellenistic culture.[193] The Song takes on some of its elements, such as the greater value given to women and to the feelings, the search for a life closer to nature, while taking its distance from others, affirming its own religious and cultural tradition.

Heinevetter and Müller stress the cultural nearness of the Song with the book of Qoheleth,[194] which recent criticism agrees in dating in the Hellenistic period. Both books can be considered as a response by Israel to the provocations of the surrounding Hellenistic culture.

Is it possible to be more precise over the date? The reflections of Graetz,[195] developed by Heinevetter,[196] seem again to be the most sensible. First of all a date later than 220 B.C., that is the accession to the throne of Antiochus III, the Great, is to be discarded. For Palestine, that was the beginning of a period of wars which continued up to the end of the Jewish state in A.D. 70: a period that was hardly propitious for the composition of love poetry. We should add that the clash between the Jewish and Hellenistic worlds assumed more radical tones at that stage (one thinks of the movement of the *ḥăsîdîm* resulting in the Maccabean Revolt). This is very far from the Song of Songs.[197]

On the other hand, a date from the early years of the dominion of the Ptolemies is also improbable: it takes time to assimilate a culture.

---

[193] Heinevetter (1988), pp. 215–220.

[194] Heinevetter (1988); Müller (1992), p. 4 (cf. Müller [1978], pp. 254–260).

[195] Graetz (1871), pp. 79–91.

[196] Heinevetter (1988), pp. 221–223. Heinevetter's proposal has been favorably received by Schwienhorst-Schönberger (2001), p. 347, and Lacocque (1998), pp. 193–194.

[197] This seems, therefore, to give a decisive blow to Garbini's hypothesis of dating the Song in 68 B.C., a date which is founded on the fantastic identification of the 'abducted bride' (this is Garbini's understanding of Song 6:8–12) with Cleopatra Selena, killed on the orders of Tigran, King of Armenia, in 69 B.C. (cf. Garbini [1992], pp. 248–251, 293–296). The supposed polemic against Simeon ben Shetach (*ibid.*, pp. 293–295) is also founded on the slenderest of elements (cf. Borgonovo, *Review* of Garbini [1994], pp. 581–582). Heinevetter (1988), p. 221, rightly observes that if the Song was not ostracised by the Maccabees, it must have been because it already enjoyed canonical authority.

The period which best corresponds to the social framework presupposed by the Song is the reign of the third Ptolemy, Ptolemy Euergetes (246–221 B.C.). In this period, the dominant figure in the land of Israel was that of Joseph, the son of Tobias, who, for twenty two years (probably from 239 to 217),[198] was the official gatherer of taxes for Ptolemy—not only for Palestine but also for Syria and Phoenicia. Joseph was the model of the emancipated Jew, open to Hellenistic customs, by contrast with the 'conservative' party headed by the sacerdotal family of the Oniads. Under Joseph, Jerusalem became a rich[199] and cosmopolitan[200] city. Contacts with Alexandria were particularly lively: the Tobiads had an official representative there.[201] The other side of the coin can be inferred from the fact that Joseph did not hesitate to have the notables of Ashkelon and Scythopolis put to death when they protested against the exorbitance of the tribute.[202]

The placing of the Song in the Ptolemaic period can account for the particular closeness with the Egyptian love songs. Even if they come from a millennium earlier, it is highly probable that they were known in the sophisticated cultural environment of Alexandria.[203] At the same time we have an explanation for the influence of Theocritus who lived at the court of Alexandria between 284 and 275 B.C. In this ambit too, it is comprehensible that the 'king' (Song 1:12) is called 'pharaoh' (Song 1:9); this is what, in fact, the Ptolemies were called.

Undoubtedly, as has been seen, an urban environment is to be claimed for the place of composition. In the past, there have been those who have thought of Alexandria, but there is no hint of this city in the Song. Today the almost unanimous choice falls on Jerusalem. It is the city most mentioned in the poem: the friends of the beloved woman are called, significantly, 'daughters of Jerusalem' (1:5; 2:7; 3:5, 10; 5:8, 16; 8:4) or 'daughters of Zion' (3:11), while 3:6–11 and 8:5 clearly refer to the topography of Jerusalem.

---

[198] Thus Jagersma (1986), p. 31.

[199] "He (Joseph, *author's note*) was a good man and high-souled, and brought the Jews out of a state of poverty and meanness to one that was more splendid" (Josephus, *Ant* 12:4,10).

[200] "Now for the first time in history Jerusalem, too, becomes an important international city" (Jagersma [1986], p. 31; cf. Hengel [1973], p. 51).

[201] Josephus, *Ant* 12:4,5.

[202] Cf. Tcherikover (1975), p. 134, and, in general, Heinevetter (1988), pp. 222–223.

[203] The Graeco-Roman epoch attests to the rebirth of the ancient Egyptian culture both in the architectural field, with the construction of numerous temples, and in the literary one. It is sufficient to think of the famous 'library' of Alexandria.

6. The Hermeneutical Problem

No book of the Bible has been so variously interpreted as the Song. The interpretations range from the most elevated mysticism to the most extreme eroticism.[204] A history of the interpretation of the Song is outside the bounds of this present study:[205] we shall limit ourselves to some background considerations in order to account for the hermeneutical choice implied in our exegesis.

In simplest terms, the two basic lines of interpretation are the 'allegorical' and the 'literal'. Our investigation into the book's canonical status allowed a glimpse of the fact that, for a time, the two readings existed alongside each other.[206] The polarisation over the allegorical interpretation in the time of Rabbi Aqiba is probably bound up with historical circumstances. The same goes for the patristic interpretation: the work of Origen, which had a determinative influence on Christian exegesis of the Song, was itself influenced by neo-Platonic philosophy which was founded on body-soul dualism.[207]

The allegory recognises two senses in the Song: the natural one which speaks of the love between two spouses, and the spiritual one which, for Israel, is the love of God for the Jewish people and, for Christians, the love of Jesus for the Church. The first sense is intended by the inspired author as only a figure for the second: the true theme of the Song is not sexual love between man and woman (something considered unworthy of the sacred text), but supernatural charity. 'Allegory' derives from *allos* ('other'): the sense of the Song is not in the text itself but elsewhere.

The allegorical interpretation is the traditional one both in Israel and in the Church. Even today, in Jewish families, the Sabbath is welcomed on Friday evening as the bride of the Song, and the Song is read on the feast of the Passover understood as the marriage between God and his people. The Song has nourished a multitude of saints who have read in it the history of their own relationship with God: from John of the Cross to Francis de Sales, to Edith Stein. It is understandable, therefore, that today, from various quarters, protests are raised

---

204 There is a contemporary view which advocates a 'pornographic' reading of the poem. Cf., for example, Boer (1998); *id.* (2000).

205 For this cf. Barbiero (2004), pp. 446–469.

206 Cf., *supra*, pp. 2–4.

207 Cf. Lacocque (1998), pp. 12–15; Ricoeur (1998), pp. 281–285.

against a type of exegesis which would seem to deny this tradition as a misunderstanding of the text.

Basing herself on the modern hermeneutic, A.-M. Pelletier has revalued the allegorical and spiritual tradition:[208] the significance of a work is not to be limited to the original sense but 'increases with the reader'.[209] In a text, one recognises one's own vital experience, recognises oneself: a book which 'says nothing' to the reader is quickly discarded. In the words of Gadamer, an aseptic reading, without any prejudices, is simply impossible. A text is important through its *Wirkungsgeschichte*, the history of its influence on the readers.[210] Significantly, Pelletier's book is subtitled: *De l'énigme du sens aux figures du lecteur*.

However, despite revaluing the 'subjective' dimension of the reading, the 'objective' one remains fundamental in order to distinguish a good from a false interpretation. In fact, not every interpretation is good. If one reader finds a legitimation of free love in the Song and another an advocacy of chastity, one of the two interpretations must be false, and, to have a criterion of value, it is necessary to refer back to the literal sense, that is, to what the text says, distinguishing that from its successive interpretations. The 'subjective' sense of a text cannot be in dispute with the 'objective' one. Gadamer speaks of the fusion of horizons, of the horizon of the text and that of the reader.[211] M. Dumais, in a recent work on hermeneutical philosophy, makes an affirmation that can be widely shared: "The spiritual sense [...] is, in my eyes, the literal sense of Scripture understood in its depth".[212]

Having examined the text of the Song of Songs, I am of the opinion that the original sense of the book, the sense intended by the author, is not of an allegorical nature. Earlier, I gave the example of Song 8:5,[213]

---

[208] Pelletier (1989); cfr. *id.* (1999), and Sonnet (1991). In the same sense, also, De Ena (2004). Beside a 'textual' sense (which takes up the traditional 'literal sense', but rightly putting the emphasis more on the text than on the author), De Ena stresses the importance of a 'directional sense', that is, of an openness in the text to a further meaning.

[209] The phrase is that of Gregory the Great: *Divina eloquia cum legente crescunt* (in *Homiliae in Hiezechihelem Prophetam* 7:8).

[210] Gadamer (1965), pp. 280, 318–319, 354.

[211] Gadamer (1965), pp. 286–290. Ricoeur proposes a similar hermeneutical circle when he speaks of 'understanding' (subjective) and 'explanation' (objective) of a text. Cf. Ricoeur (1976), p. 71. For a review of the definition of the 'literal sense' in contemporary hermeneutics, cf. Racine (1999), pp. 199–214 (the author holds that today we ought to speak simply of the 'sense' and no longer of the 'literal sense').

[212] Dumais (1999), p. 239.

[213] Cf., *supra*, p. 8.

significant because it concerns a fundamental passage in the Song: according to the MT, it is not the man but the woman who is to 'awaken' her own partner. The initiative is hers. That is incompatible with an allegorical interpretation that identifies the beloved man with God and the beloved woman with Israel. It is in fact unthinkable in the biblical tradition for the love of man for God to precede that of God for man. The continuation of the passage ("There your mother travailed, / there she travailed, and gave you to the light") confirms this incompatibility: it would actually imply that God was conceived and given birth to by a human mother! Moreover the messianic interpretation which sees in Solomon the image of the Messiah must take account of those texts in which Solomon is presented in a decidedly negative light (cf. 6:8–9; 8:11–12).[214] In my opinion, the allegorical reading, though venerable, belongs to the *Wirkungsgeschichte* of the text and not to the text itself.[215]

Looking at it another way, the fact, mentioned above, of its place among the sapiential writings, stands in support of a natural reading of the Song in its obvious sense as a poem about the love between man and woman.[216] The title (Song 1:1) attributes the book to Solomon, putting it, therefore, alongside Proverbs (Prov 1:1) and Qoheleth (Qoh 1:1). The use of the nuptial allegory to speak of the relationship between God and Israel is, of course, typical of the prophetic literature (cf. Hos 1–3; Jer 2:2; Ezek 16). It is clear in these cases, however, that the interest of the prophet is not in the concrete relationship between man and woman; this is only an image with which to speak of the other relationship, that between God and his people. It is this which is the concern of the prophet. In the sapiential books, however, the perspective is different. There, the interest is not directly in religion but in every day life, mundane reality, 'secular' matters as we would say today, although for biblical man there was no reality that did not have a relationship with God. However, God is almost never mentioned. In the Song of Songs, the name of God appears only once, in 8:6, and even there it is an abbreviated form ('a flame of Yah') which is

---

[214] One understands, therefore, why Robert—Tournay (1963), pp. 328–329, speak of 'appendices' which do not belong to the primitive text which they consider to be of an allegorical kind.

[215] According to Zunz (1991), p. 86, in the history of the interpretation of the Song of Songs "we come to a knowledge of the exegetes if not of the Song".

[216] Cf. Audet (1955), pp. 202–204; Krinetzki (1981), pp. 24–27; Childs (1979), pp. 574–576.

susceptible to misunderstanding. God is not absent, but he is not in the foreground; he is hidden behind the things, the source of wisdom, the foundation of the cosmic order. The Song is born from that wonder in the face of the mystery of love which is discernible in Prov 30:18–19:

> Three things are too wonderful for me;
> four I do not understand:
> the way of an eagle in the sky,
> the way of a serpent on a rock,
> the way of a ship on the high seas,
> and the way of a man with a maiden. (RSV)

Among all the mysteries of life, the most fascinating is the outpouring of love between two young people. There is no talk of God, but the author feels himself to be before a reality greater than he, something that man can neither understand nor control; he feels himself grasped by transcendence.

Today, the natural reading of the Song is no longer exceptional. It is the norm, even among confessional scholars. Nevertheless, this type of interpretation also reveals its limits. A.-M. Pelletier has shown how the modern, 'natural', reading was born in a polemical context aimed at the believer.[217] That is not without its consequences. Modern commentaries on the Song employ a wealth of parallels with the texts of the Ancient Orient; they exploit the latest archaeological discoveries; they are enriched with new insights deriving from psychological and psychoanalytical research;[218] they sharpen the linguistic tools; but they are poor from the theological point of view, as if theology were a secondary element in the biblical text.[219] As far as Keel is concerned, for example, it is only allegory that has transformed a book "*of dubious content* into the most holy of all books".[220] For Clines,

[217] Pelletier (1989), pp. 87–107.

[218] I am thinking in particular of the later works of Krinetzki: Krinetzki (1980), and *id.* (1981). In the latter work, the editor of the series, J. Schreiner, felt the need to add three dense pages (pp. 29–31) on the theological (not the allegorical) significance of the book.

[219] On the other hand, there has been a proliferation of little books on the Song which have no serious scientific basis, also of moralising uses of the book on the basis of theses formulated *a priori*. Cf. Heinevetter (1988), pp. 7–12, for a criticism of Thilo's commentary. Separation between critical discourse and discourse based on faith is harmful to both, even if one has to recognise the autonomy of the two approaches.

[220] Keel (1991), col. 189 (my emphasis).

> the material cause of the Song of Songs is [...] the need of a male public for erotic literature. [...] And the social context is one that approves the existence and distribution of soft pornography.[221]

If the allegorical interpretation turned the Song into a solely 'spiritual' book, eliminating the sexual aspect, the natural interpretation runs the opposite risk, that of considering only the material aspect, and eliminating the spiritual and theological dimensions.[222] Both show themselves to be incomplete. It is necessary to reconstruct the two meanings as two aspects of a single reality which is ambivalent in itself.[223] The Song is not an allegory, but it is a metaphor,[224] a symbol[225] which refers to something higher. It belongs to the logic of the Incarnation: the divine is present in the human and inseparable from it because the love between man and woman is at the same time sensual and spiritual, human and divine.[226]

The theological dimension, therefore, is not something added on to the Song on the basis of an allegorical interpretation but is inherent

---

221 Clines (1994), p. 8.

222 Cf. Lacocque (1998), p. 13: "To reduce the Song's meaning to the allegorical is unwarranted. To read it as exclusively naturalistic is another aspect of the same mistake". On this, cf. Carr (2000), p. 2, and, above all, Carr (2003), pp. 139–151. The chapter is entitled: "The erotic and the mystical. Bringing sexuality and spirituality together in reading the Song of Songs". The author describes a history of interpretation of the Song, characterised at an early stage by a spiritual reading which excluded the erotic side of the poem ("The Song as spiritual, not sexual"), to which he counterposes a second reading, characterised by a completely opposite approach ("The Song as sexual, not spiritual"). The author defends an interpretation which puts the two approaches together ("Putting sexuality and spirituality together"), without killing off either of them. Wendland (1995), p. 48, comes to similar conclusions: "a purely naturalistic reading [...], which in many instances ventures off into blatantly sexual and erotic (even Baalistic) speculation, leaves much to be desired as far as understanding this particular composition is concerned".

223 In this sense, cf. Lys (1968), p. 55: "It is not a matter of opposing the literal sense and the spiritual sense but of affirming that the spiritual sense is in the literal sense".

224 Cf. Barbiero (1991), pp. 631–648; Ricoeur (1998).

225 It is the term used by Ravasi to express this same presence of the divine in the human, of the spiritual meaning in the literal. Cf. Ravasi (1992), pp. 132–134.

226 "It is not although, but because the Song of Songs was an 'authentic,' that is to say a 'worldly' love song, that it was an authentic 'spiritual' love song of God's love for man. Man loves because, and as, God loves" (Rosenzweig [2005], p. 214). And again: "For it is not possible for love to be 'purely human'. When it begins to speak—and this it must do, for there exists no other utterance spoken besides itself than the language of love—so when love speaks, it is already changed into something superhuman; for the sensuous character of the word is full to the brim with its divine supra-sensuous meaning; like language itself, love is at once sensible and supra-sensuous. To express it in another way: the allegory is not a decorative accessory for love, but essence" (*ibid.*, p. 216). Cf., also, Loretz (1964), pp. 215–216.

in the letter itself.[227] It is the literal sense of the Song which has a theological dimension.[228] This is the challenge which has been imposed on exegesis by the developments in criticism: it is a relatively new approach, but one of which the contemporary world feels the need.[229] In a civilisation that has been strongly eroticised, listening to the Word of God on the mystery of human love is shown to have a surprising relevance.

The high road to recovering the theological dimension of the Song of Songs is to read it against the background of the entire Bible, above all the Old Testament, an approach that has been neglected in modern research.[230] This is the road taken in the works of E. Salvaneschi[231] and A. Lacocque,[232] which at times, however, go too far in putting forward an approach of a midrashic, mechanical type. In fact, it is not enough to establish a parallel simply if a term appears in another passage: it is necessary to retain the context as well. At times, this can lead to understanding the same lexeme in a way that is totally different. Undoubtedly, however, the Song of Song, like Qoheleth, is characterised by a continuous, refined intertextuality which the present work will attempt to demonstrate.[233]

---

[227] I think a criticism of Garbini's book is in place here. We must recognise that the author has a straightforward intention, that of seeing in the Song an affirming of the legitimacy and sanctity of sexual love. But, in order to do this, Garbini feels he has to change the letter of the Song as if the present text had actually been deprived of its erotic character by puritan hands. That is simply not true, and the judgements of Keel and Clines reported above are the proof (cf., *supra*, pp. 40 and 41). In its present tenor, the Song is profoundly erotic: the following study will confirm this. To understand the erotic dimension of the poem it is unnecessary to change the text: it suffices to read it as it is. The process of modifying the text handed down by tradition to propose a 'better' one is, at bottom, close to that of the allegorical exegesis from which it would like to distance itself: the message is being sought 'outside' rather than within the text itself.

[228] "The deepest interpretation here can only be the most natural" (Barth [1948], p. 355). "While you are in Italy I shall write to you about the Song of Songs. I must say I should prefer to read it as an ordinary love song, and that is probably the best 'Christological' exposition" (Bonhoeffer [1967], p. 176). On the hermeneutical presuppositions of this reading, cf. Martin (1996), p. 355.

[229] This necessity has been advanced recently with some emphasis. Cf., for example, Davis (1998); Corney (1998); Campbell (2000); Schmuttermayr (2000).

[230] Along these lines, it is instructive to note the criticism of Lacocque who addresses the work of Keel (Lacocque [1998], pp. 192–204). Cf., also, Ricoeur (1998), pp. 295–303 ("Toward a Theological Reading of the Song of Songs"), and Boyarin (1990).

[231] Salvaneschi (1982).

[232] Lacocque (1998).

[233] The recent work of E. Kingsmill (Kingsmill [2010]) is a markedly intertextual reading. Unfortunately, I have not had the time to address it in detail. By means of

The first parallel, one that has been observed many times, is the account of Paradise. D. Lys comes to the conclusion: "The Song is nothing other than a commentary on Gen 2".[234] The parallel is spoken of at length in *Die kirchliche Dogmatik* of Karl Barth[235] and has recently been developed by P. Trible[236] and F. Landy.[237] But this parallel is not the only one. P. Beauchamp has pointed out the correspondence with the prophetic texts that speak of the love of God under the spousal metaphor (or allegory).[238] Even if the approach is different in the two cases, both lead to the observation that the privileged place for discourse about God is, for the Old Testament, human love. Not less prominent is the comparison with the other sapiential books, above all with Proverbs[239] and Qoheleth,[240] but also with Sirach.[241] The relationship is not always one of convergence but often also of polemic, dialectic. While the other books tend to warn against the risks of human love and sexuality, the Song praises their positive value, bringing the relationship of man and woman back to the innocence of Paradise before sin disturbed the harmony that existed.

A Christian reading of the book would require the extension of the intertextual inquiry into the New Testament too, but this is, unfortunately, outside the scope of the present work which is restricted to the field of the Old Testament.[242] It seems that even within these limits, the hermeneutical path is clear. It is our intention, by means of a

this intertextuality, Kingsmill arrives at an allegorical reading, something from which I distance myself decidedly.

[234] Lys (1968), p. 52.

[235] "Here [in the Song] and only here—and this exception proves the rule, so to speak—Gn 2 reaches its development: one now sees that the picture of Gn 2 did not enter the OT simply by accident and as a foreign body but has a definite role, even if this is generally not evident, in the thought of Israel" (Barth [1947], p. 358).

[236] Trible (1993), pp. 100–120.

[237] Landy (1983), above all pp. 183–265.

[238] Beauchamp (1990), p. 186.

[239] On the relationship between the Song of Songs and the book of Proverbs, cf. Paul (2001); Cottini (1990).

[240] Cf., for example, Kreeft (1989).

[241] Sirach's attitude to women is certainly not that of the Song. Cf. Trenchard (1982); Gilbert (1976). However, the Song is to be understood, like Sirach (and Qoheleth) as a reply to the cultural provocation of Hellenistic culture. Cf., in this respect, Kieweler (1992); Sanders (1983), pp. 27–59.

[242] We have left some suggestions of a possible Christian reading when this has seemed appropriate for the understanding of a particular passage, but this has not been done systematically. For a deeper investigation in this direction, we refer to the original work (Barbiero [2004], 443–445).

scrupulous exegesis of the letter of the Song, to grasp its original meaning against the background of Middle Eastern and Hellenistic love poetry. At the same time, the intertextuality with the other books of the Old Testament will allow us to discover the theological, canonical dimension. This dimension is located, not on the allegorical level, but on the metaphorical, and it corresponds, at root, to the reality of human love which is, at once and inseparably, flesh and spirit.

CHAPTER TWO

TITLE

(Song 1:1)

1 [1]Song of Songs, of Solomon

Song 1:1 is generally held to be the title of the book. It is debated whether it was part of the original composition or if it is a later addition.[1] The relative particle *ʾăšer* is unusual for the Song which prefers the late *še* (cf. 1:6e). On the other hand, the links with what follows are clear (cf. the alliteration with vv. 2–3; the royal 'travesty' in vv 4, 5) and would be a strong indication of the title's belonging to the original poem.

The Hebrew *šîr haššîrîm ʾăšer lišlōmōh* conveys an untranslatable musical play on the sound 'š' which continues in v. 2. *šîr* is a common term to indicate a 'song' or 'canticle' of a joyous nature, whether liturgical or profane, usually accompanied by one or more musical instruments. The expression 'Song of Songs' is a superlative along the lines of 'holy of holies' (Exod 26:33), 'king of kings' (Dan 2:37). It is the equivalent of saying 'the most beautiful song'. The fact that 'Song' is used in the singular is a discreet suggestion of the unity of the composition. The title of the Egyptian Songs of Love, in so many ways the nearest parallel to the Song of Songs, is by contrast: "The beginning of the joyful Songs".[2]

ʾăšer lišlōmōh, 'which is of Solomon', is undoubtedly the expression, not of the dedication ('to/for Solomon'), but, as in the titles of the Psalms, of the author of the Song. This is a question of a fictional attribution. Proverbs, Qoheleth and Wisdom are also attributed to

[1] The title is originally absent from the Vulgate, while the Peshitta ("Here follows the wisdom of wisdoms, of the same Solomon") underlines the sapiential character of the book.

[2] Papyrus Harris 500C 7:3, translated by Bresciani (1990), p. 466 (cf. also pp. 453, 463, 471).

Solomon.[3] This places the book within the sapiential literature which is very much open to international influence. Solomon is the traditional model of the sage (cf. 1 Kgs 5:12), just as David is of the worshipper. Solomon has an important role in the Song (cf. 1:5; 3:7, 9, 11; 8:11–12), a role, to be honest, which is not always positive: on the one hand, he is the king (1:4, 12), the ideal lover who transfers the humble goings-on of the two young people on to a plane that is splendid and noble (1:5, 9); on the other hand, he is the personification of a love that is rich and decadent from which the author of the Song takes his distance (cf. 8:11–12). Heinevetter attributes these two different interpretations of the figure of Solomon to two different redactional levels of the book.[4] More probably they represent the complex attitude of one and the same author.

[3] The *Midrash Rabbah* notes: "He first wrote the Song of Songs, then Proverbs, then Ecclesiastes. [...] When a man is young, he composes songs; when he grows older, he makes sententious remarks; when he becomes an old man, he speaks of the vanity of things" (Simon [1977], p. 17).

[4] Cf. Heinevetter (1988), pp. 68–70.

CHAPTER THREE

PROLOGUE

(Song 1:2–2:7)

I

Woman [2]"Let him kiss me with the kisses of his mouth,
for your caresses[1] are sweet, sweeter than wine;
[3]your scents fragrant:
your name, perfume freshly poured.[2]
Therefore the maidens love you.

[4]Take me away with you,[3] let us flee!
The king has brought me into[4] his chambers.
We shall rejoice and be glad for you,
we shall proclaim your caresses[5] more than wine.
Rightly[6] do they love you!"

---

[1] So MT *dōdèkā*, followed by the Syriac (*rḥmjk*). LXX (*mastoi sou*) and Vg (*ubera tua*) read *daddèkā*, ('your breasts').

[2] The Hebrew *tûraq* is disputed: for the list of possible translations, cf. Ravasi (1992), p. 155. With *ekkennōthen* (LXX) and *effusum* (Vg), we understand the Hebrew as the imperfect *hophʿal* of *rîq* ('to pour out'); the relative particle *še* can be understood in poetry.

[3] LXX (*heilkysan se*) and Vetus Latina (*et adtraxerunt te*) make the verb 'take away' agree with the preceding statement ('[The maidens] have taken you away').

[4] Symmachus has an imperative (*eisenenke*) and Origen's Quinta a cohortative (*eisagagetō*).

[5] Cf. n. 1 of this chapter.

[6] The Hebrew *mêšārîm* is a *plurale abstractionis* with an adverbial sense ('rightly', cf. 7:10). LXX (*euthytēs ēgapēsen se*) and Vetus Latina (*aequitas dilexit te*), interpreting allegorically, make it the subject of the verb 'to love'. The Syriac, the Targum and the Vg (*recti diligunt te*), also interpreting allegorically, understand *mêšārîm* in the plural as a reference to the 'just'.

II

Woman 5 “I am black but beautiful, O daughters[7] of Jerusalem,
like the tents of Kedar, like the curtains of Solomon.[8]
6 Do not stare at me because I am dusky,
because the sun has scorched me.
My mother’s sons were angry[9] with me,
they put me in charge of the vineyards,
but my very own vineyard I have not kept!”

III

Woman 7 “Tell me, O love of my soul, where do you pasture your flock,
where do you rest it[10] at noon,
so that I may not look like a prostitute[11]
behind the flocks of your comrades”.

Chorus 8 “If you do not know, O most beautiful among women,
go out in the tracks of the flock,
and pasture your little goats
beside the tents of the shepherds”.

---

[7] Vetus Latina *filia* and Qumran (*bnty*, ‘my daughter’), understand the phrase allegorically.

[8] MT’s *šᵉlōmōh* is disputed. *NJB* (‘like the pavilions of Salmah’) repeats a recurrent conjecture; so also, among others, Ravasi (1992), p. 165, and the explanation, pp. 170–171; Garbini (1992), p. 184; Rudolph (1962), p. 123. However, the ancient versions unite in agreeing with MT.

[9] Thus MT. The versions have translated ‘fought’, but here again we have allegorical interpretation. Cf. Garbini (1992), p. 31.

[10] Thus MT (*tarbîṣ*). Generally the versions understand the *qal* (to lie down): cf. LXX, *koitázeis*; Vg, *cubes*, Syriac, *rbʿt*.

[11] Literally MT’s *ʿōṭᵉyâ* signifies ‘one who is covered’, cf. LXX, *periballomenē* (from which ‘prostitute’, cf. commentary). The Syriac, Symmachus and Vg have ‘a vagabond’ (cf. *NJB*, *CEI*, *TILC*, *TOB*, *BJ*), reading *ṭʿyh* instead of *ʿṭyh* (cf. *BHS*).

IV

Man [9]"To a mare[12] among Pharaoh's chariots
I liken you, O my friend.
[10]Your cheeks are beautiful between ear pendants,[13]
Your neck, circled by pearls".

Chorus [11]"We shall make you ear pendants of gold, studded
with silver".

Woman [12]"While the king is in his triclinium,
my nard pours forth its fragrance.
[13]My beloved is to me a bag of myrrh,
passing the night between my breasts.
[14]My beloved is to me a bunch of henna,
among the vineyards of Engedi."

V

Man [15]"How beautiful you are, my love, how beautiful!
Your eyes are doves!"

Woman [16]"How handsome you are, my love, and delightful.
Indeed our bed is fresh grass,
[17]the beams of our house[14] the cedars,
our roof[15] the cypresses."

---

[12] MT's *susātî* has been misunderstood by LXX's *tē hippō mou* and by Vg's *equitatui meo*, which have understood the final *yod* as a possessive pronoun. In fact, it is a *hireq compaginis*. Cf. Joüon (1923), §93m, as in Lam 1:1.

[13] LXX, *trygones*, Vetus Latina and Vg, *turturis*, misunderstand the Hebrew *tôr* ('thread', 'string').

[14] The Hebrew *battênû* is a plural with singular value (plural of generalisation?), cf. Joüon (1923), §136j, n. 4.

[15] MT *rāḥîṭ* is a disputed *hapaxlegomenon* (cf. *HALAT*, p. 1114). LXX *phatnōmata* and Vg *laquearia* have understood it as part of the ceiling.

VI

Woman 2[1]“I am a[16] lily of Sharon,
a lotus flower of the valleys.”
Man [2]“Like a lotus flower among the thorns,
so is my friend among the maidens.”

Woman [3]“Like an apple tree in the forest,
so is my beloved among the young men.
I am sitting in his shade for which I longed,
and his fruit is sweet to my palate.”

VII

Woman [4]“He has brought me[17] into the banqueting chamber
and his banner over me is Love.
[5]Sustain me with raisin cakes,[18]
refresh me with apples,
for I am sick with love.

[6]His left hand is under my head
and his right hand pulls me close.
[7]I charge you, daughters of Jerusalem,
by the gazelles or by the wild deer:
do not rouse, do not waken love[19]
until it wishes.”

---

[16] MT has the article here, but this does not necessarily express determination (thus also in 1:11, 13–14; 3:9; 5:13; 7:3; 8:2: cf. *GKC* §127e; Delitzsch [1875], p. 39). LXX reads without the article: *anthos* and *krinon*.

[17] LXX (*eisagagete me*), Syriac (*ʾʿlwnj*) and Vetus Latina (*inducite me*) translate as imperative plural, making the verbs of v. 4 agree with those of v. 5. But this is a *lectio facilior* to be rejected.

[18] The translation of the Hebrew *ʾăšîšôt* is disputed, as attested by LXX (*en amorais*, ‘among cakes of honey’, var. *en mýrois*, ‘with scents’) and Vg (*floribus*). But the OT parallels undoubtedly refer to a food (cf. 2 Sam 6:19; 1 Chr 16:3).

[19] With MT, *ʾahăbâ*, LXX, *agápēn*, and Vetus Latina. *caritatem*. The Syriac *rḥmtʾ* and Vg *dilectam* make the term concrete referring it to the woman (‘loved one’).

Structure

The first unit of the Song is defined by the refrains of the embrace (Song 2:6) and the awakening (2:7).[20] With M.T. Elliott, we entitle it the *Prologue*.[21] It is like an operatic overture in which the themes which are later going to be developed and the characters who play a role in the course of the opera are both introduced. Structurally it corresponds to the *Epilogue* (8:5–14): some themes and words, in fact, appear only in the *Prologue* and *Epilogue* (cf. 1:6 with 8:12; 2:3 with 8:5; 2:4 with 8:10; 1:13 with 8:6a; 1:7 with 8:13).

The literary unit in question is structured in seven songs, each with its own thematic integrity (1:2–4, 5–6, 7–8, 9–14, 15–17; 2:1–3, 4–7).[22] It is possible that they might have had an independent origin. Be that as it may, the author has brought them into a unity as the strophes of a single song. This is demonstrated both by the regularity of the strophes (each is composed of two parts, and the number of lines is almost the same for each strophe) and the subtle thematic strands which pervade the unit. Perhaps the relative autonomy of the individual strophes (which is matched in the *Epilogue*) is to be explained by the special character of the Prologue in which the separate themes are only suggested, not completely developed.

The *inclusio* between the first and last strophe is suggested first of all by the verb 'bring in' (1:4 and 2:4). The 'chambers' of 1:4 are the equivalent of the 'banqueting chamber' of 2:4: they are the place of love. Moreover, the two strophes are linked by the metaphor of wine (1:2, 4; 2:4), by the root *'hb* ('love, to love', 1:3, 4 and 2:5, 7), and by the presence of a group of females ('maidens', 1:3; 'daughters of Jerusalem', 2:7). The entrance into the place of love, which, at the beginning, is presented as a dream, comes to fruition at the end. The theme of the 'chamber' reappears at the centre of the composition (1:12); the verse forms a bridge between the first and the last strophe and expresses symbolically the desire which leads to union. As always in the Song, the compositional unit goes from the separation of the lovers to their union by way of their reciprocal admiration and desire.

[20] On the structural function of the refrains, cf., *supra*, pp. 21–22.
[21] Elliott (1989), p. 43.
[22] Cf. Heinevetter (1988), pp. 95–98.

Along with the compositional principle 'separation-union', the *Prologue* is characterised by the contrast between high burlesque, in which the two lovers are brought into a regal atmosphere (cf. 1:3, 5, 9, 12), and low burlesque which identifies the two youngsters with peasants and shepherds and immerses them in nature (cf. 1:5–6, 7–8, 16; 2:1–3). In both cases, these are not historical data (the protagonists are neither king and queen nor shepherds or peasants), but a literary device, an escape from the real situation with its prosaic limitations and an immersion in a fictitious situation which is felt to be more suitable for love.[23]

In order to grasp the structure of the unit, it is important to consider not the subject but the object of the discourse. From this point of view, the Prologue presents the following framework (cf. *Tab. 3*).

The first strophe (1:2–4) speaks of the *man*, presented in high burlesque (king). The two lovers are separated and their union is presented as a dream.

The second (1:5–6) and the third strophe (1:7–8) speak of the *woman*, presented in low burlesque (peasant, shepherdess). The lovers are still separated but there is a movement towards searching and coming together (vv. 7–8).

The fourth (1:9–14), the fifth (1:15–17) and the sixth strophe (2:1–3) are characterised by the fact that in the first part the *woman* is spoken of (key word: *ra'yātî*, 'my friend' [f], 1:9, 15; 2:2), in the second part the *man* (key word: *dôdî*, 'my beloved' [m], 1:13, 16; 2:3). The two lovers seem to be facing each other in mutual contemplation; in the second part of each strophe the desire for union is indicated (1:13, 16 and 2:3b).

Table 3

I strophe	HE
II–III strophe	SHE
IV–VI strophe	SHE + HE
VII strophe	WE

[23] Cf., *supra*, pp. 14–15.

Union is achieved in the seventh strophe (2:4–7). The refrain of the embrace (2:6) expresses the consummation of the union while that of the awakening (2:7) seeks accordingly that the union which has been reached should not be disturbed prematurely.

First Strophe: Dream of Love (1:2–4)

The first strophe is bounded by v. 4 (v. 5, in fact, is the beginning of a different topic). It is composed of two parts: vv. 2–3 and v. 4. Each of these begins with an urgent request which is also phonetically similar (v. 2a: *yiššāqēnî*, 'let him kiss me'; v. 4a: *moškēnî*, 'take me away'). Each concludes with a choral ending in which appears the key word *ʾhb* ('to love' [v. 3c: "Therefore do the maidens *love* you"; v. 4e: "Rightly do they *love* you"]). Between the beginning and the conclusion there are words of admiration whose correspondence is marked by the recurrence of the expression *dōdèkā miyyāyin* ("your caresses more than wine", vv. 2b, 4d). The beginning of the two parts is, moreover, characterised by a change of subject. V. 2 begins with a discourse in the third person ("let him kiss me") only to pass without warning to the second person ("your caresses"). The reverse happens in v. 4. It begins with the second person ("take me away") only to pass to the third ("the king has brought me"). This is a deliberate stylistic effect (note the chiasmus a-b-b'-a'), so that there is no need for recourse to textual emendations[24] or to invoke a plurality of redactions.[25] The frequent change of subject creates an effect like that of musical 'improvisation'[26] which is well attuned to the 'overture' character of the strophe.

[1:2] The Song of Songs begins *in medias res*. The 'kisses of his mouth'[27] has a clearly erotic significance. The Song highlights two aspects of the kiss, the taste (by means of the metaphor of wine) and the smell ('your scents') (cf. again 4:10–11; 7:9b-10). It may be noted how here it is the woman who desires the kiss of the man while in 4:10–11 it is the man who desires the 'wine' which is in the woman's

[24] Cf. Colombo (1975), pp. 45–47 ("Kiss me with the kisses of your mouth", v. 2; "Bring me in, O king, into your chambers", v. 4).
[25] So Heinevetter (1988), pp. 71–72.
[26] The term is used in Ravasi (1990), p. 45.
[27] Cf. Keel (1986), p. 49, Figure 2.

mouth. Finally, in 7:9b-10 the desire is reciprocal. In this connection, Elliott speaks of a 'mirroring dynamic' in which what the man refers to his woman in one passage, the woman affirms of him in another.[28] That causes us to glimpse that reciprocity of love which is described in Gen 2:23. Ravasi draws attention to the onomatopoeic effect of the word *pîhû* ('his mouth'). In order to pronounce it, one has to position the mouth as for a kiss![29] Such subtlety is not foreign to the biblical text which has a refined poetic quality. It is combined with the alliteration of the sound *š* of the first two words of the verse: *yiššāqēnî minn*ᵉ*šîqôt* ('kiss me with the kisses').

The Hebrew *dōdîm* ('caresses') indicates something more than an innocent demonstration of friendship (cf. Ezek 16:8; 23:17; Prov 7:18). It is the erotic play which accompanies sexual intercourse. The Hebrew plural is a *plurale abstractionis* derived from the root *dwd*, the same root from which is made up the substantive *dôd* (beloved). The passage from the singular *dôd* to the plural *dōdîm* has in Hebrew the same effect as the Italian *caro* ('dear')—*carezza* ('caress'). Thus *dōdîm* expresses erotic play under the aspect of tenderness, so typical of the feminine psyche.[30] By contrast with other passages of the OT where this word denotes something of moral disapproval (cf. the passages cited above from Ezekiel and Proverbs), in the Song it is employed without any negative connotation. Erotic playfulness is presented as something desirable and fulfilling.[31] The adjective 'sweet' (*ṭôb*), repeated in v. 3 ('fragrant'), has a notable spectrum of meaning which ranges from aesthetic pleasure to physical to spiritual ('beautiful, happy, pleasant, useful, good…'). In v. 2, the context ('wine') suggests a connection with joy and pleasure. But the moral aspect does not seem to be excluded. *ṭôb* is, in fact, the adjective used in Gen 1:31 to define the 'goodness' of the creation before the Fall.[32]

In the Song, as in the whole of the Ancient Orient,[33] wine is a metaphor of love bound up with the symbolism of the vineyard as an image of the female body (cf. Song 1:6). "Love and wine are comparable

---

[28] Elliott (1989), pp. 246–251 ('The Mirroring Dynamic').

[29] Ravasi (1992), p. 151.

[30] Cf. Krinetzki (1981), p. 66.

[31] For a parallel, cf. our commentary to 7:11.

[32] The adjective forms a refrain in the priestly account of creation, cf. Gen 1:4, 12, 18, 21, 25.

[33] For the parallels from Ugaritic literature and from the Greek world, cf. Ravasi (1992), pp. 152–153.

because both lead to inebriation, but the inebriation of love penetrates more deeply".[34] Sir 40:20 is also familiar with the idea, and Song 5:1 invites the lovers to get drunk with love. Wine makes glad the heart of man (Judg 9:13; Ps 104:15), but compared with the joy of love, that brought on by wine is a poor thing.[35]

[v. 3] In Egypt, the hieroglyph which expresses the kiss pictures two noses coming close.[36] The kiss is perceived here, above all, from the olfactory point of view: it actually allows one to perceive the scent of the beloved.[37] Like wine, perfume is also a metaphor for love which is recurrent in the Song (cf. 1:12; 2:13; 4:10–11; 7:9, 14). The Egyptian custom during banquets was to wear on one's head a cone of perfume (cf. Song 5:13) which melted in the heat (cf. Ps 133:2), thus spreading an intoxicating scent.[38]

What was true of wine, is also true of perfume. Compared with the intoxication of the scents of the beloved, his person (the 'name' stands often in Hebrew for the 'person', cf. Ps 9:11; 18:50) is still more inebriating, more capable of making one dizzy, of taking one out of oneself.[39] Probably this alludes to the personal odour of the beloved. Each person has his own unmistakable odour which is perceived in the intimacy of love.[40]

The term *šemen* ('[perfumed] ointment') forms an alliteration with *šem* (name) and *šᵉlōmōh* (Solomon, v. 1).[41] The king (cf. v. 4) is 'anointed', and 'the anointed' in Hebrew is 'the Messiah', in Greek 'the Christ', so that it is not to be marvelled at that both rabbinic and

---

34 Müller (1992, p. 12). A love song from Egypt goes: "When I kiss her / and her lips are open / I am drunk, / even without wine". Cf. Bresciani (1990), p. 475.

35 From this point of view, it is possible to have a better perception of the profound symbolism of wine as material for the Eucharist: in the light of the Song, the Eucharistic Supper undoubtedly appears as an encounter of love. Again: the inebriation of wine and love has its spiritual counterpart in mystical ecstasy, in the losing of oneself in the divine lover, as is well emphasised by the allegorical interpretation. However, this does not belong to the original sense of the text; rather, it is a legitimate transposition according to the principle of analogy.

36 Cf. Fox (1985), p. 22.

37 Cf. Keel (1986), p. 50. Perhaps I can be allowed a contemporary parallel: in Brazil, a friendly kiss is called *cheiro*, 'perfume'. The word expresses in a very delicate way the olfactory aspect of the kiss.

38 Cf. Keel (1986), p. 237, Figure 138.

39 Perfume is particularly intoxicating when it has just been poured out, as is shown in the gospel scene of the anointing at Bethany (cf. John 12:3 par.).

40 Cf. Ravasi (1992), p. 161.

41 According to the fiction of the Song, the 'name' of the beloved is precisely that of 'Solomon'!

patristic exegesis interpreted this passage in a messianic sense.[42] This is, however, a *relecture*; as it is, the text is to be understood in its immediate sense.

The choral conclusion of v. 3c is totally disconcerting at first: it seems as if the woman associates other admirers with herself. The return of the *motif* in v. 4e, however, advises us against taking the text as corrupt or thinking of redactional additions.[43] The *motiv* has parallels in Egyptian love poetry where both the man and the woman are described as people who cause whoever sees them to fall in love with them.[44] The 'other' women or the 'other' men are not understood to be competitors, but they confer 'objectivity', so to speak, on the admiration of the woman. She is not the only one to be infatuated with her *beau*: in fact, no one can see him and remain indifferent.[45]

The first part of the strophe concludes with the verb *ʾāhēb* (to love) which is of central importance in the Song. The Hebrew lexeme, like the English, embraces the three Greek terms *érōs, philía* and *agápē*.[46] At one and the same time, *ʾhb* expresses the theological love between YHWH and Israel (cf. Deut 6:5), the friendship between David and Jonathan (1 Sam 18:1), and the love of Samson for Delilah (Judg 16:4). Perhaps it is possible to grasp a theological component in this linguistic phenomenon: at bottom, they are three different forms of the one unique reality. The difference is to be seen not so much in the diverse forms of love as in the authenticity or not of the sentiment.

---

[42] Cf. Meloni (1975). For a recent re-examination of this type of literature, cf. Campbell (2000).

[43] *Contra* Heinevetter (1988), p. 72.

[44] In the Chester Beatty Papyrus IA, he says of her: "Look, while she approached, / the young men bowed down / through the greatness of their love for her" (3:8, cf. Bresciani [1990], p. 456). In the same papyrus, she says of him: "The hearts of all those who stop on the street, / are inflamed with love for him" (4:1, *ibid.*, p. 457). In an ostracon from Deir el-Medineh we find similar sentiments: "I say to my heart: / [Why] do [all] hearts love him?" (*ibid.*, p. 476).

[45] For a parallel in the Song, cf. 3:10 (cf., *infra*, in the commentary on the Choral Intermezzo, Song 3:6–11). A similar phenomenon is encountered in the Mesopotamian poetry of the Sumerian and Akkadian periods where the woman in love passes without deliberation from the first person singular to the first person plural. Paul speaks of 'ecstatic plural', but scholars usually think of a female group which has the function of a chorus (Paul [1995]. Cf. the numerous passages cited there). Particularly near to our text is *Ni 2461*, 12–13: "Let *us* enjoy over and over your charms and sweetnesses! O! that you would do all the sweet things to *me*" (*ibid.*, p. 589. This text can also be found in Kramer [1969], pp. 92–93).

[46] Cf. E. Jenni, *ʾhb* lieben, in *THAT*, vol. I, col. 62.

The possibility of reading the Song in a theological key is itself based on the profound analogy of the different forms of love.

[v. 4] Like the first part of the strophe, the second too begins with a strong impact. After the detached, contemplative conclusion of the first part, there is a contrasting effect. Again it is the woman who takes the initiative, as in v. 2. She is not only the object but also the subject of passion: she does not wait to be asked, she puts herself forward. The choral aspect of love ("the maidens love you") gives way to the intimacy of the two lovers.

The perfect *hĕbîʾanî* ("[he] has brought me in") seems out of place, so much so that some authors suggest reading the imperative "bring me in".[47] If the MT is retained, as the *lectio difficilior*, it can only have the meaning of a dream, a desire. In reality, the two lovers are separated: we are still at the beginning of a course of events which will bring them to union in 2:4 where the verb 'bring in' (*bōʾ* in the *hiphʿil* form) is repeated. In the Song, this verb is always used in connection with the union of love. It returns in 3:4 and 8:2. Twice it is he who 'brings' her 'into' his chamber (1:4; 2:4), the other two times it is she who 'brings' him 'into the house of her mother' (3:4; 8:2), according to that 'mirroring-dynamic' which expresses the perfect reciprocity of love in the Song. The place of love is indicated with the term *ḥeder* (chamber), the innermost and most private room of the house, the bedroom.

The male lover receives the singular title of 'king'. As we have seen, this is an example of high burlesque, a literary device which translates the lovers into a noble sphere where the social restrictions of everyday life are not in force. Love in itself is a feast; it is noble. In the Syro-Palestinian environment, even today, newly weds are fêted as 'king' and 'queen' for a whole week;[48] also in the Byzantine liturgy, the couple are crowned. In another way, the description of 'king' is consistent with the title ('Solomon', v. 1) and with the symbolism of oil (*šemen*) in v. 3.

In v. 4cd there is a change of subject: for the second time we have a passage from the third person singular to the first plural. Evidently this is a 'we' different from that of the two lovers at v. 4a ("we shall rejoice *for you*"!). It is the group of 'young women' with which the woman is

---

[47] With the Syriac and Symmachus (*supra*, n. 4). Cf., e.g., Müller (1992), p. 12, n. 5.

[48] Cf., *supra*, p. 25.

being merged, so to speak, as in v. 3c. She belongs to this group, she identifies with it according to a kind of social identity. Even if the king has brought her alone into his chambers, it is a matter of joy for the whole group. The Song thrives on this tension between the solitude of the two lovers and the recognition of society. The woman calls on the chorus to celebrate her king with her.

The two verbs employed in v. 4c 'rejoice' (*gîl*) and 'be glad' (*śāmaḥ*), and even more that of v. 4d 'proclaim' (*zākar*), have a liturgical hue. They belong to the vocabulary of messianic salvation (cf. Isa 9:2; 25:9). That does not mean that in our text the two verbs refer directly to the love between God and his people,[49] but rather that the author invests the love of the two young people with a sacral aura. Love is not only royal; it is also sacred, divine (cf. Song 8:6).

At v. 4e, the subject changes once again, from the first to the third person plural as if the woman were no longer part of the group. Some authors attribute v. 4e to the author of the poem himself, as if a voice off-stage,[50] but the evident parallelism with v. 3c prompts us to attribute even the finale of the strophe to the woman who distances herself from the group precisely as she had done in v. 3c. Now that she has experienced intimacy with her beloved in a dream, she can understand just how ('rightly') the maidens are in love with him. But the adverb 'rightly' is open to a deeper significance: it expresses an estimation of the 'goodness' of love in line with the adjective *ṭôb* of vv. 2b.3a.[51]

Second Strophe: The Keeper of the Vineyards (1:5–6)

The separation of the strophe from the preceding context is clear: the atmosphere is totally different, indeed contrasting. The first strophe transfers the reader into an atmosphere which is noble and royal: the second is set in a rural, peasant atmosphere. A low burlesque is counterposed to the previous high burlesque, the world of the country, of nature, to that of the city. Now, too, the protagonist is different: the centre of attention is no longer the man, but the woman.

---

[49] *Contra* Robert – Tournay (1963), pp. 66–67.

[50] So, e.g., Gerleman (1965), p. 95.

[51] The two adjectives *ṭôb* and *yāšār* form a pair with a high moral value, cf. Ps 25:8.

The demarcation from the following verses is not equally clear: in vv. 7–8, the woman is still the topic in a similar low burlesque.[52] However, here we are no longer with peasants but among shepherds. The atmosphere is different so that, although noting the closeness of the two compositions, we prefer to consider vv. 5–6 and 7–8 precisely as two distinct strophes.[53]

Like vv. 2–4, vv. 5–6 are divided into two parts: v. 5 and v. 6. However, the final stich (v. 6e) is detached from the others as a kind of coda in which is contained, as we shall see, the whole point of the composition.[54] Each of the two parts begins with the *motiv* of the colour of the skin (vv. 5a, 6ab). There follow, in the first part, two comparisons ("like the tents…, like the curtains…") to which correspond two explanations of the phenomenon in the second ("[they were] angry…, they put me in charge…"). The 'coda', v. 6e, is linked to two expressions in v. 6d, 'vine' and 'in charge', changing their sense, but it falls outside the symmetry of the two parts.

Notwithstanding the distinction from the preceding material, we should note some subtle structural links. The 'curtains of Solomon' (v. 5b) recall the title (v. 1) and the 'royal' atmosphere of the first strophe (cf. v. 4b). The 'daughters of Jerusalem' (v. 5a) make us think of the 'maidens' of v. 3. Finally, the metaphor of the vineyard (v. 6) matches that of the wine (vv. 2b, 4d). If vv. 2–4 represent a dream of love, vv. 5–6 are the first steps towards its realisation. Against the wishes of the 'brothers' who want to keep her at home, the young woman decides to follow her own desire for love (v. 6e).

[1:5] The adjective *šᵉḥôrâ* ('black', cf. 5:11) has an important role in this little composition. It returns in v. 6a in a slightly altered form: *šᵉḥarḥōret* ('dusky'). Taking v. 6ab at its word, it is difficult to think here of an African beauty who would have an exotic fascination:[55] it is rather a description of an Israelite lass,[56] her skin darkened by exposure to the sun. 'Black' is to be understood as hyperbole, common in some European languages like Italian. The adjective is juxtaposed with

[52] Characteristically, Ravasi joins vv. 5–8 in a single composition. Cf. Ravasi (1992), p. 167.

[53] With the majority of exegetes. Cf. the literary reasons in Heinevetter (1988), pp. 74–77; Elliott (1989), pp. 47–50.

[54] Cf. Lohfink (1983), pp. 240–241.

[55] *Contra* Keel (1986), pp. 53–56; Pope (1977), pp. 307–318.

[56] *Contra* Sasson (1989), who thinks of Pharaoh's daughter given in marriage to Solomon (cf. 1 Kgs 11:1–2).

nā'wâ ('beautiful, pretty', cf. 1:10; 2:14; 4:3; 6:4). In Hebrew, the conjunction *w*[e] which links the two adjectives can have a coordinate value ('black *and* beautiful')[57] or an adversative one ('black *but* beautiful').[58] Are the two adjectives, then, synonymous or antithetical? Considerations of racism and the like are pointless[59] because it is apparent that the girl is native to the place and, on the other hand, the OT knows how to appreciate African beauty (one recalls the queen of Sheba, 1 Kgs 10:1–13). Here, a white complexion seems to correspond to the canons of Israelite beauty. The male lover is 'radiant white, and red' (Song 5:10, cf. Lam 4:7–8). Also the woman is 'beautiful like the fair (moon)' (Song 6:10). The two adjectives, therefore, are to be understood as an antithesis: 'black but beautiful'.[60]

The 'daughters of Jerusalem' are probably the representatives of this normative type of beauty,[61] urban and a little decadent (cf. Isa 3:16–24) to which is counterposed an ideal of beauty which is rural and wholesome. The contrast between the Moorish Bedouin and the white girls of the city are a frequent topic of contemporary Arabic amorous lyrics.[62] The young woman of the Song is probably not a peasant, just as she is not a princess. In the one case as in the other, it is a literary burlesque which corresponds to a widespread tendency in the Hellenistic epoch (one thinks of the bucolic poetry).[63] The decadent life of the city gives rise to nostalgia for a life that is simpler and in contact with nature. The city-nature contrast is a recurrent *motiv* in the Song. On the other hand, for an Israelite, this return to nature had also a

---

[57] LXX (*kai*) seems to understand it thus and, among the commentators, e.g., Keel, (1986), p. 53; Heinevetter (1988), p. 77; Garbini (1992), p. 43; Elliott (1989), p. 47; Murphy (1990), p. 109; Pope (1977), p. 291.

[58] So Vg (*sed*) and the majority of commentators.

[59] So, rightly, Ogden (1996), pp. 443–444; Hostetter (1996), pp. 35–36.

[60] A confirmation of this interpretation comes from the Jewish tradition, which reads the two adjectives in a moral sense, seeing in 'black' the colour of sin and in white that of righteousness. Cf., for example, the Targum: "When the sons of the House of Israel made the calf, their faces became black like those of the sons of Kush who dwell in the tents of Kedar. But when they repented and were converted, and they were pardoned, the splendour of the glory of their face became like that of the angels".

[61] Lys (1968), pp. 70–73, translates: "filles élégantes". Cf. *TOB* in the note: "comme on dit 'c'est une Parisienne'".

[62] Cf. Ringgren (1962), p. 258; Dalman (1901), pp. 198–201, 250–251, 285, 294.

[63] As a parallel to Song 1:5, cf., for example, Theocritus, *Idylls* 10, 26–29, in the LCL (1912) translation by J. M. Edmonds: "Bambyca fair, to other folk you may a Gipsy be; Sunburnt and lean they call you; you're honey-brown to me". Cf. Pope (1977), p. 311.

Table 4

black	→	like the tents of Kedar
beautiful	→	like the curtains of Solomon

national significance. The origins of Israel were of a nomadic, not an urban, type. The patriarchs were nomads. Therefore, nostalgia for the simple life of the country had also the sense of a return to the national origins by contrast with the urban world which was largely influenced by Hellenistic models.

The two similes of v. 5b take up and develop the antithesis of v. 5a (cf. *Tab 4*).

The simile of the tents of the desert harmonises with the ideal of rural beauty outlined in v. 5a. Still today, the tents of the Bedouin stand out against the yellow/grey of the Judaean desert by reason of their black colour which comes from their being made up of goats' hair. 'Kedar' is the name of an Arab tribe (cf. Gen 25:13; Isa 21:16; Jer 49:28; Ps 120:5) and here represents the nomads of the desert in general.

The second simile carries an opposing sense. The rare term *yᵉrîʿôt* is not completely clear. Whatever it means, 'curtains',[64] 'carpets', or 'tapestries',[65] the qualification 'of Solomon' confers a precious and refined character on these products.[66] The juxtaposition of the two similes has the effect of an oxymoron, a dissonance. The meaning is: the rustic beauty ('like the tents of Kedar') of the girl is worthy of the most elegant palaces of the city ('like the curtains of Solomon').

[v. 6] The woman asks the fair 'daughters of Jerusalem' not to scorn her on account of her dark skin, bronzed by the sun. The Hebrew text puns on the 'watching' (*rāʾāh*) of her friends and that of the sun. The verb *šāzap* means, in fact, precisely 'to watch' (cf. Job 20:9; 28:7) and from there, by extension, 'to burn, to tan'.[67] The cause of the darkening

[64] My translation makes the rare term *yᵉrîʿôt* derive from the root *yrʿ*, 'to shake' (with Elliott [1989], p. 293, n. 18). Elsewhere the term is translated by *CEI* with 'sheets' (cf. Exod 26:1–13; 36:8–17; Num 4:25) or with 'tent' (Ps 104:2). *NJB* translates 'pavilions'.

[65] Thus Krinetzki (1981), p. 241, n. 68.

[66] Cf. the translation of Lys: "comme les rideaux somptueux" (so also the translation of *TOB*, edited by the same author).

[67] LXX has *pareblepsen*. Cf. *HALAT*, p. 1350; Elliott (1989), pp. 48–49. Salvaneschi (1982), pp. 46–48, detects a semantic play not only between the two terms but with the root *šḥr*, which in Song 1:6 signifies 'dusky', while in 6:10 it expresses the 'dawn': the woman 'scorched by the sun' is also the one who is 'like the sun'. Garbini's translation

is attributed to her brothers who are called, distantly, 'the sons of my mother'. This appellation recalls the 'daughters of Jerusalem' of v. 5, suggesting a likeness between the two groups. In fact, the first group represents urban society, the second, the family: both play a role that is not always positive with regard to love. The 'brothers' reappear in the *Epilogue* of the Song (8:8–9), in a very negative role. They are preoccupied with defending the 'chastity' of their sister at all costs, taking her under their protection with an attitude that is paternalistic and sterile towards love. The girl rebels claiming her own autonomy (8:10). The brothers play an analogous role in our passage. Probably they have gathered that their sister has some feeling for a young man and have taken measures accordingly. The Hebrew verb with which the 'anger' of the brothers is expressed (*ḥārar/ḥārāh*, literally, to burn),[68] forms another play on words with the 'burning-watching' (*šāzap*) of the sun at v. 6b.[69] Perhaps in order to occupy her with an activity which distracts her and to distance her from any wooers, they have thought to entrust her with the keeping[70] of the vineyards.[71]

So far so good: *In cauda venenum*. To understand the point of v. 6e, it is necessary to grasp the new significance which the term 'vineyard' assumes here. In the whole of the Ancient Orient, the 'vineyard' is a metaphor for the female body. At bottom, as in the case of the 'garden', it is "a particular application of the archaic identification of the woman with the earth and the field".[72] Like the theme of the brothers,

("he has made me of honey") is based on the supposed derivation of Song 1:5–6 from the already cited *Tenth Idyll* of Theocritus. This, however, is difficult to demonstrate.

[68] The Hebrew *niḥărû* can be read either as a *niph'al* form of *ḥārar/ḥārāh* ('to flare up, to be angry'), or, less probably, as a *pi'el* form of *nāḥar* ('to blow, to snort'). Here too Garbini's proposal to read *ḥrpwny*, "they have promised me in marriage" (Garbini [1992], p. 185), is without any textual foundation.

[69] Cf. Elliott (1989), p. 49.

[70] The verb *nāṭar*, 'watch over, keep', occurs twice in our verse and is taken up again in 8:11–12: it is an Aramaising form of the classical Hebrew *nāṣar* (cf. H. Madl, *nāṭar*, in *TWAT*, vol. V, coll. 436–437), which confirms the late dating of the Song.

[71] If this was the aim, the means was not appropriate to the end. That the vineyard was a propitious place for amorous adventures is clear from Judg 21:15–23 (cf. on this Keel [1986], p. 99). In Papyrus Anastasi I we read: "Thou art come into Joppa, and thou findest the meadow blossoming in its season. Thou breakest in *to the inside* and findest the fair maiden who is watching over the gardens. She takes thee to herself as a companion and gives thee the color of (5) her lap" (translation *ANET*, p. 47). Perhaps in our text too an equivocal sense should not be excluded.

[72] Müller (1992), p. 15. Cf. Keel (1986), Figures 63 and 97, pp. 113 and 165 respectively. In the Sumerian poem "The Courtship of Inanna and Dumuzi", Dumuzi, the shepherd, addresses Innana, the goddess of love in these terms: "O Lady, your breast is your field. / Inanna, your breast is your field. / Your vast estate pours out plants. /

that of the vineyard is also taken up again in the *Epilogue*, in 8:11–12. Three terms are common with 1:5–6: the 'vineyard', the 'keeping' and 'Solomon'. Striking is the repetition of the expression 'my very own vineyard' (1:6e and 8:12a).[73] The role of the 'keepers' in 8:11 is similar to that of the 'brothers' in 1:6: both are responsible for guarding the 'chastity' of the young woman.

"My very own vineyard I have not kept!" The woman has 'kept' the vineyards of her brothers (v. 6d), but not her own, that is her body (v. 6e). As it stands, it seems as if the woman is defending free love,[74] so much so that Lohfink has conjectured that we have here what was originally the song of a prostitute.[75] Probably the past tense applied to the verb 'keep' is to be interpreted in the same way as that of the verb 'bring in' in v. 4. The woman describes now what will come to fruition in 2:4–7. Already, however, from this very moment, she has decided not to remain in the house but to follow the voice of love which will lead her into 'not keeping her vineyard'.

The view of love which is represented here is certainly not conventional. It is strongly critical of the family and of the patriarchal and macho society. In emphasising the ownership of the vineyard ('my very own vineyard'), the woman forcibly affirms that the decision over love belongs not to her brothers but to herself. By its nature, love is free. Otherwise it is not love, but an imposition. On the other hand, the Song does not advocate 'free love' as it is understood in today's society. It knows the value of chastity. The woman is "an enclosed garden, a stopped fountain, a sealed spring" (4:12); she has "kept her precious fruits" for her lover (7:14). But the point is that chastity is not an end in itself; it is in the service of love.[76] The garden is enclosed in

---

Your vast estate pours out grain." (Wolkstein - Kramer [1985], p. 46, cf. *ANET*, p. 642). For the Hellenistic world, cf. Müller (1998), pp. 569–584; for the OT, cf. Isa 5:1–7 and Ps 128:3.

[73] From the linguistic point of view, the expression *karmî šellî* is, like the verb *nāṭar*, a typical Aramaism (cf. Müller, [1992], p. 89, note 15). The original expression is pleonastic ("*my* vineyard which is *mine*") and underlines emphatically the exclusiveness of possession ("it is mine and nobody else's").

[74] Cf., for example: "the girl declares that she has had sexual relations despite the presumed supervision of her brothers" (Garbini [1992], p. 188).

[75] Lohfink (1983), p. 240. After the peasant burlesque, there is now, according to Lohfink, a second burlesque. The girl would be portrayed as a prostitute. She would be recounting the dream of free and adventurous love, which would be realised in a fully legal form on the wedding night.

[76] St. Thomas declares something of the kind with regard to spiritual chastity: "Ratio huius castitatis consistit in caritate" (*Summa Theologica*, II.II., q. 151, art. 2, resp.).

order to be opened to the beloved (4:16); its fruits are kept so as to be given to him (7:13e). Chastity is a precious quality of love. It has no sense if it does not lead to love, and in that case is violence and inhibition against which the woman of the Song protests with justification.

Third Strophe: The Shepherdess (1:7–8)

The third strophe is separated from the following one by a change of scene. With v. 9, we are no longer with the shepherds but once again in a royal burlesque ('Pharaoh'). The woman is no more on the look-out for her love but stands before him. The two lovers contemplate each other.

The connection with the preceding strophe is not entirely clear at first. There are no exact verbal links. Beside the low burlesque ('peasant girl', 'shepherdess'), however, one can also grasp a link in content. If, in v. 6e, the girl had decided to leave the house (theme of the 'brothers') to follow her own amorous impulse, the theme continues in vv. 7–8: the woman is invited to 'go out' (v. 8) and search for her beloved in the wide world, in a social context unknown to her.

The strophe is structured dramatically as a dialogue. At v. 7, it is clearly the woman who speaks, addressing her man. Who replies at v. 8? It is not clear. It could be the beloved himself to whom the question was addressed.[77] But in his mouth, the verse would sound somewhat cynical. It could be the chorus of the 'daughters of Jerusalem' who appeared in v. 5.[78] But it seems odd that the woman would be addressing city dwellers in order to get information on the shepherds' routine. More likely we should be thinking of a male chorus of shepherds who speak again at v. 11.[79]

The two verses divide the little unit into two parts which correspond symmetrically[80] (cf. *Tab. 5*).

The two parts begin each with an impassioned address ("O love of my soul", v. 7a; "O most beautiful among women", v. 8a). To the two

---

[77] So, for example, Müller (1992), p. 17; Nolli (1967), p. 71.

[78] Thus Heinevetter (1988), p. 79. In fact, the appellation "the most beautiful among women" is used by them elsewhere (cf. 5:9; 6:1).

[79] It could also be a 'voice off-stage', that of the poet, who would be directly addressing the young woman, as in 5:1ef. Cf. Gerleman (1965), p. 102.

[80] Cf. Heinevetter (1988), pp. 77–78.

Table 5

Woman (v. 7)	A	Address	*O love of my soul*
	B	Two questions	*where...? where...?*
	C	Conclusion	*... behind the flocks of your comrades*
Chorus (v. 8)	A'	Address	*O most beautiful among women*
	B'	Two replies	*Go out... pasture...*
	C'	Conclusion	*... beside the tents of the shepherds*

questions of the woman in v. 7ab ("Where do you pasture your flock, where do you rest it?") correspond the two replies of the chorus in v. 8bc ("go out...pasture"). The two parts conclude with indications of place that clearly mirror each other ("behind [*ʿal*, literally: beside] the flocks of your comrades", v. 7d; "beside [*ʿal*] the tents of the shepherds", v. 8d). In addition to these correspondences, we should note the repetition of the verb *rāʿāh* ('pasture') in vv. 7a and 8c. The lexeme *rāʿāh* is contained a third time in the substantive 'shepherd' (i.e. 'pastor') (v. 8d) so that it is shown to be the *Leitmotiv* of the passage.

[1:7] In v. 7a here appears for the third time the verb *ʾāhēb*, 'to love' (the Hebrew text reads literally: "He whom my soul loves"). The first two times, the subject of the verb was the maidens (vv. 3c, 4e). To the love of the many is now counterposed the love of the one: it has another quality. In Hebrew, 'soul' is *nepeš*, a word which originally indicated the 'throat' as the site of life and desire. The expression 'love of my soul' recurs in 3:1–4 (4 times!) in the similar context of an impassioned quest. It expresses the agonised yearning caused by the absence of the loved one. The meaning is: "He whom I desire with all my being". The theme of searching is frequent in the Song (cf. 2:9, 14; 3:1–4; 4:8; 5:2–6; 8:1–2, 13), as in love poetry down the ages.[81]

"Where[82] do you pasture your flock?" The question situates the action in a bucolic atmosphere, as fictitious as the agricultural one in the previous strophe. The nearest parallels lead us to Hellenistic (Theocritus)[83]

[81] Gerleman (1965), p. 103, cites parallels from Egyptian love poetry, but it is a universal human theme (cf., *infra*, our commentary to 3:1–4).

[82] The two questions are introduced by the relative particle *ʾêkâ*, 'where', which is, like *šâllāmâ*, 'so that I may not', in 7c, derived from the Aramaic and bears witness to a late dating for the language of the Song. Cf. Rudolph (1962), p. 125; Heinevetter (1988), pp. 79–80.

[83] Cf. Garbini (1992), p. 190, who cites as a parallel *Idylls* 1:80–85. In any case, this is a common literary conceit, not direct dependence.

and Roman (Virgil;[84] Longus the Sophist)[85] poetry, although there are also antecedents in Amarnan Egypt.[86] It is the nostalgic dream of someone who has up until now belonged to the ambience and culture of the city. To Hebrew ears, however, the question could but not evoke that of Joseph in Gen 37:16 ("I am seeking my brothers. Where are they pasturing the flock?"), something which again confirms the impression that in the bucolic burlesque of the Song there may be a reference to the world of the patriarchs and the origins of Israel.

The second question (v. 7b) sketches a picture typical of the pastoral life. Still today, it is the custom of Palestinian shepherds to lead their flock at midday near to a place where there is water. The shepherd settles himself down in the shade under a tree or a rock. Perhaps, given that watering places are rare, he has company. The midday sun spreads a surreal glare, the air seems immobile. It is the hour of siesta both for animals (the flock is 'resting', *rābaṣ*) and for man. It is the ideal situation for an amorous encounter. Here too we recall past happenings in the history of Israel (cf. Gen 29:1–11 [Jacob and Rachel]; Exod 2:16–21 [Moses and the daughters of Jethro]).[87]

The questions are addressed to her beloved. Since he is not present, it is really a soliloquy. The woman entrusts her questions to the wind in order that it may carry them to her beloved. She does not address herself to others (she will do that later, cf. Song 3:3; 5:8: but the result will not be positive!), because, as it concerns an amorous appointment, she would be taken for a fast woman who would be an easy conquest. The 'veil' which is mentioned here is another patriarchal reminiscence, for this is exactly how Tamar is presented when she takes up her position on the street to seduce Jacob (Gen 38:14–15): the veil was the distinctive mark of prostitutes.[88]

The group of 'comrades' who begin to speak at v. 8, forms the male counterpart of the 'maidens' of the first strophe. Here too we can observe the ambivalence of the group. On the one hand, it is felt to be an obstacle to the love of the two young people (v. 7cd); on the other

[84] Cf. Pope (1977), p. 329. Also *Georgics* 3:331; *Culex* 103.

[85] To Longus the Sophist is ascribed the romance *Daphnis and Cloe*. Cf. Müller (1992), pp. 32–33.

[86] Cf. Müller (1992), p. 16.

[87] For the NT, cf. John 4:1–26.

[88] Not to be confused with the nuptial veil which is spoken of in 4:1 (cf. in this other sense Gen 24:65; 29:23, 25).

hand, it is called on to sustain this same love (v. 8) and to recognise its beauty (cf. v. 11). The love of the Song is in continual tension between the intimacy of the lovers, which society is invited to respect (cf. 2:7), and the social recognition of which love has need. The term 'comrades' (*ḥăbērîm*) will be taken up again significantly in the *Epilogue* (cf. 8:13).

[v. 8] The initial clause ("If you do not know…") allows a certain irony to show through in the original text.[89] Could this be present also in the compliment which follows ("most beautiful among women")? The parallel with 5:9; 6:1 could lead us not to exclude it.[90] But there it is a question of women, here of men. Perhaps the compliment is sincere because the admiration for the woman's beauty continues in the following strophe (cf. v. 11). As the 'maidens' were in love with the 'king' (vv. 3c, 4e), so the men are enamoured with the 'shepherdess'. The chorus confirms and extends what she herself has affirmed in v. 5 ('I am black but beautiful').[91]

The verb 'go out' (*yāṣāʾ*, v. 8b) is intensified in the Hebrew text by an ethical dative (*ṣᵉʾî lāk*, 'go out'). It is a verb of theological importance: it is the verb of the Exodus. So the woman is being advised to adopt the attitude of the Exodus, to abandon her own certainties in order to face the new situation. It is the attitude spoken of in Gen 2:24: "Therefore a man will leave his father and his mother and cleave to his wife". The leaving of one's own family and the beginning of a new life is a wrench for which love alone renders one capable. Just as in the case of Abraham (Gen 12:1), here too the destination is unknown ("If you do not know…").

In the case of Abraham, the direction is indicated by God ("Towards the country which I will show you"). Here it is indicated by the 'little goats',[92] the animals which the shepherdess is pasturing. By following the tracks of her own little goats, the woman will find her beloved.

---

[89] The Hebrew has an ethical dative ("If you do not know it for yourself…"), which perhaps holds an emphatic nuance : "If you yourself do not know". Cf. Ravasi (1992), p. 178, n. 28.

[90] Cf., in this sense, Keel (1986), p. 58.

[91] In v. 8, the Hebrew uses the adjective *yāpâ*, 'beautiful', in v. 5 the synonym *nāʾwâ*. This lexeme is resumed in v. 10a ("Your cheeks are beautiful").

[92] The Hebrew term *gᵉdiyyôt* is the feminine plural of *gᵉdî*, which indicates the young of the sheep and the goat. The lexeme returns in the *Prologue* in 1:14 (in the name 'Engedi', the 'spring of the goat').

Perhaps the phrase can also be interpreted in a realistic sense. Ravasi notes that the pathways of the bedouin are often created by the passage of goats. If one follows them, one reaches the shepherd's tent.[93] However, if the shepherdess follows the tracks of *her own* goats, they will lead her to *her* home not to that of her beloved. It is clear that the phrase is to be principally understood as a metaphor.

In the whole of the Ancient Orient, goats are the animals which accompany the goddess of love[94] perhaps because of their natural fecundity. Also in the episode of Tamar, she receives a kid or 'little goat' in recompense for her services (Gen 38:17, 20). The symbolic significance of the 'little goat' is common in the Song: the breasts of the woman are compared to 'two fawns' (4:5; 7:4), and she swears by 'the gazelles and the wild deer' (2:7; 3:5). That leads us to see the personification of the forces of love in the 'little goats' of 1:8. The woman is, therefore, advised to follow the voice of love wherever it lead her. For the guidance of YHWH (Gen 12:1), the Song substitutes that of love. Love is, in fact, a 'flame of YHWH' (Song 8:6).

The little goats lead the woman "beside the tents of the shepherds". The phrase is parallel to that of v. 7d, "behind the flocks of your comrades". If here we have a permanent 'dwelling',[95] the time indicated now is that of the evening when the shepherds bring the sheep back to the fold. The chorus invites the woman to do exactly that which at v. 7 she wanted to avoid, seeking her beloved in his social environment without any fear of gossip. In 3:2–4 she will reveal that she has learned the lesson.

The composition thus ends in a way similar to the preceding one. There the situation of departing was in evidence, the abandoning of the family protection; here we have the arrival, the new society which the young woman has to face. In poetic form, the two strophes describe the 'journey' of Gen 2:24 cited above. Significantly, in Gen 2:24 the protagonist is the 'man' (*'îš*); here, instead, it is the *woman*.

---

[93] Ravasi (1992), p. 178.

[94] Cf. Keel (1986), Figure 11, p. 61. For Mesopotamian literary parallels, cf. Pope (1977), pp. 334–335. Pope hints at a survival of this mythological tradition in the expression 'Aštart of the flock', *ʿaštᵉrōt ṣōʾnᵉkā*, in Deut 7:13; 28:4, 18.

[95] The term *miškān* usually indicates the tent (cf. LXX *epi skēnōmasin*; Vg *juxta tabernacula*).

Table 6

SHE (vv. 9–11)	A. Admiration B. Amplification	vv. 9–10 v. 11	'my friend'
HE (vv. 12–14)	B'. Royal Burlesque A'. Admiration	v. 12 vv. 13–14	'my beloved'

Fourth Strophe: Contemplation (1:9–14)

Vv. 9–14 are usually divided into two,[96] and also into three small compositional units.[97] In fact, the background to the metaphors is very different, from the stables (?) of Pharaoh (vv. 9–10), to the triclinium of the king (v. 12), to the oasis of Engedi (v. 14). However, Heinevetter has shown convincingly that we have a unitary composition.[98] As noted above, the fourth strophe is joined to the fifth and sixth by the fact of being characterised as a duet in which, in the first part, it is she who is admired (key word *ra'yātî*, ['my friend'], v. 9b), in the second part, it is he (key word *dôdî* ['my beloved'], vv. 13–14). This divides the strophe into two parts: vv. 9–11 and 12–14 (cf. *Tab. 6*).

In its turn, the first part is composed of words of admiration pronounced by the 'king' (vv. 9–10) and a brief amplification of the praise, by way of a coda, on the part of the chorus (v. 11). The second part begins with an isolated verse which acts as a pendant to the coda of the first part (v. 12) and ends with two verses in which the woman, replying to vv. 9–10, expresses her own admiration for her beloved (vv. 13–14). The parallelism between vv. 9–10 and vv. 13–14 is emphasised not only by the dual concept *ra'yātî-dôdî* but also by the use of the preposition 'among/between' (cf. *Tab. 7*).

If the connection between v. 11 and vv. 9–10 is clear (cf. the echo 'ear rings', vv. 10a, 11), the link between v. 12 and vv. 13–14 is not equally indisputable. The three verses of the second part are united

---

96 The two units would be: vv. 9–11 and 12–14 (so, for example: Colombo [1975], pp. 52–55; Elliott [1989], pp. 55–58; Garbini [1992], pp. 191–194; Lys [1968], pp. 82–92).

97 Often vv. 12–14 are, in their turn, divided into two parts: 12 and 13–14 (so, among others: Keel [1986], pp. 60–71; Krinetzki [1981], pp. 75–82; Müller [1992], pp. 17–20).

98 Heinevetter (1988), pp. 82–83; so also Ravasi (1992), pp. 188–189.

Table 7

v. 9	a mare	among *(b^{e})* the chariots of Pharaoh
v. 10	your cheeks	between *(b^{e})* your ear rings
	your neck	among *(b^{e})* chains of pearls
v. 13	a bag of myrrh	between *(bên)* my breasts
v. 14	a bunch of henna	among *(b^{e})* the vineyards

among themselves by the fact that it is the woman who speaks in them, addressing her beloved in the third person (while the first part is characterised by direct speech). Moreover, in each verse, reference is made to perfume ('nard', v. 12; 'myrrh', v. 13; 'henna', v. 14).

The fourth strophe contrasts with the two preceding ones by the fact of being a high burlesque ('Pharaoh', v. 9; 'king', v. 12).[99] From the point of view of the passage from separation to union, we note some progress in the process of coming together. If vv. 5–8 described the movement of going out of her own home and setting out on her search for the loved one, vv. 9–14 describe the next event: the search is over, the two stand before each other in mutual contemplation. Perhaps the initial comparison of the mare alludes still to the search which characterised the third strophe.[100] The fourth strophe is connected with the second one by the theme of the 'vineyard' (*kerem*, vv. 6 and 14) and by the lexeme *n'w* ('beautiful', vv. 5 and 10). Finally, the royal burlesque joins the fourth strophe with the first ('king', vv. 4 and 12). The term 'triclinium' (*mēsab*)[101] recalls the 'chambers' of v. 4; the two strophes also share the theme of 'scent' (*rêaḥ*, vv. 3, 12).

[1:9–10] The *NET* translation ("O my beloved, you are like a mare among Pharaoh's stallions") supposes that the *tertium comparationis*

---

[99] The 'vineyards of Engedi' also belong to this royal burlesque; in fact, from time immemorial, the oasis of Engedi was a royal possession. From the end of the seventh century B.C. up to the Roman epoch, the kings of Judah had aromatic plants and fruits cultivated there (cf. Keel-Küchler [1982], vol. II, pp. 418–428).

[100] So Ravasi (1992), p. 191 ("From afar, he sees his lady advancing towards him"). In this sense also tend some parallels with the Egyptian love songs, in which it is he indeed who is compared to a horse: "Oh, that you would come to me, / like a horse of the king, / chosen from among all his chargers, / the first of his stable" (Papyrus Chester Beatty IB 1:5–6; cf. Bresciani [1990], p. 458; cf. also Papyrus Harris 500A 1:8, *ibid.*, p. 460).

[101] Like the more frequent *m^{e}sibbâ* the term indicates the Greek symposium, in which the guests recline on three couches, while the fourth side is open for the service (cf. *HALAT*: 'round table'). The root *sbb* 'around' refers to the circular form of the triclinium. The term is significant for the placing of the Song in the Hellenistic epoch.

of the metaphor is sexual attraction.[102] However, the text does not support this interpretation. The term *rikbê* is an unusual plural of *rekeb*,[103] a term which has a collective value and indicates the military corps of chariots of war (the 'cavalry' of the army).[104] The emphasis is placed, in v. 10, on the aesthetic aspect, not the erotic.[105] The Egyptian war horses, like those of Assyria, are represented with rich harnessing which shows off, above all, the neck and the face,[106] precisely the elements highlighted in v. 10.

The comparison of female beauty to a horse can seem strange to our aesthetic taste, but not to that of the Egyptians[107] or that of the Greeks.[108] According to Müller, the comparison with an animal originally had a

[102] If I am correct, the first to suggest this interpretation was Pope (1977), p. 338, and it was readopted by Keel (1986), p. 62. On the basis of this reading, there is an episode in the Battle of Qadesh referred to in the *Autobiography of Amenemheb*: "The prince of Qadesh sent out a filly in front of the army in order to [...] them, it entered into the army; I followed it on foot with my sword and opened its belly" (Bresciani [1990], p. 297). Pharaoh's cavalry was composed exclusively of stallions so that the expedient of sending a filly into the midst of them made them crazy. Only by killing the filly was Amenemheb able to save the situation.

[103] Despite the proposal of Rudolph (1962), p. 127, largely followed by the translations, of reading a singular (cf. *NJB*: 'chariot'), I am retaining the MT (cf. also LXX: *en harmasin*; Vg *in curribus*). Perhaps the plural has been chosen instead of the collective singular by assimilation with the other plurals which follow the preposition 'among/between' in vv. 9–14 (cf. *supra, Tab. 7*).

[104] The lexeme returns in Song 6:12 with analogous significance ("the chariots of my noble people").

[105] That it is a 'mare' and not a 'stallion' that is being spoken of is perhaps simply due to the fact that it is she not he that is being spoken of. Thus Elliott (1989), p. 55.

[106] Cf. Keel (1986), Figures 17 and 12, pp. 66 and 63 respectively. Lys is therefore wrong to think that the comparison with the mare is made above all with regard to the woman's thighs, which, according to the Arab ideal of beauty, ought to be large, in order to be better at child-bearing. Cf. Lys (1968), p. 82. Equally unfounded, it seems to me, is the singular suggestion of Garbini (1992), pp. 191–192 of reading, instead of *lḥyyk*, 'your cheeks', *lḥyk*, 'your haunches' (from the post-biblical Hebrew *laḥ*, 'fresh'!).

[107] Cf., for example, the texts cited in note 100, or also the great stele of the sphinx of Amenopis II: "See, when he was still a little boy, he loved his horses and was pleased with them: he was happy in his heart to take care of them, since he was one who knew their nature, good at training them". His son "bred horses without equal, when he held the reins, they were tireless and did not sweat even in a long gallop". Cf. Bresciani (1990), pp. 270–271.

[108] Theocritus compares Helen with a "horse of Thessaly" (*Idylls* 18:30); as an appellation of a woman, Anacreon uses "horse of Thrace" (75:1); Alcman compares the *choregos* Hagesichora to a racehorse bred in Venetia (1:50–63, cf. Calame [1983], pp. 29–30, 270, 327–332).

magic value.[109] By means of the force of the word ("I liken you"), the person would have received the numinous quality incorporated in the animal mentioned. In the Song, the magic world has been replaced by the lyrical. But the mythical element remains in the background. Like the goats, the horse also was associated in the Ancient Orient, above all in Anatolia, with the goddess of love.[110]

The horse formed part of the chariots of war of the Pharaoh. His chariot is often represented in Egyptian bas-reliefs.[111] The context highlights above all the opulence of the harnesses (cf. vv. 10–11), transposing the woman into an aristocratic atmosphere which contrasts deliberately with the rural scenario of the two preceding strophes. Bearing in mind the highly refined equipment of Tutankhamon's chariot, the comparison cannot be said to be inappropriate. The woman is a shepherdess, but she is also a queen.[112]

For the first time, the woman is called *raʿyātî* ('my friend'), a term which is uttered solely by the man and applied uniquely to his loved one.[113] The word derives from *rʿh* II, a root which indicates originally 'friend', 'companion' and is the usual appellation for the woman in the Song. The term *kallâ* ('bride') is restricted to 4:8–12 (and 5:1) and is not typical for the woman. In doing this, the Song does not intend to glorify extra-marital relations (cf. 8:6!) but to highlight the personal rather than the institutional aspect of love. Perhaps by contrast with the patriarchal environment in which marriage was considered as a contract which left little space for love, the Song emphasises that two spouses are united primarily by love, that they are, above all, 'friends'. It is interesting to note that the root *rʿh* is the same as that of the verb

---

[109] Müller (1992), p. 17.

[110] Cf. Keel (1984a), Figures 324 and 324a, p. 216.

[111] Cf. Keel (1986), Figure 12, p 63.

[112] The comparison with Pharaoh refers also to the figure of Solomon (vv. 1, 5). Solomon had obtained his horses from Egypt (1Kgs 5:6; 10:26–29; 2Chr 1:16–17). The author of the Deuteronomistic history disapproves of this paganising conduct (cf. Deut 17:16): there is no trace of negative judgement in the Song. Every luxury is tiny in comparison with love. Along these lines, Lacocque, recalls that "the *motiv* of the Exodus from Egypt with the accompanying humiliation of the Egyptians is central in Israel's theological reflection; but now we are invited to admire the proud majesty of Pharaoh's war chariots". Cf. Lacocque (1998), p. 77.

[113] Cf. 1:9, 15; 2:2, 10, 13; 4:1, 7; 5:2; 6:4. The masculine form *rēʿî* is employed once by the woman in speaking of her beloved (5:16). On another occasion, the author uses the plural form *rēʿîm* to indicate the two lovers (5:1).

'to pasture' (*rʿh* I, cf. vv. 7a, 8c, d). A subtle word play unites the two terms: the 'shepherdess' is also the 'friend'.

The term *tôr* (v. 10a) indicates, certainly not the 'turtle dove' as understood by the LXX and the Vulgate, but a 'thread' (cf. Esth 2:12, 15)[114] and thus something like a necklace. In our context we should think of an object which frames the face just as the harness frames the muzzle of a horse: 'ear rings', 'locks of hair', 'pendants'.[115] Next to the face, the neck is mentioned. We must think first of all of the haughty necks of the Egyptian horses.[116] Already in the OT, both the horse[117] and the neck are themselves synonyms of pride. Isa 3:16 tartly scolds the daughters of Zion who have become arrogant and so "walk with outstretched necks". In our case, dignified bearing, the 'neck', is seen as beautiful, the sign of a beauty that is aware of its own worth. Just as the face is framed by 'ear rings', so the neck is embellished by *ḥărûzîm*, a *hapaxlegomenon* of the Song but one whose sense ('thread of pierced objects' and so 'necklace') is well attested.[118]

[v. 11] In the first strophe, the praise of the woman was concluded with the choral amplification by the 'maidens' (vv. 3c, 4e); so, now, the admiration of the man is amplified by a chorus (supposed by the plural 'we shall make'). Probably it is a male group,[119] the same chorus of shepherds who had spoken in v. 8. Here too the social dimension of love is brought to the fore. The two lovers are not alone. Without jealousy, the chorus shares in the admiration, as 'friends of the bridegroom'.

The friends find that the splendid jewels which adorn the face and the neck of the woman are still no match for her beauty. She deserves more: a more noble metal ('ear rings of gold') with a workmanship that is more refined ('studded with silver'). The friends themselves are involved in the work.[120]

---

[114] Cf. *HALAT*, p. 1575.

[115] Cf. Keel (1986), p. 64.

[116] Keel (cf. the preceding note) observes that the 'haughty' bearing of the Egyptian horses is connected with the fact that the bit is brought near to the neck by an additional bridle (clearly visible in Keel [1986], Figure, 12, p. 63).

[117] Cf. Isa 30:16; 31:1, 3; Zech 9:10.

[118] Cf. *HALAT*, p. 338.

[119] Note once again the 'mirroring dynamic', cf., *supra*, p. 54: at her side is the group of maidens, at his a group of shepherds.

[120] Possibly we have here a veiled allusion to the nuptial gift *(mōhar)*, to which the friends of the bridegroom also contributed (cf. Ravasi [1992], p. 194).

[v. 12] Similarly to what was noted in the first part of the strophe, in which v. 11 was distinguished from vv. 9–10, so, in the second, v. 12 is distinguished from vv. 13–14 which are constructed in marked parallelism (cf. *Tab. 6*). In this part, dedicated to 'him', it seems that the first verse is an exception, paying attention still to 'her'. A constant feature of strophes IV–VI (1:9–2:3) is that the second part, put into the mouth of the woman,[121] passes from the contemplation to the gradual fruition of love. The fourth strophe draws attention to the olfactory aspect of the enjoyment of love, the sixth to the gustatory (2:3d; cf. 2:4–5). The series scent-taste returns also in 4:16 and indicates perhaps the passage from reciprocal desire ('scent') to the consummation of the union (to 'eat' and 'drink'). In this perspective, v. 12 describes the attraction, the desire: the two lovers are still apart. In vv. 13–14, they are united in an embrace.

"While the king is in his triclinium...". The author is describing a festive, royal banquet such as is often described in the Egyptian songs of love and in numerous representations.[122] As in the first strophe, here too there is a tension between being in the group of friends (v. 12) and the intimacy of the lovers (vv. 13–14), a tension which also exists in the Egyptian parallels.[123] The 'nard' (*Nardostachys jatamansi de Candolle*) is a very precious ointment (cf. Mark 14:3), hailing from India and here looked on as an aphrodisiac.[124] It is mentioned again in the Song at 4:13 and 14 among the scents of the 'garden'. Since the 'garden', like the vineyard, is a metaphor for the female body, we should reckon that it has the same significance in our passage.[125] In 'my nard' represents the female glamour of the woman which reaches the king reclining on his couch. But the verb 'pour forth' is *nātan* ('to give') in

[121] It is the woman, therefore, who takes the initiative, not the man. Once more she is presented not only as the object, but also as the subject of desire and passion.

[122] Cf. Gerleman (1965), pp. 109–110. Keel (1986), Figures 138 & 6, pp. 237 & 51, portray scenes of a similar 'banquet of drinks', very widespread in Egypt. From Mesopotamia, however, comes the famous scene in Keel (1986), Figure 38, p. 87, which depicts an intimate banquet for the royal couple. For the literary *motiv* of 'divan', cf. Ravasi (1992), pp. 196–197. The term used in v.12, *mēsab*, 'triclinium', recalls rather a convivial gathering.

[123] Cf., e.g., the Turin Papyrus 2,7–15, according to Bresciani (1990), p. 470. Cf. also Mathieu (1996), pp. 85–86.

[124] Cf. Zohary (1995), p. 205. In the NT, nard is mentioned at the Anointing in Bethany (Mark 14:3; John 12:3). Strangely, in rabbinic exegesis, nard is considered an unpleasant odour and becomes a symbol of sin (cf., e.g., the Targum).

[125] *Contra* Elliott (1989) p. 58, according to whom the possessive refers to the (male) beloved.

Table 8

v. 13	a bag of myrrh	my beloved is to me	between my breasts at night
v. 14	a bunch of henna	my beloved is to me	among the vineyards of Engedi

Hebrew. The use of this verb is not accidental. 'To give scent' returns in Song 2:13 (the vineyards in flower) and 7:14 (the mandrakes). But perhaps the most significant parallel is 7:13 when the woman says: "There I shall give you my caresses". According to G. Krinetzki, the verb expresses the feminine way of experiencing sexuality and love, which finds its own satisfaction in giving satisfaction to its partner.[126] With her scent, the female lover gives herself.

[vv. 13–14] The two verses should be considered in their strict parallelism (cf. *Tab. 8*).

Corresponding to the term *ra'yātî* ('my friend'), the term *dôdî* ('my beloved') is introduced twice. It is the usual appellation with which the lady addresses her man. *dôd* is probably a baby word on the lines of our 'daddy'.[127] The word often designates a degree of relationship, that is, the 'uncle' or the 'cousin', two particularly popular figures in Oriental society. The cousin especially was the childhood friend of a young woman and the prime candidate to become her husband. This familial nuance of the word is retained also in the Song where, as in the Egyptian love songs, the two lovers call each other 'brother' and 'sister' (cf. 4:9, 10, 12; 5:1, 2). But the chief emphasis is on the 'affective' aspect of the term. The root *w/ydd* means 'to love' as the term *dôdîm* ('caresses', cf. vv. 2, 4) proves. Like *ra'yātî, dôdî* also does not directly signify the spouse (in Isa 5:1 it refers to a male friendship),[128] but the 'friend', the 'beloved-friend'. And again it is the voluntary, 'amicable' aspect of love which is presented.[129]

The possessive pronoun, on the other hand, is emphasised twice ("*my* beloved is *to me*") and underlines the exclusive character of this

[126] Cf. Krinetzki (1981), p. 79: "Erotic love, above all that of the woman, knows [...] that its own need of pleasure is better satisfied in thinking more of how to pleasure the partner rather than itself".

[127] Cf. J. Sanmartin-Ascaso, *dôd*, in *DTOT*, vol. III, pp. 143–156.

[128] Cf. Wildberger (1980), p. 167. One is often meant to see in *dôd* a divine appellative. Cf. Müller (1992), pp. 19–20; Lys (1968), pp. 89–90, but the matter is disputed (cf. *DTOT*, vol. III, p. 155).

[129] Cf. the name of Solomon *yᵉdîdyâ*, 'beloved of YHWH'. A 'theological' interpretation of the name is not to be excluded. The consonants of *dôd* are the same as of *dāwid*, the name of David as it is written in the titles of the Psalms, something which would favour a messianic interpretation of the term.

friendship, something typical of being in love. The formula foreshadows the 'refrain of mutual belonging' (Song 2:16, cf. 6:3; 7:11).

The beloved is compared to a 'bag of myrrh'. This is a kind of amulet of varied form and contents, worn on the neck and often documented in oriental iconography.[130] As an amulet, its function is to protect against death: this is also the function of the 'seal' in 8:6 ("Set me as a seal upon your heart [...] for love is strong as death").[131] The contents of the bag-amulet here is 'myrrh' (*Commiphora abyssinica*), a scented resin cultivated in Arabia, Ethiopia and Somalia.[132] It is mentioned frequently in the Song (cf. 3:6; 4:6, 14; 5:1, 5, 13), above all for its erotic character (cf. Prov 7:17; Ps 45:9; Esth 2:12). Just as the woman smells of nard, so her beloved is fragrant with myrrh: with this metaphor we have an indication of their mutual attraction. But myrrh has particular connotations which are perceptible in the background. It plays a part in the consecration of priests and of sacred vestments (Exod 30:23); it confers therefore a sacral aspect on love, something which will recur. Finally, myrrh was used in embalming (cf. John 19:39), something which confirms the apotropaic value of the amulet. Love is the only thing which is in some way powerful against death.

"Passing the night between my breasts". The text is pregnant: the subject of the phrase could be either the 'bag of myrrh'[133] or 'my beloved', and probably the ambiguity is deliberate. The beloved is the true amulet. In Song 8:6 the woman is an amulet for her man; here it is he who performs the role for her: the reciprocity is perfect. The two lovers, then, are in each other's arms and pass the night together.[134] Is this a dream or reality that the woman is describing? It is difficult to say. Certainly the song is approaching its conclusion where the union is consummated.

In v. 14, the beloved is compared to a 'bunch of henna'. Henna (*Lawsonia inermis*) is a shrub which can reach the height of three metres and blooms in yellow-white with a rose-like perfume.[135] Today

---

130 Cf. Keel (1986), pp. 68–70; *id.* (1984), pp. 108–114.

131 The correspondence confirms the inclusion between the *Prologue* and the *Epilogue* of the Song.

132 Cf. Zohary (1995), p. 200.

133 Cf. Keel (1984a), Figure 118, p. 185.

134 To an ear accustomed to the reading of Scripture, there is an inescapable reference to Hos 2:4: "...that she put away her adultery from between her breasts (*mibbên šadèhā*)". Except that in Hosea the expression has a clearly negative connotation (adultery!), while in the Song there is not a shade of disapproval (cf. Lacocque [1998], p. 80).

135 Cf. Zohary (1995), p. 190.

it is known for its dye (of a red-orange colour), which is used a great deal by Arab women to colour their hair and their nails, but in antiquity the flowers were certainly valued for their scent,[136] even if this has few attestations.[137] In Egypt, the scent of henna was called *ʿanch yimi* ('inner life'). Henna flowers were placed on the tombs of the dead as a symbol of life,[138] since above and beyond the erotic aspect, it was understood, like myrrh, to represent victory over death which is, as it were, the *Leitmotiv* of the Song. This aspect is intensified by the fact that the henna flower is found in a luxuriant oasis on the edge of the Dead Sea (Engedi), in an environment surrounded by the desert: the very situation speaks of the triumph of life over death.[139]

The henna-vineyard association returns again in 7:12–13. It is intended primarily in a literal sense: in fact, at Engedi, perfumes and fruit of every kind were cultivated.[140] But, as in the preceding verse, here too an apparently innocent declaration is open to a *double entendre*. The 'vineyard' is, in fact, a metaphor for the female body (cf. v. 6e). 'Among the vineyards' thus acquires a significance not very different from 'between my breasts'.[141]

Fifth Strophe: The Bed in the Grass (1:15–17)

Like the preceding strophe, this one too is characterised by a dialogue between 'him' (v. 15) and 'her' (vv. 16–17). At the centre of the first part is the figure of the woman, at the centre of the second that of the man. The parallelism between the two parts is limited, however, to vv. 15–16a. Vv. 16b–17 introduce another theme: from the contemplation of love comes the passage to its fruition, as has already happened in vv. 13–14.

---

[136] Henna *(kōper)* is mentioned in Song 4:13 together with nard (cf. also 7:12).

[137] Cf., however, the explanation of Samuel Ali Hissein: "This henna, which makes the ugly beautiful, has innumerable flowers. And its flowers are yellow and dense. But what renders it even more precious and attractive to men is its scent [...]. Sometimes women put it under their braids or under the armpits to get rid of body odour" (quotation in Gerleman [1965], p. 112).

[138] Cf. Keel (1986), p. 70.

[139] *Ibid.*, p. 71.

[140] Pliny also speaks of the vineyards of Engedi (cf. *Naturalis historia* 5:15, 73).

[141] Perhaps the name Engedi, 'spring of the kid', also has a double sense. The 'kid' has, in fact, an erotic significance (cf. *supra*, p. 68), and in 4:5 the woman's breasts are compared to 'two fawns, twins of a gazelle' (cf. also 7:4).

Stylistically, the composition is erected on the phenomenon of *enjambement.*[142] Metrically, v. 16b is linked with v. 16a: the verse is a distich like v. 15. The connection between v. 16a and v. 16b is emphasised by the fact that both stichs are introduced by the conjunction *ʾap* ('indeed'). In content, however, v. 16b does not belong any more to the reciprocal admiration of the lovers, but introduces the theme of v. 17 (love in nature).

The reciprocal admiration (vv. 15–16a) prolongs the theme of the previous strophe. Also here we have a subtle concatenation: in Hebrew, the word *ʿayin* indicates both the eye and the spring (in so far as 'eye' and 'spring of water' are similar). It links *ʿên gedî* ('the spring of the kid', end of strophe IV) with *ʿênayik* ('your eyes', beginning of strophe V). Also the theme of love in the grass (vv. 16b–17) continues the identification of the lovers with nature which was introduced before in v. 14.

[1:15] Three times in vv. 15–16a, the interjection *hinnēh* is followed by the pronoun of the second person singular (literally: 'see, you'). It has an intensive sense ('how') but also expresses wonder before an unexpected phenomenon: that wonder which is typical of someone in love in the presence of his beloved. The same declaration ("how beautiful you are") is repeated twice by him, and she takes it up a third time ("how handsome you are", v. 16a)[143]—the triplet is deliberate. In the Song, repetition often has a stylistic function. Here it expresses the stammering of a man in love who, faced with the beauty[144] of his beloved, knows only to repeat the same words, and yet they are never the same.

"Your eyes are doves!" The phrase has aroused the keen interest of exegetes. With many, Gerleman holds that the comparison refers to the form of the eyes. In Egyptian art, the outline of the eyes is strongly

---

[142] The Webster's dictionary gives this definition of *enjambement*: "Continuation in prosody of the sense in a phrase beyond the end of a verse or couplet; the running over of a sentence from one line into another so that closely related words fall in different lines" (*Webster's Third New International Dictionary of the English Language Unabridged*, Springfield MA 1966, p. 754).

[143] All the more so as v. 15 is repeated in 4:1. For this reason, Haupt suppresses the verse as a doublet Cf. Haupt (1907), pp. 10 and 76.

[144] The adjective *yāpâ*, 'fair', is the preferred term with which the man characterises his beloved (cf. 4:1, 7; 6:4, 10; 7:7). The adjective returns in substantival form in 1:8; 2:10, 13; 5:9; 6:1. The verb *yph* is employed in 4:10 and 7:2, always with reference to the woman.

highlighted and this could make one think of a dove's eyes.[145] However, the text does not say: "Your eyes are *like* those of a dove",[146] but "they are doves". On this account, Ravasi thinks that the emphasis is placed on the significance of this bird, taken as a whole ("sincerity, tenderness, love, sexual desire, innocence, faithfulness, peace, etc").[147] Keel makes the observation that in the Oriental world the term of comparison is not so much the form of an object as its function. In the present case, what would be understood would not be the external appearance of the eyes but their function in "glancing".[148]

In the whole of the Ancient Orient, including the Graeco-Roman world, the dove was the animal of the goddess of love.[149] On the other hand, the dove early assumed the role of messenger bird.[150] If the two symbolic values are united, the metaphor of the dove is understood as 'messenger of love'. In fact, Keel has produced significant iconographic examples in which a dove flies between the eyes of two people in love, fulfilling exactly this function.[151] The sense of v. 15 seems to be, therefore: "Your eyes are sending out messages of love".

[vv. 16–17] For the only time in the Song, the adjective *yāpeh* refers to the man, and so underlines the reciprocity of the admiration. The adjective is not repeated for the man but is joined with the synonym *nāʿîm* ('delightful, sweet'). If *yph* expresses the aesthetic side of love, *nʿm* expresses the enjoyable side. It is a term with a strong mythical

---

[145] Gerleman (1965), p. 114.

[146] Thus Vg (*oculi tui columbarum*), but it is clearly a *lectio facilior*.

[147] Ravasi (1992), p. 205 (who reviews some possible interpretations). We have here an example of the 'eclectic' character of the work of Ravasi, who, wishing to embrace every possible interpretation, sometimes turns out to be vague, not too precise.

[148] "Glances" (*Blicke*) is also the title of his work, rich as always with illustrations drawn from Oriental iconography. Cf., in this respect, Keel (1984b), pp. 53–62.

[149] The origin is perhaps the natural observation of two doves pecking each other, reminiscent of the kisses of two lovers. Cf. Keel (1984b), Figure 39, p. 144; also Aristotle, *Historia animalium* 6,2; 560b; 26ff.; Catullus, *Carmina* 68A:125–128 ("Nor did ever dove delight so much in her snowy mate, though the dove bites and bills and snatches kisses more wantonly than any woman, be she amorous beyond others' measure", in the LCL translation of F.W. Cornish); Ovid, *Amores* 2:6, 56; *Ars amatoria* 2:465; Pliny, *Naturalis historia* 10:79, 158; Servius, *Commentary on Virgil's Aeneid* 6:194. For further citations, cf. Keel (1984b), p. 59. If the dove is the personification of the goddess of love, the declaration: "Your eyes are doves" confers on the loved one something of the divine, almost as if the goddess of love herself is being revealed in front of the youth. This 'theomorphic' value of the metaphor in the Song is stressed in Müller (1992), p. 21.

[150] Cf. Keel (1977).

[151] Cf. Keel (1986), Figures 37, 25, 30, 26 on pp. 87, 73, and 75 respectively.

background.[152] In appraising the connection with myth, Lys and Müller go in opposite directions. The first sees in the Song a radical demythologisation of sexuality. Love is taken away from the world of the gods and restored to that of humanity. The true *nāʿîm* is not the god Adonis but this youth who stands before me.[153] Müller, on the other hand, holds that the mythological background confers on the person of the lovers a 'theomorphic' value in the sense of Gen 1:26 (man in the image of God). The sense would be: in the love of this youth, I experience God (cf. Song 8:6).[154] It seems to me that these two approaches are complementary rather than alternatives.

As in the preceding strophe, the woman is not confined to admiring but invites (yes, *she* invites!) her lover to union. 'Our bed' alludes precisely to union. The two are no longer two separate persons, an 'I' and a 'you', but a 'we'. The first person plural pronoun is repeated three times ('*our* bed', '*our* house', '*our* roof').

The term used to express the 'bed' is not the usual (*miškāb*) but a rather rare term, *ʿereś*. As the parallels show (cf. Prov 7:16; Amos 6:4–6), it is an object of luxury which contrasts with what follows. The effect is that of an oxymoron similar to that of v. 5. The bed is luxurious but the couple are lying on the grass. A similar picture is given in Song 7:12–13 (love among the henna shrubs and vineyards) and 8:5 (love under the apple tree). The Song senses a continuity between human love and the vegetative cycle, a theme which has already been introduced with the term *nāʿîm*. The word *raʿănān* ('vivid green') denotes not the colour but the 'freshness' of the plant. It is used in the prophetic literature in connection with the open-air sanctuaries of the Canaanites where fertility rites were carried out.[155] What the prophets saw as idolatry is integrated into the Yahwistic religion in the Song. In lyrical form, the Song overcomes that alienation between man and nature which characterises the modern world and which ancient man

[152] At Ugarit 'sweet and beautiful' (*nʿmm wysmm*) is the epithet of the gods Shahru and Shalimu, the stars of morning and evening (*KTU* 1.23, cf. Del Olmo Lete [1981], pp. 427–448). Naaman is the appellation of Adonis-Tammuz. The anemone derives its name from this root: among the Arabs, this flower of a fine red colour is called 'wound of Adonis'. Cf. Lys (1968), pp. 94–95. The plural *naʿămānîm* (cf. Isa 17:10) indicates the so-called 'gardens of Adonis', bowls with shoots of cereals which were intended to symbolise the return to life of the god of vegetation (cf. T. Kronholm, *naʿam*, in *DTOT*, vol. IX, p. 473), a rite still in use in Sicily, where similar bowls adorn the 'sepulchre' in Holy Week.

[153] Lys (1968), p. 95.

[154] Müller (1992), p. 21.

[155] Cf. Deut 12:2; 1 Kgs 14:23; 2 Kgs 16:4; Jer 2:20; 3:6, 13; Ezek 6:13; Isa 57:5.

overcame by means of myth.[156] Furthermore, the theme of the 'bed in the grass' constitutes an archetype of love poetry.[157]

The lovers lie on the grass in the shadow of some tree.[158] If they look up above, they see the branches of the trees which, so to speak, make up their ceiling. This is what is expressed in v. 17. The two words used here, *qōrâ* ('beam', cf. 2 Chr 3:7) and *rāḥîṭ* ('ceiling'), but, above all, the quality of the wood, 'cedar'[159] and 'cypress',[160] make one think of a luxurious dwelling. Cedar of Lebanon was the material from which the houses of kings and gods were constructed. Once again, therefore, we have the contrast between rural simplicity and the sumptuous wealth of a palace. Love is worthy of the palace of Solomon and the temple of God.

---

[156] Cf. Müller (1976).

[157] In the Sumerian texts concerning sacred marriage, the nuptial bed in the Gipar was covered with luxuriant plants (cf. *ANET*, p. 638, ll. 40–41). The Egyptian songs of love also speak of love in nature. Papyrus Harris 500B 4:7 declares: "It is good to go into the fields, / for one who is loved" (cf. Bresciani [1990], p. 463). The Turin Papyrus 1:2–3, 9–11, describes love under the trees of the garden: "What they do, the woman with her beloved, / [is hidden by] my branches, / when they are drunk with wine and must, / perfumed with oil and fragrant essences. [...] It will make you pass a happy day, / a canopy of branches is a well-guarded place. / Look, the pomegranate is right, / come, let us treat it kindly, / who lets us pass the whole day [under the tree] / who hides us" (*ibid.*, pp. 469–469). The theme is well-known in Greece. In the *Odyssey*, the love of Demeter and Jason is described on a field that has been ploughed three times (Homer, *Odyssey* 5:125–127). In the *Iliad*, Zeus copulates with Hera on the summit of Ida. As a result of this union, all sorts of herbs and flowers sprout from the earth (Homer, *Iliad* 14:346–351). Perhaps, however, the nearest to the lyrical inspiration of the Song is Theocritus. Cf., e.g., *Idylls* 7:133–136: "[...] and in deep greenbeds of fragrant reeds and fresh-cut vine-strippings laid us rejoicing down. Many an aspen, many an elm bowed and rustled overhead, and hard by, the hallowed water welled purling forth of a cave of the Nymphs" (translation of J. M. Edmonds, LCL).

[158] A. and C. Bloch (1995), p. 147, like Lacocque, (1998), p. 80, think of a love "without roof or law", that is, a clandestine encounter. But according to 8:5 'under the apple tree' is not opposed to the 'house of my mother': they are complementary dimensions of love.

[159] The cedar *('erez)* is mentioned in the Song again in 5:15 and 8:9. It is understood also in 3:9 under the expression: 'the wood of Lebanon'. In antiquity, Lebanon was considered the 'garden of the gods' and to cut down cedars was the prerogative of great monarchs. It was with this exotic wood that the palace of Solomon was constructed (cf. 1Kgs 5:24 [the *bᵉroš* is also mentioned]; 7:7, 11) and the temple (1 Kgs 6:18, 20).

[160] The term *bᵉrôt* is a poetic form of the more common *bᵉroš*. Zohary indicates under this name three kinds of trees: the cypress *(Cupressus sempervirens)*, the spruce *(Abies cilicica)* and the juniper *(Juniperus excelsa)*. His preference is for the second or third species, something supported by the Lebanese name *(brotha)*. Cf. Zohary (1995), pp. 106–107.

Table 9

v. 1	lotus flower		
v. 2	lotus flower	like...so	
v. 3ab		like...so	an apple tree
v. 3cd			its shade...its fruit

Sixth Strophe: Desire (2:1–3)

The strophe is marked off from its predecessor by the different type of discourse: the fifth strophe (1:15–17) was characterised by direct discourse, the present one (except for v. 1) by that in the third person, more detached, similar to 1:12–14. The three strophes are linked, however, by their dialogical character. In the three verses 2:1–3, the subject who speaks changes three times (v. 1 = she; v. 2 = he; v. 3 = she), but the first two verses are united by the common object (= she; cf. the term *raʿyātî* in v. 2b), and also, both together they correspond rhythmically (four stichs) to the longer v. 3 which speaks of him (*dôdî*, v. 3b). The strophe is, therefore, divided into two parts: vv. 1–2 and v. 3.

The 'concatenation' which characterised the preceding strophe continues in this one (cf. *Tab. 9*). The first distich (v. 1) is joined to the second (v. 2) by the term *šôšannâ* ('lotus flower', vv. 1b, 2a). The second distich forms a clear parallelism with the third (cf. *Tab. 10*) in which the woman repeats with regard to the man what he has said with regard to her (cf. 1:13–14, 15–16a). Although the third distich does not continue this parallelism, it is, however, joined with v. 3ab both by the subject who is speaking and by the metaphor of the apple tree.

As in the previous strophe, so in this, the part of the woman is more in evidence than that of the man. She speaks in vv. 1 and 3, that is to say in six of eight stichs (the chiastic effect is to be noted: woman-man-woman). Moreover, she is not limited to contemplation but invites to union (v. 3cd). The passage from contemplation to union seems to be indicated by the passage from 'flowers' (vv. 1–2) to 'fruits' (v. 3).

The link with what precedes is confirmed by the persistence of the theme of immersion in nature: if, in the preceding strophe, the woman was a dove, she is now a flower, and the man a tree.

[2:1] The language of flowers is a universal human language, above all among those in love. With its shape and its scent, the flower is the expression of beauty, freshness and attraction. The first flower which is named in v. 1 is called *ḥăbaṣṣelet*. The term appears in the OT only in

Isa 35:1 where it represents the eschatological splendour of the land of Israel.[161] The botanical identification is disputed.[162] At any rate, it must be a flower that is striking. It is associated with the *šārôn*. The Hebrew term in itself signifies 'plain' and is so understood by the LXX and the Vulgate. With the article, according to the Song's custom of identifying the lovers with localities typical of the land of Israel (cf. 1:14), it probably indicates 'the Sharon', the coastal plain between Tel Aviv and Mount Carmel.[163] In antiquity it was a sparsely populated area, a countryside of sandy dunes and marshes in which the most striking flower is the maritime lily (*pancratium maritimum*).[164]

The identification of the second flower, *šôšannâ*,[165] is also problematic. Generally it is understood to be the lily.[166] Keel has proposed a correspondence with the Egyptian *sšn* which indicates the water-lily, the 'lotus flower'.[167] Even if this proposal has not yet found unanimous agreement, it seems to me reasonable and coherent with the context. The lotus flower was known also in Israel, as numerous images of the biblical epoch attest.[168] By contrast with the Christian tradition with regard to the 'lily',[169] the lotus was in Egypt, as generally in the Ancient Orient, a

---

[161] A. and C. Bloch (1995), p. 148, think of a deliberate match between our passage and Isa 35, all the more so since the other flower, the *šôšannâ*, appears in an eschatological context (cf. Hos 14:6–8). Thus the eschatological glory of the promised land would be attributed to the woman. Knowing the subtle intertextuality of the Song, we think such an allusion not unlikely.

[162] LXX and Vg understand it as a common term (*anthos, flos*); *HALAT* has 'asphodelos'; Pope 'crocus'; *CEI* and *TOB* 'narcissus'; *LND, NRV, NJB* and *RSV* 'rose'; Zohary (1995), p. 176, 'lily'.

[163] Sharon is mentioned also in Isa 35:2, in connection with the *ḥăbaṣṣelet* (35:1).

[164] So Keel (1986), p. 79; Zohary (1995), p. 178, calls it: "beach narcissus".

[165] The name 'Susanna' derives from this term. The flower is often mentioned in the Song: 2:1, 2, 16; 4:5; 5:13; 6:3; 7:3 (7 times!).

[166] *Lilium candidum*, according to Zohary (1995), p. 176. So the majority of the translations, following LXX (*krinon*) and Vg (*lilium*). For Gordis (1974), p. 81, it is not the white lily, but the anemone of a fine red colour.

[167] Keel (1984b), pp. 63–78; *id.* (1986), pp. 79–84; Keel - Küchler - Uehlinger (1984), vol. I, pp. 85–88. Keel's suggestion is followed, e.g., by Heinevetter (1988), p. 90; Müller (1992), p. 23. For the discussion, cf. *HALAT*, pp. 1349–1350, and H. Schmoldt, *šûšan*, in *DTOT*, vol. XIV, pp. 552–555.

[168] Cf., e.g., the famous Megiddo ivory in Keel (1984a), Figure 233, p. 149. It is probable that the ornamental motifs used for the columns of the temple and for the sea of bronze (1 Kgs 7:19, 22, 26; 2 Chr 4:5) were also inspired by the lotus flower, not by the 'lily'. Cf. Keel (1986), pp. 80–81.

[169] But the Oriental tradition was different. According to Zohary (1995), p. 176, the lily was a symbol of beauty, often also of fecundity and wealth.

symbol of love.[170] That agrees with the passages of the Song in which the lotus flowers are associated with the most erogenous parts of the female body (breasts, 4:5; pubic area, 7:3) and also of the masculine (lips, 5:13). At the same time, this flower was the symbol of new life. According to an Egyptian myth, the sun god (Ra) was born at the beginning of time in a lotus flower floating on the waters of primeval chaos (Nun).[171] The natural spectacle of the water lily which pops out of the stagnant waters of a marsh as though by a miracle, evoked among the Egyptians the primordial victory of life over the forces of chaos and death. Gods and mortals were represented in the act of sniffing the lotus flower which was thought to have the power to renew life. The lotus flower was put into the tomb of the dead in the hope of new life.[172]

The environment indicated for the *šôšannâ* is the 'valleys'. Consequently we should think of the swamps which lie among the dunes of Sharon which are well suited to the growth of water-lilies.

[v. 2] The man confirms what the woman has said about herself. His speech is in the third person; he wants to confer an objective character on his declaration even if it is really highly subjective. For every man in love, the woman he loves has no equal (cf. 6:9).

The woman is, then, a lotus flower who bears a breath of new life and who attracts irresistibly with her charm. In comparison, the other young women (the Hebrew word is 'daughters', which echoes the 'daughters of Jerusalem', 1:5) are repellent as 'thorns'. The preposition 'among' does not express here, as in the parallel v. 3, the site of the lotus flower (it is difficult to put thorns together with a water lily), but rather the contrast of two realities.[173] To the extent that the lotus flower is attractive and life-giving, so thorns are unpleasant and, so far as associated with the desert, the symbol of death.[174]

[v. 3] V. 3 constitutes a perfect parallel to v. 2 (cf. *Tab. 10*), another example of that 'mirroring-dynamic' which is typical of the Song.

---

[170] Cf., e.g., Keel (1984a), Figure 63, p. 157 (of Israelite origin even if betraying Egyptian influences). On the significance of the lotus flower in the ancient Egyptian culture, cf. Derchain (1975), pp. 71f. For the Indian culture, cf. Pope (1977), p. 348.

[171] Cf. Keel (1984b), Figure 58, p. 154.

[172] Cf. Keel (1986), Figure 36, p. 83.

[173] For a similar association of the lotus flower and the desert, this time in positive form, cf. 2:16. The fawn that feeds on lotus flowers is not a realistic image, but symbolic (cf. further *infra*).

[174] Cf. Isa 34:13 with 35:1–2.

Table 10

2	Like a lotus flower	among the thorns	so is my beloved	among the maidens
3a	Like an apple tree	in the forest	so is my beloved	among the young men

In Oriental iconography, the fruit tree is often used as a metaphor for the woman (cf. 7:8–9). Here, as in 5:15, it is a metaphor for the man.[175] The apple tree,[176] in particular, has an erotic background in the Graeco-Roman[177] and Oriental worlds. In the Sumerian texts on sacred marriage, Dumuzi, the sacred lover of Inanna, is called by her: "My apple tree that bears fruit up to its crown".[178] In the Song, the apple tree is spoken of again in 2:5; 7:9 and 8:5. Notable, above all, is the parallel with 8:5 because it confirms the *inclusio* between the *Prologue* and *Epilogue* of the Song. The Hebrew term *tappûaḥ* indicates both the apple tree and its fruit, and literally means the 'fragrant one' (cf. in this sense 7:9, where the breath of the woman is compared to the scent of apples). The *motiv* continues the floral metaphor of vv. 1–2: this is the way that the attraction which her beloved exercises on the woman is indicated.

Just as the lotus flower contrasts with the thorns of the desert, so the apple tree contrasts with the 'trees of the forest'. The word *yaʿar* indicates not a pleasant grove but the 'dark wood' or 'selva oscura' with which Dante's *Divine Comedy* begins (cf. *Inferno* I:2, 5). Like the desert, it is a place of fear, the habitat of wild beasts, not of men (cf. Hos 2:14; Mic 3:12; Ezek 34:25). Like the thorns in the desert, so the trees of the forest, unlike the apple tree, do not bear fruit. In comparison

[175] Krinetzki sees a phallic symbol here. Cf. Krinetzki (1970), p. 415, n. 57; *id.* (1964), p. 247, n. 128. However, the matter should not be taken too rigidly, because, as has been seen, the tree is also a symbol of the woman.

[176] The identification of the *tappûaḥ* with the apple tree is not undisputed. Colombo translates 'cedar', but comments: "it can also be understood as orange, apple, pomegranate". Cf. Colombo (1975), p. 59. *Per contra*, cf. *HALAT*, pp. 1632–1633; Zohary (1995), 70.

[177] According to the Roman grammarian Servius, the apple tree was sacred to Aphrodite Cypria. Cf. Müller (1992), p. 24. In the famous Fragment 105 (= 116 Bergk) of Sappho, the woman is symbolised by an apple tree: "As the sweet-apple reddens on the bough-top, on the top of the topmost bough; the apple-gatherers have forgotten it—no they have not forgotten it entirely, but they could not reach it" (translation by D.A. Campbell, LCL).

[178] Wolkstein - Kramer (1983), p. 38, and again, p. 40: "[...], by an apple tree, I kneeled, as is proper" (texts also in Kramer [1969], pp. 95–96 and 101). In both cases, the apple tree is a symbol of the man.

with her beloved, therefore, the other young men[179] are repellent to the woman. They do not attract; they frighten.[180]

In v. 3b, the woman passes from contemplation to union, from scent to taste, from flowers to fruit. Beside the tree she first of all finds 'shade' (*ṣēl*). In the OT, 'shade' is connected essentially with the idea of 'shelter', of 'protection' from the scorching rays of the sun.[181] Perhaps it is possible to detect a double sense here too: 'to cover' can become a synonym for 'to make fruitful' (cf. Luke 1:35).[182] One could take a double sense also in 'sitting/lying' (*yāšab*), given the context. But the verb should be understood first of all in its proper sense as 'letting go', 'wasting time', 'feeling at one's ease'.[183] In the shade of her beloved, the woman feels secure; she is in no hurry. Love is "sitting in the shade of one's beloved".

It was this shade for which the woman was 'longing'. In the OT the Hebrew term *ḥmd* almost always has a negative value: it concerns desire that is sinful (cf. Gen 2:9; 3:6; Exod 20:17 = Deut 5:21). In the Song any kind of negative connotation is absent: 'desire' is seen as the fount of life and joy. We have already observed the Song's tendency to oppose the negative valuation of sexuality that is present in other parts of the OT.[184] In the *Introduction* we touched on the intertextuality between the Song and the account of paradise.[185] The verb *ḥāmad* is employed in Gen 2:9 to describe 'desire' in a positive manner before the Fall, while in Gen 3:6 it describes the desire from which sin is born. It seems as though the Song wants to return to the prelapsarian situ-

[179] In parallel with v. 2b, in v. 3a also, the term 'sons', *bānîm*, is employed with indirect reference to 1:6.

[180] Following Krinetzki, it is possible to read here a universally human side of the experience of sexuality. Sexuality arouses fear: it is the promise of life but also the threat of death (Krinetzki speaks, in Jungian terms, of "the terrible mother who devours her own children", cf. Krinetzki [1970], p. 411). And it is love which helps to overcome fear, which transforms the terrifying 'forest' into an attractive apple tree.

[181] Feuillet emphasises the parallel with Hos 14:8, understanding the passage of the Song in an allegorical sense. Cf. Feuillet (1971). If it is true that often in the prophets and the Psalms YHWH is the shade of his people (cf. Ps 17:8; 36:8; 91:1...), the Song goes in the reverse direction: it attributes to the reality of man and woman the experience which Israel has had with its God. Thus Lacocque (1998), p. 84. It is typical of the female sensibility to seek protection and security in a man. Even sexual intimacy is understood by the woman as a feeling of herself as protected, guarded, secure.

[182] Cf. also the gesture of marrying 'covering with the mantle' (Ruth 3:9; Ezek 16:8).

[183] "The verb [...] means to say that here she must allow free play to this desire, that she must devote much time to it, if she wishes to taste tenderness in all its profundity" (Krinetzki [1981], p. 91).

[184] Cf., *supra*, p. 54.

[185] Cf. p. 43.

ation when sexuality was seen as the fount of joy and human fullness (cf. Gen 2:23–25).[186]

"And his fruit is sweet to my palate". If her beloved is the apple tree, his fruit is love. The metaphor apple = love is taken up again in v. 5 (cf. under the comment on the verse); it is parallel to the other double metaphor vine-wine. The emphasis placed on the 'taste' makes one think of the kiss which is also connected with apples in Song 7:9. But the kisses of her beloved are sweeter than any apples.[187]

Seventh Strophe: Union (2:4–7)[188]

The final strophe of the Prologue readopts the construction in two parts, vv. 4–5 and 6–7, placed in parallel (cf. *Tab. 11*). The word 'love' (*ʾahăbâ*) acts as the frame both of the strophe (vv. 4b, 7c) and of the first part (vv. 4b, 5c). Each of the two parts begins with a short description (two stichs) in the third person of the union of the two lovers (vv. 4, 6). There follows a longer verse in which is made a request in the second person plural (vv. 5, 7). The request is addressed to a group which v. 7 identifies with the 'daughters of Jerusalem'. The two verses are complementary in the sense that in v. 5 the group is invited, positively, to cooperate with love, while in v. 7 it is asked, negatively, not to disturb it. Even the construction of the two verses is similar: each is composed of two imperatives ("sustain me", "refresh me", v. 5; "do not rouse", "do not waken", v. 7), followed by a subordinate clause ("for I am sick with love", "until it is ready").

Table 11

A	v. 4	*Description*	Union of the lovers	'love'
B	v. 5	*Request*	To the chorus: sustain	'love'
A'	v. 6	*Description*	Union of the lovers	
B'	v. 7	*Request*	To the chorus: do not rouse	'love'

[186] On the connection of the Song with Gen 2–3, cf. Landy (1983), pp. 183–265; Trible (1993).

[187] The 'sweetness' of the kiss is a classical *topos* of amorous literature. It also finds expression in Ugarit: "(The god El) leant down, he kissed their lips; / and their lips were sweet, / sweet as pomegranates" (*KTU* 1:23, 49–50, cf. Del Olmo Lete [1981], p. 445). In the Sumerian texts on sacred marriage, the beloved man is called 'my man of honey'. Cf. *ANET*, p. 645; for other texts, cf. Pope (1977), p. 373.

[188] The compositional unit 2:4–7 is not accepted by all the commentators: even recently, some divide the verses into two units (vv. 4–5 and 6–7, cf., e.g., Keel [1986], pp. 85–94; Müller [1992], pp. 24–26), others into three (vv. 4–5, 6 and 7, cf. Krinetzki [1981], pp. 90–98). For the unitary structure of the passage, cf. Heinevetter (1988), pp. 91–92.

The strophe is separated from the three preceding ones which were characterised by dialogue. Here it is only the woman who speaks as in the first two strophes. The *inclusio* with the first strophe (1:2–4) has already been observed.[189] The union of love, which is dreamed of in the first strophe is realised in the final one. As conclusion of the *Prologue*, the last strophe gathers up the various *motifs* developed in the preceding strophes. It is linked to the sixth strophe by way of the metaphor of the apple tree (2:3) and of the apples respectively (2:5—the Hebrew *tappûaḥ* expresses both the tree and its fruit). The theme of union, developed in 2:4, 6, has already been prepared for in the fourth strophe by the metaphors of the nard (1:12), the bag of myrrh (1:13) and the bunch of henna (1:14); in the fifth by the bed in the grass (1:16); in the sixth by the 'sitting in the shade' of the apple tree and the 'eating' of its fruit (2:3). If the theme of the apple links the seventh strophe with the sixth, that of the grape (2:5) unites it with the second (1:6) and with the fourth (1:14). Moreover, the theme of the animals (2:7) was introduced in 1:8 and 14 ('Engedi', the spring of the kid). The seventh strophe (the number is certainly not accidental: 7 is the number of perfection) represents the coherent conclusion of the entire poetic passage of the *Prologue*.

[2,4] "He has brought me in" repeats 1:4[190] to the letter. It is a recurrent expression indicating the consummation of love. Particularly close to our text is 8:2 where the verb is connected, as here, with the *motiv* of wine.

The 'banqueting chamber' (literally: 'house of wine', *bêt hayyāyin*) is certainly not a 'tavern'.[191] The biblical parallels (Esth 7:8; Dan 5:10, cf. Jer 16:8; Qoh 7:2) lead us to see here a room for banquets within a lordly dwelling. It is a place similar to the *mēsab* of 1:12, characteristic of that high burlesque which marks out strophes I and IV ('king', 1:4, 12).[192] Love is a feast, and in this feast one cannot lack wine (cf. John 2:1–10!). It has been noted[193] that wine is a symbol of love because it

---

[189] Cf., *supra*, p. 51.

[190] Some authors, following LXX [cf. *supra*, note 17], translate with the imperative: 'bring me in'. So Müller (1992), p. 24.

[191] Cf. Lys (*TOB*): 'tavern, wine shop'. Others think of a cellar (cf. Robert - Tournay [1963], p. 101: "cellier"). Pope (1977), pp. 210–229, has the singular suggestion of seeing licentious funeral banquets here (*bêt marzēaḥ*).

[192] Cf. Keel (1986), Figures 138, p. 237, 38, p. 87 & 6, p. 51.

[193] Cf., *supra*, pp. 54–55.

leads one outside of oneself and because it is the fruit of the 'vine'.[194] The 'banqueting chamber' is therefore to be understood metaphorically as the place of love.

The meaning of the term *degel* (4b) is disputed. Those who understand the 'banqueting hall' as a tavern, think here of the tavern's sign.[195] But the parallels refer to a military context.[196] Moreover, the 'sign' does not stand over the house but 'over me', which makes one glimpse at a metaphorical sense. The image is that of a conquered city. The metaphor of the city to indicate a woman is widespread in antiquity[197] (for the Song, cf. 4:4; 6:4; 8:10) and has remained even in contemporary usage: even today we speak of amorous 'siege' and 'conquest'.[198] The banner which is fluttering over this 'city' is that of her beloved ('*his* banner'): it is the sign that the beloved has succeeded in conquering the heart of his lady. The passage from the image of the banquet (4a) to that of war (4b) can seem abrupt, but in the Orient the goddess of love was also the goddess of war (cf. 6:4, 10—"terrible as a host drawn up for battle"). According to the Song, "love is strong as death and relentless as the grave" (8:6).

Keel observes that on a military banner is represented either the particular responsibility of the battalion or else the emblem of the protecting divinity.[199] Apparently, the text here refers to this second alternative.[200] The term 'love', without article, expresses a personalisation

[194] The images, which hail from the Oriental world, indicate a narrow link between wine and love, cf. Keel (1986), Figures 37, pp. 87, & 30, p. 75 & (1984a), Figure 233, p. 149.

[195] So, for example, Gerleman (1965) , p. 118; Rudolph (1962), p. 130; Nolli (1967) p. 77. For a review of the other interpretations, we refer the reader to Ravasi (1992), pp. 219–220.

[196] In Num 1 and 2 the term designates either a unit of the army of Israel or its 'banner'. The term also has this significance in Song 6:4, 10 (cf., further, *infra*).

[197] Typical is the symbolical representation of a city as a woman with a crown in the form of a wall. This crown is a sign of the 'inviolability', both of the city and of the woman (cf. Keel [1984b], Figures 5–7, pp. 126–127; also in Keel (1986), Figure 38, p. 87, the woman wears a similar crown).

[198] In this connection, the account which Wetzstein gives of the nuptial week among the peasants of Syria offers an impressive parallel. On the first day, there is constituted a kind of tribunal, where the judge asks the 'king' (the groom) if he has really 'conquered' the city (the bride) and induces him to bring the proofs of his conquest (the sheet stained by the blood from the deflowering of the bride). Cf. Wetzstein (1873), pp. 290–291.

[199] Keel (1986), p. 88. He himself opts for the first alternative: the particular responsibility of this 'batallion' would be precisely 'love'.

[200] This interpretation is confirmed by the closeness to Ps 20:6: "In the name of our God we will unfurl our banners (*nidgōl*)". Cf. Bloch (1995), p. 150; Lacocque (1998), p. 85.

as in 8:6c. The Song says of love that it is 'a flame of YHWH' (8:6f): it has in itself something of the divine.[201] The woman, therefore, has been conquered not by force but by love. On the flag of her beloved is written: 'Love'. It is because the woman recognises the divine force of love in her beloved that she lays down her arms.[202] The man will do the same before his lady-love in 6:12.[203]

[v. 5] The result of the 'conquest' is love sickness. To look on being in love as a malady is something of a universal human phenomenon.[204] In the OT, there is the tragic case of Amnon and Tamar (2 Sam 13). Amnon is sick (with love) and can be healed only with particular sweets in the form of a heart (*lᵉbibôt*) brought by Tamar.

In our case, the woman seeks to be sustained with 'raisin cakes' (*'ăšîšôt*) whose significance is analogous to Tamar's sweets. The erotic background of the raisin is clear in connection with the 'vine' and 'wine'. Hosea 3:1 speaks of 'raisin cakes' in connection with the fertility religion.[205] The same significance should also be attributed to the 'apples' as is seen in v. 3.[206] So the woman seeks to be cured of

---

[201] Cf., *supra*, p. 80.

[202] The profound theological truth of this declaration is to be found in the event of Jesus of Nazareth. The victory of the crucified is the victory of love, not of violence.

[203] Here too note the 'mirroring dynamic': in 2:4, it is he who is the 'conqueror'; in 6:12, it is she who is the 'terrible warrior'.

[204] In the Graeco-Roman world, the theme is treated by Sappho in an unforgettable way (cf., for example, Song 31 in the translation of D.A. Campbell [LCL]: "It is no longer possible for me to speak; my tongue has snapped, at once a subtle fire has stolen beneath my flesh, I see nothing with my eyes, my ears hum, sweat pours from me, a trembling seizes me all over, I am greener than grass, and it seems to me that I am little short of dying"), but also in the Romance of Longus the Sophist, *Daphnis and Cloe* 1:14, 1 ("I am sick now, but of what disease? I know not, save that I feel pain and there is no wound. I mourn, though none of my sheep is dead. I burn, and here I sit in the deepest shade", translation of J. M. Edmonds, LCL). For the Egyptian songs of love, see the seventh stanza of Papyrus Chester Beatty IA: "It is seven days / since I have seen my beloved, / and I have been penetrated by sickness, / my limbs have grown heavy / I have forgotten my very body. / If the doctors come to me, / their remedies will not avail. / The magi do not find any cures, / my sickness has not been diagnosed. / The saying: 'She is here' gives me life. / Her name lifts me up" (4:7–9, cf. Bresciani [1990], pp. 457–458); also Papyrus Harris 500B 2:11 (*Ibid.*, p. 462). As in the Song, love is the only remedy for this sickness.

[205] Pope (1977), p. 379, lists a series of parallels in the Greek and Mesopotamian worlds for these 'cakes' dedicated to the goddess of love. In Greece, they had the form of the female organ (*mýlloi*); at Mari, they represented the nude goddess. Cf. Keel (1986), Figure 41, p. 90.

[206] Pope (1977), p. 381, cites an Assyrian magical rite against impotence: "[Incan] tation. The beautiful woman has brought forth love. / Inanna, who loves apples and pomegranates, / Has brought forth potency.../ Its ritual: either <to> an apple or to

love-sickness by love itself. We can, of course, smile about this, but G. Krinetzki stresses also the profound psychological dimension of the phenomenon of love-sickness. How many maladies of the soul have their root in the frustration of the affective impulses![207]

[v. 6] V. 6 is the logical follow-up of v. 5. The woman wishes to be cured by love, and love is what she receives. Union succeeds desire (v. 3). This, in fact, is described, in a very delicate way, in v. 6.[208] The gestures speak of reception, tenderness: they represent the embrace with the same nobility as on some Etruscan tombs!

The 'refrain of the embrace' signals that the compositional unity has reached its climax. As in 8:3, here too, the narrative tension relaxes and the poetic unit rapidly reaches its conclusion.

[v. 7] Verse 7 also belongs to those refrains which announce the conclusion of a unit ('refrain of the awakening', cf. 3:5; 8:4). It is connected logically with v. 6. There the union, the 'sleep' of love was described. Here it is requested that this 'sleep' be not disturbed.

The verb 'charge' (*šāba*ʿ) indicates the 'oath' which, in ancient times, is made only in the name of a divinity; in Israel, the name of YHWH. To swear by another is held to be blasphemy by the prophets (cf. Josh 23:7; Jer 5:7; 12:16). Here the oath is made 'by the gazelles or by the wild deer'. Like the little goat, so also the deer and the gazelles belong to the sphere of the goddess of love.[209] On account of their elegance they are images of female (cf. Prov 5:19) or even male (Song 2:9, 17)

---

a pomegranate / You recite the incantation three times. / You give (the fruit) to the woman (and) you have her suck the juices. / That woman will come to you; you can make love to her". In the Mediterranean world, the apple is still considered an aphrodisiac. Stephan (1922), p. 208, cites the following Arab saying: "Apples do not satisfy the hunger. Apples only stimulate the appetite", where by 'appetite' is also understood the sexual one. Is it possible that behind the Christian representation of the Madonna with the apple or with the pomegranate there is a recollection of this connection between the apple and the goddess of love?

[207] "So ist der Liebende auf Gedeih und Verderb von seinem Partner abhängig: In seiner Hand liegt es, ob der andere (psychisch) gesund ist, sich als ausgeglichener Mensch vorkommt oder aber als vernachlässigte Opfer seiner ungestillten Sehnsüchte" (Krinetzki [1964], p. 93).

[208] Sexual relations are being spoken of here, not of sustaining someone who has fainted (*contra* Colombo [1985], p. 73)! Such an interpretation completely ignores the meaning of the verse in the unit 1:2–2:7 and the parallelism with 8:3. Cf. the parallel with a Sumerian love song: "Your right hand you have placed on my vulva, / your left hand stoked my head" (Kramer [1969], p. 105).

[209] Cf. Keel (1986), Figures 45 and 43, p. 91. Cf. also *supra*, p. 68, and in general Keel (1984a), pp. 89–100.

beauty. But also they personify the forces of love and fecundity.[210] In Mesopotamia the representation of fawns in the act of copulating or of a hind who suckles her fawn is frequent. These images express the marvel of ancient man before the mystery of life. In them the human person feels the presence of the divine.[211] Undoubtedly we find ourselves before the survival of mythical thought. Loretz reckons that the mention of the animals substitutes for that of the goddess of love which would be held to be blasphemous.[212] Probably we should think, as in 1:8, of the integration of mythical concepts into the Yahwistic religion in the sense of 8:6 for which to swear by the forces of nature is to swear by YHWH himself.[213]

The habitat of the deer are the 'fields' (*śādeh*). By contrast with cultivated nature, *śādeh* expresses nature in the wild beyond the dominion of man. In different ways, the Song emphasises that love does not originate with man. The woman comes from the 'desert' (3:6; 8:5); she comes from the "lairs of the lions and the mountains of the panthers" (4:8). Love does not hale from the city; it is not the creation of man; it bears within itself the anarchic and vital force of the wild animals. But it has to come to terms with the 'city'.[214] Not for nothing, the place of love is the 'garden' where nature and culture meet.[215]

The 'wild deer' are counterposed to the 'daughters of Jerusalem' who are precisely the representatives of urban society. The term 'daughters'

---

[210] LXX *en tais dynámesin kai en tais ischýsesin tou agrou* ('by the forces and powers of the field'), also tends to this sense.

[211] In the Romance *Daphnis and Cloe*, Daphnis swears fidelity to Cloe, holding a female goat in his right hand and a male sheep in his left, and Cloe believes him, because "she held goats and sheep to be the very divinities of the goatherds and the shepherds" (2,39,6).

[212] Loretz (1971), p. 15, n. 1.

[213] Perhaps this integration into the Yahwistic religion is also suggested by the fact that the words *ṣᵉbāʾôt* ('gazelles'), and *ʾayᵉlôt haśśādeh* ('hinds of the field'), evoke phonetically three divine names: *(JHWH) ṣᵉbāʾôt*, *ʾĕlohîm* and *šadday*. Cf. Ravasi (1992), p. 228; Gordis (1974), p. 28.

[214] Beauchamp speaks, analogously, of the tension between 'love' and 'law'. On the one hand, love "is not the law, and the law is not love. No one has to seek permission to love. A situation in which the rites of matrimony are experienced as permission end up inevitably with the rejection of these rites. Love is explained and founded only in itself. It is from the beginning" (Beauchamp [1990], p. 169). On the other hand, love "does not withdraw itself from the dominion of law purely and simply: it lives with it in a kind of rather tormented coupling. The 'others' continually record their presence: love cannot develop outside the social body, even if it does not have its origin there" (*Ibid.*, p. 170).

[215] On this theme, cf. the suggestive considerations of Landy (1983), pp. 104–105.

has already appeared in 2:2 in a general sense, but the connection is, above all, with 1:5. There the opposition was between urban and rustic beauty, here between the 'city' itself as the dominion of man, a commonwealth regulated by human laws, and the forces of nature behind which there is a glimpse of the divinity.

The position of the daughters of Jerusalem when faced with love is ambivalent. On the one hand, they are invited to help love (v. 5); on the other hand, they are asked 'not to rouse it' (v. 7c). The Hebrew juxtaposes two forms of the verb *ʿwr* (rouse) which I have sought to translate with two synonyms. The verb returns in the Song at 4:16 (*à propos* of the wind) and in 5:2. Close to our text is, above all, 8:5 where the 'rouse' has the metaphorical sense of 'arouse love'. Murphy thinks that also in 2:7 this is the sense, that is, that the daughters of Jerusalem ought not to arouse artificially the love between the two young people.[216] But that does violence to the context. Here, love has certainly no need to be 'aroused': the two lovers are united in an amorous embrace (v. 6)! The 'sleep' which is intended is not insensibility to love; on the contrary, it is the 'sleep of love' which is spoken of in 7:10c. Therefore, the sense is that of not disturbing this sleep, of not disturbing love.[217]

The object of 'rouse' is *hāʾahăbâ* ('love'). The abstract is problematic so much so that the Syriac and the Vulgate have 'the beloved woman' (thus the translations in *NJB* and *CEI*).[218] Others, though leaving the word 'love', intend it with reference to the woman ('my love').[219] But the term is used in vv. 4 and 5 in an abstract sense. Besides, speaking till now has been the woman herself and nothing indicates a change of subject. I do not see any difficulty in understanding the term in its normal sense. 'Love' is, therefore, the subject of the last phrase: "until it is ready". That supposes again a personification of love as in v. 4.

---

[216] "The woman's admonition prohibits (artificial) stimulation of love" (Murphy [1990], p. 137). In this sense also, cf. Pope (1977), p. 364 ("that you neither incite nor excite love").

[217] The theme of rousing from 'the sleep of love' is a *topos* of the amorous Egyptian lyrics. Cf. White (1978), pp. 116–117, 149. For example, Papyrus Harris 500B 5:6: "And the voice of the swallows which speaks says: / 'It is the dawn! And your way?' / Cease from reproving me, O bird!" (Mathieu [1996], p. 179; cf. Bresciani [1990], p. 465). The song of the birds warns the woman that it is time to get up and return home, but she does not want to know. Cf. Fox (1985), p. 23.

[218] So also Robert – Tournay (1963), p. 108; Colombo (1975), p. 62. The *AV* has "my love" referring to the man.

[219] So, e.g., *TOB*, *NJB*, Ravasi (1992), p. 229. Reference to the man is excluded by the feminine gender of the verb *teḥpaṣ*.

Love itself must decide when is the time that it has to be 'roused'.[220] Love has its laws which society ought to respect because love is not a social invention; it comes from elsewhere. At heart, when the chorus advises the woman to "follow the tracks of the little goats", it establishes the same principle: of trusting love. It is the 'flame of YHWH'. Augustine would say: *Dilige, et quod vis, fac.*[221]

Conclusion

The passage 1:2–2:7 has been shown to be a radical unity despite the apparently heterogeneous nature of each of the poems. The unifying factor is the coherent development of a journey of love which starts out from the initial dream (1:2–4) ending up with the realisation of union (2:4–7), passing through the stages of abandonment of the family (1:5–6), search for the beloved (1:7–8) and reciprocal contemplation and admiration (1:9–2:3). The "staccato" effect which characterises the passage is suited to its nature as a prologue, as an overture in which the motifs and characters which will dominate the stage in the body of the poem are introduced.

The analysis has allowed us to understand the poem as a programmatic pamphlet which takes its stand against a patriarchal concept of love, represented by a family (the brothers) who remove from the woman her choice of partner (1:5–6), and by a society (the daughters of Jerusalem) which claims the right to legislate concerning love (2:7). The image of the woman which is being offered is a perfect match with that of the man, thus recovering the vision of Genesis 2.

On the metaphorical level too, the prologue anticipates the body of the poem. The low burlesque (1:5–8, 14–17; 2:1–3) is juxtaposed to the high (1:2, 4, 9–13; 2:4–7), the rural world to the urban. The treasuring of nature and the nostalgia for a world that is more simple and natural is remarkable. It is as if there is a profound continuity between the

[220] Theocritus' *Eighteenth Idyll*, the Epithalamy of Helen, closes in a similar manner: "Sleep on and rest, and on either breast may the love breath playing go; sleep now, but when the day shall break, forget not from your sleep to wake" (vv. 54–55; translation of J. M. Edmonds, LCL; cf. also *Idylls* 24:9).

[221] St. Augustine, *In epistolam ad Parthos tractatus* 7:8. In this sense, cf., also, Krinetzki (1981), p. 98.

forces of life present in the animals and plants and human love (cf. the "bed of fresh grass", 1:16–17).

The metaphors, with their poetic language, are seen to be privileged tools with which to grasp the message of the Song and its unity. Thus in the lotus flowers (2:1–2), we have understood the theme of the victory over death, present also in the bag of myrrh (1:13) and the bunch of henna (1:14). This is a theme which prepares for the great revelation of 8:6.

The "little goats", the "dove" (1:15) and the "gazelles and wild deer" (2:7) have revealed a theomorphic value by means of which the author expresses the transcendent dimension of human love, thus reusing the mythological languages of the nations neighbouring Israel in a Yahwistic sense. This is certainly not allegory, but it is metaphor. In fact, basically, human love itself is a metaphor of something which transcends it, something well expressed in the profession of faith of 8:6 ("[love is] a flame of Yah").

CHAPTER FOUR

SONGS OF THE BELOVED WOMAN

(Song 2:8–3:5)

Morning Song

I

Woman 8"Listen...it is my beloved![1]
Look at him: he is coming,
leaping on the mountains,
bounding over the hills.

9My beloved is like a gazelle
or a young stag.
Look: he is standing
behind our wall;
he peers through the windows,
he is gazing through the lattice.[2]

II

10My beloved is speaking, and he says to me:
'Rise up, my love,
my fair one, and go![3]
11For, look, winter is over,

[1] LXX (*phōnē adelphidou mou*); Vg (*vox dilecti mei*); and the Syriac (*qlh dddy*) link the Hebrew term *qôl* ('voice', 'sound') to *dôdî* ('my beloved') as do the accents of MT.

[2] MT *ḥărāk* is *hapaxlegomenon*. LXX translates *díktya* ('nets'); Vg *cancelli* ('lattice', 'grille').

[3] The Hebrew joins a *dativus commodi* to the verbs 'to get up' and 'to go away' (cf. Joüon [1923], §133d): *qûmî lāk* and *lᵉkî lāk*. Some versions (LXX *anasta elthe*, Vetus Latina *surge veni*) have understood the first *lāk* as an imperative of the verb *hālak* 'to come'. So also Müller (1992), p. 27, n. 62 ["Auf, komm!"]).

the rain has ceased, it has gone.
[12]The flowers have appeared in the land,
the time for song has arrived,
the voice of the turtle dove has been heard
in our land.
[13]The fig tree reddens its early figs,
the flowering vines pour forth their fragrance.

Rise up, my love,
my fair one, and go!
[14]My dove, you who are in the rocky ravines,
concealed in the crags,
let me see your face,
let me hear your voice,
for your voice is sweet
and your face lovely'.
[15]Catch us the foxes,
the little foxes,
who are spoiling the vineyards,
for our vineyards[4] are in flower.

III

[16]My beloved is mine and I am his,
he grazes among the lotus flowers.

[17]When the day sighs
and the shadows lengthen,[5]
come, my love, be like a gazelle
or like a young stag
on the cloven mountains".[6]

---

[4] Vg reads in the singular (*vinea nostra*); so too the Targum.

[5] MT *nāsû* literally means 'flee'; so too LXX *kinēthōsin* ('move'). Vetus Latina *amoveantur* ('disappear') refers to the morning, but Vg *inclinentur*, and the Syriac *nrknwn*, understand the 'lengthening' of the shadows in the evening.

[6] MT's *'al hārê bāter* is disputed. LXX has: *epì orē koilōmátōn* ('on the mountain of the caves'). Aquila's *epì orē bathēr* understands a proper name, as does Vg's *super montes Bether*; Theodotion reads *epì orē thymiamátōn*: ('on the mountain of

Nocturn

I

Woman 3[1]"On my bed, at night,[7] I sought
the love of my soul,
I sought him but did not find him.

[2]I will rise and go through the city;
through the streets and through the squares,
I will seek the love of my soul.
I sought him, but did not find him.

II

[3]The watchmen found me,
as they made their rounds through the city.
'Have you seen
the love of my soul?'

[4]Scarcely had I passed them,
when I found
the love of my soul.
I held him tight and would not let him go,
until I had brought him into the house of my mother,
into the chamber of her who conceived me.

III

[5]I charge you, daughters of Jerusalem,
by the gazelles or by the wild deer:

---

perfumes'), the Syrohexapla *epi orē malabathrou* (a kind of perfume), and the Syriac *'l ṭwry bsmn'*. The Quinta has *epi orē dichotomēmatōn* ('on the mountains of separations'). Cf., *infra*, in the commentary.

[7] Literally: 'the nights' (so MT and all the ancient versions).

do not rouse, do not waken love
until it wishes!"

Structure

First Part (2:8–5:1)

The Prologue reached a final chord with the refrain of the embrace (2:6) and that of the awakening (2:7). The two lovers fell asleep in the sleep of love. Song 2:8 signals the beginning of a new poetic journey. The lovers are now separated once again with each one searching for the other. But where the trajectory which starts in 2:8 ends is not agreed. A first conclusion is signalled by the reappearance of the refrain of awakening in 3:5.[8] From 2:8 to 3:5, it is the woman who speaks, while, in 3:6, the subject changes: that strengthens the hypothesis of the literary unity of 2:8–3:5. Within this compositional span, two sub-units can be distinguished as we shall now demonstrate.

To the two *Songs of the Beloved Woman*, the two *Songs of the Beloved Man* (4:1–7 and 4:8–5:1)[9] correspond. The correspondence is chiastic in the sense that in the *Songs of the Beloved Woman* there is, first of all, a long song (2:8–17) and at the end a short one (3:1–5), while, in the *Songs of the Beloved Man*, the short song comes at the beginning (4:1–7) and the long one at the end (4:8–5:1) (cf. *Tab. 12*).[10] That the two compositions, 2:8–3:5 and 4:1–5:1, are not independent but complementary is suggested both by the man-woman polarity and the fact that the conclusion of the first song of the woman (2:17—"When the day sighs / and the shadows lengthen / come, my love, be like a gazelle / or like a young stag / on the cloven mountains") is taken up again at the end of the first song of the man (4:6—"When the day sighs / and the shadows lengthen, / I will leave for the mountain of myrrh / and

[8] Actually, the union of the two lovers is spoken of in Song 3:4, with the same structural function as the 'refrain of embrace' (2:6). Thus, many authors consider 2:8–3:5 as an independent unit. Cf., for example, Elliott (1989), pp. 67–82; Rendtorff (1985), p. 263; Robert – Tournay (1963), pp. 114–139 [this structure is adopted by *NJB* and *CEI*]); Delitzsch (1875), pp. 45–56 (according to Delitzsch this would be the "second act" of the drama); Exum (1973), pp. 53–56 (according to Exum, the unit runs from Song 2:7 to 3:5). It is, however, a partial, not a definitive, conclusion.

[9] For this characterisation, cf. Rendtorff (1985), pp. 262–263.

[10] For the compositional unity of 2:8–5:1, cf. Heinevetter (1988), pp. 132–134.

for the hill of incense"). The desire expressed by the man in 4:6 seems to be his reply to the invitation issued to him by the woman in 2:17.

Between the songs of the woman and those of the man, there is a composition (Song 3:6–11) which is spoken neither by her nor by him. It is a voice off-stage, that of the author himself or perhaps of a 'chorus'. The passage has the function of an intermezzo, a bridge between the two homogeneous units, 2:7–3:5 and 4:1–5:1.

Between the beginning and the end of the composition 2:8–5:1, we can note a passage from separation to union analogous to that observed in the *Prologue* (cf. *Tab. 12*). The first song of the woman (2:8–17) shows the two lovers as separated. She is shut up in the house and, from the outside, he invites her to come out. It is the theme of the exodus from the family which echoes 1:6. In the second song, the woman goes out of the house and breathlessly seeks her beloved through the streets and squares of the city. The theme of searching too appears in the *Prologue* (cf. 1:7–8). The *Choral Intermezzo* (3:6–11) speaks of the 'journey' which leads from separation to union and is connected conceptually with the 'searching' of 3:1–5. The passage from 3:6–11 to 4:1–7 is analogous to that which unites Strophes III and IV of the *Prologue*. The 'journey' has led the two lovers before each other: they gaze at each other and admire each other (4:1–7). At the end of this contemplation, the man expresses his desire of being united with the woman (4:6), and this is the theme of the last song (4:8–5:1). That 5:1 marks the conclusion of the unit is indicated also by the fact that at the end of the last song (4:16), the woman begins to speak in order to respond to the man. There is a duet similar to that which characterised 1:9–2:3 in which the blending of the voices (4:16–5:1abcd) expresses poetically the union of the bodies. Finally, in 5:1ef a voice from off-stage (that of the poet?) addresses the two lovers together, employing in the plural appellations that are typical of the woman and the man respectively ('friends' [*rēʿîm*] and 'loved ones' [*dôdîm*]): the two have become one!

Table 12

Songs of the woman	A 2:8–17	Leaving the family
	B 3:1–5	Searching
Intermezzo	C 3:6–11	Journeying
Songs of the man	B' 4:1–7	Contemplation
	A' 4:8—5:1	Union

Songs of the Beloved Woman (2:8–3:5)

The division of the poetic unit 2:8–3:5 into two songs, 2:8–17 and 3:1–5, is generally recognised. Song 3:1 clearly signals a new beginning with respect to 2:17. The distinction and, at the same time, the complementarity of the two songs results primarily from their chronological setting. Even if the Song does not present a narrative, but rather a lyrical, type of unity, a certain logic can, nevertheless, be observed in the indications of time. The Prologue ended with the 'refrain of awakening' (2:7) which evoked the idea of morning. The woman's first song returns to this hour of the day. It is imprinted with a morning atmosphere: it is the time 'to get up' and 'to go out' of the house (2:10, 13). The song closes with a hint of evening (v. 17: "When the day sighs and the shadows lengthen"), the hour of getting together and returning home. The beginning of the second song (3:1) is coherent with this indication: now we are at night.[11] The continuity between the two temporal situations sets in deeper relief the contrast between them. Evening is the time of love;[12] that is why the woman has invited her beloved to come to her in the evening (2:17). That he is not there, that the woman is alone at night (3:1), represents a discrepancy with the invitation of 2:17.

The unity of the two songs is signalled also by the *inclusio* of the theme of the 'house'. In 2:9, at the beginning of the first song, the man wishes to enter the house of his loved one but is prevented by the wall and the windows. In 3:4, at the conclusion of the second song, she reveals her desire to bring him into the 'house of my mother'. The verb *bwʾ* ('to come, to enter', 2:8; 3:4) marks this inclusion in a definite way. On the other hand, the theme of the 'house' shows itself to be a *Leitmotiv* of the composition. As has been seen, there is talk of entering the house but also, at the same time, of abandoning it, of leaving it (2:10, 13; 3:2). The summons of the man to "rise up" (*qûmî*), directed to the woman, heartbrokenly, in 2:10, 13, is accepted by her in 3:2 ("I will rise", *ʾāqûmâ*).

[11] With this indication there agrees also the 'refrain of awakening' in 3:5, which again points to morning, and the information of 3:11, which speaks of 'day'.

[12] The theme of night as the time for love is common in Egyptian love poetry. In this respect, cf. Mathieu (1996), pp. 159–160, §139. In the love songs of the Deir el-Medineh Vase, l. 15, night is invoked as a divinity: "O night, you are mine forever, since (my) lady came to me!" (= Cairo Love Songs 20E, tr. Fox [1985], p. 33).

Beside the binome 'morning-night', the two compositions are characterised by another, country-city. The first song is an invitation to immerse oneself in nature as the place of love; the second presents the city as the enemy of love. The correlation of the two *motifs* is suggested by the verb 'to pass' (*'ābar*). The winter has to have 'passed' for the woman to be able to come out (2:11). The city watchmen have to 'pass' so that she can find her beloved (3:4). Here too is a central theme of the Song which has already been outlined in the *Prologue* (cf. 1:5).

The two compositions are complementary also from the fact that the first portrays the man's searching. It is he who sets out across the mountains to go to her house (2:8). In the second it is her search through the streets and squares of the city that is described. This is a confirmation of the 'mirroring dynamic' pointed out above.[13]

Morning Song (2:8–17)

By contrast with the *Prologue*, which consists of short, separated songs, the composition 2:8—5:1 is characterised by longer and more elaborate passages of poetry. The first song of the woman is composed of ten verses. The unity of 2:8–17 is indicated by the *inclusio* between verses 8–9 and 16–17. In the two passages, the male beloved (*dôdî*, vv. 8, 9 and 16, 17) is compared to a 'gazelle or a young stag' (*liṣbî 'ô le'ōper hā'ayyālîm*, v. 17) on the 'mountains' (*'al hehārîm*, v. 8; *'al hārê bāter*, v. 17). The *motiv* of the gazelle on the mountains marks the end of a composition (cf. 4:6; 8:14). In our case it is accompanied by the refrain of mutual belonging (2:16a)[14] which also has the structural function of a conclusion (cf. 6:3; 7:11).

It is often proposed that the literary genre of the passage is the *paraklausíthyron*, a widespread genre in the Hellenistic epoch. In it, a lover is imagined before the closed door of his beloved.[15] The similarity to the situation in the Song is undeniable, but it is more appropriate to another passage—5:2–6. In our passage the swain does not seek to enter the house; rather for his beloved to come out. Perhaps more correctly, Lys entitles the passage 'Aubade', matinée, a literary genre typical of Romance poetry.[16]

[13] Cf. p. 54.
[14] On the function of the refrains in the Song, cf., *supra*, 21.
[15] Cf., *supra*, p. 14, nn. 69–70.
[16] Lys (1968), p. 112 ('L'aubade interrompue'). Canto 10 of the *Paradiso* of Dante springs to mind: "Ne l'ora che la sposa di Dio surge / a mattinar lo sposo perché l'ami"

To grasp the structure of the song it is important, first of all, to consider who is speaking. Basically, the song has been put into the mouth of the woman, but, in the central part (vv. 10b–14), she quotes her beloved. There is a problem with v. 15. Who is speaking? By analogy with vv. 10b–14, Ravasi thinks that it is a quotation from the man.[17] For one thing, however, the addressee of v. 15 is different from that of vv. 10b–14: it is not the woman who is being addressed. For another, the 'vineyard' in the Song is a metaphor for the female body (cf. 1:6e), so the woman is undoubtedly included in the 'we' ("catch *us*", "*our* vineyards"). We propose, therefore, to take v. 15 as the woman's reply to the words addressed to her by the man (cf. the commentary below). Thus, from the point of view of the subject of the discourse, the passage presents a concentric structure (cf. *Tab. 13*): the speech of the man (b: vv. 10b–14) is framed by two speeches of the woman (a: vv. 8–10a; a': vv. 15–17):

From the structural point of view, however, in analogy with the *Prologue*, the object of the discourse seems to be more important (cf. *Tab. 14*). In this way, the passage is divided into three strophes: vv. 8–9 ('the man'), vv. 10–15 ('the woman'), vv. 16–17 ('the man'). This division is confirmed by the distribution of the appellations which are typical of the lovers. The term *dôdî* ('my beloved') appears twice in the first strophe (vv. 8a, 9a) and twice in the last (vv. 16a, 17c). Within this frame, it returns once in v. 10a functioning as a link between the first and second strophes. The central strophe is characterised by the

Table 13

a	vv. 8–10a	She
b	vv. 10b–14	He
a'	vv. 15–17	She

Table 14

I	vv. 8–9	Man	*dôdî*	vv. 8a, 9a (cf. 10a)
II	vv. 10–15	Woman	*raʿyātî*	vv. 10b, 13c
III	vv. 16–17	Man	*dôdî*	vv. 16a, 17c

("At the hour when the bride of God rises to sing matins to the Bridegroom that he may love her", vv. 140–141, tr. Sinclair [1972–1978], vol. III, p. 153). In Dante, the roles are exchanged.

[17] Ravasi (1992), p. 237.

appellation *ra'yātî*, which, analogously with *dôdî*, appears twice (vv. 10b, 13c). The second strophe, therefore, is unified by the object of the discourse (the woman), while, from the point of view of the subject, it is composed of a speech of the man (vv. 10b–14) with an introduction (v. 10a) and conclusion (v. 15) spoken by the woman.

First strophe: The arrival of the man (2:8–9)

The term *dôdî* (vv. 8a, 9a) signals a division of the strophe into two parts. The two have a symmetrical structure: in each, the mention of the male 'beloved' is followed by a phrase formed from the adverb *hinnēh* ('look') and then by a participle. In the first part, the participle refers to the verb 'to come', in the second to the verb 'to stand'. Thus the first part describes the journey of the man across the mountains, the second his coming to a halt at the house of his beloved. Even phonetically, v. 8 expresses agitated movement, and the image of the gazelle illustrates it vividly.[18] In the second part, the standing still is only apparent: all the movement is concentrated in the eyes which sparkle behind the shutters. To the two verbs that illustrate the movement of the feet ('leap', v. 8c; 'bound', v. 8d) there correspond two verbs which depict the lively sparkling of the eyes ('peer', v. 9e; 'gaze', v. 9f).[19]

[2:8] The Hebrew *qôl dôdî* can be understood in two ways depending on whether the two words are considered as united in the construct state ("the voice of my beloved"),[20] or as separate ("a voice:[21]

---

[18] In content, the metaphor of the gazelle (9ab) is, therefore, connected with the 'journey' described in v. 8, although belonging to the second part of the strophe characterised by 'standing'. An analogous phenomenon appears in v. 10a. The term *dôdî* is out of place in a strophe devoted to the *ra'yātî*. In both cases we have the phenomenon of *enjambement*, or concatenation between two different literary units. An *enjambement* can also be observed in the connection between the end of the *Prologue* and the beginning of the first song. The image of the 'gazelle or young stag' (2:9) is in fact connected with the 'gazelles or wild deer' of 2:7.

[19] Like the two verbs of vv. 8b and 9c, so also the four verbs of vv. 8cd and 9ef are participles, so that the whole strophe is characterised by nominal propositions. The participle is typical of the descriptive song, or *waṣf* (cf. 4:1–7; 5:10–16; 7:2–7), which in its turn, goes back to cultic models. By means of the participle, the being, not the action of a person is highlighted. Even when a movement is described, it is the aesthetic element of it that is marked. Cf. Müller (1992), pp. 28–29.

[20] Thus, e.g., *NKJ, NRS, RWB*, Colombo (1975), p. 63 (cf. *supra*, n. 1).

[21] The Hebrew term *qôl* can in fact indicate both the 'voice' and the 'noise'.

[it is] my beloved!").[22] From the context, the second interpretation seems preferable. In fact, the rest of the verse describes the movement, not the words, of the man. So then the woman hears a noise and recognises the step of her beloved.[23]

From 'hearing' there is a sudden step to 'seeing' ("Look"). All the poetics of the passage are built on the juxtaposition of the two senses, that of hearing and that of sight. Verses 8b–d describe the agile journey of the man in a highly lyrical way (which is perceptible above all in the Hebrew text). "Look at him" expresses the jumping for joy in the presence of the loved one (cf. 1:15–16). He who 'comes' is expected.

The two stichs of v. 8cd constitute synonymous parallelism. On the one hand, 'leap' (*dālag*) and 'bound' (*qāpaṣ*)[24] correspond, on the other hand, 'mountains' (*hārîm*) and 'hills' (*gᵉbāʿôt*). The parallel with Ps 18:30 ("With the help of my God I shall leap [*dālag*] over the wall") could make one think that in our text too it is a question of overcoming obstacles (mountains and hills, in the sense of Isa 40:4).[25] But, in Song 2:8, the verb is intransitive. The 'mountains' and 'hills' are, therefore, not obstacles but the habitat of the beloved: it is the land of Israel (v. 12) with its characteristically mountainous landscape. The woman too comes from the mountains (Song 4:8) and from the desert (3:6; 8:5), that is from that realm of the forces of nature which, in 2:7, is evoked by the lexeme *śādeh* ('the wild'). It is the 'dionysiac' aspect of love which is being brought to the fore. Perhaps we can also catch a hint of a mythological reminiscence.[26] The representation of the god of vegetation who approaches over the mountains to meet the goddess of love is frequent in Oriental iconography.[27]

---

[22] Thus the majority of modern commentators.

[23] For a biblical parallel, cf. Gen 3:8–10. The Egyptian love songs present a charming picture that is extraordinarily similar: "I raised my eyes to the door: / look, he is coming to me / my beloved. / My eyes are on the street, / my ears are listening for his footsteps" (Pap. Harris 500B 5:9. We follow here Bresciani [1990], pp. 465–466; cf. Mathieu [1996], p. 63. For a different translation cf. Fox [1985], p. 24).

[24] The verb *qāpaṣ* ordinarily means 'to close'. The meaning 'bounding' derives from the Aramaic and the Arabic. Cf. Pope (1977), p. 389.

[25] So, for example, Ravasi (1992), pp. 243–244.

[26] This aspect is stressed in Müller (1992), p. 29.

[27] For biblical man, mountains have something of the numinous, bound up with the idea of fecundity (cf. Gen 49:26; Deut 33:15). In the Ancient Orient, the representation of divinity in the form of a mountain is frequent (cf. *ANEP*, Figure 528, p. 178). In the OT we should remember the cults on the high places, so deprecated by the prophets: they were cults connected with the fertility religions (cf. Hos 4:13; Deut 12:2).

[v. 9] The image of the 'gazelle or young stag', who have their habitat on the mountains (cf. Ps 104:18), fits with the mention of the latter. These animals are a good representation of the light and elegant step of the man (cf. Ps 18:34),[28] but they are also loaded with symbolic value as has already been seen in Song 1:8, 14 and 2:7. Animals of the goat and deer families are sacred to the goddess of love;[29] they personify love itself (cf. 2:7). So the metaphor confers a theomorphic value on the beloved man: it is Love in person who arrives with him.[30] Here we have a subtlety which, again, testifies to the 'mirroring dynamic': in 2:7 these same animals are mentioned in female form. In place of the masculine *ṣᵉbî* (v. 9a),[31] v. 7b has the feminine *ṣᵉbāʾôt*; instead of *ʿōper hāʾayyālîm*, 'young stag' (v. 9b), we read *ʾaylôt* ('hind') in v. 7b. Moreover, the mention of the *young* stag (2:9) is notable.[32] Instead of the adult (v. 7 has 'deer'), the young is named as if to evoke innocence, tenderness, freshness of life.[33]

Counterposed to the movement expressed by the image of the gazelle is the stationary nature of v. 9cd: "Look: he is standing behind our wall". The journey has reached its end: for the woman, this means that her beloved has come. The 'wall' (*kōtel*) is another of those rare words which characterise the passage.[34] It indicates the external wall of the house. Like the lattice, it is a symbol of the obstacles which are interposed between the two lovers. The theme of inaccessibility will be taken up again at v. 14. The woman of the Song is certainly not an easy

---

[28] The comparison recurs in the Egyptian love songs. Papyrus Chester Beatty IB 2:1 represents the journey of the man towards his woman with three similes: that of the king's messenger, that of the king's horse, and that of a gazelle: "If only you would come to (your) sister swiftly / like a gazelle bounding over the desert..." (tr. Fox [1985], p. 66; cf. also Papyrus Harris 500A 1:8–10, *ibid.*, p. 8).

[29] Cf. *ANEP*, Figure 464, p. 160; Keel (1994), Figure 47, p. 91.

[30] Hence the legitimacy of the reading of the passage as expectation of the coming of the Lord, in the sense of Rev 3:20.

[31] The term *ṣᵉbî* can also signify 'beauty', so much so that in the lament over Saul the phrase *haṣṣᵉbî yiśrāʾēl* (2 Sam 1:19) can be translated 'the gazelle of Israel' (cf. Müller [1992], p. 30, n. 73) or 'the glory of Israel' (cf. *NJB* and *RSV*).

[32] The Hebrew term *ʿōper* is a *hapaxlegomenon* typical of the Song (where it returns in 2:17; 4:5; 7:4 and 8:14). On the etymology, cf. *HALOT*, p. 862; Garbini (1992), p. 203.

[33] The image of a fawn or a calf sucking its mother's milk is frequent in the Oriental iconographical tradition. According to Keel, it is an expression of the awe of ancient man before the mystery of life (cf. Keel [1980]). Perhaps in the choice of the term 'young stag', it is possible to detect a reminiscence of this religious thought.

[34] It is a *hapax* in the Hebrew Bible. The word derives, perhaps, from the Akkadian and recurs otherwise only in the Aramaic parts of the OT (Dan 5:5; Ezra 5:8), cfr. *HALOT*, p. 1904.

conquest. In 4:4 she is described as a 'tower of David', defended by a thousand shields; in 4:12 as an "enclosed garden, a sealed fountain". Prov 30:18–19 knows that it is not easy to enter into the heart of a young woman. In the *Prologue*, it was she who desired to enter his 'house' (the theme of 'bringing in', Song 1:4; 2:4); now, in mirror fashion, it is he who wishes to enter, and who will in fact enter, into her house. But it will be the woman herself who leads him there ("Until I had brought him into the house of my mother", 3:4e; cf. 8:2).

What is the significance of the plural possessive pronoun '*our* wall'? It is certainly not the plural of the two lovers for they are still separated. Ravasi thinks of a group of women who would be in the *harem*, the part of the house reserved for them.[35] The parallel with 3:4 makes one think rather of the family of the young woman which constitutes a protective wrapping around her (cf. the function of the brothers in 1:6 and, above all, in 8:9!), a wrapping which has to be broken open, however, when love calls (cf. Gen 2:24).

The call of love is expressed by the two eyes which peer through the window. Verse 9ef is composed in strict synonymous parallelism like v. 8cd. To 'peering' (*ṣûṣ*)[36] corresponds the 'gazing' (*šāgaḥ*); 'windows' (*ḥăllōnôt*) are matched by the 'lattice' (*ḥărakkîm*). The repetition of the verbs expresses the impatience of the one who watches, on the one hand, and, on the other, the perturbation of the one who feels watched. The roles have been reversed: from spectator ("Look at him", vv. 8b, 9c), the woman becomes the object of the troubling glances of her beloved. If *ḥallôn* ('window') is the normal designation for the opening in a house, *ḥārāk* is another *hapax* the sense of which is unclear. Probably it is an opening protected by a grating in stone or wood of which Judg 5:28 and Prov 7:6 speak with another term, the antecedent of the *musharabieh* of Arab architecture.[37] The image is parallel to that of the eyes of the woman which fire arrows from 'behind the veil' (Song 4:1).

---

[35] Ravasi (1992), pp. 245–246; so too Garbini (1992), p. 202.

[36] Another OT *hapax*. The verb *ṣwṣ/ṣyṣ* generally means 'sparkle, glisten' (*ṣwṣ* I); only here does it have the sense of 'peer' (*ṣwṣ* II). Perhaps *ṣwṣ* I and II may be allowed to be taken back to the same basic significance. In this verse, therefore, it would be a 'shining' of the eyes (cf. G. Steins, *ṣyṣ*, in *TDOT*, vol. XII, pp. 366–367; *HALOT*, pp. 1013–1014).

[37] Such a kind of 'shutter' is well suited to the chamber reserved for the women. Cf. Robert – Tournay (1963), pp. 116–117. The parallels suggest a noble house.

Second strophe: "Go, it is spring outside" (2:10–15)

The second strophe is composed of a speech by the man (vv. 10b–14), introduced (v. 10a) and concluded (v. 15) by words from the woman. The term *raʿyātî* has the same function here as the parallel term *dôdî* had in the first strophe: it divides the man's speech into two parts: vv. 10b–13b (the appearance of spring) and vv. 13c–14 (the appearing of the woman). The correspondence concerns not only the appellation: the entire distich of v. 10bc ("Rise up, my love / my fair one and go") is taken up again in v. 13cd.

We may detect an analogous correspondence between vv. 12–13a and 14c–f (cf. *Tab. 15*). The description of spring is built up on the two senses of sight (*rāʾāh*, v. 12) and hearing (*qôl, šāmaʿ*, v. 12c). It is structured chiastically (a-b-b-a): vv. 12a and 13a speak of the visual, vv. 12b and 12c of the auditory aspect of the fine season. The mention of the 'land' constitutes a further theme which links v. 12a with v. 12d transversely. The sight-hearing alternation also characterises the second part of the speech. In vv. 14c and 14f, the visual aspect of the woman (key word *rāʾāh*, vv. 14c [2x] and 14f, cf. 12a) is expressed; in vv. 14d and 14e the auditory (key words *šāmaʿ*, v. 14d, cf. 12c; *qôl*, vv. 14d and 14e, cf. 12c). In the first part, v. 13b constitutes a kind of coda, in which is presented a third dimension of spring, that of smell. This aspect too is matched in the second part: precisely in v. 15 (theme of the 'vineyards in flower' [*s*ᵉ*mādar*], vv. 13b and 15d), even if this verse does not belong any more to the speech of the man. It is an *enjambement* which, moreover, confirms the structural connection between v. 15 and vv. 10–14. The correspondence of the description of spring in the first part of the speech with that of the woman in the second part, is not only a literary expedient: it expresses the integration of the lovers into nature. The woman is part of the reawakening

Table 15

A	*Sight*	12a	The flowers *have appeared* in the land	*rāʾāh*
B	*Hearing*	12b	The time for song has arrived	
B	*Hearing*	12cd	The voice of the turtle dove is being heard in our land	*qôl, šāmaʿ*
A	*Sight*	13a	The fig tree reddens the early figs...	
A	*Sight*	14c	...let me *see* your *face*	*rāʾāh* (2x)
B	*Hearing*	14d	Let me hear your voice,	*šāmaʿ, qôl*
B	*Hearing*	14e	For your voice is sweet	*qôl*
A	*Sight*	14f	and your *face* lovely.	*rāʾāh*

of nature in spring. The term 'vines', which in v. 13b has its normal, natural significance, refers in v. 15 to the bodies of the lovers: they too are in bloom.

[2:10] V. 10a has the function of linking the second strophe (vv. 10–15) with the first (vv. 8–9). Not only is the expression 'my beloved' (*dôdî*) lined up with the two *dôdî*'s of vv. 8a and 9a,[38] but also his speech ("he is speaking") is in continuity with the *qôl* ('voice-sound') of v. 8a, and with the non-verbal communication of the eyes in v. 9de: the sound of the footsteps and the sparkling of the eyes now become 'speech'.[39] The verb 'to speak' translates the Hebrew *ʿānāh* which usually means 'to reply' (cf. the LXX and the Vetus Latina). Here, however, the meaning is clearly that of 'beginning to speak' as there is not any other speech to which to respond.[40] Perhaps the repetition of the first person singular pronoun ("*my* beloved…says to *me*…*my* love…*my* fair one") is not accidental: in mirror fashion, it refers twice to the man (v. 10a) and twice to the woman (v. 10bc). This prepares for the refrain of mutual belonging (v. 16) which closes the composition.

The beginning of the man's speech (v. 10bc) is made up of a distich which is structured chiastically and which will be repeated literally in v. 13cd (cf. *Tab. 16*). On the other hand, the chiastic structure characterises the whole of the section of vv. 10–14 (cf., *supra, Tab. 15*).

'My love' is matched by 'my fair one' (*yāpātî*). The juxtaposition of the two terms is frequent (cf. 1:15; 4:1, 7; 6:4), but only in this case does the adjective have the possessive: '*my* fair one'. It is a very dense expression which says on the one hand that, for the man, the woman is beauty itself, the only beauty (cf. 6:9), on the other hand that this beauty belongs to him, forms part of his being.

Table 16

a) rise up	×	b) my love
b') my fair one		a') and come away

[38] Cf., *supra*, n. 18. Ravasi effectively makes the first strophe end at 10a. Cf. Ravasi (1992), pp. 240–241.

[39] Krinetzki (1981), p. 99, and Keel (1994), p. 99, wrongly attribute v. 10a to a redactor who would have put together two originally independent compositions. Between vv. 8–9 and v. 10 there is no break in continuity, as is recognised by the majority of commentators.

[40] Such a meaning corresponds to late, post-biblical usage. Cf. Jastrow (1903), p. 1093. Lys (1968), p. 116, translates: "Mon chéri chante" (*ʿnh* IV according to *HALOT*).

Of the two verbs, the first ("rise up") evokes the morning awakening. The woman is, therefore, still in bed, as in 5:2, even if she wakens because she hears the noise and sees the eyes. It is in this situation that she listens to the 'aubade' or 'matinée' of her beloved. The second verb, *l*^{e}*kî lāk*, is almost universally translated with the simple 'come'. But this translation is not correct. The imperative of the verb *hālak* with the *dativus commodi* recurs in the Hebrew Bible another three times: twice in Genesis in connection with Abraham (Gen 12:1 and 22:2), a third in Josh 22:4, always with the meaning of 'to go away' but never of simply 'to come'. This meaning is confirmed by the reappearance of the same term in the following verse where the significance is clearly that of 'to go away' in parallel with 'to cease'. What is being stressed, that is, is not the point of arrival but that of departure:[41] it is to 'leave', to 'come out' that the beloved summons her just as the chorus does in Song 1:8 (*ṣ*^{e}*'î lāk*, 'go out').[42] The parallel with the call of Abraham in Gen 12:1 is manifest. However, this does not lead us to consider our text as an allegory as if the young woman were a figure for the people of Israel.[43] The text is insinuating a likeness between the adventure of Abraham and that of love. To leave one's own family, to break with the familiar ties is an 'exodus'[44] which only the force of love can succeed in bringing to pass (cf. Gen 2:24). The Song calls for a trusting to the voice of love in the same way as Abraham trusted in God: to recognise in the voice of love the voice of God who calls one to go out.

[v. 11] In vv. 11–13 is given the motivation ('for...'), first in negative (v. 11), then in positive (vv. 12–13) form, for the summons issued in v. 10. But the description goes beyond a functional explanation; it opens out to an ecstatic contemplation of nature ('look...') which is an end in itself, recalling certain of Homer's similes.

To indicate winter, the Song uses a *hapax* which is, however, recurrent in post-biblical Aramaic, *s*^{e}*tāw*. In practice, the term is synonymous with that which follows, *gešem* (rain): winter in Israel is 'the

---

[41] In this sense, cf. Chouraqui (1970), p. 50 (who, however, translates slavishly: 'Va vers toi-même'); Tournay (1975), pp. 544–546; *id.* (1982), p. 66; Morfino (1996), pp. 14–16; Lacocque (1998), p. 88.

[42] Cf., *supra*, p. 67.

[43] Here we distance ourselves from the articles of Tournay and Morfino, cited *supra* (cf. n. 41).

[44] Cf. the allegorising paraphrase of the Tg: "Rise, O congregation of Israel, my love from the beginning, and fair on account of your works, *go, leave the slavery of Egypt*".

rainy season'.[45] Thus we can understand the link with the summons to come out in v. 10c: the house serves as protection from the rain. Why remain shut up in it if it is no longer raining? For Mediterranean man, the house is not the place for living. Living is done in the open. The house serves as a refuge from bad weather.

[v. 12] The positive motivation for going out is the example of nature where everything is 'coming out', an epiphany of colours, sounds and scents. "The flowers have appeared in the land". The description of spring begins with the visual aspect (*nirʾû*, 'have become seen'). Note how the author situates the blooming of the flowers in 'the land'. The Hebrew *ʾereṣ* signifies both the 'country', by contrast with the 'city',[46] and the 'land', that is, the 'land of Israel'. This local determination is adopted again in v. 12d: 'in our *ʾereṣ*'. Here the national sense seems clear even if the other cannot be excluded. It is a recurrent *motiv* in the Song. The love of which it sings is the love which is lived in the promised land. The land itself assumes the features of the beloved woman: Engedi (1:14) and Sharon (2:1) are only two examples, but the Song is full of geographical determinations. This emphasis on the national character is understood better in the Hellenistic epoch, in parallel, for example, with Sirach (cf. Sir 24). It is the affirmation of Israel's own cultural and religious identity in the face of the Greek world, which, in so many aspects, was culturally more developed.

Moreover, the description of spring has an unmistakable Palestinian colouring: in spring there is an explosion of flowers[47] throughout the hills and plains of Israel. The auditory aspect is juxtaposed to the visual: "The time for song has arrived". Qoh 3:1–8 knows that for everything there is a season: this is the season for song. The time of the winter silence is over. The term *zāmîr* is a general one for a song accompanied by musical instruments: so it is human song, not that

---

[45] Cf. the comment of *Midrash Song of Songs Rabbah* 2:11: "Are not 'rain' and 'winter' the same thing?" (tr. Simon [1977], p. 122). For a parallel with the Hellenistic-Roman world, cf. Longus, *Daphnis and Chloe* 3:3,1 and 3:12,1.

[46] Cf. *CEI* ("in the fields"); Garbini ("in the country"). But while *CEI* translates coherently in Song 2:12d ("in our country"), Garbini (1992), p. 149, changes here: "in our land". He does not recognise the evident *inclusio* between 12a and 12d, which makes it illogical to translate the same term in two different ways (within the space of one verse).

[47] The Hebrew term *nēṣ* (synonym for *niṣṣâ*, which appears in Gen 40:10; Isa 18:5; Job 15:33, cf. Sir 50:8) actually refers not to the flowers which sprout from the soil, but to plants in bloom. Cf. Keel (1994), p. 101.

of the birds, which is intended here.[48] Even if the verb *zmr* often has a religious significance (the term *mizmôr* is used to indicate a type of song in the psalms), it seems out of place to think of ritual songs in honour of Tammuz.[49] It is simply the musical aspect of life which is awakening, a dimension linked, perhaps, with the work which is in full swing in the fields and with the love which is blooming in young hearts.

The song of man is echoed by that of the birds. The term 'voice' (*qôl*) is connected on the one hand with the beginning of the composition (*qôl dôdî*, v. 8a), on the other with v. 14d where the 'voice' of 'my dove' is superimposed on that of the turtle dove. The turtle dove is a migratory bird which arrives in Palestine in early April (cf. Jer 8:7). As Nolli observes, the cooing of the turtle dove in love is characteristic of late spring (April–May), not of its beginning.[50] If even the voice of the turtle dove has made itself heard, that means that the other birds have been announcing the 'time for song', which coincides with that of love (cf. Ezek 16:8), for some time.

[v. 13ab] In v. 13ab the visual aspect is taken up again in correspondence with v. 12a. The 'flowers' (*niṣṣānîm*) are particularised in the flowering of the fig and of the vine, two plants typical of Palestine (cf. Mic 4:4; 1 Kgs 5:5; Judg 9:10–13). The fig in particular is the herald of the fine season (cf. Mark 13:28). The Hebrew text here uses a *hapax*, *pāg*, a term which is reencountered in Aramaic and Arabic where it

[48] The term has another meaning, that of 'pruning', which is followed by the ancient versions (LXX, Syriac, Vg) and is preferred by numerous exegetes. Cf., for example, Pope (1977), pp. 395–396; Murphy (1990), p. 139. Others think that it is not necessary to choose between the two meanings. It would be a case of 'Janus parallelism', by which the term, on the one hand, with reference to the preceding (the appearing of the flowers), would signify 'pruning', on the other hand, with reference to what follows (the voice of the turtle dove) would signify 'song'. In this sense, cf. Elliott (1989), p. 70; Ravasi (1992), p. 252. In a former work, I myself have followed this latter interpretation (cf. Barbiero [1997b], p. 367). But the meaning 'pruning' goes against common sense. A tree is not pruned when it is in flower (*nēṣ* has precisely this significance: it indicates the flowering of a tree, as is confirmed by the reference to 'vines in flower', in v. 13). According to Dalman there are two pruning of the vines in Palestine, one before the flowering, in February/March, the other after the flowering, in June/July. Cf. Dalman (1935), p. 330; Gordis (1974), p. 6, n. 30; Keel (1994), p. 101. The first comes too early, the second too late with regard to the 'appearing of the flowers'. Besides, the structure delineated in *Tab. 13* requires the 'auditory' dimension of the spring at this point.

[49] Against the 'cultic' theory, which would link the Song with a spring festival. Cf. Gordis (1974), pp. 6–7.

[50] Nolli (1967), p. 84.

indicates a "bitter fruit that is not ripe".[51] Another *hapax* is the verb *ḥānaṭ* which we have translated with 'reddens'[52] because of the similarity with the Arabic. The fig produces two types of fruit: the early figs bud in February and drop in June, giving way to the figs true and proper which ripen two months later. It is to the ripening ('reddening') of the former that the text refers.

If the description of the fig is linked with the visual aspect, that of the vine (v. 13b) introduces a third sense after sight and hearing: smell. For the flowers of the vine, the Hebrew text uses a term which is also exclusive to the Song where it recurs in 2:15 and 7:13: *sᵉmādar* (properly '[vine] blossom').[53] The flowering of the vines is scarcely visible; it is grasped rather by smell than by sight. They emit, in fact, a very fragrant perfume. The expression "pour forth fragrance" has already been used in 1:12 in connection with the woman ("my nard pours forth its fragrance"). From the fact that the vineyard is a symbol of the woman (cf. 1:6), here too an erotic sense is lingering in the background. It will be made explicit in v. 15 ("*our* vineyards are in flower"). At v. 13b, the term needs to retain its plain sense.

[vv. 13cd–14] V. 13cd is a literal repeat of v. 10bc, and structurally signals the beginning of a new poetic unit (vv. 13c–14) in which the 'appearing' of the woman is put alongside the 'appearance' of spring, an expression of that continuity between nature and human love which is typical of the Song. To the two appellations of v. 13cd (and 10bc), 'my love' and 'my fair one', is joined in v. 14 a third: 'my dove'. The three terms appear together in 1:15 ("How *beautiful* you are, my *love*, how *beautiful*! Your eyes are *doves*!"). A comparison between the two passages reveals a development. The woman is not only beautiful; she is beauty itself ('my fair one', with substantival value);[54] not only her eyes but she herself is a dove ('my dove', cf. again 5:2; 6:9). That is, she is the personification of beauty ('my fair one') and of love ('my dove'). As we saw above, the dove is the animal of the goddess of love. Keel comments: "The address 'my dove' [...] confesses that in the beloved

[51] Garbini (1992), p. 204.

[52] Cf. *HALOT*, p. 333. Nolli explains: "We are right here [...] between the end of April and the beginnings of May, the time in which the early figs, which for two months seem never to have grown, begin to grow, to change colour and to swell to the naked eye" (Nolli [1967], p. 84).

[53] Cf. *HALOT*, p. 759.

[54] Cf. Elliott (1989), p. 298, n. 66.

the speaker encounters love—if not the love-goddess—in person".[55] The woman becomes here 'my dove'; she is part of the reawakening of nature in spring, of the mystery of life which is greater than man.[56]

The 'rocky ravines' and the 'craggy concealments' are the natural habitat of the *columba livia* (cf. Gen 48:28).[57] In Palestine, there are two *wadis* which bear the name of *wadi ḥamam* ('wadi of the doves'), one close to Jericho and the other in Galilee, near Hirbet Arbel. The latter is described by Pope as "a wild pass closed in between two perpendicular rocky walls perforated with numerous caves".[58] It is an environment of the kind referred to in v. 14ab. It is meant to put a spotlight on the 'inaccessibility' of the woman, a recurring theme in the Song (cf., for example, 4:4; 4:12) and one which was introduced at the beginning of the present song with the image of the wall (v. 9). The woman shut up in the house, hidden behind the lattice, becomes the dove who takes refuge among the inaccessible rocks. This image contrasts with that of the *Prologue* which portrays a woman who desires love. It is one of the many paradoxes of the Song which correspond so closely to the female psyche. Every young girl, observes Lys, is torn between reserve and coquetry.[59]

"Let me see your face [...] for your face is lovely" (v. 14cf). The Hebrew text contains a word play between the verb *rāʾāh* ('to see') and the substantive *marʾeh* ('aspect, appearance, face'). It is, thus, the 'visual' aspect of the woman which is expressed as in vv. 12a and 13a. Her face is like the flowers; it is 'lovely' (*nāʾweh*, cf. 1:5, 10). Its appearing tames the barren rocks just as the flowers tame and give life to the bare trees of winter.

Just as the dove nests in her hiding places, so the woman is shut up at home. The request is the classical one of showing oneself, of appearing at the balcony: it is a universal theme common to those in love. The *motiv* of the 'lady at the balcony' recurs often in Oriental

---

[55] Keel (1994), p. 106, cf. *supra*, p. 79, n. 149.

[56] The immersing of lovers in nature is a recurrent theme in the love poetry of all ages. In an Egyptian love lyric we read: "The vegetation of the marsh (?) is bewildering. / [The mouth of] my sister is a lotus, / her breast are mandragoras, / [her] arms are [branches (?)]..." (Papyrus Harris 500A 1:11–12, tr. Fox [1985], p. 9).

[57] Even today, one can observe this in Palestine, for example in the gorge of En Avdat. Cf. Keel-Küchler-Uehlinger (1984), I, p. 137. On the habitat of the *columba livia*, cf., also, Schouten van der Welden (1992), p. 54.

[58] Pope (1977), p. 400.

[59] Lys (1968), p. 125.

iconography.[60] Perhaps the traditional image is describing a prostitute who shows herself on the balcony to attract clients, but she is portrayed with the characteristics of the goddess of love. She personifies, therefore, the *aphroditē parakyptousa*, the theophanic apparition of the goddess of love. Keel observes that the term *mar'eh* (v. 14cf) is employed in Exod 3:3 and 24:17 with reference to the vision of YHWH.[61] The word is loaded with sacral significance. It is inconceivable that to a Jew, familiar with these central passages of the Torah, the term would not evoke similar associations. The appearing of the beloved woman is surrounded with a numinous aura which in the Hellenistic environment is that of mythology but in the Song can be only that of YHWH.

"Let me hear your voice for your voice is sweet" (v. 14de). The auditory aspect of the appearing of the woman echoes that of spring. The two terms *šāma'* (to hear) and *qôl* (voice) are common to vv. 12c and 14de. The parallel with Jer 7:34[62] makes one understand the coherence of the metaphor with the desert landscape of v. 14ab: without "the cry of joy and the voice of gladness", without "the voice of the bridegroom and of the bride", the land is a desert. The voice of the bride transforms the desert into a place of life.

[v. 15] The verse is refined in construction, in four stichs. The first and second stichs, like the third and fourth, are united by anadiplosis[63] (the words *šû'ālîm* ['foxes'] and *kᵉrāmîm* ['vineyards'] are repeated). Moreover, five out of nine words end with the plural form *-îm*, forming a play of rhyme and assonance.

The passage from v. 14 to v. 15 is abrupt, so much so that from various sides it has been suggested that we have here a pre-existing love song out of context.[64] But the rupture can be explained by the change of the speaking subject: in vv. 10b–14, the woman is quoting the man's speech; now she herself begins to speak again. Moreover, in doing this,

---

[60] Cf. *ANEP*, Figure 131, p. 39. On the theme in general, cf. Fauth (1967); Horn (1967), pp. 35–40. Fauth shows how the *Venus prospiciens* is frequently represented as a dove, cf. pp. 412–413. Cf. also Shakespeare, *Romeo and Juliet*, Act II, Scene 2.

[61] Keel (1994), p. 106.

[62] Cf. also Jer 16:9; 25:10; Bar 2:23; Rev 19:23.

[63] From A. Marchese we derive the definition of anadiplosis: "It is a rhetorical figure which consists in the repeating—at the beginning of a verse or a phrase—of a word that concludes the previous verse or phrase" (Marchese [1979], p. 19).

[64] In this sense, the great majority of authors, cf., for example, Colombo (1975), p. 66: "15–17: Verses ruptured from the preceding context and difficult to interpret".

she obeys the summons addressed to her by her beloved in v. 14de ("Let me hear your voice").[65] The connection of the verse with the preceding context is marked by some precise references. The theme of the vineyards in flower (*s^{e}mādar*) clearly recalls v. 13b. Just as v. 13b adds the sense of smell to the visual and auditory aspects of spring, so v. 15 adds to the visual and auditory aspects of the woman the olfactory (*s^{e}mādar*). The 'vineyards', understood in v. 13 in their natural sense, are transposed in v. 15 into a metaphorical sense: they become symbols of the woman.[66] The parallelism between the awakening of nature and the awakening of love in the human heart is very close.

Be that as it may, the plural creates a problem. If it is the woman who is speaking, why does she use the plural? Furthermore, whom is she addressing? The addressees of the speech are also, in fact, plural ("catch *us*"). The plural addressees are not so problematic: we could have a case of the generic plural, equivalent to an impersonal form ("let them be caught", cf. 2:5).[67] More difficult is the identification of the plural speaker. Certainly the woman is part of it because the vineyard is a feminine image. Given the plural ('*our* vineyards'), one could think of a female group. Krinetzki sees here a group of the same age as the young woman,[68] Garbini the women of the *harem* in line with 'our wall' of 9d.[69] But v. 9 is too distant: between these two 'we's' there is, in fact, that of 'our land' (v. 12d) where the 'I' of the man is included.[70] The mention of a group of women is totally foreign to the context which instead is characterised by the dialogue of the two lovers. It is possible that with 'our vineyards', the woman is referring,

---

[65] We find an analogous procedure in 8:13–14, where, to the invitation of the man in v. 13c ("let me hear [your voice]"), the woman replies in v. 14 ("Flee, my beloved…").

[66] The same play between the natural and metaphorical senses took place in 1:6d and 1:6e.

[67] Cf. Krinetzki (1981), p. 107.

[68] Krinetzki (1981), pp. 107–108; in the same sense, Keel (1994), p. 108. In both cases, this interpretation starts from the principle that the verse does not have any connection with the preceding context.

[69] Garbini (1992), pp. 205, 209. According to Garbini, in the house of the young women "there live only women, who are accustomed to sing lascivious songs" (p. 209). The "lascivious" interpretation of v. 15 is bound up with the peculiar translation of *šûʿālîm* which, according to Garbini, would offer a double sense ('foxes' and 'buttocks') (p. 205). This interpretation could work for the Greek term *alōpēx*, but certainly not for the Hebrew *šûʿālîm*. To suppose that MT has been emended *causa pudoris* is a hypothesis, to be demonstrated, not asserted gratuitously.

[70] Cf. Elliott (1989), p. 299.

by extension, to the bodies of both the youngsters. The passage from the singular to the plural of the lovers expresses the desire for union (cf. 1:16–17) and forms a prelude to the refrain of mutual belonging in v. 16a.[71] It would be possible, however, to understand the plural as a rhetorical form for the singular.[72]

Throughout the Mediterranean world, foxes constitute a threat to the vineyards,[73] so much so that even today it is common in Palestine to keep watch during the grape harvest, making a noise to scare off the foxes. By contrast with the animals listed up to now, the fox has a negative connotation in the OT; it is a harmful animal (cf. Lam 5:18; Neh 3:35).[74]

The metaphorical allusion, evident in the expression 'our vineyards', leads to a metaphorical understanding of the 'foxes' also. Despite the fact that the plural refers to the two lovers, it is above all the female body which is in mind. "To spoil the vineyards" has, therefore, the sense of 'to make an attempt on the virtue' of the young women. Neh 3:35 describes foxes as animals which know how to climb over (or pass under) the walls which protect the vineyards, those walls of which Song 8:9–10 speaks. On the other hand, foxes are greedy for the grapes not the flowers (*s^emādar*), which shows that a literal understanding of this verse is to be excluded.[75]

If that is true, one can perceive an antithesis with the affirmations of v. 14. To the man, who complains of the inaccessibility of his loved one, protected "in the rocky ravines, concealed in the crags", she replies

---

[71] A similar use of the plural is detectable in 7:14: it speaks of 'our gates', where, given the contest, one would expect the singular: 'my gates'. Cf., *infra*, pp. 419–420.

[72] Cf. König (1897), §260e (poetic plural); Joüon (1923), §136j, n. 4 (plural of generalisation). The Vg reads in the singular; so too the Tg (cf., *supra*, n. 4): here, however, an allegorical reading (vineyard = Israel) is evident. *BHS* proposes to correct *k^erāmēnû*, but this is an unnecessary emendation.

[73] For the Graeco-Roman world, cf. for example, Phaedro's fable on the fox and the grape, or the *Idylls* of Theocritus. In the first *Idyll*, a boy is represented beside a vine. "And on either side of him two foxes; this ranges to and fro along the rows and pilfers all such grapes as be ready for eating [...]" (vv. 46–47, tr. Edmonds [1923], p. 13). In the fifth *Idyll*, the goatherd Comata declares: "I hate the brush-tail foxes, that soon as day declines / Come creeping to their vintaging mid goodman / Micons's vines" (vv. 111–112, tr. Edmonds [1923], p. 77).

[74] So also in the gospels, cf. Luke 13:34. Also, outside the Bible, in popular folklore the fox has the reputation of being a crafty and malicious animal (NB the figure of the cat and the fox in Collodi's Pinocchio and of Monsieur Renard in French literature).

[75] Nolli's attempt to explain realistically the connection of the foxes with the vine flowers, misunderstands the metaphorical significance of the verse (cf. Nolli [1967], pp. 85–87).

that this is not quite the case. The woman is inaccessible only in so far as sundry 'foxes' may not threaten her chastity.[76]

Undoubtedly a shadow slips in here within the idyll of love. It is one of the rare occasions when the Song speaks of the dangers connected with sexuality. Ravasi sees in the foxes "the force of violence" which rises up against "the purity of love".[77] It seems, however, that the text does not take these dangers too seriously. The 'foxes' are qualified as 'little'. Certainly they 'spoil the vineyards', but the woman watches them with detachment; she does not feel herself very threatened. Also the verb employed, *ʾāḥaz* ('to take, to seize') does not mean 'to destroy'. It is taken up again in Song 3:4, 8 in a positive sense.[78] The 'foxes' are probably her beloved's rivals who are paying court to her and, undoubtedly, trouble the couple's love. This almost jocular way of speaking of the 'lovers' is present also in an Egyptian drawing,[79] in which suitors are seen under the form of foxes paying homage to a little lady mouse. The woman is therefore seeking (perhaps with a little coquetry because to feel oneself being wooed is not displeasing to a lady) that they leave her in peace. The motive for this request (and of the jocular character with which it is made) will be revealed in v. 16: she belongs to one only. Thus v. 15 introduces the theme of the final strophe.

Third strophe: Invitation to union (2:16–17)

The last two verses of Chapter 2 are detached from the preceding composition: here spring is no longer spoken of. But for all their apparent heterogeneity,[80] they are linked by the theme of union, affirmed in principle in v. 16 and realised concretely (even if only at the level of desire) in v. 17. The theme of union marks the conclusion of the literary journey which has begun in v. 8. At the beginning of the song,

---

[76] Cf. Murphy (1990), p. 141.

[77] Ravasi (1992), p. 263. So too Ringgren (1962), p. 269.

[78] Some authors hold a positive sense for *ʾāḥaz* in v. 15, as an encouragement to love. Cf. Gordis (1974), p. 83. Recently, Garbini has turned to this interpretation ("These verses express the girls' desire for sexual intercourse", Garbini [1992], p. 205). But both the context of the Song, which certainly does not esteem sexual promiscuity (cf. v. 16!), and the negative manner in which the 'foxes' are described ("they spoil the vineyards"), render this sense highly improbable.

[79] Cf. Keel (1994), Figure 61, p. 109.

[80] The heterogeneity of the two verses is stressed by Krinetzki, who considers them actually as two independent poems. Cf. Krinetzki (1981), pp. 109–113.

Table 17

v. 16	my beloved	×	is mine...he pastures...
v. 17	come, be like		my love

the man was outside, seeking ardently to enter; at the end, the woman invites him to return and be united with her.

Like the first strophe, the third too is characterised by the image of the gazelle on the mountains. This image joins vv. 16 and 17. The "pasturing among the lotus flowers" (v. 16b) anticipates metaphorically the "gazelle or young stag on the cloven mountains" (v. 17c–e).

Like the first, the third strophe is also focused on the 'beloved' man. The mention of the *dôdî* (vv. 16a, 17c) also structures this strophe into two parallel parts. By contrast with vv. 8–9, the parallelism here is chiastic (cf. *Tab. 17*), in the sense that in v. 16 *dôdî* precedes the predicate, whereas in v. 17 it follows it.

On the other hand, the third strophe is connected logically with the preceding. The mention of the 'gazelle' in v. 17 is counterposed to that of the foxes in v. 15. Of course, the number is relevant: the gazelle is one; the foxes are many. The latter have to be 'caught' so that they do not enter into the 'vineyards'; the former on the other hand is invited to enter. What is forbidden to the foxes is requested of the gazelle.

[2:16] "My beloved is mine and I am his" (*dôdî lî waʾănî lô*). This is a particularly intense expression of the experience of love. In the Song it returns in 6:3 where, however, the order of the two propositions is inverted ("I am my beloved's and my beloved is mine"). The refrain is repeated a third time in 7:11, here too with a significant variation ("I am my beloved's, and his desire is for me").[81] In 2:16, the affirmation of the belonging of the man to the woman ("My beloved is mine") is balanced by that of the belonging of the woman to the man ("and I am his"), emphasising the perfect reciprocity of the relationship. The author intends to make clear the perfect equality of the lovers (and the parallel with 6:3 confirms it). Neither is the man the slave of the woman nor the woman that of the man. Once again one has the impression that the Song takes human love back to the time of Paradise, before the Fall.

[81] On the significance of Song 7:11, cf. further, pp. 402–403.

In this sense, the 'formula of mutual belonging'[82] of 2:16a finds its counterpart in the cry of joy of Gen 2:23: "This at last is bone of my bones and flesh of my flesh". According to the account in Gen 2, the meaning of human sexuality is that of regaining the primordial unity.[83] Man is an incomplete being who is looking for that part of himself which he is missing.[84] When he finds the woman, he finds himself again and regains his lost unity. K. Barth observes, significantly, that Gen 2:23 is put into the mouth of the man while the formula of belonging, whether in Song 2:16 or in the parallels (6:3 and 7:11), is pronounced by the woman.[85]

Ravasi lines up Song 2:16a together with the covenant formula between YHWH and Israel, a juxtaposition dear to the allegorical interpretation ("I will be your God and you will be my people", cf. Deut 26:17–18; 29:12; Hos 2:25 etc).[86] The two formulae are too different to affirm direct dependence. Certainly Hosea describes the covenant between God and Israel after the example of his matrimonial experience, something which emphasises the analogy between the two relationships. But it is different in the Song. Here the stress is not on the theological dimension but on the human. God is not described by means of human love; rather human love is described by presenting its theological dimension. In the mutual belonging of man and woman, says the Song, we have experience of that same covenant which unites God and his people.[87] Perhaps for this reason, Barth adds, the Song can speak of human love in such an exalted and pure way.[88]

---

[82] This is Feuillet's name for Song 2:16 (Feuillet [1961]).

[83] This concept seems to correspond to the etymology of the word 'sex'. The Latin term *sexus* derives from *secare* 'to cut' and expresses the division of humanity into two parts which tend naturally to unite and recreate their unity.

[84] Cf., in this respect, the Talmud: "An unmarried man is not a man in the full sense of the word, for it is written: 'Male and female he created them, blessed them and called them man (*'ādām*)'" (cf. Gen 5:2; b.*Yeb* 62b). For every man, married or not, his relationship with the opposite sex is decisive for his personal maturity.

[85] "Here one can detect a tone which was not yet present in Gen 2: here the woman stands before the man with the same enchantment which could be expressed with a similar, 'Here he is at last'. [...] Here originates precisely from her mouth the famous inversion: 'My beloved is mine and I am his' (Song 2,16) and 'I am my beloved's and my beloved is mine'" (Barth [1947], p. 358; cf. *Id.* [1948], p. 355).

[86] Ravasi (1992), p. 265, with reference, above all, to the article by Feuillet which we cited above (n. 82). Cf., also, Lacocque (1998), p. 90.

[87] Thus, in principle, also Ravasi (1992), p. 265, who speaks in this connection of the 'symbolical' interpretation of the Song. Personally, I prefer to use the term 'metaphorical', distinguishing it from that of 'allegory'.

[88] Cf. in the third volume of his *Kirchliche Dogmatik* the chapter entitled: "The covenant as the intimate foundation of creation" (Barth [1947], specially pp. 359–364).

The formula of mutual belonging is not something pre-existent which is inserted like an erratic block in a strange context. The different form which the formula presents in the three passages Song 2:16; 6:13 and 7:11 is explained by the change of context. In the present context it is aligned with the series of first person possessive adjectives which characterise the section 2:8–17: '*my* beloved' [m.] (vv. 8, 9, 10), '*my* beloved' [f.] (vv. 10, 13), '*my* fair one' (vv. 10, 13), '*my* dove' (v. 14). It seems as though the woman wishes to respond to these declarations of her belonging to the man but, on her side, placing the emphasis on the belonging of the man to the woman ("my beloved [m.] is mine").

"He pastures his flock among the lotus flowers". The Hebrew verb *rāʿāh* has two meanings: the one transitive (the shepherd *pastures* his flock), the other intransitive (the flock *pasture/graze* on the grass). In 1:7, 8, the transitive meaning is clear. In 4:5, on the other hand, the intransitive sense is equally clear: the young animals are *grazing* the lotus flowers. If the subject is the shepherd, the verb has a transitive significance; if it is the animals, the significance is intransitive.

What function does 'my beloved' (m.) assume in 2:16b? If we read the verse in isolation, the matter is not clear. The allegorical interpretation sees the figure of the divine 'shepherd'.[89] But if we keep in mind the parallelism between vv. 16 and 17,[90] it is logical to understand the 'gazelle or young stag' of v. 17 as the subject of 'pasture' in v. 16. This interpretation is strengthened by the parallel with 4:5. The (intransitive) sense is, therefore, that the beloved-gazelle 'grazes' on lotus flowers.

Of the erotic significance of *šôšannîm* we have spoken above.[91] In 4:5 the 'lotus flowers' are associated with the breasts of the woman, in 7:3 with her pubic area. In general, allusion is being made to the body of the woman as the object of the man's erotic play ('eating' is a primordial metaphor for sexual intercourse).[92] In itself, the lotus flower is connected with marshlands while the gazelle is at home in the mountainous and desert areas. At a realistic level, the two images are not in agreement; they agree, however, in significance. Just like the lotus flower so also the little goat is the symbol of fecundity; it is, in fact, an animal sacred to the goddess of love (cf. 1:8; 2:7). Moreover, it is

---

[89] Cf. for example, Robert – Tournay (1963), pp. 125–126.
[90] Cf., *supra*, p. 120.
[91] Cf., in this respect, Keel (1994), Figures 63, p. 109, and 96, p. 159.
[92] Cf. Lavoie (1995), pp. 145–146.

a symbol of freshness and vitality precisely in contrast with the desert areas in which it lives:[93] it evokes the victory of life over death like the lotus flower. The image of a deer or goat feeding on the lotus flower is frequent in Oriental iconography.[94] Interesting above all is an Egyptian funerary representation,[95] in which a gazelle with a lotus flower in its mouth is shown under the seat of the deceased: it is an augury of new life. The gazelle which grazes on lotus flowers is the man who in the course of erotic play experiences love and new life.

The image thus expresses the opposite of what has been seen by a whole tradition, namely that the "beloved who grazes among the lilies" is a metaphor for chastity.[96] However, it would be false to think that the Song is advocating sexual promiscuity. What the beloved does is forbidden to the 'foxes' because they 'spoil the vineyards'. Not every sexual experience is the bearer of new life.

[v. 17] Verse 17 is hotly disputed. Already the first phrase is problematic: "When the day sighs and the shadows lengthen". The expression lends itself to two interpretations, a morning one and an evening one. In fact the breeze (the 'sigh' of the day) blows at morning and towards evening. Twice the shadows 'flee' (so, literally, MT's *nāsû*): actually, in the morning they 'disappear', and in the evening 'they lengthen'.[97] Taken on its own, the text is ambiguous, so much so that many authors opt for the morning solution.[98] However, the context unquestionably suggests an evening situation:[99] the preceding indication of time, in fact, is placed in the morning (cf. 2:10b, 13c) and the succeeding one (3:1) at night. The same situation is implied by the OT parallels which speak of the "lengthening of the shadows" (Jer 6:4–5) and of the "breeze/cool of the day" (Gen 3:8). It is the afternoon breeze which tempers the sultriness of the day.[100] For Palestinian man who

---

[93] Cf. Keel (1984a), pp. 84–85.

[94] Cf. Keel (1984a), pp. 86–88; *id.* (1994), Figure 65, p. 116.

[95] Cf. Keel (1994), Figure 90, p. 149.

[96] The representation of Tutankhamon in the act of gathering lotus flowers in his garden also has a clearly erotic intention (cf. Keel [1984a], Figure 72, p. 164).

[97] Thus Vg and the Syriac (cf., *supra*, n. 5). But perhaps there is no need to suppose an original Hebrew *nāṭû* (cf. Rudolph [1962], p. 135). The image of 'fleeing' can express the rapid lengthening of the shadows at evening.

[98] So, for example, Ravasi (1992), pp. 268–270; Garbini (1992), p. 206; A. and C. Bloch (1995), p. 157.

[99] So also, among others, Rudolph, Krinetzki, Gerleman, Müller.

[100] The Syriac has: "When the day cools", *npwg*. Moreover, the Egyptian love songs speak of the 'North wind' as the propitious moment for love. Cf. Pap. Harris 500C

rises early in the morning, the 'evening' begins at an hour which is still considered afternoon by Western man.[101]

The Hebrew expression *'ad še* can be understood as 'before' (cf. the *JB* and *CEI* translations; *RSV* 'until'), or 'when'. The first is fitting to the morning interpretation, the second to the evening. The declining of the day is the signal the woman gives for the appointment of love. The evening is the moment to get together in the intimacy of the house. It is "the hour that turns back the longing",[102] the hour of tenderness.

Disputed too is the significance of the imperative *sōb*. The verb also means 'to go round',[103] but here the sense of 'turn', that is, 'turn round', seems to me more satisfactory. The problem is that of knowing whether the woman is asking her beloved to turn 'away from her', that is to go away, or to turn 'towards her'. If we consider the parallel in Song 4:6 ("I will go to the mountain of myrrh and to the hill of incense"), it is the second sense that is suggested. On the other hand, if we reckon on 8:14 ("Flee, my beloved, [...] on the mountains of balms"), the first meaning seems to be suggested.[104] The context of v. 16, in which the woman solemnly declares her belonging to her beloved makes one incline to a positive significance: 'turn to me', that is, 'come'.[105]

This invitation is to be understood in the light of the parallelism with the situation described in the first strophe. In the morning the man had 'come' for the first time. But she was shut up in the house, hidden behind the wall and the lattice, inaccessible like the doves among the rocks. Now she herself asks him to come another time, at evening.

The parallelism with the first strophe is underlined by the repeat of the images of the 'gazelle or young stag' (v. 17cd, cf. 9ab) 'on the

---

7:8: "I am yours like the field / planted with flowers / and with all sorts of fragrant plants. / Pleasant is the canal within it, / which your hand scooped out, / while we cooled ourselves in the north wind" (tr. Fox [1985], p. 26). As Derchain observes, "it is apparently the end of the day, because it speaks of the North wind, which always blows in the evening" (Derchain [1975], p. 73).

101 Thus Keel (1994), p. 115.

102 "...l'ora che volge il disio" (Dante, *Purgatorio* 8:1, tr. Sinclair [1972–1978], vol. II, p. 107).

103 So Garbini (1992), p. 149. But an invitation to 'go round' undoubtedly sounds bad, unless one follows the singular interpretation of Garbini.

104 This is also the understanding of Elliott (1989), p. 77 ("2:17 marks a separation after the formulation of union and mutual possession found in 2:16"). Cf., however, our comment on the controversial verse 8:14.

105 For the discussion, cf. Robert – Tournay (1963), pp. 127–128.

mountains' (*hārîm*, v. 17e, cf. v. 8c).[106] In vv. 8–9, mountains and hills are understood in a literal sense, as expressions of the Palestinian landscape. In v. 17e, the expression *ʿal hārê bāter* ('on the mountains of Beter') is an ancient *crux interpretum* on which the ancient versions are already in disagreement.[107] The interpretations proposed run in three directions:[108]

- it is a proper name for a locality, Beter (cf. Josh 15:59) or Battir (in Arabic *chirbet el-jehud*), this latter famous for the resistance of Bar Kochba, ten kilometres to the South of Jerusalem. As elsewhere in the Song, a typical Palestinian landscape is being evoked, the natural habitat of gazelles.[109] A variant of this interpretation is that of Gerleman who proposes to understand Beter as a land of dreams just as the land of Punt, made famous by the bas-reliefs of the funeral monument of Hatshepshut at Deir el-Bahari,[110] is in Egyptian poetry.
- The parallel with Song 4:6 ('mountain of myrrh, hill of incense') as with 8:14 ('mountains of balms') leads one to see in Beter a type of perfume of Indian origin, called by the Greek name *malabathron*.[111]
- The Hebrew root *btr* signifies 'to cut in two' (cf. Gen 15:10; Jer 34:18–19). This basic meaning lends itself to different interpretations. One can distinguish: (a) a *psychological* sense. So, for example, Elliott understands "mountains of separation";[112] (b) a *geological* sense, understanding "craggy, cloven mountains";[113] (g) a *theological* sense. A. Robert – R. Tournay translate "mountains of the covenant" with reference to the drawing up of the covenant effected by

[106] The repeat of the terms 'mountains' and 'hills' occurs in the parallel passage 4:6 ('mountain of myrrh and hill of incense').
[107] Cf., *supra*, n. 6.
[108] For a more complete list of interpetations, cf. Ravasi (1992), pp. 271–273, and Bartina Gassiot (1972), pp. 435–444.
[109] So already Vg. Lately, this interpretation has been favoured by Müller (1992), p. 33.
[110] Gerleman (1965), pp. 128–129. In Egyptian love poetry, the woman is compared to the land of Punt: "I'll embrace her: / her arms are opened—/ and I (am) like one in (the land of) Punt" (Deir el-Medineh Vase, l. 15 = Cairo Love Songs 20F, cf. Fox [1985], p. 33).
[111] Cf. Keel (1994), pp. 115–117.
[112] Elliott (1989), p. 77; similarly, Ceronetti (1996), p. 19 ("on the mountain which divides us"). But as we have noted, the context favours another sense.
[113] So, for example, Pope (1977), p. 409 ("on the cleft mountains"); Delitzsch (1875), p. 147 ("auf die klüftigen Berge").

> passing between "divided" animals (Gen 15:17–18);[114] and, finally, (d) an *anatomical* sense, with reference to a part of the woman's body. Thus Haupt, for example, sees here a reference to Mount of Venus,[115] Garbini to the buttocks.[116] But such crude allusions do not correspond to the eroticism of the Song. Sexuality is not seen here as something fixated on the genitals but as playfulness and tenderness. More congenial with the poetics of the Song, it seems to me, is the proposal of Lys who sees in the "cloven mountains" the two breasts, or cleavage, of the woman.[117]

The context leads us to see in the 'mountains of Beter' an allusion to the body of the woman. The parallel expressions of 4:6 and 8:14, where the scent of the mountains is described, have the same value. In 4:6, the expression follows the description of the breasts of the woman (4:5) so that the context seems to suggest here the identification of the 'mountain of myrrh' and the 'hill of incense' with the two breasts. This seems to me also the most probable identification of the 'cloven mountains' of 2:17.[118] The 'mountains' of Palestine in fact have a rounded profile which make one think of a woman's breasts (one thinks, for example, of Tabor or the smooth hills of the Judaean desert).

The *inclusio* between the beginning and the end of the song confirms that continuity between human love and nature which we have noticed in the central part. The gazelle which leaps through the mountains of Palestine becomes the beloved who 'grazes' on the body of his woman. The woman is identified with the land, maternal, receptive,

---

[114] Robert – Tournay (1963), pp. 128–129.

[115] Haupt (1907), p. 75; so too Wittekindt (1925), p. 171; Krinetzki (1981), p. 113. The problem is that here we are speaking of 'mountains' in the plural.

[116] Garbini (1992), pp. 206–207.

[117] Lys (1968), p. 136; so too Zakovitch (2000), pp. 17–18 ("The hills of spices, the hills of *bather*, the valley, are none other than her breasts", p. 18). Actually, the breasts are often mentioned in the Song (cf. 4:5; 7:4, 8, 9), while there is not any direct allusion to the genitals. Keel explains this fact, which has a parallel in the Egyptian love songs, with the different concept of sexuality compared with the Mesopotamian texts. There, sexuality is seen as fecundity, procreation, while in Egypt and in the Song sexuality is seen as erotic play (Keel [1994], p. 246). Perhaps this identification can be supported by a linguistic factor. The Hebrew *šad*, 'breast', and the Akkadian *šadû*, 'mountain' (cf. the Hebrew *šadday*, 'Most High', a divine epithet), are probably connected from the etymological point of view. Cf. Propp (1987), pp. 232–233.

[118] The image of mountains to indicate the two breasts returns also in a passage of the Mesopotamian 'sacred marriage' quoted by Kramer (1969), p. 64. Inanna says to King Shulgi: "You are fit…, / to prance on my holy bosom like a 'lapis lazuli' calf, you are fit". In the novella of the Roman epoch, *Joseph and Aseneth*, the bride is sung of thus: "Her breasts (were) like the mountains of the Most High God" (18:9, *OTP* II, p. 232).

able to nourish and to satisfy. Her initial modesty is transformed into her gift of herself. It is the inaccessible dove in her craggy hiding places who herself issues the summons to love. What in 2:9 is an observation ('being like', participle) becomes in 2:17 a command ('be like', imperative). It is the invitation to union.

Nocturn (3:1–5)

This short composition is clearly distinct from the preceding material both because of the spatial (country-city) and the temporal (morning-night) situation. If in 2:8–17 it is the man who has to seek the woman, now it is her turn to seek him. The two songs are, therefore, not only distinct but also complementary. The union of the two lovers, presented in 2:17 as a desire, is realised in 3:4. 3:1–5 is, therefore, the natural completion of 2:8–17. The 'refrain of awakening' (3:5) signals, as in 2:7, the union which has taken place and concludes, significantly, not only 3:1–5, but the entire poetic span of 2:8–3:5. The connection between the two compositions is confirmed by some literary repeats: 'to rise' (*qûm*, 3:2; cf. 2:10, 13), 'to turn, turn round' (*sābab*, 3:2, 3; cf. 2:17), 'to see' (*rāʾāh*, 3:3; cf. 2:12, 14), 'to pass' (*ʿābar*, 3:4; cf. 2:11), 'to catch, hold tight' (*ʾāḥaz*, 3:4; cf. 2:15).

Stylistically, 3:1–5 is characterised by repetitions. The expressions 'I sought' (*biqqaštî*, twice in v. 1 and twice in v. 2), 'I found' (*māṣāʾtî*, 4; cf. v. 3), and, *vice versa*, 'I did not find' (vv. 1, 2), 'the love of my soul' (*ʾēt šeʾāhăbâ napšî*, vv. 1, 2, 3, 4), are each repeated four times in the course of five verses. As H.-P. Müller stresses, these are not clumsy redactional additions but a refined poetic instrument to express the hammer of desire, like an *idée fixe*, which is satisfied only at the end when there are no more repetitions.[119]

The composition consists of two strophes (vv. 1–2 and 3–4) and a coda (v. 5).[120] The first strophe (vv. 1–2) is characterised by the *searching*. In it the verb 'to seek' (*biqqēš*, vv. 1ac, 2cd) is repeated four times. In v. 1, the search is focused on the house, in v. 2 on the city: both conclude with the desolate observation: "I did not find him" (vv. 1c, 2d).

[119] Müller (1992), p. 35. The poetic value of the repetition is noticed also in Ravasi (1992), pp. 283–284.

[120] So too Heinevetter (1988), pp. 105–106; Elliott (1989), pp. 77–80.

Table 18

I. Seeking	"I sought"—"I did not find"	house	v. 1
	"I sought"—"I did not find"	city	v. 2
II. Finding	"They found me"	city	v. 3
	"I found"	house	v. 4

The second strophe (vv. 3–4) is characterised by the finding. Twice (vv. 3a, 4b) the verb 'to find' is repeated in a positive sense. The first time, however, the woman is not the subject but rather the object of the verb: "They found me". The apparently positive 'finding' is a delusion, a delaying moment which prolongs the anxious search. The tension is resolved in v. 4bc: "I found the love of my soul".

Beside the 'searching-finding' theme, we can note the alternating scenario of 'house' and 'city'. The sequence 'house' (v. 1) + 'city' (v. 2), which characterises the first strophe is taken up again in the second in the reverse direction: 'city' (vv. 3–4d) + 'house' (v. 4ef). The action ends where it had begun (cf. *Tab. 18*).

The 'refrain of awakening' concludes the composition as in 2:7 and 8:4. It supposes that the union of the lovers has been fulfilled. If the request is 'not to rouse love', that means to say that the two have fallen asleep in the slumber of love.[121] The refrain functions as a coda for the composition. The terms which characterise the two previous strophes –'search', 'find', 'love of my soul' are missing. But the term 'love' (*'hb*), present in each verse of the song (vv. 1b, 2c, 3d, 4c, 5c), also binds the last verse significantly with the preceding context.

First strophe: Searching (3:1–2)

The song begins with the preposition 'on' (*'al*), taking up the end of the preceding verse ('on the mountains'). It is a typical example of the phenomenon of 'attraction': Semitic thought avoids abrupt transitions from one unit to another.[122] The Hebrew term *miškāb* is usual to

[121] Garbini's interpretation, according to which 3:5 expresses the charge of the woman addressed to her friends, "that they do not fall in love so as not to suffer like her" (Garbini [1992], p. 211), goes against the context which closes on the exultant note of v. 4d–f.

[122] I was able to note this principle extensively in the Psalms. Cf. Barbiero (1999), pp. 21–22.

indicate the 'bed'. It can refer to the place of love (cf. Ezek 23:17), but not necessarily. Are the two lovers accustomed to sleeping together?[123] Institutional or moralistic questions are out of place in the Song.[124] It is a lyrical situation which is being presented here, analogous to the famous fragment of Sappho: "The moon has set and the Pleiades; it is midnight, and time goes by, and I lie alone".[125]

[3:1] "At night". The Hebrew has a plural *ballêlôt* which I have translated in the singular, understanding it as a *pluralis compositionis* ("the parts of the night, the nocturnal hours").[126] The reference is to the interminable hours of a sleepless night. The coherence with 2:17 has been noted above. Morning is the time for leaving the house, going to work (cf. 2:10, 13). Evening is the time for getting together in the intimacy of one's own house, among one's nearest and dearest. It is the time for communion, the time for love. Not for nothing has the woman arranged an evening assignation with her beloved (2:17). Being alone is felt with a particularly sorrowful anxiety.[127] A similar state of mind is presented in 5:2 ("I slept, but my heart was awake"). The 'search' (*biqqēš*) has, therefore, in our verse, the sense of 'desire' as in Ps 27:4; Jer 2:33; 5:1; Esth 5:3, 6–8; 7:2–3; Ezra 7:6.

The object of the search is "the love of my soul". The expression has already appeared in Song 1:7 in a similar context of searching. There the meaning of tormenting desire which it expresses ("He whom I desire with all my being")[128] was emphasised. In content, the expression is

[123] Colombo (1975), p. 68, speaks of "lost love", probably with reference to the union described in 2:6 (cf. also *id.* [1985], pp. 78–79). But a 'narrative' continuity is not typical of the Song. One cannot think of it as a coherent 'love story': each poetic unit initiates a new lyrical journey which goes from separation to union. Lacocque (1998), p. 93, thinks of "pre-marital sex". But this is the risk of projecting a problem typical of modern Western civilisation on to the Song. From an institutional point of view, it should be noted that in the Egyptian love songs, before marriage proper, an initial stage is supposed in which the two young people are officially 'betrothed' (cf., *infra*, n. 147) and in which intimate relations between them are allowed. The same goes for Israel. Cf. De Vaux (1961), pp. 32–33.

[124] Nolli's embarrassment in tackling this passage is evident: "The vulgarity of the language remains, even in an allegorical interpretation" (Nolli [1967], p. 89).

[125] Sappho 168B (= 94 Diehl), tr. Campbell (1982), p. 173. The sketch portrayed in Keel (1994), Figure 68, p. 123, seems to evoke a situation of this kind.

[126] Cf. Joüon (1909), p. 172.

[127] Worth looking at is a parallel from Papyrus Harris 500B: "I say to my heart within (me) in prayer: / "[Give me] my prince tonight, / (or) I am like one who (lies) in her grave" (5:4–5 = stanza 13 in Fox [1985], p. 22).

[128] Cf., *supra*, p. 165.

related to the 'formula of mutual belonging' in 2:16: it is the tension which leads to the rebuilding of the lost unity.

"I sought him but did not find him". Here we observe the two complementary verbs which structure the entire song: "seek" and "find". "Searching" expresses not only the absence of an object, or, in our case, a person, but also the perception of this absence as a loss, as something or someone who ought to be here and is not. It is a fundamental experience of being human: man is essentially a searching being. In the context of the Song, the reference is naturally to the experience of love, in terms similar to Gen 2:20—"But the man did not find (*māṣāʾ*) a helper fit for him".

In this connection, the commentators often cite mythological parallels. Throughout the Ancient Orient, with different variations, there is present the myth of the goddess of love who searches for her own partner in the kingdom of the dead and brings him back to life.[129] A direct reference to the mythology, such as Schmökel would see,[130] seems, however, to be excluded by our text. The search for love (*zētēsis tou erōtos*) is a common *topos* of the love poetry of all times.[131]

In the OT, the parallel with Hosea 2:9, where the search of the unfaithful spouse is described, is significant:

> She shall pursue her lovers
> but not overtake them;
> and she shall seek (*bāqaš*) them
> but shall not find (*māṣāʾ*) them.

These are the same words used in our text, except that in Hosea they are referred to the searching for the 'lovers', in the Song, instead, to the searching for the beloved.[132] Elsewhere the verb *bqš* indicates the 'search for God' (cf. Hos 5:6; Jer 29:13, Isa 65:1). A direct reference

---

[129] In the Ugaritic myth of the battle between Baal and Mot, the desire which will lead Anat to descend into the underworld to snatch her brother and consort Baal from the prison of Mot (= death) is described thus: "Like the heart of a cow for its calf, / like the heart of a sheep for its lamb, / so beat the heart of Anat for Baal" (*KTU* 1.6 II, 6–9, 28–30, cf. Del Olmo Lete [1981], pp. 226, 227). Egypt has the parallel myth of Isis and Osiris. The 'search' of Isis is thus described: "Isis, the powerful one, the guardian of her brother, / who sought him tirelessly, / journeys through the entire country in grief / and does not stop until she finds him". Cf. Keel (1994), pp. 121–122. A singular representation of this myth is offered in *ibid.*, Figure 156, p. 273.

[130] Schmökel (1952), pp. 59–62, with reference to the Sumero-Akkadian myth of the descent of Ishtar to the underworld.

[131] Cf. Ravasi (1992), pp. 285–288.

[132] On the parallel of our passage with Hos 2, cf. Van Dijk-Hemmes (1989), pp. 79–81.

to God here, as the allegorical interpretation would have it, is to be excluded: God is not sought 'on the bed'. What the woman is seeking is her love. It is true, however, that behind this search is revealed the search for God: the search for love is, after all, an approach to transcendence (the saying of Augustine comes readily to mind: *Fecisti nos ad te, et inquietum est cor nostrum donec requiescat in te*).[133] In an analogous way, the book of Proverbs transposes the search for love to the field of wisdom, who is presented as a demanding lover (cf. Prov 1:28; 8:17). In the end, truth and love are two different aspects of the Transcendent One.

[v.2] "I will rise and go through the city". The verbs 'to rise' (*qûm*) and 'go round' (*sābab*) are a repeat of Song 2:10, 13 ("Rise up [*qûm*], my love") and of 2:17 ("Come [*sābab*]...on the cloven mountains"), respectively. In the morning, the man had invited his beloved to leave the warmth of her bed and go out to meet love (2:13). It is not said that she followed the invitation. It seems that she accepts it now, when it is night, and the time for sleeping not for 'rising'. The repetition of *sābab* is also significant. In 2:17 the woman had invited her beloved to 'turn' and to come to her. Now, instead, it is she who 'turns' towards him. Jer 31:22 comes into mind where the sign of the eschatological times is that "a woman courts (*sābab*) a man".[134] If the correspondence is relevant,[135] it is another sign of the paradisial, eschatological character of the love described in the Song. What for Jeremiah is a sign of the eschatological times is normal for the woman of the Song.

"Through the street and through the squares I will seek the love of my soul". Such behaviour would be considered madness even today. A girl who roams through the city alone at night would be judged by us too as imprudent or as a woman of the street. In Prov 7:9–12 the 'strange woman' is described in similar terms:

---

[133] *Confessions* 1:1. For a parallel between the Song and the *Confessions*, cf. Genovese (2001).

[134] The text is disputed, but this interpretation is traditional in both Jewish and Christian exegesis. Cf. McKane (1986–1996), vol. II, p. 806, who cites the Syriac, Vg, Rashi, Qimḥi, Ehrlich, *KJV*, *RV* and *RSV*; Holladay (1986–1989), vol. II, p. 195. In the case of Jeremiah, the text refers to the YHWH-Israel relationship: the woman (= Israel), against well established social custom, herself takes the initiative to court the man (= YHWH).

[135] There is a difference between the two passages, and it is that the object of *sābab* in Song 3:2, by contrast with 2:17 and with Jer 31:22, is not the woman, but the 'city' (*'ăsôbᵉbâ bāʿîr*, 'I will go through the city'). However, this too is, indirectly, a 'turning to' the man.

...in the twilight, in the evening,
at the time of night and darkness.
And lo, a woman meets him,
dressed as a harlot, wily of heart.
She is loud and wayward,
her feet do not stay at home;
now in the street, now in the squares,
at every corner she lies in wait (tr. *RSV*).

Behaviour of this kind would be absolutely unthinkable for a normal girl in the Syro-Palestinian environment;[136] it would not even be accepted in Egypt where the position of women was freer. For this reason, numerous commentators hold that the passage describes not a reality but a dream.[137] The reality described by the Song is, however, a lyrical reality: these are poetical situations which deliberately lie outside the realistic description of events. As in Song 1:7–8, here too the woman challenges social conventions and popular gossip in the name of love. It is precisely the paradox of the situation that is being presented to help in the understanding of the greatness of love. When Paul speaks of the 'foolishness' of the cross (cf. 1 Cor 1:18–30), he suggests the profound analogy which exists between the experience of faith and that of love. To the eyes of one who is not in love, love is madness just as faith is to one who does not believe. Similar behaviour which is outside the social norms is described in the book of Ruth when the heroine slips under the cover of Booz at night (cf. Ruth 3:1–14). Moreover, Lady Wisdom does not fear to appear like a prostitute attracting men to herself (cf. Prov 8:2–3).[138]

Second strophe: Finding (3:3–4)

The second strophe begins with the repetition of the word with which the first finished, changing the negative ("I did not find") into the positive ("they found me"). At this point, the reader would expect, finally,

[136] The Middle-Assyrian laws, for example, forbid women to leave the house without particular signs to indicate their status: married women, and the daughters of a free man, with the veil; the prostitute without the veil (§40, cf. *TUAT* I/1, pp. 87–88).

[137] Cf., for example, Nolli (1967) , pp. 89–90; Garbini (1992), p. 209 ("nocturnal dream"); Lys (1968), p. 139 ("rêve d'amour").

[138] "(It is necessary) to understand that the deep and incredible wisdom of this young woman consists in her having the courage to assume the air of a prostitute for the love of the man whom she loves" (Lys [1968], p. 144).

a positive result to the searching. But instead he is disappointed. The woman does not find; she is found! And not by her beloved. Parallel to the nocturnal rounds (*sābab*) of the woman, another set of rounds (*sābab*) is in course: those of the 'watchmen'. And the searching of the watchmen, by contrast with that of the woman, is successful: "They found me".

[3:3] Here we do not have the sentries who keep guard on the city walls to defend it from external dangers.[139] This institution was known in Israel even in the pre-Exilic period (cf. Ps 127:1; 130:6; Isa 21:11–12; 62:6; Neh 4:3). In the Song, on the other hand, the watchmen form a kind of police force whose job is to control disorder and internal sedition within the city. The generic *šōmᵉrîm* ('watchmen') is qualified in the text by the *hassōbᵉbîm bāʿîr* ("as they made their rounds through the city"). The expression corresponds exactly to the Hellenistic institution of the *peripoloi*. Graetz comments: "Only in the Macedonian era, in which war or armed peace reigned continually, were these *peripoloi* generally introduced in each city where there were occupying troops".[140] They constitute, therefore, an important element for dating the Song. Perhaps also the fact that they were occupying forces explains the brutal character with which they are characterised (cf. Song 5:7).

By contrast with the brute force of the guards, the question of the woman sounds frank, innocent: "Have you seen the love of my soul?" The juxtaposition is strident. The woman does not receive any reply from the guards, and it could not be otherwise. 'Love' is not a characteristic which the police tend to recognise. We have noted how the verb 'see' (*rāʾāh*) links 3:3 with 2:12 and 2:14. It will be repeated in 3:11. It seems that 'seeing' is reserved for the one who loves.

It could be that the watchmen are characterised in a particularly negative manner because they are representatives of a foreign power, but the same goes for the 'daughters of Jerusalem' who are felt to be potentially hostile to love in v. 5. It is, therefore, the 'city' itself which is represented in negative form, as hostile to the lovers,[141] by contrast

---

[139] *Contra* Ravasi (1992), pp. 290–291; Colombo (1975), p. 69.

[140] Graetz (1871), p. 63 (cf., *supra*, p. 33).

[141] Godard's film: "Je vous salue Marie" comes to mind. Each time that Joseph, Mary's fiancé, seeks to come near her, he is beaten by the sturdy 'bodyguards', who closely resemble the watchmen of the Song. The film is certainly irreverent and can be criticised, but it represents the reaction of the ordinary man in the face of the attitude of the Church towards sexuality which is so often negative.

with the representation of nature in 2:8–17 which is in itself an invitation to love.[142]

[v. 4] Verse 3 represents a slowing up in the composition which skilfully sharpens the narrative tension. The searching seems to have a negative result. Finally, after two negations ("I did not find him", vv. 1c, 2d) and a disappointment ("The watchmen found me", v. 3a), the tension is released; "I found" (v. 4b). The cry of Gen 2:23 ("This at last...") has an analogous function after the negative experiences of vv. 19–20.

The finding certainly cannot happen in the presence of the 'watchmen'. It is necessary that they 'pass on' (*ʿābar*) just as it was necessary that the winter passed (*ʿābar*) so that the spring might appear.

"I held him tight and would not let...". The verb *ʾāḥaz* takes up 2:15 ("catch us the foxes"). Here the sense is clearly positive. But it indicates not the tenderness of an embrace, rather the strength of her grasp (cf. again 3:8). And it is understandable. After the anxious searching, once the woman has found her love, she wants no one and nothing to separate her from him ("And I will not let..."). It is the same situation which is expressed with the metaphor of the seal in 8:6: "For love is strong as death". It is the indissolubility of the union which is being stressed.

"Until I had brought him into the house of my mother". The theme of 'bringing in', with its clear sexual value,[143] appeared in 1:4 and 2:4. In the *Prologue* it is he who has to bring the woman into his 'chambers' (*ḥeder*, 1:4b; cf. 3:4f), that is into his 'banqueting chamber' (*bêt*, 2:4; cf. 3:4e). Now we have the opposite (as also in 8:2): it is she who has to 'bring [him] in' to the 'house of her mother'. The parallel with 'the chamber of her who conceived me' (3:4f) leaves no doubt: it is the place of love.

We have noted above the link with 2:9d ('our wall').[144] The desire of the man to 'enter' the woman's house, described at the beginning of the composition (2:8–3:5) is now realised at the end of it. What was closed behind the wall and gratings is now open: the woman brings

---

[142] On the city-nature opposition in the Song cf. Heinevetter (1988), pp. 179–190 ("Kultur und Natur—die 'grüne' Vision des Hld"). Krinetzki's psychoanalytic interpretation, which sees in the watchmen the personification of the Freudian super-ego, is also interesting. Cf. Krinetzki (1981), p. 116.

[143] Cf. *supra*, p. 57.

[144] Cf. p. 102.

her beloved into the 'house'. G. Krinetzki sees in the house a projection of the feminine archetype of the 'vessel',[145] but we must not forget that in the *Prologue* it is the man who has to 'bring in' the woman. 'House' in Hebrew is the equivalent of 'family'.

Generally an institutional explanation is sought for this expression. According to Jewish custom, marriage is consummated in the house of the bridegroom. The bridegroom has to to lead the woman into his house, and she enters to become part of his family (cf. Ps 45:11). Already this does not agree with our text. Exceptions to this custom have been sought, in certain forms of a matriarchal type;[146] but then the passages in which it is he who has to bring her into the house (cf. Song 1:4; 2:4) are no longer explicable. The next section (3:6–11) shows precisely the nuptial procession from the house of the bride to that of the groom. An institutional explanation of this "bringing into the house of my mother" has not yet been found.[147]

There remains another type of explanation, of a metaphorical not an institutional character, reflecting the paradox of love. After love has been described as a breaking with the ties of family, a 'leaving the house' on the lines of Gen 2:24 (the 'Exodic' character of love, cf. Song 1:8; 2:10, 13), it is now described as a reconnection with the very roots of family. In 8:1, the woman dreams that her beloved becomes her brother, suckled at the breast of the same mother. The expression of Gen 2:23, "Bone of my bones and flesh of my flesh", is, at bottom, also an expression of kinship (cf. Gen 29:14; Judg 9:2, 3; 2 Sam 5:1; 19:13, 14). In fact, love leads lovers to become a part of the same family, to reconnect with the roots of their own existence.[148] The family, which

---

[145] Krinetzki (1981), p. 91, cf. p. 257, n. 232.

[146] Cf. the review of the suggestions in Ravasi (1992), pp. 293–294.

[147] A correspondence exists, perhaps, with the institutional frame supposed in the Egyptian love songs: after the young girl is 'given in marriage', her meetings with her fiancé take place in her house: only after the wedding do the two live together in his house. So Mathieu (1996), pp. 153–155; cf., *supra*, n. 123). The mythological explanation, which has recourse to the myth of Innana and Dumuzi (Inanna's mother, Ningal, offers her own house for the meeting of her daughter with Dumuzi, cf. Pope [1977], pp. 422–423), seems far from the simplicty of our text, but it is possible that it reflects social customs analogous to those of the Egyptian songs. Even in this case, however, the invitation to the woman to leave the house (2:10–14) would be poorly explained.

[148] "Absence is replaced by intimacy of the highest level through which love recaptulates in itself all the forms of relationship, even that of consanguinity" (Ravasi [1992], p. 67).

was portrayed in a negative light in Song 1:6 is now appreciated in its positive role as the necessary environment for love.

The family is indicated in Hebrew generally with the name of the *bêt ʾāb* ('house of the father'). It is unusual that in our text (the same thing happens in 8:2), it is the *bêt ʾimmî* ('the house of my mother') that is spoken of. Here too, a realistic explanation, in the sense, for example, that the woman is an illegitimate daughter, is, frankly, out of place.[149] Neither the father of the man nor that of the woman is ever mentioned in the Song. That has a parallel in the Egyptian love songs: only the brothers and the mother are mentioned among the family members of the lovers. The latter, above all, has an important role, as counsellor in matters of the heart.[150] It can be granted, therefore, that it is a phenomenon bound up with the literary genre. Personally I would like to make a link with the NT. In the list of family members which, according to Mark 10:29, the disciples must leave in order to follow Jesus there are "brothers, sisters, mother, father and children", but in that of the members of the new family which awaits them there are only "brothers, sisters, mothers and children" (v. 30). The figure of the father is missing, certainly not by accident but with a precise intention. It means to indicate that in the new family there are no "masters"; the only father is God (cf. Matt 23:9). Perhaps the absence of the father in the Song is due to similar reasons: it is a criticism of paternal authority in the family, understood as despotic and indifferent to the reasons of the heart.

"Into the chamber of her who conceived me". The term *ḥeder* designates the most intimate part of the house, the bedroom (cf. 1:4). Allusion is being made here to the procreative function of love. The

[149] Cf. the comment of Garbini (1992), p. 210: "This detail [...] shows that the woman lives alone with her mother, who is probably a prostitute". It is worth observing that even with regard to the bridegroom only the mother is spoken of, and therefore he too for the same reason would have to be considered the son of a prostitute!

[150] Cf., for example, Papyrus Chester Beatty IA. Addressing her love, the woman says: "He lives near to the *house of my mother*, / and yet I do not know how to go to him. / Could it be to my good fortune / that my mother is kind to me? / Oh, I will go to see her! [...] He does not know of my desire to embrace him, / he does not know what has made me leave my mother" (1:8–9 and 2:2–3 = second stanza in Bresciani [1990], p. 454). In the sixth stanza, on the other hand, it is his mother who is spoken of: "When I passed near to his house, / I found the door wide open: / my beloved was standing beside his mother, / all his brothers and sisters were with him. [...] Ah, if his mother had known my heart! / If this occurred to her" (3:10 and 4:3; *ibid.*, p. 457). For a different translation cf. Fox (1985) p. 52 and 54–55.

verb *hārāh* indicates conception. In 6:9, reference is made to procreation (again it is the woman's mother who is spoken of) with the term *yālad* which expresses 'giving birth'. In 8:5 (*his* mother, this time), alongside the verb *yālad* we have also *ḥābal* ('to experience the pains of labour'). The parallel is particularly significant: in both cases, the place of love is the same in which the lovers were generated (in 3:4 where she was generated, in 8:5 where he was generated). Here too the meaning is metaphorical, not the much sought after realistic one, and that is that love reconnects the lovers with the beginnings of their life. It is a finding of themselves. It is a renewal of the miracle of life. Even if the theme of procreation is not central in the Song, it is not absent. It is linked with the theme of life, of victory over death which is the *Leitmotiv* of the Song (cf. 8:6). By means of generation, love is the victor in the battle with death.[151] In this sense, we can also understand the fact that Isaac "brought [Rebecca] into the tent which had been his mother Sarah's" (Gen 24:67). The conclusion of the verse is significant: "Isaac was comforted after the death of his mother". The mother gives way to the bride. It is the unbroken flow of life.

Coda (3: 5)

V. 5 is a literal repeat of v. 2:7 (the 'refrain of awakening'). It supposes, as we have said, that the union has now taken place. This is clear if one follows the LXX in v. 4de: *ouk aphēka héōs hou eiēsgagon* ("I did not let him go until I had brought him in"). MT has an imperfect *wᵉlōʾ ʾarpennû* which in poetic language could also be translated in the past.[152] But even when translating the imperfect of *rāpāh* in the future, according to the normal usage,[153] the sense of v. 5 does not change. Verse 5 supposes that the desire expressed in v. 4 has already been fulfilled.

The city-nature contrast, expressed in vv. 1–4 in the opposition between the watchmen and the woman, is now taken up again in the antithesis between the 'daughters of Jerusalem' and the 'gazelles and

---

[151] Significant in this sense is Keel (1994), Figure 156, p. 273.

[152] Cf. Joüon (1923), §113o, p. 306. Also Vetus Latina and numerous modern translations (e.g. Colombo, Garbini, Rudolph, Ringgren, Müller, Krinetzki, Gerleman) render the verb in the past.

[153] So too Vg *nec dimittam donec introducam illum*, and the majority of commentators in Italian, French and English.

wild deer': in the name of the forces of nature the representatives of the city are charged with not troubling the union.[154]

The link between the animals described here and in 2:7 with those of 2:9 and 2:17 was noted above.[155] The 'gazelles and wild deer' are the female counterparts of the 'gazelle and young stag'. This observation helps us to understand the function of the *inclusio* which 3:5 assumes in relation with 2:9: the theme of the animals of love makes a frame not only for the first song of the woman (2:9, 17) but also for the ensemble of the two songs (2:9 and 3:5), thus significantly concluding the unit.

Conclusion

The two "songs of the beloved woman", 2:8–17 and 3:1–5 together represent the beginning of the journey of love. They do this by taking up again the two stages of "leaving the family" (2:8–17) and "the search for love" (3:1–5) which were presented in the Prologue at 1:5–6 and 1:7–8 respectively. The reference back to the Prologue is accentuated by the similar conclusion (3:5 = 2:7). In both cases, the refrain of awakening signals the conclusion of the poetic unit.

The unity of the passage is provided in the first place by the fact that both the songs are uttered by the woman (in the following song, 3:6–11, the speaker changes), then by the skilful complementarity which characterises them. If in 2:8–17 it is he who searches for her in order to invite her to leave the house, to believe in the adventure of love, in 3:1–5 it is she who is searching for him. "Rise up, my love," seeks the man (2:10, 13); and the woman, as if by way of reply, decides: "I will rise" (3:1). The reciprocity of amorous sentiment is expressed paradigmatically in the refrain of mutual belonging: "My beloved is mine and I am his" (2:16).

Another aspect of this complementarity is provided by the juxtaposition of nature (2:8–17) and city (3:1–5). This too is a theme which has already been introduced in the Prologue. Here, the city, which was represented by the "daughters of Jerusalem" in the Prologue, is represented by the "watchmen". In this case too, the potential hostil-

---

[154] Cf. *supra*, pp. 92–93.
[155] Cf. p. 138.

ity to love is brought into play. By contrast, the preceding passage, 2:8–17, emphasises the continuity between nature and human love: the beloved man is a young stag, the woman a dove, and both are vineyards in flower. The blooming of love in the hearts of the two youngsters becomes part of the reawakening of spring from the sleep of winter. We have a jubilation of colours, sounds and fragrance: all the senses are involved together in the feast of life and love.

A third aspect is the temporal complementarity: the first song is located in the morning, it is a song of awakening—the second, a nocturne. Here we are dealing not only with chronological time but with existential, poetic time. Morning is the time for going out, evening that for meeting in amorous intimacy ("When the day sighs and the shadows lengthen, come…", 2:17). All the more painful, then, is the absence of the beloved (3:1). In 3:1–5, a tragic note is introduced into the idyll of the Song: the absence of the beloved, the hostility of society. The note of pain is not absent from the Song: the poet makes clever use of all the strings of his lyre. But the poet's lyre mirrors life itself: pain is part of the adventure of love.

The theme of the house forms an *inclusio* for the passage. At the beginning, the beloved is on the outside and looks for his beloved to leave the house (2:10, 13) where she is concealed like a dove in the crags (2:14). Later, the woman makes her beloved enter the house of her mother (3:4). This *inclusio* highlights the paradox of love which is, at one and the same time, a going out and a finding again of one's own roots.

Through an intertextual reading, we have perceived an allusion to the adventure of Abraham in the first song (Song 2:10, 13, cf. Gen 12:1) against the background of Gen 2:24 ("Therefore a man leaves his father and mother and cleaves to his wife"). Similarly, in the second song, the reference to Hos 2:9 and Prov 7:12 has highlighted another characteristic of love, its apparent madness, something which only those who are in love can understand. The text speaks of human love even if it is possible also to see in delicate strands, evidenced by the parallels, the experience of Israel with her God.

CHAPTER FIVE

CHORAL INTERMEZZO

(Song 3:6–11)

Nuptial Procession

I

Chorus 6 Who is this that rises from the desert
like a pillar of smoke,
shrouded in clouds of myrrh and incense,
with[1] every fragrance of the merchant?

II

7 Look, the litter of Solomon!
Around it are sixty mighty men,
from the mighty of Israel,
8 all of them armed with the sword,
and trained for battle.
Each has his sword on his thigh,
against the terror of the night.[2]

---

[1] It would be possible also to understand the preposition *min* in a comparative sense: 'more than any…' (cf. Heinevetter [1988], p. 114, note 73). We understand it as a specification of *m^{e}quṭṭeret*, lit. 'incensed'. Cf. Joüon (1923), §133e: "material from which one makes something". Strangely, the preposition is missing before 'myrrh and incense' (for phonetic or rhythmical reasons?).

[2] Lit.: 'in the nights', *ballêlôt*.

III

[9]King Solomon made himself a litter
from the wood of Lebanon.
[10]He made its posts of silver,
its headboard of gold,
its seat of purple,
the interior adorned with the love
of the daughters of Jerusalem.

IV

[11]Go out, O daughters of Zion, and behold
King Solomon and the crown[3]
with which his mother has crowned him
on the day of his wedding,
the day of the joy of his heart.

Structure

Song 3:6–11 constitutes a kind of intermezzo between the songs of the beloved woman (2:7–3:5) and those of the beloved man (4:1–5:1). The section is declaimed by a voice from off-stage, which has the function of the chorus in the Greek tragedies.[4] The unity of the passage is not undisputed: numerous authors see it as two distinct compositions (3:6–8 and 9–11).[5] But the reasons for considering it as a unity are

[3] We understand the b^e as a *signum accusativi* by parallelism with *bammelek*. LXX has understood likewise (*ídete en tō basilei salōmōn en tō stephánō*), and so *NRS* ("Look…at King Solomon, at the crown"). *NKJ* ("see King Solomon with the crown") follows the interpretation of the Vg (*videte [...] regem Salomonem in diademate*) with the majority of the translations.

[4] With whom this voice is to be identified is not clear. One might think of the 'daughters of Jerusalem', the spectators of the procession. But they are the addressees of the speech at v. 11. The 'chorus' could assume different roles. The first two strophes, which reflect the immediate experience of the vision, go well in the mouths of the daughters of Jerusalem. The third and fourth, which are of a more meditative character, could be put in the mouth of the poet himself.

[5] In this sense, for example, Gerleman (1965), pp. 134–143; Stadelmann (1992), pp. 96–124. Keel (1994), pp. 125–134, and Krinetzki (1981), pp. 118–138, see even three independent compositions in the section: vv. 6–8, 9–10d and 10e–11.

Table 19

A. v. 6	Dialogue: admiration		
B. vv. 7–8	Description: the litter	*miṭṭâ*, 7	*šᵉlōmōh*, 7
B'. vv. 9–10	Description: the litter	*ʾappiryôn*, 9	*šᵉlōmōh*, 9
A'. v. 11	Dialogue: admiration		*šᵉlōmōh*, 11

stronger: the poem is, in fact, unified not only by the subject speaking (the 'chorus'), but also by the mention of 'Solomon' (vv. 7a, 9a, 11b) and of the litter (v. 7a and 9a). By contrast with the preceding songs, which represent the personal relationship of the two young people, love is seen here in its social context, in its 'nuptial' dimension (cf. v. 11d). Song 3:6–11 is an *epithalamium*, a genre well known in Hellenistic poetry[6] and one which finds a parallel in the OT in Ps 45. The 'procession' is still an essential part of the nuptial ceremonies today, and not just in the Orient.

As a composition, the song is structured chiastically into four strophes (vv. 6, 7–8, 9–10, 11)[7] (cf. *Tab. 19*). The two central strophes (b–b') are united by the theme of the 'litter of Solomon' (v. 7a; cf. v. 9a). The second strophe describes its escort, the third its construction. The first and the fourth strophe (a–a') are united by the excited description of the comment which the appearing of the litter arouses in the population of Jerusalem.[8] It has a 'dialogic' character. To the question of v. 6 ("Who is it?"), v. 7 ("Look...") gives the answer. V. 11 is a speech addressed directly to the 'daughters of Zion'.

At the end of the preceding song (3:1–5), the woman 'brought in' her beloved into the 'house of my *mother*' (v. 4), that is, into her own family. In 3:6–11, it is the man who has to bring the woman into his own family. The woman comes from outside, and comes to Jerusalem, the home of Solomon. This time it is the '*mother* of the bridegroom' who has to do the honours. One cannot speak of a narrative continuity (from this point of view the two songs contradict each other),[9] but

---

[6] Cf. Theocritus, *Idyll* 18 (*Epithalamium* of Helen).

[7] So Rudolph (1962), p. 140; Ravasi (1992), pp. 305–306. Heinevetter (1989), p. 109, prefers to join the first and second strophes together.

[8] Cf. Elliott (1989), pp. 83, 88.

[9] Ravasi (1992), p. 304, notes the continuity between the two sections, but not the contradiction, when he says: "The idea seems to come from the decision of the woman to bring her beloved into the 'house of her mother', thus performing the classic nuptial procession, [...] which now the chorus or a soloist sings about". In 3:4, the 'procession' goes in a different direction from that of 3:6–11!

of thematic continuity. The social aspect of love, central in 3:6–11, has already been introduced in 3:4.[10]

The nuptial theme also unites 3:6–11 with the succeeding composition, the *waṣf* 4:1–7. The 'description of the body' of the bride has, in fact, its *Sitz im Leben* in the nuptial ceremonies.[11] The theme continues in the following song, 4:8–5:1. Here we see the appellations 'bride' (4:8, 11) and 'my sister, my bride' (4:9, 10, 12; 5:1). In the light of 4:1–7, it seems clear that the one who is arriving in 3:6–11 is the woman. In the *waṣf* (4:1–7), the man sings of the beauty of the one who has come from the desert (3:6–11).

The text presents notable difficulties of interpretation. Above all, who is it, in the 'litter'? According to v. 6, it is the woman (cf. the commentary below). But at v. 11, 'the daughters of Zion' are invited to see not her but 'King Solomon'. H.-P. Müller claims that in 3:6–11 two different processions are being spoken of: in vv. 6–8, it would be the procession of the bride that is being spoken of, in vv. 9–11, that of the bridegroom.[12] Ravasi, for his part, thinks that one procession is being spoken of, but that both the bride and the bridegroom are in the litter.[13]

The problem is complicated by the fact that the text uses two different terms to indicate the 'litter': at v. 7, the classical term *miṭṭâ* ('[transportable] bed') is used, in v. 9a, the term *ʾappiryôn*, a neologism the significance of which is disputed. Those who, like Gerleman,[14] translate this term with 'throne room' naturally separate vv. 9–11 from vv. 6–8. For H.-P. Müller too, it is something different from *miṭṭâ*.[15]

---

[10] A singular analogy exists with the Egyptian love songs. As B. Mathieu notes, they have two geographic poles: the house of the woman and that of the man. Mathieu describes the role of the two 'houses' thus: a) the boy and the girl each lives in his own house; b) the boy goes to the girl's house; c) (after the betrothal) he lives (temporarily) in the girl's house; d) the woman enters the house of her husband; e) the spouses dwell (permanently) in their house (cf. Mathieu [1996], p. 155, §33). These steps find their counterpart in the first part of the Song (2:8–5:1). Step b) is described in 2:8–9. The woman alludes to step c) in 3:4 ("...until I have brought him into the house of my mother"). Step d) is evoked by the nuptial procession. Even if secondary, then, the 'social' theme of love permeates the whole of the first part of the poem coherently.

[11] Cf., for example, Wetzstein (1873), p. 291.

[12] Müller (1992), pp. 36–41; so also Garbini (1992), p. 214.

[13] Ravasi (1992), p. 317.

[14] Gerleman (1965), pp. 139–141 ('Thronhalle').

[15] Müller (1992), p. 36, nn. 98–99. According to Müller, v. 7a is in any case a gloss. In this sense, cf., already, Rudolph (1962), p. 139, and *BHS*.

As a working hypothesis, we hold the composition to be unitary: therefore we identify the *miṭṭâ* of v. 7a with the *ʾappiryôn* of v. 9a. In the litter there is one single person, the bride.

First Strophe: Appearance in the Desert (3:6)

The first three strophes describe the progressive approach of the nuptial procession to the city from the standpoint of the inhabitants of Jerusalem. The first sign, when the procession is still distant, is the raising up of clouds of dust by its passage (v. 6ab). Then, when the caravan is approaching, one perceives that it isn't dust, but clouds of incense and myrrh (v. 6cd). Then one can see the people of the retinue (vv. 7–8). In the end, the attention is focused on the heart of the caravan, the litter (vv. 9–10). This progress towards the centre also characterises the description of the litter in vv. 9–10. It is a refined, almost cinematographic, technique which passes from the long shot through intermediate levels ending up with the focus on the protagonist in close-up.

[v. 6] The initial question ("Who is this?") creates problems. If it is true that the feminine demonstrative pronoun *zōʾt* can also have a neutral sense in Hebrew, the interrogative pronoun *mî* refers exclusively to a person. From another angle, the versions have unanimously understood a feminine singular which cannot be other than the woman, a meaning confirmed by the parallels 6:10 and, above all, 8:5.[16] The problem derives from the fact that the reply in v. 7 indicates not a person but a thing ("Look, the litter of Solomon"). Rudolph has recourse to the drastic solution of eliminating v. 7a as an allegorising gloss.[17] The other solution, generally followed, is to adapt the question to the reply, changing the gender of the interrogative pronoun: "What is this which rises from the desert?" (so, for example, *RSV* and *JB*). But is it really the case that the MT does not make sense? Elliott observes, with justice, that the tenor of v. 6 is between a question and

[16] In this sense, cf. Dirksen (1989); Elliott (1989), pp. 83–84; Heinevetter (1988), p. 111; Keel (1994), pp. 125–126; Garbini (1992), pp. 211–212. It is true that this identification does not respect the realism of the scene. From a distance, in fact, one cannot perceive who is in the litter, *a fortiori* in that a litter is generally enclosed. But such questions are out of place in a lyrical description.

[17] Müller (1992), p. 36, n. 98.

an exclamation.[18] In the two parallel passages (6:10 and 8:5) the phrase remains effectively without an answer. Even if the description concerns the litter, the numinous way in which this apparition is presented is not explained by its being a material object. The litter is invested with a theophanic character because within it there is Love personified in the 'bride'.[19] The question of v. 6a finds its true response in v. 10d. But let us proceed by steps.

"That rises from the desert". Contrary to the opinion of H.-P. Müller who thinks of a lyrical countryside without concrete geographical implications,[20] the mention of Jerusalem in vv. 10e and 11a makes one think of the Judaean Desert which begins immediately outside the city, to the East. From the Mount of Olives one has an impressive view of the desert. From there runs the road which 'rises' from Jericho to Jerusalem, one of the principal arteries of the caravan trade between the Orient and the Mediterranean. Perhaps the author has in mind particular processions (the marriage of Solomon with some Oriental princess[21] or the visit of the Queen of Sheba),[22] but that remains in the background. The naming of Solomon is part of the high burlesque introduced already in the prologue (1:1, 4b, 5d, 12).[23] Under the figures of 'King Solomon' and the exotic 'princess' are to be understood the two lovers who are now presented as bridegroom and bride.

The identification of the 'desert' with that of Judaea does not exclude the symbolic significance of this passage. The symbolism of the desert is ambivalent. On the one hand, as v. 8 recalls, the desert is a place of death and dangers, an image of the kingdom of the dead.[24] On the other hand, it is also the place of the forces of life and love. At Ugarit,

[18] Elliott (1989), p. 83.

[19] From the point of view of depth psychology, Krinetzki (1970), pp. 408–411, recalls the feminine symbolism of the litter, as 'recipient', 'vessel', which welcomes and protects. Also, on the basis of mythological stereotypes, Holman (1998) proposes an identification of the woman with the litter. The description of *miṭṭâ* would be the anatomical description of the woman. But this goes clearly beyond the data in the text.

[20] Müller (1992), p. 38.

[21] Cf., in this sense, Gordis (1974), pp. 18–23; Sasson (1989).

[22] Thus Keel (1994), p. 126.

[23] Cf. *supra*, pp. 14–15, and p. 57.

[24] Pope (1977), pp. 424–426, stresses the mythological symbolism of the desert as image of the afterlife against the background of the myth of the descent of Ishtar to the underworld. The woman in 3:6 would personify the goddess of love who climbs up again from the kingdom of the underworld. Cf., already, Wittekindt (1925), p. 134; Schmökel (1956), pp. 92–95. In our case, however, it seems to me that the accent is put on the positive rather than the negative dimension of the desert.

šaḥru and *šalimu*, the 'graceful and beautiful' gods, have their dwelling in the desert (*bmdbr*),[25] and the goddess of love is called *ʿttrt šd* ('Astarte of the steppe').[26] In Song 2:7, the woman charges 'by the gazelles or by the wild deer' where by 'wild' (literally 'of the fields' [*śādeh*]) is meant uncontaminated nature, the realm of the wild animals (*ḥayyat haśśādeh*). The bride comes from the desert, just as the man came from the mountains and the hills with the vital freshness of a gazelle (2:8).

"Like a pillar of smoke". The Hebrew *tîmărôt* is a rare term (only elsewhere in Joel 3:3), which derives from *tāmār* ('palm'). The correspondence palm-pillar is facilitated by the fact that the pillars in the buildings of the monarchical epoch had a capital in the form of a palm.[27] The first impression is visual: it is probably of the dust churned up by the horses and the people of the caravan.[28] But in the background we are allowed to glimpse a memory of the "pillar of cloud and fire" which accompanied the Israelites during their march through the desert (cf. Exod 13:21–22; 14:19, 24 etc). The cloud confers on the apparition a theophanic, numinous significance.

The visual is succeeded in v. 6cd by the olfactory impression which supposes that the procession is now closer. The 'clouds' are not of dust but of 'myrrh and incense'. The first scent was mentioned in Song 1:13: myrrh has not only an erotic significance but also a sacral background. This dimension is accentuated by the verb *qāṭar* ('to burn [incense]') which belongs to the liturgical vocabulary of sacrifices. The second scent, incense, has a clear sacral significance. The term *lᵉbônâ*

---

[25] Cf. *KTU* 1.23, 4, 65, 68 (Del Olmo Lete [1981], pp. 440 and 447). Xella (1973), pp. 105–106, comments: "the desert is precisely the land that has not been cultivated, a pure and sacred place (*mdbr qdš*) in which divinities and forces which transcend man operate".

[26] Cf. *UT*, Text 1106, ll. 52, 55 (p. 235). An analogue, in Mesopotamia, is the denomination of Ishtar as *bēlit ṣēri* ('Lady of the Steppe'). Cf. Pope (1977), p. 426.

[27] Cf. Keel (1994), Figure 70, p. 127. We should point out the curious version of the Vulgate (*virgula*) and that of the Vetus Latina (*vitis propago*), the latter preferred by the translation of Garbini (1992), p. 212 ("like a vine shoot"). The two versions cited are, perhaps, an attempt to match up the similitude (*tîmărôt*, plural) with the subject in question (*mî zōʾt*, singular). Be that as it may, they have understood the interrogative pronoun as referring to the woman, to whom they have matched the similitude. In fact, the plural creates difficulties: it passes brusquely from the person of the woman to the procession (to return then to the singular, cf. 6c), with the same liberty with which v. 7a replies to the question "Who is this?" by pointing out the litter.

[28] Thus rightly Ravasi (1992), p. 315. Nah 1:3 offers a similar image speaking of the passage of God: "the clouds are the dust of his feet".

derives from *lābān* ('white') and is close semantically to *l^ebānôn* (the 'Lebanon', cf. v. 9b), called such because of the snow, just as incense is called 'white' because of the colour of its grains. Incense is a resin which is extracted from various plants of the genus *Boswellia*,[29] and is originally from the South of the Arabian peninsula ('Saba', cf. 1 Kgs 10:2) and from Somalia. It is used still today in Arabia for profane purposes, but in the OT it has a significance which is, above all, religious. Incense forms part of the daily sacrifice (Exod 30:7–8, 34–38), and the Levite controls the liturgical use of it (cf. Lev 2:1–2, 15–16; 24:7). For Ps 141:2, burning incense is synonymous with praying. The numerous censers of a cultic character in stone or in terracotta found in Palestine and almost everywhere in the Ancient Middle East attest that the sacral significance of incense was widespread.[30]

With the expression "every fragrance of the merchant",[31] the author broadens and intensifies the image in the preceding stich, conferring on it an exotic colour. The term 'merchant' (*rôkēl*) refers generally to international trade (cf. Ezek 27). In particular, perfume merchants, were those of Saba who carried their wares in interminable caravans up to the Phoenician ports of the Lebanon (cf. Ezek 27:22).

The apparition in the desert is invested, therefore, with a theophanic glow and evokes the delights of distant lands. With the bride, something foreign and precious comes to form part of the man's 'family'.

Second Strophe: The Escort (3:7–8)

The second strophe supposes that the procession is closer. At its centre we can see a litter and recognise with amazement ("Look!") that it is that of Solomon. Then the attention is drawn to the litter's escort which is described in detail. From the literary point of view, the use of anadiplosis should be noted between v. 7bc ('mighty men') and v. 8 ac

[29] Cf. Zohary (1982), p. 197; Hepper (1992), pp. 136–137.

[30] For the Egyptian world, the use of incense is attested by the expedition of Queen Hatshepshut to the land of Punt to procure trees of incense for herself, with which to provide for the needs of the cult. Cf. Robert-Tournay (1963), pp. 347–348; Ravasi (1992), pp. 315–316.

[31] The Hebrew *ʾabāqâ* is a *hapax* derived from *ʾābāq*, whose meaning of 'dust' is assured by the synonymy with the more common *ʿāpār* in Deut 28:24. The qualification 'of the merchant' stresses that it is not dust of the ground but 'aromatic dust'.

('sword'), a phenomenon already noticed in 2:15: the repetition of the same word joins two successive stichs in 'concatenation'.

[v. 7] Eventually, then, among the clouds of incense, we can make something out. Strangely, it is not a person, as was expected ("Who is this?" v. 6a) but an object. The term *miṭṭâ* usually designates a bed;[32] from the context it is a portable bed, a 'litter' (cf. 1 Sam 19:15). The use of the litter, above all for ladies of a high class, became the fashion in the Hellenistic world.[33] At all events, it is not just any litter but one well known to the inhabitants of Jerusalem: "the litter of Solomon". The description is left to the succeeding strophe which is directly linked to this one (cf. v. 7a with v. 9a). The mention of Solomon does not imply that the king is inside.[34] Lys notes that in the OT there is no example of a king who is carried on a litter: the king goes on horseback (or astride an ass), not lying in a litter.[35] 'Solomon' has, therefore, sent his personal litter with an armed escort to transport the 'Oriental princess' who is to become his bride. This custom was widespread in the Ancient East. It is recounted of Ramses II that he sent "an army, cavalry and dignitaries to accompany a king's daughter from the Hittites into Egypt where the wedding was to be celebrated".[36] In the OT a caravan which accompanies the bride to the house of the groom is mentioned in Gen 24 and in 1 Macc 9:36–41. In our case, naturally, there is no question of an historical identification but of a literary fiction, that high burlesque which is typical of the Song and which denotes an urban and bourgeois rather than a rustic origin for the poem.[37]

---

[32] Cf. Ezek 23:41; Esth 1:6; 2 Sam 3:31.

[33] In this connection, Keel (1994), p. 131, cites a passage of the Deipnosophists of Athenaeus: at the opening of the games sponsored by Antiochus Epiphanes at Daphne, a suburb of Antioch, in 167 B.C., there were 80 litters (*phoreion*, cf. v. 9a) with feet of gold and 500 with feet of silver, all with purple tops, containing the same number of richly clothed women (*Deipnosophists* 5,195c, cf. 5,212c). Keel (1994), Figure 73, p. 132, shows a similar litter of the Roman period.

[34] Also in Jewish custom, the litter was assigned to the conveying of the bride, not the groom, during the nuptial procession. Cf. b.*Sot* 49, ed. Epstein (1935–1948), Nashim VI, p. 265; S–B, vol. I, pp. 505, 509–510; Rudolph (1962), p. 141. Dirksen (1989), pp. 224–225, n. 6, offers a recent parallel from Kurdistan.

[35] Lys (1968), p. 154 (citing Winandy).

[36] Keel (1994), p. 128. The custom of the procession is, moreover, common still today among the Arabs of Palestine and Syria. Cf. De Vaux (1961), pp. 33–34.

[37] According to Müller (1992), p. 40, the passage has its *Sitz im Leben* "among an urban bourgeoisie, whose ideal of life is represented by the social class immediately superior to it".

Beside the profane, aristocratic significance of the burlesque, its religious import is also to be noted. Gerleman has drawn attention to the Egyptian feasts of the valley of the desert and of Opet in which statues of the divinity were carried in procession on a stretcher in the form of a boat.[38] Similar processions are attested also in Mesopotamia and in the Canaanite world.[39] Where Israel is concerned, one thinks of the march through the desert with the Ark of the Covenant.[40] In the litter of the Song, there is no statue of a divinity; there is simply a young woman. But she personifies love, 'the flame of YHWH' (8:6), and is therefore invested with a sacral aura.

"Sixty mighty men are around it[41]...". The preposition *sābîb* ('around') is an echo of 3:3 ("The watchmen made their rounds [*hassōb^{e}bîm*] through the city"). Just as the 'watchmen' are represented in a negative way, as enemies of love, so the 'mighty men' are presented positively. With pride, they are said to belong to the 'mighty of Israel'. This trace of nationalism is noticeable also in the expression 'daughters of Jerusalem' (v. 10de) and in the synonymous 'daughters of Zion' (v. 11a). By contrast with the passages examined so far (1:5; 2:7 and 3:5), here the 'daughters of Jerusalem' have a positive role. The 'mighty men' and the 'daughters of Jerusalem' are the representatives of society. Not of any society, but of the people of God ('Israel', 'Jerusalem', 'Zion'). The nationalistic note was perceptible also in the specification 'our land' in 2:12. Society has, therefore, a role which is not only negative but also positive in relation to love: that of protecting love from the 'perils of the night' (vv. 7–8) and of participating in the joy of the spouses (v. 11).

It is interesting to note that, close to the woman there is a male group of 'mighty men', while close to the man it is a feminine one of 'daughters of Jerusalem' (v. 11). The group of 'mighty men' represents,

---

[38] Gerleman (1965), pp. 136–137.

[39] Cf. Lys (1968) p. 154; Schmökel (1956), p. 94.

[40] Cf. Kuhn (1926), p. 528. Moreover, this is the traditional allegorical interpretation, found, for example, in the Targum: "When the children of Israel went up from the Wilderness and crossed the Jordan with Joshua, the son of Nun, the peoples of the land said: 'What chosen nation is this that goes up from the Wilderness, perfumed with the incense of spices?'" (*Targum of Canticles* 3:6, tr. Alexander [2003], p. 122).

[41] It is not clear to what or to whom the pronoun refers. Grammatically it ought to refer to the nearest feminine noun, therefore to the litter. But Müller notes the ambivalence: it would be more logical for it to refer to the bride (cf. Müller [1992], p. 37, n. 104). At any rate, the litter accommodates the bride.

so to speak, the bridegroom to the woman[42] while that of the 'daughters of Jerusalem' represents the bride to the man.[43] Moreover, the term 'mighty men' (*gibbōrîm*) in the OT evokes David's bodyguard (cf. 2 Sam 23:8–39). David had thirty 'mighty men'. The Philistines also sent thirty young men as 'friends of the bridegroom' for the marriage of Samson (Judg 14:11). 'Solomon' has ordered double the number to accompany his bride: she is well protected!

[v. 8] The text underlines that the warriors were armed with the 'sword'. Among many Oriental peoples, the sword has an important role in the nuptial ceremonies. Among the Arabs of Palestine and Syria, the bride performs to this day the 'dance of the sword'.[44] This dance has an apotropaic value, that of protection against obscure dangers. The sword in the Song has the same significance.

The sword defends "against the terror of the night". Originally, the nuptial procession had the very concrete responsibility of acting as a defence against the attacks of robbers. The road from the desert is the same one as that in the gospel episode of the Good Samaritan (Luke 10:30)! But the MT has a plural: "the terror during the nights (*ballêlôt*)", the same expression as 3:1. The link between the two passages seems intentional. In 3:1, the 'night' is understood as the time of love, but also of danger (cf. the 'watchmen'). In 3:8, the term 'terror' (*paḥad*) has a metaphorical, even numinous, significance. In fact, YHWH is called "the terror of Isaac" (Gen 31:42, 53). The 'terror of the night' makes one think of a demoniac power ('terror') which threatens human sexuality ('of the night').[45]

---

[42] Among the Arabs of Syria, the male group with the responsibility of conducting the bride into the house of the bridegroom, is called *śebâb el-ʿarîs*, 'the young men of the bridegroom'. Cf. Wetzstein (1873), pp. 288–289.

[43] Also in John 3:29 'the friend of the bridegroom' has a particular role with respect to the bride; while in Matt 25:1–13 the virgins await the arrival of the bridegroom.

[44] Cf. Wetzstein (1873), p. 288; De Vaux (1961), p. 34 ("Sometimes, during the procession, a sword is carried by the bride or in front of her, and sometimes she performs the dance of the sabres, advancing and retreating before it; [...] The brandishing of the sword is symbolic: it cuts away bad luck and drives off evil spirits"). For similar customs in Armenia and in India, cf. Ravasi (1992), p. 320.

[45] Among the numerous representations of demons (ancient man lived under the terror of devilish powers as can be seen by the number and intensity of the representations of them), cf. Keel (1978), Figures 97a and 97b, p. 84. The figure on the right represents the divinity which has the job of killing, with sword and axe, the demon pictured on the left. In another way, the 'perils of the night', are a theme of Egyptian (cf. Mathieu [1996], p. 160) and Israelite (cf. Prov 7:8–9) sapiential and didactic poetry.

The book of Tobit speaks of this kind of demon. The demon Asmodeus killed all Sara's bridegrooms on their wedding night (Tob 3:17; 6:14). In the primitive text, perhaps the legend narrated how before being able to have relations with the bride it was necessary to kill the demon with a sword.[46] The bride of the Song is protected against a similar 'terror': the sixty 'mighty men of Israel' are ready to kill the nocturnal demon with their swords. The national flavour is not chauvinistic. It intends to signify that, in the environment of Israel, human love is protected from the dangers bound up with sexuality.[47] Not only is YHWH a defence from the terrors of the night (cf. Ps 91:5–6); the 'friends of the bridegroom', the society of the people of God, perform a similar role.

Third Strophe: The Litter of Solomon (3:9–10)

After having focused on the entourage, now the attention is levelled on the centre of the procession, the litter. The description of the litter is a piece of bravura, rich in neologisms which makes one think of certain passages in Homer where the author seems to forget the action and dwells at length on minute details. Our text finds a parallel in the Odyssey in the description of the nuptial bed of Penelope.[48]

[v. 9] Since the understanding of the passage depends on the solution of numerous lexical problems, it is suitable to linger over these before giving an interpretation to the whole. Already the first word of v. 9, *appiryôn*, constitutes a problem. It is an OT *hapax*, probably a word of foreign origin. The interpretations go in two directions:

---

[46] Perhaps there is also a memory of this legend in the obscure passage of Exod 4:24–26. There is a surprising similarity to the Song. Both passages are situated in the desert, at night. In both, marriage is the subject, and the sword (or, respectively, a knife made out of flint) plays an important role. Probably, behind the figure of YHWH in the primitive text of Exod 4:24–26 was some demon of the type of Asmodeus. *4 Ezra* 9:47–10:1 speaks of a similar demon (cf. *OTP* I, p. 546). Here we have a belief that is widespread in Judaism, so much so that bridegrooms were advised to abstain from relations during the first night of marriage. Cf. Ravasi (1992), p. 320; in general, on the anthropological significance of the 'terror of the night', cf. Krauss (1936).

[47] For the second time, following 2:15 ('the foxes'), mention is made of the dangers inherent in love. This is a rare topic in the Song, which, perhaps in antithesis to the other books of the OT, highlights almost exclusively the positive aspect of love.

[48] Cf. Homer, *Odyssey* 23:190–201. For this parallel, cf. Grossberg (1981).

- Generally, the term is understood as a synonym of *miṭṭâ* (v. 7). We could look, for example, at the LXX (*phoreion*) and the Vulgate (*ferculum*). Various exegetes hold that the term *appiryôn* is none other than the Hebrew transcription of the Greek term *phoreion*.[49] Other authors come to an analogous result making the term derive from other languages, from the Iranian *upari-yāna* ('litter') or the Sanskrit *paryanka* (from which derives our 'palanquin').[50] M. Görg proposes a derivation from the Egyptian *pry* ('to appear') and sees in it a sort of *sedia gestatoria*[51] for the public appearances of the Pharaoh and dignitaries of the highest rank.[52]
- The Syriac version *kwrsy*ʾ ('throne') supposes something different from the litter, something fixed. This is the opinion of not a few exegetes who see in *appiryôn* a derivation either from the Akkadian *appadan* ('palace'; cf. Dan 11:45),[53] or from the Egyptian *pr* (*house*).[54]

We opt for the first solution. We point out, however, an inconsistency: *miṭṭâ* makes one think of a bed whereas the description of *appiryôn*, in vv. 10–11, speaks of a 'seat' which makes one suppose a kind of a chair or throne.[55]

"King Solomon made himself…". The appositional 'king' is emphasised in the Hebrew text: it will be repeated at v. 11b, and the idea is strengthened by the image of the 'crown'. Love makes a king of the bridegroom. This image does not clash with the artisan's labour implied in the verb *ʿāśāh* ('to make'). It is unnecessary to translate 'had it made for himself' (cf. the *TOB* translation): in the case of Penelope's

---

49 Thus, for example, Rundgren (1962); Garbini (1982), p. 41; Müller (1992), p. 36, n. 99; Heinevetter (1988), p. 112, n. 69. This sense is confirmed by the Jewish tradition, which indicates the nuptial litter with terms which are evidently transliterations of *phoreion*: *ʾappiryôn* (b.*Sot* 9:14), *pôryō*ʾ (ShirR 3:9); *pōryûmâ* (for *poreuma*) or *pôryôn* (BemR 12); *ʾapôryôn* (y.*Sot* 1:17c, 20). Cf. S–B, vol. I, pp. 509–510.

50 So, for example, Gordis (1974), p. 21, n. 74; Ravasi (1992), p. 323.

51 Vetus Latina translates, precisely, *gestatorium*.

52 Görg (1982). Cf. Keel (1994), Figure 72, p. 132. In the Westcar Papyrus, mention is made of a similar conveyance. It was made of ivory, with the poles in *sesenem* wood (a particularly precious wood from Africa) covered in gold. Cf. Bresciani (1990), p. 187.

53 So, for example, Robert-Tournay (1963), pp. 147–150, and Nolli (1967), p. 97.

54 Thus Gerleman (1965), p. 139.

55 Perhaps the author was not familiar with these objects of luxury, or perhaps he made use of different sources. In any case, at the level of the final redaction, the reference of v. 9a to 7a is unquestionable: it is the same object.

bed it is the king-bridegroom, Ulysses, who has constructed it. The verb *ʿāśāh* was employed in 1:11 to indicate an exquisite work of jewellery. The most delicate materials and the artistic masterpiece of the work enhance the status of whoever uses it.

The use of the 'wood of Lebanon' for the litter is in harmony with the figure of 'Solomon'. Cedar was used by Solomon in the construction of the temple and the royal palace; it confers, therefore, on the litter an atmosphere at once regal and sacral.[56] The term 'Lebanon' joins v. 9b with v. 6c ('Lebanon' and 'incense' share the same word in Hebrew, 'the white') and with 4:8. Lebanon is in fact the mountain from which the woman hails (cf. again 4:11, 15).

[v. 10] The description proceeds from the outside to within. First of all the 'pillars' are mentioned. It is not clear whether these are the little columns which support the baldacchino, or the feet of the litter. The first is more likely. The material used for the pillars is more noble than wood: it is silver. Gradually, as progress is made towards the interior, the material increases in value.

The second element described constitutes another *hapax*: *rᵉpîdâ*. Generally, the term is made to derive from the verb *rāpad* ('to support'; cf. 2:5) and translated with 'headboard'.[57] Once again, the increase in value of the material corresponds to the progress towards the centre: the silver of the columns is succeeded by the 'gold' of the headboard.[58]

The third element of the litter is also expressed with a very rare term (*merkāb*, only again in Lev 15:9 with the meaning of 'saddle'). Since the verb *rākab* is equivalent to 'to ride', the most probable translation of the substantive seems to be 'seat', which makes one think more of a throne than of a bed.[59] If it is a seat, it is understandable that the material used is not a metal. It is, in fact, 'purple', more precisely the 'red purple' (*ʾargāmān*, cf. Song 7:6), distinct from violet, which is called *tᵉkēlet*. According to Ravasi, purple was a material more costly than silver and gold: a gram of purple was equivalent to 10–20 grams

[56] Cf., *supra*, the comment at 1:17.

[57] The Syriac *tšwyth*, LXX *anakliton* and Vg *reclinatorium* make one think rather of something horizontal, and Winandy also understands it in this way: "The horizontal part of the litter, that on which one lies, the 'châlit'" (Winandy [1965], p. 106). Robert-Tournay (1963), p. 151, think rather of a "canopy" above the "throne".

[58] For the 'silver-gold' association, cf. 1:11.

[59] But cf. Delitzsch (1875), p. 62: "It is that on which one sits or lies, the cushion". For Winandy (1965), p. 107, however, they are the poles for transporting the litter.

of gold. And it is understandable: in order to obtain a gram of purple, you had to have about eight hundred sea snails.[60]

> Because of the cost, material dyed with purple was reserved for special purposes, like statues of divinities (Jer 10:9), curtains and other objects of the sanctuary (Exod 26:1, 4, 31), priests' vestments (Exod 28, *passim*; Sir 45:10) and those of the king (Judg 8:26; Esth 8:15; 1 Macc 10:63, 64; 14:44).[61]

We are, therefore, with the same royal and sacral symbolism which characterises the rest of the passage.

"The interior adorned with the love of the daughters of Jerusalem". This phrase constitutes a famous *crux interpretum*.[62] In fact, after the list of materials from which the different parts of the litter are constructed (wood, silver, gold, purple), something of the same kind is expected here, another material. Instead, the text has an abstract substantive: 'love'. Various authors have thought of a scribal error and have proposed to replace *ʾahăbâ*, 'love', with *hobnîm* ('ebony', cf. Ezek 27:15),[63] or *šenhabbîm* ('ivory', cf. 1 Kgs 10:22),[64] or again *ʾăbānîm* ('[precious] stones').[65] Driver has proposed a second root for the Hebrew *ʾhb*, by analogy with Arabic, with the meaning of 'leather',[66] a proposal which has found a notable following,[67] but which has recently been reopened for discussion.[68] The MT is substantially confirmed by all the ancient versions.[69]

On the other hand, if we respect the Hebrew text, another difficulty arises. To speak of the "love of the daughters of Jerusalem" seems out of place, precisely in an *epithalamium*. Some commentators, therefore, place a point after 'love' and associate the 'daughters of Jerusalem'

---

[60] Ravasi (1992), pp. 325–326.

[61] Keel-Küchler-Uehlinger (1984), vol. I, p. 173.

[62] Cf. Barbiero (1995).

[63] In this sense, for example, Graetz (1871), pp. 102–103; Wittekindt (1925), p. 136; Ricciotti (1928), 231; *BJ*; Nolli (1967), p. 99; Colombo (1975), p. 73.

[64] Thus, for example, Krinetzki (1981), pp. 124–125.

[65] Cf., for example, Gerleman (1965), p. 139; Müller (1992), p. 37.

[66] Driver (1936), p. 111.

[67] Cf., among others, Gordis (1974), p. 85; Hirschberg (1961), pp. 373–374; *HALOT*, p. 18; Barr (1968), pp. 154–155; Grossberg (1981); Elliott (1989), p. 88.

[68] Cf. Rudolph (1962), p. 140; G. Wallis, *ʾāhab*, in *TDOT*, vol. I, p. 102.

[69] LXX, *entos autou lithostrōton, agapēn apo thygaterōn ierousalēm*; Syriac, *gwh rṣyp rḥmtʾ mn bntʾ wršlm*; Vg *media caritate constravit propter filias Hierusalem.*

with the following phrase.[70] For his part, Ravasi suggests understanding *ʾahăbâ* as an adverbial form ('with love') and joining the 'daughters of Jerusalem' to the verb 'to adorn', as complement of the agent ("the inside lovingly inlaid by the daughters of Jerusalem").[71] But this translation on the one hand breaks the parallelism with the preceding stichs where the substantive has the value of an 'accusative of material',[72] and on the other hand contradicts the declaration of v. 9 according to which Solomon himself is the maker of the litter. Moreover, the term 'love' in the Song never has a different sense from that of the love between man and woman; to intend it in an adverbial sense would be to trivialise it.[73]

My suggestion is to translate the MT just as it is and to try to understand it in its context. V. 10 begins with the word *tôkô* ('its interior'), which is clearly connected with the preceding discourse characterised by a process from outside to inside. This descriptive technique has been noticed with regard to the nuptial procession. The same goes for the litter: the attention is shifted from the litter viewed as a whole, to the external element of the pillars, then, proceeding towards the interior, it is held on the headboard, then on the seat. The substantive *tāwek* indicates on the one hand, the 'centre', on the other hand, the 'interior' of an object. Given the poetic language of the Song, it would not be a matter of wonder if the word 'interior' had a dual significance, that is, that the author alludes with it not only to the internal walls of the litter, or to its centre, but to its 'interior dimension'.

The participle *rāṣûp* ('adorned') is a further *hapax*. Generally, it is made to derive from a supposed root *rṣp* I ('to lay out, to make up'), above all in connection with the stones of a wall or the tiles of a pavement.[74]

---

[70] So, for example, Keel (1994), pp. 130, 135; Müller (1992), p. 37; Heinevetter (1988), p. 114; Murphy (1990), pp. 148, 150; Garbini (1992), p. 151; Colombo (1975), p. 73; Pope (1977), p. 413.

[71] Ravasi (1992), p. 327. To the authors cited by Ravasi should be added: Delitzsch (1875), p. 63; *HOTTP*, vol. III, pp. 603–604. There is a pertinent criticism of this interpretation in Rudolph (1962), p. 140.

[72] Cf. Joüon (1923), §125v.

[73] Keel (1994) p. 131, points out, among other things, the philological difficulty with this interpretation.

[74] Thus *HALOT*, pp. 1284–1285 (cf. in this sense LXX *lithostrōston*; Vg. *constravit*). *HOTTP*, vol III, p. 604, concludes: "It is impossible to determine the exact sense of the word *rāṣûp*, 'manufactured'". Garbini proposes a derivation from *rṣp* II, 'to illuminate' (cf. Sir 43:8), but he has to correct the MT (Garbini [1992], p. 213).

Table 20

9	litter →	wood of Lebanon
10a	pillars →	silver
10b	headboard →	Gold
10c	seat →	purple
10d	interior →	Love

We have reached the critical point of the stich: the term *ʾahăbâ* ('love'). Gradually, as the description of the components of the litter proceeds towards the interior, an increase in the value of the material used is noticeable. We could express this parallelism by means of a chart (cf. *Tab. 20*).

The word 'love' concludes a series of terms which denote the materials with which the litter is constructed: it is connected with the word 'interior' which, in its turn, closes the analogous series regarding the parts of the litter. In both cases, the concluding term effects a passage to another plane. The 'interior', we have said, alludes to a 'spiritual' plane. The term 'love' has an analogous value in the sense that what renders the litter precious is not its external magnificence, but something of the 'interior', precisely love.[75] Love is incomparably more valuable than any precious metal (cf. 8:7!).[76] We can understand, therefore, how the litter has been presented in v. 6 with theophanic traits. Love has in itself a divine element (8:6).[77]

On the other hand, by synecdoche, the abstract term also acquires a concrete value. That is, as elsewhere in the Song (cf. 7:7), with the term 'love', the person who is loved is indicated.[78] At the 'centre' of the

[75] A similar transition from a series of material objects to an object of a different kind is present in Rev 18:12–13. After having listed 27 precious commodities, which the merchants of the earth trade (the list makes one think of Song 3:10: cf. the terms: "cargoes of gold, of silver and of precious stones, of pearls, of linen, of purple"), the author passes, in the end, to 'wares' of another kind: [...] *kai sōmátōn kai psychás anthrōpōn*, "[...] and of human bodies and souls"). The last two items in the chain are linked by means of a conjunction to the long list of material goods. Here, at the end, is the point of the passage: they are trading with what is not negotiable! The placing of the term 'love' at the end of a series of precious materials has an analogous significance.

[76] In this sense, Elliott (1989), p. 88.

[77] To think, as does Keel (1994), p. 134, that with the word 'love' are indicated erotic scenes depicted on the inside of the litter, in line with Hellenistic fashion and according to a tradition transmitted in the Talmud concerning Jezebel (b.*San* 39b [ed. Epstein [Soncino], Nezikin V, p. 251]), seems to me foreign to the Song's conception of love.

[78] In this sense, Renan (1884), p. 160 ("Au centre brille une belle choisie entre les filles de Jérusalem"); Elliott (1989), p. 88 ("Here in 3,10d it would seem that *ʾahăbâ*

litter is the personification of love, the young bride: it is she who, with her love, adorns the litter of 'Solomon'. The question of v. 6a ("Who is this") receives its total significance from this identification.

What follows, however, becomes problematic: *mibbᵉnôt yᵉrûšālāim* ('of the daughters of Jerusalem').[79] Heinevetter notes: "Here there slips in a use of the litter which has little to do with the gravity of the king or with a marriage".[80] But this passage is not the only one to speak of the love of other women for Solomon (and *vice versa*). For the first sense, 1:2–4 is a good example. We have noted in the first strophe of the Prologue the passage from the singular of the woman to the plural of the 'maidens' ("Therefore the maidens love you", v. 3c; cf. 4e; "We shall rejoice and be glad for you [sg.]...", v. 4cd). The love of the other women is seen not as an addition to but as an amplification of the love of the one who alone enters into the chamber of the king (v. 4b). The love of Solomon for other women is spoken of in 6:8 ("Sixty are the queens, eighty the concubines and numberless the maidens"), but here too this happens in order to emphasise the uniqueness of the beloved one ("My dove is unique", v. 9). One has the impression that the 'daughters of Jerusalem' have the literary function of conferring 'choral' richness on the love of the two young people.[81] S. Paul has highlighted an analogous phenomenon in the Mesopotamian love songs.[82] If they do not wholly explain our text, these observations serve to show how little it should be considered an awkward gloss.

The 'daughters of Jerusalem' fit in with other expressions in the passage which underline the 'social' and 'national' character of love: 'mighty men of Israel' (v. 7c), 'daughters of Zion' (v. 11a). In the person of the bride (undoubtedly there is only one person in the litter), all the love of the 'daughters of Jerusalem' comes to Solomon. The young bride personifies not only the theological dimension of love, the

should be recognized as an example of the rhetorical figure 'synecdoche', where the most central, interior place stands for the person of the Beloved herself"). Garbini (1992), p. 213, thinks, however, that Love is personified in the bridegroom who is in love.

[79] The preposition *min* has the sense of indicating the source of love (cf. Joüon [1923], §133e). Perhaps it could also be understood in a causal sense ('because of the daughters'). In this sense, Solomon would be not the object but the subject of love.

[80] Heinevetter (1988), p. 113, recognises in vv. 9–10 a second redaction of the Song, which is critical with regard to 'Solomon'. He distinguishes this redaction from the pro-Solomonic original, found in vv. 6–8*.

[81] In this sense also Ogden (1990), pp. 223–225.

[82] Paul (1995).

'flame of YHWH', but also its social dimension. It is the expression of the people of Israel.[83]

Fourth Strophe: The Day of Joy of the Heart (3:11)

Up to now the centre of attention has been occupied by the woman. The arch extending from v. 6a ("Who is this?") is completed at v. 10de ("The interior adorned with the love of the daughters of Jerusalem", where the word 'love' is, as has been seen, a reference to the woman). It is she who arrives at Jerusalem in the litter. It is surprising, therefore, that, in the last strophe, the 'daughters of Zion' are called on to admire not her but 'King Solomon'. Keel[84] and Krinetzki[85] opt to consider v. 11 as an independent song. We consider vv. 6–11 as a unitary composition. In this hypothesis, how do we explain the change of perspective?

Despite the fact that up to now attention has been concentrated on the woman, the reference to Solomon does not come without preparation. It characterises the beginning not only of the fourth strophe (v. 11b) but also of the two preceding ones (cf. vv. 7a, 9a). The litter which bears the beloved is that of Solomon (v. 7) and the escort which protects her is his bodyguard. The king has personally constructed this work of art (vv. 9–10).

The summons of v. 11ab supposes that he is coming from outside together with the litter. He must, therefore, be part of the procession[86] although it is only at the end that the attention is fixed on him. Analogously in 8:5, the question of the chorus concerns the woman ("Who is this that rises from the desert", cf. 3:6a), even if it is two who are rising ("Leaning upon her beloved").

---

[83] Therefore a polemic note can be detected: not with regard to Solomon (*contra* Heinevetter [1988], p. 113), but with regard to the way of conceiving love in the Hellenistic world, to which is opposed the love to be found within the people of God. On the other hand, such an interpretation leads to the exclusion of the bride as a foreign beauty (the daughter of Pharaoh or an Oriental princess, cf., *supra*, notes 21, 22): the bride comes from the desert, but she also comes from Lebanon (4:8). 'Desert' and 'Lebanon' are regions of the land of Israel, 'our land' (2:12).

[84] Keel (1994), pp. 135–137.

[85] Krinetzki (1981), pp. 127–132.

[86] According to ancient Jewish tradition, the bridegroom actually goes to take his bride together with the 'friends of the wedding', and with them accompanies the litter (where the bride is) from the house of the bride to his own house. Cf. S-B, vol. I, p. 505.

Table 21

a (v. 6)	the bride
b (vv. 7–8)	the litter (outside)
b' (vv. 9–10)	the litter (inside)
a' (v. 11)	the bridegroom

From a structural point of view (cf. *Tab. 21*), the mention of Solomon in the last strophe with everything in the masculine (*lô;ʾimmô*, 11c; *ḥătunnātô*, 11d; *libbô*, 11e) balances that of the woman in the first strophe, all of it in the feminine (*zoʾt ʿolâ*, v. 6a; *m^equṭṭeret*, v. 6c).

In terms of the macrostructure, the centrality of the bridegroom at the end of the composition prepares for the following unit which is characterised by two songs of the man. It is he, in particular, who in 4:1 intones the praise of the woman.

[v. 11] The expression 'daughters of Zion' is a synonym of the more common 'daughters of Jerusalem', with which the preceding strophe ends (v. 10e). Why has the author chosen to change the expression (this single time)? Perhaps to avoid a repetition that might not be held to be euphonious. Perhaps also because, in the two cases, the role of the group is different: the 'daughters of Jerusalem' (v. 10e) are agents (personified in the woman), the 'daughters of Zion' (v. 11a) are spectators. Even in the OT the expression is rare. It returns uniquely in Isa 3–4[87] in the context of the prophetic denunciation of the luxury of Jerusalem (cf. Isa 3:16, 17). The contrast between the two passages is significant. The refined elegance of the women of Jerusalem is seen by the prophet as a sign of pride and vanity. In the Song there is no trace of disapproval: female charm and beauty are viewed with admiration. The jewels and most precious metals are not looked on as a waste; they are the sign of the precious nature of love.

Thus, between the first and the last strophe of the song, a passage from the 'desert' (v. 6a) to the 'city' ('Zion', v. 11a), a central theme in the Song, is outlined. Love does not come from the city; it is not a creation of social conventions. It comes from nature in the wild, from 'the desert'. What was evoked by the lexeme *śādeh* ('country') in 2:7 and 3:5 is here expressed by the word *midbār* ('desert'). The same concept is taken up again in 4:8 where the woman comes "from the

[87] Precisely in Isa 3:16, 17; 4:4.

lairs of the lions, from the mountains of the panthers". Love, therefore, comes from the desert, but goes towards the city. The desert is not only positive, it is the place of solitude and of primitive forces (wild animals) which can also lead to destruction. There is need of the city. Love seeks to be lived in the environment of society, exactly as happens in marriage. Society has the job of protecting love (the sixty mighty men, vv. 7–8), but also of rejoicing, of making a feast for it. This last function is not insignificant as is proved by the gospel passage of Matt 22:1–10.[88] If the 'refrain of awakening' emphasises the negative function of the 'city' ("Daughters of Jerusalem, [...] do not rouse, do not waken love until it is ready!", Song 2:7; 3:5), Song 3:11 shows its positive function. As in the case of the 'mighty men of Israel', also in the case of the 'daughters of Zion' an affirmation of national awareness is to be noticed. 'Zion' is not any city whatsoever. It is the city of God, the holy city.

The participation of the daughters of Jerusalem is expressed by means of two verbs: 'to go out' (*yāṣāʾ*) and 'to see' (*rāʾāh*). In the Song's play of subtle references, the first verb echoes the summons to 'come out' addressed to the woman by the chorus in 1:8. But the whole of the song of the spring is an invitation to 'come out' (cf. 2:10, 14). Here too the second verb, 'to see', has appeared (2:12, 14). The woman was invited to 'appear', like the flowers and the doves. Like the woman, so too the daughters of Zion are invited to share in the feast of love, to 'come out' from the enclosure of their houses and 'to see' the bridegroom. Unlike the watchmen: they were not able 'to have seen' love (3:3).

With others before and after him, Colombo refers v. 11bc to a supposed coronation of Solomon by Bathsheba.[89] However, it does not say in 1 Kgs 1:11–40 that Solomon received the royal crown from his mother nor that the day of his coronation was that of his marriage.

---

[88] S-B, vol. I, p. 505, thus depict Jewish custom according to the rabbinic sources: "The inhabitants of the place run in crowds to demonstrate their attention to the spouses. At the roll of the nuptial drum, even the old woman hurries. To accompany a bride was held, in fact, to be a highly meritorious work. The rabbis themselves interrupted their study of the Torah to show their appreciation of the bride...". Cf. the copious rabbinic literature on the topic, *ibid.*, pp. 510–514.

[89] Colombo (1975), p. 74; cf. *id.* (1985), p. 83. In this sense also, Ricciotti (1928), p. 226; Ravasi (1992), p. 330; Stadelmann (1992), pp. 106–108 (who gives the whole passage 3:9–11 a political interpretation, as a vindication of the national monarchy at the time of the Persian domination).

Moreover, the Hebrew *ʿăṭārâ* is not the usual word to indicate the royal crown (for which the terms *nezer*[90] or *keter*[91] are used), but has a more generic significance. It is logical, therefore, to think rather of the 'nuptial crown' in use in Israel until AD 70, then discontinued as a sign of mourning.[92] This custom has been preserved in the Byzantine liturgy.[93] On the other hand, it goes well with that high burlesque which characterises the whole passage. According to the *Pirqê de-Rabbi Eliʿezer*, "the bridegroom is a king".[94]

Although we have side-stepped the 'historical' interpretation, the coronation of the bridegroom on the part of his mother remains problematic. It does not have an institutional parallel, not even in Jewish traditions. Perhaps Krinetzki is right in having recourse to depth psychology. The mother is every man's first love, the personification of the 'great feminine' to which every man, in his quest for his personal integration, is attracted. In marriage, the mother cedes this role to the bride. For this reason it must be she who is to crown her son as bridegroom.[95] Moreover, the mother is the personification of the family. In 3:4, the bride wishes to lead her spouse into the 'house of her mother', into her own family. Here, through that 'mirroring effect' which is typical of the Song, the bride 'enters the house of the mother' of the man. The father has no role in the Song: the mother is the representative of the family.[96]

Lys considers the possibility that the 'crown' is a metaphor for the bride,[97] a possibility which is accentuated if the *b*ᵉ before *ʿăṭārâ* is understood not with modal significance ("with the crown") but as

[90] Cf. 1 Sam 1:10; 2 Kgs 11:12.

[91] Cf. Esth 1:11; 2:17 (for the queen).

[92] Cf. b.*Sot* 49a (ed. Epstein [1935–1948], Nashim VI, p. 265); S–B., vol. I, pp. 505, 507–509; Hirt (1748), pp. 10–12.

[93] Cf. Ravasi (1992), pp. 330, 335.

[94] *ḥāᵃtān dômeh lᵉmelek*, *PRE* 16. Perhaps a link with the metaphor of conquest evoked in 2:4 is possible. The crown would be, like the 'banner', the sign of the conquest of the 'city' at the hands of the 'king'. In this sense, Krinetzki (1981), p. 132.

[95] Krinetzki (1981), p. 131. This interpretation is near to the mythical one, which recalls the role of Ishtar in the hymns to Dumuzi. She is at the same time mother and sister/bride of the shepherd, who is raised by her to be a god. Cf. Schmökel (1956), pp. 93–94; Wittekindt (1925), pp. 146–147. Perhaps the myth is an expression of that same archetype of the human mind which is studied by the psycho-analysts.

[96] Cf., *supra*, the comment to 3:4.

[97] Lys (1968), p. 163.

a kind of *signum accusativi*[98] in parallelism with *bammelek*.[99] Actually, *ʿăṭārâ* has a metaphorical significance in Prov 12:4 (the perfect woman); Isa 28:5 (YHWH) and Isa 62:3 (Jerusalem). The last correspondence is particularly significant. Inasmuch as she is the bride of God (vv. 4–5), "Jerusalem will be a 'crown of magnificence' (*ʿăṭeret tipʾeret*) in the hand of YHWH, a royal diadem in the hand of her God". If the identification of the 'crown' with the bride is plausible, the daughters of Jerusalem are being invited to contemplate not only Solomon but also his bride. Thus the theme of the *waṣf* of Song 4:1–7 is introduced. Also the link between v. 11 and vv. 6–10 is clearer. The mother crowns Solomon with that crown which is the bride herself: she is the splendour, the glory, the honour of Solomon. By giving herself to him, she makes him truly 'king'.[100]

"On the day of his wedding". The temporal indication 'day', repeated twice (vv. 11d and 11e), is to be noted first of all. It forms a contrast with the 'terror of the night' of v. 8, parallel to the spatial contrast of desert-city. The dark time of night, evocative of dangers and misfortunes, is replaced by the luminous time of day, the time of the wedding, where love is lived 'in the light of day', before the whole city in celebration.[101]

The word *ḥătunnâ* is a *hapax* in the OT. It derives from the term *ḥātān* which fundamentally expresses the link between two families by means of marriage: it can, therefore, designate equally the 'bridegroom', the 'father-in-law' or the 'son-in law'.[102] Here it is clear that *ḥătunnâ* indicates the 'wedding'. It is above all the institutional aspect of love which is being presented, an aspect which is not typical of the Song, but which is certainly not ignored by it, in its positive and negative aspects.

The day of his wedding is qualified as "the day of the joy of his heart". The expression is well-known in Egyptian love lyrics, where

---

[98] *rāʾāh bᵉ* denotes a "seeing with intensity or pleasure" (cf. Joüon [1923], §133c).

[99] In this sense, cf. Graetz (1871), p. 153; Chouraqui (1970), p. 56; Pope (1977), p. 413.

[100] Cf. the 'coronation' formulae of the Byzantine liturgy: "For the groom: 'The servant of God N. receives as a crown the handmaid of God N. […]'. For the bride: 'The handmaid of God N. receives as a crown the servant of God N.'" (quotation according to Ravasi [1992], p. 335).

[101] We should note the temporal coherence with the preceding song, set 'at night' (*ballêlôt*, 3:1, 8).

[102] Cf. E. Kutsch, *ḥātān*, in *TDOT*, vol. V, pp. 270–277.

Papyrus Chester Beatty IA bears the title: "Beginning of the words of the great joy of the heart" (1:1).[103] With this phrase the internal side of the feast is expressed. There is a correspondence between the 'interior' of the litter (*tôkô*, v. 10d) and the 'heart' of Solomon (*libbô*, v. 11e). The heart in the OT is not so much the seat of the affections: it expresses rather the interiority of a person in its rational, volitive and affective components.[104] Just as the interior of the litter is love, so the interior, the heart, of the feast is joy. The institutional aspect is aimed at 'joy of the heart', and joy is inseparable from love.[105]

The song finishes with this final chord. The journey which it describes is not only physical. It is the passage from the 'desert' (v. 6a) to the 'city' (v.11a, 'Zion'), from 'night' (v. 8d) to 'day' (v. 11de), from 'terror' (v. 8d) to the 'joy of the heart' (v. 11e).

Conclusion

The analysis has allowed us to discern the unity of the pericope 3:6–11. It is concerned solely with a single procession. The passage is a lyrical description of the nuptial procession which is a typical element in Jewish weddings. The author utilises the royal burlesque, here again taking up a theme introduced in the Prologue (cf. 1:1–4, 9–12). Within the royal litter comes the bride, escorted by sixty warriors of "Solomon", the bridegroom.

The opening strophe (v. 6) describes the appearance of the festive procession in the desert. The situation has a symbolic value. Negatively, the desert is the place of death and dangers, and it is to this that the presence of the armed escort alludes. Positively, it is the habitat of the uncorrupted forces of life and love. In the context of the OT, the procession in the desert cannot be other than an evocation of the Exodus journey, centred on the Ark of the Covenant. The 'apparition', therefore, is clothed in a numinous, theophanic aura, emphasised by the accompanying clouds of incense.

---

[103] Cf. Bresciani (1990), p. 453.

[104] Cf. H.-J. Fabry, *lēb*, in *TDOT*, vol. VII, pp. 399–437.

[105] Note that the Egyptian love lyrics are not bound to the celebrations of marriage. Like the Song, with whom they display a notable affinity, they sing of love, not of marriage.

The detailed description of the escort (vv. 7–8) provides a contrast to the presence of the "watchmen" in the previous passage. It is a way of pointing out the positive function which the society of the people of God ("the mighty men of Israel") has in the protection of love. In fact, love has to confront the "terror of the night": the spouses are not alone; the warriors of Israel are at their side.

The reason for investing the litter with a numinous character is explained in the third strophe (vv. 9–10): it is, in essence, love which is present in the person of the bride. Love is the centre and heart of the wedding festivities. All the rest is choreography. As in a film sequence, the author passes from the panoramic shot of the first strophe to the detail of the third. Among the precious materials of which the litter is fashioned, the most precious is the one which lies within: love.

The final verse (v. 11) pictures the bridegroom, Solomon, beside the bride. It is he whom the "daughters of Jerusalem", the representatives of the city, are summoned to admire. Now they are understood no longer as the enemies but as the allies of love. Love is born in the desert, but it does not remain there. It heads for the city and has need of it with its dual value, positive and negative. Alongside the daughters of Jerusalem, society is personified by the mother of the bridegroom. She is the positive representative of the family just as the brothers (1:6) were its negative side. The passage is thus shown to be a kind of epithalamium which celebrates the social, that is nuptial, dimension of love.

CHAPTER SIX

SONGS OF THE BELOVED MAN

(Song 4:1–5:1)

Contemplation

I

Man 4[1]"How fair you are, my friend,
how fair!

Your eyes are doves
behind your veil.[1]
Your hair, like a flock of goats
gambolling down from the mountains of Gilead.
[2]Your teeth, like a flock of ewes coming out of their bath,
ready for the shearing,[2]
all of them the mothers of twins;
none has lost her young.

II

[3]Like scarlet thread, your lips
and your speech[3] beautiful.
Like the split in the pomegranate, your cheek[4]
behind your veil.

---

[1] LXX: *ektos tēs siōpēseōs sou*, 'outside your silence' (similarly the Syriac *lbr mn štqky*, and Vetus Latina *praeter taciturnitatem tuam*) and Vg *absque eo quod intrinsecus latet* have misunderstood the Hebrew *ṣammâ*, which undoubtedly indicates the 'veil'.

[2] MT *haqqᵉṣûbôt* strictly means 'shorn' (thus LXX, the Syriac and Vg with the *RSV* and *NJB*). But the context requires the reading 'to be shorn'. In fact, the allusion is to the bath of the sheep before shearing.

[3] With the versions. MT *midbār* is a *hapax*.

[4] With LXX and Vg: MT has: 'your temple', *viz.* of the head.

[4]Like the tower of David, your neck,
fortified with bulwarks:[5]
a thousand shields are hung there,
all the quivers[6] of the mighty men.

III

[5]Your two breasts, like two fawns,
twins of a gazelle,
which graze among the lotus flowers.
[6]When the day sighs
and the shadows lengthen,
I will leave for the mountain of myrrh
and for the hill of incense.

[7]You are all fair, my friend;
in you there is no blemish!"

Encounter

I

Man [8]"With me[7] from Lebanon, my bride,
with me from Lebanon, come.
Look[8] from the summit of Amana,
from the peak of Senir and of Hermon,
from the lairs of the lions,
from the mountains of the panthers!

---

[5] With the versions of Aquila, the Syriac and Vg. MT *lᵉtalpîyôt* is a *hapax* which has not yet found a satisfactory explanation.

[6] The meaning of MT *šeleṭ* is disputed. LXX has: *bolides* ('darts'); Vg *armatura*; the Syriac *šlṭ* is not clear. The translation *quivers* leans above all on Jer 51:11, on the Akkadian *šalṭu* ('holder [in leather] for bow and arrows'), and on 1QM 6:2.

[7] With MT. LXX, the Syriac and Vg have: 'Come'.

[8] MT *tāšûrî* can derive both from *šwr* I ('to stoop down to look'), and from *šwr* II, 'to descend'. LXX and the Syriac seem to support the second translation, but the context speaks in favour of *šwr* I.

9You have driven me mad, my sister, my bride,
you have driven me mad with one of your glances,
with one pearl of your necklaces.

II

10How sweet are your caresses,[9] my sister, my bride,
how sweet are your caresses, sweeter than wine!
And the scent of your perfumes
sweeter than any balm.

11Your lips run with flowing honey, my bride,
honey and milk under your tongue,
and the scent of your garments
is like the scent of Lebanon.

III

12Garden enclosed, my sister, my bride,
stopped fountain,[10] sealed spring!

13Your shoots, a paradise of pomegranates
with delicious fruits,
henna shrubs with clusters of nard;
14nard and turmeric,[11]
fragrant calamus and cinnamon
with every tree of incense,
myrrh and aloes,
with all the most precious balms.

[9] With MT *dōdayik*. LXX, Vg and the Syriac have read *daddayik*, 'your breasts' (cf. 1:2).

[10] With MT *gal*. LXX *kēpos*, Vg *hortus* and the Syriac *gnt'* suppose the reading *gan*, 'garden'.

[11] The Hebrew term *karkōm*, a *hapaxlegomenon*, can indicate both the turmeric, or yellow root, and the crocus or saffron.

[15]Spring of the gardens,[12]
well of living water,
springing up from Lebanon."

IV

Woman [16]"Awake, North wind,
and you, South wind, come!
Make my garden breathe:
let its balms spread.
Let my beloved come into his garden
and taste its delicious fruits".

Man 5[1]"I have come into my garden, my sister, my bride.
I have gathered my myrrh with my balm.
I have eaten my honeycomb with my honey.
I have drunk my wine with my milk".

Poet "Eat, my friends,
drink, get drunk, my dears!"

Structure

The two *Songs of the Beloved Man* (4:1–7 and 4:8–5:1) correspond chiastically to the two *Songs of the Beloved Woman* (2:8–17 and 3:1–5). The span between separation and union, opened up in 2:8, is closed in 5:1, a firm point in the structure of the Song, after the unions, partial or dreamed, which have marked the conclusion of the *Songs of the Beloved Woman* in 2:17 and 3:5. With 5:2 there begins a new movement from separation to union.

The first song (4:1–7) is clearly marked out both by its literary genre (*waṣf* or description of the body), and by the *inclusio* between 4:1 ("How fair you are, my friend") and 4:7 ("You are all fair, my friend"). This is not the case for 4:8–5:1—Colombo, for example, sees here three

[12] With MT, the Syriac, Vg and some LXX mss.; LXX[B] has the singular *kēpou*, together with the Ethiopian and Armenian versions.

songs 4:7 (!)-11; 4:12–16 and 5:1.[13] In favour of the unity of this composition there speaks, among other things, the *inclusio* effected by the verb 'to come' (*bôʾ*) between 4:8 and 5:1. It is the *leitmotiv* of the song. The theme has been introduced at the end of the preceding song, in 4:6, where the man expresses the desire to 'go' (*hālak*) to the woman. At the beginning of the new song, in 4:8, he invites the woman to 'come' to him. The woman replies, at the end of Chapter 4, in her turn inviting her beloved to 'come' into her 'garden' (*bôʾ*). In 5:1, the man joyously welcomes the woman's invitation: 'I have come'. The song describes the progressive 'coming nearer' of the two lovers until concluding in their union which is described metaphorically in 5:1.

We can characterise the relationship between the two poems as the passage from 'contemplation' of the loved one (4:1–7) to the enjoyment of her in the acts of love (4:8–5:1). Beside the verb 'to come', other subtle links unite the two songs: one notices, for example, the words 'eyes', vv. 1c and 9b; 'lips', v. 3a and 11a; 'pomegranate', vv. 3c and 13a; 'incense' and 'myrrh', vv. 6cd and 14cd; 'mountains', vv. 6c and 8f. The *waṣf* concludes with the metaphor of the 'mountains'; it is with this same metaphor that the next song begins (v. 8).[14] Also, the *motiv* of the 'wind', introduced at the end of the *waṣf* ("When the day sighs…", v. 6), is taken up again at the end of the second song ("Awake, North wind, and you, South wind, come! Make…breathe", v. 16).

On the other hand, the two *Songs of the Beloved Man* are closely joined to what precedes them. We should observe the correspondence between 4:6 and 2:16–17, that is, between the conclusion of the first *Song of the Beloved Woman* (2:8–17) and the first *Song of the Beloved Man* (4:1–7).[15] More evident are the links with the *Choral*

[13] Colombo (1975), pp. 75, 88 (cf. *Id.* [1985], p. 83). Colombo is not alone in thinking this way. Keel (1994), pp. 154–184, for example, divides: 4:8; 4:9–11; 4:12–5:1; so too Müller (1992), pp. 45–53, and Gerleman (1965), pp. 151–162, roughly following the formal classification of Horst, who sees in 4:8–5:1 the following elementary forms of amorous lyricism: "Sehnsuchtslied" (4:8); "Bewunderungslied" (4:9–11); "Vergleichslied" (4:12–15); "Allegorienlied" (4:16–5:1) (Horst [1981], 176–187). For his part, Krinetzki (1981), pp. 138–158, recognises six independent poems in our passage: 4:8–9, 10–11, 12, 13–15; 4:16–5:1d; 5ef.

[14] The beginning of the *Intermezzo*: "Who is this that rises?" (Song 3:6) also agrees with the metaphor of the 'mountain'. Cf. Lombard (1992), p. 46.

[15] Cf., *supra*, p. 100. Heinevetter (1988), p. 134, notes moreover the repetition of *marʾêk nāʾweh*, "your face is lovely" (2:14) in *midbārêk nāʾweh*, "your speech is beautiful/lovely" (4:3).

Intermezzo (3:6–11), so much so that many authors join 3:6–5:1 in a unitary composition.[16] Given the difference in the subject speaking, we have preferred to distinguish 3:6–11, declaimed by the 'chorus', from 4:1–5:1, spoken mostly by the beloved man. But the connection is undeniable. The *Choral Intermezzo*, in fact, presents the two protagonists of the *waṣf*: the woman (3:6), whose beauty is described, and 'Solomon' (3:11), who sings her praise. The journey has led the two of them together: now 'contemplation' is possible. Moreover, 3:6–11 has the nuptial background in common with 4:1–5:1. The *waṣf* (4:1–7) is a literary genre typical of wedding ceremonies; the 'veil' too (vv. 1d, 3d) forms part of the adornment of the 'bride' (*kallâ*). The woman is called 'bride' in 4:8a, 9a, 10a, 11a, 12a; 5:1a. Beyond these macroscopic signals, there are precise lexical links: the words 'myrrh and incense' (3:6; cf. 4:6), 'mighty men' (3:7; cf. 4:4), 'Lebanon' (3:9; cf. 4:8, 11, 15), the adverb *hinnēh* ('look', 3:7; cf. 4:1). The lexeme *lēb* ('heart', 3:11e) is repeated in the verb *libbabtînî* ("you have driven me mad", literally: "You have made my heart weaken", 4:9ab) and forms a paronomasia with the two terms *lᵉbônâ* ('incense') and *lᵉbānôn* ('Lebanon'). From the metaphorical point of view, the 'garden', well watered (4:12–15), is opposed to the 'desert' from which the woman originates (3:6), and the clouds of perfume which accompany the litter (3:6) are evoked again in the scents emanating from the garden under the action of the wind (4:16).[17] From the temporal point of view, there is a coherence between the indication given in 3:6 ('day') and that of 4:6 ('evening'). The 'day' is the public moment of the feast; the 'evening' is the time of the intimacy of the two lovers.

Contemplation (4:1–7)

The composition 4:1–7 belongs to a well known literary genre, which, by analogy with Arab literature, is called *waṣf*. In the Song, 5:10–16; 6:4–7 and 7:2–10 also belong to this genre. We have noticed its place

[16] For example: Rendtorff (1985), p. 263; Elliott (1989), p. 83; Exum (1973), pp. 61–65; Dorsey (1990), pp. 86–87; Bosshard-Nepustil (1996), p. 50; Lombard (1992). By contrast, the statement of Murphy (1990), p. 158, is singular: "A new section begins in 4:1, which has no connection with the preceding passage".

[17] Cf. Lombard (1992), pp. 46–47.

in the nuptial ceremonies of the Syrian peasants.[18] But its use is not restricted to this context. Dalman reports some 'descriptions of the body' in the Palestinian world which are not in a nuptial context;[19] this is the case too in the ancient Arab literature.[20] In the Egyptian love songs, the description of the beloved, whether masculine or, above all, feminine, is widespread: here too, outside the nuptial context.[21] Even the two most ancient examples which come from Jewish literature do not have a *Sitz im Leben* that is directly nuptial.[22] In our case, however, such a context is suggested both by the song which precedes and that which follows. Moreover, the role of the 'veil' (vv. 1d and 3d) is stressed in it, and the significance of this will be discussed further.[23] But the title ('Contemplation') intends to leave the institutional side implicit just as the appellation 'my friend' (vv. 1, 7) invites us to do. The contemplation of the woman here is not conventional: it proceeds from the heart (3:11).

---

[18] Cf., *supra*, p. 13.

[19] Cf. Dalman (1901), p. 100.

[20] Among other things, the *waṣf* forms part of the *nasîd*, in which the poet laments the loss of his beloved, recalling her beauty. Cf. Gerleman (1965), p. 146.

[21] Cf., for example, the Papyrus Chester Beatty IA 1:1–8: "She whose excellence shines, whose body glistens, / glorious her eyes when she stares, /sweet her lips when she converses, / she says not a word too much. / High her neck and glistening her nipples, / of true lapis her hair, / her arms finer than gold, / her fingers like lotus flowers unfolding. / Her buttocks droop when her waist is girt, / her legs reveal her perfection; / her steps are pleasing when she walks the earth, / she takes my heart in her embrace" (tr. Simpson, in Pope [1977], p. 74); cf. also 3:10–4:1; and Papyrus Harris 500A 1:10–11. For the literary genre of the description of the beloved woman in Egyptian love poetry, cf. Mathieu (1996), pp. 187–188.

[22] We have here the description of Sarah's beauty made to Pharaoh (1QapGen 20:2–8, cf. García Martínez [1994], p. 233), and that of Aseneth before her marriage to Joseph. Aseneth sees her face reflected in the basin where she is washing: "She saw her face in the water, and it was like the sun, / and her eyes [were] like a rising morning star, / and her cheeks like fields of the Most High, / and on her cheeks [there was] red [color] like a son of man's blood, / and her lips [were] like a rose of life coming out of its foliage, / and its teeth like fighting men lined up for a fight, / and the hair of her head [was] like a vine in the paradise of God, / prospering in its fruits, / and her neck like an all-variegated cypress, / and her breasts [were] like the mountains of the Most High God" (18:9–10, *OTP* II, p. 232).

[23] The separating of the *waṣf* from a directly nuptial context and the making of it into 'love poetry' is not the same thing as making it into a piece of eroticism or pornography. We distance ourselves decidedly from interpretations of the type of Boer (2000). The Song is a sacred book, recognised as normative by the Jewish people and by the Church! Moreover, pornography has no place even in the Egyptian love songs. Cf. Mathieu (1996), p. 174.

Table 22

Frame (v. 1ab)	Admiration	*How fair you are, my friend*
I Strophe (vv. 1c–2)	1. Eyes → Doves 2. Hair → Goats	*... behind your veil*
	3. Teeth → Sheep	
II Strophe (vv. 3–4)	4. Thread of scarlet → Lips 5. Pomegranates → Cheeks	*... behind your veil*
	6. Tower of David → Neck	
III Strophe (vv. 5–6)	7. Breasts → Fawns	
	Desire to climb on 'the mountain'	
Frame (v. 7)	Admiration	*You are all fair, my friend*

The song is bounded by the *inclusio* between v. 1ab and v. 7 (*Tab. 22*). Within this frame are listed seven parts of the woman's body, a number which is certainly not accidental.[24] According to a scheme already recognisable in the Egyptian love songs, the description goes from high to low (so too 5:10–16 and 6:5–7; 7:2–9 is an exception). The dominant dimension is that of verticality, clinched, in the conclusion, with the image of the 'mountain' and the 'hill' (4:6; cf. 5:15b and 7:8–9).

The first strophe (vv. 1c–2) describes three parts of the body: eyes (v. 1cd), hair (v. 1ef) and teeth (v. 2). Each time, the part of the body is named first, then the corresponding term of comparison (doves, goats, sheep), followed by a short description the first two times (vv. 1d, 1f), and by a longer one the third time (v. 2bcd). The strophe shows, therefore, a bipartite structure—v. 1cdef and v. 2—which we shall find again in the succeeding strophes.

In parallel with the first, the second strophe (vv. 3–4) describes three other elements of the body: lips (v. 3ab), cheeks (v. 3cd) and neck (v. 4). As in the first strophe, here too the parts are described by a metaphor which, at the end, with the neck, assumes an autonomous development (v. 4). We should note the inversion compared with the first

[24] Egyptian love poetry also has a preference for the number seven. In it, the metre is the 'heptametric distich', consisting of one stich of four stresses, accompanied by one of three; furthermore, the majority of the compositions have seven 'stanzas'. Cf. Mathieu (1996), p. 215.

strophe: here, three times, the metaphor comes first, then the parts of the body. The repetition of the expression 'behind your veil' (v. 3d; cf. v. 1d) is not a late gloss,[25] but forms an *inclusio* which marks off exactly the parts of the face and separates v. 3 from v. 4 within the stophe.

The third strophe (vv. 5–6) consists solely of the description of the breasts (v. 5). Here the order is the same as in the first strophe: first the part of the body is named; then comes the metaphor. The description closes here: what follows (v. 6) expresses the desire to enjoy this body which till now has been admired, a theme which will be developed in the following song. On the one hand, the passage from the 'breasts' (v. 5) to the 'mountains' and 'hills' (v. 6) is coherent; on the other hand, the mention of the breasts is already an allusion to sexual intimacy and erotic play ("I will leave for the mountain of myrrh…").[26] Furthermore, with the breasts, the parts described reach seven, a number indicating fullness. In them, therefore, is described the *whole* person of the woman, as is expressed in the final refrain (here too, v. 7!): "You are *all* fair".[27]

The language of 4:1–7 is at first wholly strange to our poetic taste. In the *waṣfs* of the Song, F. Black has proposed to see an example of poetry of the 'grotesque' along the lines of certain pictures by Arcimboldo or the artists of the Flemish school, Bruegel and Bosch.[28] Perhaps the difficulty in grasping the poetry of the *waṣf* is due to the fact that we are used to understanding metaphors from the 'visual' point of view while they should be read, above all, in their 'dynamic' aspect.[29] This consideration has been made above with regard to 1:15, a verse which is taken up literally in 4:1—"your eyes are doves".[30] The *tertium comparationis* in this case is not the form of the eyes but their "sending

[25] *Contra* Müller (1992), p. 41, who eliminates the expression in v. 1 (following Siegfried, Haupt, Zapletal, Staerck, Wittekindt, Schmökel, Haller etc.).

[26] Also in the above cited *waṣf* of *Joseph and Aseneth* the description stops at the breasts (cf., *supra*, n. 22). In Song 6:4–7 the description takes in only the head, while in 7:2–9 it regards the whole body.

[27] If one observes the refined structure of the composition 4:1–7, where each word and each syllable is in the right place, as is appropriate in poetic language, one cannot but be reluctant in the face of proposals which remove a verse from the ensemble (as with Müller, cf. n. 25), or to insert there whole verses taken from other parts of the Song (as does Garbini who inserts two verses taken from the *waṣf* of Chapter 6, vv. 4–5a, between v. 1d and 1e, cf. Garbini [1992], pp. 216–217). Again, Garbini claims v. 3cd to be out of place and puts it after v. 5 (*ibid.*, p. 222).

[28] Black (2000).

[29] Cf., *supra*, p. 12.

[30] Cf. pp. 78–79.

messages of love". This meaning is confirmed by 4:9 where the Hebrew term *'ênayim* clearly has the sense of 'glances', not of 'eyes'. That is, it is not only or even mostly the exterior aspect of the things that the author wishes to place in comparison but their 'interior' aspect, their soul. Like doves, so goats, sheep, pomegranates were considered bearers of magical forces connected with the mystery of life. It is this vital force which is the term of comparison. The surrounding civilisations expressed the interpenetration between the forces of nature and the human person by means of myth. A trace of this mythical conception is perceptible in the Song, integrated naturally into the Yahwistic religion.[31] Moreover, the love lyric has always sung of the osmosis between human love and nature.[32] The Mexican poet Octavio Paz says to his beloved: "Voy por tu cuerpo como por el mundo".[33] And Nizar Qabbani, a modern Syrian poet says:

> I love you in October in the adolescence of the vineyards,
> in the throbbing of the vines and the gardens.
> I sense in you the scent of the meadows.
> In your tresses the sigh of the flocks.
> When I embrace you, I embrace the fields,
> and Spring kisses me on the lips.[34]

Through the experience of love, man enters into contact with the forces of life, with the 'soul' of the world.

First strophe: Black and white (4:1–2)

4:1abc is a literal repeat of 1:15, for the comment on which, see above. The phenomenon of repetition is typical of the Song (think of the different refrains!), as of Egyptian love poetry.[35] But this is never a slavish process: subtle variations show that each time the repetition is adapted to the new context. In 1:15, for example, v. 15b ("Your eyes are doves") is linked structurally with v. 15a, while 4:1c is separated from 4:1ab and joined with the following parts of the body with which it forms the first strophe.

---

[31] Cf., *supra*, pp. 10–11.
[32] Cf. Müller (1976).
[33] Paz, *Piedra del sol*, in Paz (2001), vol. I, p. 218.
[34] Citation in Robert – Tournay (1963), p. 400.
[35] Cf. Mathieu (1996), pp. 176–180, §§63–66.

[4:1] The phrase 'behind your veil' (v. 1d) is singular. The Hebrew *ṣammâ* is quite rare in the OT (again only in 4:3; 6:7, and Isa 47:2) which explains the lack of understanding in the ancient versions, but the translation 'veil (for the face)' is not disputed today.[36] Beside this term, the synonym *ṣāʿîp* (Gen 24:65; 38:14, 19) is also used in the OT. The significance of the veil in Song 4:1 is different from that of 1:7c where it was the distinctive note of the prostitute. In our case, the veil is the sign of the bride (cf. Gen 24:65). According to the Jewish tradition, the bride was veiled, as a result of which we can understand the switch between Leah and Rachel made by Jacob (Gen 29:21–25).[37] In Mesopotamia too the veil marks out the bride. The word itself designates the bride: the Akkadian *kallātu* (in Hebrew *kallâ*) is connected etymologically with the verb *kullulu* ('to veil') and is synonymous with *pussumtu* ('veiled').[38] The veil was the symbol of the chastity of the bride but also of her belonging to a man. Van der Toorn adds that it was also a refined instrument of feminine beauty, allowing itself to be guessed at but not shown, suggesting that what is hidden is much more than what can be seen.[39] Not for nothing was the veil the sign not only of the bride but also of the prostitute (1:7)!

The nature of the veil is not clear: whether it was transparent as a way of covering the whole face,[40] or, as Van der Toorn would have it, "a piece of material which covered the head and which concealed the face only partially, leaving the eyes and the cheeks open".[41] The second hypothesis seems more probable to me. But in the one case or the other, the text is not wholly consistent because it describes parts of the woman which are not visible in so far as they are covered either by the veil (the hair, the lips, the neck) or by the clothing (the breasts).[42]

---

[36] Cf. *HALOT*, p. 1033. Garbini's proposal ([1992], pp. 71 and 215–216), to replace *ṣammâ*, 'veil', with *šet*, 'seat, buttock' seems to us frankly gratuitous. Garbini is not consistent, because he translates the same expression in 4:1d in one way ("al di sopra dei fianchi", i.e. "above the flanks") and in 4:3d in another ("tolto il panno", i.e. "removing the veil"). However, it is to be noted that Jerome arrives at a significance similar to that of Garbini when he translates *absque eo quod intrinsecus latet*. In this case, we have, what Ricciotti (1928), p. 234, calls a "euphemistic paraphrase".

[37] Cf., in this sense, De Vaux (1933), p. 408; *id.* (1961), p. 34; van der Toorn (1995).

[38] van der Toorn (1995), p. 331.

[39] van der Toorn (1995), pp. 339–340. In the same sense also, Ravasi (1992), p. 349.

[40] So, for example, Ravasi (1992), p. 349.

[41] van der Toorn (1995), p. 328.

[42] Thus, reasonably, Lys (1968), p. 168.

Probably the description follows a fixed scheme, without paying attention to visual consistency.[43]

The description begins from the eyes which send out a message of love ('doves'). The fact that only this part of the face remains uncovered concentrates all the beauty and vivacity of the woman in the eyes, flashing behind the veil.[44] The image is parallel to that of the man who "gazes through the lattice" in 2:9. It will be taken up again in 4:9.

If it is the communicative capacity of the woman which is concentrated in the eyes, the hair exalts her vital force. One has to think of hair that is loose, thick, very black.[45] Song 7:6 ("A king is held captive in the tresses") makes explicit the erotic value of the hair. In the OT, hair is a symbol of great quantity (cf. Ps 69:5), of vital force (one thinks of Samson, Judg 16:17, or of the heroes of Judg 5:2), even of disorder and chaos (Ps 68:22; Dan 4:30).The satyr or 'hairy one' was the demon of the desert (Lev 17:7; Isa 13:21). It is the savage, the 'dionysiac' aspect of love which is being presented.

The metaphor of the flock of goats confirms this significance. Goats are unbiddable and 'wild'. They do not allow themselves to be controlled (cf. Dan 8:5, 7). They are black and numerous ('a flock'). And they 'gambol' or move riotously. The Hebrew *gālaš* (*hapax* in the OT) expresses the movement of water when it is boiling.[46] The movement, in uncoordinated leaps, of a flock of goats which descends along the slopes of a mountain becomes a poetical metaphor for the mass of wavy, undulating hair which descends from the woman's head. The mountain mentioned is Gilead: not an isolated mountain, therefore, but the mountainous region to the East of the Jordan between the rivers Yabbok and Yarmuk. It is a region on the margins of civilisation, close to the desert, traditionally associated with demons and satyrs (cf. Isa 13:21; 34:11; Gen 32:22–33!) The woman embodies the wild and vital forces of nature; she is even the personification of the earth

[43] Garbini (1992), p. 222, claims that the woman is nude. The mention of the 'veil' speaks against this hypothesis. The problem will return when the intimate parts of both lovers are described (5:10–16; 7:2–6). Actually, the *waṣf* never describes the clothes, but the body of the person (cf., further, p. 299, and 368).

[44] Just how big a role the eyes play in female charm is clear in the contrasting case of Leah, who "had weak eyes" (*rakkôt*, Gen 29:17).

[45] For an example, cf. the women's hair in Keel (1994), Figures 78 and 79, p 140.

[46] Cf. *HALOT*, p. 195. The versions have misunderstood the word: G *apekalyphthēsan* ('have been revealed, have appeared'); S *slq* ('has gone up'); Vg *ascenderunt* ('have gone up').

itself. The term *hār* ('mountain'), which in v. 1f refers to Gilead, is in fact repeated in v. 6e to indicate the woman (so repeating the *inclusio* between 2:8 and 2:17[47]).

[v. 2] From the hair, we pass on to the teeth. The passage does not obey a logical order (cheeks and lips ought to come first in descending order), but a poetic one. The two parts of the body are, in fact, associated with the idea of 'number'.[48] Therefore both are compared to a flock. With such a juxtaposition, the poet achieves a contrast.[49] Above all from the point of view of colour: the black of the hair-goats contrasts with the white of the teeth-ewes. The white colour of wool is proverbial (cf. Isa 1:18; Ps 147:16; Dan 7:9). This aspect is accentuated by the fact that the sheep are coming out of the 'bath' (*raḥṣâ*, another *hapax*, but clearly deriving from *rāḥaṣ* ['to wash']); so they have just been washed. The Hebrew *qeṣûbôt* in itself signifies 'shorn' (and so the ancient versions have, in fact, translated), but this does not make sense: it is logical that the washing takes place before, not after, the shearing. Moreover, the meaning 'to be sheared', that is, 'ready for the shearing', is perfectly possible in the Hebrew language, all the more so in a poetic text.[50]

A second contrast is offered by the fact that the goats 'come down' while the ewes 'come up'. The procession of the ewes is as calm and orderly as the rush of the goats is wild and disordered. Visually, the white procession of the sheep represents well the two paired and regular rows of the teeth. But the *NJB* translation ("Each one has its twin"), wishing to render the visual aspect, distorts the Hebrew text. *mat'îmôt* undoubtedly signifies 'mothers of twins'.[51] For a ewe to bear twins was a sign of extraordinary fertility. The shepherd Comata recalls it in the

[47] Cf., *supra*, pp. 126–127.

[48] We should also note the exquisite poetic construction in vv. 1e-2. Each of the six stichs that describe these two parts of the body begins with the letter *šin* except for the first which begins with the letter *śin*: *śa'rēk* (v. 1e); *šeggāleššû* (v. 1f); *šinnayik* (v. 2a); *še'ālû* (v. 2c); *šekkullām* (v. 2c); *šakkulâ* (v. 2d). For a similar phenomenon of alliteration in Egyptian love poetry, cf. Mathieu (1996), p. 203, §93.

[49] The contrast beween sheep and goats is traditional, cf. Ezek 34:17; Matt 25: 32–33.

[50] Cf. Joüon (1923), p. 342 §121i; Loretz (1971), p. 27; Keel (1994), p. 142, n. 2.

[51] Cf. *HALOT*, p. 1675. We have the hiph'il participle of the verb *t'm*, a *hapax* of the Song, where it appears again in 6:6; it derives from the substantive *tô'ămîm* ('twins'). All of the ancient versions have understood 'mothers of twins'.

Fifth Idyll of Theocritus,[52] and Ishtar, in order to conquer the love of Gilgamesh, promises him that "thy sheep (shall cast) twins".[53]

The idea of fertility is confirmed in the following stich: "None, among them, is *šakkulâ*".[54] Here too the *NJB* wishes to understand the metaphor in a visual sense and, thinking of the teeth, renders: "not one unpaired with another". But *šakkulâ* refers undoubtedly to a mother who loses her children either following a miscarriage or because they are killed (cf. Gen 27:45; 1 Sam 15:33). The metaphor is understood, therefore, not in the visual sense but in the dynamic. The author starts off from a visual likeness but does not stop there: the metaphor develops autonomously in its symbolic value. The procession of ewes evokes the idea of prodigious fecundity, and it associates it with the teeth of the woman, the number of which (and the absence of gaps) is seen as a sign of the divine benediction, the promise of children. Besides, sheep and goats are sacred animals of the goddess of love (cf. Song 1:8).[55] Perhaps G. Krinetzki does not go far wrong when he invokes depth psychology for which the mouth is evocative of the womb.[56]

Second strophe: Red (4:3–4)

Here too, as in the first strophe, three parts of the body are described in approximately descending order: lips (v. 3ab), cheeks (v. 3cd) and neck (v. 4). A double number of stichs is dedicated to the third part, the neck, compared with the other two parts. The first two parts, the lips and the cheeks, are joined together in many ways. The refrain 'behind the veil' (v. 3d; cf. v. 1d) separates the parts of the face (vv. 1–3) from the rest of the body (vv. 4–5). The elements of the face are described according to a skilful colour scheme. In the first strophe, the dominant colours are white and black: the eyes of the woman are white (that is why they are compared to a dove, cf. 5:12),[57] the hair

[52] *Idylls*, 5:84: "Nigh all my goats have tweens at teat; there's only two with one" (tr. Edmonds [1923], p. 73); cf., also, 1:25.

[53] *Gilgamesh* 6:18 (cf. *ANET*, p. 84).

[54] With a fine paronomasia, the Hebrew joins the beginning of 2c (*šekkullām*) with that of 2d (*šakkulâ*).

[55] Cf., *supra*, p. 68.

[56] Krinetzki (1981), p. 134, speaks in that connection of 'vagina dentata'; cf. also Krinetzki (1970), pp. 413–414.

[57] In the *waṣf* of ancient Arab poetry, the woman's eyes are often compared to the moon; in *Joseph and Aseneth* they are compared to the morning star (cf., *supra*, n. 22).

black, the teeth, again, white. In the second strophe, the dominant colour is red: the lips are scarlet, the cheeks are flesh of pomegranate. Here the symphony of colours finishes. The description of the neck proceeds according to other criteria. From the point of view of the metaphors, those regarding the face are drawn from nature, animal or vegetable, while the metaphor of the neck ('tower of David') is taken from the life of the city.

[4:3] The erotic significance of the lips is evident: the lips are the instrument of the kiss (cf. v. 11). They are compared to a 'scarlet thread'.[58] 'Scarlet' or 'crimson' (in Hebrew *šānî*) is a lively red colour, taken from the egg of a ladybird which lives on certain types of oak tree (*Quercus coccifera, Quercus calliprinos*).[59] The contrast between the white of wool and scarlet is mentioned also in Isa 1:18. Like purple, scarlet also has a sacral connotation: it is used for the curtains of the tabernacle and the vestments of the priests (cf. Exod 25:4; 28:5–6, 8). But it is, above all, the colour of love. Scarlet is the colour of the prostitute's dress in Jer 4:30 and Rev 17:3–4. A 'scarlet thread' (the same expression as Song 4:3a) was tied to the window of the prostitute Rahab (Josh 2:18). The colour scarlet is associated with blood, or, according to Philo of Alexandria, fire:[60] and since love is a 'flame of YHWH' (Song 8:6), one understands the association between scarlet and love.

In v. 3b, the significance of the noun *midbār*, which is commonly rendered with 'mouth' (cf. *NRS*), is disputed, that is, it is understood as a part of the body. But it is not clear, then, what the difference is from the 'lips' of v. 3a. Structurally, each part of the body is followed by a stich which makes a comment (cf. in the same strophe the function of v. 3d with respect to v. 3c). At v. 3b also, therefore, one would expect not a new part of the body but something which refers to the 'lips' (v. 3a). The ancient versions have understood *midbār* (a *hapax* in the OT) in a dynamic sense as 'speech', driving it from the root *dbr* ('word').[61] This is the most probable solution.[62] It is, therefore, not a new part of the body, but a comment on v. 3a: the 'lips' are described

[58] As Rudolph emphasises, the colour does not refer to the 'lipstick', but to the natural colour of the lips (Rudolph [1962], p. 146, *contra* Ravasi [1992], p. 354).
[59] Cf. Keel – Küchler – Uehlinger (1984), vol. I, pp. 91–92; Hepper (1992), p. 170.
[60] Philo, *VitMos* 2:88; Josephus, *Ant* 3:7, 6; *Bell* 5:5, 4.
[61] Thus LXX (*lalia*), Vg (*eloquium*), the Syriac *mmllky*.
[62] So too, for example, Colombo (1975), p. 77 ('your speech'); Garbini (1992), p. 219.

now not in their external form but in their function as the instrument of speech. This happens also in the *waṣf* in Chester Beatty Papyrus IA where the various parts of the body are described according to their external form while of the mouth it is said: "sweet her lips when she converses, / she says not a word too much"(!).[63] The lips of the woman are, therefore, 'beautiful' (*nāʾweh*)[64] not as instruments of the kiss but in so far as they put forth beautiful words. The portrait of the woman is not just physical: for ancient man, beauty was inseparable from intelligence and sensitivity.

The translation of v. 3c is also disputed. It is not clear, first of all, which part of the body is being spoken of. The term *raqqâ* (literally 'the thin part') is used again in Judg 4:21–22 and 5:26 to indicate the 'temple'. But the temple is never the object of particular description in the *waṣf*. The ancient versions understand 'cheek',[65] a part of the body which is usually described in the *waṣf* (cf. Song 1:10; 5:13), and which has the form of a pomegranate, so much so that in Aramaic *rummānāʾ* indicates both the pomegranate and the cheek (analogously the Greek *mēlon* indicates the fruit and the part of the body). Perhaps the author used the term *raqqâ* ('temple') in place of the more common *lᵉḥî* ('cheek') for phonetic reasons (note the alliteration on r: *kᵉpelaḥ hārimmôn raqqātēk*):[66] the two parts, moreover, are contiguous.[67] Also disputed is the significance of the term *pelaḥ*: elsewhere it

[63] Cf. *supra*, n. 21.

[64] The adjective appears again in 1:5 (the woman); 1:10 (the cheeks); 2:14 (the face) and 6:4 (the woman). 4:3 is the only case in which the adjective is applied not to something visual, but to something auditory.

[65] LXX has *mēlon*; Vetus Latina *maxillae*; Vg *genae*. The Syriac joins v. 3b with v. 4: "Your nape (*qdlky*), because of your silence, is like the tower of David".

[66] Or perhaps, as in the case of the eyes, he has wanted to respect the visual likeness. The two parts are the only ones connected directly by 'veil'. It is conceivable that the 'veil' leaves only the eyes and the temples uncovered (cf. van der Toorn [1995], p. 328). In any case, as has been noted, it is problematic that the lips and neck, which ought also to be covered by the veil, are described.

[67] Keel (1994), p. 146, prefers to translate 'palate', because of the closeness to the lips. Wholly unfounded and specious is Garbini's translation: "Come una melagrana spaccata sono i tuoi glutei, tolto il panno", i.e.: "When the veil is removed, your buttocks are as a cloven pomegranate". By what linguistic operation Garbini arrives at translating *raqqâ* with 'buttocks' is not told us. He supposes that a puritanical censorship would have changed the original term claimed to be improper (cf. Garbini [1992], pp. 70–72, 222). But this is a gratuitous supposition: what guarantees that the term censored is precisely that supposed by Garbini? If we are really talking about a later correction, it would be inexplicable how the censors would have chosen a word so problematic as *raqqâ*. Moreover, the mention of 'buttocks' is out of place in 3c. The preceding description concerns the lips, that which follows, the neck: it is clear then

indicates one of the two millstones (Judg 9:53; 2 Sam 11:21; Job 41:16), or a cake (1 Sam 30:12), which has made some think of the half of a fruit,[68] of a 'slice'[69] or a 'segment'.[70] But the pomegranate does not cut into slices nor divide into segments. Since the root *plḥ* signifies 'to dig furrows, to plough, to divide', Keel suggests that we understand the split in the mature pomegranate which allows a glimpse of the inside.[71] The seeds of the pomegranate are a vivid red, but the flesh is of a light pink which is well suited to the skin of a young girl. The term of comparison, therefore, is not the form of the fruit but its colour, by analogy with the scarlet of the lips.

But the pomegranate (the Hebrew *rimmôn* designates both the fruit and the plant) is a fruit that is deeply evocative. It is one of the fruits most mentioned in the Song: it occurs again at 4:13; 6:11; 7:13; 8:2. Like the apple, the pomegranate too was held to be an aphrodisiac throughout the Ancient Orient.[72] Perhaps because of its numerous seeds it was bound up with the fertility cult,[73] as the name of the place *Adad Rimmon* ('Adad of the pomegranate') recalls (cf. Zech 12:11). Even today, on the occasion of a marriage, the Palestinian peasants and the Bedouin crush a pomegranate at the entrance of the house or tent to wish a large family on the spouses.[74] Keel records another aspect of the pomegranate plant: on account of its being in leaf and flower throughout the year,[75] it is bound up with the idea of life. In Mesopotamia, the tree of life is presented under the form of a

---

that we are speaking of the face. Garbini resolves the problem by shifting v. 3cd after v. 5. Here too he has to work from pure imagination, for no ancient manuscript and no ancient version supports such an operation.

[68] Thus, for example, Robert - Tournay (1963), p. 162.

[69] So, for example, *HALOT*, p. 879 ('slice of pomegranate').

[70] Thus the *CEI* translation. Both *RSV* and *NJB* have "halves".

[71] Keel (1994), p. 146. In Egyptian iconography, the fruit is almost always presented with its characteristic cleavage (cf. *ibid.*, Figure 82, p. 144).

[72] Cf. the Assyrian conjuration referred to, *supra*, pp. 90–91, n. 206.

[73] Significant in this regard is a passage from the Egyptian love songs in which speech is given to the pomegranate: "My seeds are like your teeth, / my fruits are like your breasts" (Turin Papyrus 1:1, tr. Bresciani [1990], p. 468. Fox however translates "persea tree", cf. Fox [1985], pp. 46–47). The text confirms the association of the teeth with the idea of fertlilty (cf., *supra* the comment on v. 2).

[74] De Vaux (1961), p. 41.

[75] The fact is recorded in the Turin Papyrus just cited: "[I am the most beautiful tree] of the garden, / because I last through every season. [...] Apart from me, they all perish, / [the plants] of the garden. / I go through twelve months / [with my head of foliage], and I last: / when a flower falls, / its successor is already on me" (1:2, 4–5) (tr. Bresciani [1990], p. 468).

pomegranate.[76] Moreover, the pomegranate is a fruit typical of the land of Israel, a sort of national fruit (cf. Num 13:23; 20:5; Deut 8:8; Joel 1:12), used as a decorative element for the priestly robe and for the temple (cf. Exod 28:33–34; 1 Kgs 7:18, 20).[77] In comparing the cheek of the woman with a pomegranate, it is not only the material likeness which enters into play but all this symbolic background. It is, so to speak, the vital force of the pomegranate which the young man sees as being present in the woman's cheek.

[v. 4] The description of the neck is marked off from that of the two preceding parts of the body, both because it is twice as long and also because it does not stress the dimension of colour; moreover, the similitude ('tower') is drawn from the life of the city not from nature. The image of the 'tower' returns in the Song (in 7:5 [twice] and 8:10). Generally, the *tertium comparationis* is seen in the 'thin and slender' profile which is common to both the neck and the tower.[78] That is, it is always the visual aspect which is being entertained. Keel justly observes that this could work all right for the neck (4:4 and 7:5a), but not for the nose (7:5d) or for the breasts (8:10b).[79] However, the towers which are known to us through Palestinian archaeology are not slender but rather massive. He suggests, therefore, that we consider as the *tertium comparationis* not so much the visual aspect (even if this is not excluded), as the functional one. In the OT, the tower (*migdāl*) is synonymous with defence, security, inviolability. It is able to sustain attacks and sieges without capitulating (cf. Ps 61:4; Prov 18:10). Like everything which is 'high', it is also synonymous with pride (cf. Gen 11:4–5; Isa 2:15).

---

[76] Cf. Keel (1994), Figures 80 and 81, p.144.

[77] Cf. Keel (1978), Figure 224, p. 164, a tripod haling from Ugarit, which shows an example of how the pomegranate could be used as a decorative element in the temple. Not many years ago, in the antique market of Jerusalem, there appeared the ivory pommel of a sceptre in the form of a pomegranate, bearing the inscription: "Sacred offering for the priests of the temple of YHWH" (cf. Avigad [1990]). Even today, the two pommels, usually fashioned artistically, in which the two poles which support the scroll of the Torah terminate, are called *rimmônîm*, 'pomegranates', probably because they originally took the form of a pomegranate (cf. *EJ*, vol. 15, coll. 1256–1257: I am grateful for this information to Professor Ida Zatelli). It is significant that the two poles themselves are called 'trees of life' (*'ăṣê hayyîm*), perhaps a memory of the ancient identification of the tree of life with the pomegranate, to which allusion is made above.

[78] So, for example, Ravasi (1992), pp. 356–357.

[79] Keel (1984a), pp. 32–39.

These same associations are suggested by the Hebrew lexeme *ṣawwā'r* (neck). In Isa 3:16, the 'daughters of Zion' are attacked by the prophet because in their pride 'they walk with an outstretched neck'.[80] What the prophet criticises as a sign of pride is seen by the Song as awareness of self-worth, and praised. Like a solid tower, the woman knows how to defend herself; she does not yield to the first assault (cf. Song 8:10).[81] The military metaphor with reference to love, the amorous 'conquest', has already been introduced in 2:4b;[82] also the theme of the inaccessibility of the woman has been alluded to in 2:9 (*motiv* of the 'wall') and 2:14 (*motiv* of 'unattainability'). Pope sees in this interpretation a contradiction with the portrait of the woman in 3:1–5.[83] It is not a contradiction but dialectic. The woman of the Song is torn between the affirmation of herself and the gift of herself. The poetry of the Song lives off these "paradoxes": as Landy suggests, it is only those who are fully themselves who can give themselves.[84]

Nowhere else do we hear of a 'tower of David'.[85] The building which bears this name today in the citadel of Jerusalem dates from medieval times. In any case, the appellation (whether real or fictitious) links the idea of defence ('tower') with the holy city and with the history and the people of Israel ('of David'). That is, there is a taking up again of the thought expressed in 3:7 through the sixty 'mighty men of Israel' who guard the litter. The term 'mighty men' (*gibbôrîm*) reappears, moreover, in 4:4d. The people of God is ready to defend its daughter from dangers. Elsewhere, this 'defence' is felt as a burden and criticised (cf. 8:9–10). Here, with a trace of nationalistic pride, its positive value is emphasised.

---

[80] Here, in place of *ṣawwā'r*, the synonym *gārôn* is used.

[81] Krinetzki (1981), p. 136, comments: "This girl is not easy prey for the boy whom she loves; even in love, she remains 'mistress of the field', and yields to her 'conqueror' only in full liberty".

[82] Cf., *supra*, p. 89.

[83] Pope (1977), p. 465.

[84] Landy (1983), p. 108.

[85] With his customary licence, Garbini (1992), p. 219, changes 'of David' to 'of Pharos'. This time, however, he admits that it is a reading that is "purely conjectural". We must add that it is a wrong conjecture, because the tower of Pharos was a tower for signalling, not a tower of defence, as a result of which it would be difficult to understand the "thousand shields of the mighty men" hung on it (v. 4cd). Moreover, all the other indications of place in the Song refer to the land of Israel, according to a precise symbolic intention (woman = promised land).

The expression *l^etalpîyôt* is enormously controversial. Already the versions present a diverse picture: the LXX (*eis thalpiōth*) understands the term as a proper name (today, Talpiot is the name of a suburb of Jerusalem). The Vulgate (*cum propugnaculis*) agrees with the Greek version of Aquila (*eis epalxeis*, 'with merlons, with defences') and with the Syriac (*btk'*, 'with merlons'). Graetz sees in *talpîyôt* a Hebraicisation of the Greek term *tēlōpis* ('distant vision'),[86] and thinks of a watchtower; but the proposed translations are counted in scores.[87] One of these which has gathered much approval is that, advanced by A. M. Honeyman, of connecting the word with the Arab *lafa'a* ('to arrange in rows'). It would give the translation: "constructed in layers"[88] or even "constructed with superimposed elements".[89] Such a translation would allow a visual comparison between the tower and the neck, adorned with layers of necklaces. But the bases on which this is founded are tenuous as Rudolph recognises.[90] I prefer, therefore, to adhere to the ancient versions (Aquila, the Vulgate and the Syriac) which are better suited to the context.[91] It would be, concretely, a crown-like wall, a kind of parapet or battlement (like the *ṭîrâ* of 8:9b) on which the defenders are positioned. The Assyrian relief which portrays the siege of Lachish gives an idea of this kind of construction.[92]

Just as v. 4a is linked by parallelism with v. 4b, so v. 4c is linked with v. 4d. The two distichs are joined by the paronomasia between v. 4b *bānûy* (literally 'constructed') and v. 4c *tālûy* ('hung'). The understanding of v. 4cd is made difficult by the term *šeleṭ*, the significance of which is disputed. Generally it is understood as a synonym of *māgēn* ('shield', v. 4c). But R. Borger has shown convincingly, above all on the basis of an inscription from the palace of Darius I, where the represen-

---

[86] Graetz (1871), p. 156.

[87] For a review, cf. Pope (1977), pp. 465–468; Ravasi (1992), pp. 358–359; Rudolph (1962), pp. 144–145.

[88] So Ravasi (1992), p. 337, understanding the exposed blocks of stone with which the tower is constructed. In this sense, also, Keel (1994), p. 147; Gerleman (1965), p. 148; *HALOT*, p. 1741; Pope (1977), pp. 466–467.

[89] Thus Garbini (1992), p. 223, understanding the different architectural orders of the tower of Pharos.

[90] Rudolph (1962), p. 145. The translation is rejected also by Heinevetter (1988), p. 122, n. 83; Müller (1992), p. 41, n. 118.

[91] In addition to Heinevetter and Müller (cf. n. 90 *supra*), this translation is followed by *CEI* ("like a fortress"), Robert – Tournay (1963), p. 163 ("built as a fortress"). Ricciotti (1928), pp. 235–236, in the wake of Haupt, bases this translation on the Assyrian *šulbû (labu)*, 'to enclose, to fortify' (citations there).

[92] Cfr. Keel (1984a), Figure 1, p. 123 (= *ANEP*, Figure 373, p. 131).

tation of a holder for bow and arrow is accompanied by the Akkadian word *šalṭu,* that this meaning ('holder for bow', 'quiver') is suitable also for the seven biblical passages in which *šeleṭ* appears.[93] Such a meaning is evident principally in Jer 51:11 where the translation 'shield' is impossible ("Sharpen the arrows, fill the *šᵉlāṭîm*" [the LXX has *tas pharetras*; so also the Vulgate]).[94] It is confirmed further by the Aramaic Targum.[95] In *1QM* 6, 2, the term *šeleṭ* indicates something like 'javelin' or 'arrow', in fact a hurling weapon,[96] corresponding in this to the LXX (*bolides*). It would be a semantic evolution. The two terms *māgēn* and *šeleṭ*, therefore, are not synonymous but complementary,[97] the first indicating the weapons of defence, the second those of attack[98] of the 'mighty men' who are defending the tower. In the representation of the siege of Lachish, the defenders are armed predominantly with shields and bow.

Probably the description of the tower of David is inspired by the lament over Tyre in Ezek 27:10–11: "Men of war of Persia, Lud and Put were among your hosts, they hung (*tillû*) the shield (*māgēn*) and helmet in you, they gave you splendour. The men of Arvad and their army were around your walls and watched on your towers (*migdᵉlôt*); they hung (*tillû*) their quivers (*šilṭêhem*) on your walls round about; they made perfect your beauty". The shields and the quivers, therefore, have an ornamental effect (cf. 1 Macc 4:57; 2 Sam 8:7), but, above all, a practical one. They were hung up near to the place where they were being used, that is on the bastions of the wall, as is shown in Sennacherib's relief, and they display the defensive power of a city. The thousand shields and the thousand quivers hung from the tower of David are saying that there are a thousand valiant warriors (*gibborîm*) at the defence of this 'tower'. The number is symbolic: as the following stich indicates, it is 'all' (*kol*) the people of Jerusalem who are mobilised in defence of their daughter. A visual comparison is possible perhaps. It

[93] That is, in addition to Song 4:4, 2 Sam 8:7; 2 Kgs 11:10; Jer 51:11; Ezek 27:11; 1 Chr 18:7 and 2 Chr 23:9.

[94] Borger (1972). Borger's suggestion is accepted and developed by *HALOT*, pp. 1522–1523; Garbini (1992), p. 221, recognises this meaning for the term, even if he opts for the translation "armour".

[95] Cf., again, Borger (1977).

[96] *Wurfwaffe* ("projectile"), according to Maier (1960), vol. II, p. 121.

[97] And therefore 4d is not in apposition to 4c, but a second subject of the verb *tlh*, coordinated asyndetically with 'a thousand shields'.

[98] Even the sixty mighty men defending the litter are equipped with an offensive weapon: the sword (cf. 3:8).

is may be that the 'bulwarks' allude to the necklaces which adorn the neck of the woman (cf. Song 4:9c). Even today, Bedouin women are in the habit of wearing necklaces of coins which they can pass off as 'shields'. For the 'quivers', one can easily think of a kind of 'pendant'.[99] But the external likeness is not the main consideration. As in the case of the 'ewes', the metaphor is developed autonomously through its symbolic value. The symbolism of the tower is antithetical to that of the lips and the cheeks (v. 3). Just as the latter are evidence of the 'sweetness', the attraction of the woman, so equally the neck sets in relief her proud self-awareness.

Third strophe: Desire (4:5–7)

With v. 5, the third strophe of the *waṣf* begins. The syntactic order returns to that of the first strophe: the part of the body is mentioned ("your two breasts...") first and then the similitude ("...like two fawns"). The parallelism between the third strophe and the first is confirmed also by the type of similitudes used: while in the second strophe they are 'still-lifes' (scarlet, pomegranate, tower), in the first and third they are drawn from the animal world and are full of life (doves, goats, ewes, fawns). A particular emphasis is given by the theme of the 'twins' (*t'm*) which unites v. 5b with 2c. This goes for the first part of the strophe, v. 5: the description of the breasts concludes the contemplation of the parts of the body. In v. 6, the beloved expresses the desire to be united to this person, admired for so long, thus introducing the theme of the following song.

Verses 5–6 find their counterpart in 2:16–17 and 8:14 (cf. *Tab. 23*). In the three passages, the theme of the 'gazelle on the mountains' has the function of a conclusion. 2:16–17 ends the first song of the woman (2:8–17); 4:5–6 concludes the first song of the man (4:1–7); 8:14 terminates the *Epilogue* of the Song of Songs itself. The correspondence is complete only between 2:16 and 4:5–6. The four elements of the description (a-b-c-d) are found, even if in a different order, in the two passages. In the third passage, 8:14, only the elements c-d are present. The repetition is never mechanical: not only is the order different, but

[99] A necklace of little shields is represented in a sculpture from Arsos (Cyprus), of the sixth century B.C. Cf. Isserlin (1958).

Table 23

2:16–17	4:5–6	8:14
a) My beloved is mine and I am his, he grazes among the lotus flowers.	c) Your two breasts, like two fawns, twins of a gazelle...	
b) When the day sighs and the shadows lengthen...	a) ...which graze among the lotus flowers.	
c) ...*come*, my love, be like a gazelle or like a young stag...	b) When the day sighs and the shadows lengthen...	c) *Flee*, my beloved, and be like a gazelle or a young stag,...
d) ...on the cloven mountains.	d) ...I will leave for the mountains of myrrh and for the hill of incense.	d) ...on the mountains of balms.

there is always some 'variation on the theme' as in a symphonic work. The more macroscopic, between the first and second passage, is that in 2:16–17 the woman invites her man to come on to the 'mountains', while in 4:5–6 it is the man who expresses the desire to climb up there. It is another case of the 'mirroring' principle typical of the Song. Here in particular is suggested a continuity between the songs of the woman (2:8–3:5) and those of the man (4:1–5:1): the man seems now to accept the invitation given to him by the woman in 2:16–17. However, the order given by the woman in 8:14 then becomes enigmatic: "Flee, my beloved". We shall attend to that in due course.

[4:5] In Chapter 2 (as also in Chapter 8), it is the beloved man who is compared to a gazelle; here it is the breasts of the woman. The 'duality' of the breasts is underlined (the first time with the number *šᵉnê*, the second by the dual form of the noun *šādayik*) and it is confirmed in the metaphor ('twin fawns'). The author intends to express by this the visual correlation between the part of the body and the metaphor, the symmetry which characterises the form of the breasts.[100] Moreover the grazing fawns, never still but raising their heads at the slightest noise, deftly depict the movement of the breasts of a lightly clad young woman.[101] Nolli observes that Oriental women, by contrast with

[100] Rudolph removes the numeral as a superfluous gloss. Cf. Rudolph (1962), p. 145.
[101] Cf. the poetic description sketched by Rudolph (1962), p. 147.

the Roman, did not wear brassieres to keep in their breasts.[102] It is a realistic and at the same time deeply poetic observation of the female body.

That does not exclude a symbolic significance.[103] In the Ancient Orient, the breasts are, in the first place, a symbol of fertility. The representation of the *magna mater* with breasts disproportionately large is widespread everywhere, even in Israel.[104] In the OT, this symbolism is expressed in Gen 49:25 ("Blessings of the breasts and of the womb").[105] The maternal function of the woman is being presented (cf. Isa 66:11; Song 8:1). For the *puer aeternus*, the breasts evoke the nurture and the feeding of the first months of life, unconditional trust, the feeling of being protected and loved in warmth and tenderness (cf. Ps 22:10; Job 3:12).[106] But the erotic function of the breasts is also spoken of in the OT (cf. Ezek 16:7: 23:3, 21; Hos 2:4). Particularly close to our text is Prov 5:18–19: "Rejoice in the wife of your youth: a lovely hind, a graceful gazelle: let her breasts[107] satisfy you at all times, be infatuated always with her love". The erotic dimension is predominant in the Song (cf. 1:13; 7:4, 8–9; 8:8, 10), as in the Egyptian love lyrics.[108] It is no accident, therefore, that the *waṣf* concludes with the description of the breasts: here already there is allusion to sexual intimacy, seen more as erotic play than as genital activity, even if this aspect is not absent (cf. v. 2). In this sense, the description of the breasts forms a contrast with that of the tower which emphasises the pride and inaccessibility of the woman: there is a return now to the aspect of loveableness which characterised the description of the lips and cheeks. The poet composes through antitheses and contrasts.

The two breasts are compared to two 'fawns' (*ʿŏpārîm*). The lexeme evokes tenderness, vital freshness, playfulness. The fawns are 'twins of a gazelle'. We noticed above the repetition of the theme of twins

---

[102] Nolli (1967), p. 104.

[103] This aspect is stressed in Keel (1994), pp. 150–151.

[104] Cf. Keel (1994), Figures 133–134, p. 240.

[105] The blessing, it is well-known, is connected above all to the concept of fertility (cf. Gen 1:28).

[106] Cf. Krinetzki (1970), pp. 412–413.

[107] The *CEI* translation corrects MT *daddèhā* ('her breasts') with *dōdèhā* ('her embraces').

[108] Papyrus Harris 500 comes close to the text of Proverbs: "Do you go away for a beer, while I am offering you my breast? Its reservoirs are stored up for you; one day spent in my embrace is of more benefit than a hundred thousand lands" (1, 4–6), according to Mathieu (1996), p. 57; cf. Bresciani (1990), p. 460.

introduced in v. 2. We can detect an allusion to the theme of 'fertility'. Moreover, gazelles, like goats, are animals commonly associated with the goddess of love (cf. 1:8; 2:7; 3:5);[109] they personify the forces of love and life. The 'lotus flowers' have an analogous significance as symbols of the victory of life over the chaos of the swamp.[110] With regard to 2:16–17, there is a semantic evolution (there the gazelle was the metaphor for the beloved man; here the gazelles are a metaphor for the breasts), but the fundamental significance is the same.[111] The man sees in the woman's breasts a throbbing of new life, a promise of freshness, of play, of fertility which renews the victory of life over the desert and chaos.[112]

[v. 6] In v. 6, the man expresses the desire of passing from contemplation to action, from desire to enjoyment.

"When the day sighs…". In the comment on 2:17, we opted for an evening timing: here too the context points in this direction, above all the coherence with the last temporal indication in 3:11 ('day') and with that which follows in 5:2 ('night'). The evening is the time for lovers' intimacy, the moment of encounter.[113]

The 'mountain of myrrh' and the 'hill of incense' is, like the 'cloven mountains' of 2:17, a metaphor for the female body. Since the previous verse speaks of the breasts, it is probable that is to these in particular that it alludes.[114] In 1:13 the woman compares her beloved to a bag of myrrh, "passing the night between my breasts". It could be problematic that here 'mountain' is spoken of in the singular: for this reason, some authors think of the 'Mount of Venus'.[115] But perhaps 'mountain' and 'hill' are used as synonyms to indicate each of the two breasts.[116] In 7:8 too, the *waṣf* concludes with the desire of squeezing the woman's breasts: "I will climb up the palm, I will squeeze its clusters. May your breasts be like bunches of grapes…".

---

109 Cf., *supra*, pp. 91–92.

110 Cf. pp. 83–84.

111 The image of v. 5c is not at all coherent with that of 2:16–17 and 6:2–3. For this reason, Colombo (1975), p. 78, suggests eliminating this stich as an addition. However, the Song is not a philosophical, but a poetic text in which an image can be used with different significance according to the context.

112 Cf., *supra*, pp. 122–123.

113 Cf. p. 102, n. 12; pp. 123, 129.

114 The same goes for 2:17, cf., *supra*, p. 126.

115 So, for example, Haupt (1907), p. 75. Ravasi (1992), p. 363, also thinks here of "genital sexuality".

116 So too Lys (1968), p. 175.

The identification of the breasts with mountains is connected with v. 1 ('mountains of Gilead') and forms part of the archetypical identification of the woman with the land. The mountain in particular has something of the numinous in it; it is the dwelling place of mysterious forces of fertility (cf. Gen 49:26; Deut 33:15). Almost everywhere in the Ancient Orient we find figures of mountain divinities.[117] Not for nothing were the Canaanite fertility rites performed on the mountain tops (cf. Hos 4:13; Deut 12:2).

With the mountains are associated two perfumes, myrrh and incense, the very ones which accompanied the procession of the litter (Song 3:6c). Also in 4:11, the scent of the clothes of the woman is compared to the 'fragrance of Lebanon'. The breasts-mountains perfumed with myrrh and incense wrap the body in an aura which is at the same time both erotic and sacral.[118] The proposal to see behind the names of the perfumes an allusion to mountains typical of the land of Israel seems suggestive and, in this case, not misleading. Perhaps the identification of *môr* ('myrrh') with *môrîyâ* ('Moriah'), the mountain on which the Temple of Jerusalem is built (cf. 2 Chr 3:1),[119] can raise difficulties. More convincing, also because supported by the cited reference to v. 11, is the identification of *l^{e}bônâ* ('incense') with *l^{e}bānôn* ('Lebanon'), two terms also semantically related.[120] Certainly there is no question of allegory, that is, of the primary meaning of the terms, as Robert and Tournay would see: the 'mountain of myrrh' and the 'hill of incense' refer primarily to the body of the woman. However, in the background, we may be permitted to catch sight of a second sense: the identification of the land with the woman has been observed above. With these allusions, the author perhaps intends to specify that the land with which the woman is identified is the promised land. In uniting himself to the woman, the man enjoys the land which God has promised his people as their inheritance: a good land, perfumed, where "milk and honey flow" (Exod 3:8, par.; cf. Song 4:11b).[121]

---

[117] Cf. *ANEP*, Figure 528, p. 178.

[118] On the significance of myrrh and incense, cf., *supra*, pp. **00–00**. As for the erotic connotation associated with myrrh, it is worth recalling that Hator, the Egyptian goddess of love, was called 'lady of myrrh'. Cf. Keel (1994), p. 153.

[119] Thus Robert – Tournay (1963), p. 168.

[120] Cf., *supra*, pp. 147–148.

[121] For an emphasis on the equation 'woman = promised land', cf. Davis (1998). The authoress here arrives at reframing an allegorical reading of the Song. She is echoed by Brenner (1999), p. 109, who, however, is usually very far from the allegorical inter-

[v. 7] Like v. 1, which it matches, v. 7 acts as a frame to the *waṣf* and, therefore, is separated metrically from vv. 5–6 (cf. *Tab. 22*). Rudolph and Nolli are incorrect to consider it out of place, shifting it to before v. 6.[122] The universalising particle *kullāk* (literally 'all you'), which replaces the emphatic *hinnāk* (literally 'look you…'), confers a concluding function on the verse. The three strophes, in fact, are concluded by this particle: *kullām* ('all [the ewes]', v. 2c); *kol šilṭê* ('all the quivers', v. 4d); *kullāk* ('all you', v. 7a). The number of the parts of the body (seven) is, as has been seen, a symbol of perfection. But the semantic transition should be noted: from things (in the plural, vv. 2, 4) to the person (in the singular, v. 7). The 'totality' is a question more of quality than of quantity. It is the woman, not her body which is fair. For the poet there is no separation between body and soul. While he is admiring the external form of the body, he is discerning its soul; he sees the forces of life and love which confer unity on it.

In the OT, the term *mûm* ('defect, blemish') refers to both physical and moral defects.[123] In 2 Sam 14:25, the beauty of Absalom is thus described: "From the soles of his feet to the top of his head, there was no defect (*mûm*) in him". Also the three young men at the court of Nebuchadnezzar are said to have "no defect (*mûm*) in them" (Dan 1:4). The context makes clear that the young men were not only good looking but also educated and intelligent. The term recurs above all in the language of the cult[124] where it designates the 'purity' of the animal to be offered in sacrifice. To the God of life one can offer only an animal 'without blemish', that is, without 'lack of life'. M. Douglas has demonstrated the connection between the concept of 'purity' and that of 'life' in Leviticus.[125] The observation "in you there is no blemish" (*mûm ʾên bāk*, v. 7b) refers back, therefore, to that of v. 2d: "None has lost her young" (*šakkulâ ʾên bāhem*, v. 2d). In both cases there is an allusion to the fullness of life.

---

pretation: "She (= the woman of the Song, *author's note*) is the Land, the cultivated land, the Promised Land. […] If so, perhaps an argument can be made from this for a primary allegorical meaning of the SoS". In reality, this is not a question of allegory, but of the transposition to the woman of the theology of the promised land.

[122] Rudolph (1962), pp. 143–144; Nolli (1967), p. 105.

[123] In this last sense, cf., for example, Prov 9:7; Job 11:15; 31:7; Sir 11:33.

[124] Cf. Lev 21:17, 18, 21, 23; 22:20, 21, 25; Num 19:2; Deut 15:21; 17:1.

[125] "To be holy is to be whole, to be one; holiness is unity, integrity, perfection of the individual and of the kind" (Douglas [1966], p. 53).

The affirmation of wonder in v. 7 comes close to the judgement of the Creator over his works in the account of the Creation: "God saw all that he had made, and behold, it was very good" (Gen 1:31). The wonder before the woman has a similar, almost sacral, significance: it is the recognition of the pureness of the gift of God (cf. Wis 1:14).

Encounter (4:8–5:1)

To grasp the structure of this song, it is important first of all to observe its dialogic dimension. It is basically a song of the beloved man. In continuity with 4:1–7 it is still he who speaks in vv. 8–15. It is not clear who declaims v. 16. There is, in fact, a change of person in it: from 'my garden' (v. 16c) to 'his garden' (v. 16e). Garbini thinks of an oversight and both times reads the first person possessive.[126] With greater respect for the text, Heinevetter supposes that in v. 16abcd the speech of the man continues (therefore he says: 'my garden'), while v. 16ef contains the reply of the woman (therefore she says, in the third person: 'his garden').[127] But this distinction is not necessary: the woman herself can speak on one occasion of 'my garden' (that is, the garden of the lady) and another time of 'his garden' (that is, the garden of the man). The point of this verse lies precisely in this question of ownership: from being 'my body' it becomes 'his body'. It is the reply for which the man has been waiting for a long time.

Table 24

I strophe	4:8 4:9	*to come*	*Lebanon* (× 2)	*bride* *my sister, bride*	
II strophe	4:10 4:11		 *Lebanon*	*my sister, bride* *bride*	
III strophe	4:12 4:15		 *Lebanon*	*my sister, bride*	*garden* *garden*
IV strophe	4:16 5:1	*to come* (× 2) *to come*		 *my sister, bride*	*garden* (× 2) *garden*

[126] Garbini (1992), p. 80 (leaning on textual arguments that are very tenuous: "a few Hebrew manuscripts, Sinaiticus and Alexandrinus").

[127] Heinevetter (1988), p. 124; so too Keel (1994), p. 181; Nolli (1967), p. 110.

In 5:1abcd the man begins to speak again (now he is justified in saying 'my garden'). But who declaims the last distich of the song, v. 1ef? Anticipating the conclusion which I shall reach in the analysis, let me say immediately that it is not one of the two lovers but a voice from off-stage, the 'chorus' or, more probably, the poet himself who comes out of his anonymity and starts to speak in the first person.

The structure of the song is marked by key words (cf. *Tab. 24*). The lexemes which are repeated are numerous and form a mosaic rich in references which will be pointed out in the course of the analysis. Some of these also have a structural function. We have already noticed this function for the verb *bôʾ* ('to go, to come', 4:8b, 16d; 5:1; cf. 4:6).[128] The word *l^ebānôn* ('Lebanon', 4:8 [twice], 11, 15) performs an analogous role. Verse 15 closes the man's speech since the term 'Lebanon' functions as an *inclusio* for vv. 8–15. Verse 11 closes the second strophe, linked to the first in a multitude of ways: the term 'Lebanon' here too has, therefore, inclusive value for vv. 8–11.[129] These observations are confirmed by the repetition of the term *kallâ* ('bride', 4:8, 9, 10, 11, 12; 5:1). This is a term which occurs only here in the Song, and the arrangement is not accidental. In the first part of the song (vv. 8–11), its presence signals the beginning of each verse. The four occurrences form a chiasm: at the beginning and at the end, the term appears to be isolated ('bride', vv. 8 and 11); the second and third time linked with the appellation 'my sister' (vv. 9, 10). The other two occurrences of this expression ('my sister, my bride', 4:12a; 5:1a) function as a frame for the second part of the song (4:12–5:1). Moreover, this second part is unified by the *motiv* of the 'garden', so much so that 4:12–5:1 is often considered a song in itself and entitled "song of the garden".[130] In it, the word 'garden' (*gan*) has a function analogous to that of the three preceding: it returns in 4:12 and 15 with the value of an *inclusio* for vv. 12–15 (third strophe), then in 4:16 (twice) and 5:1 marking the two parts of the last strophe.

We noted above the linking of the two songs of the beloved man, 4:1–7 and 4:8–5:1.[131] To the observations made then we can add another. The *waṣf* is characterised by the vertical dimension, in fact by a descending movement from high to low (from 'eyes', v. 1, to

---

[128] Cf., *supra*, p. 195.
[129] On the unity of vv. 8–11, cf. Ravasi (1992), p. 366.
[130] Cf., again, Ravasi (1992), p. 347.
[131] Cf., *supra*, pp. 170–171.

'breasts', v. 5). A similar movement may be observed also in 4:8–5:1. In the first strophe, in fact, mention is made of the woman's 'eyes' (*'ênayik*, 4:9; cf. 4;1); in the second of her 'lips' (*śiptôtayik*, 4:11; cf. 4:3). The 'garden' which the third and fourth strophes speak of is a symbol of the female womb, of its sexual intimacy, to which the breasts in the preceding song allude. By means of this progression there is also indicated the gradual moving towards union, which begins with looks (first strophe), passes on to the kiss (second strophe) to be fulfilled in the embrace to which 5:1 clearly alludes.[132]

First strophe: The look (4:8–9)

The boundaries of this strophe are not undisputed. Those who hold the Song to be a collection of small independent songs generally consider v. 8 as a song in its own right and, on the other hand, link v. 9 with vv. 10–11.[133] The connection of v. 9 with v. 8 is not at all clear at first. Heinevetter suggests understanding v. 9 as the motivation for the urgent request made in v. 8.[134] Since the woman has driven the young man 'mad' (v. 9), he asks her to come out of her 'refuge' and to 'come' to him (v. 8). The upheaval happened, perhaps, during the contemplation of the body (4:1–7) to which the two terms 'eyes' (v. 9b; cf. v. 1c) and 'necklaces' (v. 9c; cf. v. 4) refer. The verb *tāšûrî* ('look', v. 8c) refers in any case to the 'eyes' of the woman.

From the formal point of view, the two verses are united by the paronomasia *lᵉbānôn (v. 8ab)—libbabtînî* (v. 9ab): the two words are repeated at the beginning of the first two stichs of each verse. Moreover the two verses are marked by 'staircase parallelism'.[135] In v. 8, the second stich repeats four words from the first, the fourth two from the third, and the sixth one from the fifth (cf. *Tab. 25*). G. Krinetzki comments: "The climax imitates the progressive descent from the

---

[132] On the *gradus amoris* (a typical theme of courtly literature) in the Egyptian love songs, cf. Mathieu (1996), pp. 163–175. Mathieu describes the following stages of the amorous journey: the look, the effects (desire, agitation), the *mrw.t* ('love'), the union (embrace, caresses and kisses, sexual enjoyment). It is a common theme throughout literature, but the way of treating it in the Egyptian poetry is extraordinarily close to that of the Song.

[133] Cf., *supra*, p. 171, n. 13. Paul brings a literary support to this division: in the initials of the three verses 9, 10 and 11 (*l.m.n*), he recognises an acrostic (S. Paul, *Mnemonic devices*, in *IDBS*, p. 600).

[134] Heinevetter (1988), p. 123; in this sense also, Krinetzki (1981), pp. 138–142.

[135] "Staircase parallelism", according to Watson (1984), p. 150.

Table 25

With me from Lebanon, my bride,	||	*with me from Lebanon* come!
Look *from the summit* of Amana,	||	*from the peak* of Senir and of Hermon,
from the lairs of the lions,	||	*from* the mountains of the panthers!

Table 26

You have driven me mad,	my sister, my bride,	
you have driven me mad		*with one of your* glances,
		with one pearl *of your* necklaces.

mountain".[136] The parallelism assumes a different form in v. 9. Here the repetitions form a 'concatenation' which binds together the three stichs of the verse (cf. *Tab. 26*). The second stich repeats the initial part of the first, lengthening it by a member ('staircase parallelism'); the third stich begins by repeating the last part of the second stich (anadiplosis).

[4:8] MT's *ʾittî* ('with me') seems at first glance to be without meaning. If the two lovers are together ('with me'), the invitation to 'come' seems out of place. Actually, LXX has *deuro* ('come'), as also the Syriac and the Vulgate. The majority of the commentators follow LXX, supposing an original Hebrew *ʾĕtî* (from the verb *ʾātāh*, cf. *BHS*).[137] This translation is usual in the Catholic liturgy (cf. the antiphon for the Feast of the Immaculate Conception: "*Veni, veni de Libano*"). However, it is MT, precisely as the *lectio difficilior*, which has the greater possibility of being authentic, both from a formal point of view, in which the translation 'come' would destroy the skilful syntactic construction of the verse,[138] and from the point of view of content. If one recalls the parallelism with the first song of the beloved woman (2:8–17), to which 4:5–6 already make reference, one can think of a

[136] Krinetzki (1981), p. 139.

[137] Ravasi (1992), p. 367, chooses a middle way, retaining the two meanings at the same time, and translates: "with me (come)", but frankly this solution smacks of pastiche. Krinetzki (1981), p. 138, reads *ʾotî*: "You have made *me* come". Müller (1992), p. 45, understands the preposition in a local sense: "*To me*... come". Schweizer (1991), pp. 426–427, puts a full stop after the second "from Lebanon": "With me from Lebanon, my bride, with me from Lebanon. Come!", a solution already suggested by Joüon. Justifiably, however, Robert – Tournay (1963), p. 169, reject these adjustments: there are only two possible ways, either that of LXX or that of MT.

[138] So Gerleman (1965), p. 151; Rudolph (1962), p. 147.

situation analogous to that of 2:10c, 13d. Then we translated the imperative *l^ekî lāk*, not with the verb 'to come' but with the verb 'to go', pointing out that the text expresses not the point of arrival but the point of departure. In our case the emphasis is analogous: all the complements of place in this verse are expressed by the preposition *min* ('from', a good six times). It is an invitation to 'leave', to 'go out', to 'go away'. It is the 'Exodic' situation of love to which 1:8 has already made reference and which, at bottom, echoes Gen 2:24: it is breaking out of one's shell, 'going out' from one's own defences and daring the adventure of love.

In the Song, the verb *bô'* in *qal* form occurs outside the section 4:8–5:1 only in 2:8. There it is the man who has to 'go' to his woman. Here, in conformity with the mirror symmetry of the Song, it is the woman who has to 'go' to him (but in 4:16; 5:1, the verb refers once again to the man). The movement towards union takes on the aspect of a journey. In this sense, 4:8 continues the metaphor of 3:6–11, the theme of the 'nuptial procession'. The 'desert' from which the litter comes is a symbolic place equivalent to the 'mountains of the panthers': it is the realm of the forces of nature. The journey from the desert to the city is a journey which one does not make on one's own: only love is able to see such a journey completed. Because of this, in the parallel passage, 8:5, the one who comes from the desert is not alone but 'leaning upon her beloved'. In 3:6–11, it is possible that 'Solomon', together with the sixty mighty men, is escorting the litter, if the daughters of Jerusalem are called to go out to meet him (3:11). The MT's 'with me', therefore, seems quite the opposite of 'impossible', both from the point of view of form and that of significance.

In parallel with the verb 'to go', there occurs at v. 8c the verb *šûr*. In the OT, at least two different meanings of the root are flagged up: 'to look down' (*šûr* I) and 'to journey' (*šûr* II). This second meaning seems to have been adopted by the LXX (*eleusē kai dieleusē*) and by the Syriac (*t'tyn wt'bryn*), while the Vulgate (*coronaberis*) has read differently. At first glance, the parallelism would suggest a preference for the second sense. This is in fact the position of the majority of the translations.[139] But the meaning '(stoop down) to look', is, first of all, the ordinary sense of the term (sixteen attestations in the OT

[139] Cf., for example, Lys (1968), p. 177; Murphy (1990), p. 154; Ravasi (1992), pp. 371–372; Garbini (1992), p. 229; Rudolph (1962), p. 147.

against a single one of *šûr* II: Isa 57:9). Then, it agrees semantically with the theme of 'look' in v. 9b.[140] Particularly near to our passage is Num 23:9: "From the top (*mērōʾš*) of the rocks I see him, and from the hills I look down at him (*ʾăšûrennû*)". With this verb there may be an allusion to the representation of the *dea prospiciens*, a cult hailing from the Syro-Palestinian region but widespread everywhere, in the Mediterranean area as in Mesopotamia and Egypt, to which the numerous representations of the 'woman at the window' bear witness.[141] This theme returns in the Song at 6:10 ("Who is this who leans down like the dawn?") but has already been introduced in the image of the dove hidden within the rocky ravines (2:14).[142]

The place from which the woman is summoned to 'go away from' is 'Lebanon' (v. 8ab). The chain of mountains gives its name to the modern state. In its highest peak (*Qurnat as-Sauda*), it reaches 3088 metres. In v. 8cd, three other mountains are named in parallel with 'Lebanon': Amana, Senir and Hermon. These belong to the Antilebanon chain. Amana is generally identified with Gebel ez-Zebedani, the source of the River Amana (the 'Abana' of 2 Kgs 5:12). It dominates the central part of the Antilebanon opposite Damascus. The *massif* of Hermon (Gebel ash-Sheik, 2814 metres) represents the southern section of the Antilebanon on the frontier of Israel. Senir, mentioned alongside Hermon (v. 8d), could be one of the peaks of that *massif* since according to Deut 3:9 Hermon and Senir indicate the same mountain.[143] Garbini observes that the woman could not come from so many different places. He claims, therefore, that the invitation is being made to a divinity.[144] In fact there is only one region (the Lebanon-Antilebanon) of which the different names (to those already listed must be added the

[140] In this sense, for example, the translation of Robert – Tournay (1962), p. 170 (cf. *CEI*).

[141] Cf. Keel (1984a), Figure 319, p. 213; Fauth (1967).

[142] Cf., *supra*, p. 115.

[143] Senir and Amana are also paired in *Jub* 8:21. On the other hand, 1 Chr 5:23 supposes that there are two distinct mountains. For Loretz (1991), p. 138, Senir would be located in the northern part of the Antilebanon. According to our text, it is clear, in any case, that we have either two mountains, or two peaks of the same mountainous *massif*.

[144] "We find ourselves before a kind of prayer to the goddess of love, invoked before the embrace" (Garbini [1992], p. 228; so too Meek [1956], p. 123). But the destination of the invitation is clearly designated by the term 'bride', which, in our passage can indicate no one other than the woman of the Song (cf. the other occurrences in *Tab. 24*).

two expressions in v. 8ef) present different aspects. The indications are not to be taken in a realistic sense[145] but in their symbolic value.

The symbolism of 'Lebanon' is polyvalent.[146] A first dimension is that of 'height'. It is underlined by means of the expression *mērōʾš* ('from the summit', v. 8cd). It is from the highest point of the highest mountains that the woman is invited to look down. As the metaphor of the 'tower' (v. 4) has already shown, the vertical dimension expresses the woman's inviolability. It is the same *motiv* as that of 2:14 which reappears: there the dove was harboured 'in the rocky ravines, concealed (*sēter*) in the crags'. Here she is on the summit of the highest mountains, hidden within the "lions' lairs (*mᵉʿōnôt*)". The idea of inaccessibility is expressed also in Mesopotamian sources where 'Lebanon' is not only a garden of fragrant cedars but also a mountainous region difficult of access.[147] In the epic of Gilgamesh it is the refuge of the demon Huwawa (or Humbaba).[148]

Already in v. 6, the woman was compared to a mountain, precisely the 'mountain of myrrh and the hill of incense'. The numinous dimension of this identification is to be noted. In every religion, the mountain is the point on the earth nearest to heaven. The theophanies of both Old and New Testaments often happen on the top of a mountain, far from men, close to God (Exod 19:16–20; 34:5–9; 1 Kgs 19:9–13; Matt 17:1, 7). Lebanon in particular is known in biblical (cf Ezek 31) and extra-biblical sources as the dwelling of God, just like Mount Olympus in Greece.[149] It is connected above all with the cult of Tammuz-Adonis and Ishtar, as the upholders of the mythological interpretation of the Song have not neglected to stress.[150] The text does not offer elements

---

[145] Also unsatisfactory is the attempt to explain Song 4:8 with resort to Arab folklore. Keel cites a custom of the nomads of Hejaz and the southern Sinai, according to which the bride hides herself between the mountains on the occasion of her marriage. The bridegroom sets out in search of her, and, having found her, remains with her for a time on the mountains, until her pregnancy is advanced. Keel rightly notes that in our case the woman is invited not to go to the mountains, but to abandon them (Keel [1994], p. 155).

[146] On the symbolic value of Lebanon, cf. Müller (2001a).

[147] Thus Loretz (1991), p. 139.

[148] Cf. *ANET*, pp. 78–83.

[149] Cf. M. Weippert, *Libanon*, in *RIA*, vol. VI (1980–83), pp. 541–650, especially pp. 648–649: "Der Libanon als Götterwohnsitz"; Stolz (1972).

[150] Bertholet (1918) relates the myth according to which Tammuz seduces the very beautiful wife of Ephestus (Ishtar in person) and flees with her on to Lebanon. Here he first kills Ephestus; then, in his turn, he is killed by fierce beasts. But in our text, the woman is called to come away from Lebanon, not to go there! Be that as it may,

to make us think of a mythical interpretation, but perhaps this background plays a role. The woman is undoubtedly invested with a mythical, numinous halo.[151]

The reference of v. 8 back to v. 6 is confirmed by a double paronomasia: first of all, that already noticed between *l^ebônâ* ('incense') and *l^ebānôn* ('Lebanon'); then that between *har hammôr* ('mountain of myrrh') and *har^erê n^emērîm* ('mountains of the leopards/panthers'). The parallelism leads to the understanding of a contrast between the two representations: in v. 6 it is the attractive aspect of the 'mountain' that is being presented; in v. 8 its 'terrible' aspect is being underlined. It is another case of the paradox of love. What R. Otto says of the Holy, *mysterium fascinosum et tremendum*,[152] goes for love too: the poetics of 6:4–12 is composed on the contrast between these two aspects.[153] Even today, panthers (the Hebrew term *n^emērîm* can indicate both panthers and leopards)[154] live on the mountains of Lebanon, but the habitat of the lion was the desert or the undergrowth of the Jordan, not the Lebanon.[155] The expression has, therefore, once again, not so much a realistic as a metaphorical significance.

The goddess of love is often represented together with panthers and lions,[156] at times also in association with mountains:[157] it is the classical representation of the *potnia thērōn* (cf. 2:7; 3:6). The lions, like the young stag and the gazelles, personify the primitive forces of life which do not originate in human society, and are not at home in the city but in unspoiled nature. The man in 2:8 also comes from the mountains.

---

the Lebanon was the dominion of the *oreia mētēr*, the bride of the *ba'al l^ebānôn*, to whom different local traditions refer, and whose memory is present in Jer 22:23. Cf. Schmökel (1956), p. 75; Wittekindt (1925), pp. 164–168. The myth of Tammuz/Adonis was widespread in the Hellenistic epoch, as both Lucian (*De Syria Dea* 6ff), and Theocritus (cf. *Idyll* 15) attest. It is variously recalled in the OT, cf. Ezek 8:14; Dan 11:37. On the 'gardens of Adonis' cf., *supra*, p. 80, n. 152.

151 This element is stressed in Keel (1994), p. 155. Often in the iconography of the Ancient Orient the mountain is associated with a female divinity: cf., for example, *ibid.*, Figures 92 and 93, p. 156. But also in *ANEP*, Figure 464, p 160, the goddess is seated on a throne in the form of a mountain.

152 Otto (1963), pp. 13–36, 42–52.

153 Cf. Barbiero (1997a), p. 181.

154 Cf. Schouten van der Welden (1992), pp. 110–111.

155 Robert – Tournay (1963), p. 172, observe that the mountains of Lebanon are never cited in the ancient sources as the refuge of ferocious animals.

156 Cf. Keel (1994), Figures 94 and 95, p. 157; Figure 96, p. 159; *id.* (1984a), Figure 485, p. 336.

157 Cf. Keel (1994), Figures 97 and 98, p. 160.

Compared with the gazelle, the lion emphasises the terrible aspect of love (cf. 8:6—"For love is strong as death, jealousy relentless as the grave"). It is an ambivalent element: its power can build but also destroy.[158] Like every wild force, it has to be 'domesticated'. In Keel (1986), Figures 87 & 88, p. 147, the goddess of love holds a lion on the leash. G. Krinetzki interprets on the basis of psychoanalysis. Lions and panthers would be the dark side of femininity, the 'devouring mother'. They would represent an infantile stage of affective maturity which it is necessary to overcome. The 'mother' must give place to the 'bride' (cf. 3:11)[159] for love to become a fulfilling human experience.

For the first time in the Song the term *kallâ* ('bride'? v. 8a) occurs. In Hebrew, it stands not only for the 'bride' but also the 'daughter-in-law'. Analogously with the corresponding masculine term *ḥātān* (cf. 3:11), *kallâ* describes the link which marriage establishes between two different families.[160] It is the institutional aspect of love which is being underlined, an aspect which unites 4:8–5:1 to the nuptial procession (3:6–11) and to the *waṣf* (4:1–7; *kallâ* originally signifies 'veiled', cf. 4:1, 3). Although not dominant, the institutional theme was present also in the songs of the woman in the expressions 'our wall' (2:9) and 'the house of my mother' (3:4). It is the leaving of one's own family in order to found a new one (cf. Ps 45:11). The family offers protection and acceptance, but it can also impede the maturing of love. It has to be renounced, and the breach is never painless.

[v. 9] "You have made me mad...". The Hebrew *libbabtînî* is a denominative verb deriving from *lēb* ('heart'). Beside our passage, it appears again only in Job 11:12—"The foolish man becomes sensible (*yillābēb*)". The parallel is interesting because it allows us to understand 'heart' in the OT. It is not so much the seat of the feelings as of the reason. 'Heartless' with us is someone without love while in Hebrew it is someone who has lost his head, a madman. In Job, the verb has a positive sense ('to gain one's heart', that is, 'to become sen-

---

158 Perhaps the ambivalence of love, as source of life and death, is expressed in Keel (1994), Figure 39, p. 86, where, beside a human couple, two scenes of animals are represented: in the upper level, a lion who is attacking a gazelle (symbol of violence and death), in the lower two cherubs (guardians of the tree of life, cf. Gen 3:4?) (cf., also, *ibid.*, Figure 45, p. 91). A similar ambivalence seems to be expressed in Keel (1984b), Figure 485, p. 336, where a goddess (Ishtar?) restrains a lion by the tail with one hand and supports a gazelle with the other.

159 Krinetzki (1981), pp. 140–141; cf. Krinetzki (1970), pp. 411–412.

160 Cf. J. Conrad, *kallâ*, in *TDOT*, vol. VII, pp. 164–169.

sible'); in the Song, on the other hand, the sense is negative ('to lose one's heart', that is, 'to go mad').[161] This sense is coherent with the aggressive metaphors of v. 8ef ('lions', 'panthers'). The terrible power of love makes its effects felt.

That love causes loss of self-control, that it renders one 'mad' or even 'sick' is a universal human experience. 'Love-sickness' constitutes a theme of love poetry throughout the ages.[162] In Song 2:5 the woman says of herself that she is 'sick with love' (cf. 5:8); here it is the man who 'loses his head'. The 'mirror principle' of the Song, the reciprocity of amorous feeling, is confirmed. Mention was made of the 'heart' in 3:11 where the wedding was presented as "the day of the joy of his heart". The contrast between the two passages should be noted. On the one hand, love is the 'feast of the heart', on the other it causes one 'to lose one's heart'.[163] On the theological plane, Paul says of the Cross that it is at the same time foolishness and wisdom (cf. 1 Cor 1:18–25). The dynamic of love is similar: it leads the lovers 'out of themselves'. But to 'lose one's heart' is the only way to gain the 'heart's joy'.

To the appellation 'bride' (cf. v. 8a), v. 9 adds that of 'my sister'. We must not think of a marriage between blood relations, a practice widespread in Egypt[164] and also in the extended Jewish family.[165] In our case the appellation has a symbolic character. Both in the Mesopotamian texts of 'sacred marriage' and in the Egyptian love songs, 'brother' and 'sister' are the typical appellations of two lovers. They express the

[161] The expression is common to the Egyptian love songs, in which "*to lose the heart* [...] is equivalent to losing the moral conscience, not having the normal behaviour dictated by social conventions; and so falling into madness" (Mathieu [1996], p. 168). Against the background of the parallel with the Egyptian poetry, it is difficult to interpret the verb in a positive sense, as 'to take heart' (thus the Syriac and Symmachus) or 'to excite' (so also, for example, Waldman [1970]; Pope [1977], pp. 478–480).

[162] For the Egyptian love poetry, cf. Mathieu (1996), p. 179. Cf., for example, the fourth stanza of Papyrus Chester Beatty IA: "My heart quickly scurries away / when I think of your love... / O my heart, don't make me foolish! / Why do you act crazy? / Sit still, cool down, until the brother comes to you, / when I shall do many such things (?). / Don't let people say about me: 'This woman has collapsed out of love'" (2:9–10; 3:2–4, tr. Fox [1985], p. 53). In Egyptian love lyrics as in the Song, it is the heart that goes mad. This is seen in the second stanza of the same papyrus: "My brother roils my heart with his voice, / making me take ill... / (Yet) my heart is vexed when he comes to mind, / for love of him has captured me. / He is senseless of heart—/ and I am just like him" (1:8; 2:1–2, *ibid.*, p. 52).

[163] Notwithstanding everything, a positive significance for the verb *lbb* is, therefore, implicit!

[164] So, e.g., Ricciotti (1928), pp. 45–49.

[165] Cf., in this sense, BDB, p. 27 col. 2 (referring to Gen 20:12).

particular link which love creates between two people in terms of the tie of blood.[166] With the word 'bride' (*kallâ*) it is clear that the two lovers belong to two different families, that the woman is outside the family of the man. With the term 'my sister' (*ʾăḥōtî*), belonging to the same family is expressed. As Landy points out, the terms contradict each other.[167] The same person cannot be at the same time 'bride' and 'sister'. The juxtaposition is paradoxical and is not to be explained on the institutional plane but rather on the symbolic. On the one hand, the woman belongs to another family, she comes from outside, from the desert or from Lebanon. On the other hand, she is "flesh of my flesh and bone of my bones" (Gen 2:23). This formula refers to the relationship of consanguinity (in Gen 37:27, the brothers say of Joseph: "He is our brother and our flesh").[168] Love on the one hand leads one out of oneself, is an 'exodus', on the other it is a finding again the roots of one's own existence, the lost part of one's being.[169]

The cause of the madness is the 'looks' of the woman. We have noted the metaphorical coherence with v. 8c ('look') and, further back, with v. 1c ("your eyes are doves"). The Hebrew text *bᵉʾaḥad mēʿênayik* means, literally, "with only one of your eyes". Clearly the term *ʿênayim* is to be understood not in a static but dynamic sense as 'looks'.[170] The disturbing power of the eyes is expressed again in 6:5 ("Take from me your eyes for they are driving me mad!"), and finds a precise match in the Egyptian love lyrics where the 'loss of the heart' is often caused by a look from the person who is loved.[171]

In parallel with the 'looks', v. 9c uses a rare lexeme, *ʿănāq*. In the plural, the term indicates an ornament for the neck (cf. Prov 1:9; Judg

---

[166] Cf., e.g., how the mother of Inanna portrays to her the relationship which will unite her with her future spouse (Dumuzi): "Lo, the youth, he is your father, / lo, the youth, he is your mother" (according to *ANET*, p. 639, cf. Wolkstein - Kramer [1983], p. 35).

[167] Landy (1983), pp. 97–98.

[168] Cf., *supra*, p. 135.

[169] Salvaneschi (1982), p. 109, speaks of *regressio ad uterum*, and comments: "Man and woman have become brothers in love, elective affinity which recreates itself as ancient carnal bond, ending which is beginning".

[170] Cf., *supra*, pp. 175–176. *Contra* Pope (1977), pp. 480–482, who defends the physical meaning of the term, having recourse to representations of goddesses with many eyes. A magic power is often attributed to the eyes, something attested also by the popular term 'evil eye'. But in our case this aspect is not directly in question: we have here a normal girl!

[171] Cf. Mathieu (1996), pp. 163–164. Mathieu stresses that the most frequent motif is the look from afar. But certainly the theme is not exclusive to Egyptian poetry!

8:26).[172] From this, it seems logical to understand the singular as a part of this ornament, that is, a 'pearl' or another type of jewel.[173] The following noun *ṣawwārôn* is a *hapax*, but one clearly deriving from *ṣawwāʾr* ('neck', cf. v. 4a), and so the translation 'necklace' seems appropriate. To Garbini, it seems absurd "that the eyes and something which is relative to the neck, a necklace or whatever it may be, are being put on the same plane" and he translates, changing the text: "With one trait of your image".[174] Actually, to our Western taste, the parallel is quite unrefined. But, for the Ancient Orient it was not like this. In the Mesopotamian texts relating to sacred marriage, Inanna covers her body with jewels before meeting with her bridegroom.[175] This was not only a way of demonstrating the wealth which was being given in the dowry; in the words of Westenholz, the beauty of a woman was bound more to her jewels than to physical attributes. "Jewels are the symbol of beauty, femininity, sexual attraction, fertility, love and marriage".[176] Probably they had a magic value:[177] even today, in astrology, precious stones are connected with a particular star. The Oriental representations of the goddess of love often feature a nude woman, without clothes, but never without necklaces, bracelets and other jewellery.[178] Perhaps the fact that the same Akkadian word (*īnu*) signifies 'eye' and 'jewel'[179] can explain the juxtaposition of the two words in

[172] Thus the versions have translated: LXX *enthema*, 'ornament'; the Syriac *ʿqʾ*, 'little necklace'; Vg *crinis*.

[173] Cf. Robert - Tournay (1963), pp. 174–175.

[174] Garbini (1992), pp. 78–80.

[175] Cf. *ANET*, p. 638 ("Love in the Gipar"). In another song, Inanna recounts how she has prepared herself for the meeting with her love: "A golden ring I took in my hand, / Small beads I put on my neck, / Their rear side I fixed on my neck sinews" (Alster [1985], pp. 150–151, ll. 16–18). In the Assyrian poem which sings of the love of Nabû and Tašmetu, the goddess Tašmetu asks her partner Nabû to put an earring on her before their union in the garden, and Nabû replies to her by promising to put on her bracelets of carnelian (cf. Nissinen [1998], pp. 588 [text] and 608–609 [commentary]). Examples can be multiplied: the theme of jewellery is a *topos* of Mesopotamian amorous literature.

[176] Westenholz (1992), pp. 383, 387.

[177] Cf., again, Westenholz (1992), pp. 385–387 (with regard to the stones *šuba*); Ravasi (1992), pp. 375–376.

[178] Cf. *ANEP*, Figures 464, pp. 160; 479, p. 165; Keel (1994), Figure 43, p. 90; Figure 47, p. 91. On the function of jewels in the representation of the *dea prospiciens*, cf. Fauth (1967), p. 434. According to Fauth the traits of the goddess which are most emphasised are the eyes and the jewels.

[179] Cf. Malul (1997), p. 248.

our text. Both have the characteristics of 'sparkling' and of 'emitting flashes'.

An Egyptian love song brings together the charm of the eyes with that of jewellery:

> How fine is my sister to throw a lasso,
> without being the daughter of a breeder of bulls!
> With your hair you have thrown the rope to me,
> with your eyes you have captured me,
> with your necklace you have bound me,
> your ring is your branding iron.[180]

There should be noted here, as in the Song, the continuity between the parts of the body (hair, eyes) and the jewels (necklace, ring). Thus can be grasped the continuity between v. 9c and the description of the neck in v. 4. The 'necklaces' which are hung up there are made not only of 'shields', that is, of weapons of defence, but also of 'quivers', that is, weapons of attack, filled with highly effective arrows.

Second strophe: The kiss (4:10–11)

Verses 10–11 form a small unit that has a clear poetic structure (cf. *Tab. 27*).[181] They are constructed in synonymous parallelism: both are composed of four stichs of which the first two emphasise love's aspect of taste ('wine', v. 10b; 'flowing honey', v. 11a; 'honey and milk', v. 11b), the other two the aspect of smell ('balm', v. 10d; 'Lebanon', v. 11d); these last begin in the same way: *wᵉrêaḥ*, ('and the scent…', vv. 10c, 11c). The first distich of the strophe (v. 10ab) is characterised by the repetition of the term *dōdayik* ('your caresses') linked to the sense of 'taste'; the last (v. 11cd) is characterised by repetition of the term *rêaḥ* (scent) linked to the sense of 'smell'.

Table 27

v. 10	ab	TASTE	*wine*	*caresses*	*caresses*
	cd	SMELL	*perfume, balm*		
v. 11	ab	TASTE	*flowing honey, honey & milk*		
	cd	SMELL	*Lebanon*	*scent*	*scent*

[180] Papyrus Chester Beatty IC 17:2–3, according to Mathieu (1996), pp. 33–34. Fox (1985), p. 73, has a different translation.
[181] For the structure of the unit, cf., above all, Elliott (1989), pp. 104–107.

Table 28

1:2b	...*your caresses are sweet, sweeter than wine!*	4:10b	...*sweet are your caresses, sweeter than wine!*
1:3a	*your scents fragrant*: your name *perfume* freshly poured	4:10cd	And *the perfume of your scents sweeter than* any balm.

The second strophe is united to the first by the chiastic repetition of the terms 'bride' (vv. 8a, 11a) and 'my sister, my bride' (vv. 9a, 10a), and by the *inclusio* effected by the term 'Lebanon' (vv. 8ab, 11d).[182] Moreover, the alternation of the two senses 'taste' and 'smell' determines also the poetics of the third and fourth strophe. From contemplation we pass gradually to the enjoyment of love. Again there is desire: union is reached only after the assent of the woman in v. 16. It is symptomatic that the description of amorous enjoyment in 5:1 will take up again some of the terms of our strophe ('balm', 5:1b, cf. 4:10d; 'honey', 5:1c, cf. 4:11b; 'wine', 5:1d, cf. 4:10b; 'milk', 5:1d, cf. 4:11b).

As in the first strophe, here too the continuity with the *waṣf* of vv. 1–7 is to be marked: the beginning of the strophe (*mâ yyāpû* ['how sweet are'], v. 10a) echoes the beginning of the *waṣf* (*hinnāk yāpâ* [literally 'look, you are fair'], v. 1a) and the term *śiptôtayik* ('your lips') refer to v. 3. From the eyes (first strophe) we pass to the mouth (second strophe), from 'sight' to 'taste'.

[4:10] The verse clearly refers to 1:2–3. If we look at *Tab. 28*, we see that in the space of two stichs the two passages have five terms in common: *dōdîm* ('caresses'), *ṭôb* ('good, sweet'), *yayin* ('wine'), *rēaḥ* (perfume, scent'), *šemen* ('ointment, oil').

In 1:2–3 kisses are spoken of and so both aspects, taste and smell, are brought into play.[183] The term 'kiss' does not occur in 4:10 but it is clearly alluded to by the term *dōdîm* ('caresses'). What we have here is erotic play connected with the 'lips' and the 'tongue' (v. 11ab).[184]

---

[182] Cf., *supra*, *Tab. 22*, p. 174. In observing these precise references, one is naturally loth to replace the terms of MT with hypothetical conjectures, as does Garbini, who in v. 11 changes the term 'Lebanon' (*lᵉbānôn*) for 'incense' (*lᵉbônâ*). Such a procedure would upset the structure of the passage.

[183] Cf., *supra*, pp. 54–55.

[184] It is possible that the alliteration on the consonant *m* present in v. 10 (*mâ...mâ...miyyayin...šᵉmānayik...mikkol bᵉśāmîm*) is meant to imitate the kiss: to pronounce these consonants you have to position the lips as for a kiss. Thus Elliott (1989), p. 106; Ravasi observed something of the kind for the word *pîhû* in 1:2, cf. p. 54.

If the terms are the same, it is notable, however, that in the two cases the possessive pronoun refers to two different persons: in 1:2–3, it is the woman who is speaking of the kiss of the man; in 4:10–11, it is the man who speaks of the kiss of the woman. What the woman finds in her man, the man also finds in the woman: both are the subject and object of love. The third time that the kiss is mentioned, in 7:9b-10, it will be spoken of in the plural. From 'his mouth' (1:2), to 'your lips' (4:11), to the 'lips of the sleeping ones' (7:10). The text of the Song is coherent.

The term *yph* ('fair, sweet', v. 10a) refers to v. 1a. If referred to the woman, the adjective has an aesthetic character; referred, on the other hand, to erotic play (*dōdîm*), the emphasis is different. As Keel observes, referring to one of the Amarna Letters in which *yph* is set in parallel with *ḥmd*, the term also has the meaning of 'desirable'.[185] Assuredly, any negative judgement is absent from this connotation: desire is considered a positive reality as the parallel term, *ṭwb* ('to be good', v. 10b), underlines. On love's being 'sweeter than wine', we refer to the comment on 1:2. The metaphor of wine is often used in connection with the kiss (cf. 1:2; 7:9b–10; 8:2); it probably refers to the exchange of body fluids which occurs in a 'French' kiss (cf. v. 11). If wine inebriates, transporting its recipient into a condition of drunkenness, much more the kiss. It is that 'ecstasy' to which v. 9 already alluded and which will be taken up again at the end of the song in 5:1—"Drink, get drunk, my dears".

As in 1:2–3 (and in 7:9), here too the kiss is associated with smell: "And the perfume of your scents sweeter than any balm" (v. 10cd). Balm is mentioned frequently in the Song (cf. again 4:14, 16; 5:1, 13; 6:2; 8:14): among the scents it is that which returns most often (7 times!). The term can be understood in a general sense, as a synonym of 'scent',[186] but here it refers, as usually in the Song, to the perfumed resin obtained from the *Commiphora gileadensis*. According to Zohary, there are around a hundred species of *Commiphora*; thus we can see how it is possible to speak of 'all the balms' (v. 10d;

[185] Keel (1994), p. 68. Robert – Tournay (1963), p. 175, translate: "Que ton amour a des charmes".

[186] In fact, LXX has understood it thus: *panta ta arōmata*, 'all the scents', followed by Vetus Latina and Vg. This translation is adopted, for example, by Robert – Tournay (1963), p. 175, and almost all the modern English translations (cf. *NKJ, NJB, NRS*…).

cf. 14e).[187] In the OT, balm is connected with the figure of the Queen of Sheba (cf. 1 Kgs 10:2, 10; 2 Chr 9:1, 9) and of Solomon (cf. 1 Kgs 10:25; 2 Chr 9:24). It is not native to Israel, coming from the South of the Arabian peninsula, but the balm of Judaea was famous in the Roman epoch: it was cultivated, above all, in Jericho and Engedi, near to the Dead Sea, and the plantations were a royal monopoly that was guarded jealously. According to Pliny[188] and Josephus,[189] balm was the most sought after perfume of the time and, thus, also the most costly. It forms part, therefore, of the royal atmosphere which characterises the 'wedding' (cf. Song 3:6–11). Balm was used in the temple (1 Chr 9:29–30) and also employed in the making of anointing oil (Exod 30:23). With the Arabs today, it is valued for its medicinal properties. It had an important role in the preparation of dead bodies for burial (cf. 2 Chr 16:14; Jer 34:5; Mark 16:1, par), so much so that the verb 'to embalm' is derived from it. Naturally it had its place also in the cosmetic world, above all that of women (cf. Esth 2:12). We can appreciate, therefore, Herod's gift to Cleopatra of the balm plantations in the district of Jericho.[190]

However, every balm is a poor thing compared with the 'scents' of the beloved woman (v. 10cd). Keel observes that, despite the fact that the words are similar, the affirmation made in 4:10 is different from that of 1:3. There, in fact, the 'scents' were compared with the person (the 'name'); here they are compared with 'all the balms'.[191] In fact, we have the same thought expressed in different form, as is typical of the Song. In *Tab. 29*, the attributes of the person who is loved are listed on the left (the second person possessive should be noted), on the right the 'things' with which they are compared. In 1:3, 'your scents' are seen as something 'external' to the person, identified by the metaphor of the 'name'; in 4:10, they are identified with the person and compared with something external to her ('any balm'). In the expression 'your scents', the emphasis is on the possessive more than on the noun. It is an allusion, therefore, to the personal scent of the woman,[192] the scent of her femininity which is perceptible in the kiss. In 7:9, in connection with

[187] Cf. Zohary (1982), pp. 198–199.
[188] Pliny, *Naturalis historia* 12:54, 111.
[189] *Bell* 4:8, 3.
[190] Cf. Schürer (1973), Vol. I, pp. 298–300.
[191] Keel (1994), p. 165.
[192] The same, metaphorical, sense attaches to the expression 'my nard' in 1:12.

Table 29

1:2–3	Your caresses Your name	> >	wine *your scents*
4:10	Your caresses *Your scents*	> >	wine any balm

the kiss, 'the scent of your breath' (*rêaḥ ʾappēk*) is mentioned. There is no perfume that comes close to the scent of a woman. Her kisses are more intoxicating and invigorating than any kind of balm.

[v. 11] The verse begins with a stich that has a notable sonorous quality: *nōpet tiṭṭōpnâ śiptôtayik* ("your lips drip with flowing honey"). The vocal explosives *t* and *ṭ* imitate the drops: *nōpet* is not the usual term to indicate 'honey' (which is usually called *dᵉbaš*, cf. v. 11b). It is a rare term which, from the parallel in Ps 19:11, seems to indicate "a honeycomb which allows the most precious honey to drop because it melts without having to be pressed".[193] The thought, given the context (*dōdîm*, v. 10ab) turns naturally to the kiss, the sweetness of which is being indicated. The theme is known in the love poetry of the ages from the Sumerian texts on sacred marriage[194] to the Ugaritic myths.[195] Particularly close to the Song are some modern Palestinian songs: "Her saliva is like crystal sugar (or sugar candy), / O [*sic*], how sweet is the sucking of her lips, / sweeter than sugar or honey",[196] or: "Her mouth is sweet to me / it contains a honeycomb".[197] An interesting parallel is offered in the *Twentieth Idyll* of Theocritus where a young shepherd says of himself: "This mouth trim as a cream-cheese; and the voice which came forth o' this mouth was even as honeycomb".[198] The parallel is interesting also because here the lips are the instrument not

[193] Nolli (1967), p. 107; so too Delitzsch (1875) p. 76. The sense is confirmed by 5:1, where the 'honey' (this time called *dᵉbaš*) is mentioned together with the 'honeycomb'.

[194] "O my lubi, my lubi, my lubi! / O my labi, my labi, my labi! / My delicious wine, my sweetest honey, my lovely / "mouth of her/ mother"! / [...] / The kisses of your mouth transport me" (text recorded in Lavoie [1995], p. 138). Honey is often mentioned in the sacred marriage texts: the bridegroom is here called the 'honey-man' (cf. *ANET*, p. 645), the marriage bed 'perfumed bed of honey' (*ibid.*). On the erotic significance of honey cf. the citation of Krinetzki (*infra*, p. 212, n. 206).

[195] "He leaned down, kissed their lips; / and their lips were sweet, / sweet as pomegranates" (*KTU* 1.23, 49–50. Cf. Del Olmo Lete [1981], p. 445).

[196] Stephan (1922), p. 214.

[197] Dalman (1901), p. 134.

[198] Theocritus, *Idylls* 20:26–27 (tr. Edmonds [1923], p. 241).

only of the kiss but also of the 'voice'. A similar ambivalence is also encountered in the Song if the link with the *waṣf* is remembered (cf. 4:3, "Your speech is beautiful"). Not only are the kisses of the woman sweet; her words are too.[199]

Verse 11a has a surprising parallel in Prov 5:3: *nōpet tiṭṭōpnâ śiptê zārâ* ('the lips of the stranger woman run flowing honey').[200] The match is so exact that it is difficult to imagine that it is the result of chance or of a stereotypical expression. And the dependence goes clearly from Proverbs to the Song.[201] It is not the only case in which the Song takes up a text of the OT while changing its sense. Heinevetter is probably right in detecting a polemical intention.[202] The Song intends, that is, expressly to correct a negative conception of sexuality which is present in other books of the OT. Or, perhaps, it intends to oppose the love of the 'bride' (*kallâ*, 4:11a) to that of the stranger (*zārâ*, Prov 5:3).[203] This would be to re-enter the 'nationalistic' dimension of the Song which we have already met elsewhere: the author would thus be taking his distance from the Hellenistic, pagan conception of sexuality in order to celebrate the beauty of love as lived in Israel.

"Honey and milk under your tongue". Once again, the thought goes first of all to the 'wet' kiss of the two lovers in which the tongue plays an important role.[204] Beside this significance, we may also perceive here the other which is connected to the tongue as the instrument of speech. It is to this sense that the parallels in Job 20:12; Ps 10:7 lead, in which there is mention of the knavery of the wicked which is 'under the tongue'.[205] Antithetically, 'under the tongue' of the woman are words which nourish love ('honey and milk'). Words are surely

---

[199] Cf., also, in this sense Murphy (1990), p. 156; Elliott (1989), p. 305; Müller (1992), p. 48. This was the traditional interpretation of v. 11ab (one might look, for example, at the targumic literature), which, however, perhaps through prudery or allegorical intention, excluded the allusion to the kiss. That an expression could have two senses is not such a rare thing in the Song: cf., in this regard, Malul (1997).

[200] Among other things, the parallelism here with v. 3b ("Her mouth is smoother than oil") and the antithesis with 2b ("your lips may guard knowledge") suggest that the allusion is more to the speech of the woman than to her kisses. On the intertextuality between the Song and Prov 1–9, cf. Paul (2001).

[201] Cf. Robert – Tournay (1963), pp. 176–177.

[202] Heinevetter (1988), p. 130.

[203] We come to this conclusion by comparing the two texts. The Song repeats the text of Prov 5, word for word, only replacing *zārâ* with *kallâ* at the end. The process of 'estrangement' of the text principally concerns these words.

[204] Cf. *ANET*, p. 645 ("The sated lover").

[205] Cf. Elliott (1989), p. 305, n. 124.

not less important than kisses between the two lovers! But it is again a secondary sense here because the context speaks of 'taste' and 'smell', not of 'hearing'.

Krinetzki finds in the two foods of v. 11b ('honey and milk') a value linked to depth psychology: in the honey he sees a "symbol of fertility in love and in marriage", in the milk "the expression of the maternal feeling of the bride towards the bridegroom".[206] It is possible that such archetypal symbolism is unconsciously present. At the conscious level, we can discern an allusion to the promised land, a land in which, precisely, 'milk and honey' flow (Exod 3:8, 17; Lev 20:24; Deut 6:3, etc).[207] Already, in the Ugaritic literature, a paradisial abundance is indicated by this binome (for the OT, cf. Deut 32:13–14; Isa 7:15; Job 20:17).[208] The order of the two terms in these texts ('milk and honey') is the opposite of that in the Song ('honey and milk'). Despite this, the allusion seems clear. It would be, therefore, another example of the identification of the woman with the promised land (cf. Song 2:16–17; 4:6). If the woman is identified with the land, then the gifts are also the same. In the enjoyment of his own woman, the son of Israel experiences that fullness of life which YHWH has promised to his people in the land of Israel. In her he tastes the bounty of God. The approval of the joy brought by the love of a woman thus receives a theological dimension. It is recognition of the gift of God.

As in v. 10, so in v. 11, the olfactory aspect of the kiss follows the gustatory: "And the scent of your garments is like the scent of Lebanon". Garbini finds the reference to the garments out of place in a text that speaks of the kiss.[209] Perhaps our Western taste is different from that of the author of the Song. The scent of the clothes is spoken

---

[206] Krinetzki (1981), p. 144.

[207] Cf. Brenner (1999), pp. 105, 109.

[208] Cf. Lys (1968), p. 186.

[209] Garbini speaks of a reading 'manifestly absurd'. And he adds: "The position in which the term occurs [...] and its elimination from the text make one think easily that the original word would have indicated something relative to the sex of the woman". He therefore hypothesises a replacement of the Hebrew *ślmtjk* with *šblyk* and translates 'the odour of your sex' (Garbini [1992], pp. 78, 227–228). Apart from the debatable translation of *šōbel* in Isa 47:2 with 'sex' (I have not found this translation in any of the Hebrew dictionaries that I have consulted), the ancient versions all agree with the MT. The hypothesis of a corrupt text is, therefore, gratuitous. The only argument on which it is based is that of the 'non-sense' of the text received by the tradition. But this argument is easily refuted by the parallel with Gen 27:27. Garbini's procedure, of replacing the traditional text with a hypothetical 'unexpurgated' text, shows itself to be simply an excuse for writing a new Song of Songs.

of in the *epithalamium*, Ps 45:9, where it says of the bridegroom: "All your garments are myrrh, aloes and cassia". More precise is the parallel with Gen 27:27 in which Jacob receives the blessing which he has obtained by trickery from his father Isaac: "He (= Jacob) came near to him and kissed him (= Isaac). He (= Isaac) smelled the smell (*rêaḥ*) of his garments and blessed him and said: 'See, the smell of my son is as the smell of a field which YHWH has blessed'". The correspondence with Song 4:11cd is astonishing. First of all, we should note that in both cases (a) the talk about the 'smell' (*rêaḥ*) is associated with the kiss; (b) it is the smell of the garments not of the body which is being spoken of; (c) this smell is compared to that of the earth ('field', Gen 27:27; 'Lebanon', Song 4:11). This last aspect prolongs the *motiv* of the identification of the woman with the promised land, hinted at already in v. 11b ('honey and milk'). The theme will be taken up again and developed in the following strophe by means of the metaphor of the garden.

That Lebanon is a reference to the promised land is confirmed by the parallel with the end of the book of Hosea where the eschatological Israel is compared a good three times to Lebanon (Hos 14:6, 7, 8).[210] The second is particularly close to our text: "His (= Israel's) fragrance (*rêaḥ*) will be like Lebanon" (Hos 14:7). The Lebanon with its extensive conifer woods (cf. Isa 40:16) and its flowers was considered in antiquity as the garden of God (cf. Ezek 31:8).[211] The poet sees a likeness between the woods which 'clothe' the slopes of Lebanon and the garments which cover the woman's body. Moreover, the Hebrew word *l^ebānôn* evokes the word for incense (*l^ebônâ*). The 'Lebanon' recalls the 'mountain of myrrh and the hill of incense' (v. 6cd), the perfumed body of the woman.

A refinement: we should note the parallelism between v. 10cd ("and the scent of your perfumes sweeter than any balm") and v. 11cd ("and the scent of your garments is like the scent of Lebanon"). The parallelism is not perfect, because, while the scent of the woman is superior to that of balm ('sweeter than', v. 10d), it is equal to that of Lebanon

[210] On the connections between Hos 14:6–8 and the Song, cf. Gangloff (1999).

[211] Confirmation of this reputation comes in a passage from Florus, in which Pompey's crossing of the Lebanon chain is described in these words: *per nemora illa odorata, per turis et balsami silvas* (*Epitome of Titus Livius* 1:40, 29 [LCL, p. 188]). Neither incense nor balm is found in the forests of Lebanon, so that these terms are to be taken in a general sense as synonyms of 'perfume'.

('like', 11d). In the light of Gen 27:27 and Hos 14:7, it could not be otherwise: the woman cannot be better than the promised land since she is part of it.

Third strophe: The garden (4:12–15)

The third strophe is closely connected with the fourth by the metaphor of the 'garden' (*gan*, 4:12a, 15a, 16ce; 5:1a; cf. *Tab. 24*), so that many authors consider the two strophes as a single unit.[212] Rarely is the link between vv. 12–15 and the preceding context given attention. The third strophe continues the speech of the beloved man begun in v. 8 (cf. the *inclusio* by means of the term 'Lebanon', vv. 8, 15): in v. 16 the woman begins to speak. Moreover, the description of the garden is connected directly with the mention of Lebanon in v. 11: Lebanon is the 'garden of God' (cf. Ezek 31:8–9). The theme of the promised land has been introduced already in the preceding strophe.

The third and fourth strophes are distinguished between themselves not only by the speaking subject but also by the different dynamic. The third strophe is quiet, contemplative, a musical 'adagio'. From the point of view of literary genre, we have a sort of *waṣf*, a descriptive song.[213] As is typical of description, the text is made up of nominal propositions.[214] There are only four verbs, all participles ('enclosed/stopped' [twice], v. 12ab; 'sealed', v. 12b; 'welling up', *nōzᵉlîm*, v. 15c). Vv. 13–14 are a 'list': there is no finite verb.

The fourth strophe, on the other hand, is characterised as a furious movement, an '*allegro con fuoco*'. Here we find, in only two verses, a good thirteen verbs, one per stich; the last stich (5:1f) has two. Three subjects begin to speak, one after the other: the woman (4:16), the man (5:1a–d), and the poet (5:1ef). The passage from the third to the fourth strophe is, therefore, the passage from contemplation to action. But the contemplation in vv. 12–15 is already preparing the action: the emphasising of the 'enclosed garden' in 4:12 was an urgent request to open up. The reply of the woman in v. 16 shows that she has understood it thus.

---

[212] Cf., for example, Keel (1994), pp. 167–184; Müller (1992), pp. 49–53; Gerleman (1965), pp. 157–162.
[213] Cf. Horst (1981), p. 178.
[214] Cf. Müller (1992), p. 50.

Table 30

A	v. 12	FRAME	Garden (*gan*)—spring (*ma'yān*)
B	v. 13	FOOD PERFUME	pomegranates *with* delicious fruits henna shrubs *with* clusters of nard
B'	v. 14	PERFUME { PERFUME {	nard *and* saffron, calamus *and* cinnamon *with* every tree of incense myrrh *and* aloes *with* all the most precious balms
A'	v. 15	FRAME	Garden (*gan*)—spring (*ma'yān*)

The strophe is made up of a frame (vv. 12, 15, cf. *Tab. 30*) in which the 'garden' (*gan*) and the 'spring' (*ma'yān*) are mentioned, and of a central part (vv. 13–14) in which are listed the plants of this marvellous garden. The two verses vv. 13 and 14 make up the two sections of the list. In the first section (v. 13), two fruits (v. 13ab) and two aromatic plants (v. 13c) are placed in parallel. Thus the structure of the previous strophe, which highlighted the two senses of taste and smell, is repeated. It will be seen that the fourth strophe is also structured on this binome.

The second section (v. 14) develops the theme of smell, listing other aromatic plants. In all, there are twelve plants, a number which makes one think of the tribes of Israel, thus confirming the identification of the woman with the promised land already alluded to in the third strophe. The play between singular and plural is to be noted as well as the variation between the conjunction (*w*^{e}, 'and') and the preposition (*'im*, 'with'). This last occurs four times, once for each half verse, and joins two terms in the plural or a plural with a group of terms in the singular,[215] united by the conjunction.[216] The procedure obeys a rule of sound: the sound *'im* rhymes with the plural ending *-îm*. As Müller observes, 'enumeration' is a particular genre of ancient literature which, through the accumulation of objects, creates an impression of superabundance,[217] of luxury.

[215] Only the term *'ăholôt*, literally 'plants of aloes' (14d), is in the plural.

[216] The construction here is so careful, whether from the sonorous or the syntactic and semantic point of view, that the various attempts to change the order of the plants (for example, Rudolph [1962], p. 151; Müller [1992], p. 49) appear out of place.

[217] Müller (1992), p. 50; *id.* (1988b), p. 201. In this connection, Müller cites parallels among the more ancient Greek lyrics (Alcaeus, Sappho). Some of Homer's descriptions

[4:12] Here, as in v. 15, the MT does not have any verb so that the reading in the third person ("A garden enclosed is my sister, my bride")[218] is equally possible to that in the second person ("Garden enclosed, my sister, my bride"). Since the whole song is a direct speech, it seems logical to suppose that such discourse continues in v. 12. As for the translation, again the discrepancy between the MT and the ancient versions must be signalled with regard to the term *gal* in v. 12b. Many commentators suppose an error in the Hebrew text and follow the versions which read *gan* ('garden') in parallel with v. 12a.[219] However, the parallelism with v. 15, where a duality of 'spring' and 'well' is supposed, speaks against such a correction. The term *maʿyān* ('spring', v. 15a) is repeated literally from v. 12b, while *bᵉʾēr* ('well', v. 15b) corresponds to *gal* in v. 12b. In Ugaritic, in fact, the term *gl* signifies 'cup' but also 'basin in the form of a cup', 'pool'. The root is present in the Hebrew *gullâ* (cf. Josh 15:9; Judg 1:15), in the Akkadian *gulla-tu* and in the Greek *gaulos*.[220] Both in v. 12 and v. 15, therefore, distinction is being made between the 'spring' of water (*maʿyān*) and the 'basin' (*gal*, *bᵉʾēr*) in which it is collected.

The Hebrew term *gan* ('garden', v. 12a) derives from the root *gnn* ('to close'). The lexeme already contains within itself the concept reaffirmed by the adjectives 'closed/stooped' (*nāʿûl*, v. 12ab) and 'sealed' (*ḥātûm*, v. 12b). The 'garden' is mentioned again in 6:2, 11 and 8:13, but it is in our passage that the theme is developed into a complete metaphor. It is a topic that is widespread in Oriental love lyrics: in Mesopotamia,[221] as in Egypt,[222] parallels are found very similar to the text of the Song.[223] As Keel explains,

---

also come to mind. For the biblical world, by way of example, we should look at the already cited passage of the Apocalypse, Rev 18:11–13.

[218] So, among others, Robert – Tournay (1963), p. 179 (cf. *BJ*); Müller, p. 49; Rudolph (1962), p. 150.

[219] Thus, for example, *BHS*; Robert – Tournay (1963), p. 179; Rudolph (1962), p. 150; Murphy (1990), p. 156; Garbini (1992), p. 229.

[220] Cf. Pope (1977), p. 488; Ravasi (1992), p. 384; Lys (1968), p. 188; Elliott (1989), p. 305; Heinevetter (1988), p. 126 (H. ends up supposing that *gan*, in v. 12a, is a correction for an original *gal*).

[221] Cf., in this respect, Cooper (1971), p. 161; Nissinen (1998), pp. 616–619; Watson (1995), pp. 260–261; Westenholz (1992), pp. 382–393.

[222] Cf. Niccacci (1991), pp. 71–76; Mathieu (1998), p. 152 §28.

[223] Cf., in general, Paul (1997), pp. 100–108. Paul stresses the ambivalence of the metaphor in the three cultures: it can indicate both the place of love and the body of the woman, in particular her genitals (p. 100).

> one of the most beautiful things and one of the most greatest pleasures known to the ancient Near East was a garden—a carefully enclosed and heavily watered plot of ground planted with fragrant plants, blooming bushes, and trees filled with choicest fruits.[224]

In Israel every house had its little orchard: in it were fruit trees (cf. Jer 29:5; Amos 9:14), above all the vine and the fig (cf. 1 Kgs 5:5; Mic 4:4; Ps 128:3). The more well-off families had more extensive gardens-parks for which it was necessary to have a reservoir for irrigation, something attested in the story of Susanna (cf. Dan 13). Naturally the king possessed a splendid garden (cf. Qoh 2:5–6; Jer 39:4; 52:7; Neh 3:15). Like the house of the king, the temple also, the house of God, was endowed with a garden, the 'garden of God' (cf. Gen 13:10; Ps 52:10; 92:13–16). Moreover this was also the situation in Mesopotamia[225] and in Egypt.[226] The 'garden of God' was in its turn symbol of the garden of paradise. The term 'paradise' also appears in our text (v. 13a) with allusion (at least in the LXX) to the story of Gen 2. We have already hinted at the relationship between the Song and the situation of man before the Fall: the garden of Paradise and the garden of the Song express the same nostalgia for a love that has not been contaminated. Moreover, under the symbol of the garden is represented also the eschatological situation of Israel when God will once again dwell with men (cf. Isa 58:11; Jer 31:12; Ezek 47:1, 7, 12; Rev 22:1–2). It is interesting to observe the use of the metaphor of the garden which is made in Sir 24. Wisdom makes its home in the land of Israel and grows in it like the plants of a marvellous garden (vv. 13–17). Like the woman of the Song, Wisdom is not only the garden but also the water that irrigates it (vv. 23–29; cf. Song 4:12, 15). What Sirach says of Wisdom, the Song says of Love personified in the woman. The nationalistic tone (the identification of the garden with the promised land) is common to both, and readily understandable in the Hellenistic epoch as an affirmation of Israel's own cultural identity in the face of a more developed civilisation.

---

[224] Keel (1994), p. 169.

[225] Cf. Keel (1978), Figure 191, p. 143; *id.* (1994), Figure 100, p. 169. Nissinen (1998), pp. 616–619, claims that the 'garden', in which the encounter between Nabû and Tašmetu takes place, is actually the garden of the temple, in which the statues of the two gods are to be found.

[226] Cf. Keel (1994), Figure 101, p. 171.

"Garden enclosed, my sister". The woman is not 'like' a garden. She is herself the garden just as her eyes are 'doves' (Song 1:15; 4:1). The identification of the woman with the garden is a particular case of her identification with the land, a recurrent theme in the Song. The significance of the 'vineyard' (cf. 1:6) is analogous. Throughout the Ancient Orient, the 'garden' is, on the one hand, the place of love (cf. 1:16b–17; 7:12; 8:5c), on the other, a metaphor for the sexuality of the woman. This last aspect is evoked in an Egyptian love song:

> I am yours like the field
> planted with flowers
> and with all sorts of fragrant plants.
> Pleasant is the canal within it,
> which your hand scooped out,
> while we cooled ourselves in the north wind.[227]

Keel comments:

> The 'canal' scooped out by the lover's hand can hardly be anything but the deflowered vagina, because 'hand' probably serves as a euphemism for phallus in Egyptian as it does in Ugaritic and in Hebrew.[228]

This sense is present also in Sir 26:20 (Syriac and manuscript 248 of LXX): "After having searched for the most fertile field in the land, sow it with your seed, trusting in the nobility of your race". The context makes it clear that 'field' is a metaphor for the woman.

In parallel with the 'garden' is set the 'fountain' (*gal*). The woman is, therefore, not just the garden but also the water that irrigates it. In the Middle East, a garden is unthinkable without a source of water: the plants depend totally on irrigation as is recorded in Ps 1:3; Jer 17:8; Ezek 47:12.[229] As in the case of the 'garden' so also in that of the water we can perceive a double sense. Prov 5:15–18 is a good example:

---

[227] Papyrus Harris 500C 7:7–8, tr. Fox (1985), p. 26. Among the Sumerian texts is often cited the description which Ludingira gives of her mother: "My mother is rain from heaven, water for the finest seed, / a harvest of plenty, […]/ a garden of delight, full of joy, / a watered pine, adorned with pine cones, / a spring flower, a first fruit, / an irrigation ditch carrying luxuriant waters to the garden plots, / a sweet date from Dilmun, a date chosen from the best" (tr. according to Cooper [1971], p. 161).

[228] Keel (1994), p. 174, cf. Fox (1985), pp. 26–28.

[229] Cf., for example, Keel (1978), Figure 191, p. 143; *id.*, (1994), Figures 100, p. 169; 101, p. 171.

> Drink water from your own cistern,
> flowing (*nzl*, cf. Song 4:15) water from your own well (*be'ēr*, cf. Song 4:15).
> Should your springs (*ma'yān*, cf. Song 4:12, 15) be scattered abroad,
> streams of water in the streets?
> Let them be for yourself alone,
> and not for strangers with you.
> Let your fountain be blessed,
> and rejoice in the wife of your youth.

The water which quenches one's thirst becomes a metaphor for the love with which a woman can satisfy her man. This metaphorical significance of water is present also, in the background, in the gospel story of the Samaritan woman (John 4) and in a passage, particularly crude, in Sirach (Sir 26:12): here mention is made, reciprocally, of the sexual 'thirst' of the woman. In Proverbs, the love of one's own wife is opposed to that of the 'strange' woman which, by analogy, is called 'stolen water' (Prov 9:17). The emphasis here, as in the Song, is placed on the exclusivity of love.

The 'garden' and the 'fountain' are, of course, 'closed/stopped' (*nā'ûl*). The verb describes an object (a door, for example), closed from within with a bolt. In fact the same root also expresses the 'bolt' (*man'ûl*) in 5:5: indeed, the situation described in 5:2–6 (*paraklausithyron*) can be regarded as a comment on our verse. Moreover, the theme of the inaccessibility, the enclosure of the woman has already appeared in 2:9, 14 and 4:4. If we compare our text with Prov 5:15–18, the difference in viewpoint can be observed. In Proverbs, the chastity of the woman is considered from the point of view of the man, to whom is reserved the exclusive enjoyment of the love of the woman ("Let them be for yourself alone").[230] In the Song, the point of view is that of the woman. The gate is opened from within: the man, even the woman's own husband, cannot 'enter' without seeking permission. In this sense, the stress which is emphatically placed on 'enclosure' is an

[230] The sense of Prov 5:15–18 is not so clear. The problem is the meaning of v. 16: do the 'springs' and the 'streams' refer to the love of the woman, or to the male sperm? In the latter sense, the instruction would turn on the faithfulness of the man to his wife, in order not to produce bastards (cf. Sir 26:19–21, according to ms 248 of LXX). On the other hand, by understanding the metaphor of the water in v. 15 with reference to the woman (as is more obvious, seeing that the metaphor has this sense in vv. 15 and 17–18), then the instruction would be an exhortation to satisfy one's own wife sexually, so that she will not seek satisfaction elsewhere.

indirect request for the 'opening' of the garden. Only after the woman has given her consent (v. 16) does the man enter. As the following song shows, if the woman does not open, the encounter cannot happen: and permission must be sought each time; otherwise the encounter is not love but violence.[231]

In parallel with 'fountain' in v. 12bβ is placed the term *maʿyān* (spring). As is the case also in v. 15 and in Prov 5:15–18, the woman is not only the vessel which contains the water for the irrigation but also the 'spring' which is that water's source. That is to say, as v. 15 will make explicit, that this water is not stagnant but flowing, 'living', and, furthermore, that the garden is autonomous with regard to irrigation: it does not have to obtain water from elsewhere as happened in Egypt where the water for the garden was obtained from canals.[232] That allows the garden to be well and truly 'closed'.

This fact is confirmed by the participle 'sealed' (*ḥātûm*), which forms a parallel with *nāʿûl* ('closed'). If the latter indicates closing from within, the 'seal' indicates closure from without. If one wanted to enter, one had first to break the seal: the seal set on a door prevented furtive entrances that had not been authorised. Assuming the erotic significance of 'fountain', the seal set on it makes one think of the hymen, evidence of the virginity of the young woman.[233] How important the virginity of the bride was in the Oriental mentality is witnessed by the custom of preserving the sheets from the first night with their traces of blood (cf. Deut 22:13–21).[234] The lexeme *ḥtm* returns in the *Epilogue* of the Song in 8:6 ("Set me as a seal upon your heart, as a seal upon your arm"). This time the seal is no longer set on her: she herself becomes the seal of the union which has taken place. Whoever wants to sepa-

---

[231] This aspect is very prominent in the Jewish tradition. In the *Pesikta de-Rab Kahana*, we read: "In this way, the Torah, even if only incidentally, also teaches good manners: for example, that it is not good for the bridegroom to penetrate the chamber of the bride before she has given permission for this. In fact, first it is said: 'Let my beloved come into his garden' (Song 4:16) and only then: 'I have come into my garden' (Song 5:1)" (cf. Di Sante [1985], 127–128).

[232] Cf. *ANEP*, Fig. 95, p. 28.

[233] In a modern Arab poem, a young girl declares her own virginity with these words: "A bucket has never been lowered on to me to draw water" (cf. Dalman [1901], p. 107). As Paul says, the Hebrew expression *ptḥ ptwḥ* ('an open door') and the Arab *maftûḥa(t)* ('opened') are euphemisms for a virgin who has been deflowered (Paul [1997], p. 106).

[234] Among the peasants of Syria, the day after the wedding night, there used to take place a 'judgement', in which the 'king' was invited to show his 'bloody trophies', as a sign of the conquest that had taken place. Cf. Wetzstein (1873), p. 290.

rate the two has to break the seal. Chastity is consummated in union. Be that as it may, the seal, here too, expresses the exclusivity of love. Krinetzki comments, from the point of view of depth psychology:

> In the things of erotic-sexual love, the woman is narrowly monogamous: she can truly belong to only one man. The participial style of the passage leads us to understand that here we have fundamental affirmations on the being of woman, in the biblical sense.[235]

[vv. 13–14] The translation of the term *šelāḥayik* at the beginning of v. 13 is disputed.[236] It derives from the root *šlḥ* ('to send').[237] Two meanings are possible: the first, in continuity with the metaphor of water, is: 'your canals' (cf. Neh 3:15).[238] Given the context, the reference would be to the vagina. But the plural speaks against such an interpretation. The second sense is: 'your shoots' (cf. Isa 16:8). Here the link would be with what follows: the term would have a collective significance to designate the various plants which are listed in the following text. This second alternative seems more convincing.[239] The metaphor would refer directly to the female pubic area, the hairs of which evoke the idea of the shoots in a garden.[240] There is an allusion, therefore, to the female sex: but it is a delicate allusion, expressed in

[235] Krinetzki (1981), p. 31. But, according to the mirroring dynamic of the Song, this aspect goes for the man too (cf. 6:8–9).

[236] Cf. the discussion in Görg (1993).

[237] Hence the versions: LXX *apostolai sou*, Vg *emissiones tuae*, and the Syriac *šlyḥwtky*.

[238] *šlḥ* II according to *HALOT*, p. 1517. In this sense, for example, Keel (1994), pp. 174–176; Krinetzki (1981), p. 148. Such imagery is present perhaps in Sir 24:30–31, of which, however, the Hebrew text has not come down to us.

[239] So too, among others, *HALOT*, p. 1517 (*šlḥ* II); Heinevetter (1988), p. 127, n. 91; Robert - Tournay (1963), p. 181; Gerleman (1965), pp. 159–160. Moreover, it is the traditional interpretation, supposed also by the ancient versions.

[240] So also Görg (1993), p. 23. A Sumerian song can be seen as confirmation: "My 'wool' is lettuce, he wants to water it, it is lettuce grown in a bed, he wants to water it" ("wool" and "lettuce" are metaphors for pubic hairs, text according to Jacobsen [1987], p. 93); or also the following words addressed by Innana to Dumuzi: "I poured out plants from my womb; / I placed plants before him, I poured out plants before him; / I placed grain before him, I poured out grain before him" (cf. Kramer [1969], p. 101). For a vivid representation, one could look at the four pendants in Keel (1994), Figures 104–107, p. 175. Proposals to change the MT are not lacking. Garbini, for example, associates himself with the conjecture *lḥyk*, already advanced by Dalman, Perles, Rothstein. But while they translate "your cheeks", Garbini, consistent with 1:10 e 4:3, renders: "your hips" (Garbini [1992], pp. 78, 229), seeing in the term an allusion to anal intercourse (!). But, as far as I know, the 'hips' of the woman (as also her cheeks) do not grow any 'plants' in particular!

the symbolic form typical of the Song. In itself the text could also have a general sense and indicate the body of the woman.[241]

The Hebrew term *pardēs* is the first of numerous foreign words employed in vv. 13–14. The term derives from the ancient Persian *paradidam* ('behind the wall'), in Avestan *pairi-daēza* ('walled enclosure').[242] In the OT, the lexeme is used again only in Qoh 2:5 and in Neh 2:8, and indicates a royal park. The LXX translates as *paradeisos*, as in Gen 2–3 and in Ezek 28 and 31, where the 'garden of God' is mentioned: it identifies explicitly the garden of the Song with the Garden of Eden. In both gardens marvellous plants are growing (cf. Gen 2:9).[243]

The first two plants of the series (v. 13ab) are fruit trees: thus returns the theme of 'taste' introduced in the previous strophe. The 'pomegranate' (*rimmôn*) has already been mentioned in the *waṣf* (v. 3, *à propos* of the cheeks). There the aesthetic aspect was presented, here it is rather the erotic aspect which is being alluded to, as in Song 8:2, where the expression 'the juice of my pomegranate' is placed in parallel with 'perfumed wine' to indicate the joys of love. The term 'pomegranate', moreover, is well linked with 'paradise', given that the pomegranate is often identified with the tree of paradise, 'the tree of life', in Oriental iconography.[244]

The 'delicious fruits' (*pᵉrî mᵉgādîm*) are not to be understood as the fruits of the pomegranate.[245] The preposition *ʿim* ('with'), in vv. 13–14, always unites two different types of plants (cf. *Tab. 30*): it is practically equivalent to a conjunction. This use of *ʿim* is not usual in Hebrew: it corresponds to the Greek *hama*. It is, therefore, a Graecism which should be added to the others already noted, witnessing to the Hellenistic dating of the Song.[246] Moreover, *mᵉgādîm* is not a collective

---

[241] Cf. Keel (1994), Figure 67, p. 117. But the preceding verse, with the metaphor of the fountain and of the seal, also alluded to the genital sphere. And moreover it is to the sexual relationship that the metaphors of 'eating' and 'drinking' refer in 4:16–5:1. These are 'allusions', in metaphorical language, open to other meanings, but the Oriental parallels on the one hand and the context on the other make us inclined to a 'specific' interpretation, clearly sexual, of the 'garden'.

[242] Cf. Müller (1988b), p. 195.

[243] According to a Jewish tradition, Adam, when expelled from Paradise, obtained permission from the angels to take with him some perfumed plants, precisely the plants listed in Song 4:13–14 (cf. Ginzberg [2003], Vol. I, p. 77). The tradition is attested, among other places, in the *Life of Adam and Eve* (43:4, *OTP* II, p. 274) and in the *Apocalypse of Moses* (29:6, *OTP* II, p. 285).

[244] Cf., *supra*, pp. 183–184, and Keel (1994), Figures 80 and 81, p. 144.

[245] *Contra* Keel (1994), p. 176.

[246] So Graetz (1871), pp. 58–59.

term to indicate the fruits listed in what follows: in v. 16 and in 7:14 it is used in connection with the verb 'to eat' while the plants of vv. 13b–14 are aromatic plants. The term is to be considered, therefore, in parallel with 'pomegranates', indicating other types of fruit. The 'fruit' (*p*ᵉ*rî*) has a clearly erotic connotation here (cf. 2:3).[247]

The term *m*ᵉ*gādîm* is rare in the OT. Other than in the Song it recurs only in Deut 33 (vv. 13, 14 [twice], 15, 16) where it indicates the products of the promised land. Behind the garden of the Song, then, we can catch a glimpse not only of the Garden of Eden but also of the garden of the promised land. In the fruits which his woman gives him, the man recognises the fruits with which Moses blessed the tribe of Joseph. This is not, we repeat, an allegory. The text speaks clearly of the joys involved in sexuality. But this acquires a theological dimension: they are integrated in the Yahwistic faith and in the tradition of the people of God.

There follows a list of ten aromatic plants (vv. 13c, 14). To our taste, such a list can seem dry, precisely when we would be looking for the maximum of passion.[248] The Hebrew text has an exquisite musicality. It is undoubtedly erudite poetry: foreign terms abound, from Sanskrit (turmeric, nard, aloes) and even from Malayan (cinnamon). These words create an exotic and aristocratic atmosphere: the author wishes to transport us into a fabulous world.[249]

Of henna or cypress (*kōper*) we have already spoken in 1:14 (cf. also 7:12).[250] The plural *k*ᵉ*pārîm*, here as elsewhere in vv. 13–14, seems to refer to different plants, that is to different henna 'shrubs' rather than to different species of *Lawsonia*. Henna is the only one of the plants listed that grows spontaneously in Israel: even today it can be found in Jericho and in the valley of the Jordan, just as in the coastal plain.[251]

---

[247] It is a meaning widespread in the amorous literature of the Ancient Orient, above all in Mesopotamia, where 'fruit' (*inbu*) represents sexuality, masculine or feminine. In the epic of Gilgamesh, Ishtar begs the hero: "Come, Gilgamesh, be thou (my) lover! / Do but grant me of thy fruit" (*Gilgamesh* 6:7–8, according to *ANET*, p. 83). In the ritual Maqlû III, 8–10, 'fruit' is put in parallel with female sex appeal: "She robs handsome man of his vitality. She takes the pretty girl's fruit. With her glance, she steals her sex appeal" (Paul [1997], p. 100, n. 1). Cf. also Nissinen (1998), p. 619.

[248] Garbini (1992), p. 230, speaks of a 'coldly intellectual' piece, of a 'dry list of spices', which "does not bear the least trace of poetry". Differently, Müller (1988b).

[249] Cf. Müller (1988b), pp. 200–201. Because of the rare terms, the identification of the plants is disputed, as can easily be observed by comparing the different translations.

[250] On the symbolic value of this plant, cf., *supra*, pp. 276–277.

[251] Cf. Zohary (1982), p. 190.

Nard (*nērd*) too is already known to us: in 1:12, the perfume of nard is a symbol of the erotic attraction of the woman. The plant (*Nardostachys jatamansi*) is of the valerian family, originally from the region of the Himalayas and cultivated in India, from where its perfume was imported through Arabia. The term 'nard' is repeated twice: the first time at the end of v. 13c, in the plural (*n^{e}rādîm*, 'clusters of nard'), the second, in v. 14a, in the singular. The repetition is seen as an error by some exegetes who either eliminate v. 13c as dittography[252] or exchange *nrdym* for *wrdym* ('and roses').[253] Gerleman rightly observes that "the repetition should be attributed rather to the overloaded style, full of sentimentality":[254] perhaps sonority also plays a role. To these poetic considerations it is to be added another, theological, one: the number of plants has to be twelve to fit the symbolism mentioned above.[255]

karkōm is a *hapax* in the Bible. The LXX (*krokos*) and the Vulgate (*crocus*) have understood it as the 'crocus' or 'saffron', a plant widespread throughout the Mediterranean and used as a condiment and for colouring. But the Arab *kurkum* designates both the 'crocus' and the 'turmeric' or 'yellow radish' (*curcuma longa*), a radish cultivated in China, Bengal and Java, and it too used as both condiment and colouring. Post-biblical sources attest the use of *karkōm* and other perfumes hailing from India and South East Asia in the temple in Jerusalem. Since in our passage the origin of the other perfumes is analogous, it seems more probable to identify *karkōm* with turmeric rather than with the crocus.[256]

qāneh (LXX, *kalamos*; Vulgate, *fistula*) is a common term to indicate all kinds of 'reed'. Here it must be the 'aromatic calamus' (*qāneh bōśem*, or *qāneh ṭôb*), which was used for the anointing oil together with myrrh, cinnamon and cassia (cf. Exod 30:23). According to Jer 6:20, the calamus was imported from distant countries and was very dear (cf. also Isa 43:24). In Ezek 27:19, it is one of the commercial

---

252 So, for example, Robert – Tournay (1963), p. 181.

253 Thus, following Graetz (1871), p. 164; Rudolph (1962), p. 151, and Nolli (1967), p. 110. But the term *wrd*, 'rose', never occurs in the Hebrew Bible (only in Sir 24:14, in Greek): it is typical of the Rabbinic literature (and frequent in the Talmud).

254 Gerleman (1965), p. 157. Compare this observation with the judgement of Garbini in n. 248.

255 Cf., *supra*, p. 215.

256 So Zohary (1982), pp. 206–207; Keel (1994), p. 178. Löw inclines towards the crocus, although he recognises the possibility of thinking of the turmeric (Löw [1926–1934], vol. II, pp. 7–28). H. N. and A. L. Moldenke are clearly in favour of the crocus (Moldenke & Moldenke [1952], p. 87).

products of Tyre: Pliny informs us that it grew in Arabia and in India.[257] It is disputed which plant corresponds exactly to the *qāneh bōśem*: according to Zohary, it is one of the species of the *Cymbopogon* (*Cymbopogon martinii*, still cultivated in India, from which palmarosa oil; *Cymbopogon schoenanthus* or 'camel grass'; *Cymbopogon citratus*, the 'West-Indian lemon grass').[258] Levesque proposes, less correctly, the identification with the *Acorus calamus*.[259] Misleading, however, is the often suggested identification with our cinnamon:[260] this is the spice to which we now turn.

Cinnamon (*qinnāmôn*) is precisely the tree from the bark of which the spice 'cinnamon' is extracted. Originating in the island of Ceylon and the coasts of India (*Cinnamomun zeylanicum*), it is used, even today, both as perfume and as condiment. There is another type of cinnamon, Chinese cinnamon or cassia (*Cinnamomun cassia*), from which the garments of the king-bridegroom are perfumed in Ps 45:9. In the OT, cinnamon, together with aromatic calamus, was an ingredient of the anointing oil (Exod 30:23). It is mentioned again, together with myrrh and aloes, in connection with the bed of the 'strange woman' (Prov 7:17) and, together with balm, in the praise of Wisdom in Sir 24:15. As Zohary explains,

> land and sea trade routes for drugs, perfumes and incenses not only existed between the Mediterranean and Indian coasts but also extended farther east, joining the very ancient "silk route" between India and the Far East.[261]

Such a trade is unimaginable before the Hellenistic period.[262]

We have already spoken of 'incense' (*l^ebônâ*, cf. 3:6, 4:6). Incense is an exotic fragrance. "It was imported into the land of Israel by the Phoenicians via the famous spice route across southern Arabia and some of the littoral stations of East Africa".[263]

Myrrh (*mōr*) will also be recognised (cf. 1:13; 3:6; 4:6). 4:6 speaks of the 'mountain of myrrh and of the hill of incense': 'incense' and

---

257 *Naturalis historia* 12:48, 104, 106.
258 Zohary (1982), p. 196; so also Moldenke & Moldenke (1952), pp. 39–41.
259 E. Levesque, *Roseau aromatique*, in *DB(V)*, vol. V, coll. 1206–1207; so too Robert – Tournay (1963), p. 183: for another view, cf. Löw (1926–1934), vol. I, pp. 692–697.
260 Cf. Ravasi (1992), p. 389.
261 Zohary (1982), p. 202.
262 So Müller (1988b), p. 197.
263 Zohary (1982), p. 197.

'myrrh' are now listed among the trees of the garden (4:14). The continuity between the *waṣf* and the present song should be grasped: the 'garden' is, in fact, part of the 'mountain'.[264] It is worth stressing that myrrh too is an imported product: like incense, it grows in Arabia and also in Ethiopia and Somalia.

'Aloes' is always in the plural in Hebrew (*ʾăhālôt* or *ʾăhālîm*), perhaps to indicate that the perfume was extracted from different species of the plant. This is not the medicinal aloes (*Aloe vera*) of which John 19:39–40 speaks, but the perfume extracted from *Aquilaria agallocha* ('eagle wood') as also from other species of *Aquilaria*. Aloes was imported from Northern India and Eastern Africa.[265]

The mention of 'balm' echoes v. 10d: in both cases the term has a comprehensive function which is indicated both by the plural (with which not only different plants but also different species of the plant are designated) and by the universalising particle *kol* ('all balms'). Moreover, balm is the most precious of the various perfumes listed.[266]

The list of perfumes is not realistic: in fact, it is impossible to cultivate together in one garden plants so disparate and from such different climates. It has the character of hyperbole, intends to express the unreal, the exaggerated: note the expressions 'every tree of incense' (v. 14c), 'all the most precious balms' (v. 14e). In other words, there is no garden in the world that contains in itself all the 'perfumes' which are in the woman's genital area. In the OT, we can match four parallels to the list in the Song. Two refer to erotic attraction (Ps 45:9—'myrrh, aloes and cassia'; Prov 7:17—'myrrh, aloes and cinnamon'), one to holiness (Exod 30:23–24—'balm, myrrh, cinnamon, aromatic calamus, cassia'), one to Wisdom (Sir 24:15—'cinnamon, balm, myrrh, galbanum, onyx, stacte, incense'). The longest list, that of Sirach, has seven perfumes; in the Song there are ten, this number also indicating fullness. Leaving Sirach apart, perhaps later than the Song, the parallel with Ps 45, and above all that with Exod 30:23–24, is the nearest to our text;[267] they confer on the list of perfumes in vv. 13b–14 a tone that is both regal and sacral.

---

[264] On the symbolic significance of myrrh, cf., *supra*, the comment on 1:13 (p. 76).

[265] Cf. Löw (1926–1934), vol. III, pp. 411–414; Moldenke & Moldenke (1952), pp. 47–48; Zohary (1982), p. 204.

[266] Cf., *supra*, pp. 208–209.

[267] The expression *bᵉśāmîm rōʾš*, 'the most precious balms' (Exod 30:23), makes one think directly of *roʾšê bᵉśāmîm* (Song 4:14e).

Table 31

4:12b	fountain		spring
		×	
4:15ab	spring		well

[v. 15] The verse forms an *inclusio* with v. 12: both have the words 'garden' and 'spring' in common. Not only that, in both, 'water' is mentioned by means of a similar binome of 'basin' and 'spring'. The two binomes form a chiasm (cf. *Tab. 31*). If one also bears in mind the other *inclusio* formed by the term 'Lebanon' with v. 8, it seems logical to conclude that the verse is pronounced by the man as the conclusion, on the one hand, of the third strophe (vv. 12–15) and, on the other hand, of the entire discourse begun in v. 8.

The problems arise when one observes the content. In v. 12, the 'enclosure' of the garden and of the spring was highlighted. Here, instead, it is said, on the one hand, that the fountain irrigates 'the gardens' (v. 15a), implying the opposite of its being closed, because the waters flow out of the garden; on the other hand, that the water does not spring up from the garden itself but has its source 'from Lebanon' (v. 15c). It seems as though the affirmations of v. 15 intend deliberately to contradict those of v. 12. Because of this, different authors put the verse in the woman's mouth,[268] something syntactically possible, because it is a nominal proposition to which one can attribute a subject in the first ("I am"), the second ("you are") or even the third person ("the woman is").[269] The structural reasons mentioned above speak for a continuation of the discourse in the second person, so pronounced by the man. In this sense, the contrast between the 'enclosure' of the garden in v. 12 and its 'opening' in v. 15 should be understood not as a contradiction but as one of the many paradoxes of love, which lives precisely on the tension between these two poles. Moreover, the theme of 'opening' introduces the reply of the woman in v. 16.

"Spring of the gardens". The plural is a problem. The Song always speaks of a 'garden' in the singular, alluding to the body of the woman. How, then, do we explain the plural? Some authors, basing themselves on the LXX (Codex Vaticanus) *kēpou*, think of a scribal error. Gordis,

---

268 For example: Gordis (1974), pp. 60, 88; Lys (1968), pp. 194–197.
269 So, among others, Rudolph (1962), p. 151; Müller (1992), p. 49.

for example, translates: 'of my garden', substituting *gannî* for *gannîm*.[270] Others understand the plural as a generalising one ('garden spring')[271] or think that the plural alludes to the different flower beds of the garden.[272] Taking the plural in its obvious sense ('spring of the gardens'), the text seems directly to contradict Prov 5:16–17, quoted as a parallel of Song 4:12—"Should your springs be scattered abroad, your streams of water in the street?" The metaphor of the 'garden' has evidently a broader sense here than in v. 12. Just as in the 'our vineyards' of 2:15 we recognised the plural of the two lovers, so now there is a move to the general: love gives life not only to the womb of the woman (v. 12), but has an analogous function for others, even for all.[273] *Bonum diffusivum sui*, we could say with the Latin adage. Perhaps it is a case of that 'plural of love' discovered in 1:4cd and 3:10e. Naturally the first to be 'watered' is the man, but he, by contrast with v. 12, is no longer jealous of this love. Thus the affirmation of exclusivity is found in tension with that of the sharing of love. Landy sees here an analogy with the 'river' which waters paradise in Gen 2:10–14.[274] The garden is not able to contain the abundance of water, which overflows and waters the whole earth, forming the four great rivers of the world. The myth of the rivers of paradise is widespread throughout the Orient. In the famous fresco of Mari, two female divinities support a vase from which there issue four rivers,[275] while in an ivory from Asshur the rivers issue from a god-mountain.[276]

"Well of living water". The Hebrew *mayim ḥayyîm* indicates, first of all, 'running water' by contrast with water from a cistern. That the water of the garden would have this characteristic is already implicit in the fact that the garden is provided with a spring (vv. 12, 15). If the water is running, it cannot remain in the garden; it must also over-

---

[270] Gordis (1974), p. 88.

[271] So, among others, Krinetzki (1981), p. 149; Gerleman (1965), p. 157 ('Gartenquelle'); Lys (1968), p. 194 ('fontaine de jardins'); Murphy (1990), p. 157 ('garden fountain'); Ricciotti (1928), p. 233 ('fonte da giardini'); Ravasi (1992), p. 338 ('sorgente di giardini').

[272] For example, Elliott (1989), pp. 113–114.

[273] Keel recognises an 'augmentative function' in the plural. Cf. Keel (1994), p. 180. We are in line with the hyperbolic language of vv. 13–14.

[274] Landy (1983), pp. 194–198.

[275] Cf. Keel (1978), Figure 191, p. 143; also *ANEP*, Figure 516, p 175.

[276] Cf. Keel (1994), Figure 80, p. 144. So it is also in our text, in which the spring, on the one hand, is the woman herself (Song 4:15a), on the other, Lebanon (v. 15c), cf., further, *infra*.

flow into other gardens. But the expression goes beyond its material significance, since the theme of life is fundamental to the Song (cf. 8:6). 'Water' is in itself a symbol of life in the OT. Without water, life is impossible: the land becomes a desert. Frequently, the metaphor of water is applied to YHWH: he is the 'fount of living water' (Jer 2:13; 17:13). In our passage, water is the symbol of the love which the woman can give to her man. Love, therefore, occupies the place which Jeremiah attributes to God. The matter could appear scandalous, idolatrous. It is instead another example of that theological dimension of love that has already been revealed several times: love is a 'flame of YHWH' (Song 8:6). John takes up this symbolism again. The 'well of living water' is at the centre of Jesus' discourse with the Samaritan woman (John 4), where the threefold significance of water—the concrete, bound up with natural thirst; the thirst of love; and the thirst for God—is fully present. John takes the reverse journey from that of the Song. He transposes the human experience of love on to the divine theological level. The Song transposes on to the level of human relationships all that the prophets had said of the love of God. The experience of love is experience of God because it is experience of life.

The statement of v. 15c, according to which the water "wells up from the Lebanon", is surprising. If the woman is the spring and the garden, how can the water come from outside? 'Lebanon' here clearly has a symbolic, not a realistic significance, in conformity with the whole context. The symbolism of Lebanon is manifold: in v. 8, it is the place of origin of the woman, and therefore of love. In v. 11cd, Lebanon is the woman herself according to the metaphor introduced in v. 6. In our verse, Lebanon is placed in connection with water. The parallel with Jer 18:14 helps one to understand how it is first and foremost the inexhaustibility of such a spring that is being highlighted: "Can the snow of Lebanon leave the highest rock? Can the foreign waters which well up (*nôzᵉlîm*, cf. Song 4:15) cold change their course?"[277] The perennial snows of Lebanon guarantee the perennial nature of its springs. In the passage from Jeremiah, the Lebanon becomes the symbol of YHWH (cf. v. 15: "My people have forgotten me"). A similar value is perceptible also in the text of the Song. If, on the one hand, the water originates from the woman and on the other hand from the snows of

[277] On the translation and meaning of this difficult passage in Jeremiah, cf. Barbiero (2002).

the mountain,[278] it is a sign that love, present in the woman, proceeds from something higher than her, that is from God. For this reason it is perennial; it is never exhausted ("Many waters cannot quench love", Song 8:7).

The water of the garden is indeed 'living water'—'sealed' but not stagnant. It is open to what lies downstream, since from this spring the other 'gardens' are watered, and to what lies upstream since the water that gushes out in the garden has its origin in 'Lebanon'. So it is with love: closed in on itself, it dies. Only love that is open is a love that is living.

Fourth strophe: The union (4:16–5:1)

The strophe is characterised as a conversation among different personages. We have assumed that in 4:16 it is the woman, in 5:1a–d the man, and in 5:1ef the poet (or at any rate an outside voice) that speaks. As in an operatic finale the different characters who have taken part in the action appear together on the stage: first the woman who spoke in 2:8–3:5; then the man whose song has resounded in 4:1–15; and finally the 'voice off-stage' which made itself heard in 3:6–11. The solemn finale signals the culminating moment of the poet unit 2:8–5:1.

The strophe is articulated, by the change of characters, into three parts: (a) 4:16 = the woman; (b) 5:1a–d = the man; (c) 5:1ef = the poet. The three parts are constructed in a diminishing progression: the first has six stichs, the second four, the third two. They are joined together by a careful climactic concatenation, similar to that noted for the first strophe, by which each character repeats words of the preceding one and adds to them something new (cf. *Tab. 32*).

Table 32

4:16	WOMAN	*coming into the garden*	*balm*	*eating*		
5:1a–d	MAN	*coming into the garden*	*balm*	*eating*	*drinking*	
5:1ef	POET			*eating*	*drinking*	*getting drunk*

[278] For a visual illustration of this dual nature of the origin of the water, we refer to Keel (1978), Figures 42, p. 47; *ANEP*, Figure 528, p. 178; Keel (1994), Figure 81, p. 144.

Table 33

II strophe	4:10ab	A	TASTE (drinking)	*wine*
	10cd	B	SMELL	*balm*
	11ab	A	TASTE (eating-drinking)	*honey, milk*
	11cd	B	SMELL	
III strophe	13ab	A	TASTE (eating)	*delicious fruits*
	13c–14	B	SMELL	*myrrh, balm*
IV strophe	16a–d	B	SMELL	*balm*
	16ef	A	TASTE (eating)	*delicious fruits*
	5:1ab	B	SMELL	*myrrh, balm*
	5:1c–f	A	TASTE (eating-drinking)	*honey, wine, milk*

We have spoken of the macrostructural links of this strophe with the preceding one. It is worth underlining the exact lexical hooks. Beside the double *inclusio*, by means of the terms 'garden' (4:12 and 5:1; cf. 4:16ce) and 'my sister, my bride' (4:12; 5:1), we should note the repeat of the following terms: *nzl* ('to well up, to spread', 4:15c, 16d); *bśm* ('balm', 4:14e, 16d; 5:1b); *pry mgdym* ('delicious fruits', 4:13b, 16f); *mwr* ('myrrh', 4:14d; 5:1b). Further, the repetitive use of the preposition *ʿim* ('with, together with') with the value of a conjunction (4:13bc, 14cd and 5:1bcd) is characteristic in the two strophes.

Even though the two first and the two last strophes of the song form two pairs, it should be noted how transverse links unite the first three strophes (in that it is pronounced by the man, the *inclusio* by means of the term 'Lebanon' in 4:8, 15 is to be noted). An analogous phenomenon is discernible between the last three strophes: they are structured according to the binome smell-taste and connected by precise lexical references (cf. *Tab. 33*).

Not only because of the alternation of the two senses but also because of the lexical references, a chiasm between the third strophe and the reply of the woman in v. 16 should be noted, as also an *inclusio* between the second strophe, 4:10–11, and 5:1. Along these lines, the passage 4:10–5:1 demonstrates at the level of macrostructure a chiastic arrangement which is transverse to the dominant structure: (a) 4:10–11; (b) 4:13–14; (b') 4:16; (a') 5:1.

The union of the two lovers-spouses, described in the last strophe under the metaphor of smell and taste, is already heralded in the two preceding strophes: the song shows itself profoundly unitary.

[4:16] The speech of the woman in v. 16 is to be understood as her reply to the preceding discourse of the man in vv. 8–15. In the latter an ardent desire for union was expressed. Even the description of the 'enclosed' garden in v. 12 was an urgent request to open it. But the garden was closed from within: only the woman could open it. And this is what happens in v. 16: the woman opens her garden to her beloved. The theme of opening has already been introduced in v. 15 to which v. 16 makes direct reference by means of the verb *nzl* (to well up):[279] just as water 'wells up' from Lebanon, so the hidden perfumes have been summoned to 'well up' from the garden.

Syntactically, v. 16 is composed of six short stichs. To the nominal phrases of vv. 12–15, which express contemplation and stasis, the movement of six verbs is counterposed. The last words of each stich are linked together by rhyme or assonance: *ṣāpôn* / *têmān* (a + b); *bᵉśāmāyw* / *mᵉgādāyw* (c + e); *gannî* / *gannô* (d + f).[280] From the point of view of content, two invitations 'to come' (*bwʾ*) are expressed: the first regards the winds (v. 16a-d), the second the beloved man (v. 16ef). The 'coming' of the winds is to prepare that of the beloved.

In the case of the winds, rather than an invitation, we have a conjuration, a magical rite.[281] Generally, the names of the winds are masculine. Here they are considered feminine (the imperatives are, in fact, feminine: *ʿûrî, bôʾî*), perhaps with reference to the term *rûaḥ* ('wind') which is feminine. However, the gender does not seem to be accidental. The two winds, as matrons of honour, 'friends of the bride', have to prepare for the coming of the bridegroom. Just as the sixty mighty men represented the bridegroom before the bride, so the two winds are the maidens who represent the bride before the bridegroom. The winds in question are the cool wind from the North (*ṣāpôn*)[282] and

[279] I do not see any reason for making the Hebrew *ʿizzᵉlû* derive from *zll*, 'to shake', instead of from *nzl*, as Garbini opines (1992), p. 228, who, as the only reason, adduces the fact that *zll* "contains a greater erotic weight". From the grammatical point of view, such a derivation is not sustainable (MT moreover is supported by all the versions). From the structural point of view, the reference to v. 15 would be lost.

[280] Cf. Graetz (1871), p. 166. Such a rhythmical structure speaks against the attribution of the verse to two distinct persons (*contra* Keel, Heinevetter and Nolli, cf., *supra*, p. 9).

[281] Cf. Krinetzki (1981), pp. 153–154.

[282] The term perhaps originally designates the sacred mountain of Ugarit, today *Jebel el-Aqraʿ*, but also, generally, the 'North' (cf. Gen 13:14; Jer 26:26) and, in particular, the 'North wind' (cf. Prov 25:23; Sir 43:20) (cf. E. Lipiński, *ṣāpôn*, in *TDOT*, vol. XII, pp. 435–443). In Egypt, the 'North wind' is identified with the sea breeze and is par-

the warm and impetuous wind from the South (*têmān*).[283] The name of the two winds is a merismus: it is intended to indicate the entire group of winds (cf. Isa 43:6). There is little point, therefore, in seeing hidden meanings in these two specific winds.[284] The whole cosmos is summoned to the aid of love.

The North wind has to 'awake'. In the Song, the verb *ʿwr* ('rouse, awaken') appears in the 'refrain of awakening' (2:7; 3:5; 8:4), with the negative sense of 'rousing from the sleep of love', and in 8:5 with the positive sense of 'rousing for love' ("Under the apple tree, I have *woken* you").[285] Our text comes close to this last passage. The awakening of the wind is a prelude to the awakening of the 'garden'. The garden was full of marvellous perfumes, but they were asleep like the Sleeping Beauty of the fairy story. The woman had not yet been 'awoken', opened to love.

The South wind is adjured to 'come' (*bwʾ*) to prepare for the 'coming' of the beloved man (v. 16e).[286] The task of the winds (even if the verb is, in distributive manner, in the singular, the reference is to both the winds)[287] is that of 'making the garden breathe'. The Hebrew has here a *hiphʿil*, a causative form of the verb *pwḥ* ('to breathe'). The verb appeared in *qal* form in 2:17 and 4:6—there it expressed the 'breathing' of the day, the wind of evening. Even if it is possible to understand the *hiphʿil* here too as a *qal* ('breathe on my garden'),[288] I do not see any difficulty in understanding the verb literally and considering 'my garden' as the subject of the verb 'breathe'.[289] The sense is that

---

ticularly favourable to the promenading of those in love (cf. the passage of Papyrus Harris 500 quoted *supra*, p. 218).

[283] Analogously to *ṣāpôn*, *têmān* is also at the same time: a) a specific geographical term to indicate the southern region of Edom; b) a general term to indicate the South, and c) also the 'South wind' (cf. *HALOT*, pp. 1725–1726).

[284] Delitzsch (1875), pp. 79–80, thinks that the alternating of cold and hot is favourable to the growth of the tree, and that the change of direction of the winds is good for the spreading of perfumes. As forced as ever is the erotic interpretation of Garbini, who sees in the two winds an allusion to "the double form of the embrace" (!) (Garbini [1992], p. 228, cf., *supra*, note 240).

[285] With a clear sexual connotation ('to excite sexually'), perceptible in Mal 2:12 (cf. Glazier-McDonald [1986]).

[286] Just as *ʿwr*, so too *bwʾ* has a sexual connotation, cf. *infra*.

[287] Cf. Robert - Tournay (1963), p. 186.

[288] So *NJB, NKJ, NRS*, with the majority of modern translations.

[289] Thus, for example, Delitzsch (1875), p. 80; Lys (1968), p. 198; *NAS*: "Make my garden breathe out fragrance".

of 'releasing its perfumes'.[290] Perhaps one can grasp the nuance that the release is spontaneous and not violent. Not without reason, Keel juxtaposes to this passage Ezek 37:9 where the wind, coming on to the dry bones, causes them to live again (cf. Ps 104:30).[291] The juxtaposition can seem irreverent, but perhaps it is a testimony once again to the sacred character of sexuality and of the mystery of life with which it is connected. The reference to the conclusion of the *waṣf* is evident. The 'sigh of the day' (Song 4:6) alludes to the 'breathing of the garden' (Song 4:16): it is the time for love.

The first person possessive should be noted: '*my* garden'. Verse 16e will speak of '*his* garden', that is, the garden of the bridegroom. There is no scribal error here, nor is it necessary to imagine two different subjects for the discourse.[292] The woman herself first declares that the 'garden', that is, her body, belongs to her (cf. 1:6e; 8:12a); then she makes a gift of this body to her beloved so that it becomes 'his', it belongs to him. It is another paradox of love which lives on the tension between the affirmation of oneself and the gift of oneself.[293] Only when the woman discovers her own identity (cf. the images of enclosure in v. 12) can she arrive at the gift of herself; otherwise, one cannot speak of a true gift, only violence or moral blackmail. And on the other hand, only in the gift of herself does the woman discover her true identity (cf. v. 15). What the gospel says of the following of Christ, goes also for human love: only the one who loses his own life finds it. Whoever wants to keep it loses it (cf. Luke 9:24 par.).

V. 16d ("let its balms spread") is an explanation of v. 16c, that is, of the 'breathing' of the garden. The two terms 'spread/well up' and 'balms' are linked with the preceding strophe (v. 14e: 'balms'; v. 15c: 'welling up'). Here, however, 'balms' has the generic significance of 'perfumes': it stands for all the species listed in vv. 13c–14. 'To spread/well up' (*nzl*) establishes a parallel between the perfumes and the water. Just as the water wells up from Lebanon, so the perfumes spread from the garden. The welling up of the water is bound up with the fact that it is 'living' (v. 15b); so too the spreading of the perfumes follows the

[290] Cf. the Arabic *fwḥ*, 'to shed perfume' (according to *HALOT*, pp. 916–917).

[291] Keel (1994), p. 181. The two orders given to the winds in Ezek 37:9 are similar to those given in Song 4:6: the first, *bô'î*, 'come', is the same in both texts; the second, *pᵉḥî bᵉ*, 'blow on', uses a synonym (and homonym) of *pwḥ*, the verb *npḥ*. In Ezek, the *qal* form is used, and the complement is signalled by a preposition (*bᵉ*: 'on').

[292] Cf., *supra*, p. 194, nn. 126 and 127.

[293] Cf., *supra*, p. 185.

arrival of the breath of life—it is the sign of 'breathing'. Love seeks to be given just as perfume to be 'sprinkled' (*ntn ryḥ*, 1:12; 2:13).

After the wind has 'come', the beloved can 'come' into the garden which is now 'his' (v. 16c). In the Song, the verb *bw'* expresses the union of the two lovers (cf. 1:4; 2:4; 3:4; 4:6; 8:2). Moreover, 'to go' or 'to go down' 'into the garden' are common expressions to describe sexual congress in the love literature of the Ancient Orient.[294] Here too, therefore, the reference to the union of the lovers is clear. It takes place in the environment of marriage, as is emphasised by the appellation 'my sister, my bride', which is repeated at the beginning and at the end of the song of the garden (4:12; 5:1). However, it is remarkable that the woman does not call the man by the name of 'bridegroom' but with that of 'my beloved' (*dôdî*) to confirm the fact that they remain 'friends', even after the wedding.[295] It is also interesting to note the way in which the encounter is described. At first the 'garden' is active; it pours forth its perfume; it gives itself. Then it becomes passive; it receives. This last aspect is typical of female sexuality.[296] The man in his turn 'takes possession' of that which has first been given to him: there is not a shadow of oppression. And perhaps, also, before 'entering', there has to be a time for 'the perfume to breathe', the time for desire and for being in love. The encounter is prepared for.

The sexual value of 'entering' is confirmed by the metaphor of food at v. 16f. 'Eating' and 'drinking' are archetypal metaphors for sexual

[294] Cf. the long list of texts in Paul (1997), pp. 100–108, where, together with passages from the Song, are collected Sumerian, Akkadian and Egyptian texts, as also medieval Arabic and Hebrew poetry. The theme is also developed in Westenholz (1992), p. 382; Kramer (1969), pp. 100–101. We quote some examples: "My (?) sister, I would go with you to my garden / My fair sister, I would go with you to my garden" (Ni 4171, rev. 10f., according to Westenholz [1992], p. 382); "He (Dumuzi) made me (Inanna) enter, he made me enter, / (my) brother made me enter his garden. / Dumuzi made me enter his garden, / to lie with him at his standing tree; / he made me stand with him at his lying tree. / By an apple tree, I kneeled as is proper" (CT 58, 13, according to S. M. Paul [1997] 101). In an Akkadian composition, the goddess Tašmetu replies to the god Nabû, who asks her why she is all dolled up: "So that I may [go] to the garden with you, my Nabû [*] / Let me go to the garden, to the garden and [to the Lord! *] / Let me go alone to the beautiful garden" (Nissinen [1998], p. 590); "To the garden of your lover when I/he/she [...]/ Zarpānītum will go down to the garden" (BM 41005 obv. ii, according to Lambert [1975], pp. 104–105). Each text has its particular characteristic: at times the garden is a metpahor for the man's sexuality, at times of the woman's; on other occasions, it is the place of the amorous encounter. At times, the various meanings are superimposed.

[295] Cf., *supra*, pp. 163–164.

[296] Cf. Krinetzki (1970), pp. 408–411.

union (for the OT, cf. Prov 9:17; 30:20).[297] The objects of 'eating' are those *p^erî m^egādāyw* ('delicious fruits') of which the man spoke in v. 13. The term will return in 7:14 with the same erotic connotation.

Is it possible to see behind these 'fruits' an allusion to the fruits of paradise? The term *p^erî* appears in Gen 3:2, 3, 6. In the Genesis passage, an erotic background analogous to that in the Song is discernible:[298] in the two cases, mention is made of 'eating the fruit' and it is the woman who offers this 'fruit' to the man. The allusion is rendered probable by the numerous other cross references between the account of paradise and the Song. It is interesting to note how, in the Song, any shade of sin is absent from the 'eating of the fruit'. Sexual union is looked at as a positive experience, wholly satisfying, as the observation of the poet in 5:1ef expressly underlines.[299]

[5:1a–d] The man, rejoicing, welcomes the invitation addressed to him by his bride. The four perfect tenses are to be understood as an expression of the impatience with which the man was awaiting this invitation: the woman has scarcely had time to say 'come' (4:16d) when the man has 'already come' (5:1a) into the garden. The perfect here expresses an action begun in the (near) past but not yet completed (cf. 5ef).[300] As Elliott observes, the four verbs express a logical succession: first the man 'comes' into the garden (v. 1a), then he 'gathers' something in it (v. 1b), next he 'eats' what he has gathered (v. 1c), and finally he 'drinks'. The four stichs are carefully structured. Each time, the verb is followed by two nouns, both with the pronominal suffix in the first person, and united between themselves by the preposition *ʿim* ('with, together with'). The first stich is an exception: the second noun is not the subject of the verb but a vocative ('my sister, my bride'; cf.

[297] Cf. Lavoie (1995); Brenner (1999).

[298] Cf. Müller (1992), p. 52.

[299] Here, as elsewhere, it seems that the Song intends expressly to correct a negative conception of sexuality which sees sexual enjoyment as a source of sin, highlighting, by contrast, its positive value. From a theological point of view, in the one case as in the other, we have words which the Jewish and Christian tradition have received as inspired. Truth is always dialectical. It is a question of synthesising the two aspects of sexuality, that of its fundamental good, and that of the risk of idolatry which it always involves. Precisely because the food is 'good to eat', there is the risk that from being the gift of the Creator, it becomes an idol adored for its own sake. Of this aspect the Song says nothiing, perhaps because already abundant attention had been paid to it in the other books of the OT.

[300] Joüon (1923), §112e; *GKC* §106g. For discussion on the tense of the four perfects, cf. Ravasi (1992), p. 397.

Table 34

I have come	into *my* garden, *my* sister, (my) bride,
↓ have gathered	*my* myrrh with *my* balm,
↓ have tasted	*my* honeycomb with *my* honey,
↓ have drunk	*my* wine with *my* milk.

Tab. 34). The triple repetition of the same paradigm (v. 1bcd) creates a strongly emotional effect.

The objects of the verb are, therefore, seven, the number of perfection, which recalls that of the parts of the body (cf. 4:1–7). Our text ('I have come' [*bw'*], 5:1a; 'my myrrh', 5:1b) also refers to the end of the *waṣf* ("I will leave [*hlk*] for the mountain of myrrh", 4:6c): 5:1 is the realisation of the proposal expressed in 4:6. But the verb 'go' (*bw'*) forms a direct *inclusio* with 4:8. There, it was the man who invited the woman to 'go'. Here it is the woman who invites her man to 'come' (4:16), and the latter indeed 'comes' (5:1). It is a further aspect of that mirroring dynamic which we have observed many times. Thus we can understand also the sense of the initial 'with me'. In fact, it is the two of them who are to 'come'. The overcoming of the distance has to be accomplished jointly.

There are seven objects of the verb, as we have said, but the possessive of the first person 'my' resounds eight times, twice per stich. The use of the term outside the series (the vocative 'my sister', v. 1a) is the foundation for the others: since the 'sister' is 'mine', what belongs to her, the garden with its marvellous plants, is 'mine'. By means of the emphatic stressing of the possessive pronoun, the man takes glad possession of what the bride has given to him ("Let my beloved come into *his* garden", 4:16e). It would be a mistake to see in this an affirmation of the lordship of man over woman: this is the consequence of sin (Gen 3:16). The original plan of God is that expressed in Gen 2:23—"This at last is bone of my bone and flesh of my flesh". This is, we have seen, a 'formula of relationship', to which our text also has expressly referred ('my sister'). In the woman, the man finds again 'his own flesh', that part of himself which is lacking. On the other side, the woman also uses the possessive: 'my beloved' (Song 4:16). She belongs to him (5:1) because he belongs to her (4:16). The background of the possessive pronouns in 4:16–5:1 is the refrain of mutual belonging, 2:16 (cf. 6:3)—"My beloved is mine and I am his". The man and the woman find themselves again, then, one in the other. Man has been made incomplete in order to be able to find his own unity, his own identity by means of sexual union. For this reason Paul says: "He who loves his wife, loves himself" (Eph 5:28).[301]

The four verbs all have an erotic sense; they are all different metaphors of sexual union. Here too one can observe the succession 'smell' ('myrrh and balm', v. 1b) → 'taste' ('eating' and 'drinking', v. 1cd) prominent in v. 16 and alluding, perhaps, to a progression in the union.

We have already spoken of the 'coming into the garden'. The 'gathering' of the plants of the garden also has a double sense widely known in the love poetry of the Orient.[302] 'Myrrh' and 'balm' stand for all the perfumed plants listed in 4:13c–14. Love begins with inhaling the scent of the beloved woman.

In 5:1c we pass from smell to taste. We refer to the previous verse for the erotic significance of 'eating'. This significance is underlined by the object: the 'honey' (*dᵉbaš*). The term has already appeared in 4:11 where we commented on its symbolism.[303] In 4:11, beside the term *dᵉbaš*, the synonym *nōpet* ('flowing honey') is used. This term is replaced here by *yaʿar* ('honeycomb').[304] The honeycomb is not synonymous

---

[301] Another parallel is often cited here, Hos 2:7 ("I will go after my lovers, who give me my bread and my water, my wool and my flax, my oil and my drink"). Cf. Van Dijk-Hemmes (1989), pp. 81–84; Lacocque (1998), pp. 115–116. Despite the fact that in the two parallels mention is made of gifts connected with love, the parallel seems to me a little forced: the possessive has a different sense. In Hosea, it is a sign of the illicit appropriation of the gift of God; in the Song, it is sign of the mutual belonging of the lovers.

[302] In a modern Arabic poem, a girl is asked: "Are you still a virgin, or has someone plucked your rose?" (cf. Dalman [1901], p. 69). In the poem of Nabû and Tašmetu which we have cited, the goddess Tašmetu addresses her divine lover in a context that is decidely erotic: "May my eyes see the plucking of your fruit" (*qatāpu ša inbīka ēnāya lēmurā*, according to Nissinen [1998], p. 591; on p. 619, other Ugaritic and Assyrian texts are cited). There is an ivory plate among the funerary items of Tutankhamon which depicts the Pharaoh collecting lotus flowers in his garden (cf. Song 6:2) together with bunches of grapes, two plants with clearly erotic symbolism (cf. Keel [1984a], Figure 72, p. 164).

[303] Cf., *supra*, pp. 210–211.

[304] The only other passage of the OT where the term *yaʿar*, 'comb (of honey)', appears is 1 Sam 14:26 (actually, here the term is disputed: many translations have 'wood' [cf. *NKJ*, *RWB*]) and 27. The correspondence seems significant to me: 1 Sam speaks of Jonathan, who, through eating the honey, contravenes a prohibition of Saul. In the light of other passages of the Song (cf., *supra*, note 299), it does not seem out of place to understand Song 5:1c as an allusion to this text, in order to criticise (again) a negative attitude with regard to sexuality ('honey'). The allusion seems all the more probable, from the fact that 1 Sam 14:27 speaks of an 'opening' of the eyes of Jonathan,

with honey: it is not eaten.[305] "Eating the honeycomb together with the honey" is equivalent to "eating the plant together with its fruit"; it is a paradoxical expression to express the voluptuousness with which this honey is 'eaten'. Colloquially too we talk of 'eating' a person 'to bits' to express the strong attraction which is felt. Beyond the emotion, the expression allows a glimpse of the profundity of the communion of body and soul which is created in sexual union (cf. Gen 2:24—"The two will become one flesh"). It is two persons who unite, not just two sexual organs.

The objects of the 'drinking' are the 'wine' and the 'milk'. The two drinks were mentioned in Song 4:10, 11 in connection with kisses.[306] Wine is the usual metaphor for love in the Song (cf. 1:2; 2:4; 7:3, 10) because it is the fruit of the vine-woman and because, like love, it intoxicates (this aspect will become clear in 5:1f). Milk makes one think of the woman's breasts, of her maternal function. The 'bride' has this maternal function; it takes the man back to his origins, to the womb from which he was born (cf. 3:4; 8:5). Through its connection with the mystery of life, milk in the OT has an almost sacral significance like blood (cf. Exod 23:19).[307] Wine and milk are not to be drunk together (the preposition *ʿim* ['together with'] has, as we have seen, the value of a conjunction).[308] They are associated on account of their individual metaphorical value. In this sense, 'wine and milk' represent a binome similar to that of 'milk and honey' to express the abundance of the promised land (cf. Isa 55:1).[309] Perhaps it is possible to

---

after having eaten the honey: the eating of the 'forbidden' fruit in the garden in Gen 3:7 has a similar effect. For this correspondence, cf. Lacocque (1998), p. 114.

[305] Perhaps for this reason LXX and Vetus Latina replace 'comb' with 'bread': bread can be eaten with honey. This is clearly a *lectio facilior*.

[306] The link between 'kisses' and the 'garden' is made in various Sumerian texts. Cf., for example: "My god, sweet is the drink of the wine maid, / like her drink sweet is her vulva, sweet is her drink, / like her lips sweet is her vulva, sweet is her drink, / sweet is her mixed drink, her drink" (poem dedicated to Shu-Sin, recorded in Kramer [1969], p. 94). The parallel is significant, because it reveals the different ways of speaking about the genitals in the two texts: direct, without any veiling, in the Sumerian text, indirect, through metaphors, in the Song.

[307] On this text, cf. Keel (1980).

[308] For the record, there is an example of this mixing in the romance of Longus: *Daphnis and Chloe* 2:38,3 (tr. Morgan [2004], p. 81). But the significance of this drink (*oinogala*) is far from clear.

[309] Moreover, it is a widespread expression in the ancient world to indicate in mythic form (often bound up with fertility cults) the abundance of the land. According to the Ugaritic myth *Baal and Mot*, when Baal returns from the kingdom of the dead, "the heavens will rain oil / and the streams will run honey" (*KTU* 1.6 III, 6–7;

understand once again that allusion to the land of Israel which has already been detected in the 'delicious fruits' (Song 4:13, 16).

[5:1e–f] With the images of 'eating' and 'drinking', then, allusion is being made to the 'consummation' of the union. The two lovers are, in the language of the Song, drowsy with the 'sleep' of love. The arc which was extended in 4:1 is closed in 5:1a–d. The proposal of the man to "leave for the mountain of myrrh and for the hill of incense" (4:6) has been realised ("I have come", 5:1a). With the description of the union, the *Prologue* (cf. 2:4–7) and the two *Songs of the Beloved Woman* (cf. 3:4–5) are also closed. If we compare the three endings, we note the coherence of the poetic language. In 2:4, the place of love is called 'banqueting chamber', literally, 'wine house [room]' (*bêt hayyāyin*); in 3:4, the same place receives the name of 'house of my mother' (*bêt ʾimmî*). At the end of the *Songs of the Beloved Man*, the two images fuse together: that is, the 'milk', symbol of the mother, is joined with the 'wine'.

On the other hand, we can now observe a contrast with the two preceding endings. Both 2:7 and 3:5 were characterised by the charge to the daughters of Jerusalem not to disturb love. Society was thus being understood as potentially hostile to love. Here it is different. The description of union is followed by a joyous invitation to get drunk with love. Society is represented as a friend to the two lovers. It does not impede love but encourages it: "Eat, my friends…" (5:1e).

We have assumed that it is the poet himself who is pronouncing this phrase and who thus emerges from his anonymity to address the two lovers.[310] But the question is not indisputable. Since 5:1a–d is pronounced by the man, many authors hold that it is he himself who continues to speak: the addressees of his discourse in this case would be the 'friends of the bridegroom',[311] invited to participate in the feast

---

Del Olmo Lete [1981], p. 228). The appearance of Dionysus on the earth has an analogous effect, according to the Bacchae of Euripides: "The soil flows with milk, it flows with wine, it flows / with the nectar of bees. / The Bacchic god, holding on high / the blazing flame of the pine torch / like the smoke of Syrian frankincense / let it stream from his wand" (*Bacchae* 142–146, tr. Morwood [1999], p. 48).

310 So too Gerleman (1965), p. 162; Heinevetter (1988), p. 132; Müller (1992), p. 53; Elliott (1989), p. 119; Krinetzki (1981), p. 156; Dorsey (1990), p. 95. Lys (1968), p. 204, thinks rather of a 'chorus' of guests. At any rate, it is the voice of an outsider, someone different from the two lovers, given that the invitation is addressed to the latter.

311 So the majority of interpreters. Among the most recent, we cite, for example, Keel (1994), p. 184, who refers to the parallel with Song 1:2–4; Robert – Tournay (1963), p. 189 (the invitation would have been addressed to the 'friends of the bride',

Table 35

5:1e	A.	Eat,	B.	friends,
5:1f	A'.	drink, get drunk,	B'.	my dears!

of love. Disputed too is the significance of the last word of the verse, *dôdîm*. The term can be understood as a *plurale abstractionis* and indicate erotic play ('caresses', cf. 1:2; 4:10; 7:13),[312] or it can indicate a plurality of people, whether the two lovers or their friends.[313] The ancient versions understand it in this second sense (LXX, *adelphoi*; Vg, *carissimi*; Syriac, *dwdy*), and rightly, because this is required by the parallelism (cf. *Tab. 35*).

The verbs match each other: 'drinking and getting drunk' (a') are, in fact, two aspects of 'drinking' which form a pair that is complementary to 'eating' (a). We would expect, therefore, that the nouns would also correspond. This correspondence is lost if one translates *dôdîm* (b') with 'love'. Some commentators have been aware of this and have suggested translating *rēʿîm* too as an abstract ('friendship'),[314] but examples of this usage are not found in biblical Hebrew. It remains, therefore, to understand both the nouns in a concrete sense with reference to a plurality of persons ('friends, dears'). This meaning is supported by the recurrence of the same pair of terms in the singular in 5:16. The woman calls her partner: 'my beloved' (*dôdî*) and 'my friend/my dear' (*rēʿî*). The two words are understood as synonyms.

Besides, these two terms are the respective plurals of *raʿyātî* ('my friend') and *dôdî* ('my beloved'), the appellations with which the two lovers address each other. These words are never used for persons other than the couple of the Song.[315] For the 'friends of the bridegroom'

understood in an allegorical sense); Ravasi (1992), p. 400 (invoking John 3:29); Landy (1983), p. 109; Garbini (1992), p. 229; Murphy (1990), p. 162.

[312] This is the translation of, among others, *NRS* ("be drunk with love"); Heinevetter (1988), p. 132; Murphy (1990), p. 157; Garbini (1992), p. 229 ("inebriatevi di dolcezze"); Keel (1994), p. 167; Krinetzki (1981), p. 156; Gordis (1974), p. 61; Rudolph (1962), p. 151.

[313] So, for example, *NKJ* ("drink deeply, O beloved ones"), *TOB*, *NBJ*, Ravasi (1992), p. 339; Robert - Tournay (1963), pp. 189–190; Joüon (1909), p. 228; Elliott (1989), p. 118; Lys (1968), p. 205; Colombo (1975), pp. 88–89.

[314] Thus Elliott (1989), p. 118 ("Eat of friendship; drink and become intoxicated with love!"); Colombo (1975), p. 89 ("Fill yourselves with love, drink, get drunk on caresses!"). Dahood (1964), p. 393, adduces a relevant parallel from the Ugaritic (*UT* 1019:9–11).

[315] Cf. Lys (1968), pp. 202–204.

another term is used: *ḥăbērîm* (cf. 1:7; 8:13).[316] It is logical, therefore, to think that here too the nouns refer to the two spouse-lovers. All the more so since the verbs 'eat' and 'drink' have a clear sexual value in the context. That the groom is inviting his friends to share in the sexual act is altogether improbable![317] The two lovers are not only, each for the other, 'friend' and, respectively, 'beloved': they are both 'friends' and 'beloveds' of the poet who watches them with liking and tenderness. It could be said that: so as not to offend either, he calls them first with the plural of the name of the woman ('friends') and then with the plural of the name of the man ('dears'). Once more a testimony of that 'mirroring dynamic' which is the soul of the Song.

As hinted above,[318] the poet repeats the last two verbs used by the man in 5:1cd. He had said: "I have tasted…I have drunk", and the poet comments approvingly, "My friends, eat, drink". As if to say: what you are doing is good. The phrase is not conventional: it constitutes a profession of faith in the goodness of love in its sexual, physical dimension. The sexual act, viewed elsewhere in the Bible with suspicion or tolerated as a 'lesser evil', is openly encouraged here as a 'good thing'.

The passage from the singular ("I have tasted"), moreover, to the plural ("eat") is not without significance: both the lovers must 'eat' and 'drink'. The woman is not only the object but also the subject of love. She does not only give the man pleasure, but experiences it herself: she too is invited to 'eat' and 'drink', to be satisfied with love.

Next the poet repeats the metaphor of wine, connected with 'drinking' in v. 1d, and adds his own: "And get drunk". Wine and love, we have seen, are like each other because both lead one out of oneself: the ecstasy of love is similar to that of inebriation.[319] The poet does not exhort the lovers to moderation ("Do not drink too much because wine is bad for you"), but, rather, to excess in drinking ("Do not just drink, but get drunk"). As if to say: it isn't too much 'wine' that is bad for you but too little. It is an attitude diametrically opposed to that of

---

[316] The Syriac translates *rēʿîm* with *ḥbry* ('my companions'), making the word refer, precisely, to the group of 'friends'.

[317] Siegfried (1898), p. 111, thinks precisely of this, that is, of an "invitation made to the friends, that they too should search for amorous fruition, in a word, to get married"; but that sounds rather banal. On the interpretation of 1:3–4, to which various authors refer, cf., *supra*, p. 56.

[318] Cf. p. 230, *Tab. 32*.

[319] Cf., *supra*, the comment on v. 10, p. 208.

the 'daughters of Jerusalem' who want to "rouse love before it wishes" (2:7; 3:5), worried as they are that the ecstasy of love might last too long.

This reminds us of a famous passage of Qoheleth: "Go, eat your bread with joy, drink your wine with a glad heart [...] enjoy life with the spouse whom you love all the days of your fleeting life which God has given you under the sun" (Qoh 9:7–9).[320] Like Qoheleth, the author of the Song issues an invitation to enjoy the joys of life profoundly. In both cases, this is no superficial invitation to hedonism but an act of faith in life regardless of death. By contrast with Qoheleth, the author of the Song opines that, within the transitoriness of life, if there is anything which lasts, it is precisely love (cf. 8:6).[321]

The profession of faith of 5:1f is one of the high points of the poem and is a worthy conclusion not only of the *Songs of the Beloved Man* (4:1–5:1) but of the entire first part (2:8–5:1). It finds its equal in the Song only in 8:6c-f. Quantitatively and qualitatively the poem has reached its 'centre'.[322]

Conclusion

The journey across the desert (3:6–11) has brought the two young people face to face. Now they admire each other, desire each other (4:1–7) and unite with the acts of love (4:8–5:1). With 5:1, the journey of love begun in 2:8 comes to its conclusion. The complementarity of the two songs of the beloved man (4:1–7 and 4:8–5:1), mirrors that of

---

[320] On this passage and its celebrated parallel in Gilgamesh, cf. Pahk (1996). On p. 263, Pahk notes the relationship with Song 5:1. Having pointed out the harmony of the theme, one must also observe the difference of the Song from Qoheleth and Gilgamesh. While, in fact, in these two passages 'eating' and 'drinking' are understood in their normal sense, and we have the famous trinome: 'eating, drinking, loving', well-known in the Greco-Roman world (cf. Pahk, *ibid.*, p. 263), in the Song, the 'eating' and 'drinking' are understood in a metaphorical sense, as symbols of love. And that is why we do not have the famous trinome: at bottom, only 'loving' is being mentioned.

[321] "To Qoheleth's thesis, that everything is vanity, the Song replies with the only possible antithesis" (Landy [1987], p. 318). For the NT cf. 1 Cor 13:13.

[322] Landy (1983), pp. 313, 317, speaks of 'emotional centre' of the Song. Lys (1968), p. 204, comments: "This concludes the poem. And it is strange that the consummation takes place [...] at the centre and not at the end of the Song". Heinevetter (1988), p. 133, speaks of the "particular quality of the invitation of 5:1ef, which in this way signals the centre of the book". For his part, Tromp (1982), p. 47, feels 5:1ef as "a half way house on the journey".

the two songs of the beloved woman.[323] The acts of union (the look, the kiss, the embrace, 4:8–5:1) take up again in the same order the parts of the body admired and desired at length in the *waṣf* (4:1–7). A further aspect of this complementarity is that in the first song the woman is called "my friend" (*raʿyātî*, 4:1, 7), in the second "bride" (*kallâ*, 4:8, 9, 10, 11, 12; 5:1), following the nuptial dimension of love that is introduced in 3:6–11. The lovers of the Song are at one and the same time "friends" and 'spouses". The ideal unity of the two songs is evident in the use of the verb "come" (*bôʾ*, 4:6, 8, 16; 5:1), which articulates the various steps of the union of love.

4:1–7 represents the first *waṣf* of the Song, that is, the emotional description of the individual parts of the body of the beloved. The opening words ("How fair you are, my friend") seem to be a good representation of the basic message of the poem: an act of faith in the beauty and goodness of the woman and, in her, of human love which echoes the account of the creation: "And God saw that it was good" (Gen 1:10, 12, 18, 21, 25, 31). The woman's beauty is emphasised by the frequent identification between her and the land of Israel. The woman gathers up in herself not only the vital force of nature (animals, plants), but, in particular, that of the promised land, the good gift bestowed by God on Israel. To doubt the goodness of such a gift would be a sin (cf. Num 13:32).

We have underlined the gradual nature of the acts of love in 4:8–5:1. We go from the sharing of the eyes (4:8–9), to the exchange of odours and tastes in the kiss (4:10–11), to the fusion of bodies in the embrace (4:12–5:1). This too is envisaged under the two senses of smell and taste. The delicate song of the garden, behind which we have learned to see the female body in all its intimacy, is put forward as a metaphor of the union of love. The garden is closed, and can be opened only from within; but it is closed in order to be opened. Chastity is thus completed in the gift of self, something which can happen only in freedom.

---

[323] I would like to observe some characteristic points: a) both 2:8–3:5 and 4:1–5:1 are 'included' by the verb *bwʾ*, 'to go, to come' (2:8; 3:4 and 4:8; 5:1); b) both parts begin with the theme of the 'mountains' (2:8; 4:8): in 2:8 it is the beloved who comes from the mountains; in 4:8 it is the woman who has to come down from the mountains; c) in 3:4, the journey is ended in the 'house of my mother', in 5:1 in the 'garden', which has a function analogous to the 'house of my mother' (cf. 8:5cde). This correspondence is fittingly highlighted by Elliott (1989), p. 234 (who, however, delimits the second part differently).

Here we have an echo of the garden of the temple, the garden which is the promised land and, ultimately, the garden of Eden. The water irrigating it comes from Lebanon. It is living water, not stagnant, and it is water of life because it comes from the author of life. The poet concludes with justice: "Eat, my friends, drink, get drunk, my dears!" (5:1).

CHAPTER SEVEN

NEW SONGS OF THE BELOVED WOMAN

(Song 5:2–6:3)

Separation

I

Woman [2]"I slept, but my heart was awake.
Listen[1]... My beloved is knocking:
'Open to me, my sister, my friend,
my dove, my perfect one,
for my head is dripping with dew,
my curls with the drops of the night'.
[3]"I have taken off my dress,
how can I put it on again?
I have washed my feet,
how can I dirty them again?'

[4]My beloved stretched out his hand from the opening—
my insides stirred for him.[2]
[5]I rose to open to my beloved—
My hands dripped with myrrh,
my fingers with liquid[3] myrrh,
on the handles of the bolt.

---

[1] Cf. 2:8.

[2] Some manuscripts have: *'ly*, 'for me'. Vg: *ad tactum eius*.

[3] MT *'ōbēr* signifies literally 'transient' (cf. v. 6b): it refers also to water (Job 6:15) or to wind (Job 37:21; Prov 10:15): therefore the sense of 'fluid', 'running'. LXX has *smyrnan plērē* ('abundant myrrh'?); Aquila, *smyrnan eklektēn*; Symmachus, *smyrnan prōteian*; Vg *murra probatissima*. The Syriac repeats the verb *nṭp*, 'to drip'.

II

[6]I opened to my beloved,
but my beloved had gone,[4] disappeared—
my soul gave out at his disappearance.[5]
I sought him, but did not find him.
I called him, but he did not answer me.

[7]The watchmen found me
as they made their rounds through the city,
they struck me, they wounded me,
they took away my mantle,
the watchmen of the walls.
[8]I charge you, daughters of Jerusalem,[6]
if you find my beloved,
what will you tell him?
That I am sick[7] with love!"

Remembrance

I

Chorus [9]"What makes your beloved
different from another,
you, O fairest among women?
What makes your beloved
different from another,
that you charge us so?"

---

[4] LXX omits the verb along with Vetus Latina. Vg's *declinaverat*, Aquila's *eklinen*, Symmachus' *aponeusas* and the Syriac's *ʾrkn* allow the two meanings 'to bend' and 'to turn', but the context pushes for the second.

[5] LXX *en tō logō autou*; Vg *ut locutus est*; and the Syriac *bmmllh* agree in understanding MT's *b^{e}dabb^{e}rô* in the sense of *dbr* II, 'to speak', which is the common meaning of the word. Our translation reads here a *dbr* I ('to turn round, to go away').

[6] As in 2:7 and 3:5, LXX adds: *en tais dynamesin kai en tais ischysesin tou agrou*, 'by the forces and the powers of the field'.

[7] With MT, Vg and the Syriac. LXX *tetrōmenē*, and Vetus Latina *vulnerata*, read 'wounded'.

II

Woman [10]"My beloved is white and red,
he is distinguished[8] among thousands and thousands.

[11]His head is gold, pure gold,[9]
his curls, flowers of the date,[10]
black as the raven.
[12]His eyes like doves on streams of water,[11]
bathed in milk,
placed on a full bath.[12]
[13]His cheeks like a bed[13] of balm,
towers[14] of fragrances.[15]
His lips, flowers of lotus
dripping liquid myrrh.

[14]His hands, rings[16] of gold
set with stones of Tarshish.

---

[8] MT *dāgûl* ('who stands out like a banner'). LXX has a military term: *eklelochismenos*, 'chosen from among those who make up a *lochos* (company, battalion, host)'.

[9] MT uses two different nouns *ketem* and *pāz*. These are two synonyms, juxtaposed asyndetically, with intensifying force. The ancient versions have translated *ad sensum* (LXX supplies a conjunction: *chrysion kai phaz*, but Aquila, Symmachus, Theodotion, and Origen's Quinta have read differently; the Syriac has *k'p' ddhb'*, 'stone of gold'; the Vg *aurum optimum*).

[10] The Hebrew *taltallîm* is a *hapaxlegomenon* the interpretation of which is disputed. Our translation follows LXX *elatai* ('spathes of the date flowers') and Vg *elatae palmarum*.

[11] With MT, Vg *super rivulos aquarum*, the Syriac *'l šbq' dmy'* and Aquila *ekchyseis*. LXX has *epi plērōmata hydatōn*, as at v. 12c.

[12] MT *millē't* is *hapaxlegomenon* from *ml'*, 'to be full'. Vg *iuxta fluenta plenissima* is improbable. The Syriac translates with the abstract *'l šlmwt'* ('on perfection').

[13] Thus MT. LXX reads *phialai* ('vessels'), but Symmachus has *prasiai* ('beds'); equally the Syriac *mškbt'* and Vg *areolae*. The plural is a *lectio facilior*, to harmonise with *migdᵉlôt*.

[14] MT *migdᵉlôt* means literally 'towers'. LXX *phyousai myrepsika* ('pouring out perfume'), has probably read *mᵉgaddᵉlôt*, 'which causes to grow', a conjecture followed by many modern translations. Vg has *consitae a pigmentariis* ('sown by spicers').

[15] MT *merqāḥîm* is a *hapaxlegomenon*, deriving from the root *rqḥ*, 'to blend perfumes' (cf. 8:2c), as Vg has well understood.

[16] The Hebrew term *gālîl* is uncertain: it indicates something round or cylindrical (the root *gll* signifies 'to roll'). LXX has *toreutai*, 'chiselled'; the Syriac *krk'* ('roll'); Vg *tornatiles* ('worked on the lathe').

His belly, a block[17] of ivory
studded[18] with lapis lazuli.
[15]His legs, columns of alabaster
standing upon bases of pure gold.
His appearance, like Lebanon,
imposing like the cedars.
[16]His palate, sweetness:
he is altogether desirable.

This is my beloved, this is my friend,
O daughters of Jerusalem".

Love Found Again

I

Chorus 6[1]"Where has your beloved gone,
O fairest among women?
To where has your beloved turned,
so that we can seek him with you?"

II

Woman [2]"My beloved has gone down into his garden,
among the beds[19] of balm,
to graze in the gardens,
to gather flowers of lotus.

[3]I am my beloved's, and my beloved is mine:
he grazes among the lotus flowers".

---

[17] MT *ʿešet* is a *hapaxlegomenon*. Our translation rests on the rabbinic use of the term. LXX has *pyxion* ('table').

[18] With MT *meʿullepet* (literally, 'covered'). LXX has an incomprehensible *epi lithou*; the Syriac reads *ʿl* ('on'); Vg, *distinctus*.

[19] Some Hebrew manuscripts, two fragments from the Cairo Genizah, and Vg (*ad areolam*) have the singular, but this is owing to the influence of 5:13a. The Syriac (*lmškbtʾ*) Aquila and Symmachus (*eis prasias*) support MT.

Structure

Second Part (5:2–8:4)

With respect to 5:1, 5:2 signals a break. The two spouse-lovers were united in the 'garden'. Now the woman is alone, on her bed. The two are separated and searching for each other. The woman is no longer called 'bride', but only 'friend': and, in fact, the relationship assumed in 5:2 is certainly not that of two people who are married. It could be said that the action is regressing instead of advancing. This is a sticking point for those who want to see in the Song a drama[20] or the stages of a marriage.[21] The unity of the Song is to be sought for not on the narrative but on the lyrical plane.[22] In 5:2, a new poetic unit begins which, like the preceding one, goes once more from separation to union.

Where does the unit which begins in 5:2 end? The majority of the commentators confine themselves to the tiny unit of 5:2–8 without posing the problem of the greater poetic units. Those who look for more extended compositions see, before the *Epilogue*, a series of two or three 'complex units' between 5:2 and 8:4, the first of which is often identified with 5:2–6:3.[23] However, the structure discovered in the first part (2:8–5:1) suggests that we also search for a complex design in this second part of the Song. This is the road undertaken by Rendtorff and Heinevetter with different results.[24] If I have been able to agree with the broad lines of Heinevetter's proposal in the first part of the Song, I must dissociate myself from it in this second part. The fundamental criteria on which my proposal is founded are three: the

---

[20] Cf., *supra*, p. 16.

[21] Cf., *supra*, pp. 18, 23–24. That goes, moreover, for the allegorical interpretation of Robert - Tournay, who see there a progression towards the covenant of God with his people. Cf. Robert - Tournay (1963), pp. 18–19.

[22] This aspect is, rightly, drawn attention to by Ravasi (1992), pp. 415–416.

[23] Ravasi, pp. 413–628, discovers in 5:2–8:4 the following three compositional unities: 5:2–6:3; 6:4 -7:10; 7:11–8:4; so too Lys (1968), pp. 204–276; similarly Bosshard-Nepustil (1996), p. 63 (5:2–6:3; 6:4–7:10 and 7:11–8:7). Elliott (1989), pp. 122–189, recognises two parts: 5:2–6:3 and 6:4–8:4; similarly Exum (1973) (5:2-6:3 and 6:4–8:3). The divisions in Shea (1980), are different (5:1–7:10 and 7:11–8:5); as they are in Dorsey (1990) (5:2–7:11; 7:12–8:4).

[24] Rendtorff (1985), p. 263, sees in 5:2–6:3 an 'interlude' and in 6:4–8:4 'songs of the man', concluded by a 'love scene' in 8:1–4; for Heinevetter (1988), pp. 164–165, the second part comprises a first unit sung by the woman and the chorus (5:2–6:3), a second sung by the man (6:4–9), and a third where the three actors, man, woman and chorus are speaking (6:10–8:6).

change of subject in the discourse, the passage from separation to union, and, finally, the presence of the 'refrains'.[25]

With regard to the first criterion, in 5:2 it is the woman who begins to speak, and her song, in dialogue with the 'daughters of Jerusalem', goes on until 6:3. In 6:4, it is clearly the man who is speaking. His song concludes in 7:10a when it is interrupted by the woman (see the exegesis below). This 'duet' hints at the end of the unit, as in 1:12–2:7 and in 4:16–5:1. The new song which begins in 7:12 has the woman for protagonist, as in the first song, and ends in 8:4. In 8:5, in fact, a voice from off-stage begins to speak. So, from the point of view of the subject of the discourse, we have a concentric composition: a = songs of the woman (5:2–6:3); b = songs of the man (6:4–7:11); c = songs of the woman (7:12–8:4).

The three compositional units go from an initial situation of separation to one of union. This is clear for the first section (5:2–6:3). At the beginning, the two lovers are separated and seek each other. In 6:2–3, the union of the two in the 'garden' is represented as in 5:1. Again, this is a desire not a reality, but the tension arrives at a first resolution which is stressed by the 'refrain of mutual belonging' (6:3; cf. 2:16). The woman has 'found' what she was seeking!

The song of the man begins where the song of the woman ends. The two lovers stand in front of each other and admire each other (6:4–7:11). It is the same situation as that supposed in 4:1–7. From this admiration, mutual desire is born, as is emphasised by the woman in the concluding verse which repeats, with modification, the refrain of mutual belonging: "I am my beloved's, and his *desire* is for me" (7:11). With these words, the woman sums up the content of the two (new) songs of the beloved man (6:4–7:10).

The last composition is an invitation to union, expressed once more by the woman. The union is described first in nature (7:12–14), then in the city (8:1–4). The 'refrain of the embrace' (8:3, cf. 2:6) and that of awakening (8:4, cf. 2:7; 3:5) signal that the union has been achieved and mark the end of the composition.

Despite the fact that the three compositional units have their own poetic coherence, as a group, they trace an *itinerarium amoris*, which

---

[25] Cf., *supra*, pp. 20–24; the structure of 5:1–8:4 has been sketched in a previous study. Cf. Barbiero (1997a), pp. 174–176.

goes from separation to union, by way of desire, analogous to what was described in the first part.[26]

The parallel between the first *Songs of the Beloved Woman* (2:8–3:5) and the new ones (5:2–6:3) has been observed by Exum[27] and by Elliott.[28] The initial situation in 5:2 is that of the *paraklausithyron*: the beloved man at the closed door of the woman he loves. It is the same situation as in 2:9. Even the words correspond: both compositions begin in the same way: *qôl dôdî* (5:2; cf. 2:8). The anxious search in the night of 5:6–8 corresponds to that of 3:1–5. Here too the references are exact: "I rose" (5:5a; cf. 3:2a); "I sought him, but did not find him" (5:6d; cf. 3:1c, 2d); "The watchmen found me as they made their rounds through the city" (5:7ab; cf. 3:3a 3:3ab); "I charge you, daughters of Jerusalem" (5:8a; cf. 3:8a).

A similar parallelism is discernible also between the first *Songs of the Beloved Man* (4:1–5:1) and the new ones (6:4–7:11):[29] the *waṣf* of 4:1–7 is repeated almost word for word in 6:4–7. In the two cases, contemplation gives birth to desire (6:12; 7:9; cf. 4:6). Also the metaphor of the 'garden' in 6:11 echoes 4:12–15.

Be that as it may, the parallelism between the two major parts of the Song is imperfect. The *Choral Intermezzo* (3:6–11), the journey in the desert, remains without correspondence in the second half, just as the description of the man in 5:10–16 is without a match in the first part of the poem. This is not to be wondered at: the Song is poetry, not mathematics! The repetitions are always 'variations on the theme', not cold carbon copies.

The *Final Songs of the Beloved Woman* in the second part (7:12–8:4) also do not have a parallel earlier on. Here, however, it is perhaps possible to detect another compositional principle, that is, the wish to form an *inclusio* with the first *Songs of the Beloved Woman* in 2:8–3:5 (and, naturally, with the new ones in 5:2–6:3). In fact, the two songs of 7:12–8:4 (union in nature—7:12–14; union in the city—8:1–4) do find a match—the first in the description of nature in 2:8–17 (notice the references: 'the vineyards' [*hakkᵉrāmîm*], 7:13a; cf. 2:15; 'the vine' [*haggepen*], 7:13b cf. 2:13; 'the buds' [*hassᵉmādar*], 7:13c; cf. 2:13, 15), the second, in the description of the city in 3:1–5 (here too the

[26] Cf., *supra*, p. 24, *tab. 2*.
[27] Exum (1973), pp. 49–61.
[28] Elliott (1989), pp. 229–230.
[29] Cf, again, Exum (1973), pp. 61–70; Elliott (1989), pp. 230–231.

references are precise: the theme of the 'search' [*māṣā'*], 8:1; cf. 3:1, 2, 3, 4; the 'bringing into the house of the mother', 8;2; cf. 3:4; and the refrain of 'awakening', 8:4 and 3:5). Even these last songs, then, are to be understood, like the preceding ones, in correspondence with 2:8–3:5.[30]

New Songs of the Beloved Woman (5:2–6:3)

Already by the very fact of being pronounced by the woman, the passage 5:2–6:3 is distinguished from its context. In fact, it was the man who was speaking in 5:1 and it will be he who speaks again in 6:4. The *New Songs of the Beloved Woman* are preceded and followed by songs of the beloved man. In addition to this external unity, however, the passage shows an intrinsic literary unity (cf. *Tab. 36*), perhaps one even more marked than in the other similar compositions.[31]

At the beginning, we have a song of the woman (5:2–8—Separation), which terminates in a request addressed to the 'daughters of Jerusalem' (v. 8). The woman is searching for her beloved and, for this reason, enlists the aid of her companions. In its turn, their reply in v. 9 is a question: "How can we recognise your beloved?" This question introduces the woman's second song which, in reply, describes her *dôd* (5:10–16—Remembrance). At the end of the song, the woman addresses herself once again to the 'daughters of Jerusalem' (5:16d), provoking a second question from them: "Where has your beloved gone?" (6:1). The woman's reply makes up the third song (6:2–3—Love found again). Here the composition reaches its dénouement: the beloved man has gone 'into his garden', that is, in the symbolism of the Song, he has gone to his woman. The union has been re-established: what was lost has been found again or, better, it was never really lost.[32]

---

[30] The *inclusio* between 2:10–15 and 7:12–14 has been noted in Shea (1980), p. 386.

[31] Even Keel, who is generally not very ready to recognise extended compositional units, recognises the compactness of 5:2–6:3. Cf. Keel (1994), pp. 208–209. It is also recognised by Heinevetter (1988), pp. 135–137; Elliott (1989), pp. 122–123; Ravasi (1992), pp. 419–421.

[32] Heinevetter (1988), p. 117.

Table 36

5:2–8	First song of the woman
5:9	Question of the daughters of Jerusalem
5:10–16	Second song of the woman
6:1	Question of the daughters of Jerusalem
6:2–3	Third song of the woman

The consequential logic is confirmed by literary indications. The terms 'I' (*ʾănî*)—in Hebrew the pronoun has an emphatic force which is barely perceptible in translation—and 'my beloved' (*dôdî*) have a structuring role.[33] As a pair, they form an *inclusio* between the beginning and the end of the unit (5:2 and 6:3). The first person pronoun (always with reference to the subject of the discourse, to the woman therefore) appears in addition in the structural links of the first song (5:5, 6, 8; cf. *infra, Tab. 37*), while the term *dôdî* articulates the entire unit (5:2, 4, 5, 6 [2x], 8, 9 [2x], 10, 16; 6:1 [2x], 2, 3 [2x]).

The composition is structured as a dialogue. The first dialogue unfolds between the man and the woman (5:2–3); the other two between the woman and the 'daughters of Jerusalem' (5:8–6:3). We should note a stylistic detail: the three dialogues are characterised by the repetition of the interrogative particle: *ʾêkākâ* ('how?', 5:3bd); *mâ* ('what', 5:9ac); *ʾānâ* ('where', 6:1ac). This speaks of a unity for the passage which is not simply redactional.

Having noted the structural autonomy of the composition, it is also necessary to observe its connection with the preceding context. In fact, typical of biblical poetry is the phenomenon of 'attraction' by which the passage from one unit to another is softened by hooking together words and themes. From the point of view of content, the passage from union (5:1) to separation (5:2) is the common experience of every pair of lovers. Union is never a definitive possession: it has always to be 'reconquered'. The Song ends with the exhortation: "Flee, my beloved" (8:14). Even after union has been reached, separation forms part of the adventure of love.[34]

---

[33] This is suitably pointed out in Ravasi (1992), p. 419; Elliott (1989), p. 122.

[34] This aspect is highlighted by Ravasi (1992), p. 415, who speaks of the play of 'climax' and 'anticlimax', typical of the Song.

From the literary point of view, we should note the dimension of time. The 'sighing' of the day in 4:6, 16 leads to an evening hour: it is the time of love. In the songs of the woman in the first part (2:17), this indication is followed by that of the night (cf. 3:1). The same succession is present here: 'evening' (4:6, 16) is followed by 'night' (5:2).

The hook words between the two poetic units are numerous, above all between the end of the *Songs of the Beloved Man* and the beginning of the *New Songs of the Beloved Woman*. Let us point out some of them: the verb *ʿûr* ('awake', 5:2a; cf. 4:16a), the pair of nouns *dôdî* ('my beloved', 5:2b, cf. 4:16e; 5:1e) and *raʿyātî* ('my friend', 5:2c; cf. 5:1f);[35] the verb *nāṭap* ('to drip', 5:5; cf. 4:11); the noun *môr* ('myrrh', 5:5; cf. 4:6, 14; 5:1b). The metaphor of the garden (4:12–5:1), with which the *Songs of the Beloved Man* conclude, reappears in 6:2–3 at the end of the *Songs of the Beloved Woman*. In particular, 6:2a ("My beloved has gone down into his garden") echoes 5:1a ("I have come into my garden").[36] Also, the theme of the 'enclosure' of the garden (4:12) is taken up again and developed in the opening scene, the lament before the woman's closed door (5:2–6). The root *nʿl* ('to close') appears in 4:12 (*gan nāʿûl*, 'garden enclosed'), and is taken up again in the term 'bolt' (*manʿûl*) of 5:5. The 'garden' is closed from the inside; only the woman can open it: what 4:12 says in an abstract way is now represented concretely. Again: the description of the body of the man (5:10–16) constitutes a parallel with that of the body of the woman (4:1–7). This is seen above all in the description of the eyes. He says to her: "Your eyes are doves" (4:1b); she says of him: "His eyes, like doves" (5:12).[37] Even if no 'narrative' continuity exists between the two passages, the poetic continuity is undeniable.

Separation (5:2–8)

The first song of the woman is structured like the rest of 5:2–6:3 by the two terms: *ʾănî* ('I') and *dôdî* ('my beloved').[38] Four times the two

---

[35] This correspondence confirms the translation of *dôdîm* in 5:1f in a personal sense, with reference to the two lovers (cf., *supra*, pp. 240–241).

[36] Cf. Elliott (1989), p. 233.

[37] Cf. Elliott (1989), p. 233.

[38] For these structural considerations, we refer to Elliott (1989), pp. 123–135; Heinevetter (1988), p. 136; Ravasi (1992), pp. 419–420.

Table 37

I	a (2–3)	*I* (v. 2a)	*my beloved* (v. 2b)
	b (4–5)	*I* (v. 5a)	*my beloved* (v. 4a) *my beloved* (v. 5a)
II	b' (6)	*I* (v. 6a)	*my beloved* (v. 6a) *my beloved* (v. 6b)
	a' (7–8)	*my beloved* (v. 8b)	*I* (v. 8d)

words recur in a pair (vv. 2ab, 5a, 6a, 8bd). The order is always the same: first the pronoun, then the noun. Only on the last occasion is the order reversed with a chiastic, conclusive, effect: in v. 8, 'my beloved' (v. 8b) comes first, then the first person pronoun 'I' (v. 8d).[39] Another two times, the noun 'my beloved' appears on its own (vv. 4a, 6b). The repetitions of these words are not accidental: they suggest a chiastic structure for the song: a) = vv. 2–3; b) = vv. 4–5; b') = v. 6; a') = vv. 7–8 (cf. *Tab. 37*).

From the point of view of content, two verbs are relevant: *pātaḥ* ('to open', vv. 2:5, 6a) and *māṣāʾ* ('to find', vv. 6d, 7, 8). Each of these recurs three times. Here too the arrangement does not seem to be accidental because the first verb occurs only in the first part of the song, the second only in the last (cf. *Tab. 38*). With that, the first part is characterised from the point of view of literary genre as a 'lament at the closed door' (*paraklausithyron*), the second as 'nocturnal search'.[40] These are two clearly distinct genres as the parallel of 2:8–3:5 shows. There, the *paraklausithyron* characterised the first song (2:8–17), the 'nocturnal search' the second (3:1–5). In 5:2–8, the two genres are reunited in a single song.

The division between the two parts obtained in this way does not coincide exactly with that delineated in *Tab. 37*. In the present structure, the division is placed after v. 6c, while, in the preceding structure,

[39] In the Hebrew text, the position of the pronoun at the end of the phrase is not normal (lit.: "sick with love [am] I"). Perhaps this construction is a sign of the lateness of the Hebrew (in Qoh it is used frequently: both books date from the Hellenistic epoch). But in the Song itself the normal construction is also used (cf. 1:6; 2:1; 5:2; 6:3; 8:10), so that in our case a stylistic effect seems to be present. How do we otherwise explain that the first person pronoun (*ʾănî*) is precisely the first (5:2a) and the last word (v. 8d) of the song?

[40] Cf. Heinevetter (1988), p. 135.

Table 38

I	v.2c	*to open*
	v. 5a	*to open*
	v. 6a	*to open*
II	v. 6d	*to find*
	v. 7a	*to find*
	v. 8b	*to find*

the line of demarcation is before v. 6. This verse has evidently a double function: on the one hand, it still belongs to the scene at the door (v. 6abc), on the other hand it signals the beginning of the nocturnal search (v. 6de). Once more it is a case of that principle of 'attraction' of which we spoke above. We shall follow the first structure which seems to be the dominant one.[41]

The first part of the song (5:2–5) is characterised by the initiative of the man and the consequent reaction of the woman (cf., *infra, Tab. 39*). In its turn, it is divided into two symmetrical strophes of which the first (vv. 2–3) is marked by dialogue, the second (vv. 4–5) by action. In the first strophe, the discourse of the man (v. 2c–f) is followed by the reply of the woman (v. 3); in the second, the action of the man (v. 4) is followed by the reaction of the woman (v. 5).

In the second part of the song (vv. 6–8), the woman takes the initiative: there is, therefore, an inversion of roles as a counterpoise to the first part. Like the action of the man, that of the woman is also without success. This part is divided into two strophes, in which the first (v. 6), like the two preceding ones, is characterised by the presence of the two lovers and is carried out at the door which is now no longer closed. In the last strophe (vv. 7–8), the scene is no longer occupied by the two lovers: the woman is alone and she meets up with two groups of people: first of all, the hostile group of the 'watchmen' (v. 7); then, the supposedly friendly 'daughters of Jerusalem' (v. 8). The charge addressed to the daughters of Jerusalem (v. 8) has a concluding function for the passage (cf. 2:7; 3:5; 8:4). Like v. 6, however, v. 8

[41] Different from Heinevetter (1988), p. 136, who places the caesura between the two parts after v. 6b.

also has a double function, structurally speaking, because at the same time it introduces the following song: we should note the hook words: 'charge' (vv. 8a, 9d) and 'beloved' (vv. 8b, 9a [2x], c [2x]).[42]

The four strophes present a chiastic arrangement (a-b-b'-a') which corresponds to the distribution of the key words (cf., *supra, Tab. 37*). In content, the third strophe is directly linked with the second, is indeed its natural continuation (cf. the theme of 'opening'). The fourth strophe corresponds to the first. There, it was the man who was outside, exposed to the perils of the night in the fruitless search for the woman. Here, the latter is in an analogous situation.

First part: The closed door (5:2–5)

It has often been pointed out that the scene in vv. 2–5 is not realistic. That a marriageable girl is sleeping in a room with a door on to the street, that she would have the freedom to go out into the city at night, is unthinkable in a world where premarital chastity is a fundamental value (cf. Deut 22:13–21). On the other hand, to think of a 'dream' does not resolve the problem.[43] The whole of the Song, it could be said, is a dream: one may think of the 'burlesques' towards the high or towards the low! The two youngsters are neither 'kings' nor 'shepherds'. Our passage is no different from the other passages of the Song which describe a lyrical, not a real, situation: making use of recognised topics of love poetry, it analyses a particular aspect of the relationship of the two lovers. Here the topic used is that of the 'lament at the closed door' (*paraklausithyron*), a genre known both in the Egyptian love songs and in the Greek and Roman amorous lyrics.[44] As Heinevetter has rightly noted, a fundamental element of this genre is that the door remains closed,[45] as a result of which the opening of the door in v. 6 does not form part of the *paraklausithyron* but belongs

[42] Some authors place the caesura after v. 7, not after v. 8. So, for example, Ravasi (1992), p. 421; Krinetzki (1981), pp. 158–159.

[43] "The maiden is asleep, and in the dream she hears her lover knocking..." (Gordis [1974], p. 62). The 'oneiric' interpretation of the passage is invoked by Budde to resolve the chronological incongruity between 5:1 and 5:2: the young woman would be referring here to a dream which she had had previously at night. Cf. Budde (1898), p. 26. For a review (and a criticism) of the oneiric interpretation, we refer to Pope (1977), pp. 510–511.

[44] Cf., *supra*, p. 14, n. 69, 70.

[45] Already v. 5, which prepares for v. 6, remains outside the classical *paraklausithyron*, which is always an "expression of nostalgia that cannot be satisfied" (Heinevetter

Table 39

<table>
<tr><td rowspan="5">I part, vv. 2–5</td><td rowspan="3">I strophe, vv. 2–3</td><td>Introduction (v. 2ab)</td><td></td><td>woman + man</td></tr>
<tr><td rowspan="2">Dialogue (vv. 2c–3)</td><td>v. 2cdef</td><td>man’s question</td></tr>
<tr><td>v. 3</td><td>woman’s reply</td></tr>
<tr><td rowspan="2">II strophe, vv. 4–5</td><td rowspan="2">Action (vv. 4–5)</td><td>v. 4</td><td>man’s action</td></tr>
<tr><td>v. 5</td><td>woman’s reaction</td></tr>
</table>

to another literary genre. This detail is not irrelevant for the understanding of the passage.

The parallel with 2:8–17 was noted above. There the man was ‘behind our wall’ and “he was gazing through the lattice” (2:9); here he is ‘knocking’ at the door (5:2): the situation is undoubtedly analogous. But we must also notice a difference: in 2:8–17, the man invites the woman to come out; here he wants to enter. The motif is, therefore, repeated, but with freedom.

[5:2–3] First strophe: Dialogue. The strophe is composed of an introduction (v. 2ab), in which the personages are presented (‘I’ and ‘my beloved’), and of a dialogue between the man and the woman (cf. *Tab. 38*). The man’s request is occupied by four stichs (v. 2cdef), similarly the woman’s reply (v. 3abcd).

The initial situation of the woman in bed during the night recalls 3:1. As Keel shows, it is a frequent motif in Egyptian iconography.[46] In 3:1, it was she who had to search for him; here it is he who has to search for her. The woman is, therefore, initially passive, she is ‘sleeping’. But not completely, because ‘her heart is awake’. Since the ‘heart’ is the seat of the conscience, the phrase signifies that the woman is not wholly asleep; she finds herself in a kind of half-sleep (otherwise she could not hear the knocking at the door). But the expression has a deeper intention. In fact, the verb *ʿûr*, from which derives the adjective *ʿēr* which is used here, is a significant term in the Song (cf. 2:7; 3:5; 4:16; 8:4, 5). Above all it is possible to understand here a repeat of 4:16 where the winds were exhorted to ‘awake’ so that they might ‘awaken’ the garden (cf. 8:5). The ‘heart’, seat of the feelings, is, there-

[1988], p. 139; also cf. Gerleman [1965], p. 123). Clearly the author makes free use of literary genres; he is not strictly bound by them.

[46] Cf. Keel (1994), Figure 68, p. 123; Figure 113, p. 187.

fore, 'awake', open to love. The woman sleeps, but, even in sleep, she is ready for love.[47]

[5:2] V. 2b refers to 2:8. As there, so too here, the translation is disputed, given that the Hebrew *qôl* can have the two meanings of 'voice' and 'noise'. If we understand it as 'voice', there is a reference to the words of the man, which follow in v. 2c.[48] If we understand it as 'noise', the reference is to his 'knocking'. By analogy with 2:8, we shall choose this second alternative, but the text remains open. The Hebrew is onomatopoeic: *qôl dôdî dôpēq.*[49] We seem to hear the knocks on the door. The image has become classic in the Bible so that the Apocalypse takes it up in a theological sense (Rev 3:20).[50] In our case too, it is not any old person who knocks: it is 'my beloved'. In him it is Love that is seeking to enter.

"Open to me". Three times in the passage, the verb *pātaḥ* ('to open') returns (vv. 2, 5, 6; cf. *Tab. 38*); Elliott sees in this a reply to the three-fold 'enclosure' of the garden in 4:12.[51] A metaphorical continuity certainly exists, as has been observed: the man does not have the key of the 'garden'; he has to ask the woman to open it to him from the inside. The *double entendre*, the sexual background, of the term 'open' has often been stressed.[52] The erotic significance of the scene is clear, even without recourse to double senses: to seek to open the woman's bedroom door, at night, already in itself alludes to an amorous encounter.

In order to obtain permission to enter, the man appeals first of all to the mutual belonging of the two lovers. The 'garden' belongs to him: it is 'my' garden (4:16; 5:1). The first person possessive pronominal

---

[47] Cf. a passage from the Egyptian love lyrics: "[I dwell on] your love / through day and night, / the hours I am lying down, / and when I have awakened at dawn" (Deir el-Medineh Vase, ll. 1–2 = Cairo Love Songs 20A, tr. Fox [1985], p. 31). Ravasi (1992), p. 424, adduces the parallel with 1 Thess 5:10: "...so that whether we wake or sleep, we might live with him".

[48] Thus translate, for example, Colombo (1975), p. 90; Elliott (1989), p. 125; Salvaneschi (1982), p. 25.

[49] The Hebrew *dāpaq* indicates not so much 'to knock', as rather 'to push' (cf. Gen 33:13; Judg 19:22).

[50] *Pace* Bauckham (1977), and Tait (2008), who read the allusion in Rev 3:20 as forensic rather than nuptial. On the other hand, the motif is conventional. The *paraklausithyron* in Papyrus Chester Beatty IC 17:8–12 begins in a similar way: "(I) passed by her house in a daze. / I knocked, but it was not opened to me" (tr. Fox [1985], p. 75).

[51] Elliott (1989), p. 125.

[52] Cf. Pope (1977), p. 515; Müller (1992), pp. 55–56.

adjective returns four times; "*My* sister, *my* friend, *my* dove, *my* perfect one", thus echoing the eight occurrences of 5:1a–d. The first appellation, 'my sister', is a literal repeat of 5:1 and narrowly connects the two passages. It is the last time that this term appears in the Song after the four occurrences in the preceding section (4:9, 10, 12; 5:1). Here it is no longer the noun *kallâ* that is juxtaposed with it but *raʿyātî* ('my friend'). With these two terms, the man refers not to a right which he has of entering but to the love which unites him to his woman.[53] At any rate, the fact that the term 'bride' is not used corresponds perfectly to the situation: the two young people evidently do not yet live together. The third appellation, 'my dove', identifies the woman with the goddess of love whose animal is the dove (cf. 4:1b). The fourth invocation, 'my perfect one' (*tammātî*), is repeated from 4:7. The *waṣf* ended with the exclamation: "in you there is no blemish!" Here the same thought is expressed in a positive form: the term *tmm* expresses, in fact, fullness, perfection, completeness.[54] In the context of the 'gate' and of the 'garden', there is perhaps a discernible hint of the 'chastity and virginity' of the woman,[55] a meaning underlined by the Vulgate (*immaculata mea*). The expression "my dove, my perfect one" will be repeated in 6:9 in a context where the 'uniqueness' of the woman is being emphasised, putting her on a level that is almost divine. 'Unique' and 'all' go together: they are the qualities of the love of the Song and of the love of God (cf. Deut 6:4).[56] It should be noted, in any case, that in Song 5:1, the possessives follow the gift which the woman has presented in 4:16 where 'my garden' became 'his garden'. Here they are not preceded by an analogous offering. Perhaps it is for this reason that they remain without effect. Without reciprocity, there is no union.[57]

[53] Thus Krinetzki (1981), p. 161.

[54] *HALOT*, p. 1743, records the translation of Keel ('my all'), and of König ('my ideal') (citations there).

[55] Cf. B. Kedar-Klopfstein, *tāmam*, in *TDOT*, vol. XV, p. 705 ('my faultless one'). Also Ravasi (1992), p. 694: "...at the same time, it refers to the idea of integrity and therefore of virginity, introducing the sexual theme with great delicacy".

[56] In the French translation of his work, Keel translates *tammātî* with 'mon seul amour', and comments: "ne mettant plus l'accent sur l'appartenence mutuelle, mais sur le statut quasi divin de l'aimée" (Keel [1997], pp. 201, 205).

[57] Even if a new unit begins with 5:2, the transition between 5:1 and 5:2 is nonetheless important. It leads to considerations of the type: union is never something definitive. Just because the woman has opened the way into the garden on one occasion, he cannot enter it at will. Permission to enter must be gained anew each time.

"For my head is dripping with dew". The passage has a surprising parallel in a *paraklausithyron* of the *Anacreontea*:

> Once in the middle of the night,
> at the hour when [...] all the tribes of mortals lie,
> overcome by exhaustion,
> Love stood at my bolted door
> and began knocking. [...]
> Love said, "Open up! I am a baby:
> don't be afraid. I am getting wet,
> and I have been wandering about
> in the moonless night".[58]

In our text too, there is probably an attempt to arouse compassion. It is true that in Israel the dew is very abundant (cf. Judg 6:33–40!), and that the temperature range between day and night is high (cf. Gen 31:40). But it is not a matter of rain, and certainly the man is in no danger to his life.[59] The reply of the young woman, in the following verses, shows that the words of the man are not to be taken too seriously: they belong to those pretexts which someone in love finds in order to be able to be close to the woman whom he loves.[60]

Perhaps a metaphorical significance can also be grasped here. The man arrives from outside, not from the 'city' as in Song 2:8.[61] Dew, curls, night belong to the semantic field of 'savage nature', with its dangers (cf. 3:8),[62] but also with its youthful, vital force. The dew, sign of danger, is also a sign of fertility.[63] If, in 3:6–11, the young man was represented in a 'high burlesque' (Solomon), now, to balance things, he is represented in a 'low burlesque', as a shepherd who spends the night in the open. It is a question, naturally, of projection.[64]

---

[58] *Anacreontea* 33:1–8* (tr. Campbell [1982–1993], pp. 202–205).

[59] Generally, in the OT, the dew (*ṭāl*) is synonymous with blessing (cf. Ps 133:3), but Palestinian rabbinic and Arab traditions also know of a harmful dew. Cf. Dan 4:22, 30; 5:21; BerR 13:9; Stephan (1922), p. 215; thus Keel (1994), p. 189.

[60] Thus also Murphy (1990), p. 170: "...there seems to be a deliberate exaggeration here; it is clear that this is not the real reason for seeking entrance".

[61] The thing is rightly emphasised by Heinevetter (1998), p. 185 ("The beloved comes 'from outside', from the damp night, not from another house in the city").

[62] With regard to the dew, Krinetzki (1981), p. 162, speaks of a provenance "from supernatural, fiendish regions". Cf., also, *supra*, n. 59.

[63] One can note a parallelism with the origin of the woman. She too comes from the 'desert' (3:6), or 'from Lebanon', 'from the lairs of the lions, from the mountains of the panthers' (4:8). Here we have symbolic representations of wild nature, with its death-life ambivalence.

[64] In this connection, Krinetzki (1981), p. 162, speaks of 'Animusbild'.

[v. 3] The speech of the woman (v. 3abcd) corresponds symmetrically to the speech of the young man (v. 2cdef). It might be said that the woman gives tit for tat. The reasons the man gave for entering were pretexts: so too the reasons which the woman puts forward for not getting up to open the door are excuses. Moreover, it is typical of the *paraklausithyron* that the request of the nocturnal visitor be rejected.[65] But then there is a contrast with the affirmation of v. 2a: was the heart really 'awake'?

"I have taken off my dress...". The Hebrew term for 'dress' is *kuttōnet* (from which derive the Greek *chitōn*, the Latin *tunica* and the English 'tunic'). In summer, this was the only garment which the woman wore over her naked body. The mantle (*śimlâ*) served also as a cover during the night (cf. Exod 22:25–26). An Assyrian bas-relief from Niniveh[66] shows Israelite women being deported to Assyria: they wear a tunic and a mantle, and are barefoot. The beloved, therefore, would have been naked in bed,[67] or perhaps covered with the mantle. She has washed her feet, as is the custom for one who goes around barefoot or in sandals (cf. Song 7:2). One could think here of a sense of modesty. But it would not have been so complicated to put on the dress,[68] and the same goes for the feet.[69] The reply is, therefore, an excuse. It allows laziness to show through. The woman has gone to bed and does not wish to be disturbed. It is the situation depicted in the gospel scene of the importunate friend (cf. Luke 11:5–7). One can imagine also, perhaps, that the woman has waited earlier for the man: perhaps she has waited for him a long time before going to bed. Now he comes, when she is already in bed, and demands that she open up to him as if he had a right to this. As the sequel shows, the woman is indeed disposed to open to him (her heart was, therefore, 'awake'!),[70]

---

[65] Cf. Gerleman (1965), p. 166.

[66] Cf. Keel (1994), Figure 116, pp. 190–191.

[67] Cf. Keel (1994), Figure 68, p. 123; Figure 113, p. 187.

[68] However, not without reason, Haupt (1907), p. 55, observes that the toilette of a lady, before she appears in public, lasts rather a long time. Perhaps this is why the man is tired of waiting.

[69] Some commentators think of a double sense here too. In fact, in Hebrew, 'feet' is also a euphemism to indicate the genital area, whether masculine (cf. Exod 4:25; Isa 6:2), or feminine (cf. Deut 28:57). So, for example, Pope (1977), p. 515; Müller (1992), p. 55. But this seems forced: the parallelism with the preceding stich advises in favour of retaining the normal sense.

[70] Krinetzki (1981), p. 162, takes this refusal seriously, and interprets it as the refusal of the woman to accept her 'animus', the masculine part of her being. But the rest of the song shows that her refusal is only apparent.

Table 40

a) v. 4a	Action of the man (*hand—opening*)	b) v. 4b	Emotional echo of the woman
a') v. 5a	Reaction of the woman	b') v. 5bcd	Emotional echo of the woman (*hands—bolt*)

but she wants to make him weigh things up, to show him that the opening is not to be taken for granted: it is not a right but a gift. The woman, then, plays between coquetry and modesty, just as the man had done before.

[5:4–5] Second strophe: The hands. Since his words remain without result, the man seeks to obtain his wish with deeds, with an action. The strophe is constructed in symmetrical form: to the 'action' of the man (v. 4 = a) there corresponds the 'reaction', this time positive, of the woman (v. 5 = a'). Both the action and the reaction are accompanied by the emotional echo which the deed arouses in the heart of the woman ("my insides stirred at it", v. 4b = b; "my hands dripped with myrrh...", v. 5bcd = b'; cf. *Tab. 40*). Beside this structure, we get a glimpse of another one that is chiastic (a-b'b-a'). The first part of v. 4 is, in fact, longer than the second: in it is described the hand of the man which is stretched out from the opening of the door. In v. 5, the second part is longer than the first: in it are described the hands of the woman on the handles of the bolt. The theme of hands on the door has, thus, an inclusive function.

[v. 4] The significance of the Hebrew term *ḥōr* is debated. It can indicate a cave (1 Sam 14:11; Job 30:6; Nah 2:13), the sockets of the eye (Zech 14:12), a hole in the wall (Ezek 8:7) or in a chest (2 Kgs 12:10). Since the man is at the door, it is probably an opening in the door itself. The article before the noun (*haḥōr*) indicates that this is an opening that is well known. But just what type of opening it is is hard to specify. It has been thought to be a little window (cf. Song 2:9),[71] or a chink through which one can observe from the inside who is at the door,[72] or, more often, the keyhole.[73] Such a hole, in fact, must have been quite big because the key consisted of a spar of wood which

[71] So, for example, Siegfried (1898), p. 113; Minocchi (1898), p. 89 ("the door of the house was so widely perforated on the upper side that the room might be illuminated").

[72] Cf. Zapletal (1907), p. 115 ('Guckloch, spy-hole').

[73] So, among others, Joüon (1909), p. 234; Robert – Tournay (1963), p. 200; Ravasi (1992), p. 429.

allowed one to raise from the outside the bolt (*manʿûl*) with which the door was locked. It is possible that one could pass some fingers through such a hole but it is improbable that the whole hand could go through for otherwise the lock would be useless. Of the three possibilities, the most probable seems to me to be that of the 'little window': the only one which allows the hand to pass. In Oriental dwellings, a lamp is always burning at night so that from within one can observe the scene. The text runs: *šālaḥ yādô min haḥōr* ("he stretched out his hand from the opening"). The action is described from the point of view of the one who is watching, that is the woman. What was the purpose of this action? Since the woman had not acceded to his request, was the impatient lover perhaps wanting to open the door himself, by sliding the bolt? It is possible. Or was the young man simply wanting to demonstrate his presence, giving his friend a sign of greeting? Whatever, the extended hand expresses the desire for communion: one is reminded of the two outstretched hands in the fresco of the creation of man on the ceiling of the Sistine Chapel.[74]

[74] To think, as Keel does, of a 'sexual pantomime' (Keel [1994], p. 192), or, like Haupt, of an obscene gesture (Haupt [1907], p. 55: Haupt, however, refers this interpretation to Jacob), is not appropriate to the language of the Song, which is elevated even when it speaks of sexuality (cf. the epithet *tammātî*, 'my perfect one', in 2d). The reason for this interpretation is the uncontestable fact that, in everyday language, 'hole' is often a synonym for vagina, and 'hand' (or 'arm') in Ugarit, Egypt and Israel is a euphemism for the penis. If Haupt and Keel think of an obscene gesture, others go further and think that it is the sexual act that is being described here. This interpretation, which was already that of Wittekindt (Wittekindt [1925], pp. 154–161) and of Haller (Haller [1940], p. 37), has also been taken up again recently. Cf., among others, Pope (1977), p. 519; Lacocque (1998), p. 117; Müller (1992), pp. 55–56; Ceronetti (1996), pp. 63–69. Colombo himself claims that this interpretation is legitimate (cf. Colombo [1985], p. 91). Garbini's translation, in this sense, is vulgar. He translates v. 4 thus: "When my beloved drove in his dick, my insides quivered" (Garbini [1992], p. 234). There are three objections against such a translation. The first is that the Hebrew text has *min hahōr*: 'from the opening' (so too LXX and the Syriac; differently, Vg *per foramen* and Vetus Latina *per clostrum*), not 'into the opening'. To think of 'penetration' is to distort the sense of the Hebrew text. The second objection is decisive: the door is closed! It will be opened only in v. 6. How can one think of sexual congress when he is outside and she is within the door? While other authors do not notice this incongruity, Garbini notes it, and what does he do? He shifts v. 4 after v. 6c (conveniently modified, cf. *infra*). Such a move is, however, wholly gratuitous (not supported by any version) and denied by the precise literary composition of the present text. The third objection is of a structural character. The union of the two lovers makes sense as the end of a long journey of getting near each other, not at the beginning of the poetic unit. Indeed, both Wittekindt and Garbini honestly recognise that the present text has no erotic significance. However, they suppose that the text that we have is not the original one, but has been 'expurgated' by a puritanical censor.

The young man's action arouses a positive echo in the heart of the woman who interprets it, not as an attempt at violence, but as an expression of love. It is the beloved who is extending his hand (v. 4a), therefore "her insides stirred for him" (v. 4b). The 'insides' (*mēʿîm*) are juxtaposed with the 'hands' (v. 5) and the 'soul' (v. 6): they are three corporal expressions of the emotions of the woman. The term *mēʿîm* returns again in 5:14 where it designates the external surface of the stomach. Here, as is usual, it is the inside which is intended. In the OT, the insides are the seat of the emotions, of the feelings. The noun is accompanied by the verb *hāmāh*, used to indicate the roaring of the sea, the tumult of a people in revolt, the stirring of the emotions.[75] Those authors who read our passage in an erotic sense think that there is an allusion here to an orgasm.[76] But the parallels do not lead in this direction. In fact, Sir 51:21 speaks of the stirring of the insides (*mʿy yhmw*) to express the love of wisdom; Isa 63:15 (*hămôn mēʿekā*) and Jer 31:20 (*hāmû mēʿay lô*) express the profound tenderness of God for his people in these terms; in Isa 16:11 (*mēʿay lᵉmôʾāb kakkinnôr yehemû*) and in Jer 4:19 (*mēʿay mēʿay…hōmeh llî libbî*) the grief that overcomes the prophet in the face of a disaster is spoken of.[77] The expression denotes, therefore, a profound emotion: it is never used in the OT to indicate orgasm. Moreover, even in our text, such a significance is excluded because the two are separated, the one outside the door, the other on the bed.[78] The emotion which is mentioned is a positive sign: "My insides stirred *for him* (*ʿālāyw*)". The preposition *ʿal* expresses here the amorous desire of the woman.[79] To the extended hand of the man, the deep, 'visceral' yearning of the woman for him is a reply.

[v. 5] That the emotion is a positive sign is confirmed by what follows. Contrary to the intentions expressed in v. 3, the woman rises to

It is on this, highly hypothetical, text that they base their exegesis. Goulder (1986), pp. 41–42, also pronounces against this erotic 'double sense'.

[75] Cf. *LHVT*, p. 194.

[76] Cf., *supra*, n. 74.

[77] Cf. H. Ringgren, *mēʿîm*, in *TDOT*, vol. VIII, pp. 458–460.

[78] Vg (*ad tactum eius*) envisages contact between the two, probably of the hands, anticipating v. 5.

[79] Understanding *ʿal* either in a causal sense, or, as seems more probable to me, as an equivalent of *ʾel*, something common in Aramaic and not infrequent in Late Hebrew (cf. *HALOT*, pp. 825–827, nn. 2 and 6). Others think of a sense of compassion with regard to the man in the open air, or to a feeling of fear. Cf. Haller (1940), p. 37.

open the door. Her heart is now truly 'awake' (cf. v. 2a). But perhaps not yet fully. As Elliott observes, the woman's reaction is slow. Already in v. 4b, she begins to experience sympathy for the man. However, before she opens up (v. 6a), the rising from bed and the fumbling with the bolt (v. 5) are described with a lingering over the details. The description of the hands on the bolt seems to use the cinematographic technique of the close-up, as if the author wishes to make us sense the slowness of this operation, so justifying the departure of the impatient visitor.[80]

The personal pronoun *ʾănî* is put in the emphatic position, after the verb, just as in v. 6a and v. 8d. Here there is also a rhyming effect with *dôdî* ('my beloved'). We have spoken of the structural value of these two terms. The opening of the door, like that of the garden (cf. 4:12) cannot take place from outside; that would be violence. Because of this, the attempts of the man were not able to succeed. Only when the woman rises to open up is the encounter possible (hence the emphasising of the pronoun). It is necessary to wait until the other is ready, that she is 'awake' for love. Perhaps the man did not have this patience. But with the opening of the gate (which in fact will happen in v. 6a), the author already abandons the literary genre of the *paraklausithyron* in which the gate remains closed, by definition, and introduces the theme of the 'nocturnal search'.[81]

The hands of the woman (v. 5b) correspond to the extended hand of the man (v. 4a). The theme of the 'hands' is prolonged also in vv. 5c (the 'fingers') and 5d ('the handles', literally 'palms' [*kappôt*] of the bolt). Quite deliberately, the hand of the man and the hands of the woman[82] meet on the 'hands'[83] of the bolt.[84] The man has sought in vain to reach them through the opening of the door. Now the woman reaches them, and it is as if she clasped the hand of the man.

[80] Elliott (1989), p. 127.

[81] It is clear, therefore, that the description of sexual congress, which some authors would like to see alluded to in vv. 4–5, is incompatible with the literary genre of the *paraklausithyron*.

[82] The Syriac reads the singular (*ydy*), perhaps out of symmetry with the 'hand' of the man.

[83] Here too a Hebrew manuscript (K 18) has the singular (*kpt*).

[84] The 'bolt' also occupies a very prominent position in Egyptian love poetry (cf. Chester Beatty IC 17:8–12, cited *supra*, p. 14, n. 71).

The significance of the myrrh is disputed. Is it the myrrh which he has poured out as a sign of his presence?[85] Or the myrrh left by his hand when he fumbled with the bolt? This interpretation would be supported by the parallel with 5:13 where the expression 'dripping liquid myrrh' (*nāṭap môr ʿōbēr*) is referred to the lips of the man. However in both cases, this would be to go beyond the text which speaks of neither action. It is more natural to think of the myrrh with reference to the woman as a sign of her femininity.[86] In fact, the 'dripping of the myrrh from the hands' is in parallel with the 'stirring of the insides' (v. 4c) and of the 'giving out' of the soul (v. 6c): in the three cases, we have the bodily expression of the woman's emotion. In v. 5bcd, therefore, it is the woman's emotion, perceptible in the hands, that is being described. The hands are a particularly sensitive part of the body, as lovers of all times know: in them is concentrated the openness of the woman to love ('myrrh'). Myrrh, indeed, forms part of the trees of the marvellous garden (cf. 4:14; 5:1); it belongs to the 'mountain of myrrh' (4:6). Probably the author wishes to allude to the sweat that forms on the hands when one is in the grip of a strong emotion.[87] It is natural that the emotion occurs at the touching of the bolt, for this is the decisive instrument of the opening.[88]

To think, with Lys,[89] that the 'liquid myrrh' (*môr ʿōbēr*) is meant to lubricate the bolt sounds somewhat prosaic. 'Liquid myrrh' was the most precious, the most pure, in so far as it drained from the tree by itself without need of any incisions.[90] It was used for confecting the anointing oil (*mor d^erôr*, Exod 30:23). The parallel is not accidental: it brings us back to the sacral connotation of love, observed several times already.

---

[85] Thus, for example, Robert – Tournay (1963), p. 202, who give it an allegorical interpretation, or Garbini (1992), p. 85, who reads, with a Hebrew manuscript, *w'ṣbʿtyw*, 'and his fingers'. In this regard, Lucretius is usually cited: "At lacrimans exclusus amator limina saepe / floribus et sertis operit, postesque superbos / ungit amaricino, et foribus miser oscula figit" (*De rerum natura* 4,1171–1173).

[86] It would also be possible to imagine that the woman had perfumed herself in order to meet her beloved, but this seems less plausible.

[87] So, too, Grober (1984), p. 89.

[88] It is easy to think of an erotic double sense here too. Cf., for example, Garbini (1992), p. 85. Ceronetti (1996), pp. 63, 66, allows his fantasy to fly in this direction. But this is precisely free fantasy, not exegesis: the text does not give rise to this interpretation.

[89] Lys (1968), p. 211.

[90] Cf. E. Levesque, *Myrrhe*, in *DB(V)*, vol. IV, col. 1364.

Second part: Nocturnal search (5:6–8)

The opening of the door (v. 6a) puts v. 6 outside the *paraklausithyron*. With it there begins a new literary genre, the 'nocturnal search' which has its parallel in 3:1–5. The two passages have in common the theme of the nocturnal search in the city (5:6; cf. 3:1–2) and the encounter, first with the watchmen (5:7; cf. 3:3), then with the daughters of Jerusalem (5:8; cf. 3:5). In the first part of the Song, *paraklausithyron* (2:8–17) and 'nocturnal search' (3:1–5) form two distinct songs; here, on the other hand, the two literary genres are united in one song of which they form the two parts. The passage between the first part and the second is fluid: on the one hand, v. 5 already prepares the opening of the door which takes place in v. 6a; on the other hand, v. 6abc occurs still at the door and has the same structural characteristics as vv. 4–5. The 'search in the city', which in 3:2 is described in detail, is here only hinted at (cf. v. 6de). The role of the 'watchmen' is different: in 3:3, the woman dialogues with them, seeks their help; here there is no dialogue but only brutal repression (cf 5:7). The role of the daughters of Jerusalem also does not coincide: in 3:5, it is decisively negative while here it seems to be positive (cf. 5:8). But, above all, in 3:4 the woman finds her beloved, while here the song ends without the search having obtained any results. The fact is that the song is not 'closed' but open to what follows: v. 8 functions as a transition between 5:2–8 and 5:9–16. While 3:5 is the conclusion of the unit 2:8–3:5, 5:8 is the conclusion only of the first of the three *New Songs of the Beloved Woman* which are inseparably united among themselves. Only in 6:3 has the search reached its outcome.[91]

[5:6] Third strophe: At the gate. The third strophe can be divided into two parts of which the first looks towards that which precedes it, the second towards that which follows.[92] However, the two parts are united by a common structure. By contrast with vv. 2–5, it is now the woman who takes the initiative. The action of the woman is narrated in three steps, each time concluded with the underlining of the futility of the actions undertaken: "I opened, but..." (v. 6abc); "I sought, but..." (v. 6d); "I called, but..." (v. 6e).

[91] Cf. Heinevetter (1988), p. 135.
[92] Cf., *supra*, pp. 257–258.

Table 41

Second strophe		Third strophe	
v. 4a	*action of the man*	v. 6a	*action of the woman*
v. 4b	*emotional echo (insides)*	----	---
v. 5a	*reaction of the woman*	v. 6b	*reaction of the man*
v. 5bcd	*emotional echo (hands)*	v. 6c	*emotional echo (soul)*

The verb 'to open' links v. 6abc directly with v. 5 (cf. *Tab. 38*), of which it is the natural conclusion (cf. the sequence: "I rose", *qamtî ʾănî*, v. 5a → "I opened", *pātaḥtî ʾănî*, v. 6a). The three stichs v. 6abc are constructed in a form analogous to the two verses of the second strophe (cf. *Tab. 41*): here, however, the roles are reversed. To the action of the man (v. 4a), there corresponds the action of the woman in v. 6a; to the reaction of the woman (v. 5a), there corresponds the reaction of the man in v. 6b; to the emotional echo of the woman, expressed in the stirring of the insides in v. 4b and by the sweating of the hands in v. 5bcd, there corresponds the giving out of the soul in v. 6c. 'Insides', 'hands' and 'soul' form a coherent series of elements of the person where the intense emotion of the woman reverberates. On the other hand, the verb 'to find' connects v. 6d with vv. 7a and 8b (cf. *Tab. 39*). Here, in two stichs, closely parallel (v. 6de), the theme of the 'search' which characterises the final strophe is introduced.

[v. 6] Even if the opening of the door belongs to another literary genre, the scene in v. 6 has already been carefully prepared in v. 5. The author has lingered over the details, allowing the tension to mount. First the stirring of the insides, then the 'dripping myrrh' of the hands on the bolt have cleverly led the expectation to grow. The reader is made to share in the emotion of the woman when finally she opens the door. But the greater the expectation, the more keen the disappointment: no one is there! The man has gone away.

Precisely here lies the sense of the passage. When he wanted to enter, she was not ready. Now, she is ready, but the other is no longer disposed—he is tired of waiting. Keel says that "feelings are not always synchronised".[93] It would be wrong to speak of her fault, as

[93] Keel (1997), p. 194. The original German speaks of 'Phasenverschiebung der Gefühle'. Similarly Lys (1968), p. 204, speaks of '*rendez-vous manqué*'. The point of the passage lies precisely in this, the fact that the encounter has *not* taken place! Those who see the description of an embrace in vv. 4–5 miss the point.

if it had been her prudery or her tardiness (was she lingering to give herself time to beautify herself before going out?) that was the cause of the failed encounter.[94] One could just as easily speak of the untimely nature of his visit at such an indiscrete hour, or of his impatience in not knowing how adapt to the pace of the other. In the one case or in the other, this would be to moralise while the text intends simply to portray an experience frequent in the life of a couple.

The two stichs in v. 6ab are constructed chiastically, so that *dôdî* ('my beloved') is the last word of v. 6a and the first of v. 6b. This latter stich presents some textual problems. The rare MT *ḥāmaq* ('to turn around, to depart') is confirmed from the noun *ḥammûqîm* ('curves') in 7:2 and by Jer 31:22 (in the *hithpaʿel*, 'to go roaming', in the negative sense, 'to deviate from the path').[95] The parallel with Jeremiah allows us to glimpse, perhaps, a note of disapproval on the part of the woman.[96] To this verb is united the verb *ʿābār*[97] asyndetically. A hook with v. 5c, where the verb was attributed to the 'liquid' myrrh, is discernible. Like the myrrh, so the man is 'running' from the hands of the woman, leaving his scent there.

The meaning of v. 6c is debated. To understand it, it is important to keep in mind the structural position of the stich. It is aligned to vv. 4b and 5bcd in expressing the emotional reaction of the woman in the face of an action of the man or of herself. This emotional echo,

---

[94] Von Speyr claims that it is typical of the male psychology, and therefore absolutely normal (it is to be noted that Von Speyr is a woman), that it is for the man to fix the time of love. The woman who led the man a merry dance with excuses would be culpable. "She wants to decide, and this, here, is not on. It is the man who decides, but he must also include the woman's consent in his decision" (Von Speyr [1972], p. 58).

[95] Garbini (1992), p. 84, changes a consonant, and reads *ḥbq*, 'to embrace', starting from the following assumption: "The verb must be another, phonetically similar to *ḥmq*, with a meaning that has been caused to disappear deliberately". This assumption, however, is not supported by any ancient version.

[96] Confirmed by the Arabic, where the term *chamiqa* means 'to be mad, infantile, foolish' (cf. Keel [1994], p. 183). That speaks decisively against an identification of the beloved with God, as the allegorical interpretation would wish (cf. Robert – Tournay [1963], pp. 204–205).

[97] The meaning of the Hebrew 'to pass, disappear' is confirmed, here too, by all the ancient versions (LXX *parēlthen*; Vg *transierat*; Vetus Latina *transivit*; Syriac *ʿbr*), so that it seems wholly gratuitous to change it into another verb as proposed by Garbini (1992), pp. 84, 232, who replaces *ʿbr* with *rbʿ*, 'to bend, to lie down'. Here again we have a case of making the text say what it does not say. It is understandable that Garbini comments: "The author reveals great pyschological subtlety here" (p. 232). It is necessary only to make clear of which author he is speaking!

localised in v. 4b in the 'insides' and in v. 5bcd in the 'hands', now finds its corporal, physical expression in the 'soul'. The Hebrew *nepeš* is not the spiritual soul of the Greeks but something perceptible, like the breath, the sign of life.[98] The 'giving out' of the *nepeš* is synonymous with 'expiring', 'dying' (cf. Gen 35:18; Jer 15:9; Ps 146:4; Gen 42:28).[99] It is, therefore, a lessening of the vital forces, a dying feeling that is understood here, not so much a 'going mad'.[100] As Joüon notes, *nepeš* never indicates the intelligence.[101] But the expression must be left in its pregnant state: the exit of the soul accompanies the exit of the man from the house as if the soul wished to run after the beloved who 'had...disappeared'.

Also problematic is the last word of the stich: *b^edabb^erô*. The ancient versions translate according to the normal meaning of the verb (*dābar* II):[102] 'at his speech'.[103] However, various authors rightly observe that such a translation does not make sense, whether because the man is not speaking (he has just gone away), or because his words ought to have brought life not death to the woman. Moreover, any reference to the words of v. 3 is improbable, given the distance between the two texts. The attempt to move the stich here or there[104] has no textual basis. The problem is resolved by recognising the existence of another meaning of the verb *dābar* (*dābar* I):[105] 'to turn one's back, to go away', a meaning attested in Arabic and preserved in some Hebrew words like *midbār* ('the land that is behind', the 'desert') and *d^ebîr* (the 'room which is behind', the 'holy of holies').[106] It is certainly not the

---

98 Cf. H. Seebaß, *nepeš*, in *TDOT*, vol. IX, pp. 504–505.

99 Cf. H. D. Preuß, *jāṣā'*, in *TDOT*, vol. VI, p. 230.

100 Thus, for example, Rudolph (1962), p. 154: "I was outside myself". Also improbable is the translation of Nolli, who takes *nepeš* as a personal designation "I went out" (Nolli [1967], p. 117).

101 Joüon (1909), p. 238.

102 Cf. *HALOT*, pp. 210–211.

103 So too Nolli (1967), p. 117 ("hearing him speak"); Ravasi (1992), p. 413 ("through his words"); Salvaneschi (1982), p. 25 ("at the pasture of his word"); Colombo (1975), p. 94 ("at his speaking"); *HOTTP*, vol. III, p. 607 ("when he spoke").

104 Haupt (1907), p. 8, for example, moves it after v. 4a; Ceronetti (1996), p. 30, after v. 5a.

105 *HALOT*, pp. 209–210.

106 Thus Robert - Tournay (1963), p. 204, following Hitzig; Keel (1994), p. 183; Rudolph (1962), p. 155; Krinetzki (1981), p. 158; Murphy (1990), p. 165; Hamp (1957), p. 205. Lys (1968), p. 213, reads a *dbr* I here, but translates: 'à sa suite', understanding the pronoun not as subject but as object of the verb. Joüon and Ricciotti suggest conjectural readings (*bbrḥw*, 'de sa fuite', Joüon [1909], p. 237–238; *b'brw*, "because he had gone by", Ricciotti [1928], p. 247). In line with the rest of his interpretation,

'speech' of the man which makes the woman 'die' but his 'departure', particularly painful because unexpected, unexplained, at precisely the moment when the encounter was to be realised.

The last two stichs of the verse (v. 6de) introduce the theme of the 'nocturnal search' which will be developed in the final strophe. They have a parallel in 3:1–2 where the words "I sought him, but did not find him" (5:6) form a kind of refrain (3:1c, 2d). We refer, therefore, to that place for the comment.[107] However, the parallel concerns only v. 6d: v. 6e ("I called him, but he did not answer me") remains without correspondence. The binome 'seek-find' is linked to the binome 'call-answer' only in Prov 1:28 (the verbs are the same as in our passage except that *biqqēš* is replaced by its synonym *šāḥar*) and Jer 29:12–13 (here there is the replacement of *ʿānāh* ['answer'] with *šāmaʿ* ['listen']). In the first case, the search for wisdom is spoken of, in the second the search for God. It is possible (it would not be the first time) that the author is deliberately using a vocabulary which in the OT refers to these two fields, to denote the transcendent quality of human love. Like the search for truth, so also that for love is, at heart, the search for God (cf. Song 8:6).[108] A detail is worth underlining: in the text of Proverbs and in that of Jeremiah the 'calling' comes first and then the 'seeking', and it is natural that it should be thus. First comes the calling, then, in the case of the absence of an answer, the seeking. In our text, it is the opposite. The woman first searches (v. 6d), then 'calls' (v. 6e). If one observes the structure of the song, a chiastic inversion is to be seen with respect to the man's attempts. At first, he 'called' (a: v. 2), then he 'searched' (b: v. 4). Now the woman first 'searches' (b': v. 6d), then she 'calls' (a': v. 6e). Just as the man's attempts had remained unsuccessful, so, in a kind of tit for tat, those of the woman turn out to be in vain. It could be said that the author wishes to underline the parallelism between the two 'searches'.

[5:7–8] Fourth strophe: In the city. The fourth strophe is neatly distinct from the previous one by the change of characters and place. It is no longer at the door of the house but in the city. The protagonists are no longer the two lovers as in strophes I–III. The woman falls in with two different groups: the 'watchmen' (v. 7) and the 'daughters of

---

Garbini (1992), p. 85, changes *dbr* to *ʿrb*, 'sweetness'; but 'sweetness' is something positive, which has to bear life, not 'death'.

[107] Cf., *supra*, pp. 129–130.

[108] In this sense, cf. Lacocque (1998), p. 119.

Jerusalem' (v. 8). She is not, as in v. 6, the subject of the search but, first of all, is 'found' by the watchmen (v. 7a). After her encounter with them, no longer being able to pursue her search, she invokes the aid of her companions that they may 'find' her beloved for her (v. 8). The two groups are juxtaposed for contrast: to the masculine brutality of the watchmen, incapable of grasping the reasons of the heart, is counterposed the female solidarity of the group of friends. 'Watchmen' and 'daughters of Jerusalem', belong, with different strength, to the semantic field of the 'city' (*ʿîr*, 'city', v. 7b; *ḥōmôt*, 'walls, v. 7e; *yᵉrûšālāim*, 'Jerusalem', v. 8a). The man comes from outside, from savage nature: in this sense, the *inclusio* between the first and the last strophe presents the nature-city opposition which is one of the fundamental poetic axes of the Song. The woman will not find the man in the city but in the garden (6:2–3).

[v. 7] Verse 7ab is a literal repeat of 3:3ab, to which we refer for the comment.[109] The repetition stops here, however, for, in v. 7c, the reaction of the "watchmen who make their rounds through the city" is different from that of 3:3. There, it is limited to not replying to the woman's question; here, "they strike her, they wound her, they take away her mantle". We are not told the motive for this brutality. Graetz thinks that the present difference is due to the recidivism of the woman's behaviour.[110] That would suppose a narrative logic for the entire Song, something which remains to be proved. Apart from the improbable mythological parallel with the descent of Ishtar to the underworld,[111] the most frequent explanation is that of the punishment for the prostitutes. The Middle-Assyrian laws prescribe the following punishment for a prostitute who does her rounds with the veil as though she were a married woman: "They shall not take her jewelry away, (but) the one who arrested her may take her clothing; they shall flog her fifty (times) with staves (and) pour pitch on her head".[112] In the text of the Song, the term which we have translated as 'mantle'

---

[109] Cf., *supra*, pp. 133–134.

[110] Graetz (1871), p. 175.

[111] To reach the realm of the dead, Inanna/Ishtar has to pass through seven gates, defended by infernal guards, who ask her, each time, to remove a garment so that she appears completely naked before the god of the underworld (for the text, cf. *ANET*, p. 55; Wolkstein – Kramer [1983], pp. 57–60). In this sense, cf. Lys (1968), p. 214; Pope (1977), p. 527; Ringgren (1962), p. 268; Müller (1992), p. 56.

[112] § 40, according to *ANET*, p. 183. Cf. also *TUAT* I/1, pp. 87–88 (cf., *supra*, p. 132, n. 136).

is actually disputed. The MT's *r^e^dîd* occurs only one other time, in Isa 3:23, in a series of luxury articles worn by the elegant ladies of Jerusalem. The linguistic parallels with Arabic and Syriac lead to the meaning of 'mantle' or 'veil'.[113] Probably indicated here is that kind of over-garment with hood which the ladies of Lachish are wearing in the above mentioned bas-relief from Nineveh.[114] Perhaps there is also present an allusion to Song 1:7 where the veil (contrary to the Middle Assyrian legislation)[115] was the symbol of the prostitute. Garbini, however, goes too far when he thinks that the woman in this song is being portrayed as a professional prostitute.[116] That the watchmen mistake her for a prostitute is clear, and that her behaviour would have aided such an interpretation is equally true (cf. Prov 7:9–12). But the author has taken care to show that this is only a matter of appearance.[117] We have stressed the *inclusio* between the first and the last strophe. In the first strophe, the woman's reserve, which is perhaps even a little puritanical, is prominent. She did not want to get up because she was naked (v. 3). If now she does not fear to be taken for a prostitute, this is not because of lack of modesty but of the foolish wisdom of a woman in love who is not concerned for people's gossip so long as she can reach the object of her love.[118] It is precisely to this apparently brazen attitude that the chorus exhorts her in 1:8. In any case, the balance between v. 3 and v. 7 is evident: now the mantle is taken away from the one who did not want to put on the tunic.[119]

---

[113] For the discussion, cf. Garbini (1992), pp. 233–234. The Targum speaks of a '(royal) crown', allowing a third possible meaning for the term, 'jewel', but this would not make much sense in our text. LXX's *theristron* indicates a veil or light, summer cloak. The Vg has *pallium* ('mantle').

[114] Cf. Keel (1994), Figure 105, pp. 178–179.

[115] Rudolph (1962), p. 157, thinks, on the contrary, that the sign of the prostitute was that of going without the veil, and that this is why the 'veil' was taken from the woman by the watchmen. However, this would stand in contradiction to 1:7.

[116] Garbini (1992), p. 234. According to Garbini, the woman of the Song is not just one person, but personifies three distinct figures of woman: that of a 'bride', that of a 'free woman', and that of a 'prostitute'. In our song, it would be the third type of woman that was being represented (pp. 308–313). As we have had occasion to mention, the different aspects, at times apparently contradictory, are only different facets of the paradox of love. As for the 'free woman' and the 'prostitute', they are creations of Garbini: the woman of the Song is certainly not moralistic, but, precisely for this reason, is profoundly moral.

[117] Cf., in this sense, Lacocque (1998), p. 120.

[118] Cf., *supra*, p. 132.

[119] It is possible that the woman was wearing the *r^e^dîd*, which served as covering for her naked body, and that therefore the watchmen had stripped her. This was, precisely, the punishment of the prostitute (cf. Hos 2:5; Ezek 16:37–39; Isa 47:2–3; Jer

The mention of the 'watchmen' acts as an *inclusio* for the verse (*haššōmᵉrîm*, vv. 7a and 7e). In v. 7e the term is different: 'the watchmen of the walls'. It is difficult, however, to think that this represents a different reality:[120] it is the same institution, called by two different names for poetic variation.[121] In the Song, the watchmen have a typical, symbolical function.[122] Here in particular they personify the brute force which is counterposed to the disarming innocence of the girl, the violence which is set against love.[123] It is possible to read into this a criticism of the Hellenistic forces of occupation who formed the military garrison of the city (*peripoloi*): the 'sixty mighty men of Israel' are presented in a quite other light. But the critical potential of the Song is not confined to foreigners: the Israelite institutions, the family (cf. the 'brothers' of 1:6), the monarchy (cf. the treatment of 'Solomon' in 8:11–12), society (one thinks of the 'daughters of Jerusalem' in 2:7; 3:5) are not spared either. The term 'wall' (*ḥōmâ*) is repeated twice in 8:9, 10, a passage highly critical of society. Against the brothers who wanted to erect a protective wall around their little sister, she tells them: "I am a wall, and my breasts are like towers!" The criticism of the author is directed against the demand of imposing on love laws dictated by power or force, or by economic convenience, which have nothing to do with love. Love is law to itself.

[v. 8] Misunderstood by the watchmen, the woman seeks for understanding among her girl friends.[124] It seems to me otiose to ask: Where do these come from? The 'daughters of Jerusalem' also have sometimes the function of a 'chorus' with which the woman is in dialogue. The Song is lyrical, not narrative. As in 2:7 and 3:5, Lys sees them in a negative light. They would be the opponents of the woman, the representatives of that refined and decadent city from which the woman is

---

13:22; Nah 3:5; Rev 17:16). That would form an exact retaliation for her *pruderie* in v. 3ab: she, who did not want to get up because she was naked, is now stripped! The text is not clear on this point, however: one must be content with speculations.

[120] *Contra* Ravasi (1992), pp. 437–438, cf. Van Leeuwen (1923).

[121] So, rightly, Keel (1994), p. 184.

[122] Cf., *supra*, pp. 133–134, nn. 141, 142.

[123] As in 3:1–5, here too, Krinetzki reads the passage in psychoanalytic terms. In the watchmen, he sees the super-ego, which prevents the woman from accepting her own femininity, from maturing sexually: "In these attempts at growing, she feels herself low and vulgar, like a prostitute, for which she believes herself to deserve to be punished, something the police of the city actually do in the image of vv. 7c–e" (Krinetzki [1981], p. 163).

[124] Thus, shrewdly, Lacocque (1998), p. 120 ("in the eyes of a woman, only they are able to understand the extremes to which feminine infatuation can lead").

taking her distance; in this case, 'rivals' too in love. In fact, their role is not at all clear. Their questions to her in 5:9 and 6:1 could reveal understanding and a desire to help, but also a subtle irony. However, it seems to me that here their role is prevalently positive, in counterposition to that of the watchmen.

The *incipit* of the verse is the same as 2:7 and 3:5 (the similarity is accentuated in the LXX which adds "by the forces and powers of the field"). That makes us understand that the poetic unit is to be concluded. The sequel is, naturally, different, because here it is not a union that has been described but a 'failed union'. Strictly speaking, the friends are not asked to seek the man but to give him a message. Perhaps, however, the conditional form ("if you find")[125] is a delicate way of asking them to search, as, in fact, the friends have understood it (cf. 6:1).

The question: "What will you tell him?" has evidently an emphatic, intensifying value as in Hos 9:14. Perhaps it too expresses the indecision or the desperation of the woman who no longer knows what to do. Structurally, the phrase hooks the verse on to the following one (cf. also the terms 'daughters of Jerusalem' and 'beloved'). In Song 5:9, the friends in their turn pose two questions that begin in the same form: *mâ* ('what?').

"That I am sick with love". The song ends with a repeat of 2:5, to the comment on which we refer. The theme of 'love sickness' is, moreover, perfectly in context here. The symptoms of the illness have been listed: 'stirring of the insides' (v. 4b), 'sweating of the hands' (v. 5bcd), 'giving out of the soul' (v. 6c). With 2:5, this makes two passages in which the woman's 'sickness' is spoken of. To these correspond two others in which the man's 'sickness' is mentioned (4:9 and 6:5). Again the perfect reciprocity of love in the Song is to be noted. It is not only the woman who is a victim of 'love-sickness': her beloved is equally defenceless in the face of it.

The friends are, therefore, being requested to transmit to the man that his woman is 'sick of love'. Rothstein claims that such a message

[125] The Hebrew particle *ʾim* can have a conditional value, as here, but can also introduce an oath, as in 2:7 and 3:5 (*ʾim tāʿîrû*). In this case, it has a negative value ("I charge you *not* to rouse"). Assuming this meaning in our text, the translation would have to be: "I charge you not to find", which would not make sense. The same goes for the question which follows ("not to tell him"). Cf. Lys (1998), p. 215; Joüon (1909), p. 241.

is useless and prosaic; it would have been better to leave the question without any answer.[126] Others think that the woman is making reference to the blows received from the watchmen in v. 7.[127] But, in any case, the text speaks of the wounds of 'love', not those inflicted by the watchmen. In other words, the reference is meant to be to vv. 4–6. Perhaps, the woman thinks, my beloved has gone away because he reckons that, because I did not open up to him, I do not feel anything for him. Tell him that it is not true, that, in fact, "I am sick with love". It is thus confirmed that confusion over the '*tempi*' of love is the key to an adequate reading. He is in love with her, and she with him (she was, in fact, 'awake', v. 2): and yet the encounter did not take place. The times of the maturing of desire have not coincided.

Remembrance (5:9–16)

The second song of the woman is structured as a dialogue. The question of the 'daughters of Jerusalem' (v. 9) introduces the description of the beloved (vv. 10–16) which constitutes the natural reply to such a question. The friends ask in what way the beloved is special, and the woman explains, going on to describe her man. The link between question and answer is signalled by the repeat of the term 'beloved' (*dôd*), at the beginning of the song of the woman (v. 10a). This song is, in its turn, framed by this same word (vv. 10a, 16c). To the two ironic mentions on the part of the friends correspond two mentions by the woman in a very different tone.

Within the *inclusio* formed by the term *dôd* at vv. 10 and 16cd (a-a'; cf. *Tab. 42*), ten parts of the man's body are described, a number as symbolic as the seven parts of the woman's body described in 4:1–7. The literary genre is the same, the *waṣf*.[128] Usually, however, the *waṣf*

[126] Cited in Robert - Tournay (1963), p. 208.

[127] LXX and Vetus Latina translate with 'wounded' instead of 'sick'. They are followed, among others, by Joüon (1909), p. 241; Lacocque (1998), p. 120. Such a translation makes the Hebrew *ḥôlat* derive not from *ḥālāh*, 'to be sick', but from *ḥālal*, 'to transfix, to pierce'. With this, reference would be being made to the maltreatment inflicted by the guards in v. 7 ('to pierce' could also have the sense of a rape). Others see the Hellenistic theme of the arrows of love here (thus, for example, Colombo [1985], p. 91, who, in this connection, cites Euripides [*Hippolytus*, 392]: "Since Eros has wounded me"; or Garbini [1992], p. 235 ["That I am wounded by love"]). But, although suggestive, such a derivation cannot be sustained grammatically.

[128] Cf., *supra*, pp. 172–173.

Table 42

	vv.	*parts of the body*	*metaphor*	*aspect*	*key-words*
a	10	Introduction			*my beloved*
b	11a	I. head	gold	sight	*pure gold*
	11bc	II. curls	date flowers / raven	sight	
	12ab	III. eyes	doves	sight	
c	13ab	IV. cheeks	balm / fragrance	smell	
	13cd	V. lips	flowers of lotus / myrrh	smell	
b’	14ab	VI. hands	gold / Tarshish	sight	*Gold*
	14cd	VII. belly	ivory / lapis lazuli	sight	
	15ab	VIII. legs	alabaster / gold	sight	*pure gold*
c’	15cd	IX. appearance	Lebanon	sight	
	16ab	X. palate	sweetness / desire	taste	
a’	16cd	Coda			*my beloved*

has as its object the body of a woman (so too in 4:1–7; 6:4–7 and 7:2–9): it is rare to find a description of the male body in Oriental poetry.[129] In the biblical sphere, the nearest parallels are perhaps the description of the priest Simon in Sir 50:5–10 and that of Jacob in the pseudepigraph, *Joseph and Aseneth.*[130]

The description in Song 5:10–16 is also distinguished from the other *waṣf*’s of the Song through the fact of its not being a direct discourse:

[129] Gerleman (1965), p. 66, speaks of an example in the lyrics of ancient Egypt (ostracon n. 1125 of the Hermitage); Dalman can cite only two examples from Palestinian folklore (we offer one of them: “My life and waiting and consoling / it is vanity in vanity in vanity, / and your temples and the down of your beard and the beauty of your cheeks / is half-moon in the half-moon in the half-moon, / and your mouth and your lips and your incisors / are pearls among pearls, / and your hair, also the fleck in your hair, also my fate / are as nights in the nights in the nights”, cf. Dalman [1901], p. 243).

[130] “And Aseneth saw him and was amazed at his beauty, because Jacob was exceedingly beautiful to look at, and his old age (was) like the youth of a handsome (young) man, and his head was all white as snow, and the hairs of his head were all exceeding close and thick like (those) of an Ethiopian, and his beard (was) white reaching down to his breast, and his eyes (were) flashing and darting (flashes of lightning), and his sinews and his shoulders and his arms were like (those) of an angel, and his thighs and his calves and his feet like (those) of a giant. And Jacob was like a man who had wrestled with God” (22:7, *OTP* II, p. 238).

the man is absent; he is being described to the friends.[131] It seems, therefore, that the author is making free use of this literary genre: the intent to create a parallel with the description of the woman's body in 4:1–7 is clear. Again it is the principle of reciprocity that emerges: it is not only the woman who is the object of admiration on the part of the man; the man too is the object of admiration on the part of the woman.

As in 4:1–7 and in 6:4–7, in this *waṣf* too the order is descending. The movement is regular from v. 11a (head) to v. 15b (feet). The expression 'pure gold' (*pāz*, vv. 11a and 15b) forms an *inclusio* for the first eight parts of the body: the two that follow ('appearance', v. 15cd; 'palate', v. 16ab) have a comprehensive value for the whole person. The ten parts are divided into two groups of five. The motif of the gold, which reappears, with a different term, in v. 14a, in connection with the hands marks a division between the first and the second group. The first five descriptions refer to the head, and are divided into two sections according to the aspect, visual or olfactory, which the metaphor sets in relief. Head, curls and eyes are united in the visual aspect (b). The head is shining ('gold'), the hair black ('flowers of date', 'raven'), the eyes white ('doves', 'milk'). Cheeks and lips are united under the aspect of smell (c). The passage from the contemplation to the enjoyment of love has already been revealed as a structural principle in Chapter 4.

The other five descriptions (vv. 14–16) regard the rest of the body, and they too are subdivided into two sections, of three and two elements. Descriptions VI–VIII, hands, belly and legs (b'), form a homogeneous compositional unit: they are 'included' by the theme of gold (vv. 14a, 15b), they use metaphors drawn from the work of craftsmen, and they are structured in analogous form (cf. *Tab. 42*). In parallel with the first group of three (b: vv. 11–12), the visual element, shape and colour, is presented in them. The last two descriptions (vv. 15cd and 16ab: c') have a comprehensive character. Having described individual parts of the body from the head (v. 11a) to the feet (v. 15b), the author wishes to give a global impression of the body of the beloved. He does that by drawing attention to each of the aspects with which he has structured the description. In v. 15cd, the visual aspect is stressed

[131] In this, our *waṣf* is close to the Egyptian love songs: cf., for example, Papyrus Chester Beatty IA 1:1–8, cited *supra*, p. 173, n. 21.

(*marʾeh*: literally, 'sight'), in v. 16a that of enjoyment, now no longer from the point of view of smell but from the complementary one of taste ('sweetness').[132]

Gerleman has advanced the hypothesis that the passage 5:2–6:3 is a redactional unit: the redactor's hand would be evident in the two questions of the 'daughters of Jerusalem' (5:9 and 6:1).[133] The thesis is unsustainable, at least as regards 5:9. Certainly this verse has the function of uniting the two passages 5:2–8 and 10–16: the connection with v. 8 has been noted above.[134] Another link is formed by the characteristic interrogative particle which is doubled, *šekkākâ* ('why', v. 9d), which echoes the two *ʾêkākâ*'s ('how') of v. 3b, d. But it is not only v. 9 which refers back to vv. 2–8. The first two parts of the body that are described, the head (*rōʾš*, v. 11a) and the curls (*qᵉwuṣṣôt*, v. 11b), are a repeat of v. 2ef. The metaphor of the doves to which the eyes of the beloved are compared (v. 12a) looks back to the appellation which he addresses to her ('my dove', v. 2d). The placing of the hands (*yādāyim*) with the belly (*mēʿîm*, literally 'insides') in v. 14 takes up again, in reverse order, the emotional echo of the woman's body in vv. 4b and 5b. The expression 'dripping liquid myrrh' (*nōṭᵉpôt môr ʿōbēr*, v. 13d) is taken word for word from v. 5bc,[135] where it is referred to the hands of the woman. The term *dôdî* has a unifying structural function in the whole of the passage 5:2–6:3:[136] Just as it 'includes' the preceding song of the woman, vv. 2–8, so it also frames vv. 10–16.[137] The syn-

[132] A structure which is partly alternative to this is traced out in Keel (1992), p. 194, who sees in 5:8b–16d a chiastic composition (cf. also Heinevetter [1988], p. 137). In the face of these observations, the liberty with which Garbini changes the order of the verses of this passage seems really arbitrary. He puts v. 14cd, the description of the belly, after v. 12, that is, between the description of the eyes and of the cheeks. Cf. Garbini (1992), p. 89. This movement is necessary to justify his translation (cf., *infra*, n. 183). But, structurally, the description of the belly is lined up with that of the hands and legs not that of the eyes, and even less that of the cheeks: the metaphors are of a completely different order.

[133] Gerleman (1965), pp. 170, 179; so too Müller (1992), p. 57. Another upholder of redactional theses, Heinevetter (1988), pp. 140–144, is forced to attribute to the redactor a really large part (precisely 5:5–9, 10b, 12, 13ab, 13d, 15c–16b, 16d; 6:1–3). But this reconstruction appears extremely artificial.

[134] Cf., *supra*, pp. 254–255.

[135] Therefore one cannot understand how Garbini (1992), p. 231, translates *môr ʿōbēr* in v. 5c, without problems, as 'flowing myrrh', while at v. 13d he holds *ʿbr* to be 'a useless repetition of *nṭp*', arriving at the translation: 'myrrh which satisfies' ('mirra che sazia', *ibid.*, p. 90).

[136] Cf., *supra*, p. 255.

[137] Cf. *Tab. 37*, p. 257.

onym 'my friend' (*rēʿî*) with which the *waṣf* concludes (v. 16c) forms an *inclusio* with the beginning of the preceding song (*rayāʿtî*, v. 2c). It seems, that is, that the same hand is at work in the two songs. It is interesting to note that some of these expressions refer in both cases to the man (cf. the terms *head* and *curls* in vv. 2 and 11, also the *hands* in vv. 4 and 14), as if the woman wanted to paint a picture of that young man who was at the door shortly before. Other expressions which are here referred to the man are referred to the woman in vv. 2–8. That is the case with the term 'dove' (vv. 2, 12), with the binome 'hands + belly' (vv. 4, 5 and 14), with the expression 'dripping liquid myrrh' (vv. 5, 13), with the appellation 'my friend' (vv. 2, 16). This phenomenon is not isolated in the Song so that one can speak of poetic intentionality in this interchangeability of metaphors and attributes between the lovers. In her beloved, the woman recognises herself. The same myrrh that drips from her hands, drips from his lips, and in his eyes she recognises the same flame of love ('dove') which shines in hers. Love, it was noted above, makes people brothers, makes out of the two only one flesh.

The question of the daughters of Jerusalem (5:9)

The two questions of the daughters of Jerusalem, 5:9 and 6:1, are assimilated to each other both by their form, through being composed according to 'staircase' parallelism,[138] and by content. One should note in both, in fact, an ambiguity between the desire to help and a certain irony, and it is not clear which of the two factors is predominant.

[v. 9] "What makes your beloved different from another?" The translation of this stich is controversial. Three solutions are possible according to the sense given to the preposition *min*. One can understand this preposition, as in Arabic, with the sense of 'like', and arrive at the translation: "what kind of beloved is your beloved?";[139] one can understand it in the partitive sense ('different from…'), as we have done;[140] one can understand it, finally, in a comparative sense, and reach a

[138] Cf. our commentary on 4:8 (*supra*, p. 197).

[139] In this sense, Schmökel (1956), p. 66.

[140] With *CEI* and Joüon (1909), pp. 242–243. This is also the understanding of LXX *apo adelphidou*; Vg *ex dilecto*; and the Syriac *mn dd'*. In this connection, Joüon cites the question addressed by Rabbi Eliezer to Rabbi Aqiba: *mâ yôm miyyômîm*, 'How is this day different from all other days?' (b.*BM* 59b).

broader translation: 'better than any other'.[141] The first translation is to be discarded because it does not find any support in Hebrew. The other two are both possible. The second fits better with the reply of the woman in v. 10. The third makes the ironic character of the question stand out more. In any case, the two nuances are present however one translates.

The mythological reading, of Lys for example, which sees in the daughters of Jerusalem the priestesses of Tammuz, the *dôd* par excellence, to whom the woman counterposes her *dôd*, seems improbable to me.[142] It is more probable that the author plays on the contrast between the woman in love, for whom her beloved is unique and irreplaceable, and the others who are outside this relationship, for whom the man is 'just one among so many'.[143]

The ambiguity between earnestness and irony returns in the appellation: 'fairest among women' (repeated in 6:1). The expression can be understood in an ironic sense: (from the point of view of the other women) the woman would be the fairest of them all in the same way as the man is 'better than any other beloved'. Verse 9b is a repeat of 1:8, where the expression is put into the mouth of the male chorus of shepherds. Lys wishes to understand both passages in an ironic sense.[144] But, in the one case as in the other, he is not quite convincing.[145] It is known that love increases the beauty of a woman: a woman in love radiates a particular charm.

"That you charge us so". The reference is to v. 8a. According to the question of the friends, the charge given by the woman in v. 8 would have given them to understand the extraordinary quality of the man. To what aspect of the charge is the reference here? Elliott thinks of the form: if it was an oath, it would not be for a trifle (that would be

[141] Cf., for example, Robert – Tournay (1963), p. 209.

[142] Lys (1968), p. 218. Along these lines again, Schmökel (1956), p. 66, who sees in the woman the goddess of love (Inanna-Ishtar-Aphrodite) searching for her vanished divine partner. Wittekindt (1925), pp. 82–94, translates: "Who else is your beloved if not Dôd" (where Dôd is synonymous with Ishtar's lover, the god Tammuz). Hamp (1957), p. 205, is dismissive: "*dôd* is never a proper name". According to Pope (1977), p. 530, the passage is inspired by a Sumerian composition, "The message of Lu-dingir-ra to his mother": but, there, it is a description of a woman, here, of a man.

[143] Cf. Von Speyr (1972), p. 62, who transposes to the relationship that unites Christ and his Church as against those who do not form part of the Church.

[144] Lys (1968), p. 218.

[145] For the significance of 1:8, cf., *supra*, p. 67.

sacrilege) but precisely for something out of the ordinary.[146] Keel on the other hand thinks of the content of the oath, that is of the message to be transmitted, that she is sick with love. In the intention of the daughters of Jerusalem, this would be an ironic way of saying: "It is not worth the trouble of getting sick over the loss of one's beloved: there are many other irons in the fire!"[147] Here too one picks up that ambivalence between sincere participation and irony which characterises the whole verse.

First strophe: The head of the beloved (5:10–13)

As in 4:1–7, the description of the head of the loved one takes up the greatest part of the *waṣf*. By contrast, the rest of the body is described rather summarily. In the head, the woman sees her man as if in concentrated form: outside and inside, body and soul together. After the introductory verse, in which the woman takes up her friends' question, the description is divided into two sections, the first comprising three elements of the head (head, curls, eyes), the second two (cheeks and lips). The individual elements are grouped according to the aspect, visual or olfactory, which is intended to be stressed.

[5:10] Introduction. "My beloved is white and red". The introduction presents the visual aspect of the body which will then be developed in vv. 11–12. The Hebrew term *ṣaḥ* indicates the 'radiance' of the sun or the atmosphere (cf. Isa 18:4; Jer 4:11). In our case, the meaning 'white' is ensured by the juxtaposition with the other colour, the 'red' (*'ādôm*).[148] The binome finds a precise parallel in Lam 4:7—"Her (= of Jerusalem) princes[149] were purer (*zakkû*) than snow, whiter (*ṣaḥû*) than milk, / their body was redder (*'admû*) than coral, their appearance a sapphire".[150] The correspondence is confirmed by the fact that Lam

[146] Elliott (1989), p. 135.

[147] Keel (1994), p. 198.

[148] Cf. LXX *leukos*; Vg *candidus*; Syriac *ḥwr*. Symmachus' *lampros*, 'shining', underlines the other aspect of the lexeme.

[149] MT *nᵉzîrîm*, with the ancient versions. The term indicates primarily the 'consecrated' ('nazirites'), from which, by extension, 'princes'. *BHS* proposes the conjecture: *nᵉʿārèhā* 'her young men' (cf. *CEI; NJB*).

[150] Cf. S. Talmon, *ṣaḥ*, in *TDOT*, vol. XII, pp. 321–324. In the light of this parallel, it seems that the binome 'white and red' can express not only, as in Italian, the idea of a healthy complexion, but something more. What sense would the second term, the sapphire, otherwise have? Perhaps we have symbolic colours here, cited for the associations which they evoke in the human mind. Cf. Gerleman (1965), p. 173.

4:1–2 contains three other terms characteristic of our *waṣf*, that is the three designations of gold: *zāhāb* (Lam 4:1; cf. Song 5:14), *ketem* (Lam 4:1; cf. Song 5:11), *pāz* (Lam 4:2; cf. Song 5:11, 15). Given the subtle intertextuality of the Song, it is not unthinkable that the author intends to bring together the two passages. The young man, that is, would have the characteristics of the princes of the ancient, pre-Exilic time. It is not only the aristocratic nature of the man that is being stressed with this parallel but also his sacral character (it is about Nazirites, *n*^{e}*zîrîm*). And, perhaps, it is intended to be understood that love is the way to return to the splendour of the former time. What Lamentations weeps over as lost, the Song of Songs celebrates as present.[151] With that, the woman replies tit for tat to the daughters of Jerusalem: her beloved is not any old beloved, but something very special.[152] It is not to be wondered at that one may be 'sick with love' for him.

The resentful stressing of the beloved's uniqueness is confirmed in v. 10b: "He is distinguished among thousands and thousands". Here the aspect of stature is placed alongside that of colour. The Hebrew term *dāgûl* is a denominative verb from *degel* ('standard, banner', cf. 2:4; 6:4, 10).[153] If in the parallel passages *degel* is synonymous with military power, here its 'elevated' character is in force. The banner is raised above the hosts; it stands out and is recognisable above the multitudes. In this way the beloved is recognisable among 'thousands and thousands'.[154] This aspect of stature will be taken up again in v. 15cd.

The woman thus gives the daughters of Jerusalem the information which they have requested in order to be able to recognise her beloved, to be able to distinguish him from other 'beloveds'. In reality, the

---

[151] Cf. Lacocque (1998), pp. 121–122.

[152] According to Tournay (1982), pp. 86–87, the colour red would be an allusion to David, who in 1 Sam 16:12 and 17:42 is called *ʾadmônî*, 'ruddy', and that is viewed as an element of male beauty. Tournay naturally reads the parallel in an allegorical key: the beloved would be a figure of the Messiah. In the present text of the Song, there are real instances that allow a glimpse of a possible messianic *relecture* of the figure of the *dôdî*. But, in our case, the parallel is not completely convincing. In fact, the man is called not *ʾadmônî*, 'ruddy', but *ʾādôm*, 'red', and this is the proper name of Esau, called 'Edom' because of the red colour of his skin (cf. Gen 25:25). Also, Gerleman's proposal of seeing in 'red' the ochre colour in which male flesh is portrayed in Egyptian statuary is not convincing (cf. Gerleman [1965], p. 69). Here, in fact, we do not have only one colour, but two: 'white and red'.

[153] In this case too, one can note the perfect symmetry of the genders. Twice the 'banner' metaphor is applied to the man (2:4; 5:10), twice to the woman (6:4, 10).

[154] MT *r*^{e}*bābâ* indicates, like LXX's *myriades*, the number 'tens of thousands', but stands generically for a great multitude.

points of view are different. For the one who is in love, the loved one is unmistakable; he is unique and irreplaceable. The distinctive signs of him which the woman gives are highly subjective: only one who is in a loving relationship can grasp them. Like the watchmen, so too the daughters of Jerusalem do not succeed in finding the one whom the woman seeks on the basis of this description.

[vv. 11–12] First section: Gold, black and white. The metaphor of the banner which appears among the hosts naturally evokes the 'head' of the beloved: the transition is coherent. The head of the beloved is compared with gold. *ketem* and *pāz* are two synonyms to indicate a particularly refined quality of gold. The common term *zāhāb* will be used at v. 14 while *pāz* will be repeated at v. 15b. Thus head, hands and feet of the beloved are of gold. As Keel suggests,[155] following Gerleman,[156] the author is probably inspired by Egyptian models in vv. 11a, 14–15. The process could have been as follows. Since the statues of the gods were "made of precious stones and moulded in bronze",[157] the gods themselves were imagined as being like their images. In the *Book of the Heavenly Cow*, we read *à propos* of Amon-Ra, the sun god: "His bones were of silver, his flesh of gold, and his hair of real lapis lazuli".[158] From the gods, the model passed to their earthly representative, the Pharaoh. A princess of the *harem* thus celebrates the beauty of Ramses III: "Your hair (is) lapis lazuli, your eyebrows *qa*ʿ stones, your eyes green malachites, your mouth red jasper".[159] In this last case, the likeness between the colour of the precious material and the part of the body is to be noted, but it is not always the case. At times the *tertium comparationis* is the preciousness or the pureness of the material, not its colour.[160] In antiquity, gold was called "the flesh of the gods".[161] A statue was not simply inanimate material but was considered the incarnation or personification of the divinity. In Greece, the chryselephantine statues of Zeus Olympus and Athena Parthenos sculpted by

[155] Keel (1994), pp. 202–203.

[156] Gerleman (1965), p. 69.

[157] Thus, according to the *Instruction of Merikara*. Cf. Bresciani (1990), p. 99. For the OT, cf. Jer 10:9.

[158] Cf. Bresciani (1990), p. 236.

[159] Cf. Keel (1994), p. 202, and Figure 121, p. 203.

[160] In this connection, Pope (1977), p. 547, cites an Akkadian spell over a sick person: "Like lapis lazuli I want to cleanse my body, / Like marble his features should shine, / Like pure silver, like red gold, / I want to make clean what is dull".

[161] Müller (1992), p. 60, cf. the example quoted above from '*The Book of the Heavenly Cow*'.

Pheidias in 540 B.C. were famous. They were held by contemporaries to be a "perfect representation of the divine".[162] In fact, in vv. 11 and 14–15, gold and ivory are the materials that constitute the body of the beloved.

In the OT, one thinks of the theophanies of Ezek 1:26–27 and Dan 10:5–6 (cf. Rev 1:13–15). Since, according to the account of the creation, man is in the "image (in the sense of 'statue')[163] of God" (Gen 1:27), we should not be surprised that the beloved is described according to this pattern. Müller emphasises that in this way the 'theomorphic' value of the beloved is made clear,[164] an element already noticed elsewhere in the Song. A further biblical parallel, to which we must return, is the famous dream of Nebuchadnezzar in Dan 2:31–33.[165]

Between the two expressions 'idol' and 'image of God' there runs the border between the pagan and biblical representations of the divine value of sexuality and love. For the Bible, there is only one God, and every attempt to raise created realities to divinity is an attempt on his uniqueness. On the other hand, a real reflection of the divinity can be discerned in the human being. And it is true, for the Bible, that only by looking at man does one arrive at reaching the face of God. Not for nothing do the above-cited theophanies represent God in human form.

If, in the description of the head, the colour is not a dominating element,[166] it is so in the description of the two following parts of the body, the hair and the eyes, built up, as in the woman's *waṣf*, on the 'black-white' contrast (cf. Song 4:1–2). The second and the third descriptions are also differentiated from the first by the kind of metaphor employed. These no longer suppose the description of a statue, but are drawn from nature. Such a mixing of metaphors is common in Egyptian love poetry.[167]

---

[162] We refer once more to Keel (1994), p. 204, for the citations.

[163] Cf. Zenger (1983), pp. 87–89.

[164] Müller (1992), pp. 59–60.

[165] Cf., *infra*, p. 300.

[166] Perhaps in this sense one can cite the Homeric parallel of the encounter between Ulysses and Nausicaa, in Book VI of the *Odyssey*. With regard to Ulysses, it is said: "And as when a man overlays silver with gold, [...] even so the goddess shed grace upon his head and shoulders" (*Odyssey* 6:232, 235, tr. Murray [1995], vol. I, p. 237). Similarly, in our text, the gold has a symbolic value.

[167] Cf., for example, the *waṣf* of Papyrus Chester Beatty IA, cited *supra*, p. 173, n. 21: "Her hair true lapis lazuli. / Her arms surpass gold, / her fingers are like lotuses" (tr. Fox [1985], p. 52).

"His curls, flowers of date". The Hebrew term *taltallîm* is a disputed *hapaxlegomenon*. It seems improbable to me that the derivation arises from the root *tll* I from which the term *tēl* ('hill') derives.[168] More probable is that from the root *tlh* ('to hang'),[169] or from the Akkadian *taltallū*[170] ('pollen of date flowers') to which comes close the LXX, *elatē*, designating the spathe which contains the flowers of the palm. The spathe is dark but the flowers are white. The *tertium comparationis* seems not to be the colour, which will be emphasised in the following comparison, but the form. "The 'date panicles,' 20 inches (half-meter) long even without the stem, testify to the wild and unruly character of his hair".[171] The biblical parallel which comes to mind is that of the hair of Absalom spoken of in 2 Sam 14:26:

> And when he cut the hair of his head—for at the end of every year he used to cut it; when it was heavy on him he cut it—he weighed the hair of his head, two hundred shekels by the king's weight.

The two terms 'head' (*rō'š*) and 'curls' (*qᵉwuṣṣôt*) are repeated from v. 2. The woman, that is, gives the daughters of Jerusalem the information necessary to recognise the young man who presented himself at her door. But the shepherd has now become a 'god', and been transfigured by love: his head is of gold.

If the gold transfers him into a sphere that is noble and divine, the hair, in v. 11 as in v. 2, makes us think of a force that is wild. Like that of his friend (Song 4:1), the hair of the beloved is also thick and black. The latter adjective alludes to its youthful vitality (cf. Qoh 11:10), but in the metaphor used ('black as the raven') there is also a demonic element. The raven is an unclean animal (Lev 11:15); it belongs to the world of the demons (cf. Isa 34:11; Zeph 2:14) who are incarnated in the hairy goats of the desert (Song 5:2f).[172] The contrast between the head and the hair is at the same time of an order that is both symbolic (divine-demonic) and visual (gold-black).

---

[168] Thus Delitzsch (1875), p. 91; Garbini (1992), p. 237 ("wavy hills"); Lacocque (1998), p. 122.

[169] With Rudolph (1962), p. 158. For the discussion, cf. *HALOT*, pp. 1741–1742.

[170] So Gerleman (1965), p. 174.

[171] Keel (1994), p. 199; so too Gerleman (1965), p. 174, who thinks rather of a spathe because of the colour. Similarly, Joüon (1909), p. 249, and Robert - Tournay (1963), pp. 212–214 ("palms"). The term would then be synonymous with its homophone *sansinnîm* (7:9), to which the woman's breasts are compared.

[172] Thus Keel (1994), p. 199.

The same contrast links v. 11 with v. 12, the hair with the eyes. "His eyes, like doves…". The similitude of the dove is common to both his eyes and hers (cf. 4:1; 1:15). The only difference is that in the case of the woman, we have a metaphor ("Your eyes [are] doves"), here of a simile ("Your eyes, *like* doves"). We have already spoken of the metaphorical significance of the dove as an animal of the goddess of love.[173] The dove is counterposed to the raven, just as in the account of the Flood (cf. Gen 8:6–12). Here too the symbolic aspect (demonic-divine) is associated with the visual (black-white).

The doves are 'on streams of water'. The element of 'water' is stressed with reference, perhaps, to the characteristic 'moisture' of the eyes from which tears run. Here too there is a contrast with the raven, animal of the desert. The significance of the two Hebrew terms *ʾăpîqê mayim* ('streams of water') and *millēʾt* ('full [bath]') is disputed. The first expression is known and undoubtedly indicates a 'water course', that is, the bed in which water runs or, by metonymy, the (running) water itself.[174] The second is a *hapax* deriving from the root *mlʾ*, 'to be full'. The LXX refers it to the water itself, probably understanding thereby a pool or something of the kind.[175] But then a contrast is created between the streams and the bath. The LXX is aware of this and translates both *ʾăpîqê mayim* and *millēʾt* alike: *plērōmata hydatōn*,[176] but this is a case of *lectio facilior*. Also highly hypothetical is the proposal of inserting the term *šinnāyw* ('his teeth') at the beginning of v. 12b as Ravasi, does, for example: "*His teeth* are washed in milk / and well set in their gums".[177] We can only take the MT as it is, as *lectio difficilior*, with the apparent contradiction between the 'streams' and the 'bath'. We have here two different images even if they have the element of 'water' in common. The twofold 'streams' and 'bath' refer back to the twofold 'spring' (that is, running water) and 'fountain' or 'well' (that

[173] Cf., *supra*, pp. 178–179.

[174] Cf. *HALOT*, p. 78.

[175] *epi plērōmata hydatōn*.

[176] Robert - Tournay (1963), pp. 214–216, follow it, for example. They translate *ʾăpîqê māyim* with 'basin'. Garbini (1992), pp. 92, 237–238, imagines a deliberate correction of the primitive text, which would have had the term *mlwʾ*, 'pool of water'. Vg (*iuxta fluenta plenissima*) makes an improbable synthesis between 'stream' and 'basin'.

[177] Ravasi (1992), p. 458; so too Rudolph (1962), pp. 158–159; Müller (1992), p. 58; Murphy (1990), p. 166; Nolli (1967), pp. 120–121; Colombo (1975), p. 97. There is no textual support for such an operation: the authors generally refer to Vaccari (1947).

is reservoir) in 4:12, 15.[178] Given the subtle play of references typical of the Song, it is possible to think that the parallel is not accidental: that is, that the doves set on the 'streams' and on the 'bath' are the eyes of him fixed on her who is at the same time brook and pool.

The last image, that of the full bath, is taken up again in 7:5 where the woman's eyes are compared with the 'pools of Heshbon'. By contrast with the brook, the water of the pool is still, clear, calm. It reflects the image like a mirror.[179]

The picture of the doves set on a bath underline the Apollonian aspect of love by contrast with the Dionysian represented by the raven. This contrast is accentuated, from the point of view of colour, in v. 12b: 'bathed in milk'. The expression, as the cited parallel in Lam 4:7 confirms, is meant to emphasise the whiteness of the dove. The term 'bathed' (*rōḥăṣôt*) looks back to Song 4:2 where it is said of the teeth-ewes that they "come out of their bath (*raḥṣâ*)".[180] The Apollonian element of love, personified there in the teeth of the woman, is captured here in the eyes of the man. In both cases, the colour white is linked with a picture of serenity (ewes, doves), the black with a metaphor expressing a wild, demonic dynamism (goats, raven). Perhaps the metaphors of water, milk and 'full (bath)' also allow the connotation of abundance and satiety to appear. Water and milk are primordial symbols of life.

We have already noticed some clear cases of a parallelism between the descriptions of the body of the man and that of the body of the woman in 4:1–7 and 7:2–9. We shall find others. The fact is generally judged negatively as a lack of the originality of the present *waṣf* compared with the others.[181] The examples which we have examined up to now lead us rather to recognise here an example of that reciprocity which is typical of the Song. It is perhaps a deliberate attribution of the elements characterising one of the two partners to the other. Elliott comments on v. 12a: "For the Beloved [woman] to say: 'His eyes are

---

[178] Cf., *supra*, pp. 220, 227.

[179] It is possible that the author was inspired for this image by a celebrated mosaic of the Hellenistic period, of which the fresco coming from Villa Adriana at Tivoli (cf. Keel [1994], Figure 120, p. 200) is one of numerous reproductions.

[180] The parallel with 4:2 is adopted by Ravasi and the authors cited in n. 176, to justify the insertion of 'teeth' in 5:12b. But the author can use the same metaphor for two different parts of the body. The 'dripping with liquid myrrh' is attributed to the woman's hands in v. 5bc and to the man's lips in v. 13d.

[181] So, for example, Ravasi (1992), p. 446.

like doves' is to say that she sees herself reflected in them; they mirror her presence".[182] In the same sense, Lys speaks of 'corps frères'.[183]

[v. 13] Second section: Balm, lotus and myrrh. From the visual aspect, which characterises the description of the head, the hair and the eyes, the author passes to the olfactory in his description of the cheeks and the lips. Bearing in mind the structural parallel with vv. 15cd, 16ab (b-b': *Tab. 42*), it appears clear that there is an allusion to the kiss. In 1:2 and 4:10–11, the kiss was associated with the two senses of smell and taste. In our *waṣf*, smell is presented in v. 13, taste in v. 16ab. The link with 4:10–11 is precise: we see the terms *balm* (5:13a and 4:10d), *lips* (5:13c and 4:11a), *dripping* (5:13d and 4:11a) and *Lebanon* (5:15c and 4:11d). Moreover, the 'sweetness' of his palate (5:16a) looks back to the 'honey' which is found under her tongue (4:11b). As in 4:1–5:1, the passage from sight to smell and to taste marks a progression towards the union of the lovers. In our song too, this (imagined) union will be consummated in the garden. In 6:2–3, two terms of 5:13 are repeated; 'beds of balm' (6:2b) and 'flowers of lotus' (6:2d). Here, however, the metaphors refer to the woman. Thus the perfect symmetry with which the kiss is described appears clear: in 1:2–3 (a) and 5:13, 16ab (a') the kisses of the man are spoken of; in 4:11–12 (b) and in 6:2–3 (b') the kisses of the woman. What the woman finds in him, he finds in her. Each of the two lovers finds himself/herself again in the other.

"His cheeks[184] like a bed of balm". Despite the fact that the plural is favoured both by the immediate context ('cheeks'; 'towers') and by the parallel with 6:2, the MT's singular *'ărûgat* makes sense. It alludes in fact to the beard which forms one single 'bed' on the cheeks. The parallel of body hair with vegetation has already been introduced with the metaphor of the 'garden' whose 'shoots' are the poetic transformation of the woman's pubic hairs. In this 'garden', balm has a particular place, cf. 4:10, 14, 16; 5:1. It is present also in the description of 6:2. The cheeks are brought together in the kiss; it is natural, therefore, that their odour is pointed out, all the more since the beard was often sprinkled with fragrances (cf. Ps 133:2). In the smell of the beloved,

---

[182] Elliott (1989), p. 138.

[183] Lys (1968), p. 223.

[184] Here, too, as in 1:10; 4:3 and 4:13, Garbini (1992), p. 89, translates *lᵉḥăyîm* with 'buttocks'. Again with total licence, because none of the versions reads in this sense, and the description is found between that of the eyes and that of the lips (cf., *supra*, n. 131).

then, the woman recognises her own smell. Perhaps it is not without interest to observe that the term *ʿărugôt* (in the plural) recurs in the OT only in Ezek 17:7, 10, where it refers to the land of Israel. It would not be impossible to detect in the description of the man that same association with the promised land which has been noticed several times in the description of the woman.[185] Keel thinks that the reference is, concretely, to the plantations of balm in Jericho and Engedi.[186]

The comparison with 'towers of fragrances' is, at first glance, surprising: it is not to be wondered at that easier translations have been sought. The image of the towers[187] is, however, rendered probable by recourse to Egyptian iconography. Here, in scenes of banquets or offerings, it is frequent to see men and women wearing on their heads a white cone adorned with lotus flowers.[188] According to Keel, this is not an ornament but a "cone of ointments" (*Salbkegel*), "made of fat mixed with aromatic substances (primarily myrrh)".[189] With the heat of the body, the cone liquefied impregnating the head and shoulders of the person with its inebriating fragrance (cf. again Ps 133:2). The *tertium comparationis* is probably not the shape of the cone,[190] nor its colour, but its perfume, something, after all, which is common to all the metaphors of the verse.

"His lips flowers of lotus…". The significance of the lotus flower has already been spoken of with regard to 2:1:[191] it is a symbol of love and

---

[185] Cf., for example, the comment on Song 4:11.

[186] Keel (1994), p. 201. In support of such an identification, one could adduce MT, which has the definite article: *ʿărûgat habbōśem*, '*the* bed of the balsam'. But the expression can also have an indeterminate sense (cf. *GKC* §127e).

[187] The term *migdāl* appears again in Song 4:4; 7:5 (twice); 8:10, with a different semantic connontation (tower of defence), always with reference to the woman. Perhaps it is not accidental that the 'military' significance of the term is referred to the woman, the 'aesthetic' to the man.

[188] Cf. Keel (1978), Figure 254, p. 187; *id.* (1994), Figures 6, p. 43; 101, p. 171; 150, p. 258.

[189] Keel (1994), p. 201; cf. Gerleman (1965), p. 175. The term *merqāḥîm* is suitable for this 'perfume cone', if it is true that these were made up of different perfumes (cf., *supra*, n. 15). Lacocque (1998), pp. 123–124, underlines the fact that the root *rqḥ*, 'to mix perfumes', occurs a good six times in Exod 30:22–35, where the oil of anointing and the perfume of the sanctuary are spoken of. Rightly this seems to be a connotation of that sacrality that surrounds the beloved man. His interpretation of 'towers' is also interesting: it would be a manner of speech, to express an enormous quantity ('tons of perfume'). But attestations of this meaning for the term 'tower' are lacking.

[190] Unless he wants to allude to the high cheek bones (hence the plural), but, as Keel (1994), p. 201, notes, it is not so much the figurative as the 'dynamic' aspect of the metaphor which is of interest to Oriental poetry.

[191] Cf. pp. 83–84 (moreover, pp. 122–123).

new life. In 2:1 and 2:16, it was the whole person of the woman that was being compared with this flower. In 4:5, the term of comparison was her breasts, and also in the succeeding passages where the lotus is mentioned (6:2, 3; 7:3), the reference is to the woman's body. That here the term of comparison is the body of the man confirms the principle of 'corps frères': the woman finds herself again in the man. The lotus flower has a strong perfume[192] by which it is aligned with the other metaphors of v. 13. It can also be eaten,[193] and an allusion to this significance is not to be excluded: smell and taste, in fact, belong to the description of the kiss (cf. v. 16). The woman is not only passive; she herself breathes in the perfume and nourishes herself on the sweet 'flowers of lotus' which the beloved offers her.

Probably here the metaphor has a significance that is not only functional but also visual as Grober notes.[194] He observes that the Egyptian term *sšn* indicates the lotus flower or a cup in the form of a lotus flower (the lotus flower has actually the shape of a cup). Cup and flowers are similar visually to the human lips. First of all there is the colour: the lotus flower is pink, or white with pink outlines, like the skin of the man (v. 10); then there is the fact of the characteristic drops which its petals form and which are evoked in v. 13d ('dripping liquid myrrh'). In 5:5, it was the hands of the woman that were 'dripping liquid myrrh', and the myrrh was a metaphor for the sweat of her emotional hands. Here the 'liquid myrrh' makes reference to the exchange of fluids which takes place during the kiss of two lovers (cf. 7:10). The lips are seen as the edges of that cup which is the mouth. The Hebrew word *śāpâ* has effectively the two meanings of 'edge' and

[192] Grober (1984), p. 88.

[193] Cf. Grober (1984), pp. 99–100: "Its juicy stem and the seeds are edible. In ancient times [...] the lotus was used for making bread and fermented drink". In today's China it is very common to eat cakes of lotus seeds. Grober naturally cites the text of the *Odyssey* where the 'Lotophagi' or Lotus-eaters are spoken of (*Odyssey* 9:91–96). According to Homer, whoever ate the fruit of the lotus, 'sweet as honey' (*meliēdea*), forgot his native land, thought no more of returning to it. May there be a recalling of the erotic significance of the lotus flower in this tradition as well? In the Song, the lotus flowers are actually eaten (by the fawn [2:16], and by the beloved [6:2, 3]).

[194] Grober (1984), pp. 88–93. Grober's article is notable, because it highlights the unity of the metaphor of the 'lotus flower' throughout the entire Song. Each passage is coherent with the others, and this is a special way to grasp the unity of the Song. If the poem were the work of several people, such a metaphorical coherence would be impossible.

'lip'.[195] In 1 Kgs 7:26, with regard to the great basin in the Temple, it is said: "Its brim-lip (*śᵉpātô*) was made like the brim-lip of a cup (*śᵉpat*), like the flower of a lotus (*peraḥ šôšan*)".[196] The parallel is not accidental: it is part of a series of sacral parallels which characterise the description of the man. A. Robert and R. Tournay interpret this, as always, in allegorical fashion.[197] Grober uses the term 'metaphysical poetry', understanding by this an "erotic poetry in which the limits between sacred and secular images are blurred".[198]

"Dripping liquid myrrh". The image of myrrh accents the perfume dimension already present in the lotus flower. The passage looks back first of all to Song 5:5, where it is the woman's hands that are 'dripping liquid myrrh'. The other parallel is with 4:11—"your lips drip with virgin honey, my bride". In that case, the stress is put on the 'gustatory' aspect of the kiss; in our case, decidedly on the olfactory (myrrh is not to be eaten). Here too, beside its erotic connotation, the myrrh has a sacral significance.[199] With regard to the myrrh too, the mirror principle is operative: it is mentioned eight times in all in the Song, six times with reference to the woman (3:6; 4:6, 14: 5:1, 5 [twice]), twice, the first and last times, with reference to the man (1:13; 5:13). The two lovers are made out of the same material.

Second strophe: His body (5:14–16)

Like the first strophe, the second also has two sections (vv. 5:14–15b and 15c–16), composed, respectively, of three and two elements each. The first section is marked out by the *inclusio* formed by the theme of 'gold' (*zāhāb*, v. 14a; *pāz*, v. 15b). As far as the type of metaphor is concerned, it is linked with the description of the head in v. 11a; here too it seems that the author takes the chryselephantine statue as

---

[195] Cf. the English expression: the 'lips' of a cup. With his customary fantasy, Garbini (1992), pp. 241–242, reads, instead of *śptwt*, 'lips', *šptym*, 'double elevation', which he interprets as: 'his testicles'. Once given the principle that the original text must have spoken of sex, the consequences are coherent. But the principle remains to be demonstrated!

[196] The image of the 'basin', which is evoked subtly here, is connected with the last image of v. 12, denoting the metaphorical coherence of the text.

[197] Robert – Tournay (1963), p. 219. The correspondence is also noted by Lacocque (1998), p. 124.

[198] Grober (1984), p. 109 (Grober uses the term with reference to the poetry of John Donne).

[199] On the symbolic significance of myrrh, cf. p. 76.

Table 43

14ab	*His hands*	*rings*	*of gold*	*set*	*with stones of Tarshish.*
14cd	*His belly*	*a block*	*of ivory*	*studded*	*with lapis lazuli.*
15ab	*His legs*	*columns*	*of alabaster*	*standing*	*on bases of pure gold.*

his model. The section consists of three distinct distichs arranged in a form that is strictly parallel (cf. *Tab. 43*).[200] In the first stich, each time, the part of the body (hands, belly, legs) is compared to a crafted object ('rings', v. 14a; 'block', v. 14c; 'columns', v. 15a), made from a precious material ('gold', v. 14a; 'ivory', v. 14c; 'alabaster', v. 15a). In the second stich there is added to this object a complement formed from a second precious material ('set with stones of Tarshish', v. 14b; 'studded with lapis lazuli', v. 14d; 'standing upon bases of pure gold', v. 15b).

[vv. 14–15b] First section: Gold, ivory and alabaster. "His hands, rings of gold…". The term *gālîl* indicates something 'round', a circle or a cylinder. In 1 Kgs 6:24, it refers to the 'hinges' on which the gate turns;[201] in Esth 1:6, to the 'rings' (or 'cylindrical bars') of silver on which are hung the curtains of the king's palace; in Isa 8:23 to the district or 'circumscription' of the nations (= 'Galilee'). If 'cylinders' is intended, the metaphor is better suited to the 'arms', and actually the Hebrew term *yād* can also have this meaning.[202] But the meaning *ring* is better suited to our context. The author wishes to express the fine craftsmanship of this object. The hands are a part of the body which lends itself to this comparison. In a sculpture or a picture, they reveal the skill of the artist who is portraying them: they are so fine and well proportioned in their joints that a tiny error can render them crude. The poet compares the hands to finely worked piece of jewellery, perfect in its curves and proportions. A similar metaphor is used in Song 7:2 with regard to the woman: "The curves of your thighs are like jewels, the handiwork of an artist". In an analogous sense,

---

200 Cf. Elliott (1989), p. 140.

201 But *HALOT*, p. 193, translates here with the adjective 'revolving'.

202 However, the translation of Garbini (1992), pp. 89–90 (which, in fact, remains without parallels, ancient and modern), is completely unfounded: "His penis is a golden holder". Having thus translated *yād* in v. 4, Garbini feels himself authorised to do it here too. It matters little that here the term is plural: this is evidently the camouflage of the censors, who have disguised the original text with cunning additions. However, the plural is attested not only by the Hebrew manuscript tradition, but also by the versions (only the Syriac has a singular for 'the rings of gold': here too, the 'hands' are in the plural).

Simon the priest, in one of the rare masculine descriptions in the OT, is described: "As a vessel of hammered gold, adorned with all kind of precious stones" (Sir 50:9bc).

As in Sir 50:9bc, the precious craftsmanship of the hands-jewels is increased by the fact that to the gold are added ornaments of precious stones: "set with stones of Tarshish". The complement refers directly to the metaphor, that is, to the rings. It would be extravagant to look for an exact correspondence with the hands of the man.[203] The translation 'set' corresponds to the Hebrew *m*^{e}*mullāʾîm*. The verb *mālēʾ* is a technical term to describe the setting of precious stones in Exod 28:17; 31:5; 35:33; 39:10. The context there is sacral: these are the precious stones which adorn the breastplate of the high priest, confirming the parallel with Sir 50:9. It is not easy to say what type of stone the 'stone of Tarshish' is. 'Tarshish' is the place of provenance of the stone, and the identification of Tarshish is disputed (Spain? Sardinia?[204] Cilicia?),[205] so that it remains impossible to identify what kind of stone the author is referring to.[206] The description of the hands invests the beloved man with an aura at once of nobility (Esth 1:6) and sacrality (Sir 50:9; Exod 28:17; 39:10).

"His belly, a block of ivory...". The term *mēʿîm* generally indicates the 'insides'. Given the contest, it is the external surface which is being indicated here, that is, the 'belly'. But why has the poet chosen this term instead of the more common *beṭen* (cf. 7:3)? It is possible that he wished to signal a correspondence with v. 4 where the woman's 'insides' are spoken of, emphasising the relationship of the two 'corps frères'. The term *mēʿîm* has a parallel significance in the description of the colossal statue in Dan 2. There too, as in our passage, the description of the *mēʿîm* (*m*^{e}*ʿôhî* in Aramaic) is inserted between that of the arms and the thighs (Dan 2:32).

The term *ʿešet* is a disputed *hapax*. The verb *ʿāšat* in Jer 5:28 is placed in parallel with *šāmēn* ('to be fat') and indicates the glossiness of a body that has been well fed. In Ezek 27:19, the term *ʿāšôt* indicates

---

[203] A line of authors think of 'nails'. Among others, we cite Lys (1968), p. 226; Delitzsch (1875), p. 94; Ricciotti (1928), p. 248.

[204] Robert – Tournay (1963), pp. 220, 446–447.

[205] So Garbini (1992), p. 242.

[206] Vg has *hyacinthis*; Lys (1968), p. 226, reads 'topazes'; Ricciotti (1928), p. 248, 'chrysolites', following LXX in Exod 28:20; 39:13; Ezek 28:13; but in Ezek 10:9 LXX translates *taršîš* with 'carbuncle'.

'bars' of iron.[207] In rabbinical Hebrew, *ʿešet* indicates "metal that has been forged, bar, polished block".[208] The frequent translation 'plate, sheet' goes back to the LXX (*pyxion*, 'slab').[209] Just as the metaphor of the ring expressed the fine workmanship of the hand, so that of the 'block of ivory' the stretched out expanse of the belly. Ivory has a warm white colour which matches well the colour of the human complexion. It is a block that has been manufactured, therefore glossy: the man's belly shines with extreme cleanness.[210] In the OT, ivory is synonymous with the luxury and wealth warned against by the prophets (cf. Amos 3:15; 6:4; 1 Kgs 22:39; Ezek 27:6, 15). Here there is no shadow of disapproval: the most noble materials are but a small thing for love. It is possible, perhaps, to see a reference to Solomon: in 1 Kgs 10:18–20 (cf. 2 Chr 9:17–19), the throne of ivory and gold which Solomon had constructed for himself is mentioned.

"Studded with lapis lazuli". In parallel with the term *mᵉmullāʾîm* ('set') we find the term *mᵉʿullepet*. This is a rare verb, but its meaning ('to cover') is well attested by Gen 38:14.[211] In our case, if synonymous with the previous stich, we can think of inlays, encrustations of a second material in the block of ivory. The Hebrew *sappîrîm* is not our sapphire, but lapis lazuli,[212] a mineral of a deep blue colour, frequently mentioned both in the Mesopotamian texts on sacred marriage[213] and in the Egyptian love songs.[214] It was imported from Afghanistan and was highly prized. As in the previous stich, here too commentators

---

[207] The term *ʿăšôt* appears also at Qumran, where the expression *ʿăšôt zāhāb* indicates 'ingots of gold' (3Q15 1:5; 2:4, cf. García Martínez [1994], p. 461). In antiquity, the shape of these ingots was varied, as Gerleman (1965), p. 176, explains ("In Egypt, they often had the form of a brick or were made like round or oval slices of bread with a hole in the middle"). Cf. also in this sense Garbini (1992), pp. 239–240.

[208] Thus Jastrow (1903), p. 1128.

[209] Cf. Salvaneschi (1982) p. 27 ('sheet of ivory'); Heinevetter (1988), p. 144 ('Elfenbeinplatte').

[210] In *Odyssey* 18:196, the embellishment of the sleeping Penelope at the hands of Athene is mentioned: "(The goddess) made her whiter than new-sawn ivory" (tr. Murray [1995], vol. II, p. 215).

[211] Therefore the proposals to replace the verb *ʿlp* with *ʿpl* are shown to be unnecessary. Cf. Graetz (1871) p. 179 ('elevated'); Garbini (1992), pp. 91, 239–240 ('darkened').

[212] Thus Gerleman (1965), p. 177; Robert - Tournay (1963), p. 222; Lys (1968), p. 227.

[213] Cf., e.g., the texts quoted in Kramer (1969), pp. 67–84: the beard of Dumuzi is of lapis lazuli (p. 73), the nuptial bed is covered with precious stones (p. 76), and the necklace of Inanna is made of lapis lazuli (p. 77) (cf. also *ANET*, pp. 637, 638). On the erotic significance of jewels and precious stones, cf. Song 4:9 and the related comment (pp. 205–206).

[214] Cf. the Papyrus Chester Beatty IA 1:1–8, cited in p. 173, n. 21.

often search for a visual correspondence between signifier and signified, identifying the lapis lazuli with the veins of the belly,[215] with tattoos,[216] or with hairiness.[217] This is probably not what the author intends. The *tertium comparationis* here is not the shape or the colour but the value of the material as in the case of the gold. The lapis lazuli was a "heavenly material—the stuff of the bodies of the gods".[218] As for the OT, lapis lazuli is spoken of in Exod 24:10 and Ezek 1:26, both in a theophanic context. The pavement on which the feet of God rest and the throne on which he sits, respectively, are of lapis lazuli. With that we have confirmation of the theomorphic character of the description of the man. It should be noted that this divine material is found in a part of the body near to the genital area to which it discretely alludes. We have here a veiled hint: to want to make it explicit, as Garbini does, does not correspond to the poetics of the Song.[219] At the extreme opposite are to be found those authors who understand the covering in a literal way, holding it to be unseemly for the woman to describe the naked body of the man.[220] The *waṣf* of the Song celebrates the body not its clothes. Perhaps here we can grasp another aspect of the paradisial character of the Song. Before original sin, in fact, "they were both naked, the man and his wife, and they were not ashamed" (Gen 2:25).

"His legs, columns of alabaster". The Hebrew term *šôq* can indicate both the 'thigh'[221] and the entire leg. The comparison with the columns makes us incline towards the second sense, as is confirmed by the parallel with Sir 26:18, where it is said of the virtuous woman: "Pillars of gold on a base of silver, / so are beautiful legs on well-formed feet".[222] The material of the 'columns' is alabaster (*šēš*), the colour of

[215] Thus Delitzsch (1875), p. 95.

[216] So Haupt (1907), pp. 60–61.

[217] Cf. Garbini (1992), p. 240.

[218] Keel (1994), p. 205. As an example, see the two texts cited *supra*, p. 287.

[219] Cf., *infra*, p. 396.

[220] Cf. Joüon (1909), p. 256: "The ivory here can only be metaphorical: it undoubtedly expresses the shining whiteness of the garment".

[221] In fact, this is the translation, for example, of Rudolph (1962), p. 158; Gerleman (1965), p. 171; Keel (1994), p. 196. For his part, Krinetzki (1981), p. 171, sees in the 'thighs' a phallic symbol. Against this 'monotonous and monomaniacal' tendency to see behind every image of the Song 'animus and anima, penis and vagina', see the sharp slating by Keel (1994), p. 205.

[222] The comparison between the woman's legs and pillars is traditional in Arab poetry. Lys (1968), p. 227, cites two examples: "Your legs are like the marble columns in the Omayad mosque"; "Let me see your legs! [...] My legs are columns of marble"

which, a warm yellowy tone, is well suited to that of the complexion.[223] Alabaster is mentioned in the OT only twice. The first is the passage of Esther 1:6, already cited: here the word is of 'columns of alabaster' as in our case. The second is 1 Chr 29:2, where alabaster[224] is cited among the materials which David laid up for the construction of the Temple. Like lapis lazuli, therefore, alabaster is at home in the king's palace and the Temple. The two parallels are significant because in them is listed a series of precious materials: as if the woman wanted to sum up in the person of her beloved all the most precious things of the earth. An analogous series of precious materials is contained in Song 3:9–10 in connection with the litter which contains the woman ("wood of Lebanon, silver, gold, purple"): here too one can observe the 'mirroring' effect typical of the Song.

"Standing on bases of pure gold". With this expression the feet of the man are indicated (cf. Sir 26:18).[225] The stich forms an *inclusio*, on the one hand, with the description of the hands (v. 14a), on the other, with that of the head (v. 11a). That is, it concludes both the first section of the second strophe and the list of the eight parts of the body. Head and feet form a polarity: the beloved is golden from head to foot (the correspondence here is precise: 'pure gold' [*pāz*], vv. 11a and 15b). By contrast with the statue of Dan 2, the feet here are not of clay but of the same noble material as the head. Also significant is the fact that the gold characterises the three parts of the body where its personal aspect is best expressed: head (v. 11), hands (v. 14) and feet (v. 15).[226]

The term *ʾeden* ('base, pedestal') occurs in the OT almost exclusively in the description of the sanctuary (a good 51 times out of a total of 53), and the parallel, in view of the other sacral parallels in our text,

---

(citations *ibid.*); another is quoted by Dalman (1901), p. 134: "Legs, turned like columns / of marble, tender, and they are choicest".

[223] In antiquity, according to *PW* I/1, p. 1272, two forms of alabaster were known, one with a base of gypsum, coming above all from Tuscany (Volterra), of an immaculate white colour, the other with a base of limestone, widespread in the Middle East, of a colour between white and yellow with white streaking (onyx is a particular variety of this). With this type of alabaster were made, first of all, small objects: ampoulles for perfumes, goblets, the feet of beds and chairs; later on, jars, columns and other types of ornament. Even entire statues or parts of them were sculpted from alabaster. As the place of origin for this type of alabaster, Pliny cites Arabia, Carmania (Asia Minor), Thebes in Egypt and Damascus in Syria.

[224] The term here is *šayiš*, a more recent form of the same word.

[225] Gerleman (1965), p. 177, thinks of the 'pedestal' of a statue (cf. *ibid.* p. 69). But the Hebrew term is plural; it is more appropriate for 'feet'.

[226] Cf. Müller (1992), p. 61.

seems to be intentional. A. Robert and R. Tournay see here an allegorical intention.[227] More probably it is the theomorphic reading[228] in the sense alluded to above. Like the litter of the woman, so the body of the man is a temple of love; it encloses within itself a spark of that same God who dwells in the Temple of Jerusalem.

[vv. 15c–16b] Concluding summary. With v. 15c, the last section of the second strophe (vv. 15c–16b), with its concluding character, begins. The last two descriptions do not have a single part of the body as their object but intend to give a comprehensive impression of the beloved according to the aspects of 'vision' (15cd) and 'taste' (16ab). The term *marʾeh*, deriving from the verb *rāʾāh* ('to see') refers directly to the 'visual' aspect of the man. The term has appeared already in 2:14cf with reference to the woman whose 'appearance' was invoked. There we translated 'face'.[229] Here, given the context, a general meaning ('appearance') seems more probable. But the reference to the theophany (cf. Exod 3:3; Ezek 1:28) which we noted there[230] maintains all its sense here too. The appearance of the man is that of a divinity: a phenomenon perceptible by every one in love. The infatuation of love transfigures the person who is loved, confers on him superhuman contours. Perhaps the author is smiling at this; the whole *waṣf* is a little o.t.t.; it expresses the sentiments of a girl who is in love. But one can also lay hold of a theological dimension: in the beloved man, there is present (analogously to what happened to the woman) the love which renders him an 'image of God'. In him the woman experiences transcendence, perceives the presence of the divine.

The visual aspect links v. 15c directly with vv. 11–12 and 14–15b, constituting a transverse element with respect to the structure delineated in *Tab. 42* (b-c-b'-c'). But a link with v. 13ab is not to be excluded. In fact, Lebanon, with its fragrant woods, matches the 'bed of balm', all the more since Song 4:11 spoke of the 'scent of Lebanon'.[231] After the 'statuary' metaphors of vv. 14–15ab, the poet now makes use again of metaphors drawn from nature, as if to say that the man is not only a statue but a living being. Idols "have noses and smell not; they have

---

[227] Robert – Tournay (1963), pp. 223–224.

[228] Cf. Lacocque (1998), p. 124.

[229] Here too, this is the translation of Lys (1968), p. 227 ("visage"). Ravasi (1992), p. 465, alludes to this possibility, given the nearness of 'palate' in v. 16a.

[230] Cf. p. 216.

[231] One recalls also the assonance of *lᵉbānôn—lᵉbônâ* ('Lebanon-incense'), prominent between 4:6 and 4:8 (*supra*, pp. 147–148, 192, and 201).

hands and handle not" (Ps 115:6–7), but the man is not just good to look at; he is also pleasant to smell and sweet to taste.

The 'Lebanon' metaphor is polyvalent: here, undoubtedly, it is the aspect of height that is being stressed, taking up an element presented in v. 10b.[232] That elevated stature was an element in masculine beauty is witnessed to in 1 Sam 9:2 where of Saul it is said that he was "tall (*bāḥûr*)[233] and handsome: there was none more handsome than he among the Israelites; from his shoulders upwards, he was taller than any of the people". The imposing height of the cedars of Lebanon was proverbial (cf. Isa 2:13).[234] In the Song, the cedar is spoken of in 1:17 (the beams of the nuptial chamber) and in 3:9 (the columns of the litter); there the royal-Solomonic character of this wood (cf. 1 Kgs 7:2–3, 7, 11) and its use in the construction of the Temple (1 Kgs 6:9, 10, 15, 16, 18, 20, 36; 7:12) was pointed out.[235] The juxtaposition aligns well with the preceding context (gold, ivory, lapis lazuli, alabaster) where these same dimensions are evoked.

"His palate, sweetness". The passage from a generalising term ('appearance', v. 15c) to a particular one ('palate', v. 16a) appears strange to Garbini who replaces it with one that is more explicitly erotic.[236] Here, however, the palate is considered not from the aesthetic point of view but from that of enjoyment, in parallel with v. 13, and has a conclusive sense. As in the *waṣf* 4:1–7, the desire to enjoy the body of the person loved is born from contemplation; from *sight* one passes to *smell* (v. 13) and to *taste* (v. 16ab). The allusion to erotic play, which in 4:5 was present in the 'breasts'—the last part of the woman's body to be described—is expressed here by the 'palate' with clear reference to

---

[232] Perhaps it is also possible to detect an allusion to the colour. In fact, the name Lebanon means 'white', and the man is 'white' and red (v. 10a).

[233] On this meaning of the term *bāḥûr*, cf. Joüon (1925), pp. 314–315; *LHVT*, p. 103. In 1 Sam 9:2, LXX translates *eumegethēs*, 'tall in stature'.

[234] According to Zohary (1982), p. 104, a Lebanon cedar can reach the height of thirty metres.

[235] Cf. p. 81, n. 159; p. 154.

[236] The term chosen this time is *ḥq*: "'breast', in the generic sense as the source of embraces" (Garbini [1992], pp. 90, 242). The tension between a general and a particular term remains, however! To find 'embraces', Garbini has to change MT's *mmtqym*, 'sweetness', to *mtḥmqym*, which he actually translates with 'embraces' (*ibid.*, pp. 90–91, 242–243). The textual supports for these operations are minimal ('a Hebrew manuscript', according to Garbini). Actually, the text (the canonical one, of course) alludes to the enjoyment of love, but it does so, as is typical of the Song, by concentrating attention on the breasts and on the mouth, not on the genitals (cf. the observations made above, p. 299).

Table 44

2:3	5:15cd, 16ab
Like an apple tree in the forest,	His appearance, like Lebanon
so is my beloved among the young men.	imposing like the cedars.
I am sitting in his shade for which I *longed*,	His <u>*palate*</u>, <u>sweetness</u>:
and his fruit is <u>sweet</u> to my <u>*palate*</u>.	he is altogether *desirable*.

the kiss.[237] The two senses 'smell' and 'taste' characterised the preceding descriptions of the kiss (1:2–3 and 4:10–11). They are repeated again at the end of the last *waṣf* where the two parts of the body involved in erotic play, breast and mouth, are mentioned together: "May your breast be / like clusters of vines, / the scent of your breath like apples, / and your palate (*ḥikkēk*) like good wine..." (7:9–10). The poetry of the Song shows itself to be perfectly coherent.

Another example of the metaphorical coherence of the Song is provided by the term *mamtaqqîm* which we have understood as a *plurale abstractionis* deriving from the root *mtq* ('to be sweet'):[238] the reference to the 'honey' of 4:11 is clear. The root *mtq* appears again in the Song in 2:3, a text which has various points in common with ours (cf. *Tab. 44*).

In both cases, the superiority of the beloved compared with his peers is exalted,[239] making use of the metaphor of the tree ('apple', 2:3; 'cedar', 5:15). In both cases, the noun 'palate' (*ḥēk*) is joined to the terms 'to be sweet' (*mātōq*) and 'to desire' (*ḥāmad*).[240]

"He is altogether desirable". The first term, *kullô* (literally 'all he') leads us to understand that we are at the end of the *waṣf*. This, in fact, is the way in which the description of the woman's body concluded: "You are all (*kullāk*, literally, 'all you') fair, my friend" (4:7). The universalising particle *kol* makes explicit the global dimension of

[237] Robert – Tournay (1963), pp. 224–225, emphatically deny that there is an allusion here to the kiss, claiming that the 'sweet things' are the words of the man ("Ses discours sont la suavité même"). In the comment on 4:11, it was seen that this meaning is not to be excluded (cf. Prov 16:21), but, in our case, it is certainly not the primary sense: the whole context leads in another direction.

[238] The term recurs only in Neh 8:10, where, however, it has the concrete meaning of 'sweet drinks'.

[239] The sense of *bāḥûr* is precisely that of "a superiority in relation to things of the same order" (Joüon [1909], p. 258: the Joüon himself sees a correspondence between the two passages).

[240] The parallel is noted again by Elliott (1989), p. 142.

vv. 15cd, 16ab. No longer is it the individual parts of the body that are being described but the person as a whole. And also, in analogy with 4:7, there is nothing negative in the beloved, he is 'wholly' positive. While in 4:7 it is the aesthetic side of the person of the woman ('fair') which is prominent, here the enjoyable ('desire') aspect of the beloved is being presented. The term *ḥmd* ('desire') is to be understood in its original significance of 'desire, attraction'. Now it is precisely this desire, born out of the contemplation of a beautiful person or a valuable object,[241] which is regarded in the OT with suspicion as a source of sin. In commenting on 2:3, we have observed that the Song brings about a *relecture* of Gen 2–3, reproducing man before the Fall, when desire was viewed in a positive light (cf. Gen 2:9 *contra* Gen 3:6).[242] As in Song 2:3, also in the affirmation "He is altogether desirable", there is no shadow of negativity or of guilt. 'Desire' (*maḥămaddîm*) stands in synonymous parallelism with *mamtaqqîm* ('sweetness').

[v. 16cd] Coda. The function of v. 16cd is to bind the *waṣf* to the preceding question of the daughters of Jerusalem in v. 9 (key words: 'beloved' and 'daughters of Jerusalem') and, at the same time, analogously with v. 8, to introduce the following question (6:1, 'beloved').

"Such is my beloved". The daughters of Jerusalem wanted to know how the beloved was different from others. The woman has responded, stressing the uniqueness and unmistakeability of her man (cf., above all, vv. 10b, 15cd). The emphasis of the representation lets itself be understood as a hurt, impassioned response to the irony of v. 9. Indeed the beloved is not 'any old' beloved: he has the characteristics of a king and of God himself. This is a meaningful description for one who is within a relationship of love. What do the daughters of Jerusalem know of the sweetness of his kisses? The gold and lapis lazuli of his body are also materials which only love succeeds in seeing.

"Such is my friend". This is the only time in the Song that the noun *rēaʿ* is used in the masculine singular. *raʿyātî* is the appellation reserved exclusively for the woman (cf. v. 2). That here it is placed in the woman's mouth, in the masculine, is certainly not accidental. She wishes to call him with the same appellation with which he addresses her, thus underlining the reciprocity of the amorous sentiment. The

[241] Cf. G. Wallis, *ḥāmad*, in *TDOT*, vol. IV, p. 454, who cites Sir 40:22 ("The eye desires grace and beauty") in this connection.

[242] Cf., *supra*, pp. 86–87.

Table 45

6:1	Question	v. 1ab	*your beloved (v. 1a)*
		v. 1cd	*your beloved (v. 1c)*
6:2–3	Reply	v. 2	*my beloved (v. 2a)*
		v. 3	*my beloved (v. 3a: twice)*

man is, therefore, evoked in v. 16c with the appellations typical of him (*dôdî*) and her (*rēʿî*). The poet had used the double appellation for the pair of lovers in 5:1 (*rēʿîm…dôdîm*).

Love Found Again (6:1–3)

The unity of the little composition 6:1–3 is not undisputed. Gerleman, for example, claims that vv. 2–3 are not the reply to the question of v. 1. He supposes that v. 1 is a redactional addition.[243] On the other hand, Krinetzki and Müller hold v. 3 to be a refrain which has nothing to do with the preceding verses.[244] A structural examination, however, allows us to grasp the unity of the three verses. Like the preceding one, this composition consists of a question of the daughters of Jerusalem (6:1) followed by the woman's reply (vv. 2–3). The reply matches the question: the friends ask 'where' the beloved has gone, and the woman indicates the place. The term 'beloved' has a structural value. It not only constitutes an *inclusio* for the little unit (6:1a and 6:3a),[245] but it also subdivides it into two parts, the question of the daughters of Jerusalem (6:1ab, 6:1cd), and the reply of the woman (6:2 and 6:3) (cf. *Tab. 45*).

Garbini, for his part, denies any continuity of 6:1–3 with the preceding song. The girl who begins to speak in this song would have nothing to do with that of 5:2–16; 6:1–3, in reality, would be the continuation of 4:1–7.[246] This hypothesis also is refuted by a structural examination. The question of the daughters of Jerusalem (6:1) is introduced, in fact, at the end of the preceding song (5:16d), exactly as the last verse of 5:2–8 introduced the question of 5:9. The two questions are closely

243 Gerleman (1965), p. 179.

244 Krinetzki (1981), pp. 177–178; Müller (1992), pp. 162–163.

245 The same goes for the other units of the passage 5:2–6:3, that is, for 5:2–8 and 5:9–16 (cf., *supra*, p. 255).

246 Garbini (1992), pp. 93, 244–245.

Table 46

5:9a	WHAT makes your beloved different…,	5:9b	You, O fairest among women?
6:1a	WHERE has your beloved gone,	6:1b	O fairest among women?
5:9c	WHAT makes your beloved different…,	5:9d	*that* you charge us so?
6:1c	TO WHERE has your beloved turned	6:1d	*that* we can seek him with you?

linked, not only by their tone, midway between the sincere and the ironic, but also by their construction (cf. *Tab. 46*).

The two verses are constructed according to the same staircase parallelism by which the second part of the verse repeats half of the first part and adds a new element. The part which is repeated (5:9ac; 6:1ac) is formed by an interrogative particle ("What…? What…?'; 'Where…? To where…?") followed by a phrase the subject of which is 'your beloved'. The part that varies is formed in the first part of the verse by the appellation 'fairest among women' (5:9b = 6:1b), in the second part by a phrase of consecutive value ('that…', 5:9d; 6:1d).

Earlier, we presented the notable structural coherence of the *New Songs of the Beloved Woman*, 5:2–6:3.[247] As the conclusion of this literary unit, 6:1–3 is incomprehensible outside its context.[248] Both the references to 5:9–16 and those to 5:2–8 are so numerous that we prefer to highlight them individually in the analysis.

Question (6:1)

After being informed, *how* they can recognise the beloved (5:9), the daughters of Jerusalem now ask *where* he may be found. Like the first request, the second also introduces the following song of the woman (vv. 2–3) in which she explains where her beloved has gone. The motive for the question, expressed in v. 1d, is that of helping the woman in her search. Just as in 5:9f the verb 'to charge' referred to the preceding song, 5:2–8 (cf. v. 8), so now the verb 'to seek' refers to 5:6. In itself, the friends' offer goes beyond the question made in 5:8. It lends itself to two types of interpretation consistent with the ambiguous role of the 'daughters of Jerusalem' in the Song in general and in 5:2–6:3 in particular.

[247] Cf. *supra*, pp. 254–256.

[248] Cf. Heinevetter (1988), p. 140: "6:2 would not make sense, as text, outside the composition (= 5:2–6:3, *author's note*)".

One might think that the enthusiastic description of the beloved in 5:9–16 would have convinced the friends, who now are ready to help the woman in her search.[249] Lys, however, insinuates a doubt: do they really wish to help the woman or are they not rather thinking of themselves getting to know such an extraordinary young man?[250] The question would betray a certain rivalry between the daughters of Jerusalem and the woman. The fact that the woman refuses the help which is offered to her, leaves the door at least open to this interpretation.

According to the staircase parallelism which marks the verse, the first stich (v. 1a) is repeated in the third (v. 1c). The repetition, however, is not word for word because the verb *hālak* ('to go') is replaced by *pānāh* ('to turn'). This verb is ambivalent in itself: it indicates, in fact, to turn in a definite direction, but also to leave a direction which had previously been undertaken. This second connotation of the verb is frequent, above all in an extended sense where the verb is often used to indicate the abandoning of the Yahwistic faith to 'turn' after other gods (cf. Lev 19:4, 31; 20:6; Deut 29:17; 30:17; 31:18, 20). Hos 3:1 compares this 'turning' behaviour to adultery. The verb *pānāh* refers to Song 5:6 where the woman recounted that her beloved had gone. The two verbs *ḥāmaq* ('to turn') and *dābar* I ('to turn one's shoulders') are synonyms of *pānāh*. One can see, therefore, a touch of sarcasm on the part of the friends ("So your beautiful Prince Charming has left you in the lurch: what other woman has he gone after?").[251] This interpretation is confirmed by the woman's reply which declares, by contrast, the mutual belonging of the two lovers.

Perhaps some mythological reminiscences are echoed in the question of the friends.[252] Pope claims that the entire scene of Song 6:1–3 has as its background Anat's search for Baal.[253] Meek thinks of a liturgy

[249] Thus, for example, Keel (1994), p. 209; Elliott (1989), p. 144; Ravasi (1992), p. 470.
[250] Lys (1968), pp. 231–232.
[251] In this sense, cf., for example, Lys (1968), pp. 231–232 ("Ce garçon est tellement formidable qu'il t'a laissé tomber!"); Lacocque (1998), p. 127 ("Mr. Wonderful seems to have just dropped you!").
[252] Cf., *supra*, p. 130.
[253] Pope (1977), pp. 553–554 (cf. *KTU* 1.6 IV,4, according to Del Olmo Lete [1981], pp. 228–229: "Where is Baal, the victorious, / where is the prince, lord of the earth?").

of Tammuz,[254] similarly Wittekindt.[255] Also, the expression 'fairest among women' is a title of Innana, the Sumerian goddess of love.[256] However, these are materials which the author uses freely, embracing them in his original poetic vision: it has been seen that the two protagonists of the Song have a theomorphic value.[257]

The beloved in his garden (6:2–3)

[v. 2] The response of the woman sounds strange. It seems that she knows where her beloved has gone. Why then is she searching for him with so much trouble (cf. 5:6b-8)? Improbable too is the place indicated by the woman: 'his garden'. But the garden of the beloved can be none other than the woman herself (cf. 4:16–5:1): and the beloved has gone away from her (cf. 5:6a)! The apparent contradiction between 6:2 and 5:2–16 is the reason why, as has been noted, various authors hold that these verses have nothing to do with the preceding context.[258] But the contradiction is only apparent; in reality, as Heinevetter stresses, it is a deliberate poetic effect. The author wishes to surprise with paradoxical changes:

> The redactor is always showing himself to be an able dramatist. First of all he gives an unexpected turn to the lament at the door, in the sense that suddenly it seems that the desire for union can be realised (5a). But just as one begins to believe in this new possibility, the new surprise-effect arrives: *dôdî ḥāmaq ʿābār*! And the reader is surprised for a third time at the end of the composition. The beloved "has gone down into his garden" (cf. 5:1!): right from the beginning, the unifying force of eros was the only reality in the drama of love![259]

[254] Meek (1956), p. 131 ("Whither has your brother gone, the lamented one? / Whither has Tammuz gone, the bewailed one"; so too Lys (1968), p. 231.

[255] Wittekindt (1925), pp. 171–175 (who thinks of the descent of Ishtar to the underworld).

[256] Cf. Lacocque (1998), p. 127.

[257] It is possible to understand the search of Mary Magdalene at the sepulchre (John 20) in the light of this passage (but cf. Tait [2007], 484–486). However, that belongs to later history. It is worth recording that J.S. Bach used this text in a famous aria at the beginning of the second part of his *St. Matthew Passion*.

[258] Cf., *supra*, p. 305.

[259] Heinevetter (1988), p. 140. Heinevetter speaks of a 'redactor': in my opinion, he ought to speak rather of 'author'. I see no reason for supposing a plurality of authors in the passage Song 5:2–6:3.

A similar surprise-effect is achieved at the end of the Song. In 8:14, the beloved is begged to 'flee' (*bārah̩*), that is, to go away (v. 14a). But what is the direction of his flight? The 'mountains of balms' (v. 14c), a metaphor to indicate the woman's body (cf. 4:6)! Analogously, in our song, the beloved has gone away (6:1; cf. 5:6), but only to 'go down into his garden' (6:2; cf. 6:11).[260] It is no accident that the two paradoxes come at the end of large compound units (of the Song, that is, and of the *New Songs of the Beloved Woman*, respectively): it is the climactic finale with which the author wishes to give a beautiful conclusion to his text.

"My beloved has gone down into his garden". With these words, the woman is linked to 4:16e (cf. 5:1a): "Let my beloved come into his garden". These continual cross-references with which the Song is strewn speak strongly in favour of the unity of the whole composition. The author of 6:1–3 cannot be different from that of 4:1–5:1! Every word here is important. We should note the play between the first person ('*my* beloved') and third person ('*his* garden'): since the beloved is 'mine', 'my garden' belongs also to 'him' (cf. 4:16). In this way preparation is made for the solemn declaration of the final refrain (v. 3).

The mythical school sees in the verb 'come down' (*yārad*) an allusion to the god of vegetation's 'descent into the underworld'[261] but, perhaps, as Keel observes, the explanation is simpler: "Up until the Greco-Roman era, settlements in Palestine/Israel were exclusively on the hills; thus the gardens were in the valleys, along the streams and beside the springs found there".[262] The verb 'to go down' is repeated in v. 11 where, in connection with the 'garden', mention is also made of the 'stream'.

The beloved has, therefore, gone to his woman. As in 5:1, entry into the garden signals the end of the composition. The lovers are together once again. It is difficult to say whether this happens only in the imagination of the woman, or whether it really takes place. Actually, in v. 11, the beloved confirms that the woman was right, and, moreover, if the beloved begins to speak in v. 4, that assumes that he is present.

---

[260] "Just as the remedy for sickness is the fruit of the apple tree which represents it, so the flight of the woman leads to the garden which represents her" (Salvaneschi [1982], p. 116).

[261] Cf. Pope (1977), pp. 554–556; Schmökel (1956), pp. 55–57; Wittekindt (1925), pp. 172–174.

[262] Keel (1994), p. 209.

It seems therefore that the woman pre-senses and in that sense 'presents' the reality. However, from the initial situation to the end, there takes place an evolution, a process of the maturing of love. The idyll of the garden (5:1) was succeeded by a crisis in the relationship (5:2–8).[263] Because of the man's impatience and the woman's tardiness, the two lovers did not succeed in meeting. The beloved went away, and the woman thought that she had lost him. Now, however, she comes to the conviction that that is not true, that this is only a case of misunderstanding: in reality, she never lost him. How has this conviction taken root in her? While she was describing him to the friends, she continually found in her beloved parts of her own being; she found herself again in him.[264] The wild black hair, the eyes like doves, the balm of his cheeks, the lotus flowers of his lips, the myrrh and Lebanon have reawakened in her the awareness of their mutual belonging. She belongs to her beloved and he belongs to her (6:3). The two form a single body which nothing and no one can henceforth put asunder. The bond that unites them is stronger than the misunderstandings: love triumphs over all its crises.

In this process, taking everything into consideration, the questions of the daughters of Jerusalem seem to have the role of a challenge. To their irony over the 'extraordinary' nature of the beloved (5:9), the woman has replied with the emphatic portrait of 5:10–16. To the sarcasm on the stability of their relationship (6:1), she replies by confirming the mutual belonging of the two lovers (6:3). The warmth of the reply, in both cases, allows us to understand it as a reply to the doubts advanced by the friends.

"Among the beds of balm". The expression is a clear repeat of 5:13a, confirmed also by the ensuing mention of 'flowers of lotus' (vv. 2d, 3b; cf. 5:13c) just as, after all, 5:13 was a repeat of 4:16d and 5:1b. The interchangeability of these metaphors is clear: what was referred to the

---

[263] "In love, there also exists crisis, fear is introduced, coldness comes in, sometimes one lives of nostalgia, the absence infiltrates. But the dominating component, the 'basso continuo' of communion and reciprocal giving triumphs at the end" (Ravasi [1992], p. 472). "The woman's answer [...] makes the whole painful episode of missed opportunity and frantic searching in 5:2–8 seem a mere misurderstanding; in the bright light of the solidarity formula in 6:3 it becomes a fleeting cloud that only briefly overshadows the couple's love" (Keel [1994], p. 209).

[264] "As the Beloved sings her Lover's praise, she discovers his presence within herself and her presence in him. In this way a moment of physical absence leads to the awareness that love's union is all-embracing, and cannot be so easily broken" (Elliott [1989], p. 146).

man's beard and lips in 5:13 is now referred to the body of the woman. The two bodies are made from the same material, as the refrain of v. 3 will express symbolically.

Like the garden, the 'bed' is a metaphor for the female body in its erotic-sexual power (cf. 4:12–5:1). However, the sense of 'going down into the garden' is different from that of 'coming into the garden' in 4:16 and 5:1. There, the expression indicated sexual union.[265] Here union cannot be indicated because the two are not still together, and the verb 'to go down' has the same force as the preceding *pānāh* ('to turn'). He is not yet to 'enter' the garden but to 'direct himself' towards it. Moreover, the choice of the verb in v. 11, clearly correlated with v. 2, does not yet indicate union: the beloved has gone down 'to look'. The content of the 'vision' will be made explicit in the two *waṣf*'s that follow. In 6:1, we are still at the beginning of the second part: the journey from separation to union will be concluded in 8:3. Before that, the steps of reciprocal contemplation and desire are described. The terms 'bed' and 'garden', then, have here a value that is less specifically genital than in 4:16–5:1. Ravasi has rightly warned against the "mechanical methods of certain exegetes who want at all costs to identify these beds with the various hair-covered areas of the female body".[266] They express the body of the woman globally, clearly in its erotic value, as the following expressions 'graze' and 'gather' indicate. But here it is a matter of intention ('*[in order] to* graze', '*[in order] to* gather'), not yet of realisation.

The plural ('beds') is surprising, just as the singular was surprising in 5:13: actually, the Vulgate renders in the singular following some Hebrew manuscripts. But the plural reading is confirmed by the parallel with the term 'gardens' in the following stich and is to be retained as the *lectio difficilior*. We can rule out first of all that the woman is alluding to relationships with other women (= beds, gardens):[267] that would be to contradict, on the one hand, v. 2a where 'his garden' is spoken of in the singular, on the other hand, v. 3a where the refrain of mutual belonging also has the value of exclusivity ("my beloved is mine", and no one else's!). It is possible that the choice of the plural

---

265 Krinetzki (1981), pp. 176–177, sees a description of union in 6:2–3. He interprets the man's 'going down' as the penetration of the vagina ('the beds of balsam') by the *membrum virile*.

266 Ravasi (1992), p. 474.

267 In this sense, cf., for example, Goulder (1986), p. 46.

obeys a phonetic consideration,[268] but this explanation is not sufficient. It is probable that we have here another case of that 'plural of love' that we came across in 1:3–4[269] and 3:10.[270] Of 'gardens' in the plural we have spoken also in 4:15a,[271] and the reflections made then can also be applied in this case, as is done, in an exemplary fashion, by Lacoque:

> The fact of the matter is that the Song of Songs sees the man as epitomising all the lovers: he is *the* lover. As to [*sic*] the woman, she also is all women, the whole of womankind; their mutual love summarises and surpasses all other loves.[272]

"To graze in the gardens". The verb *rāʿāh* ('to graze') will be repeated in the following verse. In both cases, it has an intransitive sense, as in 2:16 and 4:5 (differently from 1:7, 8). The beloved is here compared to a deer which is grazing in the garden, that is, he is grazing on the wonderful plants that he finds in it. By this expression, the woman is looking back to the metaphor of 'eating' in 4:16f and 5:1cd: that is, the erotic enjoyment of her body is understood.

The link with 4:16–5:1 is confirmed by the phrase which follows: "To gather flowers of lotus". The verb 'gather' (*lāqaṭ*) is a synonym of *ʾārāh* (5:1b): in both cases, 'to gather' is placed in parallel with 'to eat' (and, respectively, 'to graze') and has the same erotic value.[273] In the metaphor, the subject of the two verbs is different: in fact it is an animal that 'grazes', a human being who 'gathers', but the significance is analogous.

[v. 3] The analogy is confirmed by v. 3b where 'to gather' is replaced by 'to graze', and the subject this time is a person 'the beloved' ("he grazes among the lotus flowers"). It is worthwhile to pause a little in order to grasp the coherence of the metaphor of the 'flowers of lotus'. 6:3b is a literal repeat of 2:16b where the fawn who grazes among the flowers of lotus is the image of the beloved who is caressing the breasts of his woman (cf. 2:17). In 4:5, the breasts of the woman are themselves compared to two fawns who graze among the flowers of lotus. From being the object of eating, the breasts become its subject.

---

268 Cf. the assonance between *laʿărûgôt* and *lirʿôt*, as also the rhyme between *baggannîm* and *šôšannîm*.
269 Cf., *supra*, p. 56.
270 Cf. pp. 158–159.
271 Cf. p. 228.
272 Lacocque (1998), p. 129, referring to Landy (1983), p. 208.
273 Cf., *supra*, p. 238.

Table 47

2:16	*6:3*
"My beloved is mine, and I am his, he grazes among the lotus flowers".	"I am my beloved's, and my beloved is mine, he grazes among the lotus flowers".

To explain this anomaly, Grober has recourse to the parallel with 8:1 where the woman, like her beloved, is suckled at the breasts of the same mother.[274] Nearer to our text is 5:13 where it is the woman who is feeding on the 'flowers of lotus' present on the lips of her beloved. The breasts stand for the woman who is, at the same time, passive and active. It is precisely because she feeds on the 'flowers of lotus' (4:5; 5:13; 8:1) that the woman can, in her turn, nourish her beloved on 'flowers of lotus' (2:16; 6:2, 3).[275] Once again the theme of reciprocity, which is solemnly confirmed in v. 3a, comes to light.

"I am my beloved's, and my beloved is mine". Like v. 3b, so also v. 3a is an almost literal repeat of 2:16 (cf. *Tab. 47*). Here we have one of the Song's 'refrains', one which not only has a structural value (here it closes the unit 5:2–6:3), but also one in which a particularly important aspect of the author's vision of human love is condensed. The refrain will appear one other time at 7:11, as conclusion of the *New Songs of the Beloved Man* (6:4–7:11), with a significant variant.[276]

The comparison with 2:16 shows an inversion of the 'formula of mutual belonging'. In 2:16 mention was made, first, of the belonging of the beloved to the woman, then of the belonging of the latter to the beloved: in 6:3, the order is inverted, perhaps to confirm the perfect reciprocity of the bond of love,[277] or, perhaps, also, for structural reasons: it was important, in fact, for the last verse of the unit to have begun with the same pronoun with which the first was begun (*'ănî*, 5:2; 6:3). It is going too far to see, with Feuillet, a progression in the

[274] Grober (1984), pp. 101–102.
[275] On the symbolism of the lotus flowers, cf. pp. 83–84, 122.
[276] On the 'formula of mutual belonging', cf., *supra*, pp. 120–121.
[277] "Everything about this love is mutual" (Bergant [1994], p. 30, citing in this sense Fox [1985], pp. 305–310). In her spiritual commentary, Bergant enhances the importance of mutuality in erotic love: "Mutuality is not an easy quality to cultivate. It requires a different kind of balance than does equality. It seeks complementary involvement or reciprocal response. In a mutual relationship, one supplies what the other lacks" (Bergant 1998, p. 50).

abnegation of the woman.[278] In reality, from the point of view of content, the two formulae are equivalent: both express that recognition of 'finding oneself in the other' which characterised the cry of the first man before his woman: "Now at last, bone of my bones, flesh of my flesh!" (Gen 2:23).

In 2:16, the formula of mutual belonging is placed in connection with the mention of the 'foxes' (2:15). In them we have recognised the beloved's 'rivals' who were constituting a threat to the love of the pair. In such a context, the formula of mutual belonging had the sense of contrasting with this danger, confirming the reciprocal and exclusive belonging of the lovers. The formula of 6:3 has also to be read in context. First of all, it forms a response to the crisis of 5:2–8 when the woman thought that she had lost her love. In 6:3 she comes to recognise that true love is never lost; it overcomes every crisis and misunderstanding. In the second place, the formula of belonging is a reply to the provocations of the daughters of Jerusalem.[279] On the one hand, by denying the sarcastic supposition that the beloved had abandoned her ("To where has your beloved *turned*?", 6:1c); on the other hand, by removing from the friends-rivals all hope that they themselves may have of establishing a relationship with him ("so that we can seek him with you", 6:1d).[280] The formula has an undoubted connotation of exclusivity, present also in 2:16 (there the couple was threatened by the other men, here by the other women).

In this sense also the declaration of v. 3b acquires an exclusive significance: it expresses the privilege, which belongs only to the beloved,

[278] Feuillet (1990), pp. 212–213, sees here a parallel to Ezek 37:23, 27. Feuillet interprets the 'formula of mutual belonging' allegorically, seeing there the renewal of the covenant of YHWH with Israel after the tragedy of the Exile; similarly, Joüon (1909), p. 262. We have already alluded to the correspondence of the Song's 'formula of mutual belonging' with the 'covenant formula' of the historical and prophetic books (*supra*, p. 121). If there is a literary dependence (given the widespread intertextuality which characterises the Song, this is not to be excluded, even if the two formulae are not completely equal), this is to be interpreted in the sense of the other parallels. The Song, that is, brings back to the reality of human love categories which in the prophets and in the Torah characterise the relationship between God and Israel. The same 'new and eternal covenant' that unites God and his people, also distinguishes the union between a man and his woman!

[279] The Midrash Song of Songs Rabbah underlines this aspect, naturally in an allegorical key. Behind the 'daughters of Jerusalem' it sees the nations who seek from Israel, where her beloved, YHWH, has gone. Israel replies: "What business have you to ask about him, when you have no share in Him? Once I have attached myself to Him, can I separate from Him? Once He has attched Himself to me, can He separate from me? Wherever He is, He comes to me" (ShirR 6:1, tr. Simon [1977], p. 256).

[280] Cf. Murphy (1990), p. 173.

of enjoying the body of his woman. Since she belongs to him (v. 3a), and him alone, he can "graze among the lotus flowers".

Conclusion

The three songs, 5:2–8; 5:9–16; 6:1–3 are shown to be a coherent compositional unit, not only through being uttered by the woman but also through clear structural echoes. These form a parallel with the two first Songs of the Beloved Woman (2:8–17; 3:1–5). After the union of 5:1, the journey of love begins all over again with the mutual searching: he searches for her (5:2–5, cf. 2:8–17), she searches for him (5:6–6:3, cf. 3:1–5). Also clear are the references to the preceding song (4:8–5:1). The theme of the bolt (5:5–6) develops that of the "enclosure" of the garden (4:12), and the actual metaphor of the garden (4:12–5:1) is taken up again in 6:1–3.

The first song (5:2–8) is the one in which the tragic, elegiac motif of the poem is most resonant, an element already introduced in the parallel passage 3:1–5. The idyll of love includes within itself the dramatic, whether the brutal violence of part of society, deaf to the reasons of love (the watchmen, 5:7), or the lack of understanding in the couple's relationship, the lack of synchronisation in the readiness to love (5:2–6).[281]

The woman does not allow herself to be vanquished but reacts bravely to the obstacles. She undertakes the path of memory, the path trodden by Israel in the tragedies which marked the history of her relationship with God.[282] She traces a passionate portrait of her beloved (5:9–16). The love which feeds on him transforms him into the living statue of a divinity.[283] This is not an idol but the realisation of the words of Gen 1:27: "In the image of God he created him".

In the description of the individual parts of the body of her man, the woman discovers that they are made of the same material as her

---

[281] Cf. Chave (1998), pp. 48–49.

[282] "Human love—that of the Canticle—and that which unites Israel and its God have the same structure. For Israel too, the nuptial union takes the way of memory: the narrative evocations of Hosea, the long parables of Ezekiel (16; 23)..." (Beauchamp [1990], p. 189).

[283] That is said also, in other words, by Beauchamp (1990), p. 191: "It would be artificial to attribute the role of the God of Israel to the young man of the Canticle. We have something else going on here. What is divine in this couple is what happens between them, the relationship itself".

own body: the lotus flowers, the myrrh, the doves... a realisation of the utopia of Gen 2:23: "This at last is bone of my bones and flesh of my flesh". It is significant that here it is the woman who speaks the words that in Genesis are given to the man. This observation flows into the refrain of mutual belonging: 'I am my beloved's, and my beloved is mine" (6:3). It is this jubilant affirmation which allows the crisis to be overcome. The beloved cannot have gone elsewhere, as the daughters of Jerusalem insinuate; he has to have "gone down into his garden, among the beds of balm" (6:2). The certainty of mutual belonging allows the distance created by misunderstanding between the two lovers to be overcome.

CHAPTER EIGHT

NEW SONGS OF THE BELOVED MAN

(Song 6:4–7:11)

Contemplation

I

Man 4"You are fair as Tirzah,[1] my friend,
lovely as Jerusalem,
terrible as a host drawn up for battle.[2]

5Turn your eyes away from me,
for they devastate me![3]
Your hair like flocks of goats
gambolling down from the mountains of Gilead.
6Your teeth like flocks of mother ewes
which come out again from their bath:
all of them have borne twins,
none has lost her young.
7Like the split in the pomegranate, your cheek,
behind your veil.

---

[1] The Hebrew term *tirṣâ* can be the proper name of a city (and of a person), or an adjective, deriving from *rāṣāh* ('to be lovable'). The versions understand unanimously in this second sense (LXX, *eudokia*; the Syriac *ṣbyn'*; Vg *suavis*), but the parallel with 'Jerusalem' speaks for the first.

[2] MT's *kannidgālôt* is a participle, in the *niph'al* form, of *dāgal* and means "'bannered' (hosts)" (cf. Song 5:10). LXX has *tetagmenai* ('[hosts] drawn up'); Vg *castrorum acies ordinata*; Symmachus, *hōs tagmata parembolōn*, 'like the battalions of armies drawn up'. The Syriac translates *gbyṭ'* ('like an elect [host?]').

[3] LXX's *anepterōsan me*; Vg's *me avolare fecerunt*; the Syriac's *'prdny* ('they have made me flee') probably refer to the 'going away' of the beloved in 5:6.

[8]Sixty are the[4] queens,
eighty the concubines,
and maidens without number;
[9]unique is my dove, my perfect one,
the only one of her mother,
the darling of the one who conceived her.
The daughters saw her and called her blessed,
the queens and concubines, and praised her".

II

Chorus [10]"Who is this, who looks down[5] like the dawn,
fair as the moon,[6]
bright[7] as the sun,[8]
terrible as a host drawn up for battle?"

III

Man [11]"I went down to the nut garden,
to look at the buds by the stream,
to see if the vine had budded,
if the pomegranates had flowered.[9]
[12]Without my knowing it, my desire
had carried me on to the chariots of my noble people".[10]

---

[4] MT has a masculine plural, *hemmâ*, explicable here as poetic licence.

[5] With MT and Vetus Latina. Vg translates *ad sensum*: *quae progreditur quasi aurora consurgens*.

[6] With the versions: MT has 'the white', *hallᵉbānâ*.

[7] MT's *bārâ* has the two meanings of 'chosen/elect' (as in v. 9c), and 'pure, bright'. LXX's *eklektē*, and Vg's *electa*, follow the first meaning; the Syriac's *dky'*, the second (so too Symmachus, *kathara*).

[8] With the versions. MT has *haḥammâ*, 'the scorching'.

[9] LXX adds: *ekei dōsō tous mastous mou soi*, 'there I will give you my breasts' (cf. 7:13e); so too Vetus Latina.

[10] With MT and the Syriac. LXX's *ameinadab* reads as a proper name; so too Vetus Latina's and Vg's *Aminadab*.

Desire

I

Chorus 7 1 “Turn round, turn round, O Shulamite;
turn round, turn round: we want to admire you!”
Man “What do you want to admire in the Shulamite?”
Chorus “What a question:[11] the dance of the two camps”.

II

Man 2 “How fair are your feet
in their sandals, daughter of a noble one!

The curves of your thighs are like jewels,
handiwork of a craftsman.
3 Your navel, a rounded cup—
may it never lack spiced wine.
Your belly, a heap of corn
surrounded with lotus flowers.
4 Your two breasts like two fawns,
twins of a gazelle.

5 Your neck like the tower of ivory.
Your eyes pools[12] of Heshbon
at the gate of Bath-Rabbim.[13]
Your nose like the tower of Lebanon,
sentinel facing Damascus.

---

[11] Understanding the k^e of MT in an asseverative sense. Some Hebrew manuscripts have a b^e: ‘*in* the dance’, thus linking 1c with 1d. Also the Syriac (*dnḥtʾ ʾyk ḥdwt*, ‘who comes down like dances’), LXX (*hē erchomenē hōs choroi tōn parembolōn*) and Vg (*nisi choros castrorum*) read the two stichs as declaimed by the same person.

[12] With MT. LXX’s *hōs limnai* supposes the particle k^e, as in the other stichs of the verse. This conjecture is possible (cf. *BHS*), but not necessary (cf. v. 3a, c).

[13] Literally the Hebrew means ‘daughter of many’. LXX’s *thygatros pollōn*; Vetus Latina’s *filiarum multarum*; Vg’s *filiae multitudinis*; and the Syriac’s *dbrt sgyʾ*, read as a common noun.

6Your head, like Carmel, crowns you[14]
and the hair of your head like purple—
a king[15] is held captive in the tresses.

7How fair you are, how sweet,
O love, in (your) pleasures.[16]
8Look at your height:[17] it resembles a palm,
and your breasts the clusters of dates.

9I said to myself: I will climb up the palm,
I will squeeze its clusters.
May your breasts be
like clusters of the vine,
and the scent of your nose like apples,
10and your palate like good wine…”.

III

Woman “…which goes straight to my beloved,
and flows on the lips of the sleepers.[18]
11I am my beloved’s,
and his desire[19] is for me”.

Structure[20]

After the incident at the gate (5:2–6), the first movement towards union was undertaken by the woman (5:6–6:1). The unit 5:2–6:3 con-

[14] Vg omits ‘crowns’ (literally, ‘above you’).

[15] Vg’s *sicut purpura regis*; and the Syriac’s *ʾyk ʾrgwnʾ dmlkʾ*, link ‘king’ and ‘purple’.

[16] So MT’s *battaʿănûgîm* (cf. LXX: *en tryphais sou*; Vetus Latina *in deliciis tuis*; Vg *in deliciis*). The Syriac *brt pwnqʾ* and the version of Aquila *thygatēr tryphōn* suppose *bat taʿănûgîm* (‘daughter of delights’).

[17] With MT’s *zōʾt* (‘this’), cf. LXX’s *touto*; the Syriac’s *whdʾ*. Vetus Latina and Vg omit the adjective.

[18] With MT’s *yᵉšēnîm*. The Syriac *wšny*, LXX *kai odousin*, Vetus Latina and Vg *et dentibus* read *wšnym*, ‘and your teeth’.

[19] LXX *epistrophē*; the Syriac *pnyth*; Vetus Latina and Vg *conversio*, apparently read *šwb* instead of MT’s *šwq*.

[20] On the structure of 6:4–7:11, cf. Barbiero (1997a), pp. 176–178.

cluded with the announcement that the beloved too, on his part, was searching for his loved one, had gone 'into his garden' (6:2). The connection of 6:2–3 with the following songs of the beloved man is thus indicated. Now the man finds himself before his loved one, expresses his own admiration for her ("You are fair", 6:4) and feels the desire to unite himself with her increase within him ("his desire is for me", 7:11). To the movement of the woman towards the man which characterises the preceding song corresponds that of the man towards the woman in the present one, confirming, once more, the perfect reciprocity of love in the Song. The connection of 6:1–3 with the two *New Songs of the Beloved Man* in 6:4–7:11 is confirmed by the repeat of the theme of the garden at the end of the first song ("to go down to the garden", 6:2a and 11a) and of that of the refrain of mutual belonging at the end of the second ("I am my beloved's…", 6:3a and 7:11ab). Both of the new songs of the man end with the expression of desire (*napšî*, 'my desire', 6:12a; *t*ᵉ*šûqātô*, 'his longing, desire', 7:11b). As in 5:10–16, here too, desire is born from contemplation of the loved one (6:4–10; 7:2–6): the three *waṣfs* have an analogous function, as was already the case, moreover, in 4:1–6.

The chronological indications display a coherent succession. The only temporal indication in the *New Songs of the Beloved Woman* referred to the 'night' (*lāylâ*, 5:2). In the *New Songs of the Beloved Man* there is also only one temporal indication which tends towards morning (*šaḥar*, the 'dawn', 6:10). These two indications are repeated at the beginning of the last songs of the woman. 7:12, in fact, speaks, first, of night (*nālînâ*, 'let us pass the night'), then, of morning (*naškîmâ*, 'we shall go out early'). It seems that the final composition intends to recapitulate in itself the two preceding ones.

Like the preceding *New Songs of the Beloved Woman*, so too the *New Songs of the Beloved Man* are characterised by a dialogic structure (cf. *Tab. 48*). The man (a: 6:4–9, 11–12; 7:1c, 2–10a) dialogues here first with a chorus (b: 6:10; 7:1abd), then, finally, with the woman (c: 7:10b–11). This final intervention of the woman corresponds chiastically to that of the man at the beginning of the preceding composition (5:2).

As in 5:2–6:3, so too in 6:4–7:11, some terms have a structuring function. This is so, above all, of the adjective 'fair' (*yph*) and of the interrogative-exclamatory particles *mî* ('who') and *mâ* ('what', 'how'). These two terms appear exactly at the lynch-pins of the discourse as *Tab. 50* (p. 323) shows. The term *yph* introduces the discourse of the

Table 48

A	6:4–9	Man
B	6:10	Chorus
A	6:11–12	Man
B	7:1ab	Chorus
A	7:1c	Man
B	7:1d	Chorus
A	7:2–10a	Man
C	7:10b–11	Woman

man in the first *waṣf* (6:4), then the response of the chorus (6:10), finally the second *waṣf* (7:2) and its concluding part (7:7). The interrogative-exclamatory particles have an analogous role in 6:10 (*mî*) and in 7:1c, 2, 7 (*mâ*). Also to be noted is the *inclusio* by means of the pair of terms *raʿyātî* ('my friend', 6:4) and *dôdî* ('my beloved', vv. 10b, 11a) where the former is pronounced by him, the latter by her.

Song 6:4–7:11 is composed of two parallel songs, 6:4–12 and 7:1–11, which form a sort of diptych.[21] In each of the two, the description of the body of the woman (a: 6:4–9 and a': 7:2–6) is followed by a global consideration of wonder which repeats the beginning of the *waṣf* (b: 6:10 and b': 7:7–8) and by a movement towards union characterised by the first person singular (c: 6:11–12 ["I went down", v. 11a: "without my knowing/I did not know", v. 12a]; c': 7:9–10a ["I said to myself", "I will climb up", v. 9a; "I will squeeze", v. 9b]). The correspondence between c and c' is chiastic (cf. *Tab. 49*).

To 6:11a ("I went down"), 7:9a ("I will climb up") corresponds antithetically; another antithetical correspondence here is "without my knowing" (*lōʾ yādaʿtî*, 6:12a) and "I said to myself" (*ʾāmartî*, 7:9a): the first expresses an unintentional activity, the second a deliberate one.

Table 49

6:11a	"I went down"		7:9a	"I said to myself"
		×		
6:12a	"Without my knowing"		7:9a	"I will climb up"

[21] So, rightly, Ravasi (1992), pp. 490–495.

The structure of the two songs is not perfectly parallel since the sequence of description-admiration-movement in the first song is built up dialogically (man-chorus-man) while in the second it is characterised by a solo from the man. Here the dialogue between the man and the chorus takes place before the *waṣf*, in 7:1. There are two structures one beside the other in the composition, the one determined by the alternation of the actors, the other by the progress of the action. Between the two structures there is a displacement, a kind of *enjambement* which confers dynamism on the whole.

The two *New Songs of the Beloved Man*, 6:4–12 and 7:2–10a, are joined together by means of the dialogue of 7:1. Not only does the man-chorus alternation continue the preceding series but also the theme of 'seeing' (*ḥāzāh*, twice in 7:1) is linked with 6:11 (*rāʾāh*, twice), and the military metaphor prolongs the theme of the preceding verse (6:12 = *mark*^{e}*bôt*, 'chariots [of war]'; 7:1 = *maḥănāyim*, 'two battlefields').[22] The movement which is spoken of in 6:11–12 ("I have gone down", v. 11a; "on to the chariots of my noble people", v. 12b) leads on naturally to the dance which is mentioned in 7:1 and which will then be described in 7:2–6 (cf. *Tab. 50*).

The final intervention of the woman, which almost robs the man of speech (7:10b), underlines the exquisite, one might say modern, composition of the passage. With regard to the two frames of the diptych, Song 7:10b–11 constitutes a kind of coda. In addition to the *inclusio* we have already noted, *raʿyātî* (6:4)—*dôdî* (7:10, 11), we should note the other one: *ʾănî* + *dôdî* (5:2 and 7:11), which hold together the two compositions 5:2–6:3 and 6:4–7:11.

Table 50

I	A	6:4–9	man	a description	*yph*—my friend (v. 4)
	B	6:10	Chorus	b admiration	*mî—yph*
	A	6:11–12	man	c movement	to go down—without my knowing
II	B	7:1ab	Chorus		
	A	7:1c	man		*mâ*
	B	7:1d	Chorus		
	A	7:2–6	man	a description	*mâ—yph* (v. 2)
		7:7–8		b admiration	*mâ—yph* (v. 7)
		7:9–10a		c movement	I said to myself—to climb up
III	C	7:10b–11	woman		my beloved (vv. 10c, 11a)

[22] Cf. Keel (1994), pp. 225–226.

Contemplation (6:4–12)

The structure of this passage is highly disputed.[23] My proposal originates from the identification of the parallelism between 6:4–12 and 7:1–10a. On the basis of the observations made above, Song 6:4–12 can be structured in three parts, whether from the point of view of the alternation of the actors or from that of the progress of the action (cf., *supra*, *Tab. 50*). The first (6:4–9) and the last (6:11–12) part are put into the mouth of the beloved, the central part (v. 10) to a, probably female, chorus (introduced in vv. 8–9). The three parts denote a progressive getting closer on the part of the lovers, marked out according to the phases of 'contemplation' (vv. 4–9), 'admiration' (v. 10) and 'movement towards union' (vv. 11–12).

Despite their different literary genre (the first part is a *waṣf* with which the second and third part do not have any connection from the formal point of view), the three parts are bound together by a double alternation. On the one hand, there is a constant, ordered oscillation between the two poles 'fair' and 'terrible' (the binome is expressly mentioned in vv. 4 and 10); on the other hand, the metaphors are drawn alternately from the 'city' or from 'nature' (cf. *Tab. 51*).[24] Here also we have two superimposed structures which do not always coincide, thus creating effects of *enjambement*.

---

[23] The spectrum of suggestions goes from the seven (!) units of Haupt (1907), p. 135 (6:4a, 4b–6, 7–8, 9, 10, 11, 12), to Krinetzki's five (6:4–5ab, 5cd–7, 8–9, 10, 11–12, cf. Krinetzki [1981], pp. 178–190). Zapletal (1907), pp. 125–129, also has five (6:4–7, 8–9, 10, 11, 12), while Keel (1994), pp. 211–229, has four (6:4–7, 8–10, 11; 6:12–7:1). Many see three units here, but the way of dividing them is different: 6:4–7, 8–9, 10–12 (Ringgren [1962], pp. 285–286; Gordis [1974], pp. 65–67; Ricciotti [1928], pp. 250–258); 6:4–7, 8–10, 11–12 (Rudolph [1962], pp. 162–167; Wittekindt [1925], pp. 8, 32, 175; Müller [1992], pp. 63–71); 6:4–7, 8–11; 6:12–7:1 (Lys [1968], pp. 231–248); 6:4–7, 8–10; 6:11–7:1 (Gerleman [1965], pp. 181–193; Rendtorff [1985], p. 263); 6:4–9*, 10*, 11–12 (Schmökel [1956], pp. 88, 48, 57). Recently, various authors have recognised two units here, but once again the demarcation is disputed: 6:4–7; 6:8–7:1 (Exum [1973], p. 69); 6:4–7; 6:8–7:10 (Bosshard-Nepustil [1996], p. 59); 6:4–9, 10–12 (Colombo [1975], pp. 104–112); 6:4–9; 6:10–7:1a (Dorsey [1990], p. 88); 6:4–10; 6:11–7:11 (Beauchamp [1990], p. 167); 6:4–10; 6:11–7:1 (Elliott [1989], pp. 148–164); 6:4–10, 11–12 (Murphy [1990], p. 177; Meek [1956], pp. 132–133). The unity of the composition 6:4–12 is recognised by Ravasi (1992), pp. 490–492; Goulder (1986), pp. 48–52; Nolli (1967), pp. 123–128. Garbini's hypothesis is singular: he moves 6:4–5a between 4:1a and 4:1b, and eliminates 5b–7 as a doublet of 4:1–3 (cf. Garbini [1992], pp. 68–69): that leaves vv. 8–12 which he treats as a unit (pp. 246–252).

[24] For the details, we refer to the exegesis of the individual verses.

Table 51

A	FAIR	v. 4ab	} A	CITY
B	TERRIBLE	v. 4c		
B'	TERRIBLE	v. 5	} B	NATURE
A'	FAIR	vv. 6–7		
–	—	vv. 8–9	A'	CITY
A	FAIR	v. 10abc	B	NATURE
B	TERRIBLE	v. 10d	A	CITY
A	FAIR	v. 11	B	NATURE
B	TERRIBLE	v. 12	A	CITY

The division of the song into three parts, vv. 4–9, v. 10 and vv. 11–12, corresponds to that of the MT which places a *setumah* (little pause) both before and after v. 10. The centre of the composition is occupied by vv. 8–9 which stand outside the 'fair-terrible' pattern and so acquire a particular relevance.[25]

First part: Description (6:4–9)

The unity of the composition 6:4–9 is not undisputed. The majority of authors stop at v. 7. Heinevetter rightly defends the unity of vv. 4–9 but goes to the opposite extreme of separating v. 10 from the preceding context and making it the beginning of a new composition (6:10–8:6).[26] Now v. 10 is firmly bound up with vv. 4–9. There is, first of all, a continuity between the mention of the 'other women' in vv. 8 and 9de and the question of v. 10. Verse 10 is precisely that 'beatification' and 'praise' of which v. 9de speaks.[27] Moreover, the two expressions, 'fair' and 'terrible as a host drawn up for battle', are a clear repeat of

[25] Not for nothing, Lys (1968), p. 234, entitles the passage 6:4–7:1: 'The Unique'. The affirmation of the uniqueness of the woman is of capital importance.

[26] Heinevetter (1988), p. 145. In this, he is following a preceding line of enquiry. For Delitzsch (1875), pp. 98, 101, in fact, 6:4–9 is the second scene of the fifth act of the drama (5:2–6:9), while 6:10–7:6 is the first scene of the sixth act (6:10–8:4). Along the same lines, we find Minocchi (1898), pp. 92–101 (6:4–9; 6:10–8:4); Ringgren, Gordis, Ricciotti, Colombo, Dorsey, Zapletal, Haller, Schmökel (cf. *supra*, n. 23), and, in part, Siegfried (1898), pp. 116–118 (6:4–9 + 11–12; 6:10 + 7:1–8:4).

[27] This is not admitted by all, but it seems the best solution. Cf. the parallel of Prov 31:28, in which it is said that the sons and the husband, respectively, 'call blessed' (*'šr*) and, 'praise' (*hll*) the 'virtuous woman'. To this affirmation, there follows, in v. 29, the quotation of the speech of the sons and the husband.

v. 4. One could think of an *inclusio* signalling the unity of vv. 4–10,[28] but the parallel with 7:7 leads us to understand this repetition rather as a new beginning. From another angle, the question: "Who is this…?" constitutes almost a refrain in the Song (cf. 3:6 and 8:5) and, always, marks the beginning of a compositional unit, while the choral amplification of the praise in vv. 8–9 has a conclusive value, as is shown by the parallels at 1:2, 4; 3:10, 11.[29]

The composition Song 6:4–9 is unified by the subject who pronounces it (the beloved man). In its turn, it consists of three strophes: v. 4, vv. 5–7 and vv. 8–9 (cf. *Tab. 52*). The first strophe (v. 4) contemplates the woman as a whole. The three stichs of the verse form three similitudes, constructed in an analogous manner, of which the first two present the fair aspect of the woman (v. 4a: "fair as Tirzah"; v. 4b: "lovely as Jerusalem"), the third her terrible aspect (v. 4c: "terrible as a host drawn up for battle").

The mention of the eyes, in v. 5ab, belongs to the sphere of 'terrible', but the construction of the phrase is different since the two stichs are linked with the second strophe in which the description passes from the global to that of the individual parts of the body. After the eyes, three elements of the face are described (hair, v. 5cd; teeth, v. 6; cheeks, v. 7), which repeat 4:1–3 word for word apart from some small

Table 52

Strophe	*Verses*	*Consideration*	*Metaphor*	*Number*	
I	v. 4	whole	city	three	Tirzah (4a) Jerusalem (4b) hosts (4c)
II	vv. 5–7	individual parts	nature	four	eyes (5ab) hair(5cd) teeth (6) cheeks (7)
III	vv. 8–9	whole	city	seven	sixty… …eighty (8)

[28] Cf. in n. 23 the series of authors who make the unit close at v. 10 (Keel, Rudolph, Wittekindt, Müller, Beauchamp, Elliott, Murphy, Meek, Gerleman, Rendtorff). To these we should add Ravasi (1992), p. 491, who, although recognising the unity of 6:4–12, divides it into two parts 4–10 and 11–12.

[29] Cf. Heinevetter (1988), pp. 145–146.

variations. While the first strophe is characterised by a series of urban and military metaphors (Tirzah, Jerusalem, host drawn up), in the second the metaphors are drawn from nature (goat, ewe, pomegranate).

The third strophe returns to the 'urban' symbolism and to the global contemplation of the woman. Now, however, the woman is not considered in isolation but against the background of a royal *harem*. On the one hand, the choral background emphasises the 'uniqueness' of the woman, on the other hand, it confers a more 'objective' character on the young man's praise (cf. 1:2, 4; 3:10). The strophe is separated from the two preceding also because the discourse is no longer direct, but indirect, in the third person.

The author plays on numbers. The first strophe is built up on the number three (three stichs and three metaphors), the second on the number four (in fact, four parts of the face are described: eyes, hair, teeth, cheeks). In the third strophe, the two numbers cited in v. 8, sixty and eighty, are precisely multiples of three ($60 = 3 \times 20$) and four ($80 = 4 \times 20$), the numbers of the two preceding strophes. The sum is, naturally, a multiple of 7 ($140 = 7 \times 20$). As the number of perfection, number 7 is well placed at the end of the passage.

The literary genre is that of the *waṣf* which we have already encountered in 4:1–7 and 5:10–16. By contrast with the other *waṣf* in the *New Songs of the Beloved Man*, 7:2–6, where the woman is contemplated in the movement of the dance, here the contemplation is static. We should note that the sketch of the body is not complete. If in 4:1–7 the picture included also the neck and the breasts of the woman, here it stops at the head, highlighting an aspect already observed in the other two *waṣfs*: in the head of the woman, the man contemplates, in concentrated form, her whole person. It is interesting to observe how the Hebrew term *mar'eh* indicates both the appearance, that is, the whole person as he or she appears (cf. 5:15), and the face (cf. 2:14). In the person of the woman, the author is interested in stressing the two antithetical aspects of the *mysterium fascinosum et tremendum*: he encounters them in her face.[30]

[6:4] First strophe. [v. 4] "You are fair…my friend". The direct discourse assumes that the two lovers are located in front of each other, thus corroborating the words of the woman in 6:2. The adjective 'fair'

[30] Cf. Elliott (1989), p. 150. On the binome 'fair-terrible' cf. Landy (1983), pp. 135–179 ("Beauty and the Enigma").

(*yāpâ*) echoes the address of the daughters of Jerusalem in 5:9 and 6:1 ('fairest among women'). Here there is no trace of irony: the compliment is sincere. The two other *waṣf*s devoted to the woman also begin with this appellation (4:1; 7:2; cf. also 1:15), which expresses, in comprehensive form, the charm, the attraction she exercises. The adjective accompanies the noun 'my friend' (*raʿyātî*) as in 1:15; 2:10, 13; 4:1, 7. This is the last time in which this typical designation of the woman appears. Structurally, it recalls, on the one hand, the beginning of the *New Songs of the Beloved Woman* in 5:2 (a resonance which will be confirmed in v. 9), on the other hand, the conclusion of the same songs at 6:3 in which the complementary term *dôdî* ('my beloved') appears. The link with the passage immediately preceding is expressed by the play between *raʿyātî* (6:4a) and *hārōʿeh* ('he grazes', 6:3b; cf. 2c). The root *rʿh* has the two senses of 'to be a friend, neighbour' and 'to graze'. Thus the man once more confirms the words of the woman: indeed he belongs to her!

"As Tirzah". Even if the term Tirzah undoubtedly indicates a city, given the parallelism with Jerusalem, it is not without importance to recall that it signifies 'lovable' and is also the name of a person, alluding, therefore, to the personification of the city. Tirzah was the ancient capital of the northern kingdom before Omri constructed Samaria.[31] Today, it is generally identified with Tell el-Far'a on the homonymous Wadi.[32] In the Hellenistic epoch, the city no longer existed, but that does not mean to say that the Song comes from pre-exilic times. As A. Robert and R. Tournay suggest, we have here probably an anti-Samaritan jibe.[33] The author evidently intends to indicate the two capitals, of the northern and southern kingdoms respectively, but avoids recognising as capital of the North the schismatic Samaria and returns to the pre-'Samaritan' time when the capital was Tirzah. In fact, we have here a further testimony to the late composition of the Song.

The metaphor of the city has already been applied to the woman in 2:4b and in 4:4. It will be taken up again in 8:10 ("I am a wall and my breasts are the towers"). One certainly cannot say that it is foreign to

[31] Cf. 1 Kgs 14:17; 15:21, 33; 16:6, 8, 9, 15, 17, 23.

[32] Cf. R. de Vaux, *El-Farʿa, Tell, North*, in *EAEHL*, vol. II, pp. 395–404.

[33] Robert – Tournay (1963), p. 233. Cf. also, in this sense, Lacocque (1998), p. 130. Naturally we distance ourselves from the allegorical interpretation of R.-T. It is not the woman who becomes the symbol of the people of Israel, but, *vice versa*, the history of Israel is applied to the reality of human love; so, rightly, Lys (1968), p. 235.

the poetics of the Song![34] Keel points out the parallel with the numerous representations, widespread in the ancient world, of a city personified by a woman with the characteristic crown in the form of a wall.[35] The invincible walls are the symbol of the virginity of the woman-city. However, this image is more suitable to the three passages cited above than to ours. Here is presented, above all, the fairness of the city. This too is not foreign to the biblical (cf., for the NT, Rev 21:2) or, for that matter, the Western mentality. To take an example that is familiar to me, I think of the representation of Venice as an attractive and wealthy woman: more than her 'inaccessibility', the images of Venice underline her charm and her wealth. As Müller observes:

> For the man of antiquity, nature finds its complement in human culture, just as, *vice versa*, culture always remains a part of nature, in so far as society, by means of its cultural resources, is integrated more completely with nature than would be possible without these.[36]

Nature and culture are, it was seen above, the two poles between which the symbolism of the present composition oscillates.

"Lovely as Jerusalem". Discourse made about any city in general acquires a particular character with Jerusalem. The city is seen as a woman, abandoned but remarried by her Creator in the famous Chapter 62 of Isaiah to which different passages of the Song refer.[37] In the OT, she is claimed to be a particularly beautiful woman-city: cf. Lam 2:15 ("Is this the city which was called the perfection of beauty [*kᵉlîlat yōpî*], the joy of the whole earth?"); Ps 48:3; 50:2. Moreover, she is the 'holy city', the dwelling place of God. The comparison is aligned, therefore, with the numerous other sacral metaphors which shroud the two lovers in a religious atmosphere.

Tirzah and Jerusalem share the fact of not being just any old cities but the capitals, the former of the northern kingdom, the latter of that of the South. In this way the man intends to stress the incomparability of the woman, responding to the praise of her in 5:10 ("he is

---

[34] Cheyne, claiming the comparison to be out of place, changes the two city names into "narcissus" and "lily of the fields" (citation in Robert – Tournay [1963], p. 232). Garbini (1992), p. 216, replaces them both with the term "Grace".

[35] Keel (1994), pp. 212–215.

[36] Müller (1992), p. 64.

[37] Cf., for example, the motif of the crown, Isa 62:3 and Song 3:11 (cf., *supra*, p. 163).

distinguished among thousands and thousands").[38] Also allowed to appear is a nationalistic trace that has already been discovered elsewhere. The woman is identified not only with the holy land, with the geography of Israel, but also with its history which is indissolubly bound up with its geography. In her is condensed the history of the people. In the woman, therefore, the man is joined to the historical roots of Israel, those of the kingdom of the North as much as those of the kingdom of the South.[39]

"Terrible as a host drawn up for battle". The metaphor of the city already carries within itself the connotation of 'invincible fortress' (cf. 2:4; 4:4; 8:10).[40] Now this aspect is made explicit. But while in the other passages the 'defensive' aspect of this fortress, its inaccessibility, is emphasised, the metaphor of the 'army' stresses its offensive power. The 'army drawn up for battle' is ready to attack, to annihilate any kind of resistance. The city-woman is not being described in a passive attitude, but active: from being 'besieged' (2:4), she now becomes the 'one besieging' as the ensuing description of the eyes demonstrates in a concrete way (6:5ab; cf. 4:9).

The term *'ăyummâ* ('terrible') is attested in the OT only in the parallel 6:10 and in Hab 1:7 where it refers to the terror inspired by the Chaldean army. Much more frequent is the noun *'êmâ*, a technical term to describe the 'holy terror' which comes upon the enemies of Israel on the occasion of the holy war (cf. Exod 5:16; Josh 2:9) or that which is present at a theophany (cf. Gen 15:12).[41] The juxtaposition is significant because the two semantic fields of holy war and theophany will be taken up again later at v. 12 ("The chariots of my noble people") and at v. 10 ("Who is this who looks down like the dawn?").

---

[38] The reference of 6:4 to 5:10 is confirmed by the repeat of the term *dgl* in v. 4c (cf. *infra*).

[39] Perhaps conceivable here is the desire for the reunification of the people of Israel, along the lines of Ezek 37:15–28. We have already noted the possibility of seeing, behind the events of the Song, the events of the history of Israel (cf., *supra*, pp. 212–213, 223). Again, this is not in the allegorical sense, but *vice versa*: the Song is singing of human love, not of the relationship of Israel with its God. The history of Israel is placed at the service of human love; it is evoked in order to understand the significance of this experience. At bottom, the two viewpoints meet, but it is right to respect the autonomy and the originality of both approaches.

[40] This aspect is highlighted in Keel (1994), p. 215, who, however, stresses exclusively its defensive character.

[41] Cf. H.-J. Zobel, *'êmâ*, in *TDOT*, vol. I, pp. 219–221; Salvaneschi (1982), pp. 52–54.

Moreover, the two fields are connected: both, in fact, are manifestations of the divine with its character which, at one and the same time, is *fascinosum et tremendum*. The woman is being described, therefore, as an incarnation of transcendence. It is clear that, just as the man is not an idol, so too the woman is not a pagan divinity: it is not she, but the love that is within her, which is divine. In her, the man catches a glimpse of the divinity, the same God who dwells in Jerusalem, who is, simultaneously, 'perfect beauty' (Ps 50:2) and 'terrifying fire' (Isa 33:14).

The term *nidgālôt* is the *niph'al* participle of *dāgal*, a denominative verb deriving from the noun *degel*, 'banner' (cf. Num 1:52; 2:2) or even 'bannered host' (cf. Num 2:3, 10 etc). Here it is probably the second meaning that is to the fore: in fact this is how the LXX, the Vulgate and the version of Symmachus have understood it.[42] The plural term indicates the different battalions of an army, drawn up under their banner, ready to give battle.[43] The term was chosen perhaps to match Song 5:10 where it was said, of the man, that he was *dāgûl* (bannered), that he stood out, that is, like a banner above the crowds. The noun occurs again in 2:4 where the 'banner' is linked once more with the man (*diglô*, '*his* banner'). The same irresistible force which the woman saw in her man is now encountered by the man in the woman. The 'mirroring dynamic' of the Song is a continually recurring motif. In both cases, the banner is that of love (2:4). Here too, to an ear used to frequenting the OT, there cannot not resonate those passages where the banner is attributed to YHWH, such as Ps 20:6 ("In the name of our God we shall raise the banner [*nidgōl*])" or Exod 17:15 ("Moses

[42] Cf., *supra*, n. 2. The different conjectures proposed seem improbable to me: *kammigdālôt*, 'like the towers' (Graetz [1871], p. 182); *k^energāl*, 'like Nergal' (A. Jeremias, cf. Robert – Tournay [1963], p. 233). Rudolph (1962), p. 162, translates 'Himmelsbilder', understanding images of constellations; Gerleman (1965), p. 183, sees the phenomenon of the 'Morgan le Fay' ('Trugbilder'). Both are led to this translation by the parallel with 6:10. But in 6:4, the context is different: there is nothing here that makes us think of heavenly apparitions! The repetitions in the Song are never mechanical transposition, but each time they are inserted perfectly into their context, so that it is not to be wondered at if the same expression assumes different meanings in different contexts. In the same direction as Rudolph and Gerleman are those who, like Müller and Garbini, simply eliminate v. 4c as a useless doublet of 10d (cf. Müller [1992], p. 63; Garbini [1992], p. 68: Garbini actually omits the whole passage of 6:4–7 as a 'fragment without sense'; similarly, Wittekindt [1925], p. 32). Regalzi's proposal to see in the *nidgālôt* the 'Amazons' of Greek mythology (cf. Regalzi [2001], p. 142), is based on Garbini's emended text: it makes no sense if one accepts the MT.

[43] Thus *HALOT*, p. 213.

built an altar which he called: YHWH is my banner [*niṣṣî*]"). This is not, as Salvaneschi insinuates, 'disrespectful use' of a sacral language, but the conscious application of this language to the human-divine reality of love.[44] The banner of love is YHWH's own banner.

In the mythology of the Ancient Orient, 'terrible' is attributed to the goddess of love who is, at the same time, also the goddess of war. Anat at Ugarit and Inanna-Ishtar in Mesopotamia are represented in this way.[45] In the Song, this aspect is highlighted in 8:6 where of love it is said that it is "strong (*ʿazzâ*) as death, relentless (*qāšâ*) as the grave".[46] 'Fair' and 'terrible' are terms that are only apparently irreconcilable: they express the paradox of love, and the author of the Song composes through paradoxes deliberately. An analogous paradox is the juxtaposition of the warlike aspect of the woman ('host drawn up for battle') with Jerusalem, the city of peace (*šālôm*) (v. 4b). The same juxtaposition is made in 7:1 where the appellation *šûlammît*, in which the root *šlm* is also present, is set in a warlike context (*maḥănāyim*, 'military camp'). Also in 8:10, after being compared to a wall with towers, the woman concludes: "In his eyes I have found peace" (*k*ᵉ*môṣ*ᵉ*ʾēt šālôm*). Love is war, turning upside down the ordered and reasonable life of a person, but only by entering upon this war is peace to be found.[47]

[6:5–7] Second strophe. The *waṣf* begins with a description of the eyes, as in 4:1 (cf. 1:15). The 'fairness' of the woman is reflected first of all in her eyes. But in our case, the eyes are associated with the terrible, not the charming aspect of the woman. That is, they make concrete what v. 4c was saying in a general way. The binome fair-terrible proves to be a structuring principle of the strophe. The first two parts of the body (eyes, hair) personify, in fact, the terrible, the last two (teeth, cheeks) the charming aspect of the woman.[48] An analogous composi-

---

[44] Salvaneschi (1982), p. 50.

[45] Cf. the documentation in Pope (1977), pp. 561–563, also Keel (1978), Figures 324 and 324a, p. 237, and *id.* [1994], Figures 94 and 95, p. 147.

[46] There comes into mind a parallel from the Antigone of Sophocles: *erōs anikate machan*, 'love invincible in battle' (*Antigone* 781).

[47] A similar paradox is proposed in the Gospel: Jesus too "has not come to bring peace but the sword" (Matt 10:34); however, he leaves his peace to his disciples (John 14:27).

[48] This could be the reason why the author has not taken up again the description of the eyes from 4:1 in 6:4: in 4:1, the eyes personify the woman's beauty, in 6:4, her terrible power.

tional principle characterised the description of the head of the man in 5:11b–12: there, his hair expressed the dyonisian, savage aspect of love, his eyes the apollonian. It is understood that the author is not interested in a description of all the parts of the body: he operates a selection according to the aspects of the person which he wishes to bring forward. The description is complete even if it embraces only four parts of the body.

The alternation of the two aspects, fair and terrible, is not the only compositional principle of the strophe. Other factors can be observed (cf. *Tab. 53*). The two central descriptions, of the hair (v. 5cd) and of the teeth (v. 6), form a clear parallel. In both, the metaphor is made up of a 'flock' (*ʿeder*), the one of ewes, the other of goats. From the point of view of colour, the contrast between black and white should be noted; from that of sound, vv. 5c–6 are built up on the sound *s* which marks the incipit of each stich (*śaʿrēk, šeggalšû, šinnayik, šeʿālû, šekkullām, šakkulâ*). In both descriptions, the metaphor is introduced by the comparative particle *kᵉ*: we therefore have similes rather than metaphors. The first and last descriptions of the strophe fall outside this parallelism. The description of the eyes (v. 5ab) does not employ any metaphor: indeed, it is not even a description but a request. Nevertheless, the author connects it with vv. 5c–6 by means of the sound *š* at the beginning of the second stich (*šehem*). There begins here a series of seven stichs all beginning with the same sound. The series is interrupted at v. 7 with the description of the throat which clearly lies outside the parallelism. But here too the author is careful to bind it to the two central descriptions by means of the comparative particle *kᵉ* at the beginning of the verse. Moreover, the series of colours, black and white, continues with the 'pink' of the pulp of the pomegranate. If the strophe presents a parallel construction from the point of view of the binome fair-terrible (a-a-b-b), from the stylistic angle it presents a chiastic construction (a-b-b-a). The two structures stand in tension with each other.

Table 53

v. 5ab	EYES	a	terrible	a	—	—	*š*	—	—
v. 5cd	HAIR	a	terrible	b	flocks	goats	*š*	*kᵉ*	black
v. 6	TEETH	b	fair	b	flocks	ewes	*š*	*kᵉ*	white
v. 7	THROAT	b	fair	a	—	pomegranate	—	*kᵉ*	pink

[v. 5ab] The Hebrew verb *rāhab*, used here in the *hiph'il* form ('devastate'), has the same root as the noun *rahab* which is the name of the mythical monster of marine mayhem (cf. Ps 89:11; Job 9:13; 26:12; Isa 51:9).[49] Keel comments:

> Every great love is a new cosmos, whose birth is accompanied by life-threatening manifestations of chaos, for the birth of new world calls into question that which already exists.[50]

'To love' signifies to lose one's life, to live no longer for oneself but for the other, and it is understandable that this gives rise to fear in one's own self.

The man had already spoken of the terrible power of the glances of the woman in 4:9 ("You have driven me mad[51] with one of your glances"). Here too, the eyes are seen in their function ('glances') as messengers of love. If the 'dove' (1:15; 4:1; 5:12) presented the fascinating aspect of the eyes, Rahab expresses the terrible. However, the request to turn away the eyes is not to be taken too seriously:[52] the young man feels himself attracted by them. The force of the attraction is so strong that he is frightened of it: since they are so fair, they are terrible.[53]

[vv. 5c–7] The following three parts of the face, hair, teeth and cheeks, are repetitions of 4:1–3, to the commentary on which we refer for the details. The repetition is not mechanical, however: the text shows some small but significant variations with respect to its parallel. They lead us to understand that the verses in question are not due to a copyist's error or a late insertion but are a stylistic device used for

---

[49] The name means 'he who presses' (*Dränger*), with reference to the restlessness and assault of the sea (cf. *HALOT*, p. 1193).

[50] Keel (1994), p. 215. Krinetzki (1981), p. 179, interprets the same phenomenon in a psychological key: "Although desirable for her beauty, the woman causes the young man to retreat trembling because of her feminine difference, which for him at bottom is again something totally strange, as if it presented a threat. He has a presentiment in some way that, in the love of this young woman, he will encounter the 'terrible mother', and that it will be a mortal encounter, which will require of him the total sacrifice of his own life: the masculine nature is fearful of such an encounter".

[51] The verb used in 4:9 is *lābab*, lit. 'to cause to lose heart', that is, 'to cause to go mad' (cf., *supra*, pp. 202–203).

[52] Krinetzki (1981), p. 180, thinks, for example, of a "request for distance in the face of one's own partner in moments of too strong attraction or of too intense acts of tenderness".

[53] This is the understanding of Ibn Ezra, *ad loc.*: "Are too strong for me, or have taken away my power and my command" (tr. Mathews [1874], p. 8).

a reason envisaged by the author. The variations of 6:5c–7 compared with 4:1–3 are the following: 1) in the description of the hair (v. 5cd), the word *har* ('mountain') is omitted; 2) in the description of the teeth (v. 6), the term *haqq^{e}ṣûbôt* ('ready for the shearing') is replaced with *hār^{e}ḥēlîm* ('mother ewes'); 3) the description of the fourth element of the face, the cheek (v. 7), follows here immediately on that of the teeth, while in 4:3 it is preceded by the description of the lips (4:3a). However, repetition is typical of the language of love: the words of love are always the same.[54]

As in 4:1 and 5:11, the poet sees in the hair (v. 5cd) the dionysian aspect of love, its wild, untamed, chaotic component which is lined up with the description of the eyes.[55] The geographical indication, Gilead, accentuates the identification of the woman with the promised land, something already hinted at in the two indications of v. 4.

The apollonian aspect, expressed by the colour white, was associated, in 5:12, with the eyes: here, on the other hand, as in 4:2, it is associated with the teeth-ewes. In the three cases, the 'whiteness' is underlined ("washed [*roḥăṣôt*] in milk", 5:12; "which come out again from their bath [*min hāraḥṣâ*]", 6:6; cf. 4:2). The term *rāḥēl* ('mother ewe'), new as far as 4:2 is concerned, heightens the theme of fertility which the poet sees as present in the woman's teeth, as already in the parallel passage. To a Jewish ear, however, such a term could not avoid evoking the figure of Rachel, the matriarch of Israel (another allusion to the history of the Jewish people after those of vv. 4 and 5). In the teeth of the woman, then, the man sees a promise of fertility: his woman is fertile like the twin-bearing ewes, like the wife of Jacob, the mother of the chosen people.

After the black-white contrast which characterises the juxtaposition of hair and teeth, the third colour of love, red, is evoked in v. 7, as in 4:3: it is situated in the woman's cheek which is pink "like the split in the pomegranate". Why, of the two 'red' parts of 4:3 has the author chosen the second, leaving out the lips? The term *rimmôn* ('pomegranate and pomegranate tree') is a *Leitmotiv* in the passage: it will be taken up again in v. 11 (cf. 7:13; 8:2). The pomegranate is the national fruit of Israel, and it is a symbol of fertility because of its numerous

[54] Cf. *supra*, p. 78.
[55] Cf. *supra*, p. 178.

seeds, the pledge of numerous descendants.[56] The choice, therefore, is not accidental but fits well in the context. This stress on fertility is not typical of the Song which generally exalts the friendship aspect of love. The aspect of the transmission of life is not absent, however: a discourse on sexuality would be incomplete without this dimension. Fertility is inseparably bound up with the theme of life and the victory over death, which is central in the Song. Consequently, the affirmation which has often been made in recent commentaries, that there is no mention of procreation in the text, is too categorical. The theme is certainly not the centre of attention but has a role in the poem which cannot be passed over.

"Behind your veil". The repetition of this detail from 4:3 is surprising. There, the mention of the 'veil' made sense in parallel with 4:1. But here, up to now, there has been no mention of a 'veil'. To posit mechanical repetition does not fit with the poetics of the Song: up till now, every repetition has been shown to be coherent with the context and expressive. In the comment on 4:1, it was seen that the veil (*ṣammâ*) is a sign of the bride. It is possible that here too this connotation is present because the *waṣfs* (6:4–9; 7:2–10) and the dance (7:1) allude to such a context. As in the case of fertility, this would be a discreet allusion which will be made explicit at the end of the composition when the author resumes his discourse on the social dimension of love (cf. 8:1–4).

[6:8–9] Third strophe. The strophe is built up on the number 3 and is constructed in concentric form (a-b-a'). The mention in v. 8 of three categories of women of the *harem* (a: 'queens...concubines...maidens') is repeated in v. 9de in a form that is almost chiastic (a': 'daughters...queens...concubines'). The two series form the frame for v. 9abc where the uniqueness of the woman is praised three times in counterpoint ('unique...only one...darling'). The author wishes to counterpose the 'only one' to the 'many' (cf. *Tab. 54*). The ternary rhythm is observable in each of the individual parts: only the last (vv. 9de), as the conclusion, combines the ternary rhythm (three subjects and three verbs) with a binary one (two stichs, constructed chiastically: the first with two verbs and one subject, the second with two subjects and one verb).

---

[56] Cf., *supra*, p. 183.

Table 54

a v. 8	a b c	sixty eighty without number	the queens the concubines the maidens	MANY
b v. 9	a b c	one the only one the darling	my dove… of her mother of the one who conceived her	ONE
a' v. 9	d e	saw her and called her blessed praised her	the maidens the queens and concubines	MANY

The *waṣf* 5:10–16 was a reply to the daughters of Jerusalem's question: "What makes your beloved different from another?" The woman had claimed the uniqueness and incomparability of her man among all the men of the world ("he is distinguished among thousands and thousands!"). The man now does the same for his woman (again the mirroring principle): she is the unique one. To make this affirmation, the man has to compare her with other women: the strophe has a choral character, typical of the conclusion of a unit.[57]

The "sixty queens, eighty concubines and maidens without number" undoubtedly depict a royal *harem*. Gerleman is right to ask himself: What does the author intend with this kind of comparison?[58] Are we to think of a 'high burlesque' such as has generally taken place till now, where the man is identified with 'Solomon' or 'the king' (1:2–4, 12; 3:6–11)? Or is there here a trace of criticism in the comparison with Solomon as in 8:11–12? Gerleman opts for the second alternative, and I believe that he is right: the author wishes to take his distance from a 'quantitative' conception of love. To the many women who populate the *harem* of Solomon, he wishes to counterpose the uniqueness of his woman.

[v. 8] "Sixty…, eighty…, without number". Commentators often seek an historical counterpart for these figures. But the numbers given in the OT for the *harem*s of Solomon and Rehoboam do not coincide with these (cf. *Tab. 55*).

---

[57] According to Horst (1981), p. 183, the literary genre of 6:8–9, as of 8:11–12, is the 'Prahllied' ('boasting song'). Given its insertion in 6:4–9, however, it forms an integral part of the *waṣf*, of which it expresses the dimension of admiration ('Bewunderungslied').

[58] Gerleman (1965), pp. 184–185.

Table 55

Song 6:8		*1 Kgs 11:3 (Solomon)*		*2 Chr 11:21 (Rehoboam)*	
queens	60	princesses	700	wives	18
concubines	80	concubines	300	concubines	60
maidens	without number	—		—	

The first designation 'queens' (*m*ᵉ*lākôt*) has no match either in 1 Kgs 11:3, where, with regard to Solomon's *harem*, 'princesses' (*śārôt*) are mentioned, or in 2 Chr 11:21, where wives (*nāšîm*) are spoken of. In the OT, the term *malkâ* is confined to foreign queens: the queen of Sheba (1 Kgs 10:1, 4, 10, 13) and Vashti (Esth 1:9, 11 etc.). The author probably intends with this term to allude to the official 'wives' of the king:[59] Solomon had a good seven hundred of them, Rehoboam, eighteen. Sixty, the number of the Song, is situated between the two. The second term *pilāgšîm*[60] is common to the three texts and signifies the 'concubines', the unofficial women of the king: the number of the Song (eighty), in this case also, is less than that of Solomon (three hundred) and greater than that of Rehoboam (sixty). The third quantity, the 'maidens' (*ʿălāmot*) is without parallel. The term has appeared already in the *Prologue* of the Song in 1:3. In the context of the *harem*, which is being spoken of here, the allusion is probably to the multitude of 'maidens (*neʿārôt*), virgin (and) beautiful' who, in the book of Esther, waited to be summoned by the king (cf. Esth 2:2, 3).[61] After having spent a night with him, they passed into the rank of the 'concubines' (cf. Esth 2:14) or that of 'queen' (cf. Esth 2:17).[62]

The author, then, substitutes freely for the data of a royal *harem* (given the symbolism of the Song, the allusion to Solomon seems evident), adapting them to his own poetics. From a rhythmical point of view, the three groups of women are necessary to keep the ternary

[59] Here the mythological interpretation sees an allusion to Ishtar, the 'queen', and to her priestesses. Cf. Wittekindt (1925), pp. 10–11. It seems more probable to me to see here a hint to Solomon, the 'king' in the language of the Song.

[60] The term is not Semitic. A derivation has been proposed from the Greek *pallax, pallakis*, Latin *pellex*, 'concubine' (cfr. *HALOT*, p. 929).

[61] So Ravasi (1992), p. 506.

[62] Keel (1994), p. 218, thinks rather of 'young girls at court' ('Hoffräulein'), the service staff, of which Ps 45:10 speaks: but in our case the connection is with the king, not with the queen.

rhythm of the strophe. From the theological point of view, a negative emphasis is apparent. In 1 Kgs 11:3, there is a very severe judgement on the foreign women who made up part of Solomon's *harem*: "His women perverted his heart". It does not seem accidental, therefore, that the national character of the woman is underlined (cf. v. 4 ['Tirzah', 'Jerusalem'], v. 5 ['Gilead'], v. 6 ['Rachel']). She is one, just as the God of Israel is one compared with the gods of the nations.[63]

As has been seen, the numbers "sixty... eighty... without number" do not conform to an historic concern. They are a stylistic device: that is, they express ascending numeration, something characteristic of Semitic poetry (cf., for the OT, Amos 1:3, 6, 9, 11, 13; Prov 30:15, 18, 21, 24, 29; Job 5:19).[64] Albright notes how the sequence 'six... eight' is anomalous. In Ugaritic literature, the sequence 'seven... eight' is common.[65] Job 5:19 has the other sequence: 'six... seven'. Anyway, these are cases with two contiguous numbers. The explanation for this anomaly, already advanced by Gordis[66] and Greenfield,[67] is to consider 'six' and 'eight' as multiples of 'three' and 'four' respectively. Now the sequence 'three... four' is traditional in the OT (cf. the examples cited above from Amos and Proverbs). This explanation fits well with our song where the first strophe was characterised by the number three, the second by the number four (cf., *supra*, *Tab. 52*). Now, in the third strophe, the two numbers are repeated together with conclusive character: their sum, one hundred and forty has a significance analogous to the 'without number' of v. 8c.[68]

[v. 9abc] To the three categories of women of the *harem* corresponds the triple affirmation of the uniqueness of the woman: "unique... the only one... the darling". It is the triumph of quality over quantity.[69] In

---

[63] The correspondence is often made in an allegorical sense, when the woman is identified with the chosen people and the other women with the nations (cf. Joüon [1909], p. 267; Robert – Tournay [1963], p. 238; Ricciotti [1928], p. 253). We distance ourselves from such an interpretation. However, the profound analogy that exists between monogamy and monolatry is undeniable: it leads to that 'sacral', 'theomorphic' estimation of love which we have pointed out many times.

[64] Thus Gordis (1974), p. 94, cf. also Ravasi (1992), p. 507.

[65] Albright (1963), p. 1.

[66] Gordis (1974), p. 94.

[67] Greenfield (1965), p. 257a.

[68] Cf. Lacocque (1998), p. 132.

[69] Cf. Ravasi (1992), p. 509: "It is the defeat of multiplicity by fulness, and the triumph of qualitative perfection over quantitative accumulation, and the victory of personality over possession".

love, it is not quantity that is at stake (the more women one has, the happier one is). The 'unique' is placed on a level higher than that of the 'many'. In the case of the 'many', there is, in fact, something of the commercial, able to be acquired with money (cf. 8:11–12); in the case of the 'unique', we have love, which belongs to another order. The text intends to be a protest in favour of monogamy in a world where polygamy was normal.[70] One can love only one person with all one's heart; by its nature, nuptial love is exclusive, admitting no rivals (cf. 8:6—"Jealousy [is] relentless as the grave"). We hinted above at the correspondence between monogamy and monolatry. In the Shema it is said: "YHWH is our God, YHWH *alone* (*'eḥād*). Therefore you shall love YHWH, your God, with *all* your heart" (Deut 6:4–5). 'Alone' goes together with 'all'. If, in Deuteronomy, we can perceive a transposition of the experience of human love to the relationship with God,[71] in the Song we have the opposite phenomenon: what Israel knows of its God is transferred to the relationship between man and woman.

"My dove, my perfect one". The binome is taken up again from 5:2 (to the comment on which we refer the reader).[72] First of all, we should note the repetition of the possessive: twice the man claims that the woman belongs to him ('my'), twice that she belongs to her mother ('of her mother', 'of the one who conceived her'). The juxtaposition of the two loving relationships is significant: they are the existential locus where uniqueness is experienced.

The dove is the animal of the goddess of love: the metaphor strengthens the sacral aura which shrouds the woman. In her, the man encounters Love in person.[73] The term *tammātî* ('my perfect one') expresses, on the one hand, the fullness, the totality of the love which the man encounters in his woman, as a result of which he has no need of other loves; on the other hand, it is a discrete allusion to the woman's chastity: she belongs to him alone. Chastity is understood as the exclusivity

[70] So too, rightly, Lys (1965), p. 241: "It is the freedom of monogamous love in a polygamous society"; Krinetzki (1981), p. 185: "This turns out to be clear: that polygamy is contrary to the nature of true love. On this point, the Song is more advanced than the legislation of its time".

[71] Lohfink comments in this sense on the formula of Deut 6:4: "As the God whom Israel loves, Yahweh is Israel's *only one* and *unique one* ('*Einziger* und *Einzigartiger*' in the German original)" (N. Lohfink, *'eḥād*, in *TDOT*, vol. I, p. 196).

[72] Cf., *supra*, p. 262.

[73] The woman is compared to a dove in 2:14 and 5:2. In 1:15; 4:1 and 5:12, it is the eyes that are compared to doves.

of mutual belonging.[74] Again we grasp the coherence of the whole: the affirmation is in counterpoint with the formula of mutual belonging with which the *New Songs of the Beloved Woman* terminated (6:3). The emphasis, it should be noted, is not placed on the institution of marriage, even if a hint at it has been registered in the motif of the veil (v. 7b): it is love in itself that is strictly monogamous.

So as to underline the superiority of quality over quantity, the man places the love of the mother for her daughter beside his own. The woman is 'unique' not only as far as the man is concerned but also to her mother. It is not necessary to think of an only daughter:[75] each child is unique to its mother. It is love which renders a person unique, irreplaceable.[76] This is said in expressive form in Prov 4:3—"When I was a son with my father, tender, the only one (*yāḥîd*) in the sight of my mother". In the Song, it has been noticed, the father never figures, but the mother is often mentioned, whether the woman's (1:6; 3:4; 8:1, 2) or the man's (3:11; 8:5).[77]

The Hebrew term *bārâ* can have two correlated semantic meanings: 'favourite, darling'[78] and 'pure, shining'. This second meaning is present in v. 10c and is strengthened by Ugaritic and Akkadian parallels;[79] but, in our case, the synonymy with 'only one' impels us in the direction of the first sense, which is also that understood unanimously by the versions.[80] As a biblical parallel one can cite the figure of Joseph in Gen 37:3–4. 'Darling' places a slightly different stress from that of 'unique'. If every child is its mother's 'only one', 'darling' implies that

---

[74] Thus Krinetzki (1981), p. 185: "(The poem) expresses [...] the strong tendency of every young man who is truly in love, to have the woman alone for himself".

[75] *Contra* Garbini (1992), p. 246.

[76] There come to mind the gospel parables of the lost sheep, the lost coin and the prodigal son (Luke 15). Keel (1994), p. 219, cites the parable of Nathan (2 Sam 12:1–4). The rich man had every kind of beast, the poor man had "only one little ewe lamb", which "was like a daughter to him" (v. 3): where the "little ewe lamb" stands for Bathsheba. Ravasi (1992), p. 508, recalls the case of Isaac (cf. Gen 22:2: "Your son, your only son [*yāḥîdkā*], whom you love"): but here it is a literal case of the *only* son.

[77] Cf., *supra*, p. 136.

[78] Cf. Gordis (1974), p. 94; Gerleman (1965), p. 184.

[79] Cf. V. Hamp, *bārar*, in *TDOT*, vol. II, pp. 309–310, who holds this significant also for Song 6:9. In the same sense, cf. Zatelli (1994), p. 153.

[80] LXX *eklektē*, Vg *electa*, Syriac *gby'*. So too the majority of modern commentators. Cf., for example, Robert – Tournay (1963), pp. 239–240. Garbini (1992), p. 247, reads the substantive 'daughter', as in Ps 2:12 and Prov 31:1: the parallel with Prov 4:3, where 'son' is synonymous with 'only one' (cf. also Gen 22:2), would support this translation. It seems to me, however, that 'darling' fits the context better.

there are other children and that this is the 'most loved'. With this adjective, the man places himself, in a certain sense, outside the exclusive relationship which unites him to the woman and seeks to give an objective character to his sentiment. It is not just he who has preferred her to other women; her mother too has preferred her to her other children:[81] there must be something extraordinary about her.

[v. 9de] The objectification of the amorous sentiment continues in the last two lines of the strophe. If the mother's judgement may be suspected of partiality, that of the other women of the *harem* may certainly not be: in fact, they are the woman's rivals. If even they praise her, that means that her beauty is incontestable; it is open to the eyes of all.[82]

The three categories of women that are listed correspond to those of v. 8: only the term *ʿălāmôt* ('maidens') is replaced by *bānôt* ('daughters'), perhaps by attraction to the reference to the 'mother' in v. 9bc.[83] It is natural that the lowest and youngest category be the first to praise (cf. Ps 45:15–16; Gen 30:13). In v. 8, the maidens occupy the last place, the daughters the first in v. 9de. For them, it is enough to 'see'[84] the woman to praise her. The 'queens and concubines' come after them: for them it is more difficult to recognise the superiority of another woman.[85] Here the role of the women is not so much that of competitors, as in v. 8, but that of allies in love. The 'maidens' (*ʿălāmôt*) perform a similar role in Song 1:2, 4, and the daughters (*bānôt*) of Jerusalem[86] or of Zion in 3:10–11. There they are invited to admire the man, here, the woman.

The activity of praise is expressed by means of two verbs: *ʾšr* in *piʿel* form ('to call blessed') and *hālal* ('to praise'). The first verb finds a singular parallel in the birth of Asher (*ʾāšēr*, 'happy'). His mother, Leah, named him thus because "the daughters will call me blessed" (Gen 30:13). The second is rarely used in a profane context. In Gen 12:15 it

---

[81] Also in this sense, Esther is loved by Ahasuerus 'more than all the other women' (Esth 2:17), and Judith is blessed 'above all women on earth' (Jud 13:18 cf. Luke 1:42).

[82] In this sense, it is reasonable to consider the strophe as a 'boasting song' ('Prahllied', cf., *supra*, n. 57). In it, there is something of the excessive and the provocative.

[83] Also in Gen 30:13, it is the 'daughters' who call Leah 'blessed' (*ʾiššᵉrûnî bānôt*).

[84] However, the verb 'to see' refers, clearly, not only to the daughters, but also to the other categories of women (cf. the conjunction before 'praised her').

[85] Cf. Keel (1994), pp. 219–220.

[86] Also for 6:9, Siegfried (1898), p. 117, conjectures 'daughters of Jerusalem', but that is contrary to the parallelism with v. 8.

refers to the 'praises' which Pharaoh's official heap on Sara (*wayyirʾû ʾotâ... wayhalᵉlû ʾōtâ*): here too there is a comparison between the many foreign women (the *harem* of the Pharaoh) and the unique Hebrew woman. In Prov 31:28, at the end of the praise of the 'virtuous woman', the two verbs are used together: "Her children rise up and call her blessed (*wayʾaššᵉrûhā*); her husband also, and he praises her (*wayhalᵉlâ*)".[87]

But the verb *hālal* is a technical term for liturgical praise: it resounds very frequently in the Psalms where the expression *halᵉlûyâ* constitutes a *ritornello*. Here too, it is impossible not to seize on a link between the praise of the woman and that of YHWH, all the more since the expression *wayhalᵉlûhā* is very close phonetically to *halᵉlûyâ*. The praise of the woman, therefore, has a liturgical, sacral[88] tone which will be confirmed in the following verse where the woman will be exalted with divine prerogatives.

The discourse of the beloved man terminates at v. 9. The compositional unit of vv. 4–9[89] finds an interesting counterpart in the first stanza of the love songs of Papyrus Chester Beatty 1A. At the centre of the stanza, there is a *waṣf*, a description of the individual parts of the woman's body,[90] that corresponds to Song 6:5–7. This description is framed by two 'global impressions' of the woman which have an undoubted likeness to the first and third strophes of our song. The stanza begins thus:

> One alone is (my sister), having no peer:
> more gracious than all other women.
> Behold her, like Sotis rising
> at the beginning of a good year.

On the one hand, the uniqueness of the woman is stressed as in Song 6:9; on the other hand, she is compared to a star as in Song 6:10. The star to which reference is being made is Sotis (Sirius) the appearance of which signifies the beginning of the year. The end of the stanza goes:

[87] The parallel between our passage and these two is all the more significant in that the use of the *w* conversive is very rare in the Song (only in 6:9de and in 2:17). Another grammatical peculiarity is that all three verbs, in Song 6:9de, are masculine while the subject is feminine. But this phenomenon is not rare in the Song.

[88] In this sense, cf. Mulder (1992), p. 109; Lacocque (1998), p. 134 and n. 15; H. Ringgren, *hll*, in *TDOT*, vol. III, pp. 405–406.

[89] Cf., *supra*, *Tab. 51*.

[90] Cf., *supra*, p. 173, n. 21.

She makes the heads of all (the) men
turn about when seeing her.
Fortunate is whoever embraces her—
he is like the foremost of lovers.
Her coming forth appears
like (that of) her (yonder)—the (Unique) One.[91]

The word 'one' functions as *inclusio* for the stanza. As in Song 6:4–9, here too the conclusion is choral: the man is not alone in feeling himself attracted by his woman: she fascinates all the men. The feminine chorus of the Song is replaced by a masculine one, but the principle is analogous. We should note, finally, the theomorphic character of the woman. She is identified with Hathor, the goddess of love ('the [Unique] One'). The star Sotis was also considered a divinity.[92]

Second part: Admiration (6:10)

Verse 10 is placed between two discourses of the beloved man (vv. 4–9 and 11–12) and functions as bridge between them. It is connected with what precedes it both by the fact that the subject speaking is introduced in v. 9 and by the repetition of the expression "terrible as a host drawn up for battle" from v. 4 and the term *bārâ* ('darling, bright') from v. 9. The link with what follows is still more marked: in fact, the two binomes fair-terrible and nature-city characterise both v. 10 and vv. 11–12 (cf., *supra*, *Tab. 51*).

[v. 10] "Who is this…?" We have alluded to the parallelism with 3:6 (and 8:5). The comparison has a relevance that is not only structural but also semantic. In 3:6, in fact, mention is made of an apparition wrapped in a supernatural aura both from the fact that it takes place 'in the desert', a numinous place,[93] and from the fact that the 'pillar of

[91] Papyrus Chester Beatty IA 1:1–2 and 6–8, tr. Fox (1985), p. 52. The parallel is observed by Gerleman (1965), p. 186; Niccacci (1981), p. 70; White (1978), pp. 152–153. What is said here of the woman, is said of the man, in the sixth stanza of the same poem, with a 'mirroring effect' similar to that of the Song: "Love of him captures the heart / of all who stride upon the way—/ a precious youth without peer! / A brother excellent of character!" (4:1, tr. Fox [1985], p. 54).

[92] On the religious background of the songs of Papyrus Chester Beatty IA cf. Mathieu (1996), pp. 212–213, 240. According to Mathieu, the source of these songs is a hymn to the goddess Mut. Thus, the 'contamination' between poetry and theology that is characteristic of the Song has a parallel in Egypt.

[93] Cf. Müller (1992), pp. 112–113.

smoke' recalls the march of the Ark across the desert.[94] The theophanic character of the apparition is expressed in our case by the very fact that it is 'queens' who offer up the praise. Lys observes: "If even queens praise her, with whom can they compare her, who stands on a level higher than theirs, if not to a goddess?"[95] Until now, the metaphors have been taken either from city life or from nature, at any rate from the earthly world. The comparisons with heavenly phenomena, in v. 10, leads us on to a supernatural level. The 'many' remain on the earth; the 'unique one' surpasses the earth because in her divinity is present. The divinisation of the woman corresponds to that of the man in the *waṣf* of 5:10–16. Both representations are naturally to be understood within the ambit of the Yahwistic religion, in the sense of the 'image of God' of Gen 1:26.[96]

"Who looks down". The Hebrew verb *šāqap* probably derives from *šeqep*, the 'frame' of a window or door, and has the basic significance of 'showing oneself (at the window)'.[97] The semantic passage from 'showing oneself' to 'looking down' is comprehensible without having recurrence to a second meaning of the verb. The one who 'looks down to see' is always in a higher position relative to the one who is being watched. The verb refers to mountain tops (Num 21:20; 23:28; 1 Sam 13:18), to queens who look down from the window of the palace (Judg 5:28; 2 Sam 6:16; 2 Kgs 9:30–31), above all to God himself who looks down from heaven (Ps 14:2; 85:12; 102:20; Deut 26:15; Lam 3:50).[98] The LXX (*hē ekkyptousa*) and the Vetus Latina (*quae prospicit*) accentuate the theophanic dimension in so far as the two verbs make one think of *Aphroditē parakyptousa* and *Venus prospiciens* respectively, a very frequent representation of the goddess of love who appears at the window.[99] The motif has already been mentioned in connection with Song 2:14 and 4:8 (*šûr*).[100]

---

[94] Cf., *supra*, p. 147.

[95] Lys (1968), p. 243.

[96] This aspect is rightly underlined by Müller (1988a), p. 112: "The lyrical reproduction of representations that were originally mythical and of their iconographic equivalents leads, precisely here, to a fleeting 'theomorphisation' of the person who is the object of erotic admiration, which takes shape by means of the emphasis of the literary discourse and immediately vanishes".

[97] Cf. H.-P. Mathys, *šqp*, in *TDOT*, vol. XV, p. 462; Garbini (1992), p. 247; Müller (1992), pp. 113–117.

[98] Cf. Keel (1984b), p. 48.

[99] Cf. *ANEP*, Figure 131, p. 39.

[100] Cf., *supra*, p. 116, and 199.

"Like the dawn". The coherence of this temporal indication with that of 5:2 ('night') was noted above. 'Night' characterised the search of the woman: now that the two meet, it is day, the dawn breaks.[101] The term *šāḥar* designates the first light of morning (cf. Gen 19:15; 32:25, 27) which 'rises' in the East and colours the peaks of the mountains with its warm tones (cf. Joel 2:2; Job 38:12–15).[102] Here too, we have a term full of mythological reminiscences. At Ugarit, *šāḥaru* and *šalimu* are the gods of the twilight of morning and evening, identified in their turn with the related stars. In Mesopotamia, the morning star is Inanna-Ishtar (with us too, the memory has remained: Venus!).[103] Of the fact that the dawn and its star were considered as a divinity traces are found even in the OT:[104] here there is mention of the 'eyelashes' and the 'wings' of the dawn (Job 3:9; 41:10; Ps 139:9). It has to be 'awakened' as a person who sleeps (Ps 57:9; 108:3). In Isa 14:12, the king of Babylon is compared to Helel (Lucifer) the morning star, 'the son of the dawn (*šāḥar*)'.[105]

After the dawn are named the two 'great lights' (cf. Gen 1:16). The moon and the sun were also divinities in the surrounding world. The

[101] The passage from the 'night' of 5:2–6:3 to the 'dawn' of 6:10 is noted by Lys (1968), p. 242 ("In the night in which the heroine seeks her fiancé [...], she appears like the Dawn"). Note that the term *šḥr* is polysemic. It indicates the colour black (cf. 1:5; 5:11) and the dawn (6:10), but it is also the verb with which the amorous search is indicated in Prov 7:15, a text particularly close to Song 5:6–8 (cf. Salvaneschi [1982], pp. 46–48, 51–52). It is possible that these meanings are etymologically connected (cf. Ravasi [1992], p. 511, who thinks of a contrast between the 'dark' of the dawn and the 'white' of the moon), but it is not certain (*TDOT* refers the three meanings to three different roots, cf. vol. XIV, pp. 570–582; so too *HALOT*, pp. 1465–1469). The subtle play of references in the Song seems more probable to me.

[102] Cf. L. Ruppert, *šaḥar/mišḥar*, in *TDOT*, vol. XIV, pp. 576–577. In fact, it is not completely clear which aspect of the 'dawn' is indicated by *šāḥar*. LXX has *orthros*; Vetus Latina *diluculum* (the morning twilight), Vg reads *aurora* (the reddish light before dawn). *THAT* goes for the morning twilight ('Morgendämmerung', cf. T. Hartmann, *šemeš*, in *THAT*, vol. II, coll. 990–992: the English version [*TLOT*] is not clear); so also *HALOT* ('grayness of the morning/morning twilight', p. 1467). *TDOT* goes for the reddish glow that precedes the dawn (cf. Ruppert's article cited above vol. XIV, p. 577), with the majority of the authors (cf. Robert – Tournay [1963], p. 241; Gesenius [1835–1853], 1391–1392; Koehler – Baumgartner [1958], 962). The Job and Joel parallels apparently confirm this identification.

[103] Cf. the Sumerian hymn to Inanna and Iddin-Dagan in the role of Tammuz: "To her who appears in the sky: 'Hail', I say; / to the Lady who appears in the sky: 'Hail', I say; / to the great Mistress of the sky, Inanna: 'Hail', I say. / To the pure torch who lights up the sky, / to the shining light, Inanna of the gleam of the day, / to the great Mistress of the sky, Inanna: 'Hail', I say" (cf. Castellino [1977], p. 148).

[104] Cf. Keel (1994), p. 220.

[105] Cf. McKay (1970).

attraction which the two stars exercised on ancient man is expressed in Job 31:26–27:

> If I have looked at the sun when it shone,
> or the moon moving in splendour,
> and my heart has been secretly enticed,
> and my mouth has kissed my hand;
> this also would be an iniquity (tr. *RSV*).[106]

Both the moon and the sun are not called by their own names in our text but with a periphrasis.[107] The moon is called *hallᵉbānâ* ('the white') with allusion to the full moon. The brightness of the full moon in the Oriental sky is particularly evocative, so much so that in Arab amorous literature it is common to compare the beloved woman, especially her face, with the full moon.[108] The fascination of this celestial phenomenon is expressed by the adjective 'fair' (*yāpâ*) which echoes v. 4. Probably the comparison with the moon (and even more with the sun) is intended to stress the superiority of the woman over other women in the sense of the famous fragment of Sappho:

> The stars hide away their shining
> from around the likely moon
> when in all her fullness she shines
> (over all) the earth.[109]

"Bright as the sun". For the sun as well, the usual name (*šemeš*) is not used but a periphrasis: *haḥammâ* ('the scorching'). Like the preceding *hallᵉbānâ*, this is a rare term. Apart from Ps 19:7, where the lexeme does not directly designate the sun but precisely 'its heat' (*ḥammātô*), and the disputed Job 30:28,[110] in the other two passages (Isa 24:23 and 30:26), the term is used in a pair with *hallᵉbānâ*, in the same order:

---

[106] For other OT evidence of the astral cult, cf. 2 Kgs 23:5; Ezek 8:16; 1 Sam 20:18, 24 (on the feast of the new moon).

[107] By analogy with the Genesis account, one could conceive of a demythologising intention. Cf. Lys (1968), p. 242; but then why has *šāḥar* kept his own name?

[108] Cf. Dalman (1901), pp. 111, 124, 212, 216, 219, 227, 234, 245, 247, 251–252, 261; Stephan (1922), pp. 217–218; Keel (1984a), p. 50; Robert – Tournay (1963), p. 408 ("Where are you going my guest / O full moon, your love has burned me"); Müller (2001b).

[109] Fragment 34 (= 4 Diehl) (tr. Campbell [1982–1993], vol. I, p. 83). The famous song for Arignota (96 [= 98 Diehl]) is similar: "Now she stands out among Lydian women like the rosy-fingered moon after sunset, surpassing all the stars, and its light spreads alike over the salt see and the flowery fields" (*ibid.*, p. 121).

[110] MT's 'not by the sun', *bᵉlōʾ ḥammâ*, is conjecturally emended in *BHS* to *bᵉlōʾ neḥāmâ*, 'without comfort' (so *NAS*, cfr. also *NJB*).

first 'the white' and then 'the scorching'. These are two late texts of Isaiah referring to the eschatological inauguration of the kingdom of YHWH. Is it possible that in our text also this eschatological element is present in the sense that the beauty of the woman reflects the beauty of the future kingdom of God ("when the Lord will bind up the hurt of his people and heal the wounds inflicted by his blows", Isa 30:26)? The reference to paradise, found frequently in the Song, would be confirmed in some measure by that to eschatology.[111] At bottom, both accounts, that of the origins and that of the end, are projections of an ideal world, unharmed, as it is in the plan of God.

The adjective *bārâ* which already appeared in v. 9c is associated with the sun. If the context in that verse required the translation 'darling', here the association with the burning heat of the sun makes us opt for the other possibility, 'bright, pure'. The term refers primarily to the brightness of the sun at midday and therefore to the 'radiance' of the physical beauty of the woman.[112] But a moral nuance is not absent:[113] it is in line with the praise of the beloved in v. 9a: *tammātî* ('my perfect one').

Verse 10d passes from the 'fair' to the 'terrible' (*ʾăyummâ*) aspect of love. On the other hand, this aspect has already been preannounced to a certain extent in the metaphor 'scorching'. In fact, the sun is so bright that you cannot look at it; it damages the sight. The same goes for the woman: her beauty is so splendid that it is overwhelming; it arouses fear. Between fair and terrible there is no contradiction but continuity. The excessively fair is terrible.

The expression *ʾăyummâ kannidgālôt* is repeated from v. 4 but requires, here, to be interpreted in its new context. It does not seem necessary to have recourse to the Akkadian *dagālu* ('to see') to reach

---

[111] According to Feuillet (1984), Song 6:10 would be the basis for Rev 12, where a sign appearing in heaven is mentioned: "a woman clothed with the sun, the moon under her feet and on her head a crown of twelve stars" (v. 1). Revelation is reading in an allegorical sense, identifying the woman clothed with the sun with the eschatological people of God; but the sense of the metaphor in the Song is the reverse. The woman carries in herself the splendour of the eschatological people of God.

[112] Cf. Sir 26:16: "Like the sun that rises in the height of the sky, so beautiful is a woman in the chosen room (*bdbyr bḥwr*)" (following the Hebrew text of Sirach, according to the edition of the Academy of the Hebrew Language and the Shrine of the Book, Jerusalem 1973).

[113] It is usual, in fact, in the OT. Cf. 2 Sam 22:21, 25; Ps 18:21, 25; 19:9; 24:4; 73:1; Job 11:4; 22:30.

a translation such as 'constellations' or 'mirages':[114] the significance of 'host drawn up for battle' remains. Only it assumes a different connotation. In fact, in the OT, the stars are often represented as a disciplined army, so much so that the triad "sun, moon and heavenly host (*ṣ^{e}bāʾ haššāmayîm*)" is a technical expression to indicate the idolatrous cult of the stars (cf., for example, Deut 17:3; Jer 8:2). The expression *YHWH ṣ^{e}bāʾôt* is itself also to be understood against this background even if a reference to the ideology of the holy war is not to be excluded.[115] Our passage presents the same oscillation between the two senses (cf. v. 4). It is interesting to note that the three heavenly phenomena evoked, moon, sun and stars, are each called by a circumlocution: 'the white', 'the scorching', 'the host drawn up'.

The comparison of the woman with celestial phenomena finds a significant parallel in Mesopotamia where Inanna-Ishtar is the 'lady of heaven'.[116] Also, in the cult of the 'queen of heaven', widespread in Israel, an Assyrian influence is detectable, although it is not clear whether the texts which speak of it (Jer 7:18; 44:17–19, 25) refer to Ishtar or to a local divinity (Ashera).[117] It is typical of Inanna-Ishtar to be simultaneously goddess of love and of war, that is, fair and terrible together. One of her characteristics is the numinous aureole (*melammu*), endowed with magic power, with which the goddess vanquishes her enemies.[118]

Discourse on the invincible strength of love is a fundamental theme of the Song. The small, defenceless girl, stripped and humiliated by the 'watchmen of the walls' is, nonetheless, strong as a 'host drawn up'.

---

[114] *Contra* Gordis (1974), p. 94, Rudolph and Gerleman (cf., *supra*, n. 42). Müller (1992), pp. 119–120, retains the two derivations ('army' and 'constellations') possible and sees in *nidgālôt* a term that is polysemic. He arrives at this conclusion because he holds 6:10 to be the original location of the expression *ʾăyummâ kannidgālôt*, deleting v. 4c as pointless. In 4c, in fact, the second interpretation does not find any support. We do not feel able to follow him in this dubious operation which overthrows the structure of the passage.

[115] Cf. H.-J. Zobel, *ṣ^{e}bāʾôt*, in *TDOT*, vol. XII, pp. 215–232.

[116] Cf. the hymn to Inanna and Iddin-Dagan cited *supra*, n. 103. The parallel is naturally highlighted by the mythological school, which sees in 6:10 a hymn that originally referred to Inanna: cf. Wittekindt (1925), pp. 9–10; Schmökel (1956), pp. 48–51. For an Egyptian parallel, cf. the passage mentioned *supra*, pp. 343–344.

[117] On this, cf. Keel - Uehlinger (1992), pp. 332–335, 386–390; Schroer (1987), pp. 273–281; Winter (1983), pp. 445–460.

[118] Cf. Keel (1994), Figures 124 and 125, p. 221. For a Christian parallel, cf. Rev 12: the woman wears a crown of twelve stars on her head, and a conflict is mentioned, one which the woman wins in the end, vanquishing her enemies.

She has the same overwhelming power of divine terror (*ʾăyummâ*). The fact is that in her is present that love which is "as strong as death" (Song 8:6c). Her victory, no less than the victory of the man in 2:4, is the victory of love. One can smile, as Hellenistic poetry often does, at being the victim of the power of love, a power which makes even the strongest men surrender (the theme of 'Mars and Venus'). But there is a more profound dimension to the theme, brought into light by the event of Jesus of Nazareth. The cross is, in fact, the victory of love over violence. The discourse of Jesus about non-violence is along the same lines as the Song even if on another level. There is a profound analogy between all the different forms of love.

Third part: Movement (6:11–12)

The unity of the two verses, 11 and 12, is not clear at first sight. Verse 11 is characterised by a vegetable, v. 12 by a military metaphor. No word is common to the two verses. It is no wonder that some authors think here of two independent fragments.[119] For the unity of the two verses, there speaks, first of all, the fact that they are written autobiographically, in the first person singular. In this, they are distinguished both from the preceding verse and from the following, both characterized by the direct discourse of the chorus. Who is speaking in vv. 11–12? For some authors it would be the woman in both verses,[120] or at least in v. 12.[121] This is also, apparently, the understanding of the LXX which inserts after v. 11d: "There I will give you my breasts", anticipating 7:13a. But the 'garden' in the Song is always used as a metaphor for the woman so that the only alternative here is that it is

[119] Cf., *supra*, p. 324, n. 23.

[120] So, for example, Robert – Tournay (1963), p. 448 (correcting what they have said on p. 244); Murphy (1990), p. 179 (Murphy advances the parallel with 7:13, noted also in LXX: but the undoubted resemblance between the two verses does not necessarily speak for the fact that they must be uttered by the same person: apart from anything else, in 7:13a–d, the woman speaks in the plural, including her beloved in the discourse; the verse is to be understood rather as a sort of riposte to the desire of the man); Pope (1977), pp. 579–591; Heinevetter (1988), p. 151; Garbini (1992), p. 248 (according to Garbini, in vv. 11–12 "we have a young girl who is recounting her mishap to the other women of the harem". Garbini entitles the passage 6:8–12: 'The Abducted Bride', with improbable, fantastic allusions to the doings of Cleopatra Selene); Gerleman (1965), p. 190; Lacocque (1998), p. 136.

[121] So, among others, Lys (1968), pp. 245–248; Elliott (1989), pp. 160–162; Keel (1994), pp. 225–226.

the man who is speaking, continuing the discourse of vv. 4–9.[122] He confirms what the woman had said in v. 2 ("My beloved has gone down into his garden"). From another point of view, despite appearances, vv. 11–12 are firmly bound together, which makes us include v. 12 also in the discourse of the man.

The contrast between the two verses can be referred to the tension which runs throughout the song, on the one hand between 'fair' and 'terrible', on the other, between 'nature' and 'city' (cf. *Tab. 51*). The logic that unites vv. 11 and 12 can be evinced by some clues. In v. 11 there begins a movement towards union, implied in the verb 'to go down' (v. 11a). This movement gains acceleration in v. 12 where chariots are mentioned. It continues also in 7:1 where the woman is described in the whirling movement of the dance. A similar progression towards union is implied by the passage from the theme of 'seeing' (*rāʾāh*, v. 11bc) to that of 'desire' (*nepeš*). Desire, in fact, is born from contemplation.

On the other hand, vv. 11–12 are linked to the preceding passage, especially v. 10. If the whole song, 6:4–12 is characterised by the two binomes fair-terrible and city-nature (something that is no longer the case for the following song, 7:1–11), verse 10 initiates a double alternation (a-b-a'-b'; cf., *supra, Tab. 51*) which forms a second series after that of vv. 4–9. Also from the rhythmic point of view, the quaternary rhythm which characterises v. 10 (dawn-moon-sun-host) returns in v. 11 (nuts-buds-vines-pomegranates): v. 12, as the conclusion, is outside this rhythm.

The theme of 'seeing', if it is connected with the *waṣf* of vv. 4–9 (cf. the verb *rāʾāh* in v. 9d), corresponds directly to the verb *šāqap* ('to show oneself, to look down') in v. 10. He sees the one who has shown herself/looked down. The military theme of the 'host drawn up' (v. 10; cf. v. 4) is prolonged in the term *mark^{e}bôt* ('chariots [of war]', v. 12b). Moreover, the verb 'to go down' (*yārad*, v. 11a) forms a neat contrast with the heavenly images of v. 10: with v. 10 there begins a vertical movement that is continued in the following verse.

[6:11] On 'going down to the garden', we refer to the comment on 6:2.[123] The past of the verb (*yāradtî*) is to be taken seriously: it coincides

[122] This is the view of the majority of commentators. Cf., for all of them, Hamp (1907), pp. 207–208.

[123] Cf. pp. 308–310.

with the indication given by the woman to her friends in v. 2. He 'went down' then. 'To see' refers to what the man has just done in vv. 4–9: in fact, the term 'pomegranate' (*rimmôn*, v. 11d; cf. v. 7a) refers to the *waṣf*.

On the other hand, the 'going down into the garden' acquires, after v. 10, a new sense compared with v. 2. It is not only the material descent from the city to the valley. The comparison with the celestial bodies has raised the woman to a supernatural, heavenly level. Now the man 'goes down' to her: with that is implied a kind of incarnation of the divine.[124] The passage from heaven (v. 10) to the nut garden (v. 11) signifies that in this garden, in this simple young woman, heaven is present because love is present. In this passage one grasps well the simultaneously demythologising and theologising poetics of the Song.

The parallel with 7:13 was noted above.[125] This parallel is significant also for the fact that there the author places in comparison 'nature' and 'city', another fundamental theme of the Song which has a structural value in our passage (cf., *supra, Tab. 51*). The evoking of the women of the *harem* (v. 9) drew attention to the city. The 'going down to the garden' is also leaving the city, which is found in an elevated situation, and going to nature, in contact with the forces of life and love. The garden is not only a figure of the woman but also the place of love. Perhaps mythical reminiscences of sacred marriages on the virgin ground resonate here.[126] We have already alluded to them in the comment on 1:16–17.[127]

The 'nut' (*juglans regia*, Hebrew *ʾĕgôz*) is mentioned only here in the OT. Even if Josephus speaks of its presence in Galilee,[128] the nut has always been considered an exotic plant in Israel.[129] The fruit was held to be an aphrodisiac in antiquity, just like the pomegranate, prob-

---

[124] In Erfurt cathedral, there is a *bas-relief* of the Annunciation, in which the angel bears a scroll with the words: "I went down to the nut garden". This is allegorical interpretation indeed: but the text is open to such a reading.

[125] Cf. Murphy's comment, *supra*, n. 120.

[126] There are reminiscences, without one's being able to indicate a precise text. But, as Müller (1992), p. 70, says, they "give to the text background and depth, which are the principal components of its lyrical atmosphere".

[127] Cf. p. 81, and n. 157.

[128] *Bell* 3:10,8.

[129] Thus Keel (1994), pp. 222–223; Löw (1926–1934), vol. III, pp. 29–59; *contra* Zohary (1982), p. 64.

ably because of the shape which recalls the female organ.[130] Until the nineteenth century, in Afqa in Lebanon, one could visit a wood of imposing nut trees in the so-called 'Valley of Adonis'.[131] In the Hebrew tradition too, the nut and its fruit have an important place in the nuptial festivities.[132] One can say that this erotic dimension plays a role in the choice of the plant or, perhaps, as Keel suggests, the plant has been chosen for its exotic character;[133] at any rate, the 'garden' is the same one as that spoken of in 4:12–5:1 and 6:2.

The purpose of going down is not directly that of 'grazing' (*rāʿāh*), as the woman had announced in v. 2, but that of 'seeing' (*rāʾāh*). Graetz thinks of an error and has proposed reading *rāʿāh* here too.[134] But the time for 'grazing' has not yet been reached; it will come at the end of the composition (cf. 7:13—"there I will give you my love"). Now is the time for admiration and desire.

The 'contemplation' is expressed by means of the construction *rāʾāh bᵉ* which connotes a particular intensity of seeing ('to look with emotion', of joy or grief).[135] The object of 'seeing' is first of all the 'buds by the stream'. The Hebrew term *nāḥal* corresponds to the Arabic *wadi* and indicates a water course and the valley through which it flows.[136] For the greater part of the year, the stream is dry, but in spring, after the rains, it is the spot where the first greenery sprouts. The stream and the valley bottom are therefore particularly tied to the cycle of vegetation and the cult of fertility. In the Ugaritic myth 'Baal and Mot', the first sign of the resurrection of Baal is the fact that "the heavens rain oil and the rivers flow with honey".[137] The prophets Isaiah and Jeremiah

---

[130] Pliny, on the other hand, explains the noun *juglans* as 'Jove's testicles' (*Naturalis historia* 15:24, 91) and recalls that nuts were connected with the Fescennine songs on the occasion of nuptial feasts (*Naturalis historia* 15:24, 86).

[131] Naturally, Wittekindt and the mythological school hold this to be the true *Sitz im Leben* of the fragment. Cf. Wittekindt (1925), pp. 177–178.

[132] For this, we refer to Pope (1977), pp. 574–579, and to Löw (1926–1934), vol. III, pp. 35–59, but Löw rightly asks himself if, in their turn, these traditions may not have been influenced by our passage of the Song.

[133] Keel (1994), p. 223.

[134] Graetz (1871), p. 186.

[135] Cf. H.-F. Fuhs, *rāʾāh*, in *TDOT*, vol. XIII, p. 220 ("The sexual context, in which *rāʾâ* reaches its goal in *yādaʿ*, stands clearly in the foreground").

[136] Since, very rarely, the term also indicates the 'palm', some authors want to retain this meaning here: so, Rudolph (1962), p. 166; Gerleman (1965), p. 188; Müller (1992), p. 69. But I do not see any reason for abandoning the normal sense of the term.

[137] Cf. Del Olmo Lete (1981), p. 228 (*KTU* 1.6 III, 6–7, 12–13 [= *UT* 49 III, 6–7, 12–13]).

rebuke Israel for the cults which are performed 'in the valley', in honour of the divinities of fertility (cf. Isa 1:29; 57:5–6; Jer 2:23). The rebirth of life in spring is, moreover, a spectacle which always fascinates the human being: the metaphor is intended to be understood primarily in its literal sense.

What sprouts by the stream carries the name of *ʾēb*. The term appears again in the OT only at Job 8:12 where it indicates the buds of an aquatic plant. The sense of 'bud' is to be retained in our text also. In Akkadian, the term *inbu* has an erotic sense: it indicates, besides the 'bud', the 'fruit',[138] and connotes both the feminine attraction and the masculine sexual power.[139] But even without this correspondence, the image of 'buds' has already an erotic connotation within itself as was revealed in 4:13 ("Your shoots [*šᵉlāḥayik*] a paradise of pomegranates"). The topic is the signs of the sexual maturity of the young woman (with a discrete allusion to her pubic hairs).[140] The signs of the awakening of nature become metaphors for the 'awakening' of love in the young woman.

"If the vines had budded". Like the 'vineyard' (*kerem*, cf. 1:6; 2:15; 8:11, 12), so also the 'vine' (*gepen*, cf. Song 7:9; Ps 128:3) is an image of the woman. The verb *pāraḥ* indicates the 'budding', the reawakening of the life of a plant after winter. It is a question, then, of spring, as in Song 2:13, 15, with allusion to the 'spring of love'. Probably, with the image of the vine, the author intends to allude to the growing of breasts as an external sign of sexual maturity: in 7:9, in fact, the clusters of the vine (*gepen*) are symbols of the woman's breasts (cf. Ezek 16:7–8).[141]

"If the pomegranates had flowered". According to 4:13, the woman is a 'garden/paradise of pomegranates'. The pomegranate too is a symbol of the woman.[142] Since the pomegranate is an image of the female breasts in Oriental poetry,[143] we can perhaps understand here another

---

[138] The meaning of 'fruit' is present also in the biblical Aramaic *ʾănēb*, cf. Dan 4:11.

[139] For the documentation, we refer to n. 247, p. 223, and Pope (1977), pp. 582–583. In the Song also, the term 'fruit' has a connotation that is clearly erotic, cf. 2:3; 4:13; 7:14.

[140] Cf., *supra*, pp. 221–222, and Keel (1994), Figure 67, p. 117, and Figures 104–107, p. 175.

[141] Cf. Keel (1994), p. 223. The 'forming of the breasts' (*šādayim nākōnû*) and the 'growing of hair' (*śᵉʿārēk śimmēaḥ*) are given by Ezekiel as signs of the 'age for love' (cf. Ezek 16:7–8).

[142] Keel (1994), Figure 125, p. 221, confirms the link between the goddess of love and the pomegranate. On the metaphorical significance of the fruit, cf., *supra*, pp. 183–184.

[143] Cf. the passage from the Turin Papyrus cited in n. 73, p. 183.

allusion to this part of the body: also in 7:13, a passage parallel to ours, vine (*gepen*) and pomegranate (*rimmôn*) are evoked together. The conclusion of that verse ("There I shall give you my love") lets us see that, in both cases, the 'seeing' is a preparation for the relationship of love.

Perhaps this observing of the signs of the physical maturing of the woman is linked to the Semitic custom of betrothing two youngsters very early.[144] At any rate, here it reveals the respect which the two lovers have for each other. Love has its own seasons: to know how to recognise their signs is an art, one no less difficult than recognising the signs of the times in the history of salvation. The man thus makes up for the impatience he showed in 5:2–6. The woman cannot be forced; she must open herself from within. In 7:13–14, the woman herself offers her 'fruits' to her beloved.

[v. 12] According to the common judgement of the exegetes, v. 12 is the most difficult of the Song,[145] so much so that many authors, even recently, have abandoned the attempt to translate it.[146] In an earlier article, I proposed a new solution,[147] arising not so much from an examination of the verse in itself, as from its structural position: in my opinion, the difficulty in understanding the verse arises from a lack of consideration of its context.[148]

Verse 12 is the last verse of the compositional unit 6:4–12. It is uttered by the man.[149] As often in the Song, in the last verse we can expect a surprise-effect, that is, a sudden change, a riddle, which tends to leave the reader 'gob-smacked'![150]

The first stich of the verse (12a) is immediately problematic. The MT's *lō yādaʿtî napšî śāmatnî* is ambiguous. The term *napšî* can, in

[144] Cf. Keel (1994), p. 224.

[145] We cite Ravasi (1992), p. 524, for all: "Therefore, although translating the passage in some way, we affirm that the text as it stands is an unresolved puzzle perhaps never to be solved".

[146] So, for example, Krinetzki (1981), p. 188, who translates only: "[...] my heart has transformed me into..."; Heinevetter (1988), p. 162, who leaves the text completely blank; also Landy (1983), p. 333, n. 34; Falk (1982), p. 41.

[147] Cf. Barbiero (1997a). Three monographs have recently been dedicated to the passage: Tournay (1982) (cf. pp. 73–81: 'Les chariots d'Aminadab'); Mulder (1992); Lacocque (1995), cf. *id.* (1998), pp. 137–143.

[148] For a review of the different attempts at a solution, I refer to Ravasi (1992), pp. 520–523. Among the few who have tried to interpret the passage in its context, I cite Hamp (1957), pp. 207–208.

[149] Cf., *supra*, pp. 324–325, 350–351.

[150] Cf. 1:6, 8; 2:17; 3:10; 4:6; 6:2; 8:14 (cf. the observations made at pp. 308–309).

fact, be understood as the object of *yādaʿtî* ('I do not know my soul')[151] or as subject of *śāmatnî* ('my desire has placed me').[152] The accents of the Hebrew text favour the second translation[153] which, undoubtedly, makes more sense.[154]

The beginning of the verse *lō yādaʿtî*, therefore, expresses a surprise: "Without my knowing...". Salvaneschi observes:

> The verb *ydʿ* [...] or its synonyms sometimes occurs preceded by a negation or as second member of coordinate phrases to designate a state of passivity and amazement in the face of events neither understood nor foreseen: it is a syntactical stereotype that often occurs when the threat and power of Yahweh are described.[155]

In this sense, Salvaneschi cites Job 9:5, 11 (cf. also Isa 47:11; Ps 35:8). This 'state of passivity and amazement' before the terrifying action of YHWH is here experienced in the face of the power, it, too, terrible (*ʾăyummâ*, vv. 4, 10), of love.[156] Man is no longer the master of his own actions; he feels overwhelmed by a force that is greater than he. The parallel is suggestive and matches well the other theophoric allusions of the passage.

"My desire...". Here *nepeš* has less the sense of 'vital principle' and more that of 'longing, desire', which, according to Hebrew anthropology, is localised in the 'throat' (cf. in this sense 1:7; 3:1–4: *šeʾāhăbâ*

[151] This is the translation of Gerleman (1965), p. 190; Ricciotti (1928), p. 255; Nolli (1967), p. 127 ("I do not know my own soul, that is, I am outside myself"); Gordis (1974), p. 95; Lys (1968), p. 245 ("I did not know my own self"); S. M. Paul (1978); Lacocque (1995), p. 338. Job 9:21: *lōʾ ʾēdaʿ napšî* is cited in favour of this interpretation (cf. Salvaneschi [1982], p. 101). But this is a text that is equally ambiguous: here too *napšî* can be the object ("I do not know my soul", cf. *RWB*) or the subject of the verb ("I myself do not know it", cf. *CEI, FBJ*).

[152] So Ravasi (1992), p. 524 ("Without knowing it"); Keel (1994), p. 225; Mulder (1992), p. 110. Salvaneschi's position is interesting—she allows for both possibilities: the ambiguity would be deliberate. Cf. Salvaneschi (1982), p. 101.

[153] So too Vg (*nescivi, anima mea conturbavit me*). LXX *ouk egnō hē psychē mou: etheto me...*; Vetus Latina *Non cognovit anima mea, posuisti me...*; and the Syriac *lʾ ydʿt npšy smtny*, however, understand *napšî* as the subject of *ydʿ*.

[154] This already from a rhythmical point of view; without taking into account the fact that, by joining *napšî* with *yādaʿtî*, the other verb, *śāmatnî* would be left without a subject. Cf. Delitzsch (1875), p. 105.

[155] Salvaneschi (1982), p. 101. So too Müller (1992), p. 71 ("The whole phrase seems to want to express a surprise, but what?"), and Murphy (1990), p. 176.

[156] Catullus offers a parallel to this 'not knowing' in the face of love: "*Odi et amo, quare id faciam fortasse requiris. / Nescio, sed fieri sentio et excrucior*" (Carmina, 85).

napšî): the term is synonymous with *tešûqâ* ('yearning', 7:11).[157] The contemplation of the body of the woman (cf. the verb 'to see' in v. 11bc) has caused an irresistible desire to grow in him.

The expression that follows, *śāmatnî markᵉbôt*, is disputed. Since there is no preposition in front of *markᵉbôt* in the Hebrew text, the expression can be understood as a case of a double accusative: "My desire has made (transformed) me (into) chariots...".[158] However, one can also understand a preposition before *markᵉbôt* in the sense of an accusative of movement to a place ("My desire has set me on chariots...").[159] Perhaps the difference between the two translations is not so considerable: the second translation can be understood as a metaphor to indicate the content of the first. In both cases allusion is being made to a transformation which takes place in the man on account of his desire.[160]

The term *markᵉbôt* ('chariots, coaches') generally stands for 'chariots of war'.[161] We find ourselves, therefore, faced with a military metaphor which matches the others in the passage (cf. 4, 10: "Terrible as a host drawn up for battle"). The series will be prolonged in 7:1 ("dance of the two battlefields"). As in the other metaphors where the terrible aspect of the woman is set in relief (vv. 4c, 5, 10d), here too the power is not defensive but offensive: it is the force of love, personified in the woman by whom the man feels himself vanquished. To be rejected, therefore, are those interpretations which see in the *markᵉbôt* the 'chariot' suitable for the transport of the Ark (*ʿăgālâ*, 1 Sam 6:7, 8, 10, 11, 14; 2 Sam 6:3),[162] or even the *merkābâ*, the mobile throne

[157] Cf. Deut 12:15; Job 23:13; Ps 17:9; Prov 23:2; Isa 5:14. Cf. C. Westermann, *nepeš*, 'soul', in *TLOT*, vol. II, pp. 745–747; H. Seebaß, *nepeš*, in *TDOT*, vol. IX, pp. 505–508.

[158] Thus LXX *etheto me harmata*; Vetus Latina *posuisti me currus*; the Syriac *smtny mrkbtʾ* (a variant has *bmrkbtʾ*). Among the moderns, cf. Joüon (1909), p. 272 ("Mon désir a fait de moi un char"); Robert – Tournay (1963), p. 75 ("Il a fait de moi les chariots"); Ravasi (1992), pp. 524–525 ("He has made me like the chariots"); Murphy (1990), p. 176. For the discussion, *HOTTP*, vol. III, pp. 610–611.

[159] Cf. Joüon (1923), §125n, p. 372. Thus Origen's Quinta: *ethou me eis harmata*, and the majority of modern translations: cf., for example, Delitzsch (1875), p. 106; Robert – Tournay (1963), pp. 244–245 ("L'amour m'a jeté sur les chars").

[160] The aspect of 'transformation' is underlined, rightly, by Krinetzki (1981), p. 188.

[161] Cf. Exod 14:25; 15:4; Josh 11:6, 9; Judg 5:28; Isa 11:6, 9; 32:18; 66:15; Jer 4:13; Joel 2:5; Mic 5:9; Hab 3:8.

[162] In this sense, the allegorical tradition: cf., chiefly, Tournay (1982), pp. 75–76; but also, with a different emphasis, Lacocque (1998), pp. 337–338. In the case of *ʿăgālâ*

of YHWH according to later Jewish tradition.[163] The plural, *mark^e-bôt*, matches, phonetically and in content,[164] the other plural *nidgālôt* (literally 'bannered hosts'): the two terms function as an *inclusio* for the passage 6:4–12. In Song 1:9, the woman was compared to 'a mare among pharaoh's chariots (*rikbê*)'. Perhaps behind the two passages, there are the remains of a mythological tradition that associated the war horse with the goddess of love.[165]

With the last two words of the verse, *ʿammî* and *nādîb*, we reach the most controversial point and the one that is decisive for the interpretation. In the Hebrew text, the two words are linked by a *maqqep*. It would be possible to read them together, as the name of a person. But the name *ʿammînādîb* ('my people is noble') is not known elsewhere in the OT. The LXX, the Vetus Latina and the Vulgate read 'Amminadab',[166] a name well known in the OT[167] but one which has

---

in 1 Sam 6 and 2 Sam 6, we have only one chariot, moreover one pulled by oxen, certainly not a war chariot.

[163] Cf. Ezek 1 and 10: here, however, the term does not appear. But it appears on one occasion in reference to Ezekiel's vision in Sir 49:8 (the Hebrew text has *mrkbh*, the Greek *harma*). The allusion of *mark^ebôt* to the *merkābâ* of Ezekiel is upheld by Lacocque (1995), p. 339 (cf. *id.* [1998], p. 140), and by Mulder (1992), pp. 111–113.

[164] *mark^ebôt* could be regarded as a case of *pars pro toto*: the mention of the cavalry could be intended to evoke the entire army.

[165] Cf. *ANEP*, Figure 479, p. 165; Keel (1978), Figure 324a, p. 237. Another parallel frequently adopted (cf. Gerleman [1965], p. 191), is that of the chariot of Prince Mehi, of whom the Egyptian love songs speak. "On the way I found Mehi in his chariot, / together with the 'lovers'. / I cannot take myself away from him. / I should pass freely by him. [...] / My heart is foolish indeed! / Why would you stride freely by Mehi? / Look, if I pass before him, / I will tell him my swervings: / 'I belong to you'—I'll tell him—/ and he will boast of my name / and assign me to the chief (band of the) ensnared (?) / who accompany him" (Papyrus Chester Beatty IA, third stanza [2:5–9], tr. Fox [1985], p. 53). The figure of Mehi is controversial: for some, he is a kind of Cupid, who makes people fall in love, for others, a kind of rival in love, who hinders boys from getting near to girls. Cf., on the subject: Smither (1948); Donadoni (1986); Mathieu (1996), pp. 155–156. In any case, where Mehi is concerned, a single chariot is spoken of, not an army. Pope (1977), p. 591, advances the Mesopotamian parallel of the 'chariot of love', on which Ishtar invites Gilgamesh to mount (cf. *ANET*, pp. 83–84: the passage in question is *Gilgamesh* 6,10–12). But in our passage, war chariots are mentioned, not passenger ones.

[166] But the Syriac has *dʿmʾ dmṭyb*, 'of my noble people'; thus Aquila (*laou hekousiazomenou [archontos]*); Symmachus and Origen's Quinta (*laou hēgoumenou*); Theodotion (*laou mou hekousiazomenou*).

[167] Cf. Exod 6:23; Num 1:7; 2:3; 7:12, 17; 10:14; Ruth 4:19–20; 1 Chr 2:10; 6:7; 15:10, 11. Recently, Müller (1996) has suggested the identification of Amminadab with the name of an Ammonite king, which appears in the inscription of Tell Siran. But evidence is lacking that this personage was known in Hellenistic Israel, so that the correspondence remains highly hypothetical.

no relevance to the Song. Tournay suggests reading 'Abinadab'.[168] Abinadab is the man at whose house the Ark of the Covenant stopped before being transported to Jerusalem (1 Sam 7:1; 2 Sam 6:3, 4; 1 Chr 13:2). The 'chariot of Abinadab' would, then, be the one that transported the Ark.

It can perhaps be allowed that this is the interpretation of the LXX and the Vulgate, but it is much more difficult to accept that this is what the MT intended. In the first place, in fact, *ʾabînādāb* is too far graphically from the MT's *ʿammî nādîb* to think of an error of transcription; then the two words are written separately in the Hebrew text (so also in the Syriac version, in those of Aquila, Symmachus and Theodotion, and in the Quinta of Origen),[169] while proper names are written without any kind of separation. The Hebrew text has, therefore, understood the two words not as a proper name of a person but as two nouns connected with each other.[170] That is confirmed by the fact the term *nādîb* is taken up again in 7:2 where the Shulamite is called *bat nādîb* (here too the two words are united by a *maqqep*): 'daughter of a noble one'.

Even the two terms *ʿammî nādîb* taken by themselves are not without difficulty. *ʿām*, in fact, can have a collective significance (the usual sense of the term: people) or an individual one (relation). Correlatively, *nādîb* can be understood as an adjective ('noble') or a noun ('prince'). This second sense agrees better with the individual interpretation which goes: "(The chariots) of my relation, a prince".[171] But in the song 6:4–12, there has not been any hint of the man's family until now. Such a motif, at the conclusion of the passage, would be totally out of context. On the other hand, the composition is pervaded by

[168] Tournay (1982), pp. 73–81, following the suggestion of Buzy (1951), p. 346. Cf., also, Lacocque (1998), p. 138.

[169] They are joined by a *maqqep*, but this sign joins two different words, never the two parts of a name. Moreover, we should note that in some manuscripts the *maqqep* is lacking.

[170] So too Garbini (1992), p. 249; Delitzsch (1875), p. 106; Joüon (1909), pp. 272–273.

[171] In fact, this is the understanding of Garbini (1992), 249–251: "the chariot of the Benefactor, my relation". The translating of *nādîb* as 'Benefactor' is, frankly, forced, and is to be understood against the background of the fantastic identification of the woman with Cleopatra Selene, daughter of Ptolemy VIII Euergetes. As for the individual interpretation of the term *ʿām*, Garbini would be justified in citing the parallel of 7:2 ('daughter of a noble'), if it were the woman speaking in 6:12. However, in our opinion, it is the man who is speaking here.

a subtle national pride. This is expressed right at the beginning with the mention of the two capitals of the kingdom, Tirzah and Jerusalem (v. 4), and is confirmed with the mention of Gilead in v. 5 and of *rāḥēl* ('ewe mother [Rachel]') in v. 6. That now, at the conclusion of the passage, mention is made of a 'noble people' is perfectly in harmony with what precedes. This 'noble people' is, naturally, Israel. The expression *ʿammî*[172] *nādîb* without article is unusual. As Delitzsch stresses, to use an adjective in appositive position emphasises it (cf. Gen 37:2; Ps 143:10: Ezek 34:12).[173] The term *nādîb* generally designates the superior and ruling class.[174] With reference to a people, it exalts its superiority in comparison with others. This national awareness, noted many times in the Song, is understood particularly well in a period like the Hellenistic when the cultural identity of Israel was threatened by the superior Greek culture. For Sirach, wisdom dwells *en laō dedoxasmenō* (Sir 24:12): for the author of the Song, love is at home in a 'noble people'.

The 'chariots of my noble people' are, then, the war chariots of Israel. In the OT, these are spoken of above all in connection with Elijah and Elisha. In 2 Kgs 2:12, when Elijah is assumed into heaven, Elisha cries out after him: "My father, my father, the chariots of Israel and the horsemen thereof!"[175] The lexeme used here is *rekeb*, a collective term to indicate the entire body of the chariots of war (chariotry): the significance is identical to the *markebôt* of Song 6:12. The same expression is also employed by king Joash in his dealings with Elisha in 2 Kgs 13:14. Galling, in fact, claims that the title 'chariots of Israel and its horsemen' was originally attributed to Elisha and then transferred to Elijah. Indeed, in the stories of Elisha, there is word of the mysterious 'chariots and horses of fire' which fight on Israel's behalf (cf. 2 Kgs 6:16–17; 7:6). This is a heavenly, not an earthly host. This characteristic

[172] Understanding, naturally, the final *y* of *ʿammî* as a first person suffix ('*my* people'). It would also be possible to understand it as a *yod paragogicum* (Aquila, Symmachus and the Quinta have translated it this way, cf., *supra*, n. 166). Cf., in this sense, Joüon (1909), p. 273, following Rashi; Robert – Tournay (1963), pp. 245–246; Ravasi (1992), p. 526. But this interpretation is probably dictated by the allegorical understanding (bride = Israel).

[173] Delitzsch (1875), p. 106; cf. *GKC* §126h and 126z.

[174] Cf. J. Conrad, *ndb*, in *TDOT*, vol. IX, pp. 224–226.

[175] For this translation, cf. Galling (1956), p. 135. The German expression is: 'Kriegswagenkorps Israels und dessen Gespanne' (so too *HALOT*, p. 1234: 'Israel's war chariot corps and its horses'). The parallel with the two passages of 2 Kgs is noted in Lacocque (1995), p. 338, and Mulder (1992), p. 112.

matches well the celestial apparitions of Song 6:10 where the stars are evoked under the metaphor of a 'host drawn up'. Moreover, the term *ʾayummâ* ('terrible', Song 6:4, 10) is close, as has been noted,[176] to *ʾēmâ*, the divine terror which overcomes the enemies of Israel on the occasion of holy war. Now the holy war scenario is undoubtedly the background of the 'chariots of Israel' of Elijah and Elisha. The three verses 4, 10 and 12 are thus intimately linked and confirm the unity of the composition Song 6:4–12. The same numinous power, not only of an earthly (v. 4) but of the heavenly (v. 10) army and of Elijah's chariots of fire (v. 12) is personified by the woman. Lacoque thinks of a parody of the religious traditions of Israel:[177] the discourse of the Song is, however, serious. It is to be understood in the light of the book's confession of faith: "Love is strong as death [...], a flame of YHWH" (Song 8:6). The chariots of Israel are the chariots of love, and, therefore, the chariots of YHWH.

Despite the serious background, something playful, bound up with the surprise-effect, is perceptible. If we have understood aright, between the beginning and the end of the song 6:4–12 there takes place a development in the man who is in love, who is described as 'being conquered' by the supernatural power of love, a passing from contemplative stasis to 'movement' (even in our language one speaks of being 'transported by love'). The initial attitude of the man in the face of this attack was that of resistance. In v. 5, he prayed the woman to turn away her eyes from him. Now, finally, he lays down his arms; not only that: he himself mounts the chariots[178] of the army which is attacking him. It is 'his desire' that has completed in him this transformation without his knowing.

Desire (7:1–11)

The song 7:1–11 is subdivided into three parts, marked by change in the subjects. 7:1 (a) is a dialogue between the chorus (v. 1abd) and the man (v. 1c). 7:2–10a is a solo of the man. In 7:10b–11 (a') the woman follows on from her man, taking over his speech from him and

---

[176] Cf., *supra*, p. 330.
[177] Lacocque (1998), p. 142, n. 36.
[178] In fact, in 7:1, he himself will ask, together with the chorus, the woman to dance.

concluding with the refrain of mutual belonging. The man's solo is thus framed by two dialogues: the first with the chorus, the second with the woman. The *inclusio* between a and a' is signalled by the fact that at v. 1, the term 'Shulamite' is uttered twice, while in vv. 10b–11, the expression 'my beloved' (*dôdî*) occurs twice: the two terms appear only here in the unit. In its turn, the song of the beloved man, in vv. 2–10a, is composed of two strophes: the first (vv. 2–6: b) is a true and proper *waṣf*, a contemplative description of the woman's body; the second is characterised by the movement towards union (vv. 7–10a: b', cf. *Tab. 56*).

First part: Invitation to the dance (7:1)

The verse is structured as a lively dialogue. Unfortunately it is not clear who begins to speak and when. In v. 1ab, the subject is plural which makes one think of a chorus. Whether it is the female chorus which began to speak in 6:10[179] or a male chorus remains open. Perhaps the request to 'admire' the beauty of the woman is better understood if uttered by a group of men.[180] Who starts to speak in v. 1c? It could be the woman:[181] we would thus have an *inclusio* with the end of the song. But it is more suitable to think that it is the man, if it is the case that it is he again who is speaking in v. 2. The principal problem is v. 1d. The versions join it to v. 1c, assuming that we have here a single sentence. I prefer to look on it as the reply, on the part of the chorus,

Table 56

I	CHORUS	a. 7:1	invitation to the dance	Shulamite (2x)
II	MAN	b. 7:2–6	description	*mâ—jph* (v. 2)
		b'. 7:7–10a	movement	*mâ—jph* (v. 7)
III	WOMAN	a'. 7:10b–11	agreement	*dôdî* (2x)

179 Thus, for example, Delitzsch (1875), p. 107; Graetz (1871), p. 188; Heinevetter (1988), p. 151; Colombo (1975), p. 116; Garbini (1992), p. 253.

180 Since in 5:2–6:3 the song of the woman had entered into dialogue with the female chorus of the 'daughters of Jerusalem', it seems logical to maintain that the song of the man is in dialogue with the male chorus of 'companions' (cf. 1:7–8, 9–11; 8:13). Lacocque (1998), p. 148, thinks that the 'two battlefields' represent the two groups, the female one of the daughters of Jerusalem and the male one of the shepherds.

181 So, for example, Müller (1992), p. 75; Murphy (1990), p. 185; Gordis (1974), p. 68.

to the man's question in v. 1c.[182] We would, thus have the double alternation: chorus (v. 1ab)—man (v. 1c)—chorus (v. 1d)—man (vv. 2–10a) (cf. *Tab. 50*).

The verse performs the function of bridge between the two songs of the beloved man. The link with 6:12 has already been presented.[183] That with vv. 2–10a leaps to the attention:[184] the theme of 'admiring' (v. 1cd) introduces the *waṣf* of vv. 2–6, which represents the woman in the movement of the dance, as had been requested by the chorus (v. 1d). The beginning of the man's question, *mâ* ('what', v. 1c), is taken up again at the beginning of the *waṣf*: *mâ yāpû* ('how fair', v. 2a).

[7:1] The request of the chorus in v. 1ab is constructed elegantly both from the rhythmic and the sonorous points of view. To be noted is the alliteration of the sounds *š*, *u* and *i*: *šûbî šûbî haššūlammît, šûbî šûbî wᵉneḥĕzeh bāk*. From the rhythmic point of view, the two stichs are structured according to that staircase parallelism which we came across in 4:8:[185] the second stich takes up the first hemistich of the preceding one and prolongs it with a new element (cf. *Tab. 57*). A similar construction is found in the Song of Deborah: *ʿûrî ʿûrî dᵉbôrâ ʿûrî ûrî dabbᵉrî šîr* (Judg 5:12). We shall be returning to this parallel.

The sense of the Hebrew *šûbî* is contested. The ancient versions have understood it in the sense of to 'return', that is of a linear movement towards the point from which one has gone away,[186] and so too many modern commentators.[187] But from the context it does not appear that

Table 57

v. 1a	*Turn round, turn round,*	*O Shulamite,*	
v. 1b	*turn round, turn round:*		*we want to admire you.*

[182] Cf., *infra*, pp. 365–366.
[183] Cf. p. 323.
[184] Cf. Ravasi (1992), p. 528, which entitles 7:1 'Opening Intermezzo of the second song'.
[185] Cf., *supra*, pp. 196–197.
[186] LXX *epistrephe*; Vetus Latina *convertere* (here probably we have the other meaning of *šwb*: 'to convert'); Vg *revertere*; Syriac *twby*.
[187] This translation is dear to the allegorical interpretation, cf. Joüon (1909), p. 274; Robert - Tournay (1963), pp. 248–249. But others too, who can certainly not be suspected of allegorism, translate in this way: cf. Keel (1994), p. 228; Salvaneschi (1982), p. 33; Lys (1968), pp. 249–250 (who thinks of an allusion to the myth of the return of Ishtar from the other world); Lacocque (1998), pp. 143–150, who, along the lines of the allegorical interpretation of Robert - Tournay, but with a different value, sees a correspondence with the passages of 2 Sam 6 ('return' of the Ark); Jer 31 ('return' from the Exile); Gen 32 ('return' of Jacob).

the woman has gone away. She is in front of her beloved who has described her beauty in the preceding *waṣf* (cf. 6:11—"I went down to the nut garden"). In Hebrew, the verb *šûb* can also have the meaning of 'to turn round' in a circular manner, like a wheel (cf. Prov 20:26).[188] It is a synonym of the more usual *sābab* with which it is sometimes placed in parallel (cf. Gen 42:24; 2 Sam 6:20 with 1 Chr 16:43).[189] The term *m*^{e}*ḥôlâ* in v. 1d (cf. below) also leads us to the circular movement of the dance. The rhythmic construction of the verb, repeated four times, makes one think of the clapping of the hands with which the spectators accompany the dancer's movement.

The woman is called 'Shulamite'. The Hebrew bears an article: *haššûlammît* ('the Shulamite'): this is not, therefore, the actual name of a person but an appellation. The term is a *hapaxlegomenon* of disputed significance. The solutions suggested are: 1) *šûlammît* is the feminine form of *š*^{e}*lōmōh* ('Solomon'). The same 'high burlesque' which characterizes the man also characterises his woman;[190] 2) *šûlammît* signifies 'inhabitant of Shunem'. The city of Shunem has, in fact, the Arab name of Sulem.[191] In the OT, there are, principally, two women who hail from this city. The first is the beautiful Abishag who 'warmed up' the elderly David (1 Kgs 1:1–4)[192] and was then demanded as wife by Adonijah (1 Kgs 2:17, 21–22). The second woman is bound up with the story of Elisha (2 Kgs 4:8–37; 8:1–6). This latter correspondence takes us back to the same *Sitz im Leben* of the 'chariots of Israel' of Song 6:12; 3) since Jerusalem is also called Salem, *šûlammît* means 'inhabitant of Jerusalem';[193] 4) the term is the Hebraicising of the Assyrian *šulmānītu*, epithet of Ishtar in Jerusalem. Typical of Ishtar is the warlike character with which the dance is associated. Ishtar is called: 'The one whose dance is the battle', and she is the protectress of 'those who dance in the battle';[194] 5) *šûlammît* derives from the root

---

[188] Cf. H.-J. Fabry, *šûb*, in *TDOT*, vol. XIV, pp. 475, 478.

[189] The emendation of *šûbî* into *sōbbî*, proposed by Rudolph (1962), p. 168, among others, is, therefore, superfluous.

[190] Cf. Rowley (1939); Shea (1980), p. 392.

[191] Thus Gordis (1974), p. 68. Codex Vaticanus of LXX reads *soumaneitis*, as in 1 and 2 Kgs. In this sense, cf. Delitzsch (1875), p. 107; Robert - Tournay (1963), pp. 249–250.

[192] This parallel is particularly emphasised by Lacocque (1998), pp. 144–146, according to whom the Shulamite of the Song would be the deliberate antithesis of Abishag in 1 Kgs 1–2.

[193] Cf. Segal (1962), p. 476.

[194] Citations in Lys (1968), p. 251. This interpretation is naturally characteristic of the mythological school: cf. Pope (1977), pp. 598–600; Wittekindt (1925), pp. 4–8.

šlm ('perfection' and also 'peace').[195] The name would then indicate the 'pacified' woman. This interpretation is supported by the parallel 8:10 where the woman says of herself: "I have become in his eyes as one who has found peace (*kemôṣeʾēt šālôm*)". Perhaps none of these five explanations is to be excluded: the name is to be left in its polysemy, open to different associations.

The request of the chorus is for admiration of the Shulamite. The expression used, *ḥāzāh be*, is a synonym of *rāʾāh be* (v. 11bc), and constitutes a clear connection between the two passages. It indicates a 'looking' full of emotion (cf. Mic 4:11; Ps 27:4; Job 36:25). *ḥāzāh* is a specifically sacral term:[196] it is the technical word for prophetic vision (cf Isa 1:1; 2:1; 13:1), and has God as the object (Exod 24:11; Ps 63:3; 17:15; 11:7; 27:4; 46:9; Job 19:26–27; 36:25) or his works (Job 36:24–25); sometimes it even has God as the subject (cf. Ps 11:7; 17:2). It is not likely that such a word expresses a voyeuristic desire.[197] It is more probable that the author is deliberately transposing religious language to the contemplation of the woman's body. In the woman, something which corresponds to God himself and to his great works is being contemplated.

Verse 1c, then, is not to be understood as a reproof, but as the meeting with a good desire. The dialogic form confers vivacity on the verse.

Verse 1d is also problematic. The ancient versions[198] and the majority of modern commentators opt for linking it with v. 1c, understanding the initial *ke* as a comparative particle ('as') or correcting it with a *be* ('in').[199] But this is to force the text. Moreover, the question of v. 1c would thus remain without a reply: v. 2, in fact, makes no reference to it, even assuming, contrary to our belief, that here it is not the man who is speaking but that the discourse of the chorus is continuing. The solution seems to be to understand the *ke* as an asseverative form, an

[195] Aquila and Origen's Quinta actually have *eirēneuousa*. Cf., in this sense, Joüon (1909), pp. 274–275; Robert - Tournay (1963), p. 250.

[196] Cf. A. Jepsen, *ḥāzāh*, in *TDOT*, vol. IV, pp. 280–290.

[197] It is the term used by Keel (1994), p. 229, who claims that in v. 1ab we have the language of the barracks.

[198] Cf., *supra*, n. 11.

[199] Some Hebrew Mss. have precisely a *b* instead of the *k* (cf. *BHS*), so too Symmachus (*en trōsesin*). Numerous translators render in a pregnant sense: 'as in'. Cf. Robert - Tournay (1963), p. 252; Murphy (1990), p. 181; Keel (1994), p. 225.

unexceptionable grammatical use.[200] Verse 1d is thus the response, on the part of the chorus, to the question put by the man in v. 1c.[201]

The object of the admiration is supposed to be 'the dance of the two battlefields' (*m*ᵉ*ḥōlat hammaḥănāyim*). The term *m*ᵉ*ḥōlâ* derives from the root *ḥwl* which denotes the 'turning around', as happens in a dance.[202] The circular movement indicated here confirms the interpretation of the verb *šûb* (v. 1ab) given above: it will become a compositional principle in the *waṣf* that follows (cf. vv. 2c–4). The *m*ᵉ*ḥōlâ* was executed by women, often accompanied by musical instruments and sometimes by an antiphonal song with two choirs (cf. Exod 32:18–19; 1 Sam 21:12; 29:5).

Gruber draws attention to the link between the *m*ᵉ*ḥōlâ* and military victory.[203] In fact a *m*ᵉ*ḥōlâ* is spoken of after the crossing of the Reed Sea (Exod 15:20), after Jephtha's victory (Judg 11:34) and that of David (1 Sam 18:6–7; 21:12b; 29:5). This connection is suggested, in our text, by the term *maḥănāyim* ('two camps').[204] Perhaps the term alludes to the chorus of bystanders divided into two ranks (male and female?) between which the Shulamite is dancing. But the term *maḥănāyim* is not the only one to point to a military context: it corresponds to the 'host drawn up' of Song 6:4, 10 and the 'chariots of my noble people' of v. 6:12. In our interpretation, 6:12 concerns the victory of love described under a military metaphor. That the dance, as a celebration, follows on from the victory is perfectly logical.[205] The association

---

[200] In this sense, cf. Gordis (1974), p. 68 ('Indeed'); Gruber (1981), p. 343 ('Of course'). The possibility is allowed also by Lys (1968), p. 253. Cf. *HALOT*, p. 454, n. 5: 'seemingly superfluous, stressing, pleonastic'; *GKC* §118x; Joüon (1923), §133g (*k*ᵉ *veritatis*): citing Neh 7:2; Obad 11.

[201] Although retaining the comparative sense of *k*ᵉ, Delitzsch (1875), p. 108; Rudolph (1962), pp. 167–168; Lys (1968), p. 245, understand in this sense.

[202] Cf. *HALOT*, p. 569; Gruber (1981), pp. 341–345 ('perform a whirling dance').

[203] Gruber (1981), pp. 342–343.

[204] Mahanaim is also the name of a city, linked, above all, to the Jacob cycle (cf. Gen 32:2–3). The etymology of the name is linked here to the 'army' of angels which the patriarch met in that place while he was on his way back to Canaan. Certainly, one can find points of contact with our text (cf. the verb *šwb*), but the correspondence seems forced to me frankly (*contra* Lacocque [1998], p. 148; Lacocque links Mahanaim also with 'Abinadab', advancing 1 Kgs 4:14 [where, however, Achinadab is read!], cf. *ibid.*, p. 144). One could think of a form of dance typical of Mahanaim: but here too we would have an hypothesis that cannot be verified: there is no trace of such a dance. We prefer, therefore, to understand *maḥănāyim* as a common noun. This, moreover, is the reading of the ancient versions, which suppose a plural, in place of MT's dual: LXX *parembolōn*; Vetus Latina and Vg *castrorum*; Syriac *dmšryt'*.

[205] Wetzstein matches the dance of the Shulamite to the 'dance of the sword' in use among the peasants of Syria, a dance the bride performs on the evening of the first

dance-battle has, furthermore, a mythical background as was recalled above with regard to Ishtar.

The name of 'Shulamite' contrasts with this military context as, according to the etymology which 8:10 provides for it, it stands for the 'lady of peace'. The same contrast was noted above, in 6:4, where the name of 'Jerusalem', the 'city of peace', was juxtaposed with the image of the 'host drawn up'. It is the paradox of love that it throws a life into disorder, turns a quiet life upside down, disturbs that fragile equilibrium that one constructs for oneself and yet it is the only road by which to find 'peace', the satisfaction of the most profound desires.[206]

Second part: Song of the beloved man (7:2–10a)

The dialogue with the chorus introduces the new song of the beloved man (vv. 2–10a). Its parallelism with 6:4–9 has been noted above. In the preceding song, the dialogue with the chorus (6:10–12) marked the conclusion of the song; here (7:1) it signals the beginning: is it possible to discover a chiastic intention? The repetition, in v. 7a, of the two terms, *mâ* ('what/how') and *yph* ('fair'), which characterise the beginning of v. 2, signals a division of the song into two strophes, vv. 2–6 and vv. 7–10, which, also in content, present a thematic diversity.[207]

[7:2–6] First strophe: Contemplation. The *inclusio* between vv. 2 and 6 is marked by the fact that in v. 2b the woman is characterised as 'daughter of a noble one' (*bat nādîb*), while in v. 6 the man is called 'king' (*melek*). This double and complementary 'high burlesque' wraps the two lovers in an aristocratic aura.[208]

The literary genre of vv. 2–6 is the *waṣf*, the admiring description of the body of the two spouse-lovers, a literary genre already met with in 4:1–7 (the woman), in 5:10–16 (the man) and, just above, in 6:4–7 (the woman). In 4:1–7, the body of the woman is described from high to low; so too in 6:4–7. The first time, the description reaches the breasts; the second is limited to the head. Only the description of the man in

day of the wedding between two semicircles, one of men and one of women, in the light of the fire, and which constitutes the high point of the feast. Cf. Delitzsch (1875), p. 171. Moreover, the whole marriage feast has a 'military' character here: the amorous 'conquest' is celebrated as a military victory (cf., *supra*, p. 89, and n. 198). However, while in this case victory belongs to the groom, in Song 7:1 it belongs to the bride: it is she who 'makes her beloved surrender'.

[206] Cf., *supra*, p. 332.

[207] Cf., *supra*, p. 362, and *Tab. 56*.

[208] On the literary phenomenon of burlesque, cf., *supra*, pp. 14–15.

5:10–16 embraces the entire person, from head to foot. This happens in the last *waṣf* devoted to the woman, 7:2–6. However, in this one, by contrast with the preceding ones, the order is reversed: it starts from the feet and arrives at the head. The reason for this reversal is easy to apprehend: treating as it does of the description of a dancer, it is understandable that there is a particular spotlight on the feet.

In these two *waṣfs*, in 7:2–6 more explicitly still than in 5:10–16, the description alludes to the properly genital sphere. One has the impression that the woman is being described in her splendid nudity,[209] something which need not be marvelled at: the 'paradisial' character of the Song has frequently been mentioned. Before the Fall, man was not ashamed of his nudity (cf. Gen 2:25).[210]

Within the *inclusio* of vv. 2–6, ten parts of the body are listed as in 5:10–16. However, the list of parts in 7:2–6 is different from that in 5:10–16 and from the other *waṣfs* (cf. *Tab. 58*): it is notable that some

Table 58

4:1–7 (woman)	*5:10–16 (man)*	*6:4–7 (woman)*	*7:2–6 (woman)*
	1. Head		9. Head
			8. Nose
1. Eyes	3. Eyes	1. Eyes	7. Eyes
2. Hair	2. Curls	2. Hair	10. Hair
3. Teeth		3. Teeth	
4. Lips	5. Lips	4. Lips	(cf. 7:11)
5. Cheeks	4. Cheeks		
6. Neck			6. Neck
7. Breasts			5. Breasts
	6. Hands		
	7. Belly		4. Belly
			3. Umbelicus
	8. Legs		2. Thighs
	9. Appearance		(cf. 7:8)
	10. Palate		(cf. 7:10)
			1. Feet

[209] In 4:1–7 and in 6:4–7, the mention of the 'veil' and the fact that attention is focused on the face lessened the impression of nudity. In 7:2–6, the veil is not mentioned and attention is focused on the erotic parts. The only clothing mentioned are the 'sandals' (v. 2b). Again it is to be noted that the two are not alone: the 'chorus' is present (v. 1). On the utopian character of nudity in the Song, cf. Viviers (1999), pp. 618–619; Hunter (2000), pp. 121–122.

[210] Cf., *supra*, p. 299.

of the elements present in 5:10–16 and omitted in 7:2–6 are taken up again in 7:7–11, something that denotes the complementarity of the two strophes. Study of the structure of the preceding *waṣf* has shown that the parts of the body are not listed simply according to descending order but also according to other compositional principles. *Tab. 59* gathers some observations made from different points of view.

The first and last part described (feet and hair) form a pair by themselves: the 'high burlesque' concerns not only the terms 'daughter of a noble one' (v. 2b) and 'king' (v. 6c), but the entire description: the 'sandals' (v. 2b) and the 'purple' (v. 6b), respectively, confirm the aristocratic characterisation of the two members. While in the other descriptions the shape of the body is emphasised, here any talk of the shape is absent so as to bring forward, instead, the movement. This aspect, characteristic of the dance, is localised in the feet of the dancer, adorned with sandals, and in the hair which, with its undulating movement, is able to ensnare a king. It is possible that the aspect of movement also characterises the description of the breasts, in v. 4, at the conclusion of the first part of the *waṣf*.

By analogy with the preceding *waṣf*, where the elements were structured on the one hand by the binome fair-terrible and on the other by the type of metaphor drawn from nature or from city life, here too we can observe a contrast between the round shape which characterises parts II–V and the linear which is typical of parts VI–IX (with the

Table 59

Verse	*Member*	*Metaphor*	*Nat./Cult.*	*Form*	*Psych. Aspect*
2ab	I. Feet	(Sandals)	Culture	—	—
2cd	II. Thighs	Jewels	Culture	Round	Closeness
3ab	III. Navel	Cup	Culture	Round	Closeness
3cd	IV. Belly	Corn	Nature	Round	Closeness
4ab	V. Breasts	Fawns	Nature	Round	Closeness
5a	VI. Neck	Tower	Culture	Linear	Distance
5bc	VII. Eyes	Pools	Nature	—	—
5de	VIII. Nose	Tower	Culture	Linear	Distance
6a	IX. Head	Carmel	Nature	Linear	Distance
6bc	X. Hair	Purple	Culture	—	—

exception of the eyes).[211] That this is a compositional principle of the passage is confirmed by the fact that it too characterises the second strophe of the song, vv. 7–10a: here the linear element is expressed in the metaphor of the palm tree, the round element in that of the clusters and grapes. As Krinetzki stresses, the round shape is the archetypal symbol of the woman, not only for the external aspect of her body:

> The round form is [...] also psychologically characteristic of the 'global' way in which the woman perceives, thinks and desires, of her 'resting in herself', of her propensity to welcome and offer refuge, as also of the man's desire to 'enter' 'into' woman to 'rest' in her (like a baby).[212]

The thighs, the navel, the belly and the breasts, with their respective metaphors, are 'round' in shape. These are the tender, soft parts of the female body which express closeness and receptivity.[213] Parts VI–X are characterised instead by the 'linear' shape, that is by the straight line. Certainly a visual dimension is present here (the slender woman is a synonym of beauty: cf. the metaphor of the palm tree on which one must 'climb'), but the 'functional' dimension is prevalent. This is an important aspect for understanding the metaphors of vv. 5–6a which otherwise could appear grotesque (the nose is compared to a tower, the head to a mountain!).[214] In the tower metaphor, for example (v. 5ade), it is above all the inaccessibility, and, therefore, the pride of the woman which is being presented (cf. 4:4);[215] in the mountain, it is the imposing majesty. In other words, while parts II–V bring to attention the 'closeness' of the woman, parts VI–IX by contrast emphasise her 'distance', her aristocratic awareness of her station. The eyes constitute an exception, for their comparison, 'pools of Heshbon', does not fit in with the 'verticality' of the other metaphors. Perhaps 'distance' is being expressed here through the fact that Heshbon is located on the edges of the promised land, geographically distant from Jerusalem. Or perhaps the author wishes to set a different tone. In sum, the

---

[211] Cf. Elliott (1989), pp. 165–166. It was noted above that the 'round' aspect was introduced in v. 1 by the terms *šûbî* e *m*ᵉ*ḥōlâ*.

[212] Krinetzki (1970), p. 409.

[213] Garbini (1992), p. 104, also notes the difference between the first parts of the body and the others, but refers it to the aspect of 'fertility', an aspect that plays a secondary role in the Song.

[214] On the apparently parodying character of the metaphors in 7:2–6, cf. Segal (1962), p. 480 ("Only as playful banter can be rationally explained the grotesque description"); Pope (1977), p. 627; Soulen (1967), pp. 184–185; Brenner (1990); Black (2000).

[215] Cf., *supra*, pp. 184–185.

binome round-slender represents another of those paradoxes of love with which the poet is in the habit of structuring his poem.

As for the other binome, nature-art, the two extremes, feet and hair, are characterised by objects drawn from art ('sandals', v. 2b; 'purple', v. 6b). Parts II–V display a paired alternation (art ['jewels'] + art ['cup']; nature ['corn'] + nature ['fawns']), while parts VI–IX employ a single alternation (art ['tower of ivory'] + nature ['pool']; art ['tower of Lebanon'] + nature ['Carmel']). Within the *inclusio* between v. 2ab and v. 6bc, therefore, the remaining eight parts are divided into two groups of four: vv. 2c–4 (parts II–V) and vv. 5–6a (parts VI–IX).

Looking at it another way, parts I and X are hooked on to parts II and IX respectively. Only these four parts of the body, in fact, are designated with two terms (v. 2a: 'fair + feet'; v. 2c: 'curves + thighs'; v. 6a: 'head + above you'; v. 6b: 'hair + of your head').[216] All the other parts are designated by a single term ('your navel', v. 3a; 'your belly', v. 3c; 'your two breasts', v. 4a; 'your neck', v. 5a; 'your eyes', v. 5b; 'your nose', v. 5d). Not for nothing, in the division of the verses, the first and second part are united in v. 2, the ninth and tenth in v. 6. It is the phenomenon of 'attraction' or *enjambement*: we shall notice others in the study of the individual parts.

[v. 2ab] The woman's feet. The importance given to the feet corresponds to the fact that the woman is pictured while she is dancing. The term *paʿam*, in fact, indicates the 'feet', the 'step'[217] and, even the 'rhythm'. The link with the 'sandals' goes for retaining the first sense, but the two other connotations resonate in the background: it is the feet that move rhythmically and mark out charming figures of dance.[218] The use of sandals is uncommon: generally Jewish women went about barefoot,[219] and in Oriental iconography it is rare to see women with shoes.[220] Sandals were an object of luxury which would only have been permitted to the ladies of the aristocracy. According to Jud 16:9, Holofernes was seduced by Judith's sandals: so sandals conferred a particular fascination on a person, heightening the beauty of well formed feet. As Keel puts it, sandals "allow an authoritative way of

[216] Cf. Stadelmann (1992), p. 178.

[217] This is the understanding of LXX's *diabēmata*, Vetus Latina's and Vg's *gressus*.

[218] Among the Arabs of Palestine, there is a custom that the bride performs the parade dance wearing special clogs of wood inlaid with mother of pearl, cf. Dalman (1901), p. 257.

[219] Cf. Keel (1994), Figure 116, pp. 190–191.

[220] Cf. Keel (1997), Figure 115a, p. 246.

proceeding both in the literal and in the extended sense of the term",[221] so much so that the removal of the sandals signifies the renunciation of any juridical claim (cf. Deut 25:5–10; Ruth 4:7). Moreover, to walk barefoot is a sign of mourning (2 Sam 15:30) and submission (Isa 20:2–4), attitudes which do not become the aristocratic characterisation of the Shulamite.

The woman is called 'daughter of a noble one' (*bat nādîb*). Even today, among the Arabs of Palestine, it is the custom to call the bride with a similar appellation (*bint il ʾakbār*).[222] It corresponds, as we have noted, to the 'royal' characterisation of the man in v. 6c. The 'high burlesque' expresses the conviction that the true nobility of a person is given by his capacity to love:[223] it is love which makes the woman 'daughter of a noble one' and the man 'king'. Here, in our passage, another connotation is to be understood. The term *nādîb*, in fact, is a clear reference to 6:12b ('the chariots of my noble [*nādîb*] people').[224] Since the term there referred to Israel, it is logical to perceive a similar nationalistic emphasis here which fits in well with the numerous geographical indications of the land of Israel which characterise the passage (Heshbon, Bat Rabbîm, Lebanon [v. 5]; Carmel [v. 6]). In so far as she is a daughter of Israel, the woman is 'daughter of a noble one'. Love has its native country in the promised land.

[7:2c–4] The body. The four parts of the body that follow ('thighs, navel, belly and breasts') form a compositional subunit characterised by the theme of the roundness and the tenderness, the 'receptivity' which the female body offers. Beside the alternate structure a-a'-b-b' which characterises the type of metaphor (cf. *Tab. 59*), we can observe a chiastic structure which is transverse with respect to the preceding one (a-b-b'a'). In fact, the first and fourth part of the body are characterised by the dual form (two thighs, two breasts), the second and the third (navel, belly) by the singular. In this sense, the first part of

---

[221] Keel (1994), p. 231.

[222] Cf. Dalman (1901), p. 257; Stephan (1922), p. 219.

[223] The term *nādîb* indicates literally one who is 'generous, liberal in giving'. This is the connotation that distinguishes a 'noble' (cf. J. Conrad, *nādab*, in *TDOT*, vol. IX, p. 220).

[224] Having read *Ameinadab* in Song 6:12, LXX naturally reads here too *Nadab* (LXX^{B}) or *Aminadab* (LXX^{A}), so Vetus Latina *Aminadab*. The Syriac *mṭybʾ* and Vg *principis*, on the other hand, follow MT (so too Aquila *archontos*, or, following other Mss., *hekousiazomenou*; Symmachus *hēgemonos*).

the section (thighs) is connected with the part previously described (feet). The two central parts are linked by the binome drink-eat which characterises the two metaphors ('wine', v. 3b; 'corn', v. 3c).[225]

[v. 2cd] From the 'two feet' (*p^eāmayik*), attention is shifted to the 'two thighs' (*y^erēkayik*). The term indicates the upper part of the leg connected to the genital area (cf. Gen 24:2, 9; 47:29). The associated term *ḥammûqîm* is a *hapax* deriving from the verb *ḥāmaq* ('to turn') encountered in Song 5:6. Delitzsch thinks of the characteristic swaying of the dance,[226] but, as with the feet, the metaphor which follows leads us rather to consider the shape, a curve, even if there can be a connotation of circular movement. Be that as it may, there is semantic continuity between the verb *šûb* ('to turn') of v. 1ab, the *m^eḥōlâ* ('circular dance') of v. 1c and the 'curves' of the flanks.[227] To think, as the Vulgate does, of the 'joint' of the thighs is out of place because that is singular while the term here is plural:[228] it is quite clearly an allusion to the curves of the female buttocks. Round 'cheeks' form part of the Oriental idea of beauty,[229] but also that of the Greeks where Aphrodite was called *kallipygos* ('of the beautiful buttocks').[230] Lacoque points out the abrupt passage between the two expressions 'daughter of a noble one' and 'the curves of your thighs'. The second could make one think of a woman of easy habits. It is for this reason that the author takes pains to advise the reader: what follows is said not of a prostitute but of a 'daughter of a noble one'.[231] There is not a trace of vulgarity.

The thighs of the woman are compared to 'jewels'. The Hebrew term *ḥălî* appears again only in Prov 25:12 in parallel with *nezem* ('ring'),

---

[225] On the parallelism of 3ab with 3cd, cf. Joüon (1909), p. 281.

[226] Delitzsch (1875), p. 110. Similarly, Salvaneschi (1982), p. 33: 'The rhythms of your hips'.

[227] Cf. Lacocque (1998), p. 152.

[228] So too Ceronetti (1996), p. 39. Even if in the plural, Garbini's reading is similar: 'allacci' ('junctions'), understanding 'the lower part of the abdomen' (Garbini [1992], pp. 253–255).

[229] Cf. Rudolph (1962), p. 172.

[230] Cf. Keel (1994), Figure 76, p. 133.

[231] Lacocque (1998), p. 151. In this connection, Lacocque cites two texts: 2 Sam 6 and Jer 31. In the first, David dances before the Ark, uncovering himself before the daughters of Israel (2 Sam 6:14, 20). What is apparently an act of immorality is justified as 'making merry before the Lord' (v. 21). In Jer 31:22, Israel is reproved for 'roaming' (*ḥāmaq*) like a 'rebellious daughter' (*bat haššôbēbâ*), and the miracle of the eschatological times is foretold: "the woman encompasses, *t^esôbēb*, the man". The woman of the Song realises this miracle.

this parallel also being confirmed by the homonym *ḥelyâ* in Hos 2:15.[232] It is, therefore, a jewel of circular form, a ring or bracelet. The perfect curves of the jewel allow us to think of that masterpiece of beauty, the hips of a young woman. It is perfect craftsmanship that is being spoken of here: 'work of a craftsman'. The Hebrew term *ʾommān* ('craftsman') is another *hapax* which makes one think of the *ʾāmôn* of Prov 8:30. The subject there is creative Wisdom, and, moreover, it is to the works of the Creator that the expression 'works of his hands' often refers (cf., for example, Ps 8:7; 19:2 etc). It is being discreetly insinuated here, therefore, that the artist who has shaped the woman's hips is God. Yet, contrary to the opinion of Lacoque, there is no 'irony' in this identification:[233] rather the invitation to look at the human body with that same wondering glance, without malice, of Gen 2.

[v. 3] In v. 3, we pass from the dual to the singular, from the legs to the trunk of the body. The first term, *šorᵉrēk*, is disputed. The term occurs again in Ezek 16:4 and is lexically well attested in the sense of 'navel' or even 'umbilical cord'.[234] Such a part of the body seems out of place whether because the next part ('belly') is lower down or because the 'spiced wine' is an eloquent metaphor of the sexual relationship. For this reason, various authors translate with 'vulva'[235] or 'womb'.[236] But from the figurative point of view, Gerleman has produced significant parallels in Egyptian art in which the navel is always notably marked in such a way that the comparison with a cup fits like a glove.[237] Keel has put forward other examples from the figurative art of Syria and Mesopotamia.[238] In these last examples, the interchangeability between the navel and the womb[239] should be noted. Probably with the 'navel', the intention is to allude discreetly to the entire genital area, to which the metaphor of the wine is better suited.[240]

---

[232] Even if etymologically distinct, the term undoubtedly evokes the *mᵉḥōlâ* of v. 1.

[233] Lacocque (1998), p. 152. Landy (1983), pp. 258–259, draws attention to those passages where idols are called 'the work of men's hands', as if the author wished to express the ambivalence of human sexuality, standing between the good creation of God and the idol of man. But there is no trace of negativity in our text!

[234] Cf. *HALOT*, pp. 1650–1651.

[235] Cf. Pope (1977) p. 617; Ceronetti (1996), p. 39. Lys (1968), p. 258, translates: 'Ton sexe'.

[236] So Rudolph (1962), pp. 168–169, adducing the Arabic *sirr*, 'mystery' (= *pudendum mulieris*).

[237] Gerleman (1965), pp. 70, 197.

[238] Cf. Keel (1994), Figure 127, p. 232, and Figure 26, p. 72.

[239] Cf., in this sense, also Keel (1994), Figures 104–107, p. 175.

[240] Cf. Krinetzki (1981), p. 194.

The navel is compared to a 'rounded cup'. Here too the translation is controversial. *ʾaggān* is a rare term. It returns again only in Exod 24:6 where 'basins' of notable proportions are[241] indicated, and in Isa 22:24 where it is a question of 'small vessels'. The second sense offers a more probable parallel to the umbilical button,[242] but the first could be an hyperbole to indicate the enormous quantities of 'wine' which the 'navel' can contain. It is interesting to note how in Exod 24:6 we have the basins which contain the blood of the covenant: the lexeme is, thus, loaded with sacral significance. The term associated with it, *hassahar*,[243] is a *hapaxlegomenon*. The linguistic parallels lead us to think of something round like the (full) moon or like an enclosure wall.[244]

From the point of view of depth psychology, the feminine archetype of the 'vessel' is mentioned here.[245] Navel and vagina are complementary: both are bound up with procreation. This association is made clear in the next phrase: "May it never lack spiced wine". The Hebrew term *mezeg* is another *hapax*. It represents the Aramaic form of the Hebrew *māsak* ('to mix').[246] It can indicate the wine mixed with water, the typical drink of the Jews, but also 'resined wine', supplemented with aromatic and sweetening substances (cf. also Isa 5:22; 19:14); in Prov 9:2, 5, it is this wine that Lady Wisdom mixes for her guests.

The Song's usual metaphor for love is 'wine' (cf. 1:2; 2:4; 4:10; 5:1; 7:10). In particular, 'spiced wine' (*yayin hāreqaḥ*) is mentioned in 8:2. In the context of the navel-womb, the allusion to the pleasure which the woman knows how to give to her partner during sexual relations is clear. To go much further and to see in the resinated wine the male seed[247] or the 'love juice' given out by the vagina during sex,[248] seems to

---

[241] This is also the understanding of LXX's *kratēr*, followed by Vetus Latina and Vg. *HALOT*, p. 11: 'large and deep bowl'.

[242] Cf., in this sense, a passage from the *Arabian Nights*, referred to in Stephan (1922), p. 218, in which it is said of the beloved woman: "The navel may hold an ounce of oil, and is like the bottom of a tiny coffee cup".

[243] As in Song 5:13, the article here does not necessarily have determinative value (cf. *GKC* §127e).

[244] Cf. *HALOT*, p. 744; Joüon (1909), p. 283; Rudolph (1962), p. 169. This is also the translation of the versions: LXX *toreutos*; Vetus Latina and Vg *tornatilis*; Syriac *dkrykʾ*. Lys (1968), p. 259, and Robert – Tournay (1963), pp. 258–260, prefer the sense: 'at halfmoon'. The conjecture *ḥrwṣ*, 'chiselled, engraved, sculpted', proposed by Garbini (1992), pp. 255–256, shows itself to be unnecessary.

[245] Krinetzki (1970), p. 416.

[246] Cf. Garbini (1992), p. 256; *HALOT*, p. 564.

[247] Thus Haller (1940), p. 41.

[248] Cf. Pope (1977), p. 620.

me not to correspond to the style of the Song which uses a euphemism ('navel') to speak of the female organ.

In the description of the 'belly', compared to a heap of corn, visual and functional elements enter into play together. As Delitzsch says,

> still today, cereals, after having been winnowed and sifted are piled up in large heaps with a very regular hemispherical shape. These are often provided with objects which move in the wind to defend them from the birds.[249]

The convex shape of the heap of corn is antithetical to the concave shape of the cup, thus underlining the complementarity of the two metaphors. Perhaps not only the shape but also the colour plays a role. With the Arabs, in fact, the colour of corn is the ideal colour of a healthy complexion.[250] But more than these visual elements it is the significant function of the metaphor which is interesting. A heap of corn expresses fertility and divine blessing (cf. Gen 27:27–28). The element of fertility is underlined by the fact that the word which indicates the belly (*beṭen*) is the same one that indicates the maternal womb (cf. Judg 13:5, 7). Moreover, 'corn' is the principal food in Palestine: bread (v. 3c) and wine (v. 3b) are the fundamental elements of the Mediterranean diet (cf. Ps 104:15).[251] The aspect of 'eating', then, is evoked together with 'drinking', two activities which are metaphors of love (cf. Song 5:1).

Not very clear is the significance of what follows: "surrounded[252] with lotus flowers". From the visual point of view, allusion was made before to the objects placed on the heap of corn to fend off the birds. Others think of the hedges of thorns which were used to defend the corn from robbers.[253] Keel claims we have an ornamental motif frequent in Egyp-

---

[249] Delitzsch (1875), p. 112.

[250] According to the *Sunna*, this was the colour of the first man. Cf. Delitzsch (1875), p. 112. In Egyptian art too, yellow ochre is the ideal colour of the female complexion. Cf. Gerleman (1965), p. 70.

[251] Cf. Keel (1994), pp. 234–235. Grober (1984), p. 104, suggests a parallel with Euripides' *Bacchae* (vv. 274–280): "For, young man, there are two fundamental elements among mankind. The goddess Demeter—she is Earth, call her whichever of those names you will—she nurtures men with dry food. And the god who came next, the son of Semele, invented, to balance Demeter's gift, the liquid drink of the grape and introduced it to men" (tr. Morwood [1999], p. 52).

[252] The Hebrew *sûgâ* is another *hapax*. It is an Aramaism, whose meaning 'fenced' is well attested.

[253] Cf., for example, Keel (1994), p. 235 (citing Ruth 3:7). From the point of view of meaning, the *šôšannîm* are identified with the pubic hairs (Rudolph [1962], p. 172),

tian and Phoenician art.[254] However, Grober is right not to insist on the visual side of the metaphor.[255] It is unlikely that lotus flowers grow in a corn field, or among the thorns (cf. 2:1), just as it is improbable that a fawn feeds on such flowers (cf. 2:16; 4:5). The association has to be sought in the fact that corn and lotus can be 'eaten'.[256] "To graze on lotus flowers" is an expression indicating the experience of new life which the two partners enjoy in erotic play:[257] the 'lotus flowers' are, in fact, associated with the lips (5:13) and the breasts (4:5). To associate them now with the belly brings us to see this part of the body not only in its generative capacity but also in its erotic value as is typical of the Song. The belly, in fact, is "the seat of carnal affection, of sensuality as well as being the source of compassion and love".[258]

[v. 4] The description of the breasts in v. 4 is an almost literal repetition of 4:5,[259] but Garbini is mistaken in omitting it as a useless repetition.[260] The poetry of the Song lives off these repetitions. As usual, the repetition is not completely literal: here, Song 4:5c—"which graze among the lotus flowers"—is omitted. And one can understand the reason: the theme of the lotus flowers has already been evoked in connection with the belly (v. 3d). Belly and breasts are thus symbolically brought together: both are made of 'lotus flowers', good to smell, to eat and to drink.[261]

Belly and breasts are traditional symbols of fertility: in Gen 49:25, Joseph is blessed with "blessings of the breasts and of the womb". It has been seen that in the Song too the theme of fertility is not absent. Just as, in the description of the belly, this aspect was evoked in the metaphor of the heap of grain, so now it is present in the metaphor of the 'twins' which refers to Song 6:6 ("all have borne twins"). But

---

with the clothes (Delitzsch [1875], p. 112), or with an ornamental garland (Murphy [1990], p. 186).

[254] Cf. Keel (1994), Figures 129 and 130, p. 233.

[255] Grober (1984), pp. 102–104.

[256] In Song 2:2 ("like a lotus flower among the thorns") the two metaphors had a contrasting symbolic value; in the present case ("a heap of corn surrounded by lotus flowers"), they have the same sense: the second metaphor accentuates the meaning of the first, as in the juxtaposition of the gazelle and the lotus (2:16 e 4:5). Each time, the emphasis is placed more on the symbolic than on the visual aspect of the metaphor.

[257] Cf. pp. 122–123, and 190–191; Keel (1994), Figure 66, p. 116, and Figure 90, p. 149.

[258] Grober (1984), p. 104, citing A. De Vries, *Dictionary of symbols and imagery*, Amsterdam 1976, p. 45.

[259] Cf., for the comment, pp. 189–190.

[260] Cf. Garbini (1992), p. 105.

[261] Cf., *supra*, pp. 193–194, and n. 193.

it remains secondary: in the Song, love is seen first and foremost as a relationship between two lovers. Analogously to the kiss, the breasts are perceived in the first place, therefore, as an instrument of erotic play, communication of love through the language of the body (cf. 7:9).

In the comment on 4:5, the image of the 'two fawns' was pointed out not only in its symbolic but also in its visual aspect. One of the elements of this aspect is the mobility of the fawns-breasts, heightened by the fact that the woman is not wearing a brassiere and so her breasts are free. The 'movement' theme forms an *inclusio* with v. 2ab where the 'rhythm' of the dancing feet was evoked. The *inclusio* is confirmed by the fact of the duality, here underlined ("your *two* breasts like *two* fawns, *twins*..."), which joins v. 4 with 2.[262]

[7:5–6] The face. The description of the neck in v. 5a consists of a single stich. This has aroused the suspicions of the commentators who have proposed completing the verse by adding another stich ("founded on bases of precious stones", cf. *BHS*).[263] However, vv. 5–6a form a whole constructed in perfect parallelism (cf. *Tab. 60*). The monostich description of the neck (v. 5a) is in fact balanced by another monostich description, of the head (v. 6a).[264] The other two parts are each made up of two stichs: here the parallelism is clear, each stich being characterised by a geographic name (Heshbon, v. 5b; Bat Rabbim, v. 5c; Lebanon, v. 5d; Damascus, v. 5e).

The four parts, therefore, form a chiastic structure, transverse with respect to the alternating one, which is constituted by alternating the type of metaphor (nature-art).[265] Other transverse links unite v. 5a with v. 5d (tower) and v. 6a with v. 5b–e (the geographic name 'Carmel').

---

[262] Also phonetically *šādayik* matches *pᵉʿāmayik* (v. 2a) and *yᵉrēkayik* (v. 2c).

[263] Others suggest adding *bānûy lᵉtalpiyôt*, 'fortified with bulwarks' (cf. Colombo [1975], p. 118), a reading supported by a Hebrew manuscript. For a review of the conjectures that have been proposed, we refer to Hamp (1957), p. 208 (who states judiciously: "Metre by itself is rarely a sufficient reason for moving away from the order of the text handed down by the tradition"), and Ravasi (1992), pp. 555–556. Garbini opts for the radical solution of suppressing v. 5a, just as he suppressed v. 4 (Garbini [1992], p. 105).

[264] Nolli (1967), p. 133, following Budde, Haller and Fischer, notices the fact, but suggests shifting v. 6a after 5a, making a distich from the two monostichs ("Your neck is like a tower of ivory, your head above you is like Carmel"). But such a change upsets the careful symmetry of the strophe: in fact, v. 6a is indissolubly joined to 6bc (cf. the term *rōʾšēk* in 6ab).

[265] Cf., *supra*, *Tab. 58*, p. 368.

Table 60

a	NECK	v. 5a	tower	
b	EYES {	v. 5b v. 5c		Heshbon Bat Rabbim
b'	NOSE {	v. 5d v. 5e	tower	Lebanon Damascus
a'	HEAD	v. 6a		Carmel

[v. 5a] The neck is compared to a 'tower of ivory' (*migdal haššēn*). In 4:4 it was compared to the 'tower of David'. There it was the 'defensive' aspect of the tower that was being emphasised ("fortified with bulwarks: / a thousand shields are hung there"), here, rather, its elegance ('ivory'). One can think of a tower covered, at least in part, with carved ivory plaquettes as they are known, in large number, from the excavations at Samaria.[266] Ps 45:9 mentions 'palaces of ivory' (*hêkᵉlê šēn*), and 1 Kgs 22:39 and Amos 3:15 'houses of ivory' (*bêt haššēn*), where these buildings are expressions of magnificence and wealth. In the Song, ivory (*šēn*, literally 'tooth') is mentioned in 5:14 in the description of the man's belly ("His belly a block of ivory, / studded with lapis lazuli"). Once again the mirroring effect should be noted: the two bodies are made of the same noble material as a result of which one finds oneself in one's own partner (Gen 2:23). Here the visual aspect certainly plays a role: ivory has a warm white colour which matches well the colour of the skin.[267] And the image of the tower makes one think of the slender neck, sensual and noble, of the bust of Nefertiti.[268]

The neck-tower expresses a dimension antithetical to that of the roundness that characterised the thighs, navel, belly and breasts of the woman. The vertical dimension is being set off here and, psychologically, her aristocratic elegance ('daughter of a noble one', v. 2b), her pride, to which, moreover, the term neck (*ṣawwāʾr*) already refers.[269] The portrait of the woman lives off this tension between circularity and verticality, between gift and awareness of self.

[266] Cf. *EAEHL*, vol. IV, pp. 1032–1050.

[267] The image has a famous parallel in *Anacreontea* 17: *elephantinos trachēlos* (vv. 28–29). However, the poet is speaking of a young man's neck (tr. Campbell [1982–1993], pp. 186–187).

[268] Cf. *ANEP*, Figure 404 (from the Egyptian Museum of Berlin), p. 141.

[269] Cf., *supra*, pp. 184–185.

[v. 5bc] The description of the eyes interrupts the series of vertical images which continue later in the description of the nose and head. The breaking of the rhythm is underlined by the fact that here, uniquely in v. 5, we do not have a simile but a metaphor (lacking the comparative particle *k^{e}*). The usual metaphor for the eyes is 'doves' (cf. 1:15b [without *k^{e}*]; 4:1 [without *k^{e}*]; 5:12 [with *k^{e}*]). In the last passage, beside the metaphor of the doves, that of the sheet of water was introduced ("on streams of water... placed on a full bath"). Given the subtle intertextuality of the Song, it is not improbable that the metaphor of the pools in 7:5 is making reference to 5:12. If the 'doves' are the eyes of the man, the 'pools' in which they are reflected are the eyes of the woman. The 'mirroring dynamic' of the Song finds here an emblematic image. It relates to Gen 2 where the woman is described as the one "like his counterpart" (*k^{e}negdô*, v. 18), precisely his 'mirror'. In the eyes of the woman he finds himself, sees his own image: man needs a mirror to know that he exists and who he really is (the woman will say something similar of the eyes of the man in Song 8:10—"In his eyes, I have become like one who has found peace").

The term *b^{e}rēkâ* indicates a 'pool', that is an artificial basin of water.[270] The emphasis here is placed not on the construction but on the water, as a result of which the image can be classified among the 'natural' images. The same Hebrew vocabulary *ʿayin* expresses both 'eye' and 'spring of water'; what links the two, according to Keel, is their 'gleaming'.[271] The reflection of light on the rippling surface of a sheet of water is a spectacle of fascination for the Oriental.[272] The eyes of the Shulamite are not 'dull' like those of Leah (cf. Gen 29:17); they sparkle and shine as a pool that reflects the sun.[273] And since the water of the pool is calm, they are transparent. Just as the eye can fathom the bottom of a mirror of calm water, so the eyes of the woman reveal her mind. There is no part of the body more transparent, one might

[270] LXX *limnai* indicates rather a small lake or pool; but Symmachus has *kolumbēthrai*, and Vg *piscinae*.

[271] Keel (1994), p. 236.

[272] Cf. Delitzsch (1875), p. 113 ("Either because they sparkle like a mirror of water, or because they are so attractive to look at: in fact, for an Arab, there is no greater pleasure than to admire the movement of clear water").

[273] Ovid describes the sparkling of the eyes. Not so much in connection with 'purity' (*contra* Ravasi [1992], p. 557), but in the moment of erotic excitement: "Adspices oculos tremulo fulgore micantes, / ut sol a liquida saepe refulget aqua" (*Ars amatoria* 2:721–722).

say, more spiritual than the eyes. Perhaps that is why they are mentioned in each of the *waṣfs* of the Song (cf. *Tab. 58*). The *waṣf* does not describe just the body but the whole person, and interior beauty shines through the eyes.

With 'Heshbon' there begins a series of geographical indications which continue until v. 6a. The series is connected with the first song (cf. Song 6:4—Tirzah, Jerusalem; 6:5:—Gilead) and with the beginning of the present one (Shulamite, Mahanaim [= 'the two battlefields'], 7:1). Having been evoked in the toponyms 'Gilead' and 'Mahanaim', the Transjordan is now recalled in the central part. Heshbon (the real *ḥisbān*) is found, in fact, between Amman and Madaba on the homonymous *wadi* (*wady ḥusbon*). Still today, in the hinterland, you can observe cisterns excavated in the rock and the remains of a great reservoir:[274] but that is a common element of ancient cities. Heshbon is located on the borders of Israelite territory. It was the capital of 'Sihon, king of the Amorites' (cf. Num 21:26) from whom it passed to the tribes of Reuben and Gad (Num 32:3, 37). In the oracles against the nations, it is mentioned among the cities of Moab (Isa 15:4; 16:8, 9; Jer 48:2, 34, 45; 49:3). Perhaps it has been chosen for its exotic name like 'Kedar' in Song 1:5.[275] It is possible that the theme of 'distance', connected, in the other parts of the face, with height is here connected with geographical distance.[276] In any case, we have here a further identification of the woman with the land, the geography and the history of the people of Israel.

The following expression *ʿal šaʿar bat rabbîm* is debated. The versions understand the expression as a common noun: "At the gate of the daughter of many". Even among the commentators, numerous understand it in this way: it remains to be decided if 'daughter of many' refers to the gate (a gate through which many people pass)[277]

---

[274] Cf. Delitzsch (1875), p. 113; S. H. Horn, *Heshbon*, in *IDB.S*, p. 410; Eichner—Scherer (2001) (these last authors go for the identification of the 'pools' with two Iron Age cisterns, found on the *tell* itself, while the large reservoir, in the neighbourhood of the *tell*, is from the Byzantine epoch). On the site in general, cf. also *EAEHL*, vol. II, pp. 511–514.

[275] Thus Keel (1994), p. 236.

[276] Aquila translates *en epilogismō*, 'in the reflection', understanding *bᵉḥešbôn* as a common noun, from the root *ḥšb*, 'to think, to plan'. It would not be improbable to think that the noun was chosen also for this meaning, linked semantically with the 'eyes'.

[277] So, for example, Keel (1994), p. 218: "evoking the crowds of people who came from the steppes (cf. Num 21:16–18, 23, 25) to drink from the pools or to wash and

or to the city of Heshbon itself ("At the gate of the populous [city]").[278] The parallelism with the other stichs (v. 5def) in which a geographical indication is present (Heshbon, Lebanon, Damascus, Carmel) drives us to read *bat rabbîm* as the name of a city.[279] In Jerusalem one speaks of the 'Jaffa Gate' or the 'Damascus Gate' to mean the gate oriented towards those cities. However, a city of the name Bat Rabbim is unknown: a suggested identification with Rabbat Ammon, the capital of the Ammonites (present day Amman) is lacking in decisive arguments.[280] Be that as it may, behind the proper name, a symbolic significance is to be considered. Bat Rabbim, the 'populous city (or gate)' is a symbol of the woman whose eyes are not the exclusive property of her beloved but light up with their beauty all those (*rabbîm*) who see her (cf. 4:15—"spring of the gardens").[281]

[v. 5de] The passage from the description of the eyes to that of the nose is characterised by contrast: from an idyllic image of tranquillity ('pools'), to a warlike one ('tower', 'sentinel'). The woman, 'daughter of many', is depicted once more as one who knows how to defend herself, as in v. 5a. Open to others, but also preserving her own identity. 'Daughter of many' is to be read in counterpoint with 'daughter of a noble one' (v. 2b).

Like the neck, the 'nose' (*ʾap*) is also already in itself a symbol of pride and *hauteur*. *Hochnäsig* ('with nose in the air') signifies, in German, 'conceited, arrogant'. In Hebrew, *ʾap* indicates both 'nose' and 'anger'. Keel observes rightly that the metaphor of the 'tower of Lebanon' is not to be understood in its visual aspect (which would really be a self-parody) but in its functional dimension.[282] The 'tower', here as in 4:4, is seen in its function of impregnable fortress. In this sense

---

refresh themselves in them"; Lys (1968), pp. 262–263, who comments: "Peut-être cette désignation (imaginaire?) concerne-t-elle la 'bouche', où passent dans les deux senses en abundance mots et nourriture"; but mention of the mouth would break the parallelism of the strophe; Müller (1992), p. 72, n. 225.

278 In this sense, cf. Lam 1:1–*hāʿîr rabbātî ʿām*, 'the city of numerous people'. Among the moderns, cf. Rudolph (1962), p. 167: "am Tor der volkreichen (Stadt)".

279 Thus the majority of exegetes. Cf., for all, Robert – Tournay (1963), p. 264.

280 Advanced already by Graetz (1871) p. 195, and viewed with favour by Joüon (1909), p. 287, and Robert – Tournay (1963), p. 264, the hypothesis has been maintained recently by Brenner (1992).

281 Cf. Papyrus Chester Beatty IA 1:6: "She makes the heads of all (the) men / turn about when seeing her" (tr. Fox [1985], p. 52). On the meaning of Song 4:15, cf., *supra*, pp. 228–229.

282 Keel (1994), p. 236.

it agrees with the symbolic significance of the nose as that part of the body in which the scornful and warlike pride of the woman is situated.

After the 'tower of David' (4:4) and the 'tower of ivory' (7:5), it is now the turn of the 'tower of Lebanon'. By analogy with the two preceding ones, we are led to think in the first place of a military construction.[283] Solomon indeed had fortifications constructed on Lebanon (cf. 1 Kgs 9:19; 2 Chr 8:6). However, the expression could also indicate a natural rocky spur or a mountain (also in Italian one speaks of 'towers' to indicate certain peaks in the Dolomites).[284] With the name of 'Lebanon' is indicated not only the chain of the Lebanon proper, but also the Anti-Lebanon, the eastern chain which towers above Damascus: one's thought leaps, in particular, to the *massif* of Hermon on the borders of Israel.

"Sentinel facing Damascus". The verb *ṣāpāh* expresses observation from an elevated point.[285] It is thus the synonym of *šāqap* (cf. Song 6:10): in Num 21:20 it is said of the peak of Pisgah that it "looks towards (*nišqāpâ ʿal pnê*) the desert". The participle *ṣôpeh* is a technical term to indicate the office of a sentinel who stands on an elevated point to warn of the advance of an enemy. In a figurative sense, the task of *ṣôpeh* is attributed to the prophet (cf. Hos 9:8; Jer 6:17, and, above all, Ezek 3:16–21 and 33:2–9).[286] It is appropriate to think of Mount Hermon as a natural sentinel facing Damascus. Robert and Tournay see in 'Damascus' the traditional enemy of Israel. It is true that, from the eighth century, this danger no longer existed. But the Song re-evokes traditions from Israel's past (Solomon is an example): moreover, in the Hellenistic epoch, the war of Damascus against Israel had other protagonists but was fully real.[287] Perhaps in the expression 'sentinel facing Damascus' one can take as the background an

[283] Thus Delitzsch (1875), pp. 113–114; Keel (1994), p. 236.

[284] Thus the majority of modern commentators: cf. already Joüon (1909), pp. 287–288.

[285] Garbini's suggestion to replace *ṣph* with *ṣpḥ*, 'jug' is wholly gratuitous. Garbini thus arrives at the reading: *ʾpk kmgdl hšn ʿl ṣpḥ yyn hśwrq*, "your nose is like a tub of ivory on a basin of red wine" (Garbini [1992], pp. 105–107, 256–258). Thank goodness the author himself finds this image 'frankly unpoetic' (p. 258).

[286] Cf. G. Steins, *ṣāpāh*, in *TDOT*, vol. XII, pp. 431–433.

[287] Robert – Tournay (1963), pp. 265–266 ("La puissante et hautaine surveillance de l'Hermon est une sorte de défi jeté à ceux qui sont les successeurs de l'ennemi traditionnel et qui continuent de tenir la Palestine dans la servitude"). Cf., also, Ricciotti (1928), p. 266.

emphasis on the vindication of the national identity of Israel against the policy of Hellenisation pursued by the Seleucids with regard to the Jews.[288] Background, we say, because the attention is directed primarily to the woman, to her proud and noble carriage. In Song 5:15, the metaphor of Lebanon was evoked in respect of the man ("His appearance, like Lebanon, / imposing like the cedars"). To be noted again is the mirroring dynamic of the Song.

Elliott recalls the attention to another aspect of 'Lebanon', that of perfume (cf. 4:11: moreover, *l^e^bānôn* recalls *l^e^bônâ* ['incense']). This aspect would be underlined in the repetition of the term *ʾap* in 7:9e ("the scent of your nose like apples").[289] Such a semantic play is quite possible in the Song as other examples have shown. If, then, the term 'tower' emphasises the proudness of the nose, the term 'Lebanon' connotes, perhaps, its connection with breath and smell.

[v. 6a] Verse 6a concludes the description of the four parts of the face. As a monostich, it corresponds to v. 5a. Moreover, it matches the 'vertical' theme which characterises the description of the neck and the nose and prolongs the series of four geographical indications in v. 5bcde: Heshbon, Bat Rabbim, Lebanon, Damascus. The link with the description of the nose (v. 5de) is particularly evident: the passage from 'Lebanon' to 'Carmel' is natural, concerning, as it does, the two mountains which are geographically on the northern border of Israel. In the OT, Lebanon and Carmel are associated because of the splendour of their vegetation (cf. Isa 33:9 and 35:2; Nah 1:4). Delitzsch records, moreover, that the promontory of Carmel bears the Arab name of *anf-el-gebel* ('nose of the mountain').[290]

'Your head' (*rōʾšēk*) is to be understood here as the whole the parts of which have been described in the preceding verse: a similar usage can be observed with respect to the man's head in 5:11a. There, the description of the 'head' precedes that of its individual parts, here it follows it: in both cases, it has a summarising function.[291] The noun is followed by an expression which at first glance seems to be pleonastic:

---

[288] It is interesting to note that the three locations listed in vv. 5–6a (Heshbon, Lebanon, Carmel) are situated on the frontier, on the borders of the land of Israel, as if to define its national identity.

[289] Elliott (1989), p. 169.

[290] Delitzsch (1875), p. 114.

[291] Unnecessary, therefore, the translation 'your hair' ('Haupthaar'), proposed by Graetz (1871), p. 196.

'crowns you' (literally, 'above you' [*ʿālayik*]).[292] But it was noted above that parts I–II and IX–X are structurally united by the duality of the terms with which the part of the body is indicated.[293] The expression 'above you' is, therefore, structurally necessary. Let us add that, even if forced, it is not without sense.[294] It makes clear that the head is the crown of the body, underlining its pride. The Shulamite does not have a drooping head but one that stands well on her shoulders.

Some authors suggest reading the term *karmîl* ('crimson')[295] instead of *karmel*, although none of the versions supports this reading. The reason is that to compare the head to Mount Carmel is problematic: it seems abnormal, as does comparing the nose to Lebanon. Here again, it is necessary to distance oneself from a visual conception of the metaphor and to refer to its symbolic, functional value. The term of comparison between 'Carmel' and 'the head of the woman' is impressiveness and majesty (cf. 5:15cd). Mount Carmel is not very high (552m., approximately 1800 feet), but it stands out clearly both from the sea and from the plain of Jezreel.[296] Moreover, Carmel was famous for its vegetation (cf. Isa 33:9; 35:2; Amos 1:2) which constitutes a reference to the hair of the woman (cf. v. 6bc).

From the point of view of depth psychology, Krinetzki detects an archetypal symbol in this undoubted stressing of the size of the woman.[297] The man would see personified in the woman the *magna mater*, before which he would return to see himself as the *puer aeternus*.[298] The correspondence is suggestive, but it is relativised by the fact that

---

[292] So much that Vg omits the expression.

[293] Cf., *supra*, p. 371.

[294] So also Hamp (1957), p. 209 (*contra* Budde, Haller, Schmökel and Fischer).

[295] Thus Graetz (1871), p. 196, following Ibn Ezra. Also Gordis (1974), p. 96, and Garbini (1992), p. 258.

[296] We should remember that, in the topographical list of Tuthmosis III, Carmel is named *r-š q-d-š*, 'holy headland'. Cf. Aharoni (1979), p. 161; Stadelmann (1992), p. 178.

[297] The matter is expressed thus by Gerleman (1965), p. 199: "Like the preceding geographical similitudes, this too is characterised by a use of hyperbole which borders on the colossal-heroic, far away from any kind of realism".

[298] Krinetzki (1970), p. 414, n. 52. Krinetzki cites the Egyptian representation of Horus as a baby in his relationships with Isis-Hator, sister, spouse and mother. This would not be a regression to the infantile state, but: "in an authentic identification with the baby, the man experiences the mother and the great feminine as a symbol of life, on which he himself depends even as an adult". Krinetzki cites here Neumann (1957), pp. 132–133.

'impressiveness' also characterises the representation of the man (cf. Song 5:15cd): perhaps one can see in it an allusion to the 'superhuman' character of the two portraits.[299]

[v. 6bc] The Hair. The description of the hair is intimately linked with that of the head. The most obvious sign is the conjunctive particle *w*^{e} at the beginning of v. 6b. Also the term 'head' (*rōʾš*) unites the two stichs 6a and 6b, as well as the duality of the subject ("your head...crowns you", v. 6a; "the hair of your head", v. 6b). Moreover it has been seen that in the image of 'Carmel' are included the woods, an allusion to the hair. And, moreover, the coast to the North of Carmel was celebrated for the molluscs from which the purple mentioned in v. 6b was extracted.

At the same time, however, the metaphor of the purple is separated from the preceding which stressed the vertical dimension of the woman. In v. 6bc there is a return to the circular dimension or better to the 'movement' which characterised the description of the feet (and the breasts). The *inclusio* with v. 2ab is underlined by the fact that the two descriptions are characterised by the 'high burlesque'.[300]

The term *dallâ* is rare. It derives from the root *dll* which signifies 'to hang, to be suspended, to dangle'.[301] The name of Samson's woman, Delilah (cf. Judg 16:4), derives from the same root. Perhaps, with this term, the intention is to allude to the free movement of the hair during the dance. An idea is provided by the Egyptian representations of dancers and singers with the characteristic flowing hair.[302]

The hair is compared to purple. Here we have, as in Song 3:10, the dark red purple (*ʾargāmān*). Probably the emphasis is not being laid on the colour (as if the woman had hair dyed with henna).[303] The woman's hair is black (cf. 4:1e; 6:5d), and the purple of that time, both the red and the violet varieties, had a dark colour.[304] The stress is being

---

[299] Homer praises not only the beauty of Nausicaa, but also her stature, which makes her like a goddess (cf. *Odyssey* 6:16, 153).

[300] Cf., *supra*, pp. 306 and 369.

[301] The only other passage in which the noun returns is Isa 38:12: here the term *dallâ* refers to the threads of the cloth that remain outside the part that is woven. The fringes on the girls' hair in Keel (1994), Figure 132, p. 237, make one think precisely of the fringes of a piece of fabric.

[302] Cf. *ANEP*, Figures 208–209, p. 65; Keel (1994), Figures 78 and 79, p. 140.

[303] *Contra* Ravasi (1992), pp. 562–563. Gerleman (1965), p. 71, thinks instead that the term of comparison is not the woman herself, but certain Egyptian statues, in which golden threads are inserted into the hair.

[304] In the same ode, (Pseudo-)Anacreon calls the hairs of a girl first 'black', then 'purple' (*Anacreontea* 16:7, 11, tr. Campbell [1982–1993], pp. 182–183); Lucian speaks

placed on the characteristic sheen of the purple which make us think of those of female hair; Goulder recalls the sheen of the black hair of certain Asiatic women.[305]

The other element of the comparison is the precious nature of purple. This has already been dealt with *à propos* of 3:10. It was reserved to kings and gods.[306] The 'royal' character of purple is emphasised by the Syriac version and the Vulgate which unite the term 'king' in v. 6c with 'purple' in v. 6b (*purpura regis*). Be that as it may, even if we keep to the letter of the MT, the two terms are correlated. The Shulamite is not only 'daughter of a noble' (v. 2b) but actually 'queen' ('purple', v. 6b), just as he is king (v. 6c).

The 'high burlesque' of the man is well known (cf 1:4, 12; 3:9, 11). New here is the fact that it is the young man who calls himself 'king' (it is, in fact, to the man that the metaphor alludes). Perhaps it is possible to pick up a hint of irony here: the content of the phrase lends itself to this. With the expression, "a king is held captive in the tresses", the man is, in fact, declaring himself to be a 'prisoner' of the woman, in love with her, employing that same kind of warlike metaphor which had concluded the previous *waṣf* (cf. 6:12).

The term *rᵉhāṭîm* causes difficulty. The common meaning, 'water troughs' (cf. Gen 30:38, 41; Exod 2:16), does not make sense, nor even the correspondence with *rāḥîṭ* ('beam', Song 1:17).[307] A derivation is suggested, therefore, from the Aramaic *rhṭ*, equivalent to the Hebrew *rûṣ* ('to flow'). As far as we can see, this is the understanding of the versions.[308] To compare hair to the 'waves' of a stream which flows from the head seems an appropriate image. The plural makes one think of the different 'tresses' of the 'hair' such as we see in some figures of Egyptian dancing girls.[309]

The particular fascination exercised by female hair is a topic of the amorous literature of all ages. The Egyptian love songs have very

---

of *porphyrous plokamos* (*De saltatione* 41:2). Of Tyrian purple, Pliny says: "Laus ei summa in colore sanguinis concreti, nigricans adspectu, idemque suspectu refulgens; unde et Homero purpureus dicitur sanguis" (*Naturalis historia* 9:26, 135).

[305] Goulder (1986), p. 57.

[306] Cf., *supra*, pp. 154–155.

[307] Gerleman (1965), pp. 199–200, wants to retain this meaning: "fastened to the shafts (of the loom)". He is followed by Krinetzki (1981), p. 191.

[308] LXX *en paradromais*; Vetus Latina *in transcursibus*; Vg *canalibus*; the Syriac *brhṭ'*.

[309] *dallâ* and *rᵉhāṭîm* represent, therefore, the same reality, the first term in collective form ('comb'), the second in distributive form with reference to the individual elements of the comb ('tresses').

similar emphases to those of our passage. One could look at the passage drawn from Papyrus Chester Beatty cited above,[310] or also the following, taken from Papyrus Harris 500:

> Her brow a snare of willow,
> and I the wild goose!
> My [beak] snips [her hair] for bait,
> as worms for bait in the trap.[311]

Ricciotti cites Apuleius: "Adiuro te per dulcem istum capilli tui nodulum, quo meum vinxisti spiritum".[312] In a Palestinian love song we read: "Oh, your flowing black hair: / seven tresses takes us prisoners".[313]

In v. 6c, therefore, there is a passage from contemplation to action, to the effect, that is, that contemplation produces on the man. With that, the second part of the song is introduced, characterised by the desire to be united with the one whom till now the man has contemplated and by whom he has been definitively 'captured'.[314]

[7:7–10a] Second strophe: Desire. As in the preceding song (6:4–12), here too, after the contemplation of the woman's body, there follows the amazed, global admiration of what up to now has been described in its details, and the desire of enjoying the body that has been admired. By contrast with 6:10–12, we should observe the greater closeness of the lovers in 7:7–10a. In 6:11, the man wanted to 'see' the body of the woman; here he wants to 'enjoy' it. The man was passive in 6:12 ("Without my knowing it, my desire had carried me"): now he becomes active ("I said to myself: I will climb up the palm", 7:9). The song is strongly passionate. It is still not the moment of union, but one feels that it is near.

The strophe is structured in two movements: admiration (vv. 7–8) and desire (vv. 9–10a). Syntactically, 10a continues in 10bc, but here the subject of the discourse is someone else, the woman (cf. the appellation *dôdî*) as a result of which the distich v. 10bc forms a unity with the following one, v. 11ab, while v. 10a completes 9e, forming another distich with it. The two movements therefore are characterised by an even number of stichs: the first has four, the second six (cf. *Tab. 61*).

---

[310] Cf., *supra*, p. 206.
[311] 1:12–2:1, according to Pope (1977), p. 74, tr. Simpson.
[312] *Metamorphoses* 3:23.
[313] Cf. Dalman (1901), p. 260.
[314] The same dynamic is also characteristic of the first *waṣf*, Song 4:1–7 (cf. v. 6).

Table 61

ADMIRATION	a) person (you [sg.])	7a 7b	
	b) metaphor (she)	8a 8b	*palm* *breasts—clusters*
DESIRE	b') metaphor (she)	9a 9b	*palm*
	a') person (you [sg.])	9c 9d 9e 10a	*breasts* *clusters*

Table 62

a	v. 9cd	*your breasts*	*like*	*clusters of the vine*
b	v. 9e	*the scent of your nose*	*like*	*apples*
a'	v. 10a	*your palate*	*like*	*good wine*

Verses 7–10a present a chiastic structure in so far as at the beginning and the end of the strophe (vv. 7 and 9c–10a: a-a') the discourse is addressed directly to the woman; in the centre (vv. 8 and 9ab: b-b') the woman is described under the form of a metaphor ('palm') speaking of her in the third person. The four units thus delineated are joined among themselves. In v. 7 (a), in fact, the discourse on the 'charms' (*taʿănûgîm*) is to be understood as an allusion to what is expressed in vv. 9c–10a (a'). The three terms of v. 8 (b), 'palm' (*tāmār*), 'your breasts' (*šādayik*) and 'clusters' (*ʾaškōlôt*) are repeated, respectively, in v. 9a (b') and 9cd (a'). The four stichs that compose the fourth unit (a') are constructed in a strictly parallel pattern (cf. *Tab. 62*).

Three times, a part of the female body ('your breasts', 'your nose', 'your palate') is joined by the comparative particle (k^e) to a metaphor ('clusters of the vine', 'apples', 'good wine'). It should be noted how in a and in a' the subject is made up of one word, the predicate of two, while in b the opposite is the case: the subject is composed of two words, the predicate of one; a and a' are linked further by the type of metaphor ('vine' and 'wine').

The link between the first strophe (vv. 2–6) and the second (vv. 7–10a) is underlined by the fact that the rhythm 'round-slender' that distinguishes vv. 2–6 also characterises vv 7–10a: cf. the binome palm-clusters in vv 8–9. An analogous phenomenon was met with in the first song where the binome fair-terrible characterised not only the *waṣf* (vv. 4–8) but also vv. 10–12 (cf, *supra, Tab. 51*). The aspect of 'slenderness' (*qômātēk*, 'your height', v. 8a) is mentioned first, in continuity with the metaphors of the tower, of Lebanon and Carmel, with which the first strophe closed.

[vv. 7–8] First movement: Admiration. After having contemplated the individual parts of the body, the man breaks out into an exclamation full of amazed admiration before the apparition which is standing in front of him: "How fair you are!"[315] 'Fair' (*yph*) is attributed almost exclusively to the woman (cf. 1:8, 15; 2:10, 13; 4:1, 7; 5:9; 6:1, 4, 10). Here the verb is used, as in v. 2a, with reference to the feet of the woman, and in 4:10 to her caresses. Only once (1:16), is the term *yph* attributed to the man, and this time together with *nʿm* as in our case. The two terms express, in the first case the aesthetic aspect of love, in the second, the enjoyment of the same:[316] if the first term looks to the preceding strophe, the second introduces the theme of desire which will be developed in the following verses and has a synonym in the term *taʿănûgîm* in v. 7b. *nʿm* is a word with a strong mythological background, connected with the god of vegetation. The fact that it is attributed to the woman is another sign of the 'reciprocity' of the Song. In 1:16, an adjective typical of the woman (*yph*) is applied to the man; in 7:7, another adjective characteristic of the man (*nʿm*) is attributed to the woman, thus preparing for the refrain of mutual belonging which closes the strophe (v. 11).

"Love". MT (*ʾahăbâ*) and the LXX (*agapē*) are undoubtedly abstract. But the context suggests that here it is the woman in her concreteness that is being indicated. The 'you' to whom the man refers in v. 8 is a person not an abstract principle. Moreover, this is the understanding of both the Syriac (*rḥymtʾ*) and the Vulgate (*carissima*). Without any need to change the MT,[317] we believe that we have here a case of metonymy or synecdoche, that is, the use of the abstract for the concrete, identical to that noticed in 3:10. In Engish, the term *love*, on the

---

[315] We have the second person feminine here, not the third, *contra* Garbini ("How fair she is", Garbini [1992], p. 262).

[316] Cf. Delitzsch (1875), p. 116, and *supra*, p. 79. For the translation 'sweet', cf. Prov 9:17; Ruth 1:20 (opposition *nʿm—mrʾ*).

[317] Following the Syriac and Vg, some authors suggest reading the participle *ʾăhubâ*, 'beloved', instead of the abstract (cf. *BHS*). The conjecture is unnecessary.

mouth of a person in love, can indicate the concrete object of love.[318] Such metonymy, however, is significant: with it is expressed the idea that the loved one is the personification of love.[319] No wonder, therefore, that she is clothed with a divine aura, that she is theomorphic.

"In (your) pleasures". The reading of the MT is a little hard. It would be possible to postulate an haplography for *bat taʿănûgîm* ('daughter of pleasures'): in fact, this is the reading of the Syriac and Aquila.[320] But MT is confirmed by the LXX, the Vetus Latina and the Vulgate, and is, therefore, preferable as it is the *lectio difficilior*.[321] Naturally it does not refer to love in the abstract but to the woman: she knows how to inundate her man with pleasures. Moreover, the term *taʿănûgîm*, indicates the pleasure of the senses, the '*dolce vita*' (cf. Mic 1:16; 2:9; Qoh 2:8; Prov 19:10): it is, therefore, unequivocally the sensual, erotic aspect of love which is being presented here. It is a human experience which is almost always looked upon with suspicion in the Bible: it is unusual that here it is praised as something positive.[322] It is interesting to note that the root *ʿng* receives a positive transposition in the OT inasmuch as it is referred to YHWH (cf. Ps 37:4; Isa 58:13–14) and to his gifts (Isa 55:2; 66:11; Ps 37:11).[323] In our case, it is the woman who is the source of 'pleasure'. Not that the woman usurps the place of God; that would be idolatry. She is seen as the gift of God, part of that 'promised land' whose pleasures are destined to fill YHWH's poor, an anticipation of eschatological salvation.

In v. 8, two elements of the round-slender binome which characterised vv. 2–6 are repeated. Here the sequence is reversed: first there is the slender element ('palm'), then the round ('breasts-clusters'): thus, in the unit of vv. 2–10a, a chiastic structure is formed (a: vv. 2c–4 [round]; b: vv. 5–6a [slender]; b': vv. 8ab, 9a [slender]; a': vv. 8c, 9bc [round]), something which witnesses to the unity of the passage.

---

318 *Contra* Delitzsch (1875), pp. 115–116; Graetz (1871), p. 197; Garbini (1992), p. 260; Gordis (1974), pp. 96–97.

319 Cf. Elliott (1989), p. 171.

320 Cf., in this sense, Graetz (1871), p. 197; Joüon (1909), p. 292; Robert – Tournay (1963), p. 269; Colombo (1975), p. 121.

321 So, for example, Krinetzki (1981), p. 284; Ravasi (1992), p. 567.

322 Cf. the general statement of Fuerst (1975), p. 199: "This book has only one message: the implication that human and erotic love is a good and joyful part of God's creation. [...] The Song celebrates sexual love".

323 Cf. T. Kronholm, *ʿānag*, in *TDOT*, vol. XI, pp. 213–214; "The root *ʿng* [...] presents a semantic cluster similar to that of *ḥmd*: it transposes physical enjoyment to Yahweh, his laws, and his loving-kindness" (Salvaneschi [1982], p. 85).

We should note, first of all, in the opening of the verse, the demonstrative pronoun *zōʾt*. The position is unusual so that one should not be surprised that the majority of modern translations omit it, following the Vetus Latina and the Vulgate.[324] Actually, it indicates that the beloved is in front of the object (the woman) that he is describing.[325]

The noun *qômâ* derives from the root *qwm* ('to stand') and indicates the whole person under the aspect of height ('stature'), resuming in a certain way the description of the neck, the nose and the head in vv. 5–6. Connected with the aspect of height is the connotation of the 'distance' which must be overcome if one wants to enjoy the closeness offered by the round element (the 'clusters').

The upright tree is a phallic motif that is associated with the man in 2:3 and 5:15,[326] but it is also a feminine symbol above all when we are talking about the palm. In Odyssey 6:162–168, Nausicaa is compared to a tall palm tree.[327] Stephan cites a parallel from modern Palestinian love songs: "O you, whose height is that of a palm in a serail".[328] On the other hand, in the Song, the 'vertical' dimension is accompanied by the 'round' one: this is represented by the breasts (v. 8b; cf. v. 4) which correspond, on the metaphorical level, to the 'clusters' (*ʾaškōlôt*). These are 'clusters of palm', not of the 'vine'[329] which will be mentioned in v. 9d. In fact, the metaphor of the palm continues in v. 9a, and the parallel demands that we understand, in v. 8b as in v. 9b, the fruit of the palm, that is dates. Generally these are represented in ancient iconography in pairs which hang symmetrically from the two sides of the palm.[330] Thus the palm metaphor does not glorify the thin and linear type of beauty fashionable today: the Egyptian dancers have slender figures but well developed breasts.[331] And in Israel, between the eighth

---

[324] So Ravasi (1992), p. 569. Others make *zōʾt* the subject of a nominal phrase, the predicate of which is *qômātēk*: 'This is your height'. Cf. Müller (1992), p. 75. Garbini's suggestion of referring *zōʾt* to 'Love' and to read the verb *dāmtāh* in a *piʿel* sense ("He [= Love, *author's note*] makes your height like a palm"), is unlikely. Cf. Garbini (1992), p. 260.

[325] Cf. Joüon (1923), §143i ("ta taille que voici").

[326] Something underlined by Krinetzki (1970), p. 415.

[327] The term with which LXX translates *qômâ* in v. 8a is not, as would be expected here, *hypsos*, 'height', but *megethos*, 'largeness', the same term used by Homer in *Odyssey* 6:153 to indicate the height of Nausicaa, which makes her like a goddess.

[328] Stephan (1922), p. 275.

[329] So, rightly, Robert - Tournay (1963), p. 271, *contra* Joüon (1909), p. 292.

[330] Cf. Robert - Tournay (1963), p. 271.

[331] Cf. Keel (1994), Figure 131, p. 237, and Figure 133, p. 240.

and the sixth centuries BC, statuettes of a female divinity with enormous breasts were very widespread:[332] these are not only the sign of fertility but also the criterion of beauty and erotic attraction.

In Egypt, the tree is often represented as a female divinity which gives nourishment and life.[333] This is probably a variant of the motif of the 'tree of life'. Interesting is the fact that often this tree has the form of a palm.[334] Furthermore, throughout the Ancient Orient, the palm is the goddess of fertility and of love,[335] who is often represented with clusters of dates in her hand.[336] In Israel too this tree has a place of importance: Jericho was called 'the city of palms' (cf. Deut 34:3; Judg 1:16) and Engeddi was renowned for its palms (cf. Sir 24:14). Palms were to be found in the Temple enclosure (cf. Ps 92:13–14) and the sanctuary itself was decorated with motifs inspired by the palm (cf. 1 Kgs 6:29, 32, 35; 7:36; Ezek 40:16; 41:18–20). The name Tamar (= 'palm') is connected with women known for their attractiveness (cf. Gen 38; 2 Sam 13; 2 Sam 14:27). As Keel rightly emphasises, in order to understand the metaphor of the palm, one cannot pass over the mythical and religious background of this tree.[337]

[vv. 9–10a] Second Movement: Desire. As in Song 6:11–12, 'admiration' is followed by a monologue in which the man expresses the desire of being united to the woman, using the metaphor of movement. The correlation of the two passages was noted above.[338] The movement is expressed by two antithetical verbs: "I went down" (6:11a) and "I will climb up" (7:9a). The interior aspect of the process is indicated by two further antithetical terms: "Without my knowing" (6:12a) and "I said to myself" (7:9a). In 6:11–12, the man is passive, overwhelmed by a force greater than he (the "chariots of my noble people"); in 7:9, he is active, not conquered but the conqueror ("I will squeeze its clusters").

Like the 'garden' so the 'palm' is a metaphor of the woman, so that the one expression: 'to go down into the garden' is equivalent to the other: 'to climb up the palm'. They are both images of union, of 'taking possession'. The link between the two passages is confirmed by the use of the word *gepen*, an unusual term for the 'vine' in 6:11c and

---

332 Cf. Keel (1994), Figure 134, p. 240.
333 Cf. Keel (1978), Figure 254, p. 187.
334 Cf. Keel (1994), Figures 142 and 143, p. 248.
335 Cf. Keel (1994), Figure 93, p.156; Figure 95, p. 157; Figure 136, p. 241.
336 Cf. *ANEP*, Figure 505, p. 172; Keel (1994), Figure 127, p. 225.
337 Keel (1994), pp. 224–245.
338 Cf. p. 322, and *Tab. 49*.

7:9d. Neither in 6:11–12 nor in 7:9–10, however, is it a case of sexual union[339] but only of its preliminaries. In 6:11, it is a matter of 'seeing'. In 7:9–10, there is already mention of the enjoyment of love, by means of the classical metaphors of 'touch' (v. 9abcd), of 'smell' (v. 9e) and of 'taste' (v. 10a), but the parts of the body involved are the breasts and the mouth, not the genital organs, and, moreover, in both cases, it is a question of a 'desire', as the woman's reply in v. 11b underlines (cf. 6:12a), not of reality. The union will be described in the next passage, 7:12–8:4, which concludes with the two refrains of the embrace and of the awakening (8:3–4). As in the first part of the Song, so too in the second, the author describes a true and proper *itinerarium amoris*.

"I said to myself: I will climb up the palm". The verb *ʾāmar* ('to say') describes an interior process, which takes place in the present time. It "expresses the ardour of the desire of the Bridegroom and the energy of his decision".[340] 'To go up' (*ʿālāh*) is to be understood, primarily, in a realistic sense. In order to gather the fruits, it is necessary 'to climb' up the palm tree: the dates are to be found at the top. Numerous images of the Ancient Orient show how this was done: either by climbing[341] or by means of a ladder.[342] The gathering of dates was held to be a sacred action.[343] In the famous fresco of Mari, the palm is part of the Temple enclosure and from it issues a dove (the animal of Ishtar) while two men are climbing to gather the dates.[344] The parallel confers a religious character on the erotic action to which the metaphor alludes. It has been noticed that 'height' expresses the 'distance' and 'inaccessibility' of the woman. 'To climb up' is to overcome this distance. The verb 'to go up', and still more the ensuing' to squeeze' (*ʾāḥaz*), express a certain violence: we can perceive again an allusion to the 'warlike' nature of love. Love is a conquest, a siege (cf. 2:4), a 'war' (cf. 6:4, 10, 12). But the roles change: if now, as in 2:4, the man is on the attack and the woman is defending herself (cf. the images of the tower [4:4; 7:5; 8:10], and of

[339] *Contra* Krinetzki (1981), p. 200, and Garbini (1992), pp. 107–108, 260–262. In order to reach such an interpretation, however, Garbini has to change the text markedly. He translates vv. 9e.10a: "your buttocks like cloven pomegranates and your womb like superior wine". By means of refined linguistic acrobatics, he arrives at the reading *plḥ hrymwnym* behind *rêaḥ ʾappēk kattappûḥîm*, and *ḥyqk* behind *ḥikkēk*. However this is not exegesis but fantasy.

[340] Joüon (1909), p. 293.

[341] Cf. Keel (1994), Figure 146, p. 249.

[342] Cf. Keel (1994), Figure 141, p. 245.

[343] Cf. Wittekindt (1925), pp. 49–50; Keel (1994), p. 246.

[344] Cf. Keel (1978), Figure 191, p. 143.

the mountain [7:6a]), in 4:9; 6:4, 10, 12, the opposite took place: there it was the woman who was on the attack, "terrible as a host drawn up". In both cases, the force with which the war is conducted is not violence, the force of arms, but the force of love: in fact, this word is on the man's banner (2:4), and the 'chariots' of which the woman's army is made up are those "of my noble people" (6:12), the chariots of YHWH, the God of love (8:6).

"I will squeeze its clusters". The Hebrew term *sansinnîm* is a *hapax* understood in various ways by the versions. The LXX has *hypseōn* ('tops'), similarly the Vetus Latina, *altitudines*; Aquila reads *elatōn* ('spathes'); Symmachus (*baiōn*) and the Syriac (*swkwhy*) understand as 'branches of palm'.[345] But the Vulgate (*fructus*) sets us on the right track: if one climbs up the palm, it is certainly not to take the leaves but to gather the fruit. The parallelism with the 'clusters' (v. 8b) demands this meaning which is attested in other Oriental languages.[346] In itself, the term does not indicate the fruit but the stem with the dates, that is, to be exact, the 'cluster'.[347] The term recalls the *taltallîm* of 5:11: but there, the allusion was to the flowers, here to the fruits.

The verb *ʾāḥaz* ('to seize/to squeeze') denotes, as has been seen, a certain violence. It betrays the strong emotional tension which animates the passage.[348] In the Song, it has appeared already in 2:15 and 3:4, 8. Particularly interesting is the comparison with 3:4. There it is the woman who 'squeezes/holds tight' the man after having searched for him for a long time during the night; here it is the man who 'squeezes' the woman. The woman is not only the object but also the subject of conquest. The perfect reciprocity of the amorous sentiment will be confirmed in the refrain of mutual belonging in v. 11.

The fourth section of the strophe begins with v. 9c (cf. *Tab. 61*). We pass from the metaphor of the palm to the very person of the woman, from indirect to direct discourse, emphasising the emotion of the one who speaks. The erotic coming together is described in gradual form, by means of the three senses of touch (v. 9 cd), of smell (v. 9e) and of taste (v. 10a). The description takes an element from each of the two sections of the *waṣf*. The breasts are chosen to represent the 'round' parts of the body (v. 9c; cf. v. 4); the nose, the 'slender' ones (v. 9e;

---

345 So too Delitzsch (1875), p. 117; Rudolph (1962), p. 174; Ravasi (1992), p. 571.
346 Cf. *HALOT*, p. 761 ("panicle of the date").
347 Thus Robert – Tournay (1963), p. 272; Garbini (1992), p. 260.
348 Cf. Elliott (1989), p. 171.

cf. v. 5de). The sequence is, therefore, chiastic with respect to that of vv. 8–9b.

"May your breasts be like clusters of the vine". The choice of the breasts from among the other 'round' parts of the woman, although they were evoked extensively in vv. 2c–4, is significant. In Mesopotamia, in the myths of sacral marriage, sexuality is seen primarily as procreation and the transmission of life. In the representations of the goddess of love, it is her genitals that are in evidence; often her breasts are not even shown.[349] In the Song, on the other hand, as in the Egyptian love songs, it is the erotic, playful aspect of love that is presented: here the breasts and the mouth have a preponderant role. With regard to the breasts, they certainly have also a dimension of fertility, bound up with the mother figure,[350] but the expression 'squeeze' the breasts-clusters (v. 9b) directs the attention to the other significance, the erotic (cf. Prov 5:18–20).[351] The passage in Proverbs is unique in the OT in speaking positively about caressing the breasts: in Hos 2:4; Ezek 23:3, 21, it is spoken of in a context of prostitution. In the Bible, erotic play generally has a connotation of obscenity. That the Song speaks of it in a form not only neutral but positive, shrouding the gestures of tenderness with a sacral aura is, therefore, decidedly against the grain.

The term *ʾeškᵉlôt* ('clusters') is taken from v. 8b where it refers to the clusters of the palm. That the metaphor is changed here, and 'of the vine', *haggepen*, is added to 'clusters' seems out of place.[352] But structurally v. 9d is not connected so much with what precedes it but with what follows, as has been noted above.[353] The mention of the 'vine' precedes and prepares for that of the 'wine' in v' 10c. From another point of view, the term *gepen* is a reference to 6:11. Through superimposition, one might say, the clusters of the palm are transformed into clusters of the vine.[354] Perhaps the visual aspect plays a role here: grapes correspond to the elasticity of the female breasts better than

---

[349] Cf. Keel (1994), p. 246, and Figures 147–148, p. 250.

[350] Cf., in this sense, Keel (1994), Figure 140, p. 245.

[351] Cf. also Keel (1994), Figure 128, p. 232.

[352] Siegfried (1898), pp. 120–121, suggests that we think, in v. 8, of the clusters of a vine that is climbing on the palm; Haupt (1907), p. 37, on the other hand, suppresses the term *gepen* in v. 9d.

[353] Cf. *Tab.* 61, p. 389.

[354] Keel emphasises the continuity between the two metaphors, palm and vine, in the sense that both plants are associated with the goddess of love (Keel [1994], p. 246, and Figure 148, p. 250).

dates.[355] But the parallel with the already cited text of Prov 5:19b recalls the attention rather to the link of the grape with the wine: "Let her breasts inebriate you always". Like wine, the caressing of the breasts of the woman makes her man drunk with joy.[356]

From the tactile aspect of amorous play, we pass to the olfactory: "And the scent of your nose[357] like apples". Here and in the following stich, allusion is being made to the kiss under the olfactory and gustatory aspects, as happened already in 1:2–3; 4:10–11.[358] The term 'nose' (*ʾap*) is a repetition of v. 5 where this part of the body was compared to the 'tower of Lebanon'. Now it is the perfume (cf. 4:11) from 'Lebanon' that is put forward, as in a passage from Papyrus Harris 500. It is instructive, in this case, to compare some translations of this passage.[359] Mathieu translates: "Only *the odour of your breath*—that is what revives my heart";[360] Bresciani: "It is *your kisses*...";[361] and Fox: "Only *the scent of your nose*...".[362] From this comparison, we observe the interchangeability of the terms 'kiss', 'nose' and 'breath'. The nearness of the nose during the kiss allows the taking in of that particular, very personal smell which the breath of one's own partner has in the excitement of love: it is unique access to the intimacy of the person who is loved.[363]

The metaphor passes from the vine to apples. The Hebrew term *tappûaḥ* ('apple tree/apple') signifies literally 'fragrant': we understand, therefore, that the apple is being chosen as a metaphor for the breath of the woman.[364] The apple tree is a favourite tree of the author of the Song who mentions it again in 2:3, 5 and 8:5. It has been noted, with

---

[355] Cf. Delitzsch (1875), p. 117.

[356] A similar thought is present in Papyrus Harris 500A 1:4–5: "Is it because you are hungry that you would leave.../ (Then) take my breasts" (tr. Fox [1985], p. 8; cf., also, Mathieu [1996], p. 57, and Bresciani [1990], p. 460, who offer different versions).

[357] The Syriac has *ʾpyky*, 'your face'. Cf., also, Gordis (1974), p. 70. Vg reads 'mouth' instead of 'nose' (*odor oris tui*). The allusion to the kiss is made explicit, but the hook with v. 5d is lost: in the *waṣf* the mouth is not mentioned.

[358] Cf., *supra*, pp. 54–55, and 207–214.

[359] Papyrus Harris 500B, 5:2: it is the woman who is speaking.

[360] Mathieu (1996), p. 62.

[361] Bresciani (1990), p. 464.

[362] Fox (1985), p. 21.

[363] Pope's suggestion, on the basis of Akkadian and Ugaritic parallels, of translating *ʾap* with 'vulva' or 'clitoris' seems improbable to me. Cf. Pope (1977), pp. 636–637. Here, it would be completely out of context.

[364] By way of contrast, cf. the bitter observation of Job 19:17.

regard to 2:5,[365] that the apple, like the pomegranate,[366] was reputed an aphrodisiac, and this sense is confirmed also in 8:5—"Under the apple tree, I awakened you". Thus the perfume of the woman's nose 'awakens' love in her beloved, arouses pleasure.

Structurally, v. 10a is closely linked to v. 9c–e. This connection is underlined by the Vetus Latina which places a point after '*vinum optimum*'. In the Hebrew, the caesura is not so strong: grammatically, in fact, the two participles *hôlēk* ('which goes', v. 10b) and *dôbēb* ('which flows', v. 10c) refer to 'wine' (v. 10a). The woman continues the discourse begun by the man, but structurally and rhythmically v 10bc belong to a new composition, something that will be made clear shortly. As in v. 9e, also in v. 10a, the kiss is being spoken of, no longer under the olfactory aspect but under that of taste. The passage from smell to taste expresses an increasing closeness to union (cf. 4:16–5:1).

ḥēk is the 'palate', a term which occurs again in 2:3 (her palate) and in 5:16 (his palate): both times, the 'sweetness' (*mtq*) of this part of the body is emphasised, with evident reference to the 'French kiss', in which the tongue and the inside of the mouth of the two lovers come together.[367] Song 4:11 ("honey and milk under your tongue") also alludes to the exchange of fluids which takes place during the kiss. Here the salivary liquid is called 'wine' as in 1:2 and in 4:10. Like the wine, the woman's kisses bring the man to state of drunkenness, carry him outside himself in the abandonment of love. We can grasp a further reference to the *waṣf*: the metaphor of wine was used in connection with the woman's womb (v. 3). The parallel underlines the correspondence between the womb and the mouth as expressions of feminine intimacy.[368] It is stressed that the wine is 'good' (*ṭôb*),[369]

---

[365] Cf. p. 90, and n. 206.

[366] Actually, Vetus Latina reads *sicut mala granata*, but MT is supported by LXX, Vg, and the Syriac.

[367] In this connection, Delitzsch (1875), p. 117, cites Lucretius (*jungere salivas oris*) and Ovid (*oscula per longas jungere pressa moras*). Strangely, however, he claims that our text refers to 'words of love'. So too Joüon (1909), p. 294, and Robert - Tournay (1963), p. 273. We have recognised this possibility for 4:10–11 (cf., *supra*, p. 211): actually, the 'palate' is also, like the 'tongue', an instrument of speech (cf. Prov 5:3; Job 6:30; 20:13; 31:30). But here the context requires understanding the term in an erotic form (in continuity with touch and smell).

[368] Krinetzki (1981), p. 201.

[369] LXX (*oinos ho agathos*), Vetus Latina and Vg (*vinum optimum*), understand a superlative. MT *k^{e}yên haṭṭôb* is strange: literally, it signifies 'wine of bounty'. Joüon (1909), p. 295, would want to understand it as 'perfume', as an equivalent of the 'perfumed wine' of 8:2. But the parallel with 1:2 commends a more general sense.

where with 'good' is to be understood, primarily, praise of the quality of the wine (bouquet, taste); however, as in 1:2b and 4:10b, a moral connotation is not excluded.[370]

Third part: Agreement (7:10b–11)

Just as v. 10a forms a unit with 9cde, so 10b with 10c. This unity is indicated not only by the fact that the two stichs are uttered by the same person (the woman), but also by a clear parallelism. In fact, both begin with a participle (*hôlēk*, v. 10b; *dôbēb*, v. 10c), followed by a pair of nouns (*l^edôdî l^emêšārîm*, v. 10b; *śiptê y^ešēnîm*, v. 10c). The end rhyme (*mêšārîm—y^ešēnîm*) further unites the two stichs.

Verse 11 also belongs to this compositional unit. Contrary to widespread opinion,[371] it is not a sign of the beginning but of the conclusion of a poetic unit as is customary with the refrains (cf., with regard to the refrain of mutual belonging, 2:16 and 6:3). The link between v. 10bc and 11 is suggested by the repetition of the term *dôdî* (v. 10b and 11a, both in the first stich). As far as content is concerned, the declaration of the belonging of the woman to her beloved (v. 11a) accounts for the gift of her body made in v. 10b while the underlining of the mutual aspect (v. 11b) corresponds to the plurality of the 'sleepers' expressed in v. 10c. Rhythmically, the shorter v. 11 (2 + 2 stresses) breaks the rhythm of the previous verses: this fits in well with its concluding role.

[v. 10bc] The translation of v. 10bc offers numerous difficulties to exegetes. MT *hôlēk l^edôdî* ("which goes straight to my beloved") can only be uttered by the woman. But the procedure is unusual: the woman would be interrupting the man's speech, taking part in it by means of a subordinate clause. To various authors, this seems too modern, corresponding to an operatic duet, rather than the restrained poetry of ancient times.[372] It has been suggested, therefore, that we

---

[370] Cf., *supra*, p. 54. It is significant that the root *ṭwb* is used in the Song always in connection with the kiss (1:2b, 3a; 4:10b; 7:10a).

[371] Ravasi (1992), pp. 587–591, makes a new poetic unit begin with 7:11; so too Colombo (1975), p. 124; Lys (1968), pp. 270–271; Goulder (1986), pp. 60–61; Shea (1980), pp. 385–387; Webster (1982), pp. 74–75; Bosshard-Nepustil (1996), p. 63. Other authors claim v. 11 to be a self-standing fragment: cf. Krinetzki (1981), p. 202; Keel (1994), p. 251–252; Müller (1992), p. 77. The separation of v. 11 from v. 10 is bound up with the change of the speaking subject that is supposed by these authors.

[372] Cf. Ravasi (1992), pp. 573–575.

eliminate *l^e^dôdî*[373] or replace it with some other word which can be uttered by the man,[374] or again, as another option, attribute the whole of v. 10 to the woman.[375] Against these conjectures stands the witness of the ancient versions which agree in following the MT.[376] From a structural point of view too, this seems the best solution.[377] The woman's reply, in fact, does not come as a surprise. The passage from the third to the second person in vv. 9c–10a directly presses for it. In the first part of the Song, the description of union in 5:1 ("I have come") was preceded by the jubilant assent of the woman (4:16, "let my beloved come") to the desire expressed by the man of uniting himself with her (4:6, "I will leave"). Now also the description of union (7:12–8:5) is preceded by the agreement of the woman (7:10b–11) to the desire of the man (7:9–10a). The absence of agreement had led to the failure of the encounter in 5:6—the door can be opened only from within. Even in the *Prologue*, the description of the embrace (2:4–7) is preceded and prepared for by a duet in which the voices merge little by little (1:9–2:3). Once again, therefore, we follow the MT, leaving it to surprise us by its modernity. The woman does not allow the man to finish his speech but interrupts him, introducing herself into his phrase: the procedure expresses the spontaneity of someone who "freely anticipates the asking".[378] The 'yes' is not given unwillingly, making it burdensome: the woman allows it to be understood that the man's request corresponds to her own intimate desire.

The understood subject of the verb *hālak* ('to go') is the 'good wine', that is, the salivary liquid exchanged in the kiss.[379] The man had asked

---

[373] Thus, for example, Pope (1977), p. 639.

[374] Cf. some of the conjectures that have been proposed: *l^e^dôdîm*, 'towards the lovers' (Gordis [1974], p. 97; *l^e^dôdayi*, 'towards my embraces' (Hamp [1957], p. 209; Krinetzki, [1981], p. 198); *leḥikkî*, 'towards my palate' (Budde [1898], p. 40; Joüon [1909], p. 295). Nolli, with much fantasy, translates: "Which sweetly penetrates my lips and teeth, permeates my saliva and my very insides" (Nolli [1967], p. 135).

[375] It is the solution adopted by *JB* (1966) and *CEI*. But in the Hebrew and Syriac texts, the second person pronouns in vv. 9c–10a are feminine, and, moreover, v. 10a is inseparable from v. 9c–e.

[376] The Syriac *lddy*; LXX *tō adelphidō mou*; Vetus Latina *cum fratre meo*; Vg *dignum dilecto meo ad potandum*.

[377] In this sense also Robert – Tournay (1963), p. 273; Lys (1968), p. 269; Elliott (1989), p. 174; Heinevetter (1988), p. 152.

[378] "Liberamente al dimandar precorre", Dante, *Paradiso* 33:18 (tr. Sinclair [1972–1978], vol. III, p. 479).

[379] Garbini's highly erotic proposal, which understands the 'beloved' as the subject of 'to go', eliminating the preposition *l^e^* ("My beloved entered with ease"), seems to me

for this in v. 10a, and it is this that the woman declares herself ready to give. Perhaps we get an insight here into a typical aspect of female psychology which, even in love, is realised in the gift of itself (cf. 1:12; 4:16; 7:14). Prov 23:31 speaks of a wine which 'goes straight' (*yithallēk* *b*ᵉ*mêšārîm*): with this expression it is intended to indicate the quality of the wine. Even with us, one says of a good wine that "it goes down well": a bad wine sticks in the gullet; it does not go down well.[380]

The mention of the 'lips' in v. 10c confirms that it is kisses that are being spoken of. The meaning of the *hapaxlegomenon dābab* is not clear.[381] *HALOT* gives two roots *dbb*, one with the meaning of 'to speak',[382] the other with that of 'to slide, to flow'.[383] This second sense, supported by Aramaic, Arabic and Modern Hebrew, is better suited to the context.[384] Controversial too is the last word of the stich, *y*ᵉ*šēnîm*. The Syriac and the LXX read 'and the teeth' (*wšnym; odousin*), a translation followed by many commentators who see in the 'teeth' a parallel to the 'lips'.[385] But the MT's 'of the sleepers' is by no means impossible. In fact, in the language of the Song, 'to sleep' is a metaphor for love. It is derived, indirectly, from the 'refrain of awakening' (Song 2:7; 3:5; 8:4), where there is a request not to 'awaken' the two lovers from the sleep of love. Here too, I see no difficulty in following the MT. The plural ('of the sleepers') stresses the reciprocity of love. The 'wine' does not flow only on the man's lips but also on those of the woman. She too is inebriated by it; she too is soothed into sleep, rapt in the ecstasy of love. Inasmuch as she fills her beloved with joy ("it

completely gratuitous (cf. Garbini [1992], p. 262). The text speaks of the kiss ('lips'!), not of sexual union.

380 Cf. Delitzsch (1875), p. 118. This reading is not undisputed: Gordis (1974), p. 97, reads *l*ᵉ*mêšārîm* as a good wish ('to your health'); Goulder (1986), p. 54, understands it in an erotic sense ('to touch my love's erectness'). But the arguments, for the one interpretation as for the other, are very tenuous.

381 Cf. the versions: LXX *hikanoumenos* ('sufficient'); Vetus Latina *sufficiens*; Vg *ruminandum*; Syriac *dmzyʿ* ('which agitates').

382 So, for example, Delitzsch (1875), p. 117: "which renders eloquent the lips of him who sleeps".

383 *HALOT*, p. 208.

384 Thus the majority of commentators: cf., for example, Joüon (1909), p. 296; Robert - Tournay (1963), pp. 274–275; Rudolph (1962), p. 174; Garbini (1992), p. 261. According to this reading, however, it is necessary to understand a preposition (*b*ᵉ) before 'lips', and LXX^{A} actually has this (*en cheilesin mou*).

385 Cf. Ricciotti (1928), p. 268; Joüon (1909), p. 296; Colombo (1975), p. 122; Rudolph (1962), p. 174; Krinetzki (1981), p. 198. So too the *RSV*.

goes straight to my beloved"), she herself is satisfied ("it flows on the lips of the sleepers").[386]

[v. 11] The woman's wine goes straight to her beloved because she herself belongs to him: she is the flesh which is tending to union with that from which it was drawn (cf. Gen 2:21–24). The refrain of mutual belonging (v. 11) is a coherent insertion into the reasoning of v. 10bc. At the same time, it has a concluding function: it has been pointed out that the term *dôdî* forms an *inclusio* with *šûlammît* (v. 1),[387] demarcating the second song of the beloved man (7:1–11), and also with *raʿyātî* (6:4), marking off the section 6:4–7:11.[388]

Verse 11 has a parallel in 2:16 and 6:3. The formula recurs in each of the three passages with light, but significant, variations (cf. *Tab. 63*).

The fact that the declaration of the belonging of the woman to the man precedes its counterpart (as in 6:3, differently from 2:16) is explained here contextually, if it is true, as we have said, that 7:11 functions as justification for 10bc.

The variation in the formula of belonging—"and his desire is for me"—is also to be explained contextually. With this expression, the woman recapitulates what the man had expressed in 6:4–7:10. In particular, the reference here is to vv. 9–10a ("I said to myself..."). The parallel with 6:12 ("my desire had carried me...") was mentioned above.[389]

On the significance of the formula of mutual belonging, we refer to what was said with regard to 2:16 and 6:3.[390] It remains to comment on the singular variant in v. 11b: *ʿālay tᵉšûqātô*.[391] The term *tᵉšûqâ* appears

Table 63

2:16	*6:3*	*7:11*
My beloved is mine, and I am his.	I am my beloved's, and my beloved is mine.	I am my beloved's, and his desire is for me.

[386] Cf. the expressive relief in Keel (1994), Figure 2, p. 42.
[387] Cf., *supra*, p. 362.
[388] Cf., *supra*, pp. 321–322.
[389] Cf., *supra*, p. 322.
[390] Cf. pp. 120–122, and 313–315.
[391] It was noted above (cf., *supra*, n. 19) that the versions read *šwb*, 'convert', here instead of *šwq*, 'yearn for'. Such a reading is contrary to the allegorical interpretation of Robert – Tournay (cf. Robert – Tournay [1963], p. 276): a 'conversion' of God is, in this context, unthinkable.

only twice more in the OT, in Gen 3:16 and 4:7.[392] The rarity and importance of these occurrences renders accidental correspondence improbable. We must think rather of conscious intertextuality. In Gen 3:16, the desire of the woman for the man is seen as the origin of subordination: "your desire (*tᵉšûqātēk*) shall be for your husband, but he shall rule over you". The punishment inflicted by God after the Fall does not concern desire in itself (this was also there before the Fall),[393] but rather the lordship of the man over the woman consequent on it. This subordination did not exist before the Fall as the joyful cry of the man in 2:23 reveals. Well then, the formal of mutual belonging refers explicitly to Gen 2:23. This means to say that the Song is deliberately returning human sexuality to its paradisial position, taking away from desire the curse consequent on sin.[394] In God's plan, the Song seems to intend to say, desire is the source of reciprocal joy, not of the dominion of one sex over the other. It is interesting to observe that in Gen 3:16 the subject of the desire is the woman (*tᵉšûqātēk*) while in Song 7:11 it is the man (*tᵉšûqātô*). Already, in this change of subject, we can perceive the emphasis on reciprocity.

In Gen 3:16 and 4:7, the term *tᵉšûqâ* governs the preposition *ʾel* ('towards'), while here we have the preposition *ʿal* ('on'). Generally this anomaly is attributed to the confusion between *ʾel* and *ʿal* that is typical of Aramaic.[395] Perhaps another explanation, complementary to the preceding, is possible, that is, that the preposition *ʿal* is an echo of the verb 'to go up' (*ʿālāh*) in v. 9a. There the man expressed his desire for union, with the metaphor of 'climbing up the palm'; here, coherently, his desire is 'on me'. If we accept this correspondence, the concluding function of v. 11 appears clear: not only is the term *dôdî* a repetition of v. 10b, but also *ʿal* (v. 11b) is a repetition of v. 9a. The four terms form a chiastic structure (cf. *Tab. 64*).

---

[392] On these three texts, cf. Busenitz (1986).

[393] Something rightly emphasised by Busenitz (1986), pp. 207–208, who, however, goes too far when he holds that even man's dominion over woman corresponds to the prelapsarian situation (*ibid.*, p. 212).

[394] Cf. Keel (1994), pp. 251–252 ('Lifting the curse'). On the term *tᵉšûqâ* cf. also the stimulating reflections of Salvaneschi (1982), pp. 84–87. In this connection, Salvaneschi speaks of an "autonomous liberation of passion from judgement, an immanent song of passion itself" (p. 85). But the Song goes further than a 'neutral' presentation of passion: it presents it as a 'good' thing; it does not separate it from every ethical judgement, but confers on it a positive ethical judgement.

[395] Cf. Joüon (1909), pp. 296–297; Robert – Tournay (1963), p. 276.

Table 64

a	v. 9a	I said to myself: I will climb up (*ʿlh*) the palm,...
b	v. 10b	...which goes straight to my beloved (*dôdî*)
b'	v. 11a	I am my beloved's (*dôdî*),
a'	v. 11b	and his desire is for (*ʿal*) me.

Conclusion

As in the first part of the poem, the voice of the man responds to that of the woman. The correspondence between 4:1–5:1 and 6:4–7:11 (the first and second Songs of the Man) is underlined by the repeat of the *waṣf* 4:1–7 in 6:4–7. As in 4:1–7, the two lovers are now standing face to face. The beloved man has gone down into his garden and stands there contemplating its enthralling beauty. The time for searching, delineated in the preceding chapter, has been succeeded by that for admiration. The theme of the garden (6:11) links the Songs of the Man directly with those of the woman (6:2–3): both conclude with the refrain of mutual belonging (6:3; 7:11). The praise of her body (6:4–7; 7:2–7) responds to that of his body (5:10, 16), emphasizing the perfect reciprocity of their feelings of love.

The man's two songs make up a mirroring diptych in each part of which there is a movement from admiring contemplation of the body to the desire of being united to it by the acts of love. The first (6:4–12) is built up on the binome "fair-terrible" (6:4, 10) which corresponds to the fundamental quality of the sacred as a *mysterium fascinosum et tremendum*. Side by side with this binome is the other, "Apollonian-Dionysian". This is reflected in the disposition of the parts of the woman's body, and her character, at once "warlike and peaceful". She is *šûlammît*, the "woman of peace" and at the same time an army with banners unfurled. If, in 5:7, the maiden appeared as the helpless victim of the watchmen's brutality, now she is strong with the numinous force of the chariots of Israel (6:12). She reflects the quality of love which is defenceless as a child but "strong as death" (8,6).

Perhaps here, as in no other song there appears the supernatural dimension of love. The comparison with the heavenly phenomena (6:10) is the paradigmatic expression of the theomorphic character of the woman. There is nothing idolatrous or ironic about this, and it corresponds to the theomorphic character of the man which was displayed in 5:10–16. In 6:10, the "heavenly" character of the woman is linked to her uniqueness (6:9). To Jewish ears this can only evoke the uniqueness of the God of Israel (Deut 6:4). The Song transposes what is characteristic of the relationship between Israel and its God to the level of human love. Again, we must repeat, this is not allegory but metaphor: the emphasis is placed on monogamy in a world where polygamy was the norm.

The second song (7:1–11) is based on two characteristics of the female body, its roundedness and its height. Associated with the first, sings the author, is the welcome, the tenderness which a man finds in a woman's body, with the second, its aristocratic distance, its awareness of itself. The body appears in its splendid nakedness in correspondence with the words of Gen 2:25: "And the man and his wife were both naked, and were not ashamed". The Song brings human love back to its primal innocence before it was disturbed by sin. As proof of this paradisial nature of love, we have considered the positive use of the term *t*^{e}*šûqâ* in 7:11.

In both songs, the female body appears to be immersed not only in the geography but also in the history of Israel: the woman is beautiful like Jerusalem and Tirzah (6:4); she is Rachel, the mother ewe (6:6); she possesses the might of the chariots of Israel (6:12); she is the 'daughter of a noble one' (7:2). The markedly nationalistic character of the Song situates it close to Sir 24 with the strong self-awareness which the Jewish people assumed during the Hellenistic period.

CHAPTER NINE

FINAL SONGS OF THE BELOVED WOMAN

(Song 7:12–8:4)

Union in Nature

Woman [12]“Come, my beloved,
let us go out into the country!
We shall spend the night among the henna-bushes,[1]
[13]early in the morning, we shall go to the vineyards:
we shall see whether the vine has budded,
whether the buds have opened,
whether the pomegranate trees are in flower.
There I will give you my love.[2]

[14]The mandrakes pour forth fragrance,
and all kinds of choice fruits are at our doors
new as well as old:[3]
I have guarded them for you, my beloved.

---

[1] MT *k*^{e}*pārîm* can mean both ‘villages’ (from *kāpār*: this is the reading of the versions: LXX *en kōmais*; Vetus Latina *in castellis*; Vg *in villis*; Syr *bkpr’*), and ‘plants of henna’ (from *kōper*, cf. 1:14; 4:13).

[2] With MT’s *dōday*, lit. ‘my caresses’. As in 1:2, 4; 4:10, the versions read *dadday*, ‘my breasts’, as in Song 1:2, 4; 4:10.

[3] Symmachus (followed by the Syro-Hexaplar version) adds: *hosa edōke moi hē mētēr mou*, ‘which my mother has given me’.

Union in the City

8 [1]Oh that you were[4] like[5] a brother to me,
suckled at the breast[6] of my mother!
If I met you outside, I would kiss you,
and no one would despise me.
[2]I would lead you, I would bring you
into the house of my mother: you would be my teacher.[7]
I would make you drink spiced wine,
the juice of my pomegranate.[8]

[3]His left hand is under my head
And his right arm embraces me.
[4]I charge you, daughters of Jerusalem:
why do you want to rouse, why to awaken love,
before it wishes?"

Structure

With the two *Final Songs of the Beloved Woman*, the second part of the poem reaches its conclusion: if we have been counting correctly, there are seven (!) songs, five delivered by the woman—three at the beginning of the composition (5:2–6:3) and two at the end (7:12–8:4)—, and two by the man (6:4–7:11). Like the first part, the second also ends with the union of the two lovers in the garden (7:2–14; cf. 4:16–5:1).

---

[4] Lit.: "Who will give you to me as brother". Here we have a rhetorical question, which is intended to express a desire (cf. *GKC* §151b).

[5] The Hebrew particle *k*[e] ('as') is lacking in LXX ("Who will give you to me, my brother?", similarly also Vg and Vetus Latina). It is, therefore, omitted as dittography by some authors. Cf. Rudolph (1962), p. 178; *CEI*; *NET*; *NJB*). However, it is present in the Syriac and in Aquila.

[6] Lit. 'sucking the breasts'.

[7] Lit.: 'you would teach me', *t*[e]*lamm*[e]*dēnî*. It is also possible to understand MT: 'and she (my mother) would teach me', or 'who has taught me' (cf. Müller [1992], p. 80). LXX, the Syriac and Vetus Latina substitute: 'and into the chamber of her who conceived me' (cf. 3:4). Some authors propose correcting *t*[e]*lamm*[e]*dēnî* with *tēl*[e]*dēnî*, 'who conceived me', from the root *yld* (cf. Rudolph [1962], p. 178), but this is a *lectio facilior*. MT is supported by Vg (*ibi me docebis*) and by some codices of the Syro-Hexaplar (*didaxeis me*).

[8] With MT. Some Hebrew manuscripts have the plural *rimmōnîm* (cf. *BHS*). Some codices of LXX, Vg, Vetus Latina, and the Syriac have the plural with the suffix of the first person singular: 'my pomegranates'. MT seems preferable as the *lectio difficilior*.

The tension, begun with the woman's search for her beloved (5:2–6:3), sharpened, mirror-like, with the man's desire for his beloved woman (6:4–7:11), finds its release in the long prepared for union of the two lovers. Both the 'searches' lead to the 'garden' (6:2–3 and 6:11), which is not only a metaphor for the woman but also the place of love ("*There* I will give you my love", 7:13).

In both parts of the poem, the contemplation of the woman's body precedes the union. In fact, this explains the concatenation of the two songs of the man in the first part (4:1–7 and 4:8–5:1), just like the passage from the songs of the man (6:4–7:11) to those of the woman (7:12–8:4) in the present composition. The journey of love is analogous in the two parts. In both, the woman's assent to the man's desire (4:16; 7:10b–11) directly introduces the description of the union (5:1; 7:12–8:4). In this second part, the continuity between 6:4–7:11 and 7:12–8:4 is signalled by the repetition of the terms *gepen* ('vine', 6:11; 7:9 and 13); *yayin* ('wine', 7:10 and 8:2); *rimmôn* ('pomegranate', 6:11; 7:13 and 8:2); *šādayim* ('breasts', 7:4, 8, 9 and 8:1); *dôdî* ('my beloved', 7:10, 11 and 12, 14); *rêaḥ* ('scent/fragrance', 7:9 and 14), and *ʾahăbâ* ('love', 7:7 and 8:4).

The literary unity of Song 7:12–8:4 is not universally accepted.[9] Actually, of the two songs, 7:12–14 and 8:1–4, each presents a distinct scenario: the first unfolds in the country, in nature, the second in the city and in the 'house of my mother'. The link which binds the two pictures is not narratival but lyrical: it is precisely the counterposing of 'nature' and 'city', a *Leitmotiv* of the Song which has already been introduced in the two *waṣf*s of 6:4–12 and 7:2–6. In both the songs, union is mentioned, but in 7:12–14 the two lovers are alone, immersed in nature, while in 8:1–4, they are part of the urban society of the family. The theme of society will be taken up again and deepened in the *Epilogue* (8:5–14). The *Final Songs of the Beloved Woman* thus constitute an *inclusio* with the first two, at the beginning of the first part of the poem. In 2:8–17, in fact, it was love in nature that was being sung

[9] Apart from the fact that the majority of commentators begin the song with v. 11, there are few who observe the reciprocal relationship of the two songs 7:12–14 and 8:1–4. Among these few, cf. Ravasi (1992), pp. 588–592; Dorsey (1990), pp. 89–90; Heinevetter (1988), p. 157; Lys (1968), p. 270; Roberts (2007), pp. 292–317. Keel (1994), pp. 253–266, divides thus: 7:12–13; 7:14–8:2; 8:3–4; Krinetzki (1981), pp. 204–216: 7:12–13; 7:14; 8:1–2; 8:3; 8:4; Gerleman (1965), pp. 205–213: 7:12–13; 7:14–8:4. More frequent is the division into two independent songs: 7:12–14 and 8:1–4 (cf., for example, Rudolph [1962], pp. 175–179; Garbini [1992], pp. 263–268).

Table 65

I. Nature—7:12–14 (to go out)	A. Problem: vv. 12–13	a. *rimmônîm, v. 13d* b. *nātan, v. 13e*
	B. Response: v. 14	b. *nātan, v. 14a*
II. City—8:1–4 (to come in)	A. Problem: vv. 1–2	b'. *nātan, v. 1a* a'. *rimmōnî, v. 2d*
	B. Response: vv. 3–4	

while in 3:1–5 the search for the beloved man through the streets and squares of the city was counterposed to this idyllic picture. In both cases, love gets the better of the obstacles placed by the 'city' (3:4; cf. 8:3), but the latter is rebuked for its hostile attitude with regard to love (3:5; cf. 8:4).[10] As it is a conclusion, it is natural to find in it multiple links with what has gone before.[11]

In addition to the 'country-city' polarity, the two songs are connected also by another: 'to go out-to come in' (cf. *Tab. 65*). To the two verbs "come, let us go out" (7:12) correspond, in fact, in 8:2, two other verbs which indicate the reverse movement: "I would lead you, I would bring you in".[12] The literal links between 7:12–14 and 8:1–4 are not many: however we can note the important verb *nātan* ('to give', 7:13e, 14a; 8:1a) and the noun *rimmôn* ('pomegranate tree/pomegranate', 7:13d; 8:2d): the four terms form a chiasm (a-b-b'-a').[13]

The structure of the two songs is similar in many ways. In fact, each is composed of two parts, in which the first outlines a request or a difficulty, the second offers the response. In 7:12–13, the woman wishes to see if the plants are in flower. The response is given in 7:14: not only the flowers but also the fruits are ready. Analogously, in 8:1–2, the woman is ashamed to embrace her man in public: in 8:2–4, the embrace happens, despite the talk of the people ('daughters of Jerusalem').

[10] For the verbal references between 2:8–3:5 and 7:12–8:4, cf. pp. 253–254.

[11] Given the link between the *New Songs of the Beloved Woman* (5:2–6:3) and the earlier ones (2:8–3:5), it is natural to observe also the links between the *New Songs of the Beloved Woman* and the final ones. In the new ones also, in fact, one can note the same opposition between city (5:6–9) and nature (6:2–3). The verbal correspondences are: 'to find' (8:1 and 5:6, 7, 8) and 'daughters of Jerusalem' (8:4 and 5:8, 16).

[12] Cf. Elliott (1989), p. 176.

[13] Furthermore, the hook by means of the particle *gam*, 'also' (7:14d; 8:1d) is to be noted.

Union in Nature (7:12–14)

As we have noted, the song is composed of two strophes, vv. 12–13 and 14, which can be looked on as request and response. Within each strophe, one can observe a further bipartition in the sense that, in the beginning, the metaphor of nature is evoked (vv. 12–13d, 14a–c), in the end, mention is made of the two lovers (vv. 13e, 14d). In this sense, the structure is alternate: a-b-a'-b' (cf. *Tab. 66*).

Among the lexical correspondences we should underline first of all the *inclusio* created by the term *dôdî* (vv. 12a and 14d). The term forms a subtle paronomasia with the related *dôdîm* ('caresses', v. 13e) and *dûdā'îm* ('mandrake', v. 14a), the former at the conclusion of the first strophe and the second at the beginning of the second so as to form reciprocal *inclusio*s with *dôdî*. The root *ptḥ* offers another correspondence: it is present in v. 13bc ('to bud, to be opened') and in v. 14b ('openings, doors'). Finally, the verb *nātan* ('to give') links the end of the first strophe with the beginning of the second (vv. 13e, 14a). The four terms correspond in chiastic form (cf. *Tab. 66*).

From the beginning to the end of the song, one can observe a progression in the use of the senses. We pass from 'seeing' (v. 13b), to smelling ('fragrance', v. 14a), to eating ('fruits', vv. 14b–d), repeating the itinerary already observed in 7:1–11. Naturally the intention is to speak of amorous enjoyment. The progression continues in 8:2 where 'drinking' is mentioned. In parallel fashion, we pass from the description of 'flowers' in the first strophe, to that of 'fruits' in the second: the first strophe evokes spring, the second, autumn.

First strophe: The flowers (7:12–13)

From the rhythmic point of view, the strophe is based on ternary rhythm (cf. *Tab. 67*). After an isolated stich (v. 12a), there follow three cohortatives in the first person plural ("let us go out", "we shall spend

Table 66

A. 7:12–13	a. nature: vv. 12–13d b. love: v. 13e	*dôdî* (v. 12a); *pātaḥ* (v. 13c) *nātan*; *dôdîm*
B. 7:14	a'. nature: v. 14a–c b'. love: v. 14d	*dûdā'îm*; *nātan* (v. 14a); *pātaḥ* (v. 14b) *dôdî*

Table 67

	Come,	
let us go out	We shall spend the night	early in the morning, we shall go
	we shall see	
whether the vines have budded	whether the buds have opened	whether the pomegranates are in flower
	I will give you	

the night", "early in the morning, we shall go"), denoting a movement towards nature as the place of love (vv. 12b–13a) The fourth verb of the series ("we shall see") rules a series of three interrogative propositions (v. 13bcd). An isolated stich (v. 13e) which matches the initial one, closes the strophe.[14]

[7:12] "Come, my beloved, let us go out...". The two verbs, 'come' (*l*^{e}*kâ*) and 'let us go out' (*nēṣē'*), have their equivalent, the first in 2:10, 13, the second in 1:8 (cf. 3:11). In both cases, we have noted the link with the exodic character of love which is expressed symbolically in Gen 2:24. In the first part of the poem, it was the woman who was invited to go out (in Song 2:10, 13, on the part of the man): now it is her turn to take the initiative, to invite her man to abandon his security in order to commit himself to the adventure of love.[15] Does she thus want to make up for the hesitations of Song 5:3?

The plural ("let us go out") is not accidental. It characterises the whole song, up to the paradox of 'our doors' in v. 14b. The plural is a sign of union: it was announced in v. 10 ('sleepers'). We have detected an analogous phenomenon in 1:15–17 where the singular of the lovers, in vv. 15–16a, is transformed into the plural of vv. 16b–17 ('our bed', 'our house', 'our ceiling'). The 'I' and the 'thou/you' give place to the 'we'. In particular, as far as the 'going out' is concerned, the reference

[14] Yet again, given a careful construing of the actual Hebrew text, we have little inclination to eliminate any words or to change their order on the basis of highly hypothetical conjectures. For example, a synthesis of vv. 12c and 13a is often made, by eliminating *bakk*^{e}*pārîm* from v. 12c and replacing it with *bakk*^{e}*rāmîm*, which is consequently omitted from v. 13a; thus Wittekindt (1925), pp. 52–53; Ringgren (1962), p. 288; Haller (1940), p. 42.

[15] "The house is the familiar and the protected, the country is the rustic and the dangerous [...]. The house is the enclosed and the secluded, the country is the open and the exposed" (Alonso Schökel [1990], p. 65).

is to 4:8—"With me...come". The journey is made together, as the icon of 8:5 expresses: "Who is this who rises from the desert, *leaning on her beloved*?"

The destination of the journey is 'the country' (*śādeh*). In 2:7 and 3:5, the term expressed the habitat of the wild animals, that is, the wilderness, the desert. Here, it has another meaning, as the context indicates: in fact, *śādeh* is placed in parallel with 'henna-bushes' (v. 12c), 'vineyards' (v. 13a) and 'pomegranate trees' (v. 13d). That is, it has the same trees as the 'garden' (cf. 6:11; 4:13). Symbolically, however, the function is analogous: *śādeh* represents 'nature' by contrast with the 'city'; which will be represented in the following song.[16] To see, with Lacocque and Garbini, an intention in our text to correct Gen 4:8[17] is, perhaps, excessive;[18] rather, the parallel, which is undoubted, leads us to understand the invitation as the desire of the lovers to be alone, far from prying looks (cf. again 1 Sam 20:5–11).[19] Deut 22:23–27 catches, in paradigmatic form, how being in the country (*baśśādeh*) is a 'being alone', by contrast with being in the city (*ba'îr*). What is perceived as the 'protection' of love in the Deuteronomic legislation is seen here as an obstacle (cf. Song 8:1–4). The looks of other people take away the spontaneity from the lovers. Certainly it is necessary to confront the city, but, first, comes the encounter of the two persons in the solitude and freedom of the country where the trees are witnesses of the truth of the words and gestures of love.

What follows indicates that the purpose of the going out is not an harmless country walk but a true and real encounter of love. The verb *lîn* ('to spend the night') refers to 1:13—"My beloved is to me a bag of myrrh, passing the night (*yālîn*) between my breasts". The correspondence of the two passages is certainly intentional, for two other lexemes from 1:14 ('henna', 'vineyards') are repeated in 7:12c, 13a.

---

[16] This meaning is typical of the lexeme (cf., for example, Deut 28:3; cf. G. Wallis, *śādeh*, in *TDOT*, vol. XIV, pp. 38–39).

[17] In conformity with the Syriac, LXX, Vg and the Targum, *BHS* suggests conjecturing: *nēl^{e}kāh haśśādeh* for MT.

[18] "In the country villages the lovers will spend the night making love, not war!" (Lacocque [1998], p. 158). "[...] in order to emphasise, not without polemic, the difference between her invitation to love and that which the sacred text presents as an invitation to death" (Garbini [1992], p. 264).

[19] "One goes into the fields to be alone with someone else, unobserved by others" (Keel [1994], p. 254).

In this context, to translate *k^e^pārîm* with 'villages', following the ancient versions, seems, frankly, out of place.[20] The term is a specification of 'fields' (*śādeh*, v. 12b) and stands in parallel with 'vineyards' and 'pomegranate trees'. If the two young people wish to be alone, they are certainly not passing the night in a village where the eyes of the inhabitants are no less prying than in the city. The picture being sketched is like that of 1:16–17 ("our bed is fresh grass, and the beams of our house the cedars, our roof the cypresses").[21] The country is not only the opportunity for the intimacy of the two lovers; it is also the environment of love. However, there is no identification of the 'henna-bushes' with the woman: such an identification will come shortly in v. 13bcd. Here, in vv. 12–13a, 'fields', 'henna-bushes' and 'vineyards' are not directly symbols of the woman.[22] That is excluded by the fact that the woman is part of the plural subject of the verbs: she cannot be their subject and object simultaneously. In our song, the natural metaphors oscillate continually between two meanings: sometimes they are the place of love ("*There* I will give you my love", v. 13e), at other times they are the symbol of the woman ("If the vines have budded", v. 13b). An analogous case can be detected in the metaphor of the garden which in 4:12 is identified with the woman ("[you are] a garden enclosed"), while in 8:13, of the woman it is said that "she dwells in the gardens".

[v. 13] Verse 13a (*naškîmâ lakk^e^rāmîm*)[23] is closely connected with v. 12c (*nalînâ bakk^e^pārîm*) both from the rhythmic[24] and the logical

---

[20] *Contra*, among others, Delitzsch (1875), p. 120; Joüon (1909), p. 298; Robert – Tournay (1963), p. 278; Gerleman (1965), p. 207; Krinetzki (1981), p. 204; Colombo (1975), p. 125; Murphy (1990), p. 180; Lacocque (1998), p. 158. Also Salvaneschi's suggestion that the author might have been playing on the two senses of the word seems improbable to me in this case. Cf. Salvaneschi (1982), p. 97.

[21] On the mythological background of the 'bed in the grass' and its parallels with Hellenistic and Egyptian poetry, cf., *supra*, n. 157, p. 81.

[22] *Contra* Krinetzki (1981), p. 206, who sees the same symbols of the 'great mother' here. Cf. the biting criticism by Keel (1994), pp. 254–255: "Instead of Israel or the Church or the believing soul, now it is the *anima* or the Great Mother that is found hiding under every vine. This interpretation obliterates the rich textures of the Song and turns the wonderful variety of ingredients into a monotonous stew".

[23] The expression is an example of brachylogy, which is attested also in prose (cf. Gen 19:27; Judg 19:9), which means literally: "We shall get up early (in the morning, to go) into the vineyards".

[24] "*bkprym* is found in parallel with *bkrmym*, despite the misleading stichometric division of the text that has been handed down" (Garbini [1992], pp. 264–265). Actually, it is more logical to divide: 12ab (two statements) and 12c–13a (two further

points of view. The three places, 'fields', 'henna-bushes' and 'vineyards' are, as has been noted, synonyms to indicate the environment of love;[25] in v. 13b, the vegetable metaphor has a different significance. Moreover, the link between 'henna-bushes' (v. 12c) and 'vineyards' (v. 13a) is confirmed by the parallel with 1:14 ("My beloved is to me a bunch of henna [*kpr*] among the vineyards [*krm*] of Engeddi"). Finally, we should observe the polarity between 'passing the night' (*nālînâ*) and 'going early in the morning' (*nāškîma*). The temporal succession is coherent.

According to an ancient tradition, mentioned in the *Mishnah* and the *Babylonian Talmud*, the girls of Jerusalem used to go out twice a year, on the 15th of Ab and on the Day of Atonement, to dance among the vineyards.[26] These were propitious occasions for a young man to be able to find the woman of his life. Perhaps also we also have an echo of a similar practice in Judg 21:15–25.[27] It is possible that such traditions play a role in the background of our verse: they are, however, transformed and incorporated into the poetics of the Song.

If, on the one hand, *naškîmâ lakkᵉrāmîm* is linked with what precedes it, it also performs an immediate introduction to what follows. In fact, 'seeing' denotes a connection with light: it is necessary for morning to come if we are to be able to see. The actual object of seeing, the *gepen* (vine) is understood as a specification of the *kᵉrāmîm*, as one of the elements of the 'vineyards'. The division of the MT, which places *naškîmâ lakkᵉrāmîm* at the beginning of v. 13, is not, therefore, without reason. Here too, one can speak of *enjambement*.

The interrogative particle which follows, *ʾim* ('if/whether'), governs three parallel clauses (v. 13bcd).[28] The first and third ("whether the vine has budded" and "whether the pomegranates are in flower") are a literal repetition of 6:11. There it was the man who wished to see if the 'vine' and 'pomegranate' were in flower. As has been seen, the two

---

statements). Cf. Zapletal (1907), p. 141. However, we do not agree with Garbini on the replacement of *lakkᵉrāmîm* with *bakkᵉrāmîm*.

[25] There is no question, therefore, of successive stages in a journey. The place is the same: it is the 'country', of which the 'henna-bushes' and the 'vineyards' are a part. In this sense, 7:13a is distanced from other uses of the term *kerem* in the Song, where it is a metaphor for the woman (cf. 1:6; 8:11–12), or, by extension, for the two lovers (2:15).

[26] Cf., *supra*, p. 3.

[27] Cf. Segal (1962), pp. 485–488; Keel (1994), pp. 101–102.

[28] Cf. Elliott (1989), p. 177.

plants are symbolic of the woman whose sexual maturity the young man wishes to realise.[29] The repetition of the words of the man by the woman has the significance of agreement to the desire expressed there, along the lines of the mirroring we have noted several times. The term *gepen* was also pronounced by the man in 7:9 with reference to the woman's breasts. Probably here too, we can make out a reference to the development of the breasts as a sign of sexual maturity.

Verse 13c ("whether the buds have opened") is a reprise of 2:13, 15.[30] As in the first song of the beloved woman, the correspondence of which with the last song has been stressed, here too there is expressed a continuity between the awakening of nature in spring and the awakening of love in the body (and in the heart, cf. 5:3–6) of a young woman.[31] Love has its seasons which are not to be forced (cf. Ezek 16:7–8).

As in Song 6:11, the 'pomegranate', another metaphor for the female body, in particular of the breasts,[32] is juxtaposed with the 'vine' in v. 13d, even if an exact correspondence between the metaphor and the woman's body is ruled out by the fact that, both in the case of the vine and in that of the pomegranate, mention is made of flowers, not of fruits. Allusion is being made, therefore, in a general way, to the signs of the sexual maturity of the woman.

The adverb *šām* in v. 13e is ambivalent. Usually, it has a local value ('there'). In this sense, it would be referring to vv. 12–13a, that is to nature as the *place* of love. But the adverb can also have a temporal value ('then'),[33] and this sense would correspond better to the signs of the maturing of love expressed in v. 13bcd. This second meaning of *šām* could be paraphrased thus: "In the case of a positive response to

---

[29] Cf., *supra*, p. 354.

[30] *sᵉmādār* in the three cases expresses the 'flowers of the vines': the phrase is to be understood as synonymous with v. 13b. Garbini mistakenly shifts the stich to after the following one, seeing an allusion there to the flowers of the vine and of the pomegranate. Cf. Garbini (1992), p. 265.

[31] In the 'opening' of the shoots, Müller (1992), p. 78, sees an allusion to the opening of the womb, that is, to the deflowering of the woman (cf. also R. Barthelmus, *pātaḥ*, in *TDOT*, vol. XII, p. 183). But, in our case, the term 'to open' has a more general sense. In fact, there is an allusion to the consummation of love in v. 13e: that would not make sense if this had already taken place.

[32] Cf. p. **00**. In this connection, cf. the Turin Papyrus 1:2, 4–5 (cited in n. 73, p. 183), or even the following modern Arabic poem: "Look at the sweet one in the garden, / she is swaying like the branch of a willow; / I put out my hand to the pomegranate, / but she said: 'I am green, I am not ripe, / O light of the eye'" (cf. Dalman [1901], p. 250). On the erotic significance of the pomegranate, cf. also Lavoie (1995), p. 135.

[33] Cf. *HALOT*, p. 1547; Robert – Tournay (1963), p. 279.

the three 'whethers' mentioned in the preceding stichs...". Perhaps it is not necessary to choose between the two options and the two meanings can be retained. The local sense refers to the continuity between nature and human love, as will also be confirmed by the *Epilogue* of the Song: "Under the apple tree I have wakened you" (8:5). The 'place' of love is not the stones of the city but living nature which is born, reproduces itself and dies.[34] The temporal sense refers, not already to the eschatological age, as Robert and Tournay would see it,[35] but to that of the maturing of love. 'Then', when the vine and the pomegranate are in flower, the woman will give her love.

The terms of the promise are worthy of note. Object of the phrase is *dôdîm*, a plural of abstraction already encountered in 1:2, 4 and 4:10 (twice). Phonetically and etymologically it is bound up with *dôdî* ('my beloved', vv. 12a and 14d) and with *dûdāʾîm* ('mandrakes', v. 14a) and expresses the sexual encounter from the point of view of tenderness.[36] Here again, the term does not permit a glimpse of any negative connotation, such as is usual in the OT (cf. Ezek 23:17; Prov 7:18).

The verb is *nātan* ('to give'), a *Leitwort* in our passage (cf., again, v. 14a, lit.: "The mandrakes *give* fragrance", and 8:1, lit.: "Who will *give* you to me as a brother"). Its not superficial significance was put forward in 1:12–"My nard *gives/pours forth* its fragrance".[37] There, as in 7:14, it is *giving* fragrance; here, of *giving* love: in the language of the Song, the two things are synonymous. The way in which the woman describes the sexual encounter is, however, illuminating: as a 'giving' or, better, as a 'self-giving', because, behind the gift of one's own love, there is the gift of oneself, and this is reciprocal as 8:1 allows us to understand. Gollwitzer is right to state that *eros* is inseparable from *agape* in the Song.[38]

Second strophe: The fruits (7:14)

Not everyone accepts that v. 14 is connected with the two verses that precede it. The recent authoritative commentaries of Krinetzki and

---

[34] With that is excluded the identification of 'country', 'henna' and 'vineyards' with the woman's body. So, rightly, Rudolph (1962), p. 176.

[35] "Ce sera la consommation de l'alliance nouvelle et définitive entre Yahvé et Israël" (Robert - Tournay [1963], p. 280).

[36] Cf., *supra*, p. 54.

[37] Cf., *supra*, pp. 74–75.

[38] Casalis, Gollwitzer and De Pury (1984), pp. 59–72.

Müller treat it as a composition in itself, while Gerleman and Keel link it to 8:1–4.[39] The reasons for considering it the second strophe of the song 7:12–14, have been listed above: I would like to stress once again the relationship of the two strophes as request and response. Verse 13 closes with a conditional promise: "If the flowers have come out…, I will give you my love". Verse 14 does away with this reservation: the time of love has arrived because not only the flowers but the fruits have come. The promise can, therefore, be realised: the union can take place.

[v. 14] "The mandrakes pour forth fragrance…". The Hebrew term *dûdāʾîm* ('mandrakes') has a parallel in the Ugaritic *ddym*[40] which makes one suppose a link with the root *dd* ('love'). Actually, the only other passage in the OT in which the term appears, Gen 30:14–24, connects the mandrake with fertility. In our passage, it is not so much fertility as erotic desire which is to the fore; but the two realities are correlated. There is a widespread tradition about the aphrodisiac value of the mandrake, not only in Graeco-Roman antiquity but also in Mediaeval and Renaissance Europe.[41] Generally, however, the aphrodisiac character is attached to the roots which vaguely recall the form of a human trunk. In our text 'fragrance' is mentioned: the reference is, therefore, to the fruit of the mandrake. In spring, the mandrake already produces from three to five large berries of a yellowish colour which give off a very penetrating, but not disagreeable perfume.[42] And it is to this perfume of the 'apples of love' that numerous Egyptian representations refer where the mandrakes are associated with lotus flowers[43] or with pomegranates.[44] In a fragment of love songs from the Vase of Deir el-Medineh, the young man expresses the following desire:

> If only I were her Nubian maid,
> her attendant in secret!
> She brings <her> [a bowl of] mandragoras…
> It is in her hand,

[39] Cf. Krinetzki (1981), pp. 207–210; Müller (1992), p. 79; Gerleman (1986), pp. 208–210; Keel (1994), p. 256.
[40] Cf. *HAH*, p. 244.
[41] Cf. Pope (1977), pp. 647–649; Moldenke & Moldenke (1952), pp. 137–139; Ravasi (1992), pp. 602–603.
[42] Cf. Zohary (1982), pp. 188–189.
[43] Cf Keel (1994), Figure 150, p. 258; 151, p. 259.
[44] Cf Keel (1994), Figure 152, p. 263.

while she gives pleasure.
In other words:
she would grant me
the hue of her whole body.[45]

"And all kinds of choice fruits are at our doors". The term *p^etāḥîm* signifies literally 'openings', and is a repetition of the verb *pātaḥ* in v. 13c ("whether the buds *have opened*"). The response is, therefore, positive: the bodies are open to love. The plural ('our doors') is problematic because in v. 14d it is only the woman who is the 'guardian' of the fruits, and, moreover, the 'vine' in v. 13bc, was an image of her. As A. Robert and R. Tournay observe, it is not necessary to correct ('at our door' or 'at my door') because we could have here a poetic plural or a plural of generalisation with singular value.[46] The 'choice fruits' (*m^egādîm*) are, in 4:13, 16, the joys which the woman knows how to offer to her man in the encounter of love. Various interpreters understand the expression 'our doors' in an anatomical sense, as though indicating the female womb:[47] this was also the case with the garden in 4:12–5:1. It is, however, also possible to refer the 'doors' to that 'house in the green' which was spoken of in 1:17 ("the beams of our house the cedars, our roof the cypresses") and which will come up again in 8:5 (cf. also 2:3 with regard to the fruit). In our case, it would refer to the 'henna-bushes' and to the 'vineyards' as the place of love (vv. 12c, 13a): such a house is 'ours' (his and hers) and has many doors and windows

---

[45] Lines 18–19, according to Fox (1985), p. 37, cf. Derchain (1975), p. 77. See also l. 5 of the same collection, in which the girl speaks of the love of her beloved: "It is like a mandragora in a man's hand" (Fox [1985], p. 31). In the hymn to Ramesses IV (or V?), it is said of the Pharaoh: "Your perfume, your perfume is like that of the mandrakes" (Mathieu [1996], p. 108, n. 363). Similar tones resound in Papyrus Harris 500A 2:9: "Memphis is a jar of mandragoras / set before the Gracious One" (tr. Fox [1985], p. 12). Keel (1994), pp. 257–260, quotes a passage from another love song in which the young man in love says of his sweetheart: "Your skin is the skin of the mandrake, which induces loving".

[46] Robert - Tournay (1963), p. 281. We have encountered a similar phenomenon in 2:15 ("*our vineyards* are in flower") (cf. pp. 117–118). Perhaps here too it is possible to think in an extended sense of the bodies of the two lovers. In any case, the first person plural possessive ('our') is retained, even with reference to the 'gate' of the woman: one can encounter here that same change of ownership which was expressed in 4:16 in the passage from 'my garden' to 'his garden'.

[47] Cf. Wittekindt (1925), p. 54 ('pudendum mulieris'); Krinetzki (1981), pp. 208–209; Garbini (1992), p. 265. *Per contra*, Keel's observation: "It would be wiser not to give a Freudian interpretation to every opening and every space in the Song—seeing these as symbols of the womb" (Keel [1994], p. 260).

(the openings among the branches).[48] 'At our doors' would have here the sense of 'being within reach'.[49] This second interpretation seems to us more congenial to the metaphorical language of the Song. Perhaps, however, we do not need to choose: double meanings are a normal procedure in love poetry.[50]

With the term *m^e^gādîm*, we pass from smell (v. 14a) to taste. 'Fruit' is there to be eaten, as was said in 4:16f: it is an erotic metaphor.[51] At the comment on 4:13, 16,[52] it was observed that *m^e^gādîm* refers to Deut 33:13–16, the blessing of Joseph:

> Blessed by YHWH be his land:
> with the choicest (*meged*) of heaven, the dew [...]
> with the choicest (*meged*) of the fruits of the sun,
> with the choicest (*meged*) of what each month produces [...],
> with the choicest (*meged*) of the everlasting hills
> and with the choicest (*meged*) of the earth and all that therein is.

Song 4:13–16; 7:14 and Deut 33:13–16 are the only attestations of this word in the OT: the echo can hardly be fortuitous. The parallel cannot escape an assiduous reader of the Scriptures. This confirms that identity of the woman with the promised land which has already been encountered several times, precisely in the second part of the poem when the woman's body was compared to the cities and mountains of Israel (cf. 6:4, 5; 7:5, 6). The woman belongs to the promised land; she is its personification. Therefore, the fruits which she offers are choice and precious like the fruits of that land. They are a good gift of YHWH, given to his people to make use of with joy.[53] To despise this gift would be an act of ingratitude in one's dealings with the donor.[54]

The link of the woman with the land is confirmed by the expression that follows: "new as well as old". The two adjectives, *yāšān* and *ḥādāš*,

---

[48] This is the interpretation of Elliott (1989), p. 182; Ravasi (1992), pp. 604–605.

[49] Delitzsch (1875), p. 122, understands *ʿal p^e^tāḥênû* 'above our doors', making reference to the practice of putting out fruit to dry above and within the door of the house. But nothing indicates that the two are in a normal house: the encounter takes place in nature.

[50] Cf. Lys (1968), p. 275. On 'double entendre' as an essential element of the poetry of the Song, cf. Ricoeur (1998), pp. 273–274; Alter (1985), pp. 185–203. Ricoeur sees a kind of 'poetic sublimation' of eroticism in this procedure.

[51] This meaning is emphasised by Symmachus and by the Syro-Hexapla which add, after 'old': "which my mother has given me" (cf., *supra*, n. 3).

[52] *Supra*, p. 223.

[53] Cf. Luther's aphorism: "Appetitus ad mulierem est bonum donum Dei" (according to Ravasi [1992], p. 596).

[54] Cf. Num 13–14; Deut 1:19–33.

appear, in fact, in Lev 26:10 with reference to the fruits of the promised land. One of the blessings connected with the observance of the Torah goes: "You shall eat old (*yāšān*) store long kept, and you shall clear out the old (*yāšān*) to make way for the new (*ḥādāš*)". The expression indicates the prodigious abundance of the fruits of the land. 'New' and 'old' form a merismus to indicate the totality of the harvest.[55] But here the intention is to say more than just 'all the fruits': the intention is to express the miracle of love, old as the world, but always new, which never repeats itself. A woman who loves is able to surprise her partner with inventions that are always new.[56] In an analogous way, Augustine calls on God: "O beauty so old and so young".[57]

"I have guarded them for you, my beloved". Here the woman evidently passes from the signifier to the signified: the fruits are the symbol of the joys which she wishes to give to her man in the intimacy of love. Structurally, the phrase stands in parallel with the conclusion of the first strophe: "There I will give you my love" (v. 13e). The two sentences express an antithesis which has already been revealed in connection with the garden which is 'enclosed' (4:12), only 'to be opened' to the beloved (4:16).[58] Analogously here, the 'fruits' are first of all 'guarded' (the Hebrew verb *ṣāpan* properly signifies 'to hide'): the term is a discreet allusion to the chastity and the restraint which is the fundamental quality of female fascination. The Song certainly does not champion sexual promiscuity. Chastity is not seen as a privation, however: it is a quality of love, and it is in the service of love. Just as in the case of the garden, here too the 'fruits' are 'guarded' (*ṣāpan*, v. 14) in order to be given (*nātan*, v. 13) to the loved one. In this context, Krinetzki speaks again of the 'mystery' (*ṣāpan*) which each lover remains for his own partner. In sexual intimacy, the mystery is unveiled, but always partially, never wholly:

> Only in so far as each person, especially the woman for the man and *vice versa*, remains a mystery for the other can the two lovers attract each other and come together with ever new surprises which render their relationship interesting and, in the long term, worthy of being maintained.[59]

---

[55] So Keel (1994), p. 260; Gerleman (1965), p. 211 (citing Matt 13,52).
[56] Cf. Krinetzki (1981), p. 209.
[57] *Confessions* 10:27 (38).
[58] Cf., *supra*, pp. 219–220.
[59] Krinetzki (1981), p. 209.

Union in the City (8:1–4)

This small song is clearly marked off from its predecessor by the different scenario: the two pictures, 'love in the country' and 'love in the city' are juxtaposed with each other without apparent continuity. The transition is not narratival but logical, and it is that of an antithesis: just as nature is the ally of love, the city is hostile to it. Verse 1a ("Oh that you were like a brother to me") places the realisation of the dream of love under the mark of impossibility: what is described in vv. 1–2 is seen as something unattainable.

Less clear is the boundary with the following context. Various authors separate vv. 1–2 from vv. 3–4: this would be a slavish repetition of 2:6–7 and 3:5 which would not take account of the preceding verses.[60] Actually, the passage from v. 2 to v. 3 is rather abrupt: there are no direct lexical links between vv. 1–2 and vv. 3–4. But it has been remarked several times that the refrains of the Song are never a mechanical repetition: they fit in logically with their context. We have suggested above[61] the possibility of considering the two verses as the response to the difficulties raised by vv. 1–2: what appeared impossible in vv. 1–2 is now realised (love overcomes the difficulties put in its way by society).

From another angle, the two refrains of vv. 3 and 4 mark the conclusion of a unit (cf. 2:6–7 and 3:5). Therefore, differing from Lacoque,[62] we connect v. 5 with what follows not with what goes before, although it presents clear lexical and thematic links with vv. 1–4.

Even if precise lexical repetitions are lacking, an *inclusio* between the beginning and the end of the song can be seen in the polarity 'mother' (v. 1b; or 'brother', v. 1a) and 'daughters (of Jerusalem)' (v. 4a). The theme of the city appears at the beginning ('outside', v. 1c) and at the end of the song ('daughters of Jerusalem', v. 4a), while in the two central verses the scene unfolds in the 'house of my mother'. This is clear for v. 2, but it is implicit also for v. 3 if, in fact, it is describing the embrace (cf. the parallel with 3:4, immediately before

[60] Cf., in this sense, among the more recent commentators: Krinetzki (1981), pp. 213–216; Keel (1994), p. 264; Elliott (1989), p. 186. Some commentators even eliminate the two verses as a late addition, for example Müller (1992), p. 81; Garbini (1992), pp. 113, 266; Ricciotti (1928), pp. 273–274.

[61] Cf., *supra*, p. 410.

[62] Lacocque (1998), pp. 160–168.

Table 68

A. Obstacles to love (vv. 1–2)	a. in the city (v. 1) b. in the house (v. 2)	*brother, mother* *mother*
B. Victory of love (vv. 3–4)	b'. in the house (v. 3) a'. in the city (v. 4)	*daughters*

the 'refrain of awakening'). Like the preceding song, therefore, 8:1–4 is also formed of two strophes, divided in their turn into two parts: the arrangement here is chiastic (cf. *Tab. 68*).

The criticism of society will be taken up again in the *Epilogue* of the Song where vv. 8–10 take aim at the family (the 'brothers') while vv. 11–12 refer to urban society ('Solomon'). However, society does not have only a negative aspect: despite the opposition, the union takes place, no longer among the vineyards but in the city and in the house of the mother. As in the first part of the poem, the theme of the institution receives a discreet allusion (cf. 3:6–11 and 4:1–5).[63]

First strophe: Obstacles put in the way by society (8:1–2)

[8:1] "Oh that you were like a brother to me…". The initial phrase offers various interpretative difficulties. The principal one arises from the term 'brother' (*'āḥ*). The question here is whether the young woman's desire is reasonable, given that if her beloved were her brother, she would no longer be able to marry him. An attempt has been made, therefore, to understand the term in a broad sense, as equivalent to 'fiancé', or to find ethnographic parallels where marriage between siblings is permitted.[64] The theoretical possibility of understanding the term in this sense is undeniable because the woman herself is called 'sister' (4:9, 10, 12; 5:1, 2). But then it would not make sense to express as a desire what was already a reality. The desire is formulated as an impossible one; it is essential, therefore, to understand the term in the physical sense, as 'carnal brother'. It is impossible, in the eyes of

---

[63] *Contra* Keel (1994), p. 262, who thinks that this concerns the impossible dream of an incestuous love. Similarly too Landy (1983), p. 97. Such a reading is possible only by isolating 8:1–2 from what follows: not only 8:3–4 but also 8:5–14 speak of a love that is experienced in the city and in the family.

[64] For a review of the different possible interpretations, we refer to Lys (1968), pp. 277–278; Pope (1977), pp. 655–657; Ravasi (1992), pp. 610–613.

the woman, that her beloved be at the same time her brother, but it would be wonderful if it could be thus. The preposition 'like' in front of 'brother', which is present in the MT and wrongly omitted from translations as dittography, confirms the woman's awareness that her dream is unrealisable.

The carnal significance of the word 'brother' is confirmed by the phrase that follows: "Suckled at the breast of my mother". Here it is clear that the desire is an impossible one: the two youngsters belong to two different mothers (cf. 3:11; 8:5). The term 'breasts' (*šādayim*) refers to 7:8, 9, where the breasts of the woman are mentioned. The passage from the beloved woman to the mother is significant: the two images are superimposed. In the breast of his own woman, a man finds his own mother again: and, on the other hand, the woman herself will become a mother. This continuity of the generations will be underlined in the following verse where the union of the two lovers takes place "in the house of my mother". The desire for 'fraternity', therefore, is not only practical, with reference to the outside world, as will be expressed in v. 1cd; it manifests a profound aspect of love, already indicated by the appellation 'sister' with which the man addresses his woman. It is the 'consanguinity' established in the relationship of love[65] as it is expressed in the formula of Gen 2:23—"Bone of my bones, flesh of my flesh". The two lovers become one same flesh; they make part of the same family; they suck the milk of the same mother.[66] It is the supreme image of trust and equality between two persons to the point of identification:[67] it naturally has to be complemented with the antithetical image of their otherness, expressed in the 'exodic' character of love. We noticed above the tension between "let us go out" (7:12a) and "I would bring you into the house of my mother" (8:2).[68]

---

[65] Cf. in this connection, Landy (1983), pp. 99–100.

[66] Krinetzki (1981), p. 212, interprets this process in the light of Jung's depth psychology: "In the beginning, the young woman who is in love loves not a concrete young man, but the image of her 'animus', which she projects on to the young man" (Krinetzki [1970], p. 412, n. 43).

[67] Lacocque (1998), p. 160, rightly insists here on the inappropriateness of an allegorical reading: one cannot really apply the image of Song 8:1b to the divine lover. Joüon (1909), pp. 301–304, and Robert – Tournay (1963), pp. 284–286, apply the image to the Messiah, but even this reading seems forced, frankly. Von Speyr (1972), pp. 80–83, makes a more convincing Christological and ecclesial reading of the passage: here, however, it is clear that we have a case of transposition, not of the primary sense of the text.

[68] Cf., *supra*, p. 410.

The reason the woman adduces to explain her desire for consanguinity is of the social order: "If I met you outside, I would kiss you, and no one would despise me" (v. 1cd). The verb 'to find/meet' (*māṣāʾ*) links our song with 3:1–5 and 5:2–8, the two nocturnal searches. Also, the term 'outside' makes us think of the 'streets and squares' of 3:2, and, behind the verb 'despise' (*bûz*),[69] one can see an allusion to the 'watchmen of the walls' of 3:3 and 5:7. In the three cases, society is represented as an obstacle to love. Love is not comprehensible to those who stand outside this relationship; it is felt as disorder, an upsetting of the social conventions. According to Wetzstein, with the Arabs, not even the bridegroom can kiss his own bride in public, but only her brother or her cousin.[70] If the young woman dared to kiss her beloved in the street (note that it is the woman's initiative, an unthinkable reality in the Oriental world), she would be taken for a good-for-nothing (cf. 1:7). Actually, the 'strange woman' of Prov 7:6–27 behaves in a similar way (the two terms *ḥûṣ* ['outside', Prov 7:12] and *nāšaq* ['to kiss', Prov 7:13] appear also in Song 8:1). But this is, precisely the case of a dissolute woman whose conduct is severely censured by the author of Proverbs.

Such a problem did not arise in Song 7:12–14—there the two young people were alone, surrounded by friendly nature. But love cannot remain like this. It has to confront society,[71] even if the latter is potentially hostile, does not understand the pair in love because it is outside their relationship, reasons with other parameters (cf. 8:8–12). The author's sympathy is certainly not with society; on the contrary, he prays it not to disturb love (v. 4).[72] However, he is not proposing a flight from it. Despite its limitations, society has an unavoidable role

[69] The term indicates something stronger than a 'mocking' or a 'leg-pulling'. As Keel (1994), p. 261, rightly observes, it is that social disapproval which marks a woman as an adulteress or a prostitute.

[70] Citations in Robert - Tournay (1963), p. 283; in this sense also, cf. Buzy (1951), p. 355; Lys (1968), p. 278.

[71] Krinetzki (1981), p. 210, entitles the passage 8:1–2: "Desire for the end of the subterfuges" ("Sehnsucht nach einem Ende der Heimlichkeiten"). It is to be noted, however, that the author of the Song does not depict the encounter in nature as something reprehensible, a kind of clandestine love.

[72] The critical aspect of the Song with regard to society is emphasised, perhaps a little unilaterally, by Heinevetter (1988), p. 188: "It is clear [...] that the redactor is not interested in an idyll in nature as an end in itself, a kind of refuge from the world of the 'city'. He presents nature in an active role of opposition to the 'city', in order to be able, in the face of such a clear contrast, to criticise the latter in a still more radical way".

in the realisation of the union. The nuptial context which preceded the union in the first part of the Song (cf. the nuptial procession in 3:6–11 and the appellation 'bride' in 4:8, 9, 10, 12; 5:1, not to mention the theme of the 'veil' in 4:1, 3) is evoked again at the end of the second. It is alluded to in the repetition of the theme of the veil in 6:7. In our song, the social dimension of the union can be picked up in the allusion to the 'house of my mother' (8:2) and to the 'daughters of Jerusalem' (8:4).[73]

[v. 2] After having criticised the society that prevents the two lovers from living their love in the light of the sun, the author goes on to criticise the family. Verse 2, then, is also critical: the verbs express the conditional of impossibility, straight from the protasis of v. 1ab: "If you were my brother…". Consanguinity would allow not only the appearing together in public (v. 1cd), but also the living in the same house (v. 2), sharing the daily life and the intimacy of the home. This is now presented as impossible: the family tends to close in on itself, not allowing a stranger, which is what the beloved man evidently is, to be introduced within it. However, the realisation of the union passes through this difficulty: only when the woman succeeds in making her beloved accepted by her own family as a 'brother' will the union be able to be realised.

From the 'open space' ('outside') which characterises v. 1, the author passes now to the enclosed, protected space of the house: the union cannot take place in public but only in the 'house of my mother'. As a member of the family, the woman has the responsibility of 'doing the honours of the house',[74] that is of 'looking after/leading' (*nāhag*)[75] the guest. The second verb, 'to bring in' (*bôʾ* in *hiphʿil* form), is generally

[73] Song 8:2 has a frequently cited parallel in the Egyptian love songs. Here too is the woman who sees her beloved in the company of his relations. She desires that his mother would agree to their love: "Then I would hurry to (my) brother / and kiss him before his company, / and not be ashamed because of anyone. / I would be happy to have them see / that you (the beloved, *author's note*) know me" (Pap. Chester Beatty IA 4:4–5, sixth stanza, according to Fox [1985], p. 55). In both cases, it is a question of challenging society in order to be able to live one's own love openly, in the sight of the family and of the city.

[74] "To this house, he is a stranger—she brings him and guides him there—and there he receives hospitality" (Landy [1983], p. 100).

[75] The verb *nhg* is used with reference to 'livestock' (Gen 31:18; Exod 3:1; Ps 80:2) either to animals in general (Isa 11:6; 2 Sam 6:3), and, in a derived sense to prisoners (Isa 20:4; Lam 3:2). It is employed in a metaphorical sense to indicate God as 'guide' in the desert (Ps 78:52) and in the return to Zion (Isa 49:10; 63:14). Here too Lacocque (1998), p. 163, observes the impertinence of an allegorical interpretation, in which God is the object of the verb.

used in the Song to indicate the place of love (cf. 1:4; 2:4; 3:4). "To bring into the house of my mother", in particular, is a repetition of 3:4 where it is followed by the expression: "into the chamber of her who conceived me".[76] In our case too, the 'house of my mother' is to be understood in this sense: what follows, in fact, speaks of an intimate encounter. *À propos* of 3:4, the singularity of the expression 'house of my mother' was mentioned.[77] The theme of the 'mother' has already been introduced in v. 1b and will be taken up later in v. 5d: she is the only member of the family who is spoken of in positive terms. The text suggests, again, an identification between 'mother' and 'bride'. It is significant that the union always takes place in 'the house of the mother' (in 3:4 and 8:2 of her mother; in 8:5 of his). It is a finding again of one's own 'matrix', the primordial roots of one's own existence.[78] It is an immersing of oneself in the flow of life, received and given, a binding of oneself to the chain of generations which renews the victory over death.

The verb that follows, *tᵉlammᵉdēnî*, is ambiguous. It could refer to the second person singular, the beloved (literally: 'you would teach me') or to the third person singular feminine, the mother ('she would teach me'). In that the context is speaking of an intimate encounter, the first reading would seem preferable.[79] The abrupt change of subject perhaps reveals the author's concern to express the 'mirror-nature', the reciprocity of the relationship of love: in 'leading', the initiative lies with the woman; in 'teaching', it lies with the man. But not only with him, for in 8:5 it will be she, once again, who is to 'waken' her man. As for the significance of the verb 'teach', it is clear that the implied object is 'love'. This is the initiation into love-making.[80] The teaching of love has to belong to the man, not the mother. In Hebrew, the sexual act is expressed with the verb *yādaʿ* ('to know', cf. Gen 4:1); this 'knowledge' can be transmitted only by one's own partner.[81]

---

[76] The phrase is repeated in 8:2 by some codices of the Syro-Hexapla.

[77] Cf., *supra*, pp. 134–135.

[78] Referring to the theory of C.G. Jung, Krinetzki speaks in this connection of a 'process of individuation' (Krinetzki [1970], p. 406).

[79] Landy (1983), pp. 100 and 308, prefers to think of deliberate ambiguity: the phrase would intend to retain a double sense.

[80] Often taken up in this sense is Jer 13:21, a controversial text, where Jerusalem's flirtations with the nations is mentioned: "What will you say when they set as head over you those whom you yourself have taught (*limmadt*)?"

[81] As is also the case with Jer 13:21, an Arabic poem attributes the 'teaching' to the woman: "If my breast interests you / and you are a Moslem and not a Jew, / I will

The metaphor of 'eating' to indicate love, which was introduced in the previous song (Song 7:14cd), is now complemented with that of 'drinking' (*šāqāh*, 8:2c): this coherence of the amorous journey witnesses to a continuity between the two songs, the differences in environment notwithstanding. Also in 5:1, the metaphor of 'drinking' follows that of 'eating': in both cases it is the 'consummation' of love[82] that is being expressed. The Hebrew *ʾašqᵉkā* ('I would make you drink') is assonant with *ʾeššāqᵉkā* ('I would kiss you', v. 1c): the consonants of the two verbs are the same. The correspondence makes one think that the author sees, in 'drinking', the kisses, taking up the image of 7:10. The link between the two texts is confirmed by the object of drinking in 8:2, *yayin hāreqaḥ*[83] ('spiced wine') which makes one think of the *jên haṭṭôb* ('good wine') of 7:10. Here too there is probably an allusion to the exchange of fluids during a kiss. The technical term *yayin hāreqaḥ* designates a wine mixed with spices like the *mezeg* of 7:3.[84] Just as, nay more than, wine, the caresses of the woman and her kisses know how to 'inebriate' the man, transforming him in the ecstasy of love (cf. 1:2–3; 4:10–11).

With the 'wine', there is juxtaposed the 'juice of my pomegranate'. If you squeeze pomegranates, you get a sweet and refreshing juice which has to be drunk immediately before it ferments.[85] But the expression '*my* pomegranate' (*rimmônî*)[86] leads one to an unequivocal understanding of an erotic significance. The reference is to 7:13d ("whether the pomegranate trees are in flower"). The 'pomegranates', then, are not only in flower; they have yielded their fruit (7:14), and the juice is being offered to the beloved man. The metaphorical play is coher-

---

let you rest on my arms, / which will teach you the job of love, / O light of my eyes" (Dalman [1901], p. 250).

[82] Cf. Prov 5:15, 19; 9:17; 20:17; 30:20; Sir 23:17; 26:12. On the subject, cf. Lavoie (1995), p. 145.

[83] The construction is anomalous, since the term *yayin* is not in construct state. Here we would expect *yēn*, as in 7:10 (cf. *BHS*).

[84] The root *rqḥ* is present in the term *merqāḥîm*, 'fragrances', of 5:13.

[85] Cf. Ravasi (1992), p. 618; Hepper (1992), p. 116.

[86] MT reading, *rimmōnî* ('my pomegranate'), is preferable to the plural ('my pomegranates'), proposed by *BHS*, not only as the *lectio difficilior*, but also because of an another observation: the four distichs, that make up vv. 1–2, all terminate with the first person suffix *-î* (*ʿimmî, lî, tᵉlammᵉdēnî, rimmōnî*), suggesting a rhyming effect. Since the term *rimmôn* can indicate both the tree and the fruit, it is uncertain to which allusion is being made here. If we read the plural, it is clearly a question of the fruits (the breasts are two): for the singular, it is more logical to think of the tree. Joüon's proposal reading *mon vin de grenade* (Joüon [1909], p. 307) does not allow the allusion to the woman's body to be grasped.

ent all the more in that in 7:13 the pomegranate is associated with the vine whose fruit, the wine, is being offered along with the pomegranate juice. Thus the literary unity of the two songs, 7:12–14 and 8:1–4, is confirmed.

In commenting on 7:13d, we mentioned that the pomegranate is a classical metaphor for the breasts: perhaps it is to the 'squeezing of the breasts' (cf. 7:9) that the 'juice of my pomegranate' refers. What the man longed for, 'to squeeze the breasts' (7:9) and to 'drink the wine' (7:10), is now offered in the kisses and caresses of the woman. The woman has 'learned', in the school of the man.

Second strophe: The triumph of love (8:3–4)

The description of the union in the house of the mother is so passionate that we forget that it is only a dream, directly following on the impossible condition of v. 1a: "If you were my brother…". Only after the woman has made the city and her family accept her beloved as 'brother' will it possible for this dream to become a reality. In fact, this reality is presented in vv. 3–4. The union which was declared impossible is described in vv. 3–4. That means to say that the obstacle has been overcome, that the beloved man has truly become her 'brother' in some way. The union is realised, therefore, in the 'house of the mother' as v. 5cde also confirms (there indeed it is his mother, but the two images are superimposed: it is the family context that matters), and in the city: the 'daughters of Jerusalem' are prayed in v. 4 not to disturb this union, while in v. 5ab they watch the embrace of the couple with admiration, certainly not 'despising' them. Verses 3–4, which have been wrongly considered extraneous to the composition, show themselves instead to be closely connected with it; something, moreover, which is common to all the 'refrains' we have examined up to now. Yes, they signal the conclusion of a larger compositional unit (thus is explained the absence in them of direct verbal echoes with the preceding passage), but at the same time they are the conclusion of the song 8:1–4 (and this explains the variations in the refrains compared with the parallel passages).

[8:3] If one excepts a difference that can be overlooked,[87] the 'refrain of the embrace' is repeated literally from 2:6, to the commentary on

[87] In 2:6 we read *taḥat lᵉrōʾšî*, in 8:3 *taḥat rōʾšî*: the particle *lᵉ* before *rōʾš* is lacking, but the meaning does not change. We should note the fact that various Hebrew manuscripts read, *lᵉrōʾšî* as in 2:6.

which we refer the reader.[88] In it, the embrace of the two lovers is described in a way that is modest and full of tenderness, typical of the Song.[89] It therefore signals the conclusion of a poetic unit which goes from separation to union. Just as 2:6 closed the *Prologue* (1:2–2:7), so 8:3 concludes the second part of the poem (5:2–8:4). In the course of this second part, no other unions are described: it is towards this moment that the compositional unit has been tending: searching (5:2–6:3), contemplation (6:4–12), desire (7:1–11). The union in nature (7:12–14) is also shown to be a kind of preliminary with regard to what is being described here.

The verse is meant to be understood as the antithesis of v. 2. What seemed to be an impossible dream is now represented as reality. This brief but intense announcement is to be understood as pronounced in a triumphal tone by someone who has won a battle. The woman is describing here the victory of love over the obstacles put in the way of the realisation of her dream by her family: not for nothing will she later say that love is 'strong as death' (8:6).

[v. 4] Verse 4 takes up 2:7 (= 3:5) but with some differences worthy of note. First of all, in the MT, there is no mention of the 'gazelles' or of the 'wild deer'.[90] The reason for this omission is not clear.[91] Ravasi observes that the metaphors of the animals appeared for the last time in 6:5–6 and 7:4, while, in the two 'songs of the woman' (7:12–8:4), they are completely absent.[92] Mention of the animals is absent too from the charge of 5:8, whose *incipit* is identical to that of 8:4, *hišbaʿtî ʾetkem bᵉnôt yᵉrûšālāim*.

---

[88] Cf., *supra*, p. 91.

[89] "The poem [...] does not describe, or show the moments of mutual possession, but only evokes, in the strongest sense of this word [...]. Carnal love [...] is not said in a descriptive mode. Rather it is sung" (Ricoeur [1998], p. 272).

[90] This mention is present in four Hebrew manuscripts, LXX and Vetus Latina. But MT, followed by Vg and the Syriac, is certainly the *lectio difficilior*, and should be retained.

[91] The reasons employed up to now are not satisfactory. Delitzsch thinks that the omission is explained by the fact that "the natural aspect of love is overcome here, and eros tends to become agape" (Delitzsch [1875], p. 125). Pope (1977), p. 661, claims that in 8:4 we do not have an oath, but a simple prohibition, hence the absence of the divinity through whom one swears. But the use of the verb *šbʿ* makes one hold 8:4 too as an oath. Keel (1994), p. 264, thinks of Yahwistic censorship in the face of an oath sworn through something other than YHWH. But, in that case, why has the mention of the animals of the goddess of love been retained in Song 2:7 and 3:5?

[92] Ravasi (1992), p. 620.

More significant is the other modification, that is the change of the particle *ʾim*, typical of an oath, to the question *mâ* ('why')[93] (here too we should note the parallel with 5:8!). Certainly, in 8:4, we have a rhetorical question, with a negative value, but it does not simply have the effect of a negation: there is a different nuance here from 2:7. The question, that is, is first of all denouncing behaviour that is felt to be negative, seeking indirectly to stop it. In our case, it expresses the conviction that the daughters of Jerusalem are wakening love prematurely: they are, therefore, being exhorted to put an end to this attitude.[94] As Thilo underlines, the rhetorical form suggests a triumphant certainty, on the part of the woman, of being in the right. Thilo places this certainty against the background of the two other reproaches of 2:7 and 3:5.[95] The structure delineated above (cf. *Tab. 68*) also suggests a link with 8:1. There, the potentially hostile attitude of the city in its relations with the two lovers was presented: the text speaks of 'despising' (*bûz*). Now this attitude is being reproached. The woman no longer has any fear of the disdain of the city of which the daughters of Jerusalem are the representatives: she addresses them directly, reproaching them. It is not the two lovers who should be ashamed. It is the city which should be; it is in the wrong because it does not understand the logic of love.

The author seems to wish to create an *inclusio* with the beginning of the second part of the poem, 5:2–6:3, where the woman's search ran into the hostile attitude of the 'watchmen' and the ambiguous attitude of the 'daughters of Jerusalem'. The woman did not speak with the guards; it would have been useless. But with the daughters of Jerusalem, yes (5:8; cf. 8:4). They too are women. They can change: actually, the 'chorus', which begins to speak in 8:5 shows a different attitude from that of v. 1 in its relations with the two lovers.

As in 2:7, so in 8:4, the meaning of the verb *ʿûr* is debated.[96] Two interpretations are possible: to understand it as 'to excite, to kindle'

---

[93] Here too it should be marked that LXX, Vg and the Syriac have kept the same particle as in 2:7: again we have a *lectio facilior*, through harmonisation with the two preceding texts. MT is supported by Vetus Latina.

[94] "It is supposed that the daughters of Jerusalem wake up love prematurely, and the poet wishes to censure this" (Graetz [1871], p. 204).

[95] "(The phrase reads) like a triumphant self-justification of the opportunity to repeat the warning ('...wie eine triumphierende Selbstrechtfertigung für die Berechtigung der wiederholten Mahnung')" (Thilo [1921], p. 33).

[96] Cf., *supra*, p. 93.

love, or, the opposite, 'to disturb' it. In the first case, 'sleep' is a metaphor for the lack of awareness of love, in the second case it is a metaphor for love itself. The fact that in 8:5 ("Under the apple tree I have wakened you [*ʿôrartîkā*]"), the verb is used in the first sense has led various authors to keep this meaning also in 8:4.[97] But that works against the context. Both in 2:7 and in 3:5, as in 8:4, the refrain of 'awakening' is immediately preceded by the indication of the union of the two lovers (cf. 2:6; 3:4; 8:3). In these three cases, love has certainly no need of being 'kindled'! In 8:4, the metaphorical coherence of the text is confirmed by 7:10 where mention is made of the 'sleepers' to indicate the couple in love with each other united in a kiss. Here too, therefore, as in the two previous cases, we ought to retain the meaning of 'disturbing the sleep of love'.[98]

With the word *love*, significantly, the second part of the poem ends just as the *Prologue* had ended. As in 2:7 and 3:5, we have the personification of love, Love with a capital letter, because it is the subject of the verb 'to like/to wish' (*ḥāpēṣ*). Love personified will also be the subject of the great profession of faith of 8:6.[99]

Conclusion

By contrast with the first part, where the voice of the man concludes the journey of love, here, at the end of the second part, it is the woman who has the last word: the two final songs are entrusted to her. In them, the searching (5:2–6:3) and the contemplation (6:4–7:1) flow into union. Thus the two songs 7:12–14 and 8:1–4 correspond to 4:8–5:1 in the description of the various steps in the intercourse of love, by means of the sense of sight, smell and taste (eating and drinking). From another point of view, they form an *inclusio* with the first songs of the woman 2:8–3:5 in their juxtaposition of the two locales of love, nature (7:12–14, cf. 2:8–17) and the city (8:1–4, cf. 3:1–5). The parallelism is emphasised by the similar conclusion (8:4, cf. 3:5).

---

[97] In this sense, cf. Murphy (1990), p. 189; Pope (1977), p. 653 (cf., *supra*, p. 93, n. 216); Graetz (1871), p. 205 ("warum wollt ihr erwecken, warum erregen die Liebe?"); Landy (1983), p. 117.

[98] Cf. Viviers (1989).

[99] Something that confirms the correctness of the MT against the Syriac (*rḥmtʾ*) and the Vg (*dilectam*), which, as in 2:7, read a passive participle.

7:12–14 describes the union in nature, taking up again a constant motif in the poem, that of the continuity between the forces of nature and human love. Nature is at the same time the place of love (cf. 2:8–17) and a metaphor for the female body (cf. 4:12–5:1). From nature, the two lovers learn to respect the times of love, the time of flowers and that of fruit ("I have guarded them for you", 7:14). In any case, the encounter takes place first in nature, amid the vines and the bunches of henna, because love takes its origin not from society but from nature. We may detect here an echo of the bucolic poetry, the flight from the city, the nostalgia for the world of shepherds and peasants so typical of the Hellenistic world. However, nature acquires here a theological dimension: it becomes the voice of the Creator (cf. 8:6).

8:1–4 describes the difficulties which society puts in the way of realizing the union of love: difficulties on the part of the family (8:1–2) and on the part of society ("daughters of Jerusalem", 8:4). As in 3:1–5, however, the woman overcomes these difficulties and introduces her beloved into the house of her mother. The refrain of the embrace (8:3, cf. 2:6) bears witness to this. Love is not born from society but has need of it, as the song of the litter (3:6–11) has already made clear. Significantly, the next passage will take up again the opening of that song (8:5, cf. 3:6). The Song is not advancing the notion of an adolescent flight into secrecy: rather, it is seeking to confront society, bringing in it the critical instance of love (8:4).

CHAPTER TEN

EPILOGUE

(Song 8:5–14)

I

Chorus [5]"Who is this who rises from the desert,[1]
leaning on her beloved?"[2]

Woman "Under the apple tree, I awakened you,[3]
there your mother travailed,[4]
there she travailed, and gave you to the light.[5]
[6]Set me as a seal upon your heart,
as a seal upon your arm,

---

[1] Instead of 'from the desert', LXX has, 'made white' (*leleukanthismenē*, cf. Vetus Latina *candida*). This is probably a case of derivation from 6:10, therefore a secondary reading, *contra* Garbini (1992), pp. 117–118. Vg adds to 'desert' *deliciis affluens*, probably understanding in an allegorical sense.

[2] The Hebrew *mitrappeqet* is an *hapax*, but the root *rpq* with the sense of 'to lean' is attested in rabbinic Hebrew, Arabic and Ethiopic (cf. *HALOT*, p. 1279). Moreover, the versions also understood it thus (LXX *epistērizomenē*; Vetus Latina *incumbens*; Vg *nixa super*; the Syriac *mstmk'*).

[3] Throughout the verse, the MT has a masculine object, for which the subject of the verb is undoubtedly the woman. In the Greek and the Latin, the gender of the pronoun is not determined, but G^A (Codex Alexandrinus) and G^S (Codex Sinaiticus) are provided with a marginal note which puts the phrase into the mouth of the bridegroom: *ho nymphios (tade pros tēn nymphēn)*. The Syriac has the suffixed object in the feminine. But in the case of the two LXX codices and the Syriac, we have a *lectio facilior*, dictated by an allegorical interpretation of the text. MT is incompatible with this interpretation which identifies the bridegroom with YHWH. Precisely for this reason, it is less suspect of manipulation.

[4] MT's *ḥibbᵉlatkā* means literally: 'She had had the pains (of childbirth) for you' (cf. LXX's *ōdinēsen*). Vetus Latina omits the double mention of the verb and translates simply: *illic parturivit te mater tua*. Aquila's *diephtharē* and Vg's *corrupta est*, understand, both times, a *ḥābal* III, 'to corrupt, to ruin', as in Song 2:15.

[5] With MT's *yᵉlādatkā* (there, however, the two verbs *ḥbl* and *yld* are joined asyndetically). LXX *hē tekousa sou* and Vg *genetrix tua* have read a participle instead of a perfect, something which better respects the parallelism with 'your mother' in the preceding stich. But thus we would have a tautology, while MT reflects the various phases of childbirth.

for Love is strong as death,
Jealousy relentless as the grave.
Its darts[6] are darts of fire,
a flame of Yah.[7]
[7]The great waters are not enough
to quench love,
no rivers sweep it away.
If a man were to give all the wealth of his house
in exchange for love,
scorn is all he would obtain".

II

Chorus [8]"We have a little sister,
and she does not yet have breasts.
What shall we do for our sister,
in the day that she is spoken for?
[9]If she is a wall, above her
we shall build battlements of silver.
If she is a door,
we shall bar her[8] with a board[9] of cedar".

Woman [10]"I am a wall,
and my breasts are like towers:
but, in his eyes, I have become
like one who has found peace".

---

[6] The Hebrew term *rešep* is primarily the name of a divinity (cf. the commentary). LXX has *períptera*, 'sparks'; Vg *lampades*; the Syriac *zlyql*, 'rays'.

[7] Thus MT *šalhebetyâ*. Along with numerous manuscripts, Ben Naphthali's reading actually separates the two words *šalhebet-yâ*. The ancient versions have understood differently: LXX has *phloges autēs* ('its flames'), reading *šalhăbōtèhā*, in parallelism with *r*^{e}*šāpèhā*; similarly Vg *atque flammarum*, and the Syriac *wšlhbt'*, 'the flames'.

[8] The verb *ṣwr* has three possible meanings (cf. *HALOT*, pp. 1015–1016). The context recommends *ṣwr* I (= *ṣārar*), 'confine'. The versions have understood otherwise. LXX *diagrapsōmen* and Vetus Latina *describamus* have read *ṣwr* III (= *yāṣar*), 'to form, cast'. Perhaps at the base of this interpretation there is an allegorical intention, which is made explicit in the Targum ("Law, [...] which is written on the table of the heart", cf. Garbini [1992], p. 280). Vg's *compingamus* probably reflects *ṣwr* II, 'to attack, fight'.

[9] With MT and LXX. The Syriac, Vg, Vetus Latina and Symmachus have the plural.

III

Chorus [11]"Solomon[10] had a vineyard, at Baal Hamon;[11]
he gave this vineyard to keepers,
each one brings him, for its fruit,
a thousand shekels of silver".

Woman [12]"My vineyard, my very own, is before me:
yours the thousand shekels, Solomon[12]—
and two hundred for the keepers of its fruit!"

IV

Man [13]"You who dwell in the gardens,[13] my companions[14]
are attentive to your voice,[15]
let me hear it".

Woman [14]"Flee, my beloved,
be like a gazelle
or a young stag,
on the mountains of balms".

---

[10] Vg's *Pacifico* probably understands in an allegorical sense.

[11] With MT, considering the expression as a toponym (cf. 7:5: 'Bat Rabbim'). In itself, the term means 'lord of a multitude' or 'master of wealth' (so Gordis [1974], p. 101). The Syriac *w'bh sgy*, 'its fruit is abundant'; Aquila *en echonti plēthē*; Symmachus *en katochē ochlou*; Vg *in ea quae habet populos*, understands the expression in a common sense. LXX has different versions of the name: *Beethlamōn* (Codex Vaticanus, cf. Vetus Latina *Bethlammon*), *Beellamōn* (Codex Sinaiticus), *Beelamōn* (Codex Alexandrinus). The Targum understands Jerusalem.

[12] As in v. 11, Vg translates *Pacifice* (cf. note 10).

[13] MT (with Vg, Aquila and Symmachus) has a feminine (*hayyôšebet*), while LXX, Theodotion and the Quinta of Origen have a masculine, *ho kathēmenos*. The Syriac (*'ylyn dytbyn*) reads in the plural. So too Vetus Latina (*qui sedent*).

[14] LXX's Codex Sinaiticus has 'others' (*heteroi*). The Syriac omits the term.

[15] The Syriac has a conjunction before the participle (*wṣytyn*, 'and who pay attention'). While MT, LXX, the Syriac, and Vetus Latina join 'your voice' to 'to be attentive' (v. 13b), Vg joins it to 'make me hear' (*amici auscultant, fac me udire vocem tuam*); so too Codex Sinaiticus of the LXX.

Structure

The structure of the last section of the Song is not easily recognisable. At first sight, Song 8:5–14 gives the impression of an heap of small compositions piled up without any order at the end of the book. Robert and Tournay make the Song proper close at 8:7—what follows they entitle 'Appendices'.[16] Heinevetter gets as far as 8:6. According to him, after this 'confession of faith', the Song has nothing more to say.[17] Although admitting the integrity of the passage 8:5–14, Ravasi divides it into two distinct songs (8:5–7 and 8:8–14) which have nothing to do with each other.[18] For Garbini, there are four songs (8:5–7, 8–10, 11–12 and 13–14);[19] for Gerleman, five (8:5, 6–7, 8–10, 11–12, 13–14);[20] for Keel, six (8:5ab, 5cde, 6–7, 8–10, 11–12, 13–14).[21]

It is our belief that Song 8:5–14 is an integral part of the Song in its original form, and that it consists of a unitary composition.[22] Several times a correspondence with the beginning of the book has been

[16] Robert - Tournay (1963), pp. 308–329, cf. *CEI.* In this sense also Joüon (1909), p. 318, who entitles vv. 8–14: 'Trois appendices'; and Murphy (1990), p. 195, for whom the entire passage 8:5–14 would be 'a collection of disparate poems or fragments of poems'.

[17] "8:7–14 represent [...] a later re-elaboration of the Song, on the basis of which the critical potential of the poem has had to be reduced" (Heinevetter [1988], p. 169, citing in this sense Landy [1983], p. 133). Heinevetter treats vv. 7–14 cursorily in four short pages (pp. 166–169), while devoting a good thirty two of them (pp. 67–98) to the *Prologue* (1:1–2:7). Salvaneschi (1982), p. 115, rightly protests against such 'cop-outs', confirming the importance of the *textus traditus*: "For the final verses, criticism speaks of appendices, successive additions, according to the customary—misused but perennial—philological cop-out which claims to have resolved the textual problem when it believes that it has identified a possible stratification, on the basis of aseptic canons of what is logical. [...] What is important is the textual reality, confirmed by centuries of tradition; we place ourselves before it synchronically, not before one of its possible but debatable etiologies".

[18] Ravasi (1992), pp. 629–634.677–687; so too Rendtorff (1983), pp. 261–262.

[19] Garbini (1992), pp. 268–289; similarly also Budde (1898), pp. 43–48; Rudolph (1962), pp. 179–186.

[20] Gerleman (1965), pp. 214–223.

[21] Keel (1994), pp. 265–283. Thus Krinetzki (1981), pp. 214–233, and Müller (1992), pp. 81–90, also divide.

[22] Delitzsch (1875), pp. 125–142, also reaches this conviction. For him, 8:5–14 constitute the sixth act of the drama, divided, in its turn, into two scenes: 8:5–7 and 8–14. From a literary point of view, cf., however, Elliott (1989), p. 189, who entitles the passage precisely 'epilogue' and shows its connection both with 1:2–2:7, and with the rest of the book (pp. 216–228); and Dorsey (1990), p. 90.

noted:[23] just as the Song has a *Prologue* (1:2–2:7), it also has an *Epilogue* (8:5–14). The typical 'staccato' which characterised the *Prologue* returns in the *Epilogue*. If the *Prologue* had the function of introducing the different themes of the Song, the *Epilogue* has that of gathering them up: this explains the apparent lack of links between the different scenes. Just as in a symphonic finale, the disparate *motifs* are repeated and brought together into a unity.[24] The *Epilogue* can be understood only as the conclusion of a text, against the background of what has gone before.

The precise references to the various passages of the Song will be noted in the course of the analysis. We will content ourselves now with the *inclusio* between the *Prologue* and the *Epilogue*. The most obvious correspondence is that of the theme of the 'vineyard', 1:6 and 8:11–12. In both cases, it is spoken of in an ambiguous way, first in the usual sense of the term, then in a figurative sense (*karmî šellî*, "my vineyard, my very own", 1:6e; 8:12—only here in the Song). The theme of the brothers, preoccupied with the chastity of their sister (1:6), is repeated in 8:8–9. The 'custody' (*nāṭar*) of the vineyard, which in 1:6 was entrusted to the young woman, is now committed to the officials of Solomon (8:11, 12). The name of Solomon is something else that links 1:5 and 8:11, 12. The metaphor of the 'apple tree' as the place of love (8:5c) is repeated from the end of the *Prologue* (cf. 2:3). The image of the 'seal upon the heart' (8:6a) refers back to that of the 'bag of myrrh between the breasts' (1:13). The 'companions' (*ḥăbērîm*) appear only in the *Prologue* (1:7) and in the *Epilogue* (8:13). The term 'love' (*ʾahăbâ*) which returns three times in the *Epilogue* (8:6–7), appears in the *Prologue* also three times (2:4, 5, 7), while the verb *ʾāhēb* also appears there another three times (1:3, 4, 7).[25]

Like the *Prologue*, the *Epilogue* is also characterised by direct discourse with frequent change of subject. Who is speaking from time to time is not clear. Verse 5ab is a repetition (one of so many in the *Epilogue*)[26] of 3:6 and of 6:10. In the two previous passages, the text is

[23] Cf., for example, Rendtorff (1983), pp. 261–262; Exum (1973), pp. 74–77; Shea (1980), pp. 381–385; Dorsey (1990), p. 92.

[24] "What Krinetzki considers a collection of fragments is really a recapitulation of motifs" (Exum [1973], p. 74).

[25] For a complete list of the verbal correspondences, we refer to Elliott (1989), pp. 226–228 (*Chart III*).

[26] For a complete table of the links between the *Epilogue* and the rest of the Song, cf., again, Elliott (1989), pp. 223–226 (*Chart II*).

put into the mouth of a chorus. That is also probable for 8:5ab; it is clear, in fact, that it cannot be uttered by either of the two protagonists from the fact that they are spoken of in the third person. Since the 'daughters of Jerusalem' were referred to in v. 4, it is reasonable to think that it is they who begin to speak. In v. 5c, the subject changes. According to the MT, which we are following as the *lectio difficilior*, the object of the 'awakening' is the man: the subject is, therefore, the woman. It is she who utters vv. 5c–7: there are, in fact, no signals of a change in person.

The subject changes at v. 8. Here we have a plural subject; once again, therefore, a 'chorus'. From the fact that a 'sister' is being spoken of (v. 8), it is logical to think of the woman's 'brothers'. She replies in v. 10.

Verse 11 is spoken by another voice, impersonal as in v. 5ab. Here we have, for the third time, the voice of a chorus which could be identified with the keepers of the vineyard or even, by analogy with v. 5ab, with the daughters of Jerusalem. The woman replies in v. 12.

In v. 13, an individual addresses the woman. Since her reply in v. 14 is directed to the beloved man (*dôdî*), it is clear that it is he who was speaking in the previous verse.

We have, then, four dialogues in which the reply is always put into the mouth of the woman (vv. 5c–7, 10, 12, 14) while the question is entrusted to different people. In the first three dialogues, it is uttered by a chorus which represents different social groups ('daughters of Jerusalem' [?], vv. 5ab; 'brothers', vv. 8–9; 'keepers of the vineyard' [?], v. 11), in the fourth, by the man (v. 13) (cf., *supra*, *Tab. 69*).

This dialogue structure reveals itself fundamental for understanding the arrangement of the *Epilogue*. The division which it presup-

Table 69

I	v. 5ab vv. 5c–7	Chorus (daughters of Jerusalem?) Woman
II	vv. 8–9 v. 10	Chorus (brothers) Woman
III	v. 11 v. 12	Chorus (watchmen?) Woman
IV	v. 13 v. 14	Man Woman

Table 70

	Verses	Theme	Key-words	Metaphor
A	5–7	I-THOU RELATIONSHIP	*ʿālāh, dôd* (v. 5a)	nature
B	8–10	CRITICISM OF THE FAMILY	*kesep* (v. 9b)	city
B'	11–12	CRITICISM OF THE 'CITY'	*kesep* (v. 11)	nature/city
A'	13–14	I-THOU RELATIONSHIP	*dôd, ʿal* (v. 14)	nature

poses is, in fact, confirmed by other observations[27] (cf. *Tab. 70*). The first and last strophe are united between themselves by the word *dôdî* ('beloved', vv. 5b, 14a—only here in the *Epilogue*), and by an ascending movement (*ʿālāh*, 'to come up', v. 5a; *ʿal*, 'on, above', v. 14c). The two correspondences function as an *inclusio*.

In the first and last strophes, the relationship between the two lovers is spoken of, and the discourse is in the second person singular: I-thou. In v. 5ab, the two embrace, and what follows theorises on this fact. The difficult v. 14 treats again of the relationship between the two: the 'gazelle on the mountains' is, in fact, a clear metaphor for the union (cf. 2:17; 4:5–6). In the two central strophes, the discourse is in the third person. The theme here is the relationship of the couple with society, with the family (vv. 8–10) and with the 'city' (vv. 11–12). The two strophes are linked by the term *kesep* ('silver', vv. 9 and 11). In them, therefore, we have the attempt of the family and of the 'city' to replace the logic of love with that of commerce, a theme introduced at the end of the first strophe (v. 7cde).[28]

Perhaps we can also observe an alternation in the use of metaphors. In v. 5, the metaphor is vegetable, drawn from nature ("Under the apple tree, I awakened you"); this is also the case in vv. 13 ('gardens')[29] and 14 ('gazelle on the mountains'). The second strophe is characterised by urban symbolism ('walls, towers', vv. 9–10). The third juxtaposes an exquisitely natural metaphor ('vineyard'; cf. 7:13) with an urban one ('pieces of silver'), with deliberate dissonance.

---

[27] Cf. Dorsey (1990), pp. 90–92.

[28] This link was already pointed out by Ricciotti: "It seems to me that the piece (that is, vv. 8–14, *author's note*) is intimately connected with the composition itself, and that the hook is found precisely in that 8:7 which the critics have overlooked, considering it only as the conclusion of what goes before and not also as the starting point of what follows" (Ricciotti [1928], p. 281).

[29] Cf. Budde's observation at v. 13: "The closest relationship is with v. 5" (Budde [1898], p. 48).

First Strophe: Set Me as a Seal upon your Heart (8:5–7)

If the structure of the *Epilogue* in general is disputed, that goes above all for the first strophe, vv. 5–7. As has been seen, some authors hold that the Song ends at v. 6; others break vv. 5–7 into two units (v. 5 and vv. 6–7) or even into three (v. 5ab; v. 5cde; vv. 6–7).[30] Actually, between v. 5ab and v. 5c there exists a break in continuity: the question of the chorus requires a reply, but this is not found in v. 5cde. Also, there exists no apparent relation between v. 5cde and v. 6: there are no verbal correspondences, and the metaphors are of a different order (in v. 5cde, they belong to the natural world; in v. 6ab, we have a product of civilisation). Again: vv. 6c–7 have a different tone from the rest of the strophe, a tone that is unique in the Song: here we have philosophical disquisitions on the nature of love which are often seen as an independent section.[31] Indeed, the strophe has a structure that is anomalous as far as the others are concerned. It can be conceded that this may reveal redactional working. But it is more probable that the anomaly is due to the particular character of this strophe; it is the theological synthesis of the entire book.

In favour of the unity of vv. 5–7, there speaks, first of all, the rhythm. Under this aspect, the Hebrew text[32] displays a notable regularity (cf. *Tab. 71*). The two rhythmic verses that compose v. 5 (v. 5ab and 5cde) are different in length: the first is a distich (3 + 2 accents), the second a

Table 71

A	*5ab*	3 + 2
B	*5cde*	3 + 3 + 3
A'	*6ab* *6cd* *6ef*	3 + 2 3 + 3 3 + 2
B'	*7abc* *7def*	3 + 2 + 2 2 + 3 + 3

[30] Cf., *supra*, p. 438.
[31] Cf. Tromp (1979), pp. 90–92.
[32] The translation has sought to preserve the colometric division of the Hebrew text, so that it is possible in some way with it to follow the rhythmic discourse.

Table 72

Stich	*Repetitions*	*Concatenation*
5ab	*ʿālāh* ('to rise'), *ʿal* ('on')	*ʿal*
5cde	*šāmmâ ḥibbᵉlâ* ('there she travailed') (2x)	
6ab	*kāḥôtām ʿal* ('as a seal upon…') (2x)	*kᵉ*; *ʿal*
6cd	*kᵉ* ('as') (2x)	*kᵉ*; *ʾahăbâ* ('love')
6ef	*rᵉšāpîm* ('darts') (2x)	
7abc	*lōʾ* ('not') (2x)	*ʾahăbâ*
7def	*bûz* ('scorn') (2x)	*ʾahăbâ*

tristich (3 + 3 + 3). The three rhythmic verses of v. 6 (6ab, cd, ef) are all distichs (3 + 2; 3 + 3; 3 + 2). On the other hand, the two rhythmic verses of v. 7 (7abc and 7def) are tristichs (3 + 2 + 2; 2 + 3 + 3). So v. 5 functions as an introduction: it summarises within itself the rhythm of the two following verses.

A second characteristic of vv. 5–7 is the repetitions of words, both within the same rhythmic verse and between different verses, resulting in concatenation (cf. *Tab. 72*). The phenomenon of repetition can be observed immediately in v. 5ab: in the Hebrew text, the verb *ʿālāh* ('to rise', v. 5a) has the same root as the preposition *ʿal* ('above, on', v. 5b, "leaning *on* her beloved").[33] The repetition in v. 5cde is obvious: "there…travailed". In v. 6ab the expression "as a seal upon" is repeated twice: the preposition 'as' (*kᵉ*) is repeated four times in two rhythmic verses (v. 6a, b, c, d).[34] Also v. 6ef is characterised by the repetition of the word 'darts' (v. 6e). In v. 7abc the repetition of the negative particle *lōʾ* (v. 7a, c) is to be noted, and in v. 7def that of the verb 'scorn', with its reinforcing infinitive absolute (*bôz yābûzû*, v. 7f). The repetition, far from being a sign of unauthenticity,[35] shows itself to be a fundamental stylistic tool. Not only does it produce sonorous effects of alliteration; it also confers unity on the strophe, a unity also underlined by the

[33] Here we should note also the alliteration of the sound *mi* (*m̲î̲ zōʾt ʿōlāh m̲i̲n̲ ham̲m̲i̲d̲bār m̲i̲t̲rappeqet*) and *t* (*t̲aḥat̲ hat̲t̲appûaḥ ʿôrart̲îkā*).

[34] Five times, if the particle *kî* ('for'), at the beginning of v. 6c is counted.

[35] *Contra* Garbini (1992), pp. 119–120, who expunges and changes almost all the repetitions as a sign of textual corruption. Let us give one example: "[…] the word *ḥblh* appears superfluous and the parallelism with *ʾmk* disappears; that signifies an improving of the text, avoiding the repetition (not certainly the work of the author) of the verb *ḥbl*". At least Garbini himself admits, here and there, the hypothetical nature of such a procedure!

Table 73

v. 5	Representation of the union
v. 6ab	The union cannot be broken
v. 6cdef	Motivation: love is a flame of YHWH
v. 7	Consequence: superiority over death and over money

repetition of a few, but significant, lexemes which 'concatenate' among themselves the different parts of the composition.

From the point of view of content, the various statements are linked among themselves by a logical connection which it is important to understand before becoming immersed in the detailed analysis (cf. *Tab. 73*). Verse 5 presents the union of the two lovers ("leaning on her beloved", v. 5b; "I awakened you", v. 5c). Coherently, in v. 6ab, it is sought that this union never be broken (image of the seal). Verse 6cdef, in its turn, is linked with 6ab by means of the causal particle *kî*: it explains why the bond that unites the two lovers cannot be broken, culminating in the declaration that love is a flame of YHWH (v. 6f). Basing itself on this premise, v. 7 can finally proclaim the superiority of love over death (v. 7abc) and over money (v. 7def), considered as enemies of love.

Even if a new composition begins in 8:5, the links with the preceding one are undeniable.[36] The union referred to in v. 5a is in fact described as a past event ("I awakened you"), on which the lovers are now reflecting.[37] It is logical to think that the intention is to allude to what was described in the two preceding poems. Various indications contribute to supporting this. The theme of the desert (v. 5) echoes that of the country (7:12).[38] If, there, the two lovers went out (*yāṣā'*, 7:12), here they are going up (*'ālāh*, 8:5), that is, going up to the city, towards Jerusalem (cf. 3:6): it is the same movement shown as a dream in 8:2. It should be noted that the place of love, expressed

[36] So much so that various authors link 8:5 with what precedes, not with what follows, cf., in addition to Lacocque (cf., *supra*, p. 422, n. 62), also Shea (1980), pp. 385–387; Robert - Tournay (1963), pp. 291–292.

[37] "The present picture begins (v. 5) with a recalling of previous scenes, especially 3:6 (6:10), followed by a brief allusion to past events. [...] The paraenesis is contained in vv. 6–7, but it is based on the historical allusion contained in v. 5, from which the teaching originates" (Ricciotti [1928], p. 275). Naturally we distance ourselves from the allegorising interpretation of Ricciotti on the content of this "historical retrospective".

[38] On the *midbār-śādeh* correspondence, cf. Elliott (1989), p. 191.

in the binome 'apple tree' (8:5c) and 'chamber of the mother' (8:5de), reflects the content of the two songs 7:12–14 and 8:1–4 ('union in nature—union in the city'). The adverb *šām* ('there') links 8:5de with 7:13e ("there I will give you my love"). The term *ʾēm* ('mother', 8:5d) refers back to vv. 1b and 2a. The expression "leaning on her beloved" (v. 5b) makes one think of the description of the embrace in v. 3 ("His left hand is under my head, and his right arm embraces me") which is then also evoked in the metaphor of the seal upon the heart and upon the arm (v. 6ab). The verb 'to scorn' (*bûz*) in 8:7f clearly echoes v. 1 where the young woman was afraid of the 'scorn' (*bûz*) of society: now instead it is society, which understands only the language of money, that is to be scorned in the name of love. The attitude of the daughters of Jerusalem in v. 5ab is different: the people who, in v. 4, were requested not to disturb love, now watch the embrace of the two lovers with admiration and respect. The theme of 'love', central in the strophe (*ʾahăbâ*, 8:6c, 7b, 7e), has already been introduced at the end of the preceding song (v. 4c). That of 'awakening' (*ʿûr*) joins v. 5 to v. 4 even if, as we shall see, the sense of the verb is not the same. But precisely this change of sense is revealed as a deliberate semantic play which demonstrates the link between the two verses. We should note that the references to the preceding song concern not only vv. 5–6 but also v. 7,[39] which therefore is shown to be an integral part of the poem, quite different from a posthumous appendix.

[8:5] Retrospective glance at the union. The verse is divided clearly into two parts, the first spoken by the 'chorus' (v. 5ab), the second by the woman (v. 5cde). There are no apparent links between the two parts: the woman does not reply to the question posed by the chorus. This is not surprising: rather than a question, properly speaking, we have here, as also in the parallel passages (3:6; 6:10), an exclamation of admiration, i.e. a rhetorical question. There is a link between the first and the second parts of the verse, and it is of the order of content in that in both parts there is a looking back to the union described in 7:12–8:4—first by the chorus (v. 5ab), then by the woman (v. 5cde). Elliott suggests that the exclamation of the chorus might have the

[39] To the references indicated above, we can also add the significant lexemes: *nātan*, 'to give', 8:7d and 7:13e, 14a; 8,1a; *bêt*, 'house', 8:7e and 8:2b.

function of fixing attention on the woman who will then become the protagonist of the verses that follow.[40]

[8:5ab] "Who is this who rises from the desert?" In 3:6 and 6:10 (the repetition confirms the concluding character of the *Epilogue*), the phrase marks the beginning of a new poetic unit: here too it is possible to understand the same function. The question is always put into the mouth of a chorus which, in 3:6, we identified with a voice off-stage, while in 6:10 the context made us think of the women of the *harem* evoked in the previous verse. Perhaps in 8:5, we can think of the daughters of Jerusalem,[41] who have been mentioned in v. 4, and consider the phrase as an indirect riposte to the reproof which was directed to them there. The representatives of the city would, therefore, have taken in the words of the woman, assuming a more positive attitude towards the two lovers.

The parallel with 3:6 makes one think of the same geographical situation. The daughters of Jerusalem are looking towards the Judaean desert which extends to the immediate East of the city. Because Jerusalem enjoys a high location, to journey towards Jerusalem is an ascent (*ʿālāh* [cf. the Psalms of 'Ascents'!]). In 3:11, the 'daughters of Zion' were invited to go out to admire King Solomon with his nuptial crown. Perhaps also in 8:5, we can imagine a similar context. We saw, above, the parallel between the desert and the country (7:12). Love is born in the desert, in the intimacy of a personal encounter. Robert and Tournay detect there a reference to Hos 2.[42] The reference is suggestive (cf. above all Hos 2:16—"Therefore, behold, I will allure her, / and bring her into the wilderness, / and speak tenderly to her"), but it is not to be interpreted in an allegorical way, rather as a re-transposition of the Hosea metaphor into its original nuptial context.[43] The entry into Jerusalem is reconnected, therefore, to that entering into the house of the mother which was spoken of in v. 2. After the description of the union (v. 3), this entry is represented no longer as a dream but as a reality.

[40] Elliott (1989), pp. 190–191.

[41] In this sense, cf. Minocchi (1898), p. 102; Ricciotti (1928), p. 276; Elliott (1989), p. 190; Colombo (1975), p. 129.

[42] Robert – Tournay (1963), p. 292.

[43] This 're-transposition' is not without consequences, however, as Lacocque (1998), p. 176, emphasises: "It is not sheer retrogression, however, for the discourse is now charged with the meaning it acquired by being used theologically. [...] For the Torah and the Prophets, God's love was to be described in terms of human love. The Song now models human love on God's love".

The house of the mother will be spoken of expressly in v. 5cde: now it is the urban dimension of love that is being underlined. The woman no longer has any fear of showing herself in public with her beloved (cf. v. 1): love is being lived out before the city. There is no reason to change the difficult *mitrappeqet*. The sense of 'leaning', backed up by the ancient versions, is supported linguistically.[44] The verb does not describe the supporting of someone who is weak, but the embrace of the two people in love.[45]

In the 'rising from the desert', the theme of the journey from nature to the city, which was expressed in 4:8, is repeated. What was signified there by the 'lairs of the lions' and by the 'mountains of the panthers' is evoked here by the desert. The desert is not only the place of the heart to heart, where the lovers are alone, but also the domain of the uncorrupted forces of nature, where love is at home,[46] a home which love must abandon, however, to go to the 'city', to give it life and to be 'domesticated' by it. And the desert is also the symbol of death.[47] If the litter which transported the woman along the desert in 3:7–8 was escorted by sixty mighty men armed with swords against the terror of the night, here the woman is accompanied by her beloved. And this is sufficient: because, as v. 6c will say: "Love is strong as death". Verse 5ab, therefore, introduces the central theme of the passage: the love-death relationship.[48] The journey of the two lovers across the desert is iconic of the love that conquers death. A last aspect deserves to be mentioned. *À propos* of 3:6 and 6:10, the numinous character which clothed the apparition in the desert was noted. It is logical to see here too the same characterisation: this is a theophany. That accords well with the profession of faith in v. 6f. Love is a flame of YHWH: its apparition brings the sign of transcendence.

---

[44] *Contra* Garbini. Cf., *supra*, n. 2, p. 435.

[45] Cf. Rudolph (1962), p. 181: "I believe that the poet would have placed v. 5a at the beginning to make clear that he was dealing with a married couple; if, indeed, the woman arrives leaning on her beloved or being supported by him, that is possible only for married people, given the huge reserve emplyed by Orientals with regard to expressions of tenderness between people in love (cf. v. 1)". In the *Megillat Judit*, Judith asks Holofernes to send away the servants 'so that they do not see us leaning on each other (*mtrpqym*)' (Dubarle [1959], p. 527, n. 1). In rabbinic Hebrew, *rpq* signifies 'to join one's self; [...] to endear one's self' (so Jastrow [1903], p. 1491).

[46] Cf. 2:7. On the desert as place of love, cf., *supra*, pp. 146–147.

[47] Cf., *supra*, n. 24, p. 146.

[48] Moreover, the journey made by the two lovers in 4:8 is also made jointly ("With me from Lebanon, come").

[v. 5cde] The exclamation of the chorus has drawn attention to the woman ('this'). Now she begins to speak. She does so, addressing herself, surprisingly, not to the chorus but to her beloved. If we look closely, however, this dialogue also was introduced in 5ab because the woman was presented 'leaning on her beloved'. Now the dialogue of the two is expressed, precisely while they are close in their embrace. It extends to v. 7, and is characterised, in vv. 5c–6b, by direct discourse, in 6c–7f, by statements in the third person, which are of a more universal character but which are nevertheless closely bound to the preceding discourse by means of the causal particle *kî* ('for').

It has been noted that the *Peshitta* has the pronominal object of the verb 'to awaken' in the feminine (*ʿyrtky*),[49] supposing, therefore, that it is the man who is speaking. This reason is easily to be explained by the intention of making the text agree with the allegorical interpretation according to which the man is the symbol of YHWH.[50] The MT has instead a masculine object (*ʿôrartîkā*) for which the subject is necessarily the woman. In this case, an allegorical interpretation is impossible: it would imply not only that it was for Israel, or somebody on its behalf, to arouse love in God, but also that God was conceived and generated by a mother.[51] Here the MT absolutely contradicts any allegorical interpretation, and it is the most clear proof of the originally literal significance of the text of the Song.[52]

The verb 'to awaken' links v. 5c with 4bc. There the daughters of Jerusalem were prayed not to disturb the two lovers who had fallen asleep in the slumber of love. Here, clearly, the sense of the verb is different: it is the waking up of a love which is sleeping, that is, which has not

---

[49] Cf. *BHS*.

[50] Cf., *supra*, n. 3, p. 435. Of course, all the authors who interpret the Song allegorically follow the Peshitta, cf., for example, Joüon (1909), p. 310; Ricciotti (1928), p. 276; Robert – Tournay (1963), p. 296. So too *CEI*, very much bound up with the commentary of Robert – Tournay. We should note the singular interpretation of Garbini, who translates the verb in intransitive form ('I awoke'), understanding personified 'Love' as the subject. Cf. Garbini (1992), pp. 118–119, 269. For this operation, Garbini has to eliminate the pronominal suffix and read *htʿwrrty*, without any textual support. With equal liberty, he suppresses the mention of the mother in 5d, again understanding Love as the subject of 'travailing' and 'giving light to' (p. 119). Here, it is true, he produces the witness of a Hebrew manuscript that omits *ʾmk*, and four others that read *yldtyk* instead of *yldtk*. But this use of textual documentation smells of preconception. First, Garbini formulates his thesis, then he searches for support, however minimal, among innumerable textual witnesses.

[51] So, rightly, Pope (1977), p. 663; Lacocque (1998), p. 166.

[52] Cf., *supra*, pp. 8, 38.

yet become aware of itself, which has not yet been kindled.[53] It is singular that it is the woman who does this: perhaps for this reason, even authors who follow a literal reading of the Song prefer the reading of the *Peshitta*.[54] For a woman to take the initiative in love is incomprehensible in a patriarchal society. In the OT, the figure of Ruth comes to mind (cf. Ruth 3). Keel thinks of Lot's daughters (Gen 19:30–38) and Tamar (Gen 38).[55] But these are extreme cases. Normally one who acted thus was considered a prostitute (cf. Prov 7:5–27). Jer 31:22 sees in the fact that "the woman pays court to the man" the unequivocal sign of the eschatological age. Certainly, Jeremiah is speaking in an allegorical sense of the love of God in his relationship with his people: but the analogy remains.[56]

The verb is in the perfect (*ʿôrartîkā*), which makes one think of a past action.[57] The woman is evoking something that has already happened; she is not describing an action which is taking place now. It is logical to hold that it refers to the union described in 7:12–8:4, even if, since this is the Epilogue, one can think of the entire content of the Song, the whole story of love described there.

The place of the awakening is emphasised. The three local indications, 'under the apple tree' (v. 5c), 'there' (v. 5d), 'there' (v. 5e) are placed emphatically at the beginning of the three stichs. It is difficult to say what place is intended. In fact, it is only one place ('there'), although two indications are given, which do not agree between themselves. On the one hand, the place is 'under the apple tree', that is, in nature; on the other, it is 'where your mother gave birth to you', that is, in the house. To think that in the garden of the house there would have grown an apple tree as a result of which the mother's chamber could

---

[53] Tromp observes, suggestively, that in current language people in love are passed off as 'dreamers', cut off from reality, up in the clouds, while for the Song they are 'awake', the only real persons in the world who exist. Cf. Tromp (1982), p. 48.

[54] Cf., for example, the comment of Krinetzki (1981), pp. 216–217, who certainly does not follow the allegorical interpretation, or also Rudolph (1962), p. 180; Colombo (1975), p. 130.

[55] Keel (1994), p. 269.

[56] On the correspondence of the Song to Jer 31:22, cf., also, *supra*, p. 131.

[57] From a merely syntactic point of view, a reference to the present would also be possible, as in 5:1. But the context here is different. In the Song, union takes place at the end, not at the beginning of a poetic unit. 5:1 is situated at the end of a composition: there, the union of the lovers makes sense; it has been prepared for by the whole of the preceding context. 8:5, on the other hand, is at the beginning of the *Epilogue*. If union is spoken of here, we must assume that it refers to an event in the past (so too Colombo [1975], p. 129, who thinks that the words are uttered "on return from an encounter of love").

really have been located 'under the apple tree'[58] is a pious forcing of the text. Equally forced is the other supposition, that the mother gave birth in the open, under an apple tree.[59] Delitzsch rightly observes:

> The Shulamite is not a daughter of the Bedouin so as to be able to be born under a tree. Among the Bedouin a girl is called Munehil, Ruhela, Talla or Thelga according to whether she was born at a watering place, or on the road, or on the dew or on the snow.[60]

With regard to the object of the birth, Delitzsch evidently follows the *Peshitta*, but the observation is easily transferable to the MT. There is no 'realistic' explanation of this apparent contradiction.[61] The only solution is to understand the two indications in a symbolic sense as referring to the same place under two different aspects.

So then, love took place 'under the apple tree'.[62] We observe, first of all, the preposition 'under', *taḥat*. It forms an antithesis to the preposi-

---

[58] Renan's interpretation run in this direction ("L'amant dépose sa bien aimée sous le pommier de la ferme", Renan [1884], p. 57). Ginsburg's is similar (Ginsburg [1970], p. 186).

[59] The mythological school, above all, interpret in this sense. In ancient mythology, in fact, mention is often made of childbirth under a tree. Thus, Adonis was born under a tree of myrrh, Tammuz under a cedar, Diana under an olive at Delos, Apollo and Artemides under a palm. According to the Koran, Jesus himself would have been born under a palm. Cf. Wittekindt (1925), pp. 56–57; Schmökel (1956), p. 78. Albright (1963), p. 7, has recourse, instead, to Ugaritic mythology. Murphy (1990), pp. 195–196, n. 5, observes judiciously: "There is simply no analogy for such a notion elsewhere in the literature of the Hebrew Bible".

[60] Delitzsch (1875), p. 127.

[61] Cf. Murphy's conclusion: "It must be admitted that the emphatic reference to the place ('there'—under the apple tree) where the mother conceived remains very obscure" (Murphy [1990], p. 195).

[62] In this localisation, a reference to the account of Paradise has been detected. Cf. Garbini (1992), p. 270; Landy (1983), p. 214. This interpretation has a long history behind it. Cf. St. John of the Cross: "Beneath the apple tree: / there I took you for My own, / there I offered you My hand, and restored you, / where your mother was corrupted" (*The Spiritual Canticle*, 23). In the apple tree, the Spanish mystic sees the tree of the Cross, as antithesis to the tree of the garden. Such a correspondence is certainly legitimate. Disputed is the fact that the correspondence of Song 8:5c and Gen 3 is intended by the text itself. It is generally objected that in Gen 2–3 the 'apple tree' is not mentioned. Certainly the identification of the tree of the knowledge of good and evil with the apple tree is post-biblical. However, it seems to me that the objection is not decisive. It has been seen that in some way the whole of the Song has been written using Gen 2–3 as a model. Here too, it seems to me that the correspondence is pertinent. In fact, the 'awakening' (Song 8:5c) could well refer to the 'opening of the eyes' after the eating of the forbidden fruit (cf. Gen 3:7). If the parallel exists, then the Song's *relecture* of Gen 3 is similar to that of 7:11. Here the 'eating of the fruit' does not lead to death, but to the exact opposite, that is, to the overcoming of death (cf. Song 8:6c–7).

tion 'above/on' (*ʿal*), which characterised the two preceding stichs. A similar antithesis was noted in the juxtaposition of 6:10 with 6:11.[63]

The mention of the apple tree refers to 2:3. There the apple tree is a symbol of the man. The woman desires to sit 'under its shadow' and to eat of its fruit. The description clearly alludes to the amorous relationship, also because the apple tree, like the pomegranate tree, bears erotic symbolism (cf. 2:5; 7:9).[64] The link between the two passages is not accidental: the *inclusio* between the *Prologue* and the *Epilogue* was noted above.[65] 'In the shadow of the apple tree' and 'under the apple tree' are two equivalent expressions to indicate the place of love. It is the theme of 'love in the green', evoked in the *Prologue* also at 1:16–17.[66] There, the two zones, that of nature and the domestic one, harmonise: 'our bed' is 'of fresh grass', and 'the beams of our house' are made of 'cedars' and 'cypresses'.

In the context immediately preceding the *Epilogue*, the theme of nature is developed in 7:12–14. The relationship between this passage and ours is suggested by the emphatic adverb *šām* ('there'). 'There' (7:13e), that is, in the midst of nature, among bushes of henna, vineyards and pomegranates in flower, the woman promises to give the man her love. Once again, 'there' (8:5de),[67] under the apple tree, she declares, now, that she has awakened him. She thus declares that she has kept her promise. It is to be noted also that in 7:14, as in 1:16–17, the metaphor of nature is contaminated by a domestic element ('at our gates', 7:14b).

Also in 8:5bc, nature is transformed into a domestic ambience. The mention of the mother is, in fact, connected with the 'house of the mother' of 8:2 and 3:4. In 3:4, the 'house of the mother' is qualified by the apposition: 'the chamber of her who conceived me' (*hôrātî*).[68] Even

---

[63] Cf., *supra*, p. 352.
[64] Cf., *supra*, p. 85.
[65] Cf. p. 439.
[66] For the cultural background to this representation, we refer to p. 81, n. 157.
[67] In 8:5ef the adverb has a paragogic *-āh*, which Delitzsch interprets as indicating movement towards a place (cf. Delitzsch [1875], p. 127): the tree would not indicate the place, but would signal the direction of the house. However, it is perfectly possible to understand it as a synonym of *šām*. Cf. Joüon (1923), §93e.
[68] Probably under the influence of 3:4, the versions change the perfect of MT in 8:5e (*yᵉlādatkā*) with a participle. Here too, MT is the *lectio difficilior* which should be retained (cf., *supra*, n. 5, p. 435). We should observe that the repetition of a text is never wooden: just as in a musical score, the Song likes to introduce ever new variations, adapting the *ritornello* to its new context.

if there is no mention of a 'chamber' in 8:5, it is natural to think that the reference is to this place. Compared with 3:4, however, there are two variations in 8:5. First of all, here it is not the woman's mother that is being spoken of, as in 3:4 and 8:2, but the man's. That lets us understand that the continuity between 8:2 and 8:5 is of a symbolic, not a narrative, type. Even if 8:1–4 speaks of her family and 8:5 of his, the two passages are united by the family symbolism. Probably we should register once more an emphasis of that mirror technique which is typical of the Song.

In the second place, in 3:4, there is mention of 'conceiving' (*hārāh*), that is, of a process bound up with the act of love, while in 8:5 the emphasis is on 'childbearing'. The term *ḥābal*, repeated twice, in connection with *yālad* ('to give birth'), clearly has the meaning of 'to have the pains of labour'.[69] The three verbs, *hārāh, ḥābal* and *yālad* describe successive phases of the generative process: the first, the initial phase, the other two, the final phase.

In the three passages (Song 3:4; 8:2; and 8:5), love links up the two lovers with their roots, with the succession of the generations,[70] but here the emphasis is particular and must be underlined. In 'awakening' her man, the woman renews the moment of his generation, makes him born anew. She replaces his mother in giving him a new existence. The act of love is a new birth in which the bride is the mother.[71]

The place where this generation takes place is the same in which it happened before; therefore it is the 'chamber of her who conceived me' (3:4). Here too, as in the case of the apple tree, we have a symbolic place. Symbolically, the two locations, nature and 'the house of the mother', are intended to express the place of love. Verse 5cde summarises the two preceding songs, uniting in a sole place the natural and familial dimensions of love. The urban dimension has already been evoked in 5ab.

---

[69] The verb can also indicate conception (cf. Ps 7:15, in synonymous parallelism with *hārāh*), but here the closeness to *yālad* leads one to think rather of 'birth pangs' (*ḥăbālîm*). Cf. H.-J. Fabry, *ḥbl*, in *TDOT*, vol. IV, p. 191 (*contra* Gerleman).

[70] Cf., *supra*, pp. 136–137.

[71] In this sense, cf. Lys (1968), p. 284 ("Je t'ai enfin éveillé à une nouvelle naissance, celle de l'amour"); Elliott (1989), p. 193 ("In the embrace of the love, she has given him a new birth"). Less convincing is Lys's reference to the myth of the descent into the underworld ("Comme la déesse, elle aurait d'abord réveillé son chéri dans le sol du sommeil de la mort pour ensuite monter ensemble des enfers", p. 284). In the Song, the 'awakening' has another sense!

[8:6] The union must never be broken. Verse 6 is composed of a request (v. 6ab = direct discourse), followed by a reason (v. 6cdef = sapiential axioms in the form of nominal propositions). Contrary to the opinion of Tromp, according to whom the two parts are all but independent of each other,[72] it is my conviction that the *kî* (v. 6c) indicates a relationship of causality between the first and second part, just as is also the case with 1:2; 2:5, 10–11, 14, 15; 5:2. Verse 7 is distinguished from v. 6, both from the point of view of rhythm (tristichs instead of distichs) and from the point of view of syntax (we have, in fact, no longer nominal but verbal propositions). Even if one can consider it as part of the motivation, we prefer to treat it separately.[73]

Like v. 5, v. 6 is composed, therefore, of two parts, the first of one (v. 6ab), the second of two distichs (v. 6cdef). The second distich (v. 6cd), although syntactically linked to the third, is joined to the first by the repetition of the preposition *k*ᵉ ('as'):[74] v. 6ef, detached rhythmically from the two preceding ones, assumes the value of a conclusion.

[v. 6ab] "Set me as a seal upon your heart, as a seal upon your arm". The 'seal' (*ḥôtām*) was generally worn on the neck, fastened to a cord (cf. Gen 38:18—in this case, it was a cylindrical seal),[75] or it was set in a ring and worn on the finger (cf. Jer 22:24—in this case, the seal was a disc and functioned as a stamp).[76] For this reason, some authors understand 'arm' here as a synonym of 'hand'. W. W. Hallo has demonstrated, however, the possibility that a (cylindrical) seal might be fastened to the wrist, tied with a kind of bracelet.[77]

The root *ḥtm* appears on another occasion, in 4:12, in a verbal form where the woman is described as a 'sealed spring'. The function of the seal, it was noted, is that of preventing something closed from being

---

72 Cf. Tromp (1979), pp. 90–91. As Tromp emphasises, it is true that the motivation of 8:6 is of a particular character compared with the others. In any case, it is motivation. Tromp's position has been taken up by Loretz (1993), who leans upon a debatable 'colometric' analysis.

73 Here too, *contra* Tromp (1979), who joins v. 7abc to v. 6cdef, leaving v. 7def out of the unit.

74 A similar phenomenon is also encountered between the second tristich of v. 5 and the first tristich of v. 6, united between themselves by direct discourse. The entire strophe is charcterised by careful concatenation (cf., *supra*, *Tab. 71*, p. 442).

75 Cf. Keel (1997), Figure 142, p. 283.

76 Cf. Keel (1994), Figure 155, p. 271.

77 Hallo (1983), p. 10; *id.* (1985), pp. 25–26; cf. also Keel (1994), pp. 245–246; Moscati (1949), p. 319.

opened surreptitiously.[78] Here too the function is basically analogous. The seal is to bear witness to the lasting nature of the union described in v. 3.[79] Hallo underlines the inseparability of a seal from the person who bears it. Mesopotamian archaeology has confirmed that both types of seal were placed in the tomb together with the dead person,[80] that is, they accompanied him even after death. Such a symbolic value of the seal is also adduced in Jer 22:24, *à propos* of the rejection of Jechoniah: "Even if you were a ring (*ḥôtām*) on my right hand, I would tear you off". There, by the contrast, it can be inferred that the seal is the most precious item from which it would be most difficult to separate.[81]

On the seal was impressed either a design or the name of the person who wore it. It had the legal function of attesting the ownership by the proprietor of the seal of the object on which it was impressed.[82] This is clear from the episode in Gen 38 when Tamar seeks Judah's seal as a pledge (v. 18). It will then be easy to trace its proprietor with it (cf. vv. 25–26). With reference to the relationship between the lovers, the symbol of the seal expresses something like the refrain of mutual belonging (Song 2:16; 6:3; 7:11). The woman is the profound identity of the man, the sign of his personality: in her, the man finds himself.[83]

Keel[84] and Pope[85] stress a further significance of the seal. It was often worn as an amulet. The parallel with 1:13 confirms this dimension: the bag of myrrh, which passes the night between the breasts of the woman, has the same significance as the seal on the heart of the man. The two images are reciprocal: in 1:13, it is the man who is to be an amulet for the woman (the myrrh alludes, in fact, to the victory over

[78] For an example, cf. Keel (1994), Figure 103, p. 173.

[79] Once again, we can note the mirroring play: in 4:12, it is the woman who is sealed, in 8:6, it is rather the man. The woman here acts as 'seal' for the man.

[80] Hallo (1993).

[81] In positive form, cf. Hag 2:23. The motif of the closeness of the seal to the person who carries it, is transposed also in Egypt to the relationship of the two lovers: "If only I were her little seal-ring (*ḥtm*), / the keeper of her finger! / I would see her love each and every day, / … [while it would be I] who stole her heart" (Deir el-Medineh Vase, second cycle, l. 21 = Cairo Love Songs 21C, tr. Fox [1985], p. 38). The translation of the second part is disputed. For an alternative, cf. Bresciani (1990), p. 476.

[82] Cf. B. Otzen, *ḥtm*, in *TDOT*, vol. V, pp. 263–269.

[83] Cf. Elliott (1989), p. 195.

[84] Keel (1994), pp. 272–274.

[85] Pope (1977), pp. 666–667. In this sense also, Hallo (1993), p. 46, *pace* Loretz (1993), p. 240–244, who denies any connection between v. 6ab and 6c.

death);[86] in 8:6, it is the woman who is to fulfil this function for the man (vv. 6c–7 will speak of the victory over death).

The iconographic parallels show that the two positions of the seal (on the heart and on the arm) have a realistic significance. The seal was actually worn on the neck and on the wrist. At the same time, with reference to the woman ("set *me* as a seal"), they refer to the embrace of the couple as it has just been described in 8:3. In the embrace, the woman finds herself literally on the heart and on the arm of her beloved. She now seeks, therefore, that this union (the two are still embracing according to v. 5) will never be dissolved, that it will last for ever.[87]

To an ear attuned to the Scriptures, the seal on the heart and on the arm cannot not evoke some central texts for the faith of Israel. The first is Ex 28 and 39: of the fifteen occurrences of the noun *ḥôtām* in the OT, a good six refer to the ephod and to the breastplate of the high priest (Ex 28:11, 21, 36; 39:6, 14, 30) on which were inscribed the names of the sons of Israel. The Israelites were thus placed, literally, 'on the heart' of the high priest. The other text is Deut 6:6–8 (cf. 11:18), a passage which forms part of the daily prayer of every Jew, the *Shema*:

> And these words which I command you this day shall be upon your heart (*ʿal lebābekā*)..., you shall bind them as a sign upon your hand (*ʿal yādekā*), and they shall be as frontlets between your eyes.

In view here is an indissoluble bond between the Israelite and the law of YHWH: every action and every thought must be prompted to it. That is seen as a consequence of the love that binds Israel to its God (Deut 6:5—"You shall love YHWH your God with all your heart, with all your soul and with all your strength"). The correspondence makes one think of an intentional reference to the *Shema* by Song 8:6ab.[88] What the Shema says of the relationship between Israel and its God, the Song transfers to the relationship between the two lovers. It thus

[86] Cf., *supra*, p. 76.

[87] Elliott (1989), p. 195, proposes a symbolic interpretation of 'heart' and 'arm'. 'Heart' would stand for the interior of the man, 'arm' for his external activity. "She would become a type of enclosure for him, for all his thoughts, affections and deeds". The interpretation seems suggestive to us: it would cause the connection between our text and the *Shema* to be highlighted still more, on which cf. further *infra*.

[88] On the relationship between the Shema and the Song, cf. N. Lohfink, *ʾeḥād*, in *TDOT*, vol. I, p. 196.

brings back the metaphor of love, that was transferred by Deuteronomy to the supernatural plane, to its primary significance. But this operation, as Lacocque opportunely observes,[89] is not without consequences. In being transferred to the theological plane, the reality of human love had gained a divine value: and this still remains in the re-transferring to human love. The formula of v. 6f will make this dimension explicit.

[v. 6c–f] The great profession of faith of the Song of Songs is put down as the reason for the request made in v. 6ab.[90] Only a love like that expressed in v. 6ab can justify the claim of being 'flame of YHWH'.[91] It is true that the statements of v. 6c–f are separated from their context by their abstract, universal character, but that does not take away their connection with what goes before. Here, in a few lines of extraordinary density, is concentrated the whole of the content of the Song.

"For Love is strong as death". The subject of the phrase is *ʾahăbâ* ('Love'). The noun is without article, as in 7:7, indicating a personification of love: the same goes for the parallel *qinʾâ* in v. 6d.[92] Moreover, 'love' (with the article) also took on this character in v. 4c: the repetition of the term underlines the continuity between the last song of

---

[89] Lacocque (1998), p. 176: "*Eros* will never be the same again after having been transfigured by *agape*".

[90] "This clause motivates the preceding demand that her lover bind her to him as tightly and permanently as a seal. To do anything else would be to defy love's power, which is no less than death's irresistible force" (Fox [1985], p. 169).

[91] Cf. Harper (1907), p. xxxi: "The praise of such love (in his exclusiveness) cannot but become a satire upon what usually passes for love in a world in which polygamy is practised".

[92] To think, as Garbini (1992), p. 269, does, that love is presented as a god, is to go beyond the textual data. The correspondence with *qin'â* already speaks against this identification. Love, then, is spoken of in 8:4 too in a personal form, but here the noun bears the article as is usual in the book. We ourselves have emphasised, many times, the theological character of love, but it is another thing to make a god of it, in the same way as the Greek gods: that is unthinkable in the Jewish world. 8:6f will say that it is a 'flame of Yah', a formula which is perfectly a part of the ambit of Israelite theology. Cf. the criticism of Garbini raised by Sacchi (1993), p. 297; and Borgonovo (1994), p. 579. The OT knows of a similar personification with *ḥokmâ*, 'Wisdom' (also here without article, cf. Prov 8:1, 12), who is not God, but his creature (cf. Prov 8:22). Garbini rightly juxtaposes the two personifications, even if I do not share the idea of substitution ("The author wanted a female figure to substitute for Wisdom […], which someone considered almost an hypostasis of Yahweh", p. 269). Wisdom and love are two flashes of God into our world: they are two different ways by which to reach him. If wisdom is the way to God for the sages, for the Song the way is love, but the two ways are not incompatible between themselves. Cf., in this regard, the suggestive pages of Schäfer (2002).

the beloved woman and the *Epilogue*. The noun is the *Leitwort* of the strophe, recurring three times (vv. 6c, 7b and 7e).

Of Love (the term in Hebrew is feminine) it is said that it is 'strong' (*'azzâ*). At first sight, the adjective is surprising, so much so that Joüon proposes to understand it as 'insatiable'.[93] But the parallel with *qāšâ* ('hard, relentless', v. 6d) makes one think rather of the context of strife. Love, then, is not a faint-hearted little boy, but a terrible warrior.[94] This characterisation of love is not new in the Song. In 2:4, the man is represented under the metaphor of a warrior who conquers a city (cf. also 8:10). Reciprocally, the woman is 'terrible as a host drawn up' (6:4, 10) and has the irresistible, supernatural strength of the 'chariots of Israel' (6:12): her glance is sufficient to overwhelm (4:9; 6:5). Now, at last, the enigma is explained: behind the superhuman power of the two lovers is the power of Love. In fact, the banner of the conqueror bears this very name (2:4).

The only warrior who can be compared with love is death (*hammāwet*). In the face of death, every power surrenders: there is no physical power, no intelligence, no astute diplomacy which can match it with equal weapons. The 'Triumph of Death', so dear to medieval art, expresses this context. The comparative particle *k*ᵉ ('as') is the *mot juste*: it should not be replaced with a *min* ('more than'):[95] this will be said later. At the moment, the author wishes to affirm the immeasurable, irresistible power of love without giving a value judgement on it. Just as one cannot resist death, so one cannot resist love.

---

[93] Joüon (1909), p. 314. Graetz (1871), p. 207, has: 'painful' (*schmerzlich*).

[94] The motive is widespread in Graeco-Roman literature. Often cited as a parallel is this passage from Sophocles' Antigone: "Love invincible in battle, Love who falls upon men's property, you who spend the night upon the soft cheeks of a girl, and travel over sea and through the huts of dwellers in the wild! None among the immortals can escape you, nor any among mortal men, and he who has you is mad. You wrench just men's minds aside from justice, doing them violence. [...] Victory goes to the visible desire that comes from the eyes of the beautiful bride, desire that has its throne beside those of the mighty laws; for irresistible in her sporting is the goddess Aphriodite" (ll. 781–800, tr. Lloyd-Jones [1994], pp. 77–79). Plato too speaks of the invincible and savage power of love: "Thirdly comes our gratest need and keenest lust, which, though the latest to emerge, influences the soul of men with most raging frenzy—the lust for the sowing of offspring that burns with utmost violence" (*Laws* 6:783A, tr. Bury [1926], vol. I, pp. 493–495).

[95] *Contra* Garbini (1992), p. 278, who translates: "Love is stronger than Death". Such an operation has no textual support.

Actually, love and death form a binome which has been dwelt on by the literature of every age.[96] To love is, in some measure, to die. This is true even of the physical experience of love:

> Love and death in conjunction offer a powerful shortcut expressing the paradoxical amorous mix of deathlike self-abandonment and life-full self-achievement reached at the peak of the sexual act. Both partners are dealing to each other life and death. Ecstasy, rapture and release are contiguous.[97]

But love and death also go together in a more general sense that is not directly sexual. Whoever loves, loses his own freedom and his own time, and ends up sacrificing his own life for the person he loves. "Greater love has no man than this, that a man lay down his life for his friends" (John 15:13). To love means, definitively, to die, to lose one's own life, no longer to live for oneself. What Jesus says to his disciples, is true for every authentic experience of love: "Whoever loves his life will lose it, and who loses it [...] will find it" (Matt 10:39; cf. 16:25; Mark 8:35; Luke 9:24; 17:33; John 12:25). Love and death, says Landy, are alike because both "offer fusion, final integration. For the ego, then, they are equally threatening".[98]

But they are also enemies, rivals, at war with each other (the term *ʿāz* refers to this contest). If the war is won by death, then it separates the two lovers: the seal is broken. If Love is truly strong, it has to win the war with the last enemy. In this connection, Ravasi quotes a phrase of Gabriel Marcel: "To say: 'I love you' is to say: 'You shall not die'".[99]

Loretz claims that the thought of a victory over death is foreign to the Song.[100] However, it is true, as Heinevetter has shown,[101] that the theme of the victory of love and life over death is the theological centre of the book. Until now, the Song has not expressed itself in philosophic

---

[96] For the theme of Eros-Thanatos in Greek literature, we refer to Ravasi (1992), p. 648, n. 21.

[97] Lacocque (1998), p. 171.

[98] Landy (1983), p. 123. Similarly, Linafelt (2002), p. 325, referring to the thought of G. Bataille: "The commingling of selves exists only in the violation of borders, only in the state of being affected by an external agent, which, though we may know such violation as an experience of ecstasy, is noneless an experience of anguish".

[99] Ravasi (1992), p. 648.

[100] "It is impossible that it would occur to an Israelite that he could confront death on equal terms with his love or even that he could hold on to his state of loving in the grave" (Loretz [1993], p. 228).

[101] Heinevetter (1988), pp. 190–198: "Death and life—the theology of the collection".

terms but with the language of metaphors. The *Epilogue* formulates in theoretical terms what the rest of the book has expressed in poetic terms. It is worth remembering some of these metaphors: first of all the lotus flower (2:2, 16; 4:5; 6:2, 3; 7:3),[102] then the myrrh (1:13; 3:6; 4:6; 5:5),[103] the henna (1:14; 4:13; 7:12),[104] the gazelle (2:7, 9, 17; 3:5; 8:14).[105] In the immediate context of our verse, we have read the image of the two lovers close together against the background of the desert (v. 5ab) as an icon of the victory of love over death.[106] We have also recognised an apotropaic value to the 'seal on the heart' (v. 6a).[107] If it is true, finally, that the 'apple tree' (v. 5c) recalls the tree of paradise, something that seems highly probable, then it is possible to understand a polemical aim against Gen 3. There, in giving him the fruit of the forbidden tree, the woman led the man to death.[108] Here, instead, 'awakening him' under the apple tree, the woman gives him life (cf. v. 5de: "There she travailed, and gave you to the light").[109] The likelihood of the parallel is strengthened by the fact that in the 'garden-paradise' of the Song (Song 4:12–15), there is a well of 'living water' (*mayim ḥayyîm*, v. 15), which makes one think of the 'tree of life' of Genesis (*ʿēṣ haḥayyîm*, Gen 2:9; 3:22).[110] The woman's love, according to the Song, is the source not of death but of life for man.

[102] On the connection between the metaphor of the lotus flower and the theme life-death, cf., *supra*, pp. 83–84.

[103] Here too we are reminded of p. 76.

[104] Cf. pp. 76–77.

[105] Cf. pp. 122–123.

[106] *Supra*, p. 447.

[107] Cf. pp. 454–455.

[108] At least in the primitive intention of the myth, the eating of the fruit had a sexual connotation. "Gen 3—in its most ancient significance, still that of a fairy tale—connects the birth of love with the loss of immortality. According to the epic poem of Gilgamesh, when Enkidu dies, he curses the prostitute who has taught him about the sexual relationship; undoubtedly it was this that led to his death" (Müller [1992], p. 86; cfr. *ANET*, p. 86). Another passage from Gilgamesh, suggested by Watson, also leads to this interpretation: "The fine young man, the beautiful girl / when making love, together they confront death" (*Gilgamesh* 10,7 ll. 11–12, according to Watson [1997], p. 386; cf. *ANET*, p. 507).

[109] Cf., *supra*, p. 137.

[110] "When he is in love, the man snatches from the cherub the flaming sword that bars access to the earthly paradise and to the tree of life. Because only in the state of grace which is falling in love does the world appear to us as it was before the Fall, without suffering, without evil, without death. [...] Those in love have no fear of death because there is no death in the Garden of Eden" (F. Alberoni, *Gli innamorati hanno paura della solitudine, non della morte*, in *Corriere della sera*, 20.08.2001, p. 1; cf. *id.* [2001], pp. 49–55).

Verse 6c finds a surprising parallel in the Ugaritic literature. In the myth of the war between Baal and Mot, there is a description of the scene of the combat between the two rival divinities, the god of vegetation and life, and that of drought and death. Three times the refrain resounds: "Mot is strong (*'z*), Baal strong (*'z*)".[111] At the bottom of this myth lies the seasonal alternation of the cyclical death and rebirth of the vegetation; but the myth goes beyond this alternation, setting itself as a reflection on the reality of death and its link with life.[112] What is interesting is the role played by the sister-spouse of Baal, Anat. She seeks Mot, the god of death, in the underworld, tears him to pieces, and leads Baal back to life. The myth of the descent of the goddess of love into the underworld is present in all the cultures of the Ancient Orient, under different names: Inanna and Dumuzi,[113] Ishtar and Tammuz,[114] Isis and Osiris. Keel shows a surprising figurative version of this myth.[115] On the coffin of the dead Osiris, his wife-sister Isis is represented under the form of a female falcon in the act of being fertilised by the erect penis of the dead male. By means of generation, love conquers death. Certainly here, as in the Song, we are faced with anticipations, attempts to decipher the mystery of death.[116] At bottom, there is the intuition that if ever anything can confront the ancient enemy of humanity with equal weapons, it is love. For Christians, this intuition has been confirmed in the death and resurrection of Jesus Christ. In them the true profundity of the saying that "love is strong as death" has been revealed. It has been observed that the Fourth Gospel

---

[111] "They push (?) the pachyderm (?): / Mot is strong, Baal strong; / They gore like buffalo: / Mot is strong, Baal strong; / They bite like serpents: / Mot is strong, Baal strong; / They kick like steeds: / Mot is down, Baal down" (tr. according to Pope [1977], p. 668; cf., also, Del Olmo Lete [1981], p. 233). Watson (1997), p. 384, cites another passage, *KTU* 2.10,12–13: *kmtm 'z m'id*, which he renders: "for Death is very strong". But this translation is much debated.

[112] Del Olmo Lete (1981), p. 149.

[113] Cf. Kramer (1969), pp. 107–133; Wolkstein – Kramer (1983), pp. 155–169.

[114] Cf. Schmökel (1956), p. 79; Wittekindt (1925), pp. 115–133.

[115] Keel (1994), Figure 156, p. 273.

[116] In this sense, perhaps Garbini is right to see in our passage a polemic against the pessimistic statement of Qoheleth: "Their love (*'hbh*), and their hatred, and their envy (*qn'h*) have already perished [...]: for there is no work, or thought, or knowledge or wisdom in Sheol" (Qoh 9:6, 10, cf. Garbini [1992], p. 274). On the other hand, the affirmation of the Song is not isolated in the Old Testament. Hope in the resurrection is widespread in the Hellenistic epoch: now it concerns not only the people, but also separate individuals. In fact, the books of Daniel, Maccabees and Wisdom, where the affirmation of a life after death is clear, are from this epoch. Cf. also Tait (2008).

Table 74

v. 6c	*strong*	*as death*	*Love*
v. 6d	*relentless*	*as the grave*	*Jealousy*

presents the death of Jesus and the events of the morning of Easter under the symbolism of the Song.[117]

Verse 6d is constructed in precise synonymous parallelism with v. 6c (cf. *Tab. 74*).

The two nominal propositions have to be read together. If the first can be idealised, the second clarifies that here we are not dealing with something romantic but with love as a primordial force, a passion that overwhelms. In fact, the term *ʾahăbâ* is lined up with *qinʾâ* ('jealousy, passion'). The original significance of the root is thus specified by Reuter: "In the human domain *qnʾ* refers primarily to a violent emotion aroused by fear of losing a person or object".[118]

In our case, the link with the 'seal' is clear. It is, precisely, the fear that the seal will be broken, that the union will be dissolved, that the woman will lose the object of her love. It is interesting to note that in the OT jealousy is spoken of exclusively with regard to man in his relation to woman: it is always the woman who is considered to the 'possession' of the man, never *vice versa*. The classic case is Num 5:11–31, 'the jealousy offering'. In our verse, the statement has a general character, but it is put into the mouth of the woman, as a result of which it is primarily female jealousy that is being referred to. *qinʾâ* is usually connected with anger and revenge (Prov 6:34–35; 27:4); it leads, therefore, to violence, and 'consumes' those who are possessed by it (cf. Ps 69:10; John 2:17).

But *qinʾâ* is not only negative. In the OT 'jealousy' is spoken of with reference to YHWH whether as object (cf. 1 Kgs 19:14) or as subject. The classic place in this last sense is Ex 34:14—"You shall not prostrate yourself before another god, for YHWH bears the name of *Jealous*: he is a *jealous* God" (cf. also Ex 20:5, the second of the Ten Commandments; Deut 4:24; 5:9; 6:15). Behind this text, one glimpses, again, the preaching of Hosea who has transferred to God his relationship with Gomer. The Song operates in the reverse direction: the exclusiveness

---

[117] Cf. John 20:15 and Song 3:1; John 20:2; 21:7, 15–17, 20 and Song 8:6.

[118] E. Reuter, *qnʾ*, in *TDOT*, vol. XIII, p. 49.

of the relationship between God and his people is brought back to its original context, the man-woman relationship. But now human jealousy bears a theological value: between monolatry and monogamy there is a reciprocal relationship. We should note that the indissolubility does not concern the matrimonial bond,[119] the institution (even if this is not denied, it has been seen), but love itself.[120] If one thinks that divorce and polygamy were current practices in the society of the time, the statement of the Song appears as a protest against such customs in the sense of the gospel saying: "What God has joined together, let no man put asunder" (Matt 19:6; cf. 5:21–22). Like the gospel passage, the Song refers back to the 'beginning', to the time of paradise.

If Love is 'strong', Jealousy is *qašâ* ('relentless'). The adjective usually has a negative sense. In Gen 49:7, the two terms, *qn'* and *qšh* describe the anger of Simeon and Levi, an anger which does not know compassion. In 1 Sam 25:3 and in Isa 19:4, the term *qšh* designates a master without mercy. Just as the kingdom of the dead (*šᵉ'ôl*), heedless of human feelings, is not disposed to share its victims with others (cf. Prov 30:15–16), so jealousy will not tolerate sharing the object of its own love with others.[121] There are no value judgements here: the intention is to represent the primordial force of passion. Dante comes to mind: "Love, which absolves no beloved from loving...".[122] G. Krinetzki sees here an allusion to the dark side of the female archetype. According to depth psychology, the woman is simultaneously the welcoming mother who gives life and the terrible mother who devours her sons.[123]

Like the two preceding distichs, the last one (v. 6ef) also consists of parallel expressions (cf. *Tab. 75*). Not only does v. 6f take up again

---

[119] Cf. Krinetzki (1962), pp. 270–271. However, he refers the indissolubility to marriage, not to love. In more recent works, Krinetzki no longer adopts this idea.

[120] Between a kind of love that is spontaneous and free from any chains, which seems understood by Lacocque (cf. the commentary cited many times: Lacocque [1998]) and that sanctioned by the marriage bond, Ricoeur (1998), p. 268, introduces the category of 'nuptial bond' to speak of the love of the Song, a love that is 'free' and 'faithful' at the same time.

[121] Cf. Lys (1968), p. 287.

[122] "Amor, ch'a nullo amato amar perdona", Dante, *Inferno* 5:103 (tr. Sinclair [1972–1978], vol. I, p. 77).

[123] Cf. Krinetzki (1981), pp. 220–221; *id.* (1970), pp. 411–412. In a similar sense, D. Wolkstein sees personified in the myth of the descent of Inanna the two aspects of feminine psychology, the first, that of the goddess of love and life, Inanna, and, the second, that of the queen of the underworld, Ereshkigal. Cf. Wolkstein – Kramer (1983), pp. 156–158.

Table 75

v. 6e	*Its darts*	*are darts of fire,*
v. 6f	—	*a flame of Yah*

the image of fire, introduced in v. 6e, but also, in terms of sound, *šalhebetyâ* (v. 6f) forms a word play with *rᵉšāpehā rišpê ʾēš* (v. 6e: NB the sounds *š*, *a* and *e*). The parallelism is not perfect, however: the first part of v. 6e has no match in v. 6f. This fact, far from being a sign of corruption in the text,[124] isolates the stich 6f from the preceding stichs, underlining its distinctiveness: it is the solemn conclusion of the verse.

The term *rešep* refers primarily to a divinity known throughout the Ancient Orient and equivalent to the Greek Apollo.[125] He is first and foremost a chthonic and warlike divinity who spreads around himself plagues and diseases. But he is also a god of fertility whose weapon is the lightning.[126] From the fact that the term is plural here, it has clearly been demythologised, but the mythological background is perceptible. The meaning of the noun oscillates between 'flames'[127] and 'arrows, darts':[128] what is made explicit by the second part of the stich ('darts of fire') is already contained in the term *rešep*. It is not, therefore, the graceful bow of Cupid that is being evoked here, but the thunderbolts of the god of the storm who unleashes death and life. Because the aspect of 'fire' is highlighted in the second part of the stich, we prefer to translate as 'darts'[129] in order to make clear the link with the preceding context where war ('strong', 'relentless') was mentioned.

It is not clear to whom the possessive ('*his* darts') refers. It could refer to either 'Love' or 'Jealousy', even if the proximity with v. 6d makes one think more of the latter term, the dark, terrible aspect of love. In this it reminds us of Prov 6:27–29:

---

[124] "Has a predicate dropped out, before or after *šlhbtyh*, which would be a parallel expression to 'his flames' or, respectively, to 'are flames of fire'?" (Müller [1992], p. 84, n. 261, cf. *BHS*). Ricciotti (1928), p. 275, translates: "His flames, flame of Yahweh". Such a supposition is nourished by LXX's *phloges autēs* (cf., *supra*, n. 7, p. 436).

[125] For an iconographic representation, cf. *ANEP*, Figure 476, p. 164.

[126] Cf. *HALOT*, p. 1297–1298; M.G. Mulder, *rešep*, in *TDOT*, vol. XIV, pp. 10–16.

[127] So *HALOT*, p. 1298, and the majority of modern translations.

[128] Thus Robert – Tournay (1963), p. 301; Garbini (1992), p. 275; *TDOT*, vol. XIV, p. 15: "The ardor of passion is like Resheph's 'fieriness', whose flashing arrows ignite an irresistible fire".

[129] Cf., in this sense also, Ps 76:4 (*rišpê qāšet*).

> Can a man carry fire in his bosom
> and his clothes not be burned?
> Or can one walk upon hot coals
> and his feet not be scorched?
> So is he who goes in to his neighbour's wife;
> none who touches her will go unpunished (tr. *RSV*).

One does not play with fire: so one cannot play with love.[130]

Like Jealousy, fire is ambivalent. On the one hand, it is a consuming force, destructive. On the other hand, it is beneficent: it warms, it purifies, it establishes in unity what has been separate. This latter aspect allows us to grasp the link with the 'seal'. As Landy suggests, only if the lovers are united is there no place for jealousy.[131] Separation, on the other hand, unleashes the negative, destructive aspect of passion: destructive in relation to both its subject and its object.

The positive aspect of fire is outlined in the last stich. If in v. 6e the demonic, dark aspect of love was put forward, in 6f it is its divine aspect that is being presented ('a flame of Yah'). The reference here is to 'Love', v. 6c, rather than to 'Jealousy', v. 6d. By simplifying, one can, therefore, discern a chiastic scheme in the exposition of the positive and negative (or, perhaps, better divine and luminous, and demonic and dark aspects, respectively) of love (cf. *Tab. 76*).

The ancient versions did not understand the term *šalhebetyâ*.[132] In itself the MT is clear. The term is composite, made up of two words: the first is *šalhebet* ('flame'), the second *yâ*, an abbreviation of YHWH (as in *halᵉlû-yâ*).[133] The attempts to emend the text, supported by the ancient versions, are not convincing.[134] What does 'a flame of YHWH' signify? For many authors, it is simply a sort of superlative ('a violent flame').[135] Others see there the description of 'lightning' as in 1 Kgs

---

[130] Significantly, Lys (1968), pp. 282–308, entitles the passage 8:5–14: "On ne badine pas avec l'amour".

[131] "Only by being inseparable can they never be jealous" (Landy [1983], p. 126). This aspect is expressed in Song 2:15–16, where the lovers can watch the rivals (the 'little foxes') with detachment, because they feel themselves united ("My beloved is mine and I am his", v. 16).

[132] Cf., *supra*, n. 7, p. 436.

[133] According to R. Tournay, the spelling *-yâ* may have its origin in Aramaic influence (cf. Robert – Tournay [1963], p. 453), which would confirm the Hellenistic dating of the poem.

[134] Cf., *supra*, n. 124, p. 463.

[135] So, for example, Krinetzki (1981), p. 291 (‚gewaltige Flamme'); Gerleman (1965), p. 217; Müller (1992), p. 85, n. 264. Generally, however, the word *ʾĕlōhîm* is used in this sense (cf. Gen 1:2; 23:6; Jonah 3:3).

Table 76

v. 6c	Love	+
v. 6d	Jealousy	–
v. 6e	*rešep*	–
v. 6f	YHWH	+

18:38 (*ʾēš* YHWH); 2 Kgs 1:12; Job 1:16 (*ʾēš ʾĕlōhîm*).[136] But in this case it would be a tautology because the same concept is already expressed in v. 6e. Although being linked to the preceding stich by the image of fire, *šalhebetyâ* cannot be considered simply as a synonym of *rᵉšāpehā* and *rišpê ʾēš*, if only from the fact that there we have a plural, here a singular. Also, as has been seen, v. 6f is detached from v. 6e from the rhythmic point of view.

The objection generally adopted to a literal understanding of the expression is that in the Song God is never named. The Song would thus be a deliberately 'lay' writing. On the lay character of the Song we are in agreement, treating it as a sapiential writing. However, even if the divine name is not mentioned, the Song presents love as something with theological characteristics. The woman, for example, is represented with theomorphic features in Song 3:6[137] and in 6:10,[138] and the man, likewise, in 5:10–16.[139] When the woman charges the daughters of Jerusalem 'by the gazelles and by the wild deer' (2:7; 3:5), she makes an oath in the name of love, which can be explained only by the divine character of this reality.[140] The Song constantly retransfers to human love traits that are characteristic of the relationship of Israel with its God (we noted, for example, the relationship of Song 8:6ab to Deut 6:5–8;[141] of Song 8:6d to Ex 34:14).[142]

Certainly Lys is right to declare: "The OT battles against this 'prostitution' to the great foreign goddess. It avoids reducing YHWH to the limitations of human sexuality or divinising sexuality".[143] So Garbini's

[136] Cf. Lys (1968), p. 282 ('un sacré coup de foudre'); Keel (1994), p. 270 ('flaming bolts of lighting [*flammende Blitze*]'); Ricciotti (1928), p. 278; Colombo (1975), p. 132.
[137] Cf., *supra*, pp. 146–147.
[138] Cf. pp. 344–345.
[139] Cf. pp. 287–288.
[140] Cf. pp. 91–92.
[141] *Supra*, pp. 455–456.
[142] *Supra*, pp. 461–462.
[143] Lys (1968), p. 290.

simplification of seeing in Song 8:6 the "theophany of the Love God"[144] is not acceptable. In Israel there is only one God, and he is called YHWH. The Song certainly is hospitable to the cultural heritage of the surrounding mythology, but it reinterprets it in the ambit of the Yahwistic religion. Love is not a god which is meant to be substituted for YHWH, but is a 'flame of Yah'. It is not 'of God'[145] but of *YHWH*, that is, of the God of Israel. It is possible to grasp an antithesis in the juxtaposition of *rišpê ʾêš* and *šalhebetyâ*: love is not a fiendish flame of which one must be afraid; it is the fire of the God of liberation, the God of the Exodus. The 'flame of YHWH' recalls, in fact, the episode of the burning bush (cf. Ex 3:2), as also the column of fire which accompanied the Israelites during the Exodus (Exod 13:21–22) and, above all, the theophany of Sinai (cf. Exod 19:18; Deut 4:11–12). Deut 4:24 connects the fire of the Exodus with the divine jealousy: "For YHWH your God is a devouring fire, a jealous God" (cf. also Isa 33:14).

"Love is a flame of Yah". The text, then, has to be taken literally. Here, at the end of the Song, the veil is lifted and the profession of faith that undergirds the whole poem is confessed.[146] It was for this that the woman was invited to abandon her securities and to entrust herself to the summons of love, as Abraham had followed the call of God (cf. Song 1:8), as the Israelites had followed the call of Moses (cf. Song 2:10, 13). The adventure of love is the same adventure as that of faith.

The affirmation of Song 8:6f finds a singular confirmation in the NT. In 1 John 4:7, it is said that "love is from God", and it is the equivalent expression to Song 8:6f. Significantly, in the following verse, the subject changes. Not "love is God", but: "God is love" (*ho theos agapē estin*, 1 John 4:8), which is not the same thing. There is a profound continuity between the Song and the New Testament: it is the same revelation.[147]

---

[144] "Ahavah appears as a Greek goddess and speaks as a god who reveals himself to man" (Garbini [1992], p. 275).

[145] Again *contra* Garbini (1992), p. 269 ("Given the context, it is to be excluded that the author intended to refer to Yahweh").

[146] The expression is taken from Robert – Tournay (1963), pp. 302–303: "It ought [...] to be questioned how a book, which has always spoken of God and of God's love, could wrap its thesis in uninterrupted mistery, to lift the veil only at the conclusion". Naturally we distance ourselves from the allegorical interpretation of the two authors. The human, sexual character of the love of the Song has been pointed out in 8:5. It is precisely this love which is 'flame of Yah'.

[147] In this connection, cf. the profound reflections of F. Rosenzweig in the second

"Love is a flame of Yah". Even if the phrase has a universal value, it has to be read in its context as the reason for the request of v. 6ab with which the woman seeks that the union with the man be never dissolved. Love is presented as an all encompassing, global reality: unique (cf. the emphasis on jealousy) and indissoluble, such that not even death can destroy it. It is this love that is called 'flame of Yah'. At this point we could realistically enquire: does this love exist among men? Once again, we are seeing with our own eyes the paradisial character of the love of the Song.[148]

[8:7] Superiority of love over its enemies. Verse 7 is composed of two parts, 7abc and 7def which, at first sight, have no connection between them.[149] On closer examination, however, both can be understood as a development of the profession of faith of v. 6f. There, the divine character of love was declared. Verse 7abc draws a positive consequence from this declaration; if love is present, nothing will be able to overwhelm it, neither the forces of chaos nor death. Verse 7def draws the converse conclusion from the same declaration: if love is not present, nothing and no one, not even all the riches of this world, can buy it. So v. 7 continues the 'treatise' on love begun in v. 6c: the term *ʾahăbă* (v. 7b, e) unites both parts of v. 7 between themselves and with v. 6c. In both parts, love is confronted with something of great magnitude, but of a different order, in order to demonstrate its superiority: the '*great* waters' are not sufficient to quench love (v. 7abc); 'all the wealth of a man's house' is not sufficient to obtain it (v. 7def). The greatness of love is not in the order of quantity.[150]

---

chapter of his *Star of Redemption*, which bears precisely the title of 'Revelation', and is devoted in large part to the Song of Songs. Cf. Rosenzweig (2005), pp. 169–220.

[148] The utopia of paradise with regard to human love, on the other hand, is brought up again in the Gospel (cf. Matt 19:3–9: "In the beginning it was not so!").

[149] So much so that Ravasi (1992), p. 633, joins 7abc to v. 6, and makes v. 7def the third strophe of the compositional unit 8:5–7. In this he follows Tromp (1979), pp. 90–92, who isolates vv. 6c–7c as an autonomous unit.

[150] Such a meaning is completely distorted by understanding v. 7def as a rhetorical question: "If one were to give all the riches of his house in exchange for love, / could one scorn him?" So Müller (1992), p. 84. The text intends to declare the impossibility of such an exchange, not to encourage the selling of everything in order to buy love. It is true, however, that the Tg also understands 8,7def in a positive form: "And if a man should give all the wealth of his house to acquire wisdom in exile, I shall return to him double in the world to come" (*Targum of Canticles* 8:7, tr. Alexander [2003], 198). Garbini's interpretation is similar: "Whoever gives his life for love will save it and not lose it" (Garbini [1992], pp. 120–122, 278). Garbini bases himself on LXX, which renders MT's *hôn*, 'wealth', with *bion*, 'life'. But in Greek *bios* has also the value

Despite the fact that v. 7 is rhythmically and syntactically separated from v. 6, in another way, it is intimately joined to it, not only from the logical but also from the metaphorical point of view. The image of water (v. 7abc) is, in fact, directly connected, by contrast, with that of fire in v. 6ef. The theme of the battle between Love and Death (v. 6cd) is continued in the strife between love and the powers of chaos (v. 7abc): both the passages evoke mythological reminiscences. However, v. 7abc is not a simple repetition of v. 6cd. If there it was said that "Love is strong *as* death", now the superiority of love over death is affirmed,[151] making explicit and precise what was there only implicit.

[v. 7abc] The expression 'the great waters' (*mayim rabbîm*) has a strong mythological colouring, referring primarily to the war of the creator god with the waters of chaos: a myth attested not only in Mesopotamia and Ugarit,[152] but also in the Hebrew Bible (cf. Job 38:4–12).[153] There, this war is often historicised as victory over the historical enemies of Israel (cf. Ps 77:17–21; Hab 3:8–9; Isa 17:12–13). In the Psalms, all that threatens the life of man is expressed with this metaphor: the 'great waters' thus often become a synonym of 'death' (Ps 18:5–6, 17; Jonah 2:3–7). Even without recourse to the idea of the infernal river,[154] the association of the 'great waters' with the underworld and death is obvious in the OT.[155]

It is said of the 'great waters' that they 'cannot quench love'. The juxtaposition of the adjective 'great, many' (*rab*) with the verb 'to be able' (*ykl*) is not accidental; it expresses a contrast which we have tried to render with the translation 'are not enough'. Although the waters are 'great', they are not 'enough'. The link between v. 7a and v. 6ef is clear: only if it has been said that love is a 'fire' (v. 6ef), can one now understand the metaphor of water. And only if it has been said that it

---

of 'substance' (cf. Mark 12:44: *holon ton bion autēs*), a meaning supported, in addition to MT, by the other versions with the exception of Vetus Latina (Tg *māmôn*; Syr *'tr'*; Vg *substantiam*; Aquila *hyparxin*). From where Garbini obtains the fine phrase: "will save it and not lose it" is difficult to know. Certainly not from the text of the Song.

[151] Cf. Lacocque (1998), p. 170.

[152] The myth is frequently represented in Oriental iconography. Cf., for example, Keel (1978), Figure 42, p. 47, and Figure 48, p. 52.

[153] Cf. May (1955).

[154] A parallel with the Hubur, the infernal river of Mesopotamian literature, has been suggested by the mythological school, cf. Wittekindt (1925), p. 57; Schmökel (1956), p. 79.

[155] Cf. Munro (1995), pp. 113–114; Pope (1977), p. 673 (by contrast with May, cf. n. 153).

is a 'flame of Yah' (v. 6f), can one understand that all the water in this world is not capable of extinguishing it.

The term 'river' (*nāhār*, v. 7c) indicates a perennial watercourse: only the great rivers of antiquity bear this name. But here the plural is synonymous with the 'great waters'; these are the rivers which feed the abyss. At Ugarit, in the myth of the war of Baal and Yam, the god who personifies the watery chaos, the latter is called 'sea prince' and 'river judge'.[156] In the Hebrew Bible too, such a correspondence is usual (cf. Ps 24:2; 93:3–4; Hab 3:8–9). In parallel with the verb *kābāh* ('to quench', v. 7b), the verb *šāṭap* is used ('to sweep away, submerge'). This verb usually occurs in connection with running water, referring, therefore, to the destructive action of a river in flood (cf. Matt 7:24–27).[157] As in the case of the 'great waters', also in that of the 'rivers', the link with death and the subterranean world is clear (cf. Ezek 31:15; Hab 3:8–10; Ps 18:5–6).

In the Old Testament, it is said that the love that unites YHWH to his people is able to overcome the powers of chaos (cf. Ps 46:3–4; Isa 54:10). There is a passage of Isaiah which is remarkably close to our text:

> If you have to pass through the waters (*mayim*), I shall be with you,
> the rivers (*nehārôt*) will not drown you (*yišṭepûkā*),
> if you have to pass through the midst of fire (*'ēš*), it will not burn you,
> and the flame will not consume you,
> for I am YHWH your God (Isa 43:2).

The Psalms transpose this conviction to the individual; Ps 16:9–11 is a good example. The bond that unites the psalmist with his God is so strong that he confronts death serenely, knowing that: "you will not leave my life in the grave" (Ps 16:10). One has the impression that the Song transfers this conviction to the love between man and woman.[158] If it is the 'flame of YHWH', then not even death can stand in its way. What remains a presentiment in the OT (it is always possible to interpret the salvation from death as the prolonging of this life), receives confirmation in the NT (cfr. Rom 8:35–39). The reasoning is similar

---

[156] *zbl ym* and *ṯpṭ nhr*, cf. L. A. Snijders, *nāhār*, in *TDOT*, vol. IX, pp. 269–270.

[157] Cf. R. Liwak, *šṭp*, in *TDOT*, vol. XIV, pp. 599–606.

[158] And therefore we can make out the link, a profound one, with the request for indissolubility in v. 6ab. Not even death can separate the two lovers! What in our time is often felt as a burden, is presented in the Song as good news.

to that of the Song: love belongs to the divine order, everything else to that which is creaturely and of this world.

[v. 7def] The second part of v. 7 is seen by Robert and Tournay as an addition,[159] and it is easy to see why: it does not agree with the allegorical interpretation of the poem. Often a falling off in the tone is detected here as if the passage did not reach the heights of what has gone before.[160] Against the 'additional' character of the passage stands the above-mentioned fact of the repetition of the terms 'to scorn' (*bûz*), 'house' (*bêt*) and 'to give' (*nātan*) from the *Final Songs of the Beloved Woman* (*bûz* = 8:1; *bêt* = 8;2; *nātan* = 7:13, 14 and 8:1); against the 'falling off of the tone' speaks the fact that the theme of wealth is developed in the two following strophes (*kesep*, 'silver', vv. 9, 11), telling how much this theme is dear to the author.[161]

The declaration is to be placed against the background of the speculation on the character of wisdom. It is a widespread principle in the OT that wisdom has no price; it is superior to all the wealth in the world, cf. Prov 3:14–15; 4:7; 8:10–11. The prayer of Solomon in Wis 7:8–14 exalts Wisdom over all the goods of the world (cf. Matt 13:44–46). For Prov 8, although it is a creature, hypostasised Wisdom is both anterior and superior to the creation: it belongs to the sphere of divinity. The 'supernatural' character of Wisdom is underlined in Job 28. Since it is superior to man, it is not to be obtained with the riches of this world:

> It cannot be gotten for choicest gold,
> neither can silver be weighed for the price thereof... (Job 28:15).

Man has no access to Wisdom; only God knows the way to arrive at it (v. 23).

---

[159] V. 7def would be an isolated 'aphorism of a sage' (so Robert – Tournay [1963], pp. 304–305).

[160] Pope (1977), p. 676, places v. 7def between parentheses with the note: "Such a statement following the eloquent praise of the power of love strikes one as an anti-climax". Similarly Ravasi (1992), p. 669: "Thus ends, in a minor key, in a didactic, everyday tone a hymn which had reached the heights in a titanic duel between Life and Death, Love and the grave, and which had drawn the man in love towards heaven and towards the divine'; Landy (1983), p. 133: 'Following the credo, the Song has nothing more to say".

[161] According to Graetz (1871), p. 209: "Here (in v. 7def, *author's note*) we have the most important truth that the author wishes to impress on the heart of his contemporaries". Harper (1907), pp. 58–59, is also of the same opinion.

What Job says of Wisdom, the Song says of love. The link between the hypostasisation of Wisdom and that of love was noted above. For the sage, Wisdom is the reflection of God on earth, the way to reach him; for the Song, this is the role of love. One might say that the Song deliberately attributes to love what the sages say of Wisdom. Like Wisdom, love too is not at man's disposal. Aristotle speaks of *eutychia* (fortuitousness) with regard to the bond of love.[162] OT man knows that the birth of love in a young woman's heart is a mystery known only to God (cf. Prov 30:18–19).[163] In Gen 24:21, Abraham's servant, charged with finding a wife for his master's son, assumes a religious demeanour before Rebecca: "The man gazed at her in silence to learn whether YHWH had prospered his journey or not".[164]

For the OT there exists a third reality which is not for purchase: human life (cf. Ps 49:8–10). Life, wisdom, love are the areas where man experiences his own limits. What is human can be bought with money. What is divine has no price. It cannot be bought; it can only be given.[165]

Often v. 7def is seen as a protest against the social custom of the *mōhar*, the bride-price.[166] That is certainly possible, and it would match up well with the protest against divorce and polygamy which we have read between the lines in the comment on v. 6. Here too, however, the historical concreteness does not take away the universal value of the declaration which lies perfectly in line with the other considerations of principle on the nature of love.[167] In the OT, as generally in the

[162] Cf. the chapter devoted to love by the contemporary philosopher Tidemann (1979), pp. 74–81. I cite at random: "That we are loved depends on the subjectivity, the particularity and the irrepeatability of the situation and on personal destiny. One can do nothing here, no effort, no trick. In the depth of love, even the lightest activism has absolutely fatal consequences" (pp. 79–80).

[163] Cf. also Prov 19:14 ("House and wealth are inherited from fathers, / but a prudent wife is from the Lord"); 18:22 ("He who finds a wife finds a good thing, / and obtains favour from the Lord").

[164] In the Egyptian love songs, it is always the divinity who assigns his sweetheart to a young man (and *vice versa*). Cf., for example, Papyrus Harris 500B, 5:2–3: "I have obtained forever and ever / what Amon has granted me" (tr. Fox [1985], p. 21; for other similar passages, cf. Mathieu [1996], pp. 232–233).

[165] Perhaps at v. 7d the repeat of the verb *nātan* is not accidental. It is a *Leitwort* of the two preceding songs: in 7:13 and 14 it is for the woman 'to give' love; in 8:1, she herself receives her beloved as a gift (lit.: "who will *give* you as a brother to me?"). The 'wealth' that one light want to 'give' in 8:7 is not of the same order.

[166] Cf. Robert—Tournay (1963), pp. 305–306; Krinetzki (1981), pp. 221–222.

[167] So, rightly, Keel (1994), p. 276.

Ancient Near East, and still in our days, marriage was agreed by the parents of the two spouses. Money was paid out to the family of the bride as compensation for the loss of the work of a family member, but it is reasonable to think that this was often the main reason to arrange a marriage: love passed into second place.[168] The two following strophes continue on the same line of protest against fossilised social customs, in the name of the nature of love. Love is 'a flame of YHWH', not a contract agreed by the families for economic reasons.[169]

Second Strophe: Criticism of the Family (8:8–10)

The second and the third strophe can be considered a development of the theme put forward in the second part of v. 7:[170] the superiority of love over money. In fact, the word 'silver, money' (*kesep*) links the two passages (vv. 9b, 11). The connection with 1:5–6 also brings together the two strophes. In 8:8–10, the theme of the brothers preoccupied with guarding their sister's chastity (cf. 1:6c) is taken up again, while in 8:11–12 the play on the double meaning of the 'vineyard' to be 'guarded' returns (cf. 1:6de).

In the name of the divine nature of love (v. 6), then, a society which claims to dictate the law to love is criticised: one might say that the author is again taking up the rebuke directed to the daughters of Jerusalem for 'rousing' love (v. 4). The criticism has two aspects, anticipated in the previous song (8:1–4).[171] The second strophe (vv. 8–10) takes aim at the family ('brothers', cf. vv. 2–3), while the third (vv. 11–12) is addressed to the urban society ('Solomon', cf. vv. 1, 4). Already, v. 7def showed clear links with vv. 1–4 ('house', v. 7d, cf. v. 2b; 'love', v. 7e, cf. v. 4e; 'spurn', v. 7f, cf. v. 1d). These links continue in vv. 8–12:

[168] "This obligation to pay a sum of money, or its equivalent, to the girl's family obviously gives the Israelite marrage the appearance of a purchase" (De Vaux [1961], p. 27).

[169] Less probable, it seems to me, is the reference to the practice of cultic prostitution suggested in Wittekindt (1925), p. 58. In Hebrew, the term *bayit*, 'house' (v. 7d), can also indicate the 'family', and it is precisely to the family that the following strophe refers. But certainly the protest extends to any time of 'love for payment'.

[170] Ricciotti (1928), p. 281, considers vv. 8–10 as a development of v. 7abc, while vv. 11–12 would be the development of v. 7def. To me it seems rather that v. 7abc looks to what precedes, while v. 7def is directed to what follows.

[171] Cf., *supra*, p. 423, *Tab. 68*.

Table 77

BROTHERS (vv. 8–9)	v. 8b v. 9a	a b	*breasts* *wall*
WOMAN (v. 10)	v. 10a v. 10b	b' a'	*wall* *breasts*

thus the lexeme 'sister' (v. 8a) refers to the parallel 'brother' of v. 1a; the mention of 'breasts' (vv. 8b, 10b) takes up v. 1b; the verb 'find' (v. 10cd) echoes v. 1c; the verb 'to bring in/gain' (*bwʾ* in *hiphʿil* form, v. 11c) takes up v. 2a.

Another characteristic brings the two strophes together, and that is their obscure character which makes them look like two riddles.[172] As Landy suggests, here, as elsewhere in the Song, we have a case of deliberate obscurity.[173] Stylistically, the sententious tone of vv. 6–7 gives way to a lighter, more sparkling tone.[174] We move from the principles to their practical application, from philosophical dispute to social satire.

The second strophe (vv. 8–10) is, therefore, characterised by the theme of the family, introduced already in v. 7d (*bayit*). The strophe is structured dialogically into two parts: to the plans of her 'brothers' (vv. 8–9), the woman responds (v. 10). Her response, in v. 10, refers expressly to the words of the brothers, taking them up again chiastically (cf. *Tab. 77*). Three moments are to be noticed rhythmically, one per verse: v. 8 is characterised by binary rhythm (3 + 2; 3 + 2), while v. 9 is formed out of two terzains (2 + 2 + 2; 2 + 2 + 2). Verse 10 returns to the binary rhythm (3 + 2; 3 + 2).

---

[172] Colombo thinks of the literary genre of the *middôt*, or nuptial riddles (cf. Judg 14:14), or again of the erotic or convivial epigram typical of the Hellenistic world. Cf. Colombo (1985), p. 120. Also *CEI*, entitles vv. 8–12: 'Two epigrams'. In our case, however, there is no question of isolated fragments: as we have extensively demonstrated, the two strophes are integrated into the context of the *Epilogue*.

[173] Landy (1983), pp. 135–179: 'Beauty and the enigma'.

[174] "However, the tone undoubtedly changes (in relation to vv. 5–7, *author's note*): it becomes provocative and light, leavened with a malicious irony, and apparently illogical with respect to the exhausting emotional pitch of the preceding verses" (Salvaneschi [1982], p. 115).

[8:8–9] The plans of the brothers.[175] *[v. 8]* If the mother represents the positive side of the family (cf. v. 5),[176] the brothers represent its negative aspect. Their role is analogous to that in 1:6. They embody the patriarchal, male-dominated family.

The fact that the 'sister' is presented as still a child without breasts is problematic. Until now, the woman has been presented as mature with well formed breasts (cf. 4:5; 7:4, 8–9). Lys, for example, thinks of a flashback, which would take the action back to a time before 1:6.[177] Perhaps, however, it is not necessary to have recourse to this literary device. The author wishes to stress the fact that the brothers are not able to recognise the maturity which the girl has achieved.[178] It is typical of parents, in our families, to treat adult sons as if they were forever minors. This tutelary, paternalistic role is attributed to the 'brothers' in the Song.[179] From the woman's reaction in v. 10, it appears that the brothers' observation is false. Actually, in 7:13, the two lovers wanted to assure themselves that their bodies were ready for love, "that the buds had opened, that the pomegranates had flowered" (cf. 6:11). They had recognised that the time of love had arrived (7:14). Only the brothers have not perceived it.

If v. 8ab holds up the paternalistic attitude of the brothers to ridicule, in that they are not able to recognise the sexual maturity of their sister, v. 8cd reveals another aspect, connected with the first, that is, that of wanting to replace her in the management of her body. "What shall we do for our sister, in the day that she is spoken for?" (v. 8cd).

---

[175] Since the subject is plural and a 'sister' is spoken of, it seems clear that those who are speaking are the 'brothers' of the beloved woman, who responds angrily in v. 10. For Delitzsch (1875), pp. 133–134, however, v. 8 would concern the woman who speaks of a sister who is still a baby: the brothers would begin to speak in v. 9. Keel (1994), p. 278, for his part, puts vv. 8–9 into the mouth of the woman's older sisters. For Müller (1992), pp. 86–87, it would be the brothers speaking in v. 8, in v. 9 the suitors referred to in v. 8d. Lacocque (1998), p. 180, rightly objects: "But why the intervention in extremis of a new personage in the Song?" The point of the *Epilogue* is to gather up the motifs already developed in the poem, not to bring in new ones.

[176] Cf., *supra*, p. 136, and 417.

[177] Lys (1968), p. 294; so too Rudolph (1962) p. 183; Krinetzki (1981), pp. 225–226.

[178] It is true that in Israel, young girls were married off at a very young age, and this also explains that it was the parents or brothers who had to decide for her (cf. De Vaux [1961], pp. 29–32). But, in the Song, the woman is never portrayed as a child.

[179] Murphy (1990), p. 49, marks a parallel in the Sumerian literature. When Dumuzi wants to go to the house of Inanna, Geshtinanna, his older sister replies: "To my paternal eye / you are verily still a small child, /—yonder Baba [Inanna] may know you for a man. / I shall let you go to her" (citing Jacobsen [1987], pp. 8–9).

Table 78

v. 9ab	*If she is a wall,*	*above her we shall build*	*battlements*	*of silver.*
v. 9cd	*If she is a door,*	*we shall bar her*	*with a board*	*of cedar.*

With the expression 'spoken for' (*dābar b*[e]), there is an allusion to the negotiations in view of marriage (cf. 1 Sam 25:39). Taking for granted that the time of love has not yet arrived, plans are being made for the future. That, along with the father, the brothers are those who conduct the matrimonial negotiations is evident from Gen 24 (cf. also Gen 34). The one who decides if Rebecca can or cannot be given as wife to Isaac is not so much her father, Bethuel, but her brother Laban (Gen 24: 29, 50–51, 55). The reasoning of the brothers in v. 8b is in no way extraordinary: it was the usual practice of the traditional Israelite family. It was normal for the patriarchal mentality that it was not for the woman to decide whom she wanted to take as husband but for the male members of her family, her father and her brothers.[180] They had to decide, on the basis of criteria which had nothing to do with love, when and with whom the young woman was to be married. The Song opposes such an attitude. Perhaps it reflects the new awareness that the woman had of herself in Hellenistic society.

[v. 9] To the question which the brothers have posed in v. 8cd, they themselves give the answer in v. 9. Like the previous one, this verse also consists of two parts. The parallelism between them is particularly marked. The correspondence is exact: every word of v. 9ab finds its match in 9cd (cf. *Tab. 78*).[181] The question that will occupy us shortly is to know whether this is a synonymous or an antithetical parallelism.

The term 'wall' (*ḥōmâ*) recurs in 5:7: it indicates not the wall of a house (*kōtel*, 2:9), but the wall of the city. It carries within itself, therefore, the connotation of defence and enclosure. It is the metaphor of the city, already introduced in 2:4. The city that victoriously resists sieges is symbolic of the woman's chastity.[182] "If she is a wall" is

180 "Neither the girl nor, often, the boy was consulted" (De Vaux [1961], p. 29).

181 The aim of putting the two parts in parallel is clearly evident, above all in the verb. To *nibneh ʿālèhā* (lit.: 'we shall build above it' ['wall' is feminine in Hebrew]) corresponds *nāṣûr ʿālèhā* (lit.: 'we shall press on it'). Cf. Rudolph (1962), p. 182.

182 Cf., *supra*, p. 89.

equivalent, then, to saying: "If she knows how to keep herself chaste, if she knows how to defend her virginity".[183]

The meaning of the term *ṭîrâ* in v. 9b is disputed. Elsewhere, it designates an encampment surrounded by a wall of stone (Gen 25:16) or a layer of stones along a wall (Ezek 46:23). Being constructed above the city wall, it is logical to think of the 'battlements', with the function of strengthening the defence provided by the walls themselves. The Greek version of the LXX translates *epalxeis*, which is the term used by Aquila's version in 4:4 to translate the Hebrew *talpîyôt*.[184] Actually, the two passages are similar: in both it is a question of defences constructed above the city wall. As in 4:4 (cf. Ezek 46:23), the function of the battlements is not only defensive but also ornamental: in fact, the battlements are made of 'silver' (*kesep*).[185]

If, by itself, the wall already indicates the defence of virginity, the battlements reinforce this significance. As in 1:6, the brothers think themselves responsible for the chastity of their sister. This brotherly function receives confirmation in the tragic stories of Dinah (cf. Gen 34) and Tamar (2 Sam 13:32) in which the brothers avenge the violence done to their sister with blood. But the term *kesep* ('silver, money') makes us remember that the brothers' concern is not so noble. The term returns in fact in v. 11: it is the *Leitmotiv* in vv. 8–12, being introduced already in v. 7def. The author disapproves of this attitude, and the response of the woman in the following verse expresses this clearly. The preoccupation with protecting the sister's chastity is dictated by economic interest, not by real love towards their sister. How is this 'battlement of silver' to be represented in concrete terms? One can think of a high price for the bride which holds off the less affluent young men, claiming rather the attention of those who have good financial prospects;[186] or a whole series of attentions, aiming at keeping

---

[183] It seems to me misleading to think that 'wall' is referring to the girl's flat breast (so Goulder [1986], p. 66). If it were so, she would certainly not boast of being a wall in v. 10a!

[184] Cf. p. 186.

[185] "The idea that [the author] wants to express does not seem to be simply that of solidity but also and above all that of wealth: the construction which is mentioned has involved considerable expense" (Robert – Tournay [1963], p. 310).

[186] "They want to gain a high bride price (*mōhar*) with it (= the virginity of their sister, *author's note*): they consider it a good investment" (Rudolph [1962], p. 183); "By means of a highly inflated 'bride price', (the brothers wish, *author's note*) to draw the attention of parents of young men of marriageable age to the shy and not very prepossessing girl" (Krinetzki [1981], p. 225).

the girl shut up at home.[187] We would speak of a 'gilded cage', which, although it is made of gold, remains nonetheless a prison. This is, at bottom, 'to quench' love (against v. 7abc),[188] to impose on it foreign laws (against v. 4), to barter love with money (against v. 7def).

In parallel with 'wall', the term 'door' (*delet*) is used in v. 9c. Various exegetes see an antithesis in the two terms.[189] If the 'wall' denotes enclosure, inaccessibility, and, therefore, in an extended sense, chastity, the door indicates openness, passage, and, therefore, sexual freedom. In this case, it is understood that the brothers are concerned to block this opening with drastic counter-measures.

However suggestive this interpretation, it does not correspond to the sense of the term *delet*. By contrast with *petaḥ*, which indicates an opening in the wall, *delet* indicates the door of the gate;[190] it, therefore, expresses the same idea of 'enclosure', synonymously with the 'wall'.[191] Both the images are metaphors for the chastity of the young girl.

The 'board of cedar' is put in parallel with the 'battlements of silver'. Like the battlements, the board too has the primary function of strengthening the defence provided by the door. The brothers are apparently obsessed with the idea of preserving their sister's chastity at any price. The board, it is stressed, is 'of cedar', and so of a wood that is not only solid but also particularly precious, used for the temple and for the king's palace. In its symbolic value, the term is equivalent to the 'silver' of v. 9b. Significantly, Solomon's litter is made of 'wood of Lebanon', that is, of cedar, and of 'silver' (cf. 3:9–10). Landy comments: "The woman is an attractive fortress: attractive but barred so probably worth the trouble of defending",[192] where 'worth' is to be taken literally, in an economic sense. The girl's chastity is seen by the family as capital, an investment with juicy returns. On the market, a virgin is worth more.

---

[187] "The virtuous sister will be praised and rewarded by her brothers" (Gerleman [1965], p. 220); "A chain that binds the ankles, as in Flaubert's Salambo, can be of gold" (Lys [1968], p. 297).

[188] So Ricciotti's opinion, cited in n. 170, *supra*, is not without foundation.

[189] Cf., for example, Delitzsch (1875), p. 135; Joüon (1909), p. 323; Colombo (1985), p. 121; Gerleman (1965), p. 220; Krinetzki (1981), p. 225.

[190] The Hebrew consonant *dalet* [ד] is an ideogram, which "probably meant originally a door that turned on a hinge" (A. Baumann, *delet*, in *TDOT*, vol. III, p. 231).

[191] So, rightly, Keel (1994), p. 279; Robert – Tournay (1963), p. 310; Gordis (1974), p. 100; Lys (1968), p. 296; Ravasi (1992), p. 692.

[192] Landy (1983), p. 161.

[v. 10] The woman's response. With the phrase: "I am a wall", the woman takes her stand with regard to the plan of the brothers unfolded in v. 9. In the metaphor of the 'wall' the synonymous one of the 'door' is also included. By means of the two images, the brothers have put forward doubts about their sister's chastity ("If…"). Preoccupied with the holding of her defences, they themselves wanted to add others to them. With the emphatic stress of the personal pronoun in the first person ("*I* am a wall"), the woman declares that she is able to defend herself on her own; her chastity has no need of supports.

This declaration finds an echo in the other images of enclosure which characterise the woman. At the beginning of the poem, she was presented closed behind the wall of the house (2:9), inaccessible as the doves "in the rocky ravines, concealed in the crags" (2:14). Her litter was escorted by sixty mighty men armed with the sword "against the terror of the night" (3:8). Her neck is "like the tower of David", reinforced with bulwarks, protected by all the arms of the mighty men (4:4), and her nose, "like the tower of Lebanon, sentinel towards Damascus" (7:5). She is an "enclosed garden, stopped fountain, sealed spring" (4:12). The woman of the Song is decidedly not a lady of easy virtue. Chastity is the sign of the exclusiveness of love, expressed through the metaphor of the seal in 8:6: one can belong to only one person 'entirely'. When it is true, says the Song, love is chaste by nature: it has no need of external supports.

With the second phrase: "And my breasts are like[193] towers", the woman responds to the words of her brothers in v. 8 ("And she does not yet have breasts"). The reply denotes a hurt point of pride against the disrespectful insinuation of the brothers. Her breasts are as imposing as two towers![194] You would have to be blind not to notice them. She is no longer a child, needing protection: she can look after herself. But the phrase is ambivalent: on the one hand, the breasts form part of the woman's system of defence, linking in with the image of the

---

[193] Vetus Latina *turres*, and Syr *mgdl'*, omit the comparative particle k^e. But the parallelism with v. 10d leads us to prefer MT (which is followed by LXX and Vg).

[194] There is a curious parallel in the Egyptian love songs: "I found my beloved by a fountain, / his feet above the water. / He built an altar to make of the day a feast / and put beer above it: / its form is that of my breast, / higher than broad" (Papyrys Chester Beatty IC [Nakhtsobek Songs] 17:5–6 [= n. 45], tr. Bresciani [1990], p. 472, cf. Schott [1950], p. 63; for other translations, cf. Mathieu [1996], p. 34; Fox [1985], p. 74).

'wall' (v. 10a);[195] on the other hand, they show that the young woman is ready for love, attracting with their fascination.[196] In this sense, the theme of v. 10cd is introduced.

Verse 10cd forms the conclusion of the strophe in which the author concentrates all the verve of the passage with a deliberate effect of surprise. If till now the images have developed a context of defence and war, the conclusion speaks of peace. However, the interpretation of the passage is controversial.

The difficulty begins with the initial particle, *ʾāz* (v. 10c). It can have a temporal value ('then')[197] or a consequential one ('so, therefore, then'),[198] or, finally, an antithetical one ('and yet, nevertheless, notwithstanding which').[199] The translation depends on the meaning of what follows.

The principal problem comes with the interpretation of *kᵉmôṣᵉʾēt šālôm* (v. 10d). *môṣᵉʾēt* can be understood, in fact, as *qal* participle of *māṣāʾ* ('to find': 'like one who has found peace') or as *hiphʿil* participle of *yāṣāʾ* ('to make go out'). In this second case, the passage should be matched up with texts like Deut 20:10–11 or Josh 9:15 in which the population of a besieged city makes an embassy 'go out' to seek peace, that is to negotiate the surrender.[200] The image is the same as that in 2:4 ("His banner over me is Love"). In this context, the introductory particle *ʾāz* has an antithetical value: despite the fact that the young woman is a city defended by walls and towers, she has nevertheless capitulated. Between v. 10ab and v. 10cd, one catches sight of the tension, typical of the Song, between the affirmation of oneself (v. 10ab) and the gift of oneself (v. 10cd).[201] Or even: what for others is an unscalable wall (v. 10ab) is not so for the beloved (v. 10cd) because he embodies love (cf. 2:15, 16; 4:12, 16). The phrase has a similar sense to

---

[195] Cf. a popular Palestinian song: "Her breast—when she undid the sash, / I gazed at its contours with admiration, / the pair of bosoms made me go mad, / they were jewels, they made desire within me increase—, / on it are sentries, on it soldiers, / like a lioness when she is angry" (Dalman [1901], p. 134).

[196] In this sense, the juxtaposition 'towers-breasts' is antithetical. Cf. Song 4:4–5 (cf., *supra*, p. 190).

[197] Thus, for example, Colombo (1975), p. 135 ('now').

[198] So Ricciotti (1928), p. 280 ('therefore'); Ravasi (1992), p. 33 ('thus'); Nolli (1967), p. 143 ('for this reason').

[199] Cf. Garbini (1992), p. 282 ('but').

[200] Thus Keel (1994), p. 277: "[...] yet in his eyes, I am / as one who has surrendered". Similarly, Gerleman (1965), p. 219; Garbini (1992), p. 281.

[201] Cf. p. 234.

the piquant conclusion of the parallel passage, 1:5–6—"My very own vineyard I have not kept!" It is a confirmation of the axiom of v. 6c: "Love is strong as death". Before the assault of love there is no wall or door which will hold!

If, on the other hand, with all the ancient versions and with the majority of exegetes, the first alternative is chosen, then 'peace' (*šālôm*) does not have a military but a personal significance: in her deep trouble, the woman has found peace. In this sense too, we can detect a contrast with the preceding warlike metaphor, as a result of which it is justifiable to understand the initial particle in an adversative way. Following this interpretation, the text falls into line with the declarations of vv. 6–7 on the nature of love. Every word has echoes in the rest of the poem.

First of all, the verb *hāyîtî* ('I have become'). The perfect indicates that this is not a present action but one which is past. The 'surrender' or the 'finding peace' has already taken place. When? If it is true that v. 6cde constitutes a looking back over the union that has taken place, then it is logical to think that, here too, there is a reference to what was described in 7:12–8:4. Like vv. 6–7, so too v. 10cd is a theorising on the meaning of union.

The expression that follows, *bᵉʿênāyw* (literally, 'in his eyes'), scarcely has the diminished sense of a preposition (Vulgate: *coram eo*):[202] the eyes play an important part in the language of love. Here it is evidently the eyes of her beloved, the one who has assailed the fortress.[203] The young woman, Elliott notes, no longer lives under the eyes of her brothers[204] but under those of her beloved. The phrase is constructed by imitating the more common expression: 'To find grace (*ḥēn*) in the eyes of someone'.[205] This parallel helps us to understand that 'in his eyes' is linked to the verb 'to find'. That is, the woman finds

---

[202] *Contra* Keel (1994), p. 279.

[203] In conformity with their allegorical interpretation, Robert – Tournay, naturally think that God is in question here. The text certainly lends itself also to this interpretation; in fact it finds here its profoundest truth (the saying of Augustine, cited in p. 131, should be remembered). But it is a matter of transposition, not of the primary meaning of the text (in fact, it would be difficult to fit vv. 8–9 into this interpretation).

[204] LXX^B has *en ophthalmois autōn*, referring to the eyes of the brothers. Always in this line, Buzy (1951), p. 361, suggests *bᵉʿênêkem*, 'in your eyes'. The text would require this reading, because, until now, only the brothers have been spoken of without the beloved's being mentioned: to name him now, therefore, signals a break.

[205] So much so that LXX^S reads *charin*, 'grace', instead of *šālôm*. Cf. Garbini (1992), p. 124.

peace 'in the eyes' of her beloved. The encounter of love is seen as a meeting of looks, a communion of eyes, not of bodies.[206] There comes to mind the experience described in 5:12 with regard to the eyes of the man: "His eyes like doves [...] placed in a full bath". The 'bath', it was noted, are the woman's eyes (cf. 7:5).[207] In her eyes, the beloved finds himself, sees his own image reflected. Here, the reciprocal affirmation is made: in his eyes, the woman finds herself, finds peace.[208]

The verb 'to find' (*māṣā'*) is rich with cross-references. Throughout the poem, the two lovers are on the search for one another, but the verb is used above all in relation to the woman: it is she who searches (*biqqēš*, 3:1, 2; 5:6) and who, therefore, 'finds' (3:1, 2, 3, 4; 5:6, 7, 8). In the preceding song, the 'finding' was presented as a desire that could not be realised (*'emṣā'ăkā*, 8:1). If now 'finding' is being spoken of as an experience that has taken place (*hāyîtî*, v. 10c), it is because between 8:1 and 8:10 there is the description of the union in 8:3.

The object of finding is 'peace' (*šālôm*). The lexeme is suggestive because it forms part of the name of the man, Solomon, and of that of the woman, Shulamite.[209] The lovers are people who have been 'pacified'. As in 7:1,[210] the *motiv* of peace is juxtaposed with images of war (vv. 8–10b), expressing the paradox of love which is, at one and the same time, mortal combat (cf. v. 6cd) and profound peace: only by accepting the 'war' borne by love can one enter into peace.[211] The sense of *môṣᵉ'ēt šālôm* is, therefore, broader than that of a surrender. *šālôm* in Hebrew is full of life, health, satisfaction of the most profound needs of man. Man's deepest need is love. For this reason, the beloved

[206] "The beauty of eyes is especially interesting, for they can only unite without touching, at a psychic distance; their objective separateness is the condition for their fusion" (Landy [1983], p. 165).

[207] Cf., *supra*, p. 380.

[208] Cf. Landy (1983), p. 165: "She looks at his eyes that look at her/hers; in him she finds a refleciton of herself, of their mutual reciprocity". Krinetzki (1981), p. 226, speaks of the process of integration and individuation which is fulfilled in the encounter with the opposite sex.

[209] "The Beloved's saying that she found *šālôm* in his eyes, is another way of saying that she found herself, *haššûlammît*, reflected there, even as he would find himself, *šᵉlōmōh*, reflected in hers" (Elliott [1989], p. 203).

[210] Cf., *supra*, p. 367.

[211] Murphy (1990), p. 199, rightly opposes the 'peace' involved in the brothers' plans to that borne by the beloved: "With him she has found welcome or well-being [...], a totally satisfying relationship that goes far beyond the protective desires of her brothers'. One could say that the brothers' peace excluded war by excluding love. However, peace without love is not peace but inhibition.

woman is a woman at peace, fulfilled: she has found 'the love of my soul' (1:7; 3:1, 2, 3, 4).[212]

Perhaps it is not necessary to choose between the two interpretations. Both have been shown to be coherent. The first corresponds more directly to the immediate, the second to the broader context. The ambivalence of expression confirms the hermetic character of vv. 8–12.

Third Strophe: Criticism of Society (8:11–12)

The third strophe is also presented as a development of the theme of v. 7def: there is no comparison between love and riches. The scorn deserved by the one who wishes to purchase his love for money (v. 7def) is demonstrated concretely in the reply of v. 12. The thematic link between the two passages is confirmed by the repetition of the terms 'to give' (*nātan*, vv. 7d and 11b) and 'one, each one' (*'îš*, vv. 7d and 11c), not to mention the synonymity between *hôn* ('patrimony, wealth', 7d) and *hāmôn* ('riches', v. 11a).

Lacocque is incorrect, however, to claim that the preceding strophe "breaks the flow of the development between verse 7 and verse 11".[213] In fact, the second and third strophe are intimately connected. To the arguments rehearsed above,[214] others can be added. From a structural point of view, both the strophes are made up of two parts: in the first part there is a declaration, probably made by a 'chorus', to which, in the second, the woman replies in hurt tones, affirming her own identity with emphatic use of the first person pronoun ('*I*', '*my* breasts', v. 10; '*my* vineyard, *my very own*', v. 12). In both cases, the reply takes up the key words of the preceding declaration literally. If, in the second strophe, the order of these words forms a chiasm (cf. *Tab. 77*, p. 473), in the third, the correspondence is parallel (cf. *Tab. 79*): the terms 'vineyard', 'Solomon, 'keepers' and 'fruit', which characterise v. 11, are repeated in v. 12 in the same order.

The important term *kesep* ('money, silver', vv. 9b and 11c), functions as word-echo between the two strophes, and so too does the root

[212] The book of Ruth has a similar expression: "YHWH grant that you find rest (*mṣ' m^e^nûḥâ*) each in the house of her husband" (1:9, cf. 3:1). Cf. Zakovitch (2000), p. 22.
[213] Lacocque (1998), p. 185.
[214] *Supra*, pp. 472–473.

Table 79

v. 11	a	*kerem*, 'vineyard' (11a)
	b	*š^{e}lōmōh*, 'Solomon' (11a)
	c	*nōṭ^{e}rîm*, 'keepers' (11b)
	d	*piryô*, 'the fruit' (11c)
v. 12	a'	*kerem*, 'vineyard' (12a)
	b'	*š^{e}lōmōh*, 'Solomon' (12b)
	c'	*nōṭ^{e}rîm*, 'keepers'(12c)
	d'	*piryô*, 'the fruit' (12c)

šlm present in v. 10d in the term *šālôm* ('peace') and in v. 11a in the term *š^{e}lōmōh* ('Solomon'; the Vulgate translates 'the Peaceful One'). Moreover, from the point of view of content, the role of the 'keepers', posted to guard the chastity of the young woman (v. 11), corresponds to that of the 'brothers' in vv. 8–9. If one observes this precise interplay of references, one is less inclined to introduce emendations such as those which abound in the less recent exegetical literature, particularly with regard to v. 11.[215]

We have taken for granted that v. 11 is put into the mouth of a chorus, and v. 12 that of the woman. But both these attributions are far from obvious.[216] For many authors, it is the same person who is speaking in both verses; for some, this is the man, for others, the woman. By itself, v. 12 would also go well in the mouth of the man who would thus be counterposed to the picture of Solomon portrayed in v. 11.[217] In favour of the attribution of v. 12 to the woman, there is first of all the parallel with 1:6 where the expression 'my vineyard, my very own' is uttered by her; secondly, the parallel with the preceding strophe in

[215] Robert - Tournay state concerning v. 11: "There is no part of this verse for which suppressions or other modifications have not been proposed on the basis of metre" (Robert - Tournay [1963], p. 317). More recent commentators are generally more respectful of the text.

[216] Cf. Alden (1988).

[217] According to Horst (1981), p. 183, 8:11–12 would be a man's 'boasting song' (*Prahllied*) corresponding to 6:8–9. Of the same opinion, Krinetzki (1981), pp. 227–231 ("A happier man than Solomon"); Budde (1898), pp. 47–48; Rudolph (1962), pp. 184–185 ("I will not change places with Solomon"); Gerleman (1965), p. 222; Keel (1994), p. 283; Müller (1992), p. 88; Lys (1968), p. 300; Murphy (1990), pp. 199–200 (who also admits the possibility, however, that it may be the woman who is speaking in v. 12); Falk (1982), p. 133; Colombo (1975), pp. 136–137.

which the first person pronoun refers clearly to the woman.[218] Indeed, each strophe of the *Epilogue* is concluded by a reply by the woman (cf. vv. 5c–7, 10, 14).[219] From the point of view of content, Pope rightly observes that

> if the groom speaks, declaring dominion over his spouse's body, it is classic male chauvinism. If the female here asserts autonomy, this verse becomes the golden text for women's liberation.[220]

On the other hand, the analogy with the other strophes helps us to recognise here too a dialogue in which the person who is speaking in v. 12 is replying to the declaration made by another in v. 11. Actually, the 'vineyard' is spoken of impersonally in v. 11 ('*a* vineyard'), while in v. 12 it has become '*my* vineyard'; Solomon is spoken of in v. 11 in the third person, while, in v. 12, direct discourse is employed. In v. 11 we have a voice off-stage (as in 3:6–11), which could be identified with the chorus or with the author himself.[221]

[v. 11] The vineyard of Solomon. The beginning of the verse copies the beginning of Isaiah's 'song of the vineyard': "My beloved had a vineyard / on a fertile hill" (Isa 5:1). The correspondence is too exact to be accidental. Given the tone of social satire in the passage, it is possible to understand the correspondence as a criticism of contemporary Jewish society. In Isaiah, in fact, the 'vineyard' is a metaphor for "the house of Israel and the inhabitants of Judah" who, rather than producing *justice*, commit violence and oppress the weak (Isa 5:7). Perhaps the author wishes to reproach this society ('Solomon') for offensive behaviour with regard to feminine sexuality ('vineyard'). In doing this, he brings the metaphor of the vineyard back to its original sense. In Isaiah too, in fact, the vineyard is primarily a symbol of the woman: it is a song of love (*šîrat dôdî*, Isa 5:1) transposed to the God-people

---

[218] Lacocque (1998), p. 186, points out that, in the Song, the emphatic first person singular pronoun is always characteristic of the woman (cf. *'ănî*, 'I', 1:5–6; 2:1, 5, 16; 5:2, 8; 6:3; 7:11; 8:10; and the synonyms: *napšî*, 'my soul', 1:7; 3:1–4; 5:6; 6:12; *libbî*, 'my heart', 5:2; *karmî*, 'my vineyard', 1:6).

[219] Cf., *supra*, p. 440.

[220] Pope (1977), p. 690. The authors who attribute v. 12 to the woman are not many: we recall Alden (1988), p. 277 (we refer to this author for further bibliography); Ricciotti (1928), p. 285; Ravasi (1992), p. 702 (not so Ravasi [1990], pp. 160–161); Elliott (1989), p. 206; Tournay (1982), p. 20.

[221] Also in the parallel Isa 5:1–7, the text begins and ends with the impersonal voice of the poet ('*his* vineyard', v. 1, cf. v. 7), while the central part (vv. 3–6) is characterised by direct discourse ('*my* vineyard', vv. 3, 5).

relationship. As is its custom, the Song makes the reverse procedure: it reapplies the metaphor to the man-woman relationship, without forgetting the theological dimension which it has acquired in the tradition of Israel.[222]

The parallel with 1:6 has been noted. There, the author plays with the double sense of the term 'vineyard': in v. 6d, the term is used in its literal sense, while, in v. 6e, it is a metaphor for the body of the woman.[223] For Alden, similarly, the term would have a literal sense in 8:11, while in 8:12 it would pass over into the metaphorical sense.[224] It is true that Solomon, like the kings of Israel in general (cf. 1 Chr 27:27; 1 Kgs 21; 2 Kgs 21:18; 25:4) had famous gardens and vineyards (cf. Qoh 2:4–6), but it is also true that he had innumerable women, something regarded as a source of sin by the author of the Deuteronomic History: "He had seven hundred wives, princesses, and three hundred concubines" (1 Kgs 11:3).[225] Song 6:8–9 is also inspired by this text as was mentioned in the appropriate place.[226] The double sense is, therefore, present already in the expression 'vineyard of Solomon': on the one hand, it refers to his vineyards, on the other, to his *harem*.

Certainly the light in which Solomon is being presented is not positive: on the other hand, this image is not new; already in 6:8–9 we noticed a strongly critical tone in his regard. One understands the difficulty of the allegorical school in admitting a negative aspect in relation to a person

[222] It is to be noted, however, that whereas in Isaiah the blame falls on the 'vineyard', that is on the woman (and it cannot be otherwise, because the vinedresser, the man, is YHWH himself), in the Song, the vineyard is innocent: it is the vinedressers who are to blame, that is, Solomon and the keepers. An allegorical interpretation of the passage is impossible, and it is for this reason that Robert – Tournay consider it spurious. Cf. Robert – Tournay (1963), pp. 322–323: here they give a 'political' interpretation of the passage, seeing, behind Solomon, John Hyrcanus; cf. the criticism of Lacocque (1998), pp. 185–186.

[223] A similar play between the literal and metaphorical senses is present also in 7:13, where the plural *kᵉrāmîm* is to be understood in a concrete sense, while the *gepen* that follows has a figurative value.

[224] Alden (1988), p. 273.

[225] The sum of 700 + 300 equals 1000, a number that is encountered in our text, where mention is made of the 'thousand shekels' due to Solomon (v. 12). Is it possible that the 'thousand shekels' refer to Solomon's 'thousand women'? Cf. Tournay (1982), p. 27.

[226] Cf., *supra*, p. 338. The correspondence between the two texts is undeniable, but the fact that they are pronounced by two different persons (6:8–9 by the man, 8:11–12 by the woman) produces a change of emphasis: while in 6:8–9, the contrast between the one and the many is highlighted, in 8:11–12, the stress is more on the autonomy of the woman and the non-commercial nature of love.

who is seen as a cipher for YHWH or the Messiah. Clearly this passage is not to be thought of in an allegorical sense. If we admit a Hellenistic date for the poem, it is possible that there is a veiled reference to the Ptolemaic court and to the sympathisers which this mode of life found among the Jewish upper classes.[227] But the significance of the passage goes beyond a specific historical moment: it is valid for all time. Like the daughters of Jerusalem, Solomon personifies urban society with its ambiguous value. At times, he represents the ideal king with whom, in a 'high burlesque', the beloved man is identified (cf. 1;1, 4, 5, 13; 3:7, 9, 11); at other times, as here and in 6:8–9, he becomes the symbol of the pagan[228] conception of love from which the author takes his distance. In this light, the juxtaposition of *šālôm* and *šᵉlōmōh* (v. 11) acquires the sense of a counter-position: they are two different ways of seeking peace. The woman seeks it in love and finds it. Solomon seeks it in wealth (and does not find it).

The meaning of the following expression, *baʿal hāmôn* is debated. It seems natural to understand it as a toponym, but no record of such a place has come down to us. Given also the textual uncertainty (the ancient versions have understood the name in different ways),[229] the exegetes have proposed various conjectures: *Balamōn*, near to the present Jenin (cf. Judith 8:3);[230] *baʿal ḥermôn* in Upper Galilee (cf. Judg 3:3; 1 Chr 5:23);[231] *baʿal ḥammôn*. The last designation is dear to the mythological school: *ḥammôn* (literally, 'the scorching one', cf. 6:10) designates the sun. A divinity with the name *baʿal ḥammôn* is known in Asia Minor, at Ugarit and at Carthage.[232] There would be an allusion here to sacred marriage between Bel Ḥammon and Ishtar, and to the prostitution which was performed in their temple. The 'keepers of the fruit' would be the priests who collected the profits of prostitution. Putting everything under the name of Solomon, the author would be

[227] "Perhaps there is present, in the third century BC, a polemic against certain values, which the ancient Jewish society, in sympathy with Hellenistic fashion, could have adopted from the Ptolemaic court of Alexandria, which was in all respects superior". Cf. Müller (1992), p. 89. As has been noted, Robert – Tournay think of John Hyrcanus (cf., *supra*, n. 222).

[228] As underlined by the text of 1 Kgs 11:1–8, Solomon's women were 'foreigners' (*nokrîyyôt*, v. 1), just as the depraved woman of Prov 7 is a 'foreigner' (*zārâ*, *nokrîyyâ*).

[229] Cf., *supra*, n. 11, p. 437.

[230] Thus Delitzsch (1875), p. 138.

[231] Cf. Graetz (1871), pp. 213–214.

[232] Cf. Haupt (1907), pp. 45–46.

intending to say that such a trade was being practised in the Jerusalem Temple, and that Solomon, the constructor of the Temple, was naturally the one who controlled this trade.[233]

But neither the text nor the context offers footholds for such fanciful elucubrations. Perhaps we have here a locality whose name has become lost; or perhaps the expression has a symbolic value (the Syriac, the Vulgate, the Greek version of Aquila and that of Symmachus have understood it in this sense).[234] The term *baʿal* can signify 'lord, master', or 'place'. *hāmôn*, not to be confused with either *ḥāmmôn* or *ʾāmôn*, or even less with *ḥermôn*, can indicate 'multitude' or even 'wealth' (cf. the parallelism with v. 7d). Understood in the personal sense, the expression 'lord[235] of a multitude' or 'master of wealth' would be an allusion to Solomon and to his *harem* or to his riches. In the local sense (something suggested by the locative *bᵉ*, 'in'), it would be: 'place of the multitude (or of riches)', which could allude to Jerusalem, the city of Solomon (it would be a similar case to *bat rabbîm*, 'daughter of many', 7:5).[236]

"He gave this vineyard to keepers". The term 'keepers' (*nōṭᵉrîm*) refers back to 1:6. There the brothers were preoccupied with keeping their sister's vineyard. The parallel leads us to understand this guarding in an allegorical sense: this is probably a case of eunuchs to whom is entrusted the supervision of the ladies of the *harem* (cf. Esth 2:3).[237] The verb 'to give' casts a negative shadow on the operation. As in the case of the brothers, the guarding is not an act of love. The verb

[233] Cf. Wittekindt (1925), pp. 109–113; Pope (1977), pp. 687–688; Garbini (1992), pp. 283–285. Garbini goes further, seeing in *baʿal hāmôn* (gaily corrected by him into *byt lʾmwn*, 'temple of the god Amon') an allusion to the term *ʾāmôn* ('architect, artificer') of Prov 8:30 and therefore a satire against the misogynist concept of the Jerusalem clergy (!).

[234] Cf., *supra*, n. 11, p. 437.

[235] The term *baʿal* can also indicate the 'husband', and 'husband of a multitude' would be very suitable in the light of Solomon's *harem*.

[236] Cf. *HALOT*, p. 144. It is also the interpretation of the Targum, dictated, however, by an allegorical intention. Madl matches the text to Gen 17:4, 5, where Abraham is called *ʾab hāmôn*, 'father of a multitude', understanding the people of Israel, metaphorically, as the 'vineyard of Abraham' (H. Madl, *nāṭar*, in *TDOT*, Vol. IX, p. 405). In this case, one could think of an antithesis between Solomon (*baʿal*) and Abraham (*ʾab*).

[237] Unquestionably, the Mesopotamian sources speak of eunuch offcials, but attestations are lacking for Egypt: Keel insinuates that the supervisors figured in the *harem* scene in Keel (1994), Figure 158, p. 281, do not have the characteristics of eunuchs. In Israel too, such a custom is not mentioned (cf. Keel [1994], p. 282).

'to give' (*nātan*) refers in fact to v. 7d: "If a man were to give all the wealth…". In v. 7d, it is a question of material things, here of the 'vineyard': something that lets us perceive the commercialisation to which Solomon is subjecting his 'vineyard'. She 'has given' the beloved her love (7:13; cf. 1:12), but this same Solomon 'gives' her to keepers: he gives to others[238] the one who has given herself to him.

"Each one brings him, for its fruit, a thousand shekels of silver". Even the verb 'to bring' (*bw'* in *hiph'il* form) is dense with cross-references: generally it indicates the 'bringing into' the place of love (cf. 1:4; 2:4; 3:4; 8:2). Like the verb 'to give', so the verb 'to bring in' is suddenly degraded into a commercial sense.[239] What is being brought into the house is not the woman or her beloved but 'a thousand pieces of silver'. Money is replacing love.

The fruit of the vineyard (*piryô*, v. 11d) is wine which, in the language of the Song, is a metaphor for love (cf. 8:2). For love, therefore, each of the keepers must bring 'a thousand shekels of silver' into the house. This is a concrete illustration of what was said in v. 7d: there it was a question of giving money for love, here of giving love for money, but the sense remains the same. Solomon looks at the women of his *harem* as an investment from which he is expecting an adequate return. The 'thousand shekels of silver' is an enormous sum, like 'all the wealth of his house' in v. 7: it is quantity that is being opposed to quality. In Isa 7:23, 'a thousand shekels of silver' (*'elep kesep*) is the price of 'a thousand vines' (the number of women in Solomon's *harem* according to 1 Kgs 11:3!). Calculating that *each* keeper must bring him this sum, and that it is calculated net, without counting the payment due to the keepers, it is an enormous figure. At this level, the 'keepers' have become tenant farmers, 'vine-dressers' as in the gospel version of the metaphor (cf. Mark 12:1–2 and pars.).

How this commercialisation of love is to be understood concretely is not said. As we saw above, different exegetes have thought of high class prostitution, perhaps under the form of the sacred variety. But no information has reached us that Solomon did anything of this

[238] Is it possible to think of sexual relations between the guardians and the women of the *harem*? Certainly, if we are talking of Solomon, a single man could not hope to satisfy a thousand women. One can perhaps read here a reference to Isaiah's second 'song of the vineyard': "I, Yahweh, am its keeper (*nṣr*), every moment I water it; lest anyone harm it, I guard it (*nṣr*) night and day" (Isa 27:3, cf. H. Madl, *nāṭar*, in *TDOT*, Vol. IX, p. 404). God himself guards his vineyard; he does not *give* it to keepers.

[239] Cf. Lys (1968), p. 301.

kind, and, moreover, the parallel with vv. 8–10 leads us to look not for something extraordinary but rather for a practice that was common in Jewish society in the time of the author. It is natural to think of polygamy,[240] widespread among the upper ranks of the bourgeoisie of which Solomon would be the symbol. With the allusion to Solomon, there come to mind the political and economic advantages which such marriages gained for him, or his sons:[241] there are ways—and they are not remote, even in our society—in which a 'marriage of convenience', not of love, is often realised. It is always a making of love into a tool for ends that are foreign to it.

Solomon's attitude is similar to that of the brothers. Both are preoccupied with the chastity of the woman ('wall', 'door', v. 9; 'keepers', v. 11). Both the brothers and Solomon depersonalise the woman, taking away from her the possibility of making decisions about her own body ("What shall we do for our sister?", v. 9; "He gave this vineyard to keepers", v. 11). Both are moved not by love but by the lust for gain ('silver', v. 9 and v. 11).

[v. 12] My vineyard. The woman's reply, like the preceding one, follows closely the plans expressed by her 'guardians'.[242] In fact, the first declaration: "My vineyard, my very own" (*karmî šellî*, v. 12a) takes up v. 11a: "Solomon had a vineyard" (*kerem hāyāh lišlōmōh*). The emphatic underlining of the first person personal pronoun ("*My* vineyard, *my very own*") is a hurt protest against Solomon's claim to be himself the proprietor of the 'vineyard'. The woman affirms that her vineyard, that is, her body, her sexuality, is her own property and belongs to no one else: she alone has the right to make decisions about herself. Neither the family (vv. 8–10) nor Solomon, with all his wealth, can make decisions for her. Love is an act of liberty: without the latter there can be no love.

The meaning of the expression: "is before me" is controverted. Many exegetes consider it as the principal argument for attributing the verse to the man.[243] In fact, if 'my vineyard' is standing 'before me', this means that it is different from me. This observation would gain support from

---

[240] "It is not a question of money to be gained, but of trust in love, which chooses monogamy for itself in a polygamous society" (Lys [1968], p. 303).

[241] "As far as authentic love is concerned, the text places the emphasis not on a product (son, fertility), but on exclusive mutual belonging" (Lys [1968], p. 304).

[242] Cf., *supra*, p. 483, and *Tab. 79*.

[243] Cf., *supra*, n. 217.

the fact that, in v. 10, the analogous expression 'in his eyes' refers to the man. But *lipnê* often has an extended sense, equivalent to (being) 'at one's disposal' (cf. 1 Sam 19:7; 29:8; 2 Kgs 5:2), 'under the supervision of' (cf. 1 Sam 3:1) or 'in the power of' (cf. Judg 11:9)[244] someone. So then it can be properly uttered by the woman who thus declares that the control over her own body belongs to her because she is the owner of it. Thus understood, the declaration opposes v. 11b: "He gave this vineyard to keepers". The keeper of the vineyard, the woman says, is she herself: she has no need of other guardians. The declaration is similar to that of v. 10 where she rejected the 'defences of chastity' suggested for her by her brothers, stating that she was able to defend herself.

If we compare v. 12a with the parallel Song 1:6, we observe a tension. In 1:6 the woman says that she 'has not kept' her own vineyard. Apparently there is a contradiction with our verse where she declares that she is its keeper. Actually, what we have here are two complementary statements, as v. 10 shows. There the woman affirms simultaneously that she is a defence (v. 10ab), and that this defence has surrendered in the face of love (v. 10cd). The woman of the Song is torn between the two poles of the keeping of herself and the gift of herself. Both take place, necessarily, in freedom: the door of the fortress can be opened only from within. Only if the woman has the keys of the door can she close and also open it. Both actions obey the logic of love. On her part, Elliott observes: "The experience of love [Song 1:6, *author's note*] has given her possession of herself [8:12, *author's note*]; to be possessed [...] has meant self-possession".[245] That would be to contest certain aspects of the modern movement of women's liberation: only by losing the control over her own body does the woman truly gain it (cf. 1 Cor 7:4).[246]

At this point, the woman mocks at Solomon,[247] making real that 'scorn', pre-announced in v. 7def, for whoever wishes to give his wealth

---

[244] Cf. Alden (1988), p. 274; H. Simian Yofre, *pānîm*, in *TDOT*, vol. XI, pp. 608–611.

[245] Elliott (1989), pp. 207–208.

[246] We have pointed out a similar tension between 'my garden' and 'his garden' in 4,16: the garden is 'mine' in so far as it becomes 'his', and *vice versa* (cf., *supra*, p. 234).

[247] LXX^B omits the *soi*, 'to you', before 'Solomon', transforming the direct discourse into indirect ('Solomon's thousand'), but MT is closer to the epigramatic character of the passage. Vetus Latina transforms the derision into a compliment: *mille Salomoni sodales et ducenti servantes fructus eius*. Garbini (1992), p. 125, rightly recognises there "some retouching to lessen the sneering at Solomon".

Table 80

v. 11a	SOLOMON	*Solomon had a vineyard...*
v. 11b	KEEPERS	*he gave this vineyard to keepers.*
v. 12aα	SOLOMON	*My vineyard, my very own,*
v. 12aβ	KEEPERS	*is before me.*
v. 12b	SOLOMON	*Yours the thousand shekels, Solomon,*
v. 12c	KEEPERS	*and two hundred for the keepers...*

in exchange for love. The enormous sum of 'a thousand shekels',[248] on which the whole serious discourse of v. 11 hinges, is merrily flung into Solomon's face; this is not what the woman is interested in: her vineyard is not to be purchased with money. Love can only be 'given' (*nātan*, 7:13). With all his gold, Solomon can acquire a *harem* or a brothel, not love.

Once the owner of the vineyard has been got rid of, the discourse passes on to the 'keepers'. From the fact that the woman herself keeps good watch over her own vineyard ("My vineyard is before me"), the keepers are superfluous. They enjoy the wages, however, which Solomon gives to the keepers of *his* vineyard. If a thousand shekels went to Solomon, a lot less would be enough for his officers: two hundred shekels almost correspond to the rate for a tenant.[249] But Garbini is right to see here "a smiling and, all things considered, a gentle irony",[250] a witticism such as is typical of the classical epigram.[251]

The strophe shows a constant oscillation between 'Solomon', the proprietor of the vineyard, and its 'keepers'. The binome, introduced in v. 11ab, is taken up twice in v. 12 (cf. *Tab. 79*). The observation is added to that made above (cf. *Tab. 78*) and confirms the precise construction of vv. 11–12.

[248] There is much speculation on the 'thousand shekels' (cf. Delitzsch [1875], pp. 139–140). The amount does not seem to correspond to the one that was mentioned in v. 11cd, where a 'thousand shekels' was the amount that each keeper had to bring. Perhaps the number is understood here distributively, but Ravasi (1992), p. 703, rightly warns against any mathematical logic that is foreign to the poetry of the Song: 'thousand' is a round number to indicate an enormous quantity.

[249] According to the Talmud, a half, a third or a quarter of the fruits of the farm belong to the tenant (cf. b.*BB* 110a; b.*Git* 74b). A fifth (200/1000) or a sixth (200/1200) is envisaged for Solomon's keepers. So Gordis (1974), pp. 101–102.

[250] Garbini (1992), p. 286.

[251] Müller (1992), p. 89, speaks of an 'anticlimax', which softens the animosity of the protest of v. 12ab.

Fourth Strophe: "Flee, my Beloved" (8:13–14)

Verses 13–14 form the conclusion not only of the *Epilogue* but of the entire poem. This is an enigmatic passage in the face of which the commentators have often opted for a change of text since—they say—it is incomprehensible. The observation made by the New Jerusalem Bible is significant: "Verse 13[252] is probably the beginning of a poem that has not been preserved to which someone has added a verse inspired by 2:17".[253] That is, not only would the two verses be out of context,[254] but they would also have nothing to do with each other, originating in two different compositions. To the first hypothesis we have replied above by marking out the structure of the *Epilogue*.[255] It is worth returning to some observations made there. The last strophe forms an *inclusio* with the first (vv. 5–7): that is shown by the repeat of the term *dôd* (vv. 5, 14), by an ascending movement (*ʿālāh*, 'rises', v. 5; *ʿal*, 'on', v. 14), by the natural symbolism ('under the apple tree', v. 5; 'gardens', v. 13). In the first and the last strophe, the subject is the relationship of the two lovers while, in the second and third, the theme is the criticism of society. Significantly, the first and the last strophe are characterised by 'you' (sg.) (vv. 5c–6b; vv. 13–14), while in the central strophes the lovers are spoken of in the third person.

It is to this double nature of the addressees of the woman's discourse that the man refers in v. 13. Here we have, as in v. 5, a flashback to the preceding context. In the 'companions' (v. 13ab), we can recognise the society which the woman addressed in vv. 10 and 12. The man, who was the object of address of the woman's first word (vv. 5–6), claims for himself also the last one (v. 13c).

Against this background, one can also understand the coherence of the two verses (and so reply to the second objection): what the man seeks in v. 13, that is, to hear the woman's voice, actually happens in v. 14: in fact, the woman addresses the last word of the Song to him.

Even if direct verbal references between the third and fourth strophes are missing, a correspondence can be recognised in the relationship

---

[252] *NJB* has 'v. 11', but this is clearly a mistake: the note is set at v. 13. The French edition of 1973 has the same mistake; the new edition deleted the note.

[253] *NJB*, p. 1041, note *m*.

[254] We should note the futility of wishing to make a new poem begin in the penultimate verse of the Song!

[255] Cf., *supra*, pp. 438–441.

between the metaphor of the 'vineyard' (*kerem*, vv. 11ab, 12a) and that of the 'garden' (*gan*, v. 13): the natural symbolism unites the fourth strophe not only with the first but also with the third. Moreover, the term *ḥăbērîm* ('companions') recalls the *nōṭᵉrîm* ('keepers'): in both cases, this is 'society' presented in its negative aspect in the third strophe but in its positive one in the fourth.

Verses 13–14, then, are not a foreign body in the *Epilogue* but form its natural conclusion. Not only that, but in them are echoed continuously precise references to the themes and motive of the Song, above all of the *Prologue*. Look at the term *ḥăbērîm*, for example; it occurs again only in 1:7, or the macroscopic reprise of the theme of the 'gazelle on the mountains' (v. 14) from 2:17 and 4:6. The passage is placed as a conclusion not only to the *Epilogue* but to the entire poem. It is to be expected, therefore, that the author condenses his message in it in a particularly pregnant form.

The strophe is composed, like the preceding ones, of two parts, the first one (v. 13) characterised by the discourse of the man, the second (v. 14) by the woman's reply. The first part is composed of a tristich, the second of two distichs: the sum of the stichs, seven (!), is surely not accidental. Stylistically, the strophe is aligned more with the two preceding ones than with the first: with these it shares its enigmatic character, with the peak of the enigma in the last verse.

[v. 13] "Let me hear your voice". The textual problems are concentrated in this verse. Not so much because the MT is corrupt but rather because the sense which it offers does not satisfy the exegetes. As usual, we prefer to stick to the MT, accepting the challenge of its apparently enigmatic character.

The problems begin with the first phrase: "You who dwell in the gardens". The MT has a feminine participle, referring the phrase to the woman, while the Greek version of the LXX reads in the masculine (*ho kathēmenos*), and the Syriac translates in the plural, with reference to the 'companions'.[256] Of the companions, however, it is never said that they live in the garden: the garden is the place of love reserved for the lovers. The reading of the LXX certainly makes sense: in 5:1 and in 6:2, the man goes to 'his' garden. Since the garden is a metaphor for the woman, it seems more logical to refer the phrase to the man. But it is precisely as the *lectio difficilior* that the MT must be retained:

[256] Cf., *supra*, n. 13, p. 437.

moreover, it would not make sense for the request (v. 13) and the reply (v. 14) to be uttered by the same person.

In the Song, the garden is not only a symbol of the woman (cf. 4:12–5:1; 6:2), but also the sphere of love, as was noted *à propos* of 7:12–14.[257] This is the sense of the parallel expression in v. 5: "Under the apple tree". The apple tree could also be a symbol of the lovers (cf. 2:3; 7:9), but here the context leads us to understand it as the place of love. If the woman has to awaken the man 'under the apple tree', that means to say that this is not to be identified with either him or her: it is simply the place of love, in opposition to the city that is cold and without life, and also to the desert (v. 5a), place of death.

Of the woman it is said that she "dwells (*yāšab*) in the gardens". The verb *yāšab* can have the sense of 'sitting' (cf. 2:3), of 'lying, resting' (cf. 5:12), but also, more generally, of 'dwelling', as in this case. An erotic interpretation of the term[258] is not recommended by the woman's reply in the following verse: "Flee!"

The plural—'in the gardens' (*baggannîm*) is surprising. This is not a unique case in the Song: the term recurs at 4:15 ('spring of the gardens') and in 6:2 ('…to graze in the gardens'). Here too there is certainly present a sonorous effect (note the assonance with *ḥăbērîm*). It is also possible to think of a plural of generalisation or of indetermination.[259] But the parallels invite us to take the plural seriously. In 4:15, the term is counterposed to the images of enclosure in 4:12, alluding to a universal function for the garden.[260] Similarly, in 6:2, the term assumes a function that made universal the experience of love.[261] In our passage too, the last strophe forms a parallel complementary to the first where the exclusiveness of love is affirmed. The woman of the Song is at home in all the gardens of the world, wherever the experience of love is lived. Her voice has value not only for her beloved man but also for his 'companions'. Perhaps we have here a case of that 'plural of love' which we noted in 1:3c, 4cde[262] and in 3:10e.[263] The Oriental goddess of love is not only 'lady of the steppe' (cf. the commentary on 2:7 and

[257] Cf., *supra*, p. 414.

[258] So, for example, Garbini (1992), p. 286: "clearly referring to a woman who is stretched out in expectation of an embrace".

[259] Cf. Joüon (1923), §136j. Gerleman (1965), p. 223, suggests understanding "Gartenbewohnerin".

[260] Cf. pp. 227–228.

[261] Cf. pp. 311–312.

[262] Cf., *supra*, p. 56.

[263] Cf. pp. 158–159.

3:5), but also 'lady of the gardens'.[264] In Greece, she is venerated under the name of *aphroditē en kepois* (note the plural here too!).[265]

The term that follows, *ḥăbērîm*, is very debated. MT is without the article which has led some to suppose that there is no specific group of people here ('*the* companions'), but some people who had infiltrated the garden in secret ('companions').[266] Graetz reads here: 'My companions'.[267] But Joüon notes that the use of the article in Hebrew is very free, above all in poetry.[268] It is clear, however, that the Hebrew term was already troubling the ancient versions: the Syriac omits it;[269] the codex Sinaiticus of the LXX replaces it with *heteroi* ('others').[270] The modern commentators indulge in fantastic conjectures to which the text offers no support.[271] Generally, the 'companions' are understood as rivals of the beloved man. This is Krinetzki's comment:

> [The request characterises] the girl as a being naturally ingenuous and infantile, unaware of her own attractiveness: she sees nothing wrong in the fact that, beside her beloved, his 'companions' are also approaching her and that they, with him and like him, are listening, transported, to the beloved 'voice' [...]. Something which, in the judgement of the young man, is rather the exclusive privilege of the one who loves, which he claims for himself.[272]

---

[264] Noticeable, therefore, is a correspondence between the 'desert' of v. 5 and the 'garden' of v. 13: the journey begins in the desert and ends in the garden. The inclusion between *midbār* (v. 5a) and *gannîm* (v. 13a) is underlined by Elliott (1989), p. 211.

[265] Cf. Wittekindt (1925), p. 72. Naturally, in the woman, the mythological school sees the goddess of love, personified by a priestess or a sacred prostitute, who offers her love in the gardens of the temple. It is possible that this motif is present in the background; in the Song, however, it is reinterpreted in the sphere of the Yahwistic religion. Cf. Müller (1976), 23–41.

[266] Cf. Lys (1968), p. 305 ("*des camarades sont attentif à ta voix*"); Keel (1994), p. 284 ("Companions are listening").

[267] Graetz (1871), p. 217; so too Robert – Tournay (1963), p. 324.

[268] Joüon (1923), §137f (cf. *id.* [1909], p. 332: "*les compagnons*").

[269] So too Haupt (1907), pp. 105–106.

[270] Cf., *supra*, n. 14, p. 437. The reading 'others' is followed by Rudolph (1962), p. 186, and Gerleman (1965), p. 223.

[271] Wittekindt (1925), p. 72, translates the term with *Zaubersprüchen*, 'incantations', admitting that this is a rather audacious hypothesis: 'Let me hear your incantations'. For Pope (1977), pp. 693–694, the 'companions' would be the members of a kind of 'confraternity' which organised licentious funeral banquets (*marzēaḥ*) (cf. *ibid.*, pp. 210–229). Garbini (1992), pp. 286–288, for his part, sees, in the 'companions', some old Peeping Toms, who are spying on the two lovers as in the story of the chaste Susanna. Naturally these voyeurs would be priests, whom the author of the Song would be wishing to ridicule mercilessly. It is legitimate to ask oneself if this 'anticlerical' intention is indeed that of the author of the Song, and not rather that of its commentator!

[272] Krinetzki (1981), p. 232; so too Lacocque (1998), p. 189.

This would be then a case of jealousy, a declaration of the exclusivity of the relationship of love. The Vulgate is of a different opinion: translating with 'friends', it sees there those 'friends of the bridegroom' of which John 3:29 speaks ("He who has the bride is the bridegroom; the *friend of the bridegroom*, who stands and hears him, rejoices greatly at the bridegroom's voice"). Here the function of the companions is viewed positively.[273] The term *ḥăbērîm* in itself is open to two meanings, whether positive (cf. Qoh 4:10) or negative (cf. Ps 45:8):[274] a decision between the two can only come from the context.

The only parallel to the term is in the *Prologue* (1:7). The companions are presented here under a rather negative light. The woman does not wish to seek her beloved 'behind the flocks of his comrades', for fear of being taken for a prostitute. But the image changes in the following verse, where the companions reply wisely to the young woman's question. Their role in 1:11 is also positive: they declare themselves ready to make precious jewellery to heighten the beauty of the bride: here, they are certainly not 'rivals' but 'friends' of the bridegroom. It seems that we can recognise in the *ḥăbērîm* the representatives of society, that is to say, the male parallel to the 'daughters of Jerusalem' in their ambivalent role. On the one hand, they can disturb love (cf. the 'watchmen' in 3:3–4; 5:7, or the 'keepers' in 8:11–12), on the other hand, they can help it (cf. the 'mighty men of Israel' in 3:7). Like the 'maidens' in 1:3–4, they confer on love a social, shared character.

That in our case the companions' function is seen in a positive sense is gained above all from the verb *qāšab*, which expresses a particular mode of 'hearing':

> [*qāšab*] means heightened alertness and attentiveness to something impending, with the express intention of perceiving it completely and comprehensively, being ready and willing to incorporate it into and allow it to determinate one's conduct.[275]

In the prophetic books, the verb *qāšab* expresses the attentive and obedient listening to the word of God (cf. Isa 32:3; Jer 6:10, 17, 19; Hos 5:1; Mic 1:2; Zech 1:4; 7:11). In the Psalms, it is used of the attention

[273] In this sense Murphy (1990), p. 200, also understands the term ("They are simply the friends of the lover, whom he associates with his own desire to hear her voice"), and Ravasi (1992), pp. 707–708.
[274] Cf. H. Cazelles, *ḥābar*, in *TDOT*, vol. IV, pp. 193–197.
[275] R. Mosis, *qšb*, in *TDOT*, vol. XIII, p. 185.

that God lends to the cry of the poor (cf. Ps 5:3). Interesting also is the use made of it by Prov 1–9 where Lady Wisdom claims for herself that same attention which is afforded to the word of God (cf. Prov 1:24; 2:2; 4:1, 20; 5:1; 7:24). This, then, is not morbid voyeurism (among other things, the text speaks of 'listening' not of 'seeing'), but a highly positive disposition: the disposition with which one receives the word of God and that of Wisdom.[276] The words of the woman of the Song are not words of men, but 'word of God'. When Israel first, and then the Church, received the Song into the canon of inspired books, they were 'attentive to the voice' of the beloved woman.[277]

The woman addressed herself to the *ḥăbērîm*, that is to society, in the two previous strophes (cf. vv. 10, 13): they received positively (*qāšab*) the critical words which the woman directed to them. But now the man seeks the last word for himself. The social polemic has to give way to the dialogue of the two lovers which is the characteristic language of the Song of Songs.[278]

The request (*hašmîʿînî*, 'let me hear it') is a repetition of 2:14—"Let me see your face, let me hear your voice" (*hašmîʿînî ʾet qôlēk*).[279] In 8:13 MT, the verb 'to hear' remains without an object in Hebrew, but clearly has the same object as the preceding *maqšîbîm*: that is, it is a case of ellipsis.[280] As is typical of the Song, the repetitions are inserted each time into the new context. If in 2:14 the text made 'seeing' conspicuous alongside 'hearing', here there is no hint of 'seeing': attention is completely on the 'hearing', that is, on the 'word'. This is verbal communication: what the woman has said until now to the companions and what she is going to say to her beloved in the following verse.

---

[276] "On the basis of the sapiential terms contained in our verse, it is conceivable that the redactor is identifying the bride with the *ḥokmâ* of Sir 24 (cf. Wis 8:2)" (Robert—Tournay [1963], p. 326).

[277] Landy (1983), pp. 206–207, understands in a similar sense: "To us the beloved's voice is indissolubly linked with that of the Song whose audience we are".

[278] "The word 'I' is [...] the keynote which is integrated now in one voice, and now, when it passes to the You, in the other voice, and blends like a pedal-note with all the melodic and harmonic texture of the middle and high voices" (Rosenzweig [2005], pp. 216–217).

[279] In 8:13, Vg (*fac me audire vocem tuam*) renders the parallelism with 2:14 still more evident. It is, however, a reading of accommodation: the other versions rightly join 'your voice' to 'are attentive' (cf., *supra*, n. 15, p. 437).

[280] Cf. Watson (1984), pp. 303–304. Dahood (1966–1970), vol. III, pp. 429–444, prefers to speak of *double duty*.

[v. 14] "Flee, my beloved". The last verse of the Song is paradoxical. At the conclusion of the poem, one would expect the representation of the union of the two lovers. Instead, the author surprises us with an enigmatic "Flee!"[281] One can understand how the exegetes have tried in every way to attenuate the provocative sense of the verb. Bringing forward the parallelism, which is very evident,[282] with 2:17 and 4:6, some have seen in 8:14, an invitation by the woman to an encounter of love.[283] But the Hebrew verb *bāraḥ* does not allow such an interpretation: it always expresses the 'going away' from a place.[284] Recognising this meaning, others have interpreted this 'fleeing' not in relation to the woman ("Flee from me"), but in relation to the companions. The woman would be inviting her beloved to distance himself from the indiscreet group of his comrades and to come to her.[285] The problem for this interpretation, however, is the fact that the two lovers have not separated: in v. 5 they are represented in a close embrace, and v. 6 seeks that this embrace never be broken ("Set me as a seal upon your heart").[286] The 'fleeing' cannot express a coming towards the woman because the two are united: the only movement that can be intended is therefore a distancing from her.[287] In this, the situation supposed in 8:14 is different from that of the parallel passages where the two are apart, and the movement indicated, whether by the verb *sābab* (2:17)[288] or by *hālak ʾel* (4:6), leads to union.

---

[281] Gordis (1974), p. 102, notes, following Ibn Ezra: "The verse is best taken as a quotation of what the lover wants to hear". I am very doubtful that the beloved would expect to hear: "Flee"!

[282] Cf., *supra*, pp. 188–189, and *Tab. 23*.

[283] So, for example, Joüon (1909), p. 333 ("Accours"); Rudolph (1962), p. 186 ("Eile fort"); Müller (1992), p. 90 ("Komm schnell"). In this sense, Garbini's translation: "Penetrate" is drastic (Garbini [1992], p. 288). It is true that the sense of 'penetrate' is sometimes present in the OT, but it is an anomalous use (only twice, in a technical context, Exod 26:28 and 36:33: it is a denominative use of *bᵉrîaḥ*, 'bolt'). Such an eroticism is foreign to the discreet and allusive language of the Song.

[284] Thus, rightly, Ricciotti (1928), p. 288; Robert – Tournay (1963), p. 327.

[285] "This flight far from prying eyes must actually be a flight towards her" (Lys [1968], p. 307); so too Krinetzki (1981), p. 233; Fox (1985), p. 177.

[286] Also v. 10 ("but, in his eyes, I have become like one who has found peace") confirms that the situation presupposed throughout the *Epilogue* is that of the union of the lovers, portrayed in 8:3.

[287] Thus Elliott (1989), p. 210; Poulssen (1989), p. 73.

[288] Cf., *supra*, p. 124.

As in 2:17, the invitation is directed to the *dôdî*.[289] The term *dôd* appears here for the last time: in the whole of the Song, it occurs 33 times.[290] More significant, from a symbolical point of view, is the tally of places in which this appellation appears in the mouth of the woman, and so with the first person possessive: 26 times.[291] Now 26 is the numerical value of the divine name YHWH.[292] Perhaps there is already present here an element of allegorical interpretation: it is well-known that, according to the allegory, the beloved man is God himself.[293]

The image of the 'gazelle' or the 'young stag' is common to the parallels 2:17 and 4:5. Once again, the comparison makes the mirroring dynamic of the Song prominent: in 4:5, in fact, the woman's two breasts are compared with these animals. The 'gazelle on the mountains' is an image of liberty and openness which is counterposed to the enclosure of the 'garden' in the previous verse. It recalls the metaphor of the desert which characterises the beginning of the *Epilogue*[294] and well accords with the verb 'to flee'.

In the light of 2:17 ('cloven mountains')[295] and of 4:6 ('mountain of myrrh and hill of incense'),[296] so too the 'mountains of balms' are to be understood in a metaphorical way with reference to the female body. With his taste for variation, the author replaces the myrrh and

289 The term *dôdî* returns twice in 2:16–17. It does not appear in 4:16, because here it is the beloved himself who is speaking.

290 According to Tournay (1982), p. 89, this would be an allusion to the years in which David reigned in Jerusalem. Tournay is reading here an identification of the beloved with the Davidic Messiah, an identification suggested by the fact that the consonants of the word *dwd* are the same as the ones the titles of the Psalms use for 'David'.

291 This is also observed by Ravasi (1992), p. 708, who does not notice its symbolic value however.

292 On the importance of this number in the OT, cf. Hutmacher (1993), p. 12; Schedl (1974), pp. 46, 51. I myself have noticed how the MT of the Psalms alludes to this number several times. Cf. Barbiero (1999), pp. 192, 335, 548.

293 It would be the Song's only allusion in this sense, in a text, moreover, which has a wholly coherent literal sense. In fact, it is difficult here to imagine that the woman (= Israel, soul) would say to God: "Flee".

294 "These enclosed images (i.e. the embrace [8:5], the seal [8:6], the fortified city [8:7], the vineyard [8:11–12], and the garden, *note of the author*) are framed by two open images of *midbar* (8:5a) and *hārê bᵉśāmîn* (sic!) (8:14d)" (Elliott [1989], p. 211. Also, in another way, the image of the gazelle on the mountains (8:14) recalls that of the two lovers who rise from the desert (8:5): in both cases there is an image of life triumphing over death ('desert').

295 Cf., *supra*, pp. 125–126.

296 Cf. p. 191.

the incense of 4:6 with 'balms'.[297] Balm is the most precious perfume of antiquity: it is the one most mentioned in the Song (4:10, 14, 16; 5:1, 13; 6:2). Only once is it referred to the man (5:13): usually it is the scent of the woman, characteristic of her 'garden' (4:10, 14, 16; 5:1; 6:2) In the OT, balm is connected with Solomon (cf. 1 Kgs 2:25; 2 Chr 9:19), something which perhaps is not fortuitous, because Solomon was spoken of in the previous strophe (cf. vv. 11, 12). In an historical sense, an allusion to the royal plantations of balsam at Jericho and Engedi is conceivable.[298] In this sense, the expression of v. 14d would be continuing the opposition between the two vineyards in vv. 11–12: the true land of balm is 'my vineyard', not the plantations of Solomon!

If 'the mountains of balm' indicate the woman's body, however, the verb 'to flee' seems out of place. The apparent contradiction of the two terms is noted by Keel who resolves the contradiction by having recourse to a kind of shrewdness on the part of the woman. She would be using a coded language here: what for the companions is to be understood as an invitation to flight ("Flee on the mountains"), is intended to express an invitation to love ("Come to me") for the man.[299] Frankly, though, such an interpretation sounds artificial.[300]

Rather, the contradiction is to be taken seriously, and forms part of those paradoxes on which the poetics of the Song live. Perhaps the nearest parallel is the finale of the *New Songs of the Beloved Woman* (5:2–6:3). There, we hear of the sudden departure of the man, after his knocking in vain, and the woman's anguished search for him in the night with the hostility of the watchmen and the irony of the daughters of Jerusalem. The finale, we noticed, is surprising. To the question of the daughters of Jerusalem: "Where has your beloved gone?" (6:1), the woman replies: "My beloved has gone down into his garden" (6:2), that is to say: he has come to me.[301] The 'garden' of 6:2 has the same significance as the 'mountains of balms' of 8:14. In reality, the

---

[297] The versions understand MT's *bᵉśāmîm* as a generic term (cf. LXX's *epi orē arōmatōn*), as do also the majority of modern translations. But the plural also occurs in 4:10, 14, 16, where the term clearly has a specific sense, indicating the balsam plant (cf. p. 208).

[298] Cf., *supra*, p. 209.

[299] Keel (1994), p. 285.

[300] Hardly probable seems to me also the proposal of A. and C. Bloch, to see here the summons to a departure before sunrise, so as to avoid discovery (Bloch & Bloch [1995], p. 221). The love of the Song is not surreptitious!

[301] Cf., *supra*, p. 308. The correspondence is noted by Salvaneschi (1982), p. 116.

man had gone away from his garden; otherwise the nocturnal search would not have taken place. But now the woman has reached the certainty that the direction of 'flight' can only be the 'garden'. The refrain of mutual belonging ("I am my beloved's, and my beloved is mine", 6:3) expresses this certainty. When one is sure of mutual belonging, absence is no longer anguish.

Both things, therefore, are to be taken seriously: on the one hand, the request for taking distance ('Flee!'), on the other, the affirmation that this distance is aimed at a fuller union ('on the mountains of balms'). Union cannot last for ever: love has also a need for distance to allow each partner to be himself. A union that leads to a fusion that cancels out the differences is not authentic. Only when one is oneself, only when the otherness between the two lovers is safe, is the gift of self possible.[302]

The *inclusio*, mentioned above, between the first and fourth strophe of the *Epilogue* expresses precisely this polarity between nearness and distance. In the first strophe, the two lovers were represented as united in an embrace, and the woman sought that this union would never be broken. But perhaps one could also read (in the stress on jealousy, for example) a fear of loss, an obsessive attachment to the other.[303] The woman is liberated from this fear in the last strophe when, in apparent contradiction to the first, she seeks for the union to be broken. But, she adds, it is to be broken only to allow itself to be renewed. Love lives of this diastolic-systolic movement, between nearness and distance.[304]

---

[302] Cf. Kristeva (1983), pp. 88–89; Lévinas (1983), p. 89: "What is presented as the failure of amorous communication, constitutes precisely the positive nature of the relationship; this absence of the other is precisely his presence as other". And the comment of A.-M. Pelletier ("What Emmanuel Lévinas explores concerning alterity, femininity and love with the language of the philosopher, the Song says directly, by means of the springing up of a word that celebrates, establishes subjects, far from any form of deadly fusion", Pelletier [1999], p. 194).

[303] "The other, who builds up and participates in this union, remains other; one never reaches where he is, he remains, so to speak, foreign to all knowledge of him, to every power over him, to all manipulation. He remains, so to speak, transcendent, that is, outside and above, since he provokes responsibility toward him" (Abécassis [2002], p. 190).

[304] "It seems better to retain the tension in the Beloved's imperative, and to allow the Song to conclude in an open-ended way. She is telling him to go off quickly, but implies that his going is a way of coming again; that absence is a way of presence; that their love is never static and meant to linger long in one embrace, but dynamic and continuously developing" (Elliott [1989], p. 210). Poulssen (1989), p. 75, has a similar understanding. Cf. also Lavoie (1995), p. 145: "Actually, for the Song, the place

So, at the end of the Song, we are referred back to the beginning.[305] The story can commence anew. The two can search for each other again, find each other and then leave each other. This is the circular movement that is proper to the Song,[306] with its refrains and repetitions, which are never really such since love does not repeat itself but is ever new, even if it is as ancient as the world.

Conclusion

The Epilogue of the Song has been shown to be a unitary composition which it is important to consider in its entirety in order to understand its message. In it, the whole content of the poem is summarized as in a final synthesis. In particular, the *inclusio* with the Prologue (1:2–2:7) is clear, for it is to this that the themes of vineyard, brothers and Solomon refer. In another respect, it is linked with the song that immediately precedes it (7:12–8:4) in that it takes up again the theme of encounter-conflict between love and society. Significantly, the two passages are placed in the mouth of the woman.

The four strophes which make up the Epilogue are arranged in chiastic form in such a way that in the first and last strophes the theme is the relationship between the two lovers while in the two central ones the subject is the relationship between love and society, represented by the two elements of the family (the brothers) and civil society ("Solomon").

In 8:5–7, the Song reaches its peak, theorizing on the nature of love for the only time in the whole poem, and in a few dense lines. Looking

---

where the lovers can best find themselves is the distance that separates them: in it and through it the desire for the other is developed" (also Lavoie [1993]).

[305] Actually, the same tension between union and distance, implied in the *inclusio* between the first and last strophe of the Epilogue, can be noticed between the end and the beginnng of the Song. Just like the *Epilogue*, the Song also begins with an overwhelming desire for union: "Let him kiss me with the kisses of his mouth" (1:2).

[306] "The Song does not bring the adventure of love to a final point, but to the end of the last poem. The adventure continues. [...] Authentic love is always a search for the other; it is the constant pull towards union of him who is the beloved *par excellence* and of his companion who is the 'only one'" (Lys [1968], p. 308). "Verses 13–14 of Canticle 8 build an end that is, at the same time, a rebound of the whole poem, a return to the beginning. And thus the Canticle is an endless song [...]. The Song of Songs is indeed a *round*, the *rondeau* of the Middle Ages, that is, a endlessly repeated song" (Lacocque [1998], p. 190).

back on the union that has been achieved (8:5), the woman seeks that nothing and no one may ever separate the two lovers (theme of the "seal", v. 6). The two motivations given for this are fundamental. The first is that love is "strong as death", and it does not accept separation. In the context, it is then made clear that love is stronger than death (v. 7): not even death can divide the two lovers. Here we find expressed clearly what has already been spoken of symbolically in various images (the lotus flower, the henna, the little goat, the bag of myrrh). Love has won the battle with death.

The second reason is that love is a "flame of Yah". For the first and last time in the Song, the name of God, the God of Israel, is uttered. Here too something is being said which is a key to understanding the whole poem. Only and precisely because love is a "flame of Yah" can it be represented in the poem with numinous characteristics, and the two lovers assume a theomorphic character. To experience love is to experience God.

On the basis of this divine nature of love, the Song mounts a ruthless attack on two customs of the time which tended to reduce love to a financial transaction: the custom of the *mōhar*, or bride price (vv. 8–10) and that of polygamy, practised by the affluent classes ("Solomon", vv. 11–12). Against such practices, the woman claims for herself, and powerfully, the responsibility for her own choices. By means of these two concrete examples, there comes a realization of the affirmation of 8:7—"If a man were to give all the wealth of his house in exchange for love, scorn is all he would obtain" (8:7).

The final strophe of the Epilogue (vv. 13–14) is surprising and incomprehensible if read in isolation from its context. It is to be read as complementary to the opening strophe which brings into prominence a union which not even death can dissolve. In such union, however, there lurks the risk of fusion which constitutes a mortal threat to love. For this reason, the final strophe points out the contrasting necessity of separation ("Flee, my beloved"). In order to love, one must be oneself. Otherness is a part of love. The separation is not aimed at a break in the loving relationship but in its renewal. The direction of the flight is in fact "the mountains of balms", precisely a metaphor for the beloved woman!

CHAPTER ELEVEN

EIGHT CONCLUSIVE THESES

To conclude this work, we shall briefly summarise the results of our research, and will do so schematically in eight theses.

1. A first result bears on the *text*. Against the various proposed emendations and against the temptation to have recourse to the ancient versions, the MT is shown, in every case, to be the most reliable, even, and above all, in those places where it offers the *lectio difficilior*, as in the *cruces interpretum* of 3:10 and 6:12. Moreover, the MT does not suggest an allegorical reading; in some cases, it excludes it categorically. Furthermore, it rejects attempts like those of G. Garbini who, starting out from the hypothesis that the present text has been the object of puritanical censoring, reconstructs a "primitive" text which is more explicitly erotic. Operations of this kind lend themselves to preconceived readings. In every case, the MT has been shown to be perfectly coherent and comprehensible.

2. The study of the structure has allowed us to grasp the *literary and poetic unity* of the Song. This is no anthology of love songs but a unitary poem that has been cleverly constructed with a Prologue, an Epilogue and a main section consisting of two symmetrical parts in each of which there is a journey from initial separation to final union, with intermediate stages of abandoning the home, searching and reciprocal admiration. The changes of voice between the two protagonists mark the major divisions of the poem. The author knows how to enter into the voice of his characters who show a real correspondence with male and female psychology.[1] The unity in question is a lyrical, not a narratival one: there is no coherent love story here. Undoubtedly, however, the sequence of the individual songs is not accidental; rather it obeys a clever compositional design. We hold, therefore, that a study

[1] "The differences in the way the poet portrays the female and male lovers reveal the poet's remarkable sensitivity to differences between women and men" (Exum [2005], 14).

of the context is unavoidable in an attempt to grasp the significance of the individual songs.

3. The study of the literary parallels has allowed us to grasp the profound links between the Song and the *love poetry of the Ancient Near East.* Despite notable affinities with the Mesopotamian poems of sacred marriage, the Song distances itself from them by its conception of love and sexuality not as fecundity and procreation, but as the personal relationship between the two partners. In this respect, there is a greater closeness to the Egyptian love songs of the Ramesside epoch from which the Song clearly draws the inspiration for its vision of love and its poetic language. On the other hand, our study has confirmed the historical location of the poem in the Hellenistic period. From the conception of love prevalent then, the Song frequently takes its distance. At the same time it draws some positive values from this source such as the valuation of the woman and the nostalgia for nature with the consequent flight from the city.

4. Perhaps precisely on account of its situation in the Hellenistic period, we can understand the *nationalistic emphasis* put on love. The woman is identified with the land, not in general, but with the land of Israel with its flowers, its fruits, its history. She has the beauty of Jerusalem and Tirzah, her head is like Carmel and Gilead, she comes from Lebanon and the desert. Here the Song is close to the book of Sirach which sees Wisdom pitching its tabernacle in the land of Israel (Sir 24). For the Song, it is love which pitches its tabernacle in Israel.

5. The Song is in dialogue with the other books of the Old Testament as well as with the surrounding cultures. From time to time, *intertextuality* has been revealed as the key to the poem's understanding, and this should not surprise us given the rather late date of composition of the book (the second half of the third century B.C.). Here too, the study of the biblical parallels, as in the case of the extra-biblical parallels, has sometimes revealed affinities, but sometimes a deliberate taking of distance. Symptomatic is the case of *t*[e]*šûqâ* 7:11 in which there is a clear echo of polemic with Gen 3:16. The Song brings human love back to its paradisial state before sin disturbed the harmony between the sexes. In a general way, one can say that Gen 2 is the filigree against which the Song should be read. Thus it shows itself to be the unconditioned exaltation of the positive nature of human love, echoing the jubilant cry of the first man: "This at last is bone of my bones and flesh of my flesh" (Gen 2:23). The reciprocity of love, the perfect parity of the sexes finds its most profound expression in the

refrain of mutual belonging: "My beloved is mine and I am his" (Song 2:16; 6:3 cf. 7:11). The garden of the Song (Song 4:12-5:1), where the water of life which wells up from Lebanon flows, is the image of the garden of Eden.

6. From the hermeneutical point of view, our study has confirmed the initial hypothesis of a metaphorical, not a materialistic or an allegorico-spiritual reading of the Song. The analysis of the individual verses has shown the perfect coherence of the literal sense of the poem. Moreover, an examination of Song 8:5 MT has led us to exclude an allegorical interpretation. The Song is speaking of human love, of the relationship between man and woman. It is a sapiential, not a prophetic book. Human love has its own value, not simply as a symbol of the relationship between God and Israel. It is true, however, that, in the vision of the Song, human love is not merely human but has in itself a supernatural dimension which is evident throughout the book. The numinous character of love, which, among the neighbouring peoples, is expressed by means of mythology, is brought in the Song into the sphere of the Yahwistic religion and finds its explanation in the final revelation: "Love is a flame of Yah" (Song 8:6). This permits us to understand how it is that the appearance of the two lovers is constantly wrapped in a numinous, theomorphic aura. Basically, this corresponds to every true experience of love.

7. The study of the Epilogue has set in relief the polemic of the Song against a type of patriarchal family, represented by the "brothers" (Song 8:8–10, cf. 1:6), and against a commercial conception of love represented by the harem of Solomon (Song 8:11–12, cf. 6:8). These are not the only polemical points. As far as society is concerned, these are linked to the polemic against the "watchmen" (3:3; 5:7), who represent the brute force which represses love, and to that against the "daughters of Jerusalem" who would like to dictate laws to love (2:7; 3:5; 8:4). To these, the woman of the Song retorts that love is a law to itself because it comes from God. The Song thus shows itself to be a great deal more than a harmless literary diversion: it is a polemical pamphlet with a programme that is revolutionary with regard to contemporary customs. We have seen, however, that it is not proposing a type of love that is outside all law. Love does not originate in society, but it must interact with it, with its limitations but also with its disciplinary potential: the garden, which is the place of love, is both nature and city. The woman is not only "friend": she is also "bride", and she introduces the man into the "house of her mother" (3:4; 8:2, 5). Alongside the watchman,

we find arrayed in the field the "mighty men of Israel" who defend love from "the terror of the night". The people of God is invited to watch the feast of love with sympathy, to welcome and protect the springing up of love in young hearts.

8. Beside the revelation of the divine nature of love, the Song makes its other great affirmation: "Love is strong as death" (Song 8:6). Here we find the condensation of the deepest conception of human love entertained by the Song. Love is not a joke; one does not play with it. It is the force of life and death. It demands everything from the one who loves. He who loves loses his freedom and his life: to love means to die to oneself, to give one's own life to the beloved. Love is therefore *strong as death*. But love is also *stronger than death*. It has won the battle with death, the ancient adversary of man. Here too the final revelation is in continuity with the rest of the poem where the theme "death-life" is revealed as a *Leitmotiv*, present in almost all the vegetable and animal metaphors, just as in the "water of life" and in the perfumes. Paradoxically, it is precisely by losing one's life that one finds it. This is the truth inherent in the seasonal myths of the Ancient Near East, and it is this which finds paradigmatic expression in the Paschal mystery of Christianity. It is the woman, whom the narrative of Paradise indicts as the cause of death to man (cf. Gen 3:12), who is presented in the Song as the fountain of life (Song 4:15).

BIBLIOGRAPHY

Abécassis, A., "Espaces de lecture du Cantique des Cantiques en contexte juif", in J. Debergé and P. Nieuviarts (eds.), *Les nouvelles voies de l'Exégèse; En lisant le Cantique des Cantiques. XIX congrès de l'ACFEB (Toulouse 2001)*, LD 190 (Paris, 2002), pp. 185–196.

Abot de Rabbi Natan, The Fathers according to Rabbi Natan. Translated from the Hebrew by J. Goldin, Yale Judaica Series 10 (New Haven, 1955).

Abot de Rabbi Natan, The Fathers according to Rabbi Natan, Version B. A Translation and Commentary by A. J. Saldarini S. J., SJLA 11 (Leiden, 1975).

Aharoni, Y., *The Land of the Bible: A Historical Geography* (London, 1979).

Alberoni, F., *Innamoramento e amore* (Milano, 2001).

Albright, W. F., "Archaic Survivals in the Text of Canticles", in D. Winton Thomas and W. D. McHardy (eds.), *Hebrew and Semitic Studies presented to G. R. Driver* (Oxford, 1963), pp. 1–7.

Alden, R. L., "Song of Songs 8,12a: Who Said It?", *JETS* 31 (1988), pp. 271–278.

Alexander, P. S., *The Targum of Canticles*, Aramaic Bible 17a (London, 2003).

Alonso Schökel, L., *Estudios de poética hebrea* (Barcelona, 1963).

——, *Manuale di poetica ebraica* (Brescia, 1989).

——, *Il Cantico dei Cantici. La dignità dell'amore* (Casale Monferrato, 1990).

Alster, B., "Sumerian Love Songs", *RA* 79 (1985), pp. 127–159.

Alter, R., *The Art of Biblical Poetry*, Basic Books (New York, 1985).

"Anacreon, Anacreontea", in *Greek Lyrik*. With an English Translation by D. A. Campbell, 5 vols., LCL (Cambridge, MA, and London, 1982–1993), vol. II, pp. 1–258.

Angénieux, J., "Structure du Cantique des Cantiques en chants encadrés par des refrains alternants", *ETL* 41 (1965), pp. 96–142.

——, "Le Cantique des Cantiques en huit chants à refrains alternants", in H. Cazelles (ed.), *De Mari à Qumran. FS J. Coppens*, BETL 24 (Gembloux, 1969), pp. 65–83.

Audet, J.-P., "Le sens du Cantique des Cantiques", *RB* 62 (1955), pp. 197–221.

Augustin, M., "Schönheit und Liebe im Hohenlied und dessen jüdische Auslegung im 1. und 2. Jahrhundert", in M. Augustin and K.-D. Schunk (eds.), *'Wünschet Jerusalem Frieden'—JOSOT Congress Jerusalem 1986*, BEAT 13 (Frankfurt, Bern and New York, 1988), pp. 395–408.

Augustine, *Confessions*, H. Chadwick (tr. and ed.) (Oxford, 1991).

Auwers, J.-M., "Les septante, lecteurs du Cantique des Cantiques", *Graphé* 8 (1999), pp. 33–47.

Avigad, N., *The Inscribed Pomegranate from the "House of the Lord"*, in *BA* 53 (1990), pp.157–166.

The Babylonian Talmud, ed. I. Epstein (London [Soncino], 1935–1948).

Barbiero, G., "L'ultimo canto dell'amata (Ct 7,10b–8,7): saggio di lettura 'metaforica'", *Sal.* 53 (1991), pp. 631–648.

——, "Die Liebe der Töchter Jerusalems. Hld 3,10b MT im Kontext vom 3,6–11", *BZ* 39 (1995), pp. 96–104.

——, "Die ‚Wagen meines edlen Volkes' (Hld 6,12): eine strukturelle Analyse", *Bib* 78 (1997a), pp. 174–189.

——, "'Senti! È il mio diletto!' (Ct 2,8–17)", in A. Bonora, M. Priotto *et al.* (eds.), *Libri sapienzali e altri scritti*, Logos 4 (Torino, 1997b), pp. 357–377.

——, *Das erste Psalmenbuch als Einheit. Eine synchrone Analyse von Psalm 1–41*, ÖBS 16 (Frankfurt a. M., 1999).

——, "Vom Schnee des Libanon und fremden Wassern: Eine strukturorientierte Interpretation von Jer 18,14", *ZAW* 114 (2002), pp. 376–390.
——, *Cantico dei cantici*, I Libri Biblici. Primo Testamento 24 (Milano, 2004).
Barr, J., *Comparative Philology and the Text of the Old Testament* (Oxford, 1968).
Barth, K., *Die kirchliche Dogmatik*, Vol. III/1 (Zürich, 1947); Vol. III/2 (Zürich, 1948).
Barthélemy, D., *Les devanciers d'Aquila*, VT.S 10 (Leiden, 1963).
——, "Comment le Cantique des Cantiques est-il devenu canonique", in A. Caquot, S. Légasse and M. Tardieu (eds.), *Mélanges bibliques et orientaux en l'honneur de M. Delcor*, AOAT 215 (Neukirchen-Vluyn, 1985), pp. 13–22.
Bartina Gassiot, S., "Los montes de Béter (Ct 2,17)", in *EstBib* 31 (1972), pp. 435–444.
Bauckham, R., "Synoptic Parousia Parables and the Apocalypse", *NTS* 23 (1977), pp. 162–176.
Beauchamp, P., *L'un et l'autre testament, Vol. II: Accomplir les Écritures* (Paris, 1990).
Bentzen, A., "Remarks on the Canonisation of the Song of Solomon", in F. Hvidberg (ed.), *Studia Orientalia Johanni Pedersen* (Hauniae, 1953), pp. 41–47.
Bergant, D., "'My Beloved Is Mine and I Am His' (Song 2:16): The Song of Songs and Honor and Shame", *Semeia* 68 (1994), pp. 23–40.
——, *Song of songs: The Love Poetry of Scripture*, Spiritual Commentaries (Hyde Park, N. Y., 1998).
Berlin, A., *The Dynamics of Biblical Parallelism* (Bloomington and Indianapolis, 1992).
Bertholet, A., "Zur Stelle Hohes Lied 4,8", in W. Frankenberg and F. Küchler (eds.), *Abhandlungen zur semitischen Religionskunde und Sprachwissenschaft, FS W. W. G. von Baudissin, BZAW* 33 (1918), pp. 47–53.
Billerbeck, P., and H. L. Strack, *Kommentar zum Neuen Testament aus Talmud und Midrasch,* 6 vols. (München, 1922–1969).
Black, F. C., "Beauty or the Beast? The Grotesque Body in the Song of Songs", *BibInt* 8 (2000), pp. 302–323.
Bloch, A., and C. Bloch, *The Song of Songs* (New York and Toronto, 1995).
Bloch, J., *A Critical Examination of the Text of the Syriac Version of the Song of Songs, AJSL* 38 (1921–1922), pp. 103–139.
Boer, R., "King Solomon Meets Annie Sprinkle", *Semeia* 82 (1998), pp. 151–182.
——, "The Second Coming: Repetition and Insatiable Desire in the Song of Songs", *BibInt* 8 (2000), pp. 276–301.
Bonhoeffer, D., *Letters and Papers from Prison* (ed. E. Bethge) (London, 1967)
Bonora, A., "Cantico dei Cantici", in A. Bonora, M. Priotto *et al.* (eds.), *Libri sapienziali e altri scritti*, Logos 4 (Torino, 1997), pp. 135–153.
Borger, R., "Die Waffenträger des Königs Darius. Ein Beitrag zur alttestamentlichen Exegese und zur semitischen Lexikographie", *VT* 22 (1972), pp. 385–398.
——, "Hiob 39,23 nach dem Qumran-Targum", *VT* 27 (1977), pp. 102–105.
Borgonovo, G., Review of Giovanni Garbini, *Cantico dei Cantici, Bib* 75 (1994), pp. 576–582.
Bosshard-Nepustil, E., "Zu Struktur und Sachprofil des Hohenliedes", *BN* 81 (1996), pp. 45–71.
Bossuet, J. B., *Libri Salomonis, Proverbia, Ecclesiastes, Canticum Canticorum, Sapienta, Ecclesiasticum* (Venezia, 1732).
Boyarin, D., "The Song of Songs: Lock or Key? Intertextuality, Allegory and Midrash", in R. M. Schwartz (ed.), *The Book and the Text. The Bible and the Literary Theory* (Oxford, 1990), pp. 214–230.
Brenner, A., "Come Back, Come Back the Shulammite", in *On Humor and the Comics in the Hebrew Bible* (Sheffield, 1990), pp. 251–276.
——, "A Note on Bat-Rabbîm (Song of Songs 7:5)", *VT* 42 (1992), pp. 113–115.
——, "The Food of Love: Gendering Food and Food Imagery in the Song of Songs", *Semeia* 86 (1999), pp. 101–112.
Bresciani, E., *Letteratura e poesia dell'Antico Egitto*, I Millenni (Torino, 1990).

Budde, K., "Das Hohelied", in K. Budde, A. Bertholet and D. G. Wildeboer, *Die fünf Megillot*, KHC 17 (Freiburg, 1898), pp. I–XXIV and 1–48.
Busenitz, I. A., "Woman's Desire for Man: Genesis 3:16 Reconsidered", *GTJ* 7 (1986), pp. 203–212.
Buzy, D., "La composition littéraire du Cantique", *RB* 49 (1940), pp. 169–194.
——, "Le Cantique des Cantiques", in L. Pirot and A. Clamer (eds.), *La Sainte Bible* (Paris, 1951), pp. 281–363.
Calame, C., *Alcman, Introduction, texte critique, témoignage et commentaire*, Roma 1983.
Campbell, I. D., "The Song of David's Son: Interpreting the Song of Solomon in the Light of the Davidic Covenant", *WTJ* 62 (2000), pp. 17–32.
Carr, D. M., "Ancient Sexuality and Divine Eros: Rereading the Bible through the Lens of the Song of Songs", *USQR* 54 (2000), pp. 1–18.
——, *The erotic word.* Sexuality, Spirituality, and the Bible (Oxford, 2003).
Casalis, G., H. Gollwitzer and R. De Pury, *Un chant d'amour insolite. Le Cantique des Cantiques* (Paris, 1984).
Castellino, G. R., *Testi sumerici e accadici* (Torino, 1977).
Catullus, *Poems*, translated by F. W. Cornish in *Catullus, Tibullus, Pervigilium Veneris*, LCL (Cambridge, MA and London, 1988), pp. 7–184.
Ceronetti, G., *Il Cantico dei Cantici*, Gli Adelphi 42 (Milano, 1996).
Chave, P., "Toward a Not Too Rosy Picture of the Song of Songs", *Feminist Theology* 18 (1998), pp. 41–53.
Childs, B. S., *Introduction to the Old Testament as Scripture* (London, 1979).
Chouraqui, A., *Le Cantique des Cantiques suivi des Psaumes* (Paris, 1970).
Cicognani, L., *Il Cantico dei Cantici. Un melodramma antichissimo* (Torino, 1911).
Clines, D. J. A., "Why is there a Song of Songs and what does it do to you if you read it?", *Jian Dao* 1 (1994), pp. 3–27.
Colombo, D., *Cantico dei Cantici*, NVB (Roma, 1975).
——, *Cantico dei Cantici*, LoB.AT (Brescia, 1985).
Cooper, J. S., "New Cuneiform Parallels to the Song of Songs", *JBL* 90 (1971), pp. 157–162.
Corney, R. W., "What Does 'Literal Meaning' Mean? Some Commentaries on the Song of Songs", *ATR* 80 (1998), pp. 494–516.
Cottini, V., "Linguaggio erotico nel Cantico e in Proverbi", *SBFLA* 40 (1990), pp. 25–45.
Dahood, M., "Hebrew-Ugaritic Lexicography II" *Bib* 45 (1964), pp. 393–412.
——, *Psalms*, AB, 3 vols. (New York, 1966–1970).
Dalman, G. H., *Palästinischer Diwan* (Leipzig, 1901).
——, *Arbeit und Sitte in Palästina*, SDPI 003.1 (Gütersloh, 1935).
Dante Alighieri, *The Divine Comedy.* With translation and comment by J. D. Sinclair, 3 vols. (New York, 1972–1978).
Davidson, R. M., "The literary structure of the Song of Songs *redivivus*", *JATS* 14 (2003) 44–65.
——, *Flame of Yahweh.* Sexuality in the Old Testament (Peabody, MA, 2007).
Davis, E. F., "Romance of the Land in the Song of Songs", *ATR* 80 (1998), pp. 533–546.
De Ena, J. E., *Sens et interprétation du Cantique des Cantiques. Sens textuel, sens directionnel et cadre du texte*, LD 194 (Paris, 2004).
De Vaux, R., "Sur le voile des femmes dans l'Orient Ancien", *RB* 44 (1933), pp. 397–412.
——, *Ancient Israel: Its Life and Institutions* (London, 1961).
Del Olmo Lete, G., *Mitos y leyendas de Canaan según la tradición de Ugarit* (Madrid, 1981).
Delitzsch, F., *Hoheslied und Kohelet*, BC IV,4 (Leipzig, 1875).
Derchain, P., "Le lotus, la mandragore et le perséa", *CÉg* 50 (1975), pp. 65–86.

Di Bianco, N., "Un'interpretazione drammatica del Cantico dei Cantici", *Aspr.* 47 (2000), pp. 27–42.
Dirksen, P. B., "Song of Songs 3,6–7", *VT* 39 (1989), pp. 219–225.
Di Sante, C., *La preghiera di Israele* (Casale Monferrato, 1985).
Donadoni, S., "Al seguito di Mehi", in H. Altenmüller *et al.* (eds.), *Hommages Fr. Daumas* (Montpellier, 1986), pp. 207–212.
Dorsey, D. A., "Literary Structuring in the Song of Songs", *JSOT* 46 (1990), pp. 81–96.
Douglas, M., *Purity and Danger: An Analysis of the Concepts of Pollution and Taboo* (London, 1966).
Driver, G. R., "Supposed Arabisms in the Old Testament", *JBL* 55 (1936), pp. 101–120.
Dubarle, A.-M., "La mention de Judith dans la littérature ancienne, juive et chrétienne", *RB* 66 (1959), pp. 514–549.
Dumais, M., "Sens de l'Écriture. Réexamen à la lumière de l'herméneutique philosophique et des approches littéraires récentes", *NTS* 45 (1999), pp. 310–331.
Eichner, J., and A. Scherer, "Die 'Teiche' von Hesbon. Eine exegetisch-archäologische Glosse zu Cant 7,5bα", *BN* 109 (2001), pp. 10–14.
Eissfeldt, O., *The Old Testament: An Introduction*, tr. P. R. Ackroyd (Oxford, 1965).
Elliott, M. T., *The Literary Unity of the Canticle*, EHS (Frankfurt, 1989).
Euringer, S., *Die Bedeutung der Peschitto für die Textkritik des Hohenliedes*, in O. Bardenhewer (ed.), *Biblische Studien*, vol. VI (Freiburg I. B., 1901), pp. 115–128.
Euripides, *Iphigenia among the Taurians, Bacchae, Iphigenia at Aulis, Rhesus. Translated with explanatory notes by J. Morwood, with introduction by E. Hall* (Oxford, 1999).
Ewald, H., *Das Hohe Lied Salomos, übersetzt mit Einleitung, Anmerkungen und einem Anhang über den Prediger* (Göttingen, 1826).
Exum, J. C., "A Literary and Structural Analysis of the Song of Songs", *ZAW* 85 (1973), pp. 47–79.
——, *Song of Songs*, OTL (Louisville, KY, 2005).
Falk, M., *Love Lyrics from the Bible: A Translation and Literary Study of the Song of Songs*, BLS (Sheffield, 1982).
Fauth, W., *Aphrodite parakyptousa. Untersuchungen zum Erscheinungsbild der vorderasiatischen Dea Prospiciens*, AAWLM.G 1966 6 (Mainz, 1967).
Feuillet, A., "La formule d'appartenance mutuelle (2,16) et les interprétations divergentes du Cantique des cantiques", *RB* 69 (1961), pp. 5–38.
——, "S'asseoir à l'ombre de l'époux (Os 14,8a et Cant 2,3)", *RB* 78 (1971), pp. 391–405.
——, "La femme vêtue de soleil (Apoc 12) et la glorification de l'Épouse du Cantique des Cantiques (6,10). Réflexions sur le progrès dans l'interprétation de l'Apocalypse et du Cantique des Cantiques", *NV* 59 (1984), pp. 36–67.
——, "Perspectives nouvelles à propos de l'interprétation du Cantique des Cantiques. Les formules de possession mutuelle de 2,16; 6,3–4; 7,11", *Div.* 31 (1990), pp. 203–219.
Fisch, H., *Poetry with Purpose: Biblical Poetics and Interpretation* (Bloomington and Indianapolis, 1990).
Flavius Josephus, *Against Apion*, translation and commentary by J. M. G. Barclay, in S. Mason (ed.), *Flavius Josephus Translation and Commentary*, vol. 10 (Leiden and Boston, 2007).
——, *Antiquities of the Jews.* Whiston's Translation Revised by A. R. Shilleto, Bohn Standard Library—The Works of Flavius Josephus, 2 vols. (London, 1911–1912).
Fokkelmann, J. P., *Reading Biblical Poetry: An Introductory Guide* (Louisville, London and Leiden, 2001).
Fox, M. W., *The Song of Songs and the Ancient Egyptian Love Songs* (London, 1985).
Fuerst, W. J., *The Books of Ruth, Esther, Ecclesiastes, the Song of Songs, Lamentations*, CBC (Cambridge, 1975).
Gadamer, H.-G., *Wahrheit und Methode. Grundzüge einer philosophischen Hermeneutik* (Tübingen, 1965).
Galling, K., "Der Ehrenname Elisas und die Entrückung Elias", *ZThK* 53 (1956), pp. 29–148.

Gangloff, F., "YHWH ou les déesses-arbres? (Osée XIV 6–8)", *VT* 49 (1999), pp. 34–48.
Garbini, G., "La datazione del Cantico dei Cantici", *RSO* 56 (1982), pp. 39–46.
——, *Cantico dei cantici*, Biblica 2 (Brescia, 1992).
García Martínez, F., *The Dead Sea Scrolls Translated: The Qumran Texts in English* (Leiden, 1994).
Garrett, D. A., *Proverbs, Ecclesiastes, Song of Songs* (Nashville, TN, 1993).
Garrett, D., and P. R. House, *Song of Songs/Lamentations*, WBC 23B (Nashville, 2004).
Gebhardt, C., *Das Lied der Lieder* (Berlin, 1931).
Genette, G., *Introduction à l'architexte*, in G. Genette - T. Todorov (eds.), *Théorie des genres* (Paris, 1986), pp. 89–159.
Genovese, A., "La ricerca di Dio: il Cantico dei Cantici e le Confessioni", *RVS* 55 (2001), pp. 685–696.
Gerleman, G., *Ruth, Das Hohelied*, BK 18 (Neukirchen-Vluyn, 1965).
Gilbert, M., "Ben Sira et la femme", *RTL* 7 (1976), pp. 426–442.
Ginsburg, C. D., *The Song of Songs and Cohelet* (New York, 1970).
Ginzberg, L., *The Legends of the Jews*, 2 vols. (Philadelphia, 2003).
Glazier-McDonald, B., "Malachi 2,12: *'er w^{e}'ōneh*—Another Look", *JBL* 105 (1986), pp. 295–298.
Goodman, M., "Sacred Scripture and 'Defiling the Hands'", JTS 41 (1990), pp. 99–107.
Gordis, R., *The Song of Songs and Lamentations: A Study, Modern Translation and Commentary* (New York, 1974).
Görg, M., "Die 'Sänfte Salomos' nach HL 3,9f", *BN* 18 (1982), pp. 15–25.
——, "Travestien im Hohen Lied. Eine kritische Betrachtung am Beispiel von Hld 1,5f", *BN* 38/39 (1983), pp. 101–115.
——, "'Kanäle' oder 'Zweige' in Hld 4,13", *BN* 72 (1993), pp. 20–23.
Goulder, M. D., *The Song of Fourteen Songs*, JSOT.S 36 (Sheffield, 1986).
Graetz, H., *Schir Ha-Scirim oder das salomonische Hohelied* (Wien, 1871).
Greenfield, J. C., Review of D. W. Thomas and W. D. McHardy (eds.), *Hebrew and Semitic Studies Presented to G. R. Driver*, *JAOS* 85 (1965), pp. 256–258.
Greenspahn, F. E., *Hapax Legomena in Biblical Hebrew: A Study of the Phenomenon and Its Treatment Since Antiquity with Special Reference to Verbal Forms*, SBL.DS 74 (Chico, 1984).
Gregorius Magnus, *Omelie su Ezechiele*, vol. I, in M. Adriaen, V. Recchia and E. Gandolfo (eds.), *Opere di Gregorio Magno* 3/1 (Roma, 1992).
Grober, S. F., "The Hospitable Lotus: A Cluster of Metaphors. An inquiry into the problem of textual unity in the Song of Songs", *Semitics* 9 (1984), pp. 86–112.
Grossberg, D., "Canticles 3:10 on the Light of a Homeric Analogue and Biblical Poetics", *BTB* 11 (1981), pp. 74–76.
——, *Centripetal and Centrifugal Structures in Hebrew Poetry* (Atlanta, 1989).
——, "Two Kinds of Sexual Relationship in the Hebrew Bible", *HebStud* 75 (1994), pp. 7–25.
Gruber, M. I., "Ten Dance-Derived Expressions in the Hebrew Bible", *Bib* 62 (1981), pp. 328–346.
Haller, M., "Das Hohe Lied", in K. Galling and M. Haller, *Die fünf Megillot*, HAT 18 (Tübingen, 1940), pp. 21–46.
Hallo, W. W., "'As the Seal upon thine Arm': Glyptic Metaphors in the Biblical World", in L. Gorelick and E. Williams-Forte (eds.), *Ancient Seals and the Bible* (Malibu, 1983), pp. 7–17.
——, "'As the Seal upon Thy Hearth': Glyptic Roles in the Biblical World", *BiRev* 1 (1985), pp. 20–27.
——, "For Love Is Strong as Death", *JANES* 22 (1993), pp. 45–50.
Hamp, V., "Zur Textkritik am Hohenlied", *BZ* 1 (1957), pp. 197–215.

Harper, A., *The Song of Solomon, with Introduction and Notes* (Cambridge, 1907).
Haupt, P., *Biblische Liebeslieder. Das sogenannte Hohelied Salomos* (Leipzig, 1907).
Heinevetter, H.-J., *'Komm nun, mein Liebster, Dein Garten ruft Dich!'. Das Hohelied als programmatische Komposition*, BBB 69 (Frankfurt, 1988).
Hengel, M., *Judentum und Hellenismus*, WUNT 10 (Tübingen, 1973).
Hepper, F. N., *Pflanzenwelt der Bibel. Eine illustrierte Enzyklopädie* (Stuttgart, 1992).
Hermann, A., *Altägyptische Liebesdichtung* (Wiesbaden, 1959).
Hirschberg, H. H., "Some Additional Arabic Etimologies in Old Testament Lexicography", *VT* 11 (1961), pp. 373–385.
Hirt, J. F., *De coronis apud ebraeos nuptialibus* (Jena, 1748).
Holladay, W. L., *Jeremiah*, 2 vols., Hermeneia (Philadelphia, 1986–1989).
Holman, J., "A Fresh Attempt to Understand the Imagery of Canticles 3:6–11", in K.-D. Schunk and M. Augustin (eds.), *'Lasset uns Brücke bauen...'*, BEAT 42 (Frankfurt, 1998), pp. 303–309.
Homer, *Iliad. With an English translation of A. T. Murray revised by W. F. Wyatt*, LCL 170–171, 2 vols. (Cambridge, MA, and London, 1999).
——, *The Odyssey. With an English translation by A. T. Murray, revised by G. E. Dimock*, LCL 104–105, 2 vols. (Cambridge, MA, and London, 1995).
Horn, H.-J., "Respiciens per fenestras, prospiciens per cancellos", *JAC* 10 (1967), pp. 30–60.
Horst, F., "Die Formen des althebräischen Liebesliedes" in Id., *Gottes Recht. Studien zum Recht im Alten Testament*, TB 12 (München, 1981), pp. 176–187.
Hostetter, E. C., "Mistranslation in Cant 1,5", *AUSS* 34 (1996), pp. 35–36.
Hunter, J. H., "The Song of Protest: Reassessing the Song of Songs", *JSOT* 90 (2000), pp. 109–124.
Hutmacher, H. A., *Symbolik der biblischen Zahlen und Zeiten* (Paderborn, 1993).
Hwang, A., "The New Structure of the Song of Songs and Its Implications for Interpretation", *WTJ* 65 (2003) 97–111.
Isserlin, B. S. J., "Song of Songs 4,4: An Archaeological Note", *PEQ* 90 (1958), pp. 59–60.
Jacobsen, T., "Religious Drama in Ancient Mesopotamia", in H. Goedicke and J. J. M. Roberts (eds.), *Unity and Diversity: Essays in the History, Literature, and Religion of the Ancient Near East* (Baltimore and London, 1975), pp. 65–97.
——, *The Harps That Once...: Sumerian Poetry in Translation* (New Haven and London, 1987).
Jagersma, H., *A History of Israel from Alexander the Great to Bar Kochba* (Philadelphia, 1986).
Jastrow, M., *A Dictionary of the Targumim, the Talmud Babli and Jerushalmi, and the Midrashic Literature* (Philadelphia, 1903).
St. John of the Cross, *The Collected Works, translated by K. Kavanaugh and O. Rodriguez, with introduction of K. Kavanaugh* (Washington, DC, 1973).
Joüon, P., *Le Cantique de Cantiques. Commentaire philologique et exégétique* (Paris, 1909).
——, *Grammaire de l'hébreu biblique* (Roma, 1923).
——, "Notes de lexicographie hébraique", *Bib* 6 (1925), pp. 311–321.
Kaiser, O., *Introduction to the Old Testament: A Presentation of its Results and Problems* (Minneapolis, MI, 1975).
Keel, O., *Vögel als Boten*, OBO 14 (Fribourg and Göttingen, 1977).
——, *The Symbolism of the Biblical World.* Ancient Near Eastern Iconography and the Book of Psalms (New York, 1978).
——, *Das Böcklein in der Milch seiner Mutter und Verwandtes: im Lichte eines altorientalischen Bildmotivs*, OBO 33 (Fribourg and Göttingen, 1980).
——, *Deine Blicke sind Tauben. Zur Metaphorik des Hohen Liedes*, SBS 114/115 (Stuttgart, 1984a).

——, *Die Welt der altorientalischen Bildsymbolik und das Alte Testament. Am Beispiel der Psalmen* (Zürich and Neukirchen-Vluyn, 1984b).
——, "Hoheslied", in M. Görg (ed.), *Neues Bibel Lexikon* (Zürich, 1991–), coll. 183–191.
——, *The Song of Songs*, A Continental Commentary (Minneapolis, MI, 1994) (French tr., *Le Cantique des Cantiques* [Fribourg, 1997]).
Keel, O., and M. Küchler, *Orte und Landschaften der Bibel. Ein Handbuch und Studien-Reiseführer zum Heiligen Land. Band 2: Der Süden* (Zürich and Göttingen, 1982).
Keel, O., M. Küchler, and C. Uehlinger, *Orte und Landschaften der Bibel. Ein Handbuch und Studienreiseführer zum Heiligen Land, Band 1: Geographisch-geschichtliche Landeskunde* (Zürich and Göttingen, 1984).
Keel, O., and C. Uehlinger, *Göttinnen, Götter und Gottessymbole. Neue Erkenntnisse zur Religionsgeschichte Kanaans und Israels aufgrund bislang unerschlossener ikonographischer Quellen*, QD 134 (Freiburg, Basel, and Wien, 1992).
Kieweler, H. V., *Ben Sira zwischen Judentum und Hellenismus*, BEAT 30 (Frankfurt, 1992).
Kingsmill, E., *The Song of Songs and the Eros of God. A Study in Biblical Intertextuality*, OTM (Oxford, 2010).
König, E., *Historisch-comparative Syntax der hebräischen Sprache* (Leipzig, 1897).
Kramer, S. N., *The Sacred Marriage Rite. Aspects of Faith, Myth, and Ritual in Ancient Sumer* (London, 1969) (cf. also → Wolkstein).
Krauss, S., "Der richtige Sinn von 'Schrecken in der Nacht' Hld 3,8", in B. Schindler and A. Marmorstein (eds.), *Occident and Orient, FS M. Gaster* (London, 1936), pp. 323–330.
Kreeft, P., *Three philosophies of life. Ecclesiastes: life as vanity; Job: life as suffering; Song of Songs: life as love* (San Francisco, 1989).
Krinetzki, G., "Hoheslied" in W. Dommershausen and G. Krinetzki, *Ester, Hoheslied*, NEB.AT (Würzburg, 1980).
——, *Kommentar zum Hohenlied. Bildsprache und theologische Botschaft*, BET 16 (Frankfurt, 1981).
Krinetzki, L., "Die Macht der Liebe. Eine ästhetisch-exegetische Untersuchung zu Hld 8,6–7", *MTZ* 13 (1962), pp. 256–279.
——, *Das Hohelied. Kommentar zu Gestalt und Kerygma eines alttestamenltichen Liebesliedes*, KBANT (Düsseldorf, 1964).
——, "Die erotische Psychologie des Hohen Liedes", *TQ* 150 (1970), pp. 404–416.
Kristeva, J., *Histoires d'amour* (Paris, 1983).
Kugel, L., *The Idea of Biblical Poetry. Parallelism and Its History* (New Haven and London, 1981).
Kuhn, G., "Erklärung des Hohenliedes", *NKZ* 37 (1926), pp. 501–10, 521–572.
Kuhn, P., "Jüdische Hoheliedexegese seit dem Beginn der Aufklärung", *Nordisk Judaistik - Scandinavian Jewish Studies* 12 (1991), pp. 83–92.
Lacocque, A., "La Shulamite et les chars d'Aminadab. Un essai herméneutique sur Cantique 6,12–7,1", *RB* 102 (1995), pp. 330–347.
——, *Romance, She Wrote. A Hermeneutical Essay on Song of Songs* (Harrisburg, PA, 1998).
Lambert, W. G., "The Problem of the Love Lyrics" in H. Goedicke and J. J. M. Roberts (eds.), *Unity and Diversity: Essays in the History, Literature and Religion of the Ancient Near East* (Baltimore and London, 1975), pp. 98–135.
Landy, F., *Paradoxes of Paradise: Identity and Difference in the Song of Songs*, BLS 7 (Sheffield, 1983).
Lavoie, J.-J., "Le Cantique des Cantiques ou quand l'amour habite la distance", *Revue Scriptura* 14 (1993), pp. 73–91.
——, "Festin érotique et tendresse cannibalique dans le Cantique des Cantiques", *SR* 24 (1995), pp. 131–146.

Levinas, E., *Le temps et l'autre* (Paris, 1983).
Linafelt, T., "Biblical Love Poetry (...and God)", *JAAR* 70 (2002), pp. 323–345.
Lohfink, N., Review of R. E. Murphy, *The Wisdom Literature*, *TP* 58 (1983), pp. 239–241.
Lombard, D., "Le Cantique des Cantiques (3,6 – 5,1)", *Sémiotique et Bible* (1992), pp. 45–52.
Longman, T., *Song of Songs*, NICOT (Grand Rapids, MI, and Cambridge, UK, 2001).
Longus, *Daphnis and Chloe. Translated with an introduction and commentary by J. R. Morgan*, Aris & Phillips Classical Texts (Oxford, 2004).
Loretz, O., "Zum Problem des Eros im Hohenlied", *BZ* 8 (1964), pp. 191–216.
——, *Das althebräische Liebeslied: Untersuchungen zur Stychometrie und Redaktionsgeschichte des Hohenliedes und des 45. Psalms*, AOAT 14/1 (Neukirchen-Vluyn, 1971).
——, "Cant 4,8 auf dem Hintergrund ugaritischer und assyrischer Beschreibungen des Libanons und Antilibanons", in D. R. Daniels, U. Glessmer and M. Rosel (eds.), *Ernten, was man sät, FS K. Koch* (Neukirchen-Vluyn 1991), pp. 130–137.
——, "Siegel als Amulette und Grabbeigaben in Mesopotamien und HL 8,6–7", *UF* 25 (1993), pp. 237–246.
Löw, I., *Die Flora der Juden*, 4 vols. (Wien and Leipzig, 1926–1934).
Löwysohn, S., *melisat jeshurun* (Wien, 1816).
Lundbom, J. R., "Song of Songs 3:1–4", *Int* 49 (1995), pp. 172–175.
Luzarraga, J., "El Cantar de los Cantares en el Canon bíblico", *Greg.* 83 (2002), pp. 5–63.
——, *Cantar de los Cantares.* Sendas del Amor (Estella, 2005).
Lys, D., *Le plus beau chant de la création. Commentaire du Cantique des Cantiques*, LD 51 (Paris, 1968).
McKane, W., *A Critical and Exegetical Commentary on Jeremiah*, 2 vols, ICC (Edinburgh, 1986–1996).
McKay, J. W., "Helel and the Dawn-Goddess. A Re-examination of the Myth in Isaiah 14,12–25", *VT* 20 (1970), pp. 451–464.
McWhirter, J., *The Bridegroom Messiah and the People of God* (Cambridge, 2006).
Maier, J., *Die Texte vom Toten Meer*, 2 vols. (München and Basel, 1960).
Malul, M., "Janus Parallelism in Biblical Hebrew: Two More Cases (Canticles 4:9, 12)", *BZ* 41 (1997), pp. 246–249.
Marchese, A., *Dizionario di retorica e di stilistica* (Milano, 1979).
Mariaselvam, A., *The Song of Songs and Ancient Tamil Love Poems. Poetry and Symbolism*, AnBib 118 (Roma, 1988).
Martin, F., *Pour une théologie de la lettre. L'inspiration des Écritures*, Cogitatio Fidei (Paris, 1996).
Mathews, J., *Abraham ibn Ezra's Commentary on the Canticles, After the First Recension: Edited with Two Mss., with a Translation* (London, 1874).
Mathieu, B., *La poésie amoureuse de l'Égypte Ancienne.* Recherche sur un genre littéraire au Nouvel Empire (Cairo, 1996).
May, H. G., "Some Cosmic Connotations of Mayim Rabbîm 'Many Waters'", *JBL* 74 (1955), pp. 9–21.
Mazor, Y., "The Song of Songs or the Story of Stories? The Song of Songs: Between Genre and Unity", *SJOT* 4 (1990), pp. 1–29.
Meek, T. J., "Canticles and the Tammuz Cult", *AJSL* 39 (1922–1923), pp. 1–14.
——, "Babylonian Parallels to the Song of Songs", *JBL* 43 (1924), pp. 245–252.
——, "The Song of Songs and the Fertility Cult", in W. H. Schoff (ed.), *A Symposium on the Song of Songs* (Philadelphia, 1924), pp. 48–79.
——, *The Song of Songs*, in *The Interpreter's Bible*, vol. V (New York and Nashville, 1956), pp. 89–148.

Meloni, P., *Il profumo dell'immortalità. L'interpretazione patristica di Ct 1,3* (Roma, 1975).
Midrash Rabbah Song of Songs, tr. M. Simon, in *The Midrash Rabbah* vol. IV, *Lamentations, Ruth, Ecclesiastes, Esther, Song of Songs*, eds. H. Freedman and M. Simon (London, Jerusalem and New York, 1977).
Minocchi, S., *Il Cantico dei cantici di Salomone tradotto e commentato con uno studio sulla donna e l'amore nell'Antico Oriente* (Roma, 1898).
The Mishnah. A New Translation by Jacob Neusner (New Haven and London, 1988).
Moldenke, H. N., and A. L. Moldenke, *Plants of the Bible* (Waltham, 1952).
Morfino, M. M., "Il Cantico dei Cantici e il patto elettivo. Possibili connessioni", *Theologica et Historica* 5 (1996), pp. 7–42.
Morla, V. A., *Poemas de amor y de deseo. Cantar de los Cantares* (Estella, 2004).
Moscati, S., "I sigilli nell'Antico Testamento", *Bib* 30 (1949), pp. 314–338.
Mulder, M. J., "Does Canticles 6,12 Make Sense?", in F. García Martínez, A. Hilhost and C. J. Labuschagne (eds.), *The Scriptures and the Scrolls, FS A. S. Van der Woude*, VT.S 49 (Leiden, 1992), pp. 104–113.
Müller, H.-P., "Die lyrische Reproduction des Mythischen im Hohenlied", *ZTK* 73 (1976), pp. 23–41.
——, "Neige der althebräischen 'Weisheit'", *ZAW* 90 (1978), pp. 238–264.
——, *Vergleich und Metapher im Hohenlied*, OBO 56 (Fribourg and Göttingen, 1984).
——, "Begriffe menschlicher Theomorphie. Zu einigen cruces interpretum in Hld 6,10", *ZAH* 1 (1988a), pp. 112–121.
——, "Hld 4,12–5,1: ein althebräisches Paradigma poetischer Sprache", *ZAH* 1 (1988b), pp. 191–201.
——, "Das Hohelied", in H.-P. Müller, O. Kaiser and J. A. Loader, *Das Hohelied, Klagelieder, Das Buch Ester*, ATD 16/2 (Göttingen, 1992), pp. 1–90.
——, "Kohelet und Amminadab", in A. A. Diesel, R. G. Lehmann, E. Otto and A. Wagner (eds.), *'Jedes Ding hat seine Zeit...'. Studien zur israelitischen und altorientalischen Weisheit, FS D. Michel*, BZAW 241 (Berlin and New York, 1996), pp. 149–165.
——, "Travestien und geistige Landschaften. Zum Hintergrund einiger Motive bei Kohelet und im Hohenlied", *ZAW* 109 (1997), pp. 555–574.
——, "Eine Parallele zur Weingartenmetapher des Hohenliedes aus der frühgriechischen Lyrik", in M. Dietrich and I. Kottsieper (eds.), *'Und Mose schrieb dieses Lied aus...'. Studien zum Alten Testament und zum Alten Orient, FS O. Loretz* (München, 1998), pp. 569–584.
——, "Der Libanon in altorientalischen Quellen und im Hohenlied. Paradigma einer poetischen Topographie", *ZDPV* 117 (2001a), pp. 116–128.
——, "Der Mond und die Plejaden. Griechisch-orientalische Parallelen", *VT* 51 (2001b), pp. 206–218.
Munro, J. M., *Spikenard and Saffron: A Study in the Poetic Language of the Song of Songs*, JSOT.S 203 (Sheffield, 1995).
Murphy, R. E., *The Song of Songs*, Hermeneia (Minneapolis, 1990).
Neumann, E., *Die große Mutter. Der Archetiyp des Großen Weiblichen* (Darmstadt, 1957).
Niccacci, A., "Cantico dei Cantici e canti d'amore egiziani", *SBFLA* 41 (1991), pp. 61–85.
Nissinen, M., "Love Lyrics of Nabû and Tashmetu: An Assyrian Song of Songs?", in M. Dietrich and I. Kottsieper (eds.), *'Und Mose schrieb dieses Lied auf', Studien zum Alten Testament und zum Alten Orient, FS O. Loretz* (Münster, 1998), pp. 585–634.
Nolli, G., *Cantico dei Cantici*, SB[T] (Torino and Roma, 1967).

Ogden, G. S., "Some Translational Issues in the Song of Songs", *BT* 41 (1990), pp. 222–227.

——, "'Black but beautiful' (Song of Songs 1:5)", *BT* 47 (1996), pp. 443–445.

Origen, *The Song of Songs Commentary and Homilies. Translated and annotated by R. P. Lawson*, Ancient Christian Writers 26 (Westminster and London, 1957).

Otto, R., *Das Heilige* (München, 1963).

Pahk, J. Y. S., *Il canto della gioia in Dio. L'itinerario sapienziale espresso dall'unità letteraria in Qohelet 8,16–9,10 e il parallelo di Gilgames Me. Iii*, Istituto Universitario Orientale, Dipartimento di Studi Asiatici, Series Minor 52 (Napoli, 1996).

Paul, M., "Die 'fremde Frau' in Sprichwörter 1–9 und die 'Geliebte' des Hohenliedes. Ein Beitrag zur Intertextualität", *BN* 106 (2001), pp. 40–46.

Paul, S. M., "Unrecognized Medical Idiom in Canticles 6:12 and Job 9:21", *Bib* 59 (1978), pp. 545–547.

——, "The 'Plural of Ecstasy' in Mesopotamian and Biblical Love Poetry", in Z. Zevit, S. Gitin and M. Sokoloff (eds.), *Solving Riddles and Untying Knots* (Winona Lake, 1995), pp. 585–597.

——, "A Lover's Garden of Verse: Literal and Metaphorical Imagery in Ancient Near Eastern Love Poetry", in M. Cogan *et al.* (eds.), *Tehillah le-Moshe* (Winona Lake, 1997), pp. 99–110.

Paz, O., *Obra poética I* , Obras completas 11 (México, 2001).

Pelletier, A.-M., *Lectures du Cantique des Cantiques. De l'énigme du sens aux figures du lecteur*, AnBib 121 (Roma, 1989).

——, "Petit bilan herméneutique de l'histoire du Cantique des Cantiques", *Graphé* 8 (1999), pp. 185–200.

Plato, *Laws. With an English translation by R. G. Bury*, 2 vols., LCL (London and New York, 1926).

Pope, M. H., *Song of Songs. A New Translation with Introduction and Commentary*, AB 7C (New York, 1977).

Pouget, G., and J. Guitton, *Le Cantique des Cantiques*, EtB (Paris, 1934).

Poulssen, N., "Vluchtwegen in Hooglied 8,14. Over de meerzinnigheid van een slotvers," *Bijdr.* 50 (1989), pp. 72–82.

Propp, H. W., "On Hebrew *śade(h)* 'Highland'", *VT* 37 (1987), pp. 230–236.

Provan, I., *Ecclesiastes and Song of Songs*, NIVAC (Grand Rapids, 2001).

Rabin, C., "The Song of Songs and Tamil Poetry", *SR* 3 (1973), pp. 205–219.

Racine, J.-F., "Pour en finir avec le sens littéral de l'Écriture", *EeT* 30 (1999), pp. 199–214.

Ravasi, G., *Cantico dei Cantici* (Cinisello Balsamo, 1990).

——, *Il Cantico dei Cantici. Commento e attualizzazione*, Testi e Commenti 4 (Bologna, 1992).

Regalzi, G., "'Bella come una Grazia, terribile come…'. A proposito di Ct 6,4", *Henoch* 23 (2001), pp. 139–145.

Renan, E., *Le Cantique des Cantiques* (Paris, 1884).

Rendtorff, R., *The Old Testament: An Introduction* (London, 1985).

Reventlow, H. Graf, "Hoheslied, I Altes Testament", *TRE* 15 (Berlin, 1986), pp. 499–502.

Ricciotti, G., *Il Cantico dei cantici. Versione critica del testo ebraico con introduzione e commento* (Torino, 1928).

Ricoeur, P., *La métaphore vive* (Paris, 1975).

——, *Interpretation Theory.* Discourse and the Surplus of Meaning (Forth Worth, TX, 1976).

——, "The Nuptial Metaphor", in A. Lacocque and P. Ricoeur, *Thinking Biblically* (Chicago, 1998), pp. 265–303.

Riedel, W., *Die Auslegung des Hohensliedes in der jüdischen Gemeinde und der griechischen Kirche* (Leipzig, 1898).

Ringgren, H., "Das Hohe Lied", in H. Ringgren, A. Weiser and W. Zimmerli, *Sprüche, Prediger, Das Hohe Lied, Klagelieder, Das Buch Esther*, ATD (Göttingen, 1962), pp. 255–293.
Robert, A., and R. Tournay, *Le Cantique des Cantiques. Traduction et commentaire*, EtB (Paris, 1963).
Roberts, D. Ph., *Let me See your Form. Seeking Poetic Structure in the Song of Songs*, Studies in Judaism (Lanham, MD, *et al.*, 2007).
Rosenzweig, F., *The Star of Redemption*. Tr. by B. E. Galli, Modern Jewish Philosophy and Religion (Madison, WI, 2005).
Rousset, J., *Leurs yeux se rencontrèrent. La scène de première vue dans le roman* (Paris, 1984).
Rowley, H. H., "The Meaning of 'The Shulammite'", *AJSL* 56 (1939), pp. 84–91.
Rudolph, W., *Das Buch Ruth, Das Hohe Lied, Die Klagelieder*, KAT 17 (Gütersloh, 1962).
Rundgren, F., "*'appirjon* 'Tragsessel, Sänfte'", *ZAW* 74 (1962), pp. 70–72.
Sacchi, P., "Il Cantico dei Cantici. Riflessioni sulla recente edizione di Giovanni Garbini", *Henoch* 15 (1993), pp. 291–298.
Sæbø, M., "On the Canonicity of the Song of Songs", in M. V. Fox *et al.* (eds.), *Texts, Temples, and Traditions, FS M. Haran* (Winona Lake, 1996), pp. 267–277.
Salvaneschi, E., *Cantico dei cantici. Interpretatio ludica* (Genova, 1982).
Sanders, J. T., *Ben Sira and Demotic Wisdom*, SBL.MS 28 (Chico, 1983).
"Sappho", in *Greek Lyric*. With an English Translation of D. A. Campbell, 5 vols., LCL (Cambridge, MA, and London, 1982–1993), vol. I, pp. 2–205.
Sasson, V., "King Solomon and the Dark Lady in the Song of Songs", *VT* 39 (1989), pp. 407–414.
Schäfer, P., *Mirror of His Beauty. Feminine Images of God from the Bible to the Early Kabbalah* (Princeton, 2002).
Schedl, C., *Baupläne des Wortes. Einführung in die biblische Logotechnik* (Wien, 1974).
Schmökel, H., "Zur kultischen Deutung des Hohenliedes", *ZAW* 64 (1952), pp. 148–155.
——, *Heilige Hochzeit und Hoheslied*, AKM 32/1 (Wiesbaden, 1956).
Schmuttermayr, G., "Ohne Gott und ohne Religion? Anmerkungen zur theologischen Relevanz des Hohenliedes", in E. Mode and T. Schieder (eds.), *Den Glauben verantworten. FS H. Petri* (Paderborn *et al.*, 2000), pp. 29–40.
Schott, S., *Altägyptische Liebeslieder* (Zürich, 1950).
Schouten van der Welden, A., *Tierwelt der Bibel* (Stuttgart, 1992).
Schroer, S., *In Israel gab es Bilder. Nachrichten von darstellender Kunst im Alten Testament*, OBO 74 (Fribourg and Göttingen, 1987).
Schürer, E., *The History of the Jewish People in the Age of Jesus Christ (175 B.C.–A.D. 135)*, vol. I (Edinburgh, 1973).
Schweizer, H., "Erkennen und Lieben. Zur Semantik und Pragmatik der Modalitäten am Beispiel von Hld 4", in W. Gross *et al.* (eds.), *Text, Methode und Grammatik, FS W. Richter* (St. Ottilien, 1991), pp. 423–444.
Schwienhorst-Schönberger, L., "Das Hohelied", in E. Zenger *et al.*, *Einleitung in das Alte Testament*, Studienbücher Theologie 1,1 (Stuttgart, 2001[4]), pp. 344–351.
Segal, M. H., "The Song of Songs", *VT* 12 (1962), pp. 470–490.
Shea, W. H., "The Chiastic Structure of the Song of Songs", *ZAW* 92 (1980), pp. 73–93.
Siegfried, C., "Hoheslied" in W. Frankenberg and C. Siegfried, *Die Sprüche, Prediger und Hoheslied*, HKAT 2/3 (Göttingen, 1898), pp. 78–126.
Smither, P. C., "Prince Mehi of the Love Songs", *JEA* 34 (1948), p. 116.
Sonnet, J.-P., "'Figures (anciennes et nouvelles) du lecteur'. Du Cantique des Cantiques au Livre entier", *NRT* 113 (1991), pp. 75–86.

——, "Le Cantique, entre érotique et mystique: sanctuaire de la parole échangée", *NRT* 119 (1997), pp. 481–502.
Sophocles, *Antigone—The Women of Trachis—Philoctetes—Oedipus at Colonus.* Ed. and tr. by H. Lloyd-Jones, LCL 21 (Cambridge, MA, and London, 1994).
Soulen, R. N., "The *waṣf* of the Song of Songs and Hermeneutic", *JBL* 86 (1967), pp. 183–190.
Stadelmann, L., *Love and Politics. A New Commentary on the Song of Songs* (New York and Mahwah, 1992).
Stephan, St. H., "Modern Palestinian Parallels to the Song of Songs", *JPOS* 2 (1922), pp. 199–278.
Stolz, F., "Die Bäume des Gottesgartens auf dem Libanon", *ZAW* 84 (1972), pp. 141–156.
Stoop-van Paridon, P. W. T., *The Song of Songs.* A Philological Analysis of the Hebrew Book *šîr haššîrîm*, Ancient Near Eastern Studies Supplement 17 (Louvain, Paris and Dudley, MA, 2005).
Tait, M. B., Review of McWhirter (2006) in *RRT* 14 (2007), pp. 484–486.
——, "Till Death do us Join: Resurrection as Marriage in Ps 49:16", *RivB* 56 (2008), pp. 177–198.
——, "Jesus, the Divine Bridegroom, in Mark 2:18–22—Mark's Christology Upgraded", unpublished doctoral dissertation (University of Manchester, 2008).
Targum on the Song of Songs, cf. →Alexander.
Tcherikover, V., *Hellenistic Civilization and the Jews* (New York, 1975).
Theocritus, "The Poems", in *The Greek Bucolic Poets.* With an English translation by J. M. Edmonds, LCL (London and New York, 1923), pp. 1–381.
Thilo, M., *Das Hohelied* (Bonn, 1921).
Tidemann, W., *Philosophie des Schicksals* (Bremen, 1979).
The Tosefta. Translated from the Hebrew with a New Introduction by J. Neusner, 2 vols. (Peabody, MA, 2002).
Tournay, R., "Abraham et le Cantique des Cantiques", *VT* 25 (1975), pp. 544–552.
——, *Quand Dieu parle aux hommes le langage de l'amour. Études sur le Cantique des Cantiques*, CRB 21 (Paris, 1982).
Tov, E., "Three Manuscripts (Abbreviated Texts?) of Canticles from Qumran Cave 4", *JJS* 46 (1995), pp. 88–111.
Trenchard, W. C., *Ben Sira's Wiew of Women: A Literary Analysis*, BJSt 8 (Missoula, 1982).
Trible, P., "Love's Lyric Redeemed", in A. Brenner (ed.), *A Feminist Companion to the Song of Songs* (Sheffield, 1993), pp. 100–120.
Tromp, N. J., "Wisdom and the Canticle. Ct 8,6c–7b: Text Character, Message and Import", in M. Gilbert (ed.), *La sagesse de l'Ancien Testament*, BETL 51 (Leuven, 1979), pp. 88–95.
——, *Mens is meervoud. Het hooglied*, Cahiers Voor Levensverdieping 38 (Altiora and Averbode, 1982).
Urbach, E. E., "The Homiletical Interpretations of the Sages and the Exposition of Origen on Canticles, and the Jewish-Christian Disputation", *Scripta Herosolymitana* 22 (1971), pp. 247–275.
Vaccari, A., "Note critiche ed esegetiche (Ct 5,12)", *Bib* 28 (1947), pp. 398–401.
——, "La Cantica", in *La Sacra Bibbia: I libri poetici*, vol II (Firenze, 1959).
Van der Toorn, K., "The Significance of the Veil in the Ancient Near East", in D. P. Wright (ed.), *Pomegranates and Golden Bells, FS J. Milgrom* (Winona Lake, 1995), pp. 327–339.
Van Dijk-Hemmes, F., "The Imagination of Power and the Power of Imagination", *JSOT* 44 (1989), pp. 75–88.
Van Leeuwen, N. D., "De mishandeling der vrow in Hooglied 5:7", in *GThT* (1923), pp. 201–203.

Viviers, H., "Die Besweringsrefrein in Hooglied 2,7; 3,5 en 8,4", *Skrif En Kerk* 10 (1989), pp. 80–89.
——, "Clothed and unclothed in the Song of Songs", *OTE* 12 (1999), pp. 609–622.
Von Speyr, A., *Das Hohelied* (Einsiedeln, 1972).
Wagner, M., *Die lexikalischen und grammatikalischen Aramaismen im alttestamentlichen Hebräisch*, BZAW 96 (Berlin, 1966).
Waldman, N. M., "A Note on Canticles 4:9", *JBL* 89 (1970), pp. 215–216.
Watson, W. G. E., *Classical Hebrew Poetry*, JSOT.S 26 (Sheffield, 1984).
——, *Some Ancient Near Eastern Parallels to the Song of Songs*, in J. Davies, G. Harvey and W. G. E. Watson (eds.), *Words Remembered, Text Renewed, FS J. F. A. Sawyer*, JSOT.S 195 (Sheffield, 1995), pp. 253–271.
——, "Love and Death Once More (Song of Songs 8:6)", *VT* (1997), pp. 384–387.
Webster, E. C., "Pattern in the Song of Songs", *JSOT* 22 (1982), pp. 73–93.
Webster's Third New International Dictionary of the English Language Unabridged (Springfield, MA, 1966).
Wendland, E. R., "Seeking the Path through a Forest of Symbols: A Figurative and Structural Survey of the Song of Songs", *JOTT* 7 (1995), 13–59.
Westenholz, J. G., "Metaphorical Language in the Poetry of Love in the Ancient Near East", in D. Charpin and F. Joannès (eds.), *La circulation des biens, des personnes et des idées dans le Proche Orient ancien, Actes de la XXXVIII Rencontre Assyriologique Internationale, Paris 1991* (Paris, 1992), pp. 381–387.
Wetzstein, J. G., "Die syrische Dreschtafel", *ZE* 5 (1873), pp. 270–302.
——, "Bemerkungen zum Hohenliede", in F. Delitzsch, *Hoheslied und Koheleth*, BC IV,4 (Leipzig, 1875), pp. 162–177.
White, J. B., *A Study of the Language of Love in the Song of Songs and Ancient Egyptian Poetry*, SBL.DS 38 (Missoula, 1978).
Wildberger, H., *Jesaja*, BK (Neukirchen-Vluyn, 1980).
Winandy, J., "La litière de Salomon (Ct 3,9–10)", *VT* 15 (1965), pp. 103–110.
Winter, U., *Frau und Göttin. Exegetische und ikonographische Studien zum weiblichen Gottesbild im Alten Israel und in dessen Umwelt*, OBO 53 (Fribourg and Göttingen, 1983).
Wittekindt, W., *Das Hohe Lied und seine Beziehungen zum Istarkult* (Hannover, 1925).
Wolkstein, D. and S. N. Kramer, *Inanna, Queen of Heaven and Earth.* Her Stories and Hymns from Sumer (New York *et al.*, 1983).
Xella, P., *Il mito di šḥr e šlm* (Roma, 1973).
Zakovitch, Y., "Song of Songs—Riddle of Riddles", in K. Modras (ed.), *The Art of Love Lyrics, FS B. Couroyer et H. J. Polotski*, CRB 49 (Paris, 2000), pp. 11–23.
Zapletal, V., *Das Hohelied kritisch und metrisch untersucht* (Fribourg, 1907).
Zatelli, I., "Bar: a sample entry for a database of the semantic of classical Hebrew", *Quaderni del Dipartimento di Linguistica—Università di Firenze* 5 (1994), pp. 149–155.
Zenger, E., *Gottes Bogen in den Wolken*, SBS 112 (Stuttgart, 1983), pp. 87–89.
Zohary, M., *Plants of the Bible* (Cambridge *et al.*, 1982).

INDEX OF AUTHORS

INDEX OF HEBREW WORDS

INDEX OF ANCIENT SOURCES

1. Biblical Texts

1.1 *Old Testament*

1.2 *New Testament*

2. Ancient Near Eastern Literature

2.1 *Egyptians Texts*

4. Latin Authors

5. Jewish Sources

5.1 *Apocrypha*

5.2 *Rabbinic Literature*

5.3 *Qumran*

5.4 *Philo*

5.5 *Josephus*